Fun, interactive exercises reinforce newly-learned concepts.

Videos provide an engrossing introduction to each concept.

Students can test their understanding with a multiple-choice quiz for every topic area.

TOPIC TACKLER

This software is a complete tutorial focusing on those areas in the principles of accounting course that give students the most trouble. Providing help on two key topics for every single chapter, this program delves into the material via the following:

- Video clips

- PowerPoint slide-shows that sometimes include animations and/or audio

- Drag-and-drop, fill-in-the-blank exercises

- Self-test quizzes

- Website hotlinks

This highly engaging presentation will put your students in control of the most fundamental aspects of principles of accounting. Volume 1 covers Chapters 1-13; Volume 2 covers Chapters 13-26.

Concepts appearing in the text that receive additional treatment in **Topic Tackler** are marked with a unique icon.

System Requirements

Windows® 95, Windows® 98 Version 1, SE, 2000, NT, ME, or Equivalent

Pentium Processor (133MHz minimum)

32MB of RAM or greater

PC Compatible sound card
(Topic Tackler only)

Internet connection (Topic Tackler only)

6x CD-ROM or higher

16 bit, 640x480 video card (minimum)

Volume 1 Chapters 1–13

Fundamental Accounting Principles

Volume 1 Chapters 1–13

16 edition

Fundamental Accounting Principles

Kermit D. Larson
University of Texas at Austin

John J. Wild
University of Wisconsin at Madison

Barbara Chiappetta
Nassau Community College

McGraw-Hill
Irwin

Boston Burr Ridge, IL Dubuque, IA Madison, WI New York
San Francisco St. Louis Bangkok Bogotá Caracas Kuala Lumpur
Lisbon London Madrid Mexico City Milan Montreal New Delhi
Santiago Seoul Singapore Sydney Taipei Toronto

To my wife **Nancy.**

To my wife **Gail** and children, **Kimberly, Jonathan, Stephanie,** and **Trevor.**

To my husband **Bob,** my sons **Michael** and **David,** and my **mother.**

McGraw-Hill Higher Education 🖉

A Division of The McGraw-Hill Companies

FUNDAMENTAL ACCOUNTING PRINCIPLES

Published by McGraw-Hill/Irwin, an imprint of The McGraw-Hill Companies, Inc. 1221 Avenue of the Americas, New York, NY, 10020. Copyright © 2002, 1999, 1996, 1993, 1990, 1987, 1984, 1981, 1978, 1975, 1972, 1969, 1966, 1963, 1959, 1955, by The McGraw-Hill Companies, Inc. All rights reserved. No part of this publication may be reproduced or distributed in any form or by any means, or stored in a database or retrieval system, without the prior written consent of The McGraw-Hill Companies, Inc., including, but not limited to, in any network or other electronic storage or transmission, or broadcast for distance learning.

Some ancillaries, including electronic and print components, may not be available to customers outside the United States.

This book is printed on acid-free paper.

domestic   5 6 7 8 9 0 VNH/VNH 0 9 8 7 6 5 4 3
international   2 3 4 5 6 7 8 9 0 VNH/VNH 0 9 8 7 6 5 4 3 2 1

ISBN 0-07-242339-0 (complete text)
ISBN 0-07-246466-6 (Volume 1)
ISBN 0-07-246467-4 (Volume 2)
ISBN 0-07-246495-X (Volume 1, Instructor's Edition)
ISBN 0-07-246468-2 (Financial Chapters, Chapters 1–18)

Publisher: *Brent Gordon*
Sponsoring editor: *Melody Marcus*
Developmental editors: *Tracey Douglas/Kristin Leahy/Jackie Scruggs*
Editorial assistant: *Kelly Odom*
Marketing manager: *Rich Kolasa*
Senior project manager: *Kimberly D. Hooker*
Senior production supervisor: *Michael McCormick*
Senior designer: *Jennifer McQueen*
Photo research coordinator: *Judy Kausal*
Photo researcher: *Charlotte Goldman*
Lead supplement coordinator: *Becky Szura*
Media technology producers: *Edward Przyzycki/Todd Labak*
Cover illustration: *Tom Nemoda/Asylum Studios*
Compositor: **TECH**BOOKS
Typeface: *10.5/12 Times Roman*
Printer: *Von Hoffman Press, Inc.*

Library of Congress Cataloging-in-Publication Data

Larson, Kermit D.
   Fundamental accounting principles / Kermit D. Larson, John J. Wild, Barbara
Chiappetta.—16th ed.
     p. cm.
   Includes bibliographical references and index.
   ISBN 0-07-242339-0 (alk. paper)
   1. Accounting. I. Wild, John J. II. Chiappetta, Barbara. III. Title.
HF5635.P975 2002
657—dc21   2001030128

INTERNATIONAL EDITION ISBN 0-07-112222-2
Copyright © 2002. Exclusive rights by The McGraw-Hill Companies, Inc. for manufacture and export. This book cannot be re-exported from the country to which it is sold by McGraw-Hill. The International Edition is not available in North America.

ABOUT THE AUTHORS

KERMIT D. LARSON is the Arthur Andersen & Co. Alumni Professor of Accounting Emeritus at the University of Texas at Austin. He served as chairman of the University of Texas, Department of Accounting and was visiting associate professor at Tulane University. His scholarly articles have been published in a variety of journals, including *The Accounting Review, Journal of Accountancy,* and *Abacus.* He is the author of several books, including *Financial Accounting* and *Fundamentals of Financial and Managerial Accounting,* both published by McGraw-Hill/Irwin.

Professor Larson is a member of the American Accounting Association, the Texas Society of CPAs, and the American Institute of CPAs. His positions with the AAA have included vice president, southwest regional vice president, and chairperson of several committees, including the Committee of Concepts and Standards. He was a member of the committee that planned the first AAA doctoral consortium and served as its director.

Professor Larson served as president of the Richard D. Irwin Foundation. He also served on the Accounting Accreditation Committee and on the Accounting Standards Committee of the AACSB. He was a member of the Constitutional Drafting Committee of the Federation of Schools of Accountancy and a member of the Commission on Professional Accounting Education. He has been an expert witness on cases involving mergers, antitrust litigation, consolidation criteria, franchise taxes, and expropriation of assets by foreign governments. Professor Larson served on the Board of Directors and Executive Committee of Tekcon, Inc., and on the National Accountants Advisory Board of Safe-Guard Business Systems. In his leisure time, he enjoys skiing and is an avid sailor and golfer.

JOHN J. WILD is a professor of business and the Vilas Research Scholar at the University of Wisconsin at Madison. He has previously held appointments at Michigan State University and the University of Manchester in England. He received his BBA, MS, and PhD from the University of Wisconsin.

Professor Wild teaches courses at both the undergraduate and graduate levels. He has received the Mabel W. Chipman Excellence-in-Teaching Award and the departmental Excellence-in-Teaching Award at the University of Wisconsin. He also received the Beta Alpha Psi and Roland F. Salmonson Excellence-in-Teaching Award from Michigan State University. Professor Wild is a past KPMG Peat Marwick National Fellow and is a recipient of fellowships from the American Accounting Association and the Ernst and Young Foundation.

Professor Wild is an active member of the American Accounting Association and its sections. He has served on several notable committees of these organizations, including the Outstanding Accounting Educator Award, National Program Advisory, Publications, and Research Committees. Professor Wild is author of *Financial Statement Analysis* and *Financial Accounting: Information for Decisions,* both published by McGraw-Hill/Irwin. His research publications appear in *The Accounting Review, Journal of Accounting Research, Journal of Accounting and Economics, Contemporary Accounting Research, Journal of Accounting, Auditing and Finance, Journal of Accounting and Public Policy,* and other business periodicals. He is associate editor of *Contemporary Accounting Research* and has served on several editorial boards including *The Accounting Review.*

Professor Wild, his wife, and four children enjoy travel, music, sports, and community activities.

BARBARA CHIAPPETTA received her BBA in Accountancy and MS in Education from Hofstra University and is a tenured full professor at Nassau Community College. For the past 20 years, she has been an active executive board member of the Teachers of Accounting at Two-Year Colleges (TACTYC), serving 10 years as vice president and 5 years as president. As an active member of the American Accounting Association, she has served on the Northeast Regional Steering Committee, chaired the Curriculum Revision Committee of the Two-Year Section, and participated in numerous national committees. In April 1998, Professor Chiappetta was inducted into the American Accounting Association Hall of Fame for the Northeast Region. She received the Nassau Community College dean of instruction's Faculty Distinguished Achievement Award in the spring of 1995. Professor Chiappetta was honored with the State University of New York Chancellor's Award for Teaching Excellence in 1997. As a confirmed believer in the benefits of the active learning pedagogy, Professor Chiappetta has authored *Student Learning Tools,* an active learning workbook for a first-year accounting course, published by McGraw-Hill/Irwin.

In her leisure time, Professor Chiappetta enjoys tennis and participates on a U.S.T.A. team. She also enjoys the challenge of bridge. Her husband, Robert, is an entrepreneur in the leisure sport industry. She has two sons—Michael, a lawyer, currently practicing in New York City, and David, formerly lead guitarist in the rock band Blindman's Sun and currently pursuing a career in film scoring.

PUTTING THE STUDENT
ON A PEDESTAL

A WORD TO THE STUDENT

WHEN we set about revising FAP, we spoke to hundreds of educators throughout the country, listening to their thoughts about what worked in previous editions and what they felt could be improved. The experience they brought to us was born of countless hours of teaching, of helping students just like you to master what can be a challenging subject. They had a great deal to tell us and we listened.

NOW, after nearly two years of work, we present to you the SIXTEENTH EDITION of FAP. It is the result of a simple, guiding principle: THE STUDENT COMES FIRST. Every change to this edition, from the ENTREPRENEURIAL FLAVOR to the extensive use of helpful STUDY AIDS, is designed to make the principles of accounting easier for you to learn—and more fun too! You will encounter chapter-opening vignettes and "Did You Know" boxes containing names like eBay, FUBU, Birdhouse, NetLedger, Freeplay and Red Hat, YOUNG COMPANIES helping to shape the NEW ECONOMY in which you will soon COMPETE FOR WORK. You'll also notice a boxed feature entitled "You Make the Call" that challenges you to apply your understanding to a real-world situation.

And we haven't stopped with the text. A new, 2-volume CD-ROM called FAP Partner offers additional help for the most challenging topics in the principles course while NetTutor gives you free, real-time access to an accounting expert ready to help you with any questions you have.

There's a great deal more to this edition of FAP as you'll discover when you read the following pages. We hope you'll agree that Fundamental Accounting Principles by Larson, Wild, and Chiappetta provides you with everything you need to master the principles of accounting.

Sincerely,

The McGraw-Hill/Irwin FAP Team

TECHNOLOGY SOLUTIONS TO MEET EVERY NEED

TODAY, nearly   college instructors use the **INTERNET** in their respective courses.   Some are just getting started, while others are the very latest advances in educational **CONTENT DELIVERY** and

That's why we at McGraw-Hill/Irwin offer you a complete range of digital solutions. Your students can use **FAP**'s complete Online Learning Center (OLC), NetTutor, and PowerWeb on their own or we can help you create your own course Web site using McGraw-Hill's PageOut. We can even help you achieve dot-com nirvana with your entire principles course online.

In addition to Web-based assets, **FAP** boasts CDs for students and instructors alike. Students in particular will be grateful for **FAP Partner,** the two-volume CD-ROM that offers special assistance for the most demanding principles of accounting topics. Instructors have access to nearly every crucial supplement, from the Instructor's Resource Manual to the PowerPoint slides, on both CD and the Internet.

McGraw-Hill is a leader in bringing helpful technology into the classroom. And with **FAP,** your class gets all the benefits of the digital age.

Concept 1-1

ONLINE LEARNING CENTER (OLC)

www.mhhe.com/FAP16e

More and more students are studying online. That's why we offer an **Online Learning Center**

(**OLC**) that follows FAP chapter by chapter. It doesn't require any building or maintenance on your part.

It's ready to go the moment you and your students type in the address.

As your students study, they can refer to the OLC Web site for such benefits as:

- Internet-based activities
- self-grading quizzes
- links to text references
- links to professional resources on the Web and job opportunity information
- learning objectives
- chapter overviews

A secured Instructor Resource Center stores your essential course materials to save you prep time before class. The Instructor's Manual, Solutions, PowerPoint, and sample syllabi are now just a couple of clicks away. You will also find useful packaging information and transition notes.

The OLC Web site also serves as a doorway to other technology solutions like PageOut, NetTutor and PowerWeb which are free to **FAP** adopters.

COURSE MANAGEMENT

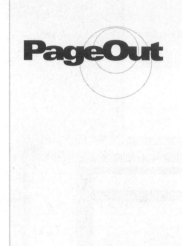

PAGEOUT

McGraw-Hill's Course Management System

PageOut is the easiest way to create a Web site for your accounting course.

There's no need for HTML coding, graphic design, or a thick how-to book. Just fill in a series of boxes with plain English and click on one of our professional designs. In no time, your course is online!

Should you need assistance in preparing your Web site, we can help you. In addition to many pre-built course Web sites, we offer a team of product specialists ready to help. Just send them your course materials, and after a brief phone consultation, they will build your PageOut Web site from scratch. (For information on how to do this, see "Superior Service" on the next page.)

PageOut is free when you adopt **FAP**! To learn more, please visit **http://www.pageout.net**.

THIRD-PARTY COURSE MANAGEMENT SYSTEMS

For the ambitious instructor, we offer **FAP** content for complete online courses. To make this possible, we have joined forces with the most popular delivery platforms currently available. These platforms are designed for instructors who want complete control over course content and how it is presented to students. You can customize the **FAP** Online Learning Center content and author your own course materials. It's entirely up to you.

Products like WebCT, Blackboard, eCollege, and TopClass (a product of WBT) all expand the reach of your course. Online discussion and message boards will now complement your office hours. Thanks to a sophisticated tracking system, you will know which students need more attention – even if they don't ask for help. That's because online testing scores are recorded and automatically placed in your grade book, and if a student is struggling with coursework, a special alert message lets you know.

Remember, **FAP**'s content is flexible enough to use with any platform currently available. If your department or school is already using a platform, we can help. For information on McGraw-Hill/Irwin's course management services, including Instructor Advantage and Knowledge Gateway, see "Superior Service" on the next page.

SUPERIOR SERVICE

No matter which online course solution you choose, you can count on the highest level of service. That's what sets McGraw-Hill apart. Once you choose FAP, our specialists offer free training and answer any question you have through the life of your adoption.

PAGEOUT

Now you can put your course online without knowing a word of HTML, using either our OLC content or your own content.

If you want a custom site but don't have time to build it yourself, we offer a team of specialists ready to help. Just call 1-800-541-7145, and ask to speak with a **PageOut** specialist. You will be asked to send in your course materials and then participate in a brief telephone consultation. Once we have your information, we build your Web site for you, from scratch.

INSTRUCTOR ADVANTAGE and INSTRUCTOR ADVANTAGE PLUS

Instructor Advantage is a special level of service McGraw-Hill offers in conjunction with WebCT and Blackboard. A team of platform specialists is always available, either by toll-free phone or e-mail, to ensure everything runs smoothly through the life of your adoption. Instructor Advantage is available free to all McGraw-Hill customers.

Instructor Advantage Plus is available to qualifying McGraw-Hill adopters (see your representative for details). **IA Plus** guarantees you a full day of on-site training by a Blackboard or WebCT specialist, for yourself and up to nine colleagues. Thereafter, you will enjoy the benefits of unlimited telephone and e-mail support throughout the life of your adoption. **IA Plus** users also have the opportunity to access the **McGraw-Hill Knowledge Gateway** (see below).

KNOWLEDGE GATEWAY

Developed with the help of our partner Eduprise, the **McGraw-Hill Knowledge Gateway** is an all-purpose service and resource center for instructors teaching online.

The First Level of **Knowledge Gateway** is available to all professors browsing the McGraw-Hill Higher Education Website, and consists of an introduction to OLC content, access to the first level of the Resource Library, technical support, and information on Instructional Design Services available through Eduprise.

The Second Level is password-protected and provides access to the expanded Resource Library, technical and pedagogical support for WebCT, Blackboard, and TopClass, the online Instructional Design helpdesk and an online discussion forum for users. The **Knowledge Gateway** provides a considerable advantage for teaching online—and it's only available through McGraw-Hill.

To see how these platforms can assist your online course, visit **www.mhhe.com/solutions**.

NetTUTOR

NetTutor allows students and tutors to communicate with each other in a variety of ways:

- The **Live Tutor Center** via NetTutor's WWWhiteboard enables a tutor to hold an interactive online tutorial with several students whose questions are placed in a queue and answered sequentially.

- The **Q&A Center** allows students to submit questions at any time and retrieve answers within 24 hours.

- The **Message Center*** is where students will be able to send questions, messages, and comments to other students and teachers.

- The **Archive Center** allows students to browse for answers to previously asked questions. They can also search for questions pertinent to a particular topic. If they encounter an answer they do not understand, they can ask a follow-up question.

- The **Management Center*** will make it easy to create, update, and delete groups and members as well as to customize the site to suit the needs of the group.

Students are issued 10 hours of free **NetTutor** time when they purchase a new copy of **FAP**. Additional time may be purchased in 5-hour increments. Live tutor availability will vary throughout the course of the term with a peak availability of around 60 hours a week.

*Note: Certain **NetTutor** features marked by an asterisk (*) may not be available at the time of the book's initial publication.

TECHNOLOGY SOLUTIONS

FREE With Adoption!

POWERWEB

Keeping your course current can be a job
in itself and now McGraw-Hill does that job
for you. **PowerWeb** extends the learning
experience beyond the core textbook by offering all of the latest news and developments
pertinent to your course, brought to you via
the Internet without all the clutter and dead
links of a typical online search.

PowerWeb offers current articles related to principles of accounting, weekly
updates with assessment tools, informative and timely world news culled by an
accounting principles expert, refereed Web links, and more.

In addition, **PowerWeb** provides a trove of helpful learning aids, including self-
grading quizzes and interactive glossaries and exercises. Students may also access
study tips, conduct online research, and learn about different career paths.

Visit the **PowerWeb** site at **http://www.dushkin.com/powerweb**
and see firsthand what **PowerWeb** can mean to your course.

SOLID ACCOUNTING COVERAGE...

WE LISTENED! IN ADDITION to a number of reviewers, we held focus groups in cities around the country to learn what **INSTRUCTORS LIKE YOU** are thinking about in the principles of accounting course and the materials you use to teach it. John Wild attended every session to listen and ask questions. We got FANTASTIC FEEDBACK and our authors have integrated that feedback into this new edition of the text. We think you'll like what you see.

THROUGHOUT THE TEXT:

Increased coverage of e-business, the Web, and entrepreneurship as related to accounting is integrated throughout the text as appropriate. Following are *some* content revisions:

Chapter 1

JobDirect **NEW opener**

New, early introduction to financial statements

Revised motivation on the relevance of accounting

Revised section on accounting and related careers

New table on compensation in accounting careers

Chapter 2

Simplified transaction analysis with accounting equation

Early introduction to statement of cash flows

Revised Nintendo financials

Top 10 list of key entrepreneurial qualities

Chapter 3

Creative Assets **NEW opener**

Streamlined section on using T-Accounts

Shortened section on posting of transactions

New discussion of using entries to analyze transactions

Chapter 4

CrossWorlds **NEW opener**

Revised presentation on accounting adjustments

Streamlined discussion of the adjusting process

Chapter 5

Red Hat **NEW opener**

Shortened section on closing entries

New Excel screen captures with acetates for work sheet

Streamlined section on account numbering system

Chapter 6

Wooden Ships of Hoboken **NEW opener**

Simplified presentation of income statement formats

Streamlined section on merchandising cash flows

Chapter 7

FUBU **NEW opener**

Streamlined presentation of gross profit method

Toys "R" Us **Updated**

Chapter 8

NetLedger **NEW opener**

More discussion on Web-based accounting

New simplified visuals for special journals (using PeachTree screen captures)

Revised special journals using perpetual inventory system

Streamlined coverage of special journals

New analysis of Harley-Davidson segments

Chapter 9

eBay **NEW opener**

New feature on cyber fraud

Shortened discussion of voucher system of control

Chapter 10

Tarina Tarantino **NEW opener**

Streamlined discussion on full disclosure principle

Dell and Apple **Updated**

Chapter 11

Papa John's **NEW opener**

Streamlined discussion of partial-year depreciation

Shortened and simplified section on "Revenue and Capital Expenditures"

Deleted section on exchange of dissimilar assets

Coors and Anheuser-Busch **Updated**

Chapter 12

Sector 9 **NEW opener**

New section on employee bonus plans

Shortened section on "Income Tax Liabilities"

Best Buy **Updated**

Revised appendix on payroll records

Chapter 13

AltiTUNES **NEW opener**

Expanded discussion of limited liability companies

New section on partnership return on equity

Boston Celtics revised feature

Chapter 14

World Wrestling Federation **NEW opener**

Deleted section on "Issuing Stock through Subscriptions"

Streamlined section on participating and nonparticipating preferred stock dividends

Deleted the Dividends Declared account to streamline journal entries for cash (and stock) dividends

Deleted the section on "Liquidating Cash Dividends"

Shortened section on "Discontinued Segments"

Simplified section on "Changes in Accounting Principles"

Streamlined section on diluted earnings per share

Shortened sections on book value per share and dividend yield

Chapter 15

David Bowie Bonds **NEW opener**

Streamlined Appendix on "Present Values of Bonds and Notes"

New Appendix 15B on "Leases and Pensions"

Chapter 16

Freeplay **NEW opener**

New illustrations on adjustments for unrealized gains and losses on securities

Chapter 17

Interactive Sports **NEW opener**

Simplified preparation of the statement of cash flows

Shortened section on "Analyzing Cash Sources and Uses"

Chapter 18

Nike vs. Reebok **Updated**

Revised discussion on comparative analysis (benchmarking)

Streamlined section on "Working Capital and Current Ratio"

Chapter 19

American Paper Optics **NEW opener**

New section on "Lean Business Model"

Shortened discussion on manufacturing management principles

Expanded discussion of service businesses

New presentation of manufacturing statement

Chapter 20

i-FRONTIER **NEW opener**

Moved manufacturing statement to Chapter 19

Simplified section on "Overapplied and Underapplied Overhead"

Deleted section on "Multiple Overhead Allocation Rates"

New section on costing and pricing for service businesses

Moved Appendix 20A on General Accounting System to the Web

Chapter 21

INCA **NEW opener**

New footnote illustration of process costing using weighted-average method

Deleted section on "Spoiled Units of Production"

New section on "Hybrid Costing"

Chapter 22

Kate Spade **NEW opener**

Simplified discussion of "Activity-Based Costing"

Streamlined sections on "Departmental Accounting"

Chapter 23

Latham Entertainment **NEW opener**

Streamlined section on "Assumptions of CVP Analysis"

Chapter 24

Birdhouse **NEW opener**

Deleted section on "Zero-Based Budgeting"

Streamlined section on the budgeted balance sheet

New section on "Activity-Based Budgeting"

Chapter 25

Toes on the Noes **NEW opener**

New discussion of service applications

Chapter 26

Leading Edge Aviation Services **NEW opener**

New applications to service businesses

INNOVATIVE PEDAGOGY

...SET IN A MODERN FRAMEWORK

e

An Entrepreneurial Icon calls out all relevant material within the chapters, whether an opening vignette, box, or end-of-chapter assignment.

ENTREPRENEURIAL CHAPTER-OPENERS

These opening vignettes focus on young entrepreneurs and the relevance of accounting in their business decisions. We highlight companies like eBay, FUBU, Red Hat, NetLedger, JobDirect, Sector 9, Kate Spade, INCA, Birdhouse, Freeplay, and WWF—names that students will recognize from magazines, newspapers, television, and the Internet. The openers discuss how accounting information and an understanding of it aided these start-ups in successfully launching and running their operations. They serve as excellent motivators—showing the importance of accounting in business.

ENTREPRENEURIAL FLAVOR – NEW

Today's students live in a world where start-up companies have redefined traditional notions of success in business. To reflect this shift, FAP integrates ideas and practices followed by today's entrepreneurs, speaking more directly to students and better preparing them for the workforce they will enter. **This approach is distinctive in the accounting principles market.**

FAP weaves the entrepreneurial flavor throughout the text in a variety of ways.

9 Cash and Internal Control

"I hope to make it easier to conduct business with strangers over the Net." —Pierre Omidyar

A Look Back

Chapter 8 focused on accounting information systems. We explained the fundamental principles and components of information systems, the use of special journals and subsidiary ledgers, and technology-based systems. We also discussed the analysis of segment data.

A Look at This Chapter

This chapter extends our study of accounting to the area of internal control and accounting for cash. We describe procedures that are good for internal control. We also explain the control of and accounting for cash.

A Look Ahead

Chapter 10 focuses on receivables and short-term investments. These items are the most liquid assets other than cash. We explain how to account and report for these assets.

350   Chapter 8   Accounting Information Systems

Entrepreneurial Decision

P1

e

BTN 8-8 Dakota Rice has operated a local gift shop for two years. Initially, she handled all aspects of the store's accounting manually. Over the past year, she has focused on upgrading the store to a computerized system and has successfully installed software to handle billing, purchasing, and payroll. Dakota hopes this year to move from a periodic inventory system to a perpetual one. She is thinking of investing in a bar code labeler and scanner system to help manage inventory.

Required

1. What are the cost-benefit considerations of a bar code system?
2. How would a bar code system work with the accounting information system to accomplish perpetual inventory accounting?

Part Three

ENTREPRENEURIAL DECISION PROBLEM

A new Entrepreneurial Decision problem is included at the end of each chapter (in the "Beyond the Numbers" assignment section). These problems focus on small businesses and the relevance of accounting in helping solve business problems or guide business strategy. No other text offers such assignments specifically directed at small businesses.

Learning Objectives

Define internal control and its purpose.

Identify principles of internal control.

Define cash and cash equivalents and explain how to report them.

Identify control features of banking activities.

Analytical

A1   Compute the days' sales uncollected ratio and use it to analyze liquidity.

Procedural

P1   Apply internal control to cash receipts.

P2   Apply the voucher system to control cash disbursements.

P3   Explain and record petty cash fund transactions.

P4   Apply the net method to control purchase discounts.

P5   Prepare a bank reconciliation.

ENTREPRENEURIAL BOXES

A selected number of new *Did You Know?* and *You Make The Call* boxes focus on entrepreneurial issues and decisions. The *Did You Know?* boxes provide current and informative observations relevant to business start-ups. The *You Make the Call* boxes engage students to apply accounting to decisions confronting entrepreneurs. These boxes are especially effective at engaging students interested in small business and start-up possibilities.

Flea Market in Cyberspace

e   SAN JOSE, CA—Who ever thought a flea market could be worth $12 billion? Paris-born entrepreneur Pierre Omidyar started his Net auction service, **eBay** (a combination of the words *electronic* and *Bay Area*), five years ago to help his girlfriend collect Pez candy dispensers (**eBay.com**). Omidyar, then 27, saw a need for a Web site where people could buy and sell all kinds of items such as computers, antiques, toys, and music. eBay is now the largest person-to-person auction site on the Web. It creates the marketplace, but buyers and sellers do their own work. eBay never touches the goods or the money. Its earnings derive from commissions, between 1 and 5%, depending on the item's value.

Omidyar calls eBay an experiment in e-commerce. But how does he persuade strangers to trust one another enough to hand over merchandise or cash? "Most people are honest, trustworthy people," says Omidyar. Still, he set up basic controls to establish responsibilities of each party to a trade and to monitor and record transactions. When complications still arose between buyers and sellers, Omidyar had to install a better control system.

Omidyar's response was fourfold. First, he devised a control system whereby buyers and sellers rate their experiences with the other party. This *Feedback Forum* is a public record of past eBay dealings of buyers and sellers. Omidyar says, "It's become a kind of virtuous cycle that's encouraged good behavior." Second, he brought in escrow services to assist traders in making deals. Buyers can have their goods delivered to an escrow service before their money is sent to the seller. Likewise, sellers can require that a buyer send money to the escrow service before sending the goods. Third, he gave traders free i...

up SafeHarbo...
dependent re...

Omidyar is...
creating an o...
hope to make...
Omidyar's cu...
$3 billion fro...
[Sources: Busi...
Web Site, Dec...

Did You Know?   *e*

Entrepreneurial Giving   Many entrepreneurs donate 10% or more of their pretax income to charities. Consultants cite evidence that socially conscious behavior brings tangible financial rewards. A recent survey found 76% of respondents saying they'd switch from their current store to one with a good cause if price and quality are equal.

You Make the Call   *e*

Entrepreneur   As a small retailer, you are considering allowing customers to purchase merchandise using credit cards. Until now, your store accepted only cash and checks. What form of analysis do you use to make this decision?

Answer—p. 421

The CAP Model

The Conceptual/Analytical/Procedural (CAP) Model allows courses to be specially designed to meet instructional and learning needs. This model identifies learning objectives, textual material, assignments, and test material by C, A, or P, allowing different instructors to teach from the same materials, yet easily customizes their courses toward a conceptual, analytical, or procedural approach (or a combination thereof) based on personal preferences.

Quick Check

These short question/answer features reinforce the material immediately preceding them. They allow the reader to pause and reflect on the topics described, then receive immediate feedback before going on to new topics. Answers are provided at the end of each chapter.

Marginal Student Annotations-NEW

These annotations provide students with additional hints, tips, and examples to help them more fully understand the concepts and retain what they have learned. They also include notes on global implications for accounting.

Did You Know?

These relevant, topical items are useful for preparing, analyzing and using accounting information. Strategically placed throughout the text, these items help students understand and effectively apply accounting.

Quick Check

7. Why are sales discounts and sales returns and allowances recorded in contra-revenue accounts instead of directly in the Sales account?

8. Under what conditions are two entries necessary to record a sales return?

9. When merchandise is sold on credit and the seller notifies the buyer of a price reduction, does the seller send a

Answers—p. 244

Point: To understand the closing process, it can help to focus on its *outcomes—updating* the capital account balance to its proper ending balance, and getting *temporary accounts* to show *zero balances* for purposes of accumulating data for the next period.

An income statement ai accounting period. It is counts. The statement of capital account for a sp with amounts in the wit counts accumulate infor balances.

To close revenue and called *Income Summary.* for the sum of all reven income or net loss and i withdrawals account bal posted, the revenue, exp

170

MORE INNOVATIVE PEDAGOGY

You Make the Call boxes develop critical thinking and decision-making skills by asking students to render decisions using accounting information. Each chapter contains 2-4 of these features. They reflect the needs of many different kinds of users: investors, consultants, programmers, financial planners, engineers, appraisers, and political and community activists. Guidance answers for all **You Make the Call** boxes are provided at the end of each chapter.

Using the Information

This section concludes each chapter and draws upon the key material presented in the chapter to introduce one or more tools of analysis. It then applies these tools to analyze and interpret the performance of actual companies and their competitors.

Beyond the Numbers, as its name suggests, is a section designed to encourage your students to look at numerical information as involving more than just mathematical calculations. These end-of-chapter exercises show your students how accounting data applies to a variety of business situations, divided into 8 sections:

Reporting in Action
Comparative Analysis
Ethics Challenge
Communicating in Practice
Taking It to the Net
Teamwork in Action
Business Week Activity
Entrepreneurial Decision

Comprehensive and Serial Problems are included in several chapters and focus on multiple learning objectives from multiple chapters. They help integrate and summarize key concepts.

---

142   Chapter 4   Accrual Accounting and Financial Statements

Using the Information   **Profit Margin**

A2 Compute profit margin and describe its use in analyzing company performance.

Business decision makers want financial statements to reflect relevant information about a company's financial performance and condition. A useful measure of a company's operating results is the ratio of its net income to net sales (revenues). This ratio is called **profit margin,** or *return on sales,* and is computed as shown in Exhibit 4.23.

Exhibit 4.23
Profit Margin

$$\text{Profit margin} = \frac{\text{Net income}}{\text{Net sales}}$$

This ratio is interpreted as reflecting the percent of profit in each dollar of sales. To illustrate how we compute and use profit margin, let's look at the results of **Ben & Jerry's Homemade Ice Cream** in Exhibit 4.24. Profit margin is one measure we can use to help evaluate Ben & Jerry's performance during the past four years.

Exhibit 4.24
Ben & Jerry's Profit Margin

	1999	1998	1997	1996
Net income (in mil.)	$ 3.4	$ 6.2	$ 3.9	$ 3.9
Net sales (in mil.)	$237.0	$209.2	$174.2	$167.2
Profit margin	1.4%	3.0%	2.2%	2.3%
Industry profit margin	2.2%	1.6%	2.0%	2.1%

Ben & Jerry's average profit margin is 2.2% over this period. Year 1999 especially stands out as poor. This is mainly due to special charges tied to the discontinuance of a manufacturing plant. The profit margin is expected to increase in subsequent years. Also note the

---

Chapter 12   Current Liabilities   **523**

3. Present journal entries to record the adjustments entered on the six-column table. Assume BeGone's adjusted balance for Merchandise Inventory matches the year-end physical count.

4. Prepare a single-step income statement, a statement of changes in owner's equity, and a classified balance sheet.

Check   Net income, $23,370; Total assets, $98,271

Beyond the Numbers

BTN 12-1   Refer to the financial statements for **Nike** in Appendix A to respond to the following:

1. Compute times interest earned for the years ended May 31, 2000, 1999, and 1998. Comment on Nike's ability to cover its interest expense for this period.

2. What evidence can you identify for an indication that Nike has temporary differences between income reported on its income statement and income reported on its tax return?

Swoosh Ahead

3. Access Nike's annual report for fiscal years ending after May 31, 2000, at its Web site [www.nike.com] or the SEC's EDGAR database [www.sec.gov]. Compute Nike's times interest earned for years ending after May 31, 2000, that you have access to.

Reporting in Action
C3 A1
NIKE

BTN 12-2   Key comparative figures ($ millions) for both **Nike** and **Reebok** follow:

	NIKE			Reebok		
Key Figures	Current Year	One Year Prior	Two Years Prior	Current Year	One Year Prior	Two Years Prior
Net income	$579.1	$451.4	$399.6	$11.0	$23.9	$135.1
Income taxes	340.1	294.7	253.4	10.1	11.9	12.5
Interest expense .	45.0	44.1	60.0	49.7	60.7	64.4

Comparative Analysis
A1
NIKE
Reebok

Required

1. Compute times interest earned for the three years' data shown for each company.

2. Comment on which company appears stronger in its ability to pay interest obligations if income should decline.

BTN 12-3   Mike Gates is a sales manager for an automobile dealership. He earns a bonus each year based on revenue from the number of autos sold in the year less related warranty expenses. Actual warranty expenses have varied over the prior 10 years from a low of 3% of an automobile's selling price to a high of 10%. In the past, Mike has tended to estimate warranty expenses on the high end to be conservative. He must work with the dealership's accountant at year-end to arrive at the warranty expense accrual for cars sold this year.

1. Does the warranty accrual decision create any ethical dilemma for Gates?

2. Since warranty expenses vary, what percent do you think Gates should choose for this year? Justify your response.

Ethics Challenge
P4

BTN 12-4   Matthew Stafford is the accounting and finance manager for a manufacturer. At year-end, he must determine how to account for the company's contingencies. His manager, John Harris, objects to Matthew's proposal to recognize an expense and a liability for warranty service on units of a new product introduced in the fourth quarter. John comments, "There's no way we can estimate this warranty cost. We don't owe anyone anything until a product breaks and is returned. Let's report an expense if and when we do repairs."

Communicating in Practice
C3

Required

Prepare a one-page memorandum for Matthew to send to John defending his proposal.

INSTRUCTOR SUPPLEMENTS

Instructor's Resource CD-ROM
007246500X

This is your all-in-one resource. It allows you to create custom presentations from your own materials or from the following text-specific materials provided in the CD's asset library:

- Instructor's Resource Manual
- Solutions Manual
- Test Bank
- Ready Shows (PowerPoint® Slides)—Ready Shows is a multimedia, lecture slide package using Microsoft® PowerPoint 7.0 to illustrate chapter concepts and procedures. It allows revision of lecture slides and includes a viewer, allowing screens to be shown with or without the software.
- General Ledger Applications Software (GLAS)
- Spreadsheet Applications Template Software (SPATS)
- Tutorial Software
- Link to PageOut
- Video Clips

Ready Show Slides
Volume 1: 0072468408
Volume 2: 0072468432

Prepared by Jon A. Booker, Charles W. Caldwell, Susan C. Galbreath and Richard S. Rand of Tennessee Technological University

An overhead presentation package including color teaching transparencies selected from the Ready Shows (PowerPoint®) slides, as well as a booklet of black and white masters for all of the Ready Show slides.

Financial and Managerial Accounting Video Library
Financial Videos: 0072376163
Managerial Videos: 0072376171

See next page for more information

Instructor's Resource Manual
Volume 1: 0072464836
Volume 2: 0072465034

Written by Barbara Chiappetta.

These manuals contain (for each chapter) a Lecture Outline, a chart linking all assignment materials to Learning Objectives, a list of relevant active learning activities, and additional visuals with transparency masters.

Instructor's Manual for *Student Learning Tools*
0256256470

Textbook Options
The textbook is published in several variations, including (1) Complete Edition—Chapters 1–26 (2) Volume 1—Chapters 1–13, (3) Volume 2—Chapters 13–26, (4) Financial Chapters 1–18, (5) Volume 1 w/Working Papers (paperback), and (6) Volume 2 w/Working Papers (paperback).

Solutions Manual
Volume 1: 0072464852
(Solutions Transparencies 0072464895)
Volume 2: 0072465042
(Solutions Transparencies 0072465069)

Written by John J. Wild, Suresh Kalagnanam, Jo Lynne Koehn, and Marilyn Sagrillo

Test Bank
Volume 1: 0072464909
Volume 2: 0072465050

Written by Marilyn Sagrillo and John J. Wild

Brownstone Test Bank
0072464925

Available for Windows only.

Instructor Booklet for Student Software CD-ROM
0072465204

This contains the solutions to the SPATS and PeachTree problems.

Practice Sets
Manual Practice Sets

Instructor	Student
Cogg Hill Camping Equipment	
007246450X	0072464577
Republic Lighting Company	
0072464496	0072464550
Freewheel Corporation, Inc.	
Prepared by Christie W. Johnson, Montana State University	
0072464526	0072464615
Understanding Corporate Annual Reports	
Prepared by William R. Pasewark, University of Houston	
0072387165	0072387149

Computerized Practice Sets
Prepared by Leland Mansuetti and Keith Weidkamp, Sierra College

Instructor	Student
Granite Bay Jet Ski, Level 1	
0072426896	0072426942
Granite Bay Jet Ski, Inc., Level 2	
0072426209	0072426950
Wheels Exquisite, Inc., Level 1	
0072427531	0072428457
Thunder Mountain Snowmobile	
0072341157	0072341149
Gold Run Snowmobile, Inc.	
0072341092	0072341076
Ramblewood Manufacturing, Inc.	
0072346426	0072348151

STUDENT SUPPLEMENTS

FAP Partner (Topic Tackler and Mastering the Accounting Cycle)

Topic Tackler developed by Jeannie M. Folk, College of DuPage

Mastering the Accounting Cycle developed by Carol Yacht (content) and Rick Birney, Arizona State University (shell)

See inside front cover for a complete description.

Student Software CD

0072463422

GLAS, SPATS, and PeachTree templates prepared by Jack E. Terry, ComSource Associates, Inc.

Tutorial software prepared by Leland Mansuetti and Keith Weidkamp, Sierra College

Not to be confused with **FAP Partner**, this CD contains four separate software applications:

* General Ledger Applications Software (GLAS)
* Spreadsheet Applications Template Software (SPATS)
* PeachTree Templates
* Tutorial Software

GLAS, SPATS, and PeachTree allow students to use various software programs to help solve selected text assignments. The Tutorial Software gives students a chance to review each chapter's material using journal entries, glossary review, true/false questions, multiple choice questions, and fill-in-the-blank exercises.

Study Guide

Volume 1: 0072464860
Volume 2: 0072465107
Chapters 1-18: 0072465158

Prepared by Barbara Chiappetta, Nassau Community College and Linda J. Schain, Hofstra University

Covers each chapter and appendix with reviews of the learning objectives, outlines of the chapters, summaries of chapter materials, and additional problems with solutions.

Working Papers

Volume 1: 007246481X
Volume 2: 0072464992
Chapters 1-18: 0072465166

Written by John J. Wild

Working Papers are available to help direct students in solving all assignments. In addition, each chapter contains one set of papers that can be used for either the A or B series of problems.

Ready Notes

Volume 1: 0072464941
Volume 2: 0072465085

Telecourse Guide

Volume 1: 0072464933
Volume 2: 0072465077

Student Learning Tools

0256255776

Prepared by Barbara Chiappetta

This workbook helps students develop and use critical thinking and learning-to-learn skills in a collaborative team environment. It contains class activities, writing assignments, and team presentation assignments.

Building an E-Business: From the Ground Up

0072426365

Written by Elizabeth Reding

Steeped in hands-on experience, this book was written specifically for those who want to develop Web skills and business plans for use in starting an e-business.

VIDEOS

Financial and Managerial Accounting Video Library

These short, action-oriented videos, developed by Dallas County Community College for the *Accounting in Action* distance-learning course, provide an impetus for lively classroom discussion. Tied closely to **FAP**'s pedagogical framework, these videos avoid talking-head footage in favor of dynamic, documentary-style explorations of how businesses use accounting information. For a complete listing of topics covered in this library, visit the FAP Web site at **www.mhhe.com/FAP16e**.

Video Telecourse

To acquire the complete telecourse, call Dallas TeleLearning at 972-669-6666, send them a FAX at 972-669-6668, or visit their Web site at **http://www.lecroy.dcccd.edu/prodsvcs/catalog/courseList/aia.htm**.

FOCUS GROUP PARTICIPANTS

We are thankful for the suggestions, comments, and counsel of the following:

Thomas Badley, Baker College

Edward Banas, Northern Virginia
Community College/Woodbridge

Scott Barhight,
Northampton Community College

Daniel A. Bayak,
Northampton Community College

Shifei Chung, Rowan University

Anthony Cioffi,
Lorain County Community College

James L. Cosby,
John Tyler Community College

Sid Davidson, Foothill College

Victoria Doby, Villa Julie College

Roger Dufresne,
Northern Essex Community College

James Forcier, Las Positas College

J. Thomas Franco,
Wayne County Community College

James S. Gale, Northern Virginia
Community College/Alexandria

Shirley Glass, Macomb Community College

John J. Godfrey, Springfield Technical
Community College

Jennifer Gregorski,
Bristol Community College

Gloria Halpern, Montgomery College

Robert J. Hardin,
Henry Ford Community College

Richard Howden, Delta College

Jill Kolody, Anne Arundel Community College

Lawrence Kreiser, Cleveland State University

Christopher Kwak, Ohlone College

Phillip Landers,
Pennsylvania College of Technology

Betty Lipford, Community College
of Baltimore County

Paul Lospennato, North Shore
Community College

Andrea M. Murowski,
Brookdale Community College

Christopher Myers, Yuba College

Ramesh Narasimhan,
Montclair State University

Leah O'Goley, Holyoke Community College

Rochelle Olive, College of Alameda

Douglas R. Pfister,
Lansing Community College

George M. Roy, Concordia College

Alphonse Ruggiero,
Suffolk County Community College

Jill Russell, Camden County College

Steve Schaefer, Contra Costa College

Linda Schain, Hofstra University

Sara Seyedin, Foothill College

Charles A. Spector, SUNY Oswego

Mary Ston, Oakland Community College

Joseph Tabet,
North Shore Community College

Steven Teeter, Utah Valley State College

Leslie Thysell, Richard Bland College

John C. VanSantvoord,
New Hampshire College

Jan Williams, Morgan State University

Orville Wright, Morgan State University

REVIEWERS

REVIEWERS

We also thank the following for their valuable comments and suggestions:

Vernon Allen, Central Florida Community College

Abdul Daten, Northern Virginia Community College/Manassas

Peggy A. Boerman, Madison Area Technical College

Bob Coburn, Franklin Pierce College

Ali M. El-Gawhary, Tanta University/Egypt

Ellen Goldberg, Northern Virginia Community College/Loudoun

Susan Hamlen, SUNY—Buffalo

Jerry C.Y. Han, SUNY—Buffalo

Sara Harris, Arapahoe Community College

Frank Heflin, Purdue University

Yvonne Phang-Hatami, Borough of Manhattan Community College

Barbara Houchen, Anne Arundel Community College

Stephen Kerr, Hendrix College

Tom Kimberling, Ventura College

Shirly Kleiner, Johnson County Community College

Eddy McClelland, Roanoke College

William Mundy, Columbus State Community College

Lynn Pape, Northern Virginia Community College/Alexandria

Susan Pope, University of Akron

Delta Heath-Simpson, Lewis Clark State College

Daniel Small, J. Sargeant Reynolds Community College

K.R. Subramanyam, University of Southern California

Thomas Thompson, Madison Area Technical College

Theron Ray Wurzburger, New River Community College

In addition to the helpful and generous colleagues listed above, we would like to thank the entire McGraw-Hill/Irwin FAP team, including Melody Marcus, Tracey Douglas, Kristin Leahy, Jackie Scruggs, Edward Przyzycki, Kimberly Hooker, Michael McCormick, Jennifer McQueen, Judy Kausal, Becky Szura, and Kelly Odom. We also owe thanks to a great marketing and sales support staff, including Kurt Strand, Rich Kolasa, and Melissa Larmon. We would also like to thank our accuracy checkers, Barbara Schnathorst, CPA, of The Write Solution Inc., and Beth Woods, CPA, of Accuracy Counts. In addition, many talented educators and professionals worked hard to create the supplements for this book, and for their efforts we're grateful to Rick Birney, Jon A. Booker, Charles W. Caldwell, Jeannie M. Folk, Susan C. Galbreath, Suresh Kalagnanam, Jo Lynne Koehn, Leland Mansuetti, Richard S. Rand, Marilyn Sagrillo, Jack E. Terry, Keith Weidkamp and Carol Yacht. Finally, many more people we either did not meet or whose efforts we did not personally witness nevertheless helped to make this book everything that it is, and we thank them all.

ABOUT THE CONTRIBUTORS

Jo Lynne Koehn is an associate professor at Central Missouri State University. She received her PhD and Master's of Accountancy from the University of Wisconsin—Madison. Her scholarly articles have been published in a variety of journals including *Issues in Accounting Education, The CPA Journal, The Tax Advisor,* and *Accounting Enquiries.* Professor Koehn is a member of the American Accounting Association and the American Institute of CPAs. She also holds a Certified Financial Planning license and is active in promoting a financial planning curriculum at Central Missouri State University. In her leisure time, Professor Koehn indulges her passion for golf and participates in the Executive Women's Golf Association of Kansas City. Professor Koehn also enjoys reading, traveling, and visiting bookstores.

Suresh Kalagnanam is an associate professor of accounting at the University of Saskatchewan. He received his B.Eng. from the University of Madras, MBA from Gujarat University (both in India), MBA and MSc in Accounting from the University of Saskatchewan, and PhD from the University of Wisconsin at Madison. His scholarly articles have been published in *Accounting, Organizations and Society, The Journal of Cost Management,* and *Management Accounting.* He has also written a teaching case which has been published by the Institute of Management Accountants. Dr. Kalagnaman is a member of the American Accounting Association, American Society for Quality, Canadian Academic Accounting Association, and the Institute of Management Accountants, and is an associate member of the Society of Management Accountants of Saskatchewan. Dr. Kalagnaman has two children, Pallavi and Siddharth. His wife, Viji, is a homemaker and a part-time university student.

Marilyn Sagrillo is an associate professor at the University of Wisconsin – Green Bay. She received her BA and MS in Accounting from Northern Illinois University and her PhD from the University of Wisconsin – Madison. Her scholarly articles have been published in *Accounting Enquiries, Journal of Accounting Case Research,* and the *Missouri Society of CPAs Casebook.* She is a member of the American Accounting Association and the Institute of Management Accountants. In 1989 she received the UWGB Founder's Association Faculty Award for Excellence in Teaching. Professor Sagrillo is an active volunteer for the Midwest Renewable Energy Association, an organization devoted to promoting renewable energy and energy conservation. She also enjoys reading, traveling, and hiking.

Jeannie M. Folk teaches financial and managerial accounting at College of DuPage and mentors accounting students working in cooperative education positions. In addition, she is active in the area of online, distance education. Professor Folk serves on the Scholarship Committee of TACTYC (Teachers of Accounting at Two-Year Colleges) and the Illinois CPA Society's Outstanding Educator Award Committee. She is also a member of the American Accounting Association and the American Institute of Certified Public Accountants. She was honored with the Illinois CPA Society Outstanding Educator Award and was a recipient of the Women in Management, Inc., Charlotte Danstrom Woman of Achievement Award. Before entering academe, Professor Folk was a general practice auditor with Coopers & Lybrand (now PriceWaterhouseCoopers). She received her BBA from Loyola University Chicago and MAS in Accountancy from Northern Illinois University. Professor Folk enjoys travel, camping, hiking and community activities with her three children.

Carol Yacht received her MA in business and Economic Education from California State University, Los Angeles and BS in Business Education from the University of New Mexico. She is the author of McGraw-Hill/Irwin's *Computer Accounting with PeachTree for Microsoft Windows* books, and is a recognized expert in payroll accounting and reporting. She has worked as an educational consultant for IBM corporation, an accounting instructor at Yavapai College, and a business education department chair at Beverly Hills High School in California. She chairs the Distance Learning Committee of the Computer Education Task Force, National Business Education Association. Professor Yacht's son, Matthew, is completing his accounting degree at Northern Arizona University. Her husband, Brice Wood, is an artist and part owner of a fine arts gallery. She is active in community activities and chairs the Planning and Zoning Commission of her town.

Tarina Tarantino Designs Crea

CrosSWorlds

Tees on the Nose

Freeplay Netledger i-FRONTIER

Papa John's

Kate Spade

FUBU eBay

WWF JobDirect Sector 9 INCA

AltTUNES Red Hat Birdhouse

Wooden Ships of U

Wooden

orts

Brief Contents

Contents

Volume 1 Chapters 1–13

Fundamental Accounting Principles

Volume 1 Chapters 1–13

Fundamental Accounting Principles

1

Accounting in the Information Age

A Look at This Chapter

Accounting plays a crucial role in the information age. In this chapter, we discuss the importance of accounting to different types of organizations and describe its many users and uses. We see that ethics and social responsibility are crucial to accounting, and that the information age provides many new accounting opportunities.

A Look Ahead

Chapter 2 explains financial statements and the principles underlying them. It also describes and analyzes business transactions. More generally, Chapters 2 through 5 focus on the accounting cycle and show how financial statements reflect transactions and events.

Learning Objectives

Conceptual

C1 Explain the aim and influence of accounting in the information age.

C2 Identify forms of organizations and their characteristics.

C3 Identify and describe the three major activities in organizations.

C4 Identify users and uses of accounting.

C5 Explain why ethics and social responsibility are crucial to accounting.

C6 Identify opportunities in accounting and related fields.

Analytical

A1 Describe income and its two major components.

A2 Explain the relation between return and risk.

A3 Explain and interpret the accounting equation.

A4 Compute and interpret return on investment.

Procedural

P1 Identify and prepare basic financial statements.

Have Résumés, Will Travel

e STAMFORD, CT—Four years ago, 21-year-old college students Rachel Bell and Sara Sutton were in a Boston taxi "stressing" about finding jobs. Sutton was frustrated by her fruitless searches on the Net for openings. Bell remembered her father's advice: "You don't have to work for a company. You can start one yourself." Their idea was a Web-based service for job seekers. "We were so fired up and excited about the concept," Sutton recalls. "We could reach out to students like us, and we could help our friends."

Bell and Sutton's plans led to the launch of **JobDirect** (**www.JobDirect.com**). First, they raised $60,000 in financing from family and friends as start-up money. Then, Bell and Sutton invested in a school bus and hired graffiti artists to paint it to look like their Web site. They equipped the bus with 15 laptops for students to type in résumés and drove off on their first promotional tour of campuses. Forty-three campuses later, their database contained the résumés of 5,000 job seekers. "We knew it would work. There was just no way it couldn't," says Bell.

JobDirect's revenues exceeded $1.3 million for its first full year of service, all from fees paid by employers to use the service. Over 500 clients currently subscribe, including IBM, Charles Schwab, and Chase Manhattan. Students use JobDirect for free. It now has three graffiti-decorated buses, and they travel with the summer's H.O.R.D.E. music festival, where Blues Traveler fans can launch job searches. JobDirect was recently acquired by Korn/Ferry International, the world's largest executive recruitment firm.

Bell and Sutton marvel at the direction their careers have taken. "Rachel and I didn't expect to go into business," says Sutton. "We weren't techies." Yet they formed a company, managed business activities, and prepared, analyzed, and used accounting reports. Bell and Sutton admit it sometimes takes starting a company to see the importance of accounting in business. [Sources: *Business Week*, May 1998; *JobDirect Web Site*, March 2001.]

An opening vignette launches each chapter showing the relevance of accounting for a real entrepreneur.

Chapter Preview

Accounting in the information age is about people like Rachel Bell and Sara Sutton from the opening vignette. Today's world is one of information—its preparation, communication, analysis, and use. Accounting is at the heart of this information age. Knowledge of accounting gives us opportunities. It also gives us the insight to benefit from these opportunities. By studying this book, you will learn about concepts, procedures, and analyses that are useful in our everyday activities. This knowledge will help us make better financial decisions throughout our lives. In this chapter we describe accounting, the users and uses of accounting information, the forms and activities of organizations, and the importance of ethics and social responsibility. We also explain several important accounting principles. This chapter provides a foundation for those who have little or no understanding of business. Chapter 2 will build on this foundation when we consider business transactions.

A **Preview** opens each chapter with a summary of topics covered.

Information Age

Key **terms** are printed in bold and defined again in the end-of-chapter **glossary**.

We live in an **information age**—a time of communication, data, news, facts, access, and commentary. The information age encourages timeliness, independence, and freedom of expression. Access to and understanding of information affect how we live, whom we associate with, and the opportunities we have. We use information to pick and choose among products and services. Examples are product rankings (*Consumer Reports*), medical advice (*American Medical Association*), and credit ratings (*Standard & Poor's*).

Communication with others and access to data make up much of the *information superhighway*. The information superhighway has redefined communication, especially business communication. Global computer networks and telecommunications equipment allow us quick access to all types of business information. To fully benefit from this information, we need knowledge of the information system. An information system involves the collecting, processing, and reporting of information to decision makers. Knowledge of the information system means personal opportunities and real increases in pay. Studies show that two-year degree graduates with this knowledge can make upward of 30 to 40% more than high school graduates, and bachelor degree graduates can make at least 50 to 75% more than high school graduates. This added pay is for an ability to understand and process information.

Check out this book's Web site created especially for you.

Concept 1-1

C1 Explain the aim and influence of accounting in the information age.

Understanding and processing information is the core of accounting. To get the most from our education and opportunities in life, we must know accounting. Your instructor will provide you with many assignments from this book and related materials to help you master accounting. We also encourage you to join us on the information superhighway to explore the opportunities. For your help, we devote an entire Web site solely for your use with this book **[www.mhhe.com/FAP16e]**.

Influence of Accounting

One of the most important roles of the information superhighway is the reporting of business activities. Providing information about what businesses own, what they owe, and how they perform is the aim of accounting. **Accounting** is an information and measurement system that identifies, records, and communicates relevant, reliable, and comparable information about an organization's business activities. It helps us make better decisions, including assessing opportunities, products, investments, and social and community responsibilities.

Completing this course will help you apply information in a way you can use in your everyday life. The use of information is not limited to accountants or even to people in business. Often the greatest benefits from understanding accounting come to those outside of accounting and business. We can use accounting to get better terms for a loan, to start a business, and to make better investment decisions. We will use accounting knowledge in whatever career we choose.

Business and Investment

A **business** is one or more individuals selling products or services for profit. Products such as athletic apparel (**Nike, Reebok, Converse**), computers

(**Intel, Cisco, Apple**) and clothing (**Levis, Limited, Gap**) are part of our lives. Services such as information communication (**Yahoo!, Microsoft**), dining (**McDonald's, Wendy's**), and car rental (**Hertz, Budget, Alamo**) make our lives easier. A business can be as small as an at-home-Web service provider or as massive as **Wal-Mart.** Nearly 1 million new businesses are started in the United States each year, no different than **JobDirect** in the opening vignette. Most of these are started by people who want freedom from ordinary jobs, a new challenge in life, or the advantage of extra money.

Business Income

A common feature of all businesses is the desire for income. **Income,** also called **net income, profit** or **earnings,** is the amount a business earns after subtracting expenses from its sales. **Sales,** also called **revenues,** are the amounts earned from selling products and services. **Expenses** are the costs incurred with producing sales. For **JobDirect,** income is the amount earned from client fees less expenses such as travel, salaries, advertising, and promotion. Not all businesses make income. A **loss** arises when expenses are more than sales. Many new businesses incur losses in their first several months or years of business. **Amazon.com** is one example. No business can continually have losses, however, and survive.

A1 Describe income and its two major components.

Nike's income breakdown is in Exhibit 1.1. If we pay $100 for a pair of Nike athletic footwear, $6.44 is income to Nike. The rest goes to cover expenses such as materials and labor ($60.08) and advertising ($10.87). Nike also pays $3.78 in total taxes. One question confronting our society today is what is the "right" amount of profit. Also, should business pay more for charitable giving or community services? Are taxes too high or too low? For us to seriously consider important questions like these, we must understand accounting.

Return and Risk

Income is often linked to **return.** The term return derives from the idea of getting something back from an investment, referred to as a return on investment. **Return on investment** is commonly stated in ratio form as income divided by <u>amount invested</u>. For example, banks or savings and loans often report our return on investment from a savings account in the form of an interest return. For example, we might have a 4% savings account or invest our college money in an 8% money market fund.

We can invest our money in many ways. If we invest it in a savings account or in U.S. government treasury bills, we get a return of around 3% to 7%. We could also invest in a company's stock, or even start our own business. How do we decide among these investment options? The answer depends on our trade-off between return and risk.

Risk is the uncertainty about the return we expect to earn. All business decisions involve risk, but some decisions involve more than others. The lower the risk of an investment, the lower is our expected return. The reason that savings accounts pay such a low return is the low risk of our not being repaid with interest (the government guarantees most savings accounts from default). Similarly, U.S. government bonds pay a low return because of the low risk that the U.S. government will default on its

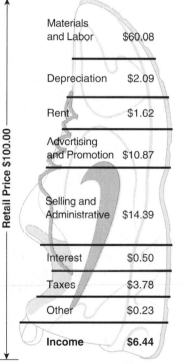

Retail Price $100.00	
Materials and Labor	$60.08
Depreciation	$2.09
Rent	$1.62
Advertising and Promotion	$10.87
Selling and Administrative	$14.39
Interest	$0.50
Taxes	$3.78
Other	$0.23
Income	**$6.44**

Exhibit 1.1
Where Our Money Goes When We Buy a Pair of Nikes

Did You Know? is a feature that highlights relevant items from practice.

Did You Know?

Celebrity Investment How do fame and fortune translate into return and risk? A poll asked people which celebrity is the best investment. Similar to business investments, people named performers with years of earning power ahead—see listing to the right.

Oprah Winfrey	27%
Steven Spielberg	19
Tiger Woods	15
Michael Jordan	14
Tom Cruise	8
Rosie O'Donnell	5
Jerry Seinfeld	4
Madonna	2

A2 Explain the relation between return and risk.

payments. If we buy a share of **Nike** or any other company we might obtain a large return, however, we have no guarantee of any return. There is even the risk of loss.

The bar graph in Exhibit 1.2 shows recent returns for bonds with different risks. **Bonds** are written promises by organizations to repay amounts loaned with interest. U.S. treasury bonds provide us a low expected return, but they also offer low risk since they are backed by the U.S. government. High-risk corporate bonds offer a much larger expected return but with much higher risk.

Exhibit 1.2

Returns for Bonds with Different Risks

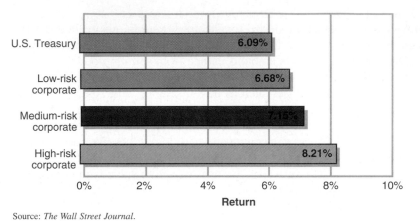

Source: *The Wall Street Journal.*

You Make the Call are role-playing exercises that stress the relevance of accounting for people in and outside of business.

You Make the Call

Programmer   You are considering two job offers. Both require your computer programming skills. One is with a new start-up Internet provider at an annual salary of $41,000; the other is with an established insurance company for $34,500 a year. Which offer do you accept? [*Answers are at the end of each chapter.*]

Answer—p. 23

Exhibit 1.3

Accounting Activities

Identifying and measuring

Recording

Reporting and analyzing

The trade-off between return and risk is a normal part of business. Higher risk implies higher, but riskier, expected returns. To help us make better decisions, we use accounting information to measure both return and risk.

Focus of Accounting

We need to guard against a narrow view of accounting. The most common contact with accounting is through credit approvals, checking accounts, tax forms, and payroll. These experiences are limited and tend to focus on the recordkeeping parts of accounting. **Recordkeeping,** or **bookkeeping,** is the recording of financial transactions and events, either manually or electronically. While recordkeeping is essential to data reliability, accounting is this and much more.

The primary objective of accounting is to provide useful information for decision making as shown in Exhibit 1.3. Accounting activities include identifying, measuring, recording, reporting, and analyzing business transactions and events. *Transactions* are exchanges between businesses. Examples are product sales, money lending, and payment of expenses. *Events* are incidents affecting a business's financial position. Examples are bankruptcies, labor strikes, and casualties. Accounting also involves interpreting information and designing information systems to provide useful reports that monitor and control a company's activities.

We benefit our careers by understanding how accounting information is prepared and used. To gain this understanding, we need to learn certain recordkeeping skills. This book provides these skills and the skills for us to read and interpret financial data.

Setting Accounting Rules

There are rules for reporting on a business's performance and financial condition. These rules increase the usefulness of reports, including their reliability and comparability. The rules are determined by many individuals and groups and are referred to as **generally accepted accounting principles,** or **GAAP.** Since accounting is a service activity, these rules reflect our society's needs, and not those of accountants or any other single constituency. Congress has charged the **Securities and Exchange Commission (SEC)** with the authority to set accounting rules for companies that issue stock to the public. For the most part, the SEC has passed authority to set accounting rules to the **Financial Accounting Standards Board (FASB).** Many interested groups and individuals lobby the FASB in their self-interests. They include unions, investors, government agencies, lenders, and politicians.

Global: Another important group in setting GAAP is the International Organization of Securities Commissions (IOSCO), a group of regulators representing about 90% of global financial markets.

Margin notes further enhance the textual material.

Accounting and Technology

Technology is a key part of modern business and plays a major role in accounting. Computing technology reduces the time, effort, and cost of recordkeeping while improving clerical accuracy. Some smaller organizations continue to perform various accounting tasks manually, but they are still impacted by information technology.

As technology has changed the way we store, process, and summarize large masses of data, accounting has been freed to expand its field. Consulting, planning, and other financial services are now part of accounting. These services require sorting through masses of data, interpreting their meaning, identifying key factors, and analyzing their implications. Technology is increasingly important in accounting information systems, and is encouraged by advances in computer technology, networks, and enterprise-application software.

Point: Computing technology is only as good as the accounting data available, and users' decisions are only as good as their understanding of accounting. The best software and recordkeeping cannot make up for lack of accounting knowledge.

Quick Check

1. What is the purpose of accounting?
2. Describe income, sales, and expenses.
3. Explain the trade-off between return and risk.
4. What is the relation between accounting and recordkeeping?
5. Who sets accounting rules?
6. Identify some advantages of technology for accounting.

Quick Checks offer a chance to stop and reflect on key points.

Answers—p. 23

Organizations can be classified as either business or nonbusiness as shown in Exhibit 1.4. Typically, businesses are organized for profit; nonbusinesses serve us in ways not always measured by profit.

Forms of Organization

C2 Identify forms of organization and their characteristics.

Exhibit 1.4
Forms of Organizations

Business   **Nonbusiness**

Proprietorship   Partnership   Corporation   Government   Nonprofit   Private

Nearly all organizations engage in some types of business activities. These can include the usual business activities of purchasing materials and labor and of selling products and services. They can also involve nonbusiness activities such as collecting money through taxes, dues, contributions, investments, or borrowings, and providing free services. A common feature in all organizations is the influence and use of accounting.

Business Organization

A business is organized and operated to make a profit. It can take one of three legal forms: *sole proprietorship, partnership,* or *corporation.* Exhibit 1.5 shows the proportion of these different forms in business today.

Sole Proprietorship

A **sole proprietorship,** or simply **proprietorship,** is a business owned by one person. No special legal requirements must be met to start a proprietorship. It is a separate entity for accounting purposes, but it is *not* a separate legal entity from its owner. This means, for example, that a court can order an owner to sell personal belongings to pay a proprietorship's debt. An owner is even responsible for debts that exceed an owner's net investment in the proprietorship. This *unlimited liability* of a proprietorship is sometimes a disadvantage.

Tax authorities do not separate a proprietorship from its owner. This means the income of a proprietorship is not subject to a business income tax but is reported and taxed on the owner's personal income tax return. The rate of tax on a proprietorship's income depends on the level of total income from all sources that the owner had for the year. Proprietorships are by far the most common form of business organization in our society. Its characteristics are summarized in Exhibit 1.6.

Partnership

A **partnership** is a business owned by two or more people, called *partners.* Like a proprietorship, no special legal requirements must be met in starting a partnership. The only requirement is an agreement between partners to run a business together. The agreement can be either oral or written and usually indicates how income and losses are shared. A written agreement is preferred because it can help partners avoid or resolve disputes. A partnership, like a proprietorship, is *not* legally separate from its owners. This means that each partner's share of profits is reported and taxed on that partner's tax return. It also means *unlimited liability* for its partners.

Two types of partnerships limit liability. A *limited partnership* includes a general partner(s) with unlimited liability and a limited partner(s) with liability restricted to the amount invested. A *limited liability partnership* restricts partners' liabilities to their own acts and the acts of individuals under their control. This protects an innocent partner from the neg-

Exhibit 1.5

Different Forms of Businesses

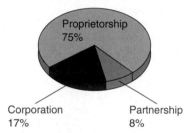

Proprietorship 75%

Corporation 17%

Partnership 8%

Source: *Statistical Abstract of the United States.*

Point: Boston Celtics Limited Partnership (BCLP) directs Celtic basketball. It has 2,703,664 ownership units. Based on recent transactions, each unit is worth about $11 to $12.

Point: Sole proprietorships and partnerships are usually managed on a regular basis by their owners. In a corporation, the owners (shareholders) elect a board of directors who appoint managers to run the business.

Exhibit 1.6

Characteristics of Businesses

Characteristic	Proprietorship	Partnership	Corporation
Business entity	yes	yes	yes
Legal entity	no	no	yes
Limited liability	no	no	yes
Unlimited life	no	no	yes
Business taxed	no	no	yes
One owner allowed	yes	no	yes

ligence of another partner. Yet all partners remain responsible for partnership debts.[1] **Nike** began as an entrepreneurial partnership and was originally called **Blue Ribbon Sports.** The partners, Philip Knight and Bill Bowerman, each contributed $500 and shipped shoes out of Knight's basement. They represent one of many entrepreneurial success stories.

Corporation

A **corporation** is a business legally separate from its owners, meaning it is responsible for its own acts and its own debts. It can enter into contracts, and it can buy, own, and sell property. It can also sue and be sued. Separate legal status means that a corporation can conduct business with the rights, duties, and responsibilities of a person. A corporation acts through its managers, who are its legal agents. Separate legal status also means that its owners, who are called **shareholders** (or **stockholders**), are not personally liable for corporate acts and debts. Shareholders are legally distinct from the business, and their loss is limited to their net investment in purchased shares. This limited liability lowers shareholder risk and is a key reason that corporations can raise resources from shareholders. It also encourages riskier investment with higher expected returns.

A corporation is legally chartered (*incorporated*) under state or federal law. Separate legal status results in a corporation having unlimited life. Ownership, or *equity,* of all corporations is divided into units called **shares** or **stock.** A shareholder can sell or transfer shares to another person without affecting the operations of a corporation. When a corporation issues only one class of stock, we call it **common stock** (or *capital stock*).

A corporation is subject to *double taxation.* This means that it is taxed on its net income, and any distribution of corporate income to its owners (through dividends) is also taxed as part of their personal income. An exception to this is an *S corporation*, a corporation with certain characteristics that give it special tax status. This special tax status removes its double taxation. Shareholders of S corporations report their share of corporate income or loss as part of their personal income.

Real company documents are often shown to enhance learning.

Nonbusiness Organization

Nonbusiness organizations plan and operate for goals other than profit. These goals include security, health, education, transportation, judicial, religious, cultural, and social. A list of nonbusiness organizations often includes museums, libraries, fraternities, utilities, roadways, hospitals, shelters, prisons, churches, parks, schools, transportation, security, and airports. Roughly one-third of U.S. business activity is done by nonbusiness organizations. Some of these organizations, such as hospitals, can operate as private, nonprofit, or government operations.

Nonbusiness organizations lack an identifiable owner. Still, the demand for accounting information in nonbusiness organizations is high because they are accountable to their sponsors. Sponsors include taxpayers, donors, lenders, legislators, regulators, or other constituents. Accounting for these organizations usually follows a *fund-based* system, but the basic principles are similar to accounting for business organizations. In all of these organizations, accounting captures and reports key information about their activities.

You Make the Call—Ethics are role-playing exercises that stress ethics in accounting and business.

You Make the Call—Ethics   *e*

Entrepreneur   You and a friend develop a new design for in-line skates that improves speed and performance by 25% to 40%. You plan to form a business to manufacture and market these skates. You and your friend want to minimize taxes, but your prime concern is potential lawsuits from individuals who might be injured on these skates. What form of organization do you set up?

Answer—p. 23

---

[1] **Limited liability companies (LLCs)** are usually organized as a form of partnership (they can also be set up for a proprietorship). LLCs represent the fastest growing form of business organization, which has led to a renewed interest in accounting for partnerships. LLCs offer the limited liability of a corporation and the tax treatment of a partnership (or proprietorship). Chapter 13 describes LLCs in more detail.

Activities in Organizations

C3 Identify and describe the three major activities in organizations.

Organizations carry out their activities in many different ways. These differences extend to their products, services, goals, organization form, management style, worker compensation, and community giving, yet the major activities of organizations are similar. We discuss the three major types of business activities: financing, investing, and operating. Each of these activities requires planning, and it is discussed first.

Planning

All organizations begin with planning. **Planning** involves defining an organization's ideas, goals, and actions. Strategies and tactics must be laid out. Employees must be informed and motivated. Managers must be credible and display leadership and vision. All of these tasks are part of planning and are the duties of *executive management*. Executive management sets the organization's strategic goals and policies that are captured in an *organization plan*. The owner(s) leads executive management in most organizations. This responsibility often carries with it the title of president, chief executive officer, or chairman of the board of directors. In nonprofit organizations the title for the top manager often is executive director.

Point: Management must understand accounting data to set financial goals, make financing and investing decisions, and evaluate operating performance.

External parties benefit from knowledge of an organization's plans. They look for clues on tactics, market demands, competitors, promotion, pricing, innovations, and projections. Much of this information appears in accounting reports. Most public corporations use the *Management Discussion and Analysis* section in their annual reports for this purpose. For example, **Nike** declares in its annual report that "management believes there is tremendous opportunity for growth in markets outside the United States. The Company continues to invest in infrastructure and local marketing and advertising to capitalize on these opportunities." Planning also involves change and reaction to it. It is not cast in stone. This adds *risk* to both the setting of an organization's plans and analysis of them. Accounting information can reduce this risk with more informed analysis and decision making.

Financing

An organization requires financing to begin and operate according to its plans. **Financing activities** are the means organizations use to pay for resources such as land, buildings, and equipment to carry out plans. Organizations are careful in acquiring and managing financing activities because of their potential to determine success or failure.

The two main sources of financing are owner and nonowner. *Owner financing* refers to resources contributed by the owner along with any income the owner chooses to leave in the organization. *Nonowner* (or *creditor*) *financing* refers to resources contributed by creditors (lenders). Creditors often include banks, savings and loans, and other financial institutions. *Financial management* is the task of planning how to obtain these resources and to set the right mix between the amounts of owner and creditor financing. **Nike**'s total financing at May 31, 2000, equaled $5,856.9 million. It comprised $3,136.0 million in owner financing and $2,720.9 million in creditor financing.

Investing

Real company names are printed in red when referred to in the text.

A3 Explain and interpret the accounting equation.

Investing activities are the acquiring and disposing of resources (assets) that an organization uses to acquire and sell its products or services. **Assets** are resources that are expected to possess current and future benefits and are funded by an organization's financing. Assets include land, buildings, equipment, inventories, supplies, cash, and all investments needed for operating an organization. **Nike**'s assets, at May 31, 2000, totaled $5,856.9 million. Organizations differ on the amount and makeup of their assets. Some organizations require land and factories to operate. Others might need only an office. Determining the amount and type of assets for operations is called *asset management*.

The concept that an organization's investing and financing totals are *always* equal is important. Invested amounts are referred to as *assets,* and financing is made up of creditor and owner financing. This implies creditors and owners hold claims on assets. Creditors' claims are called **liabilities** and the owner's claim is called **owner's equity** (or simply *equity*). This equality can be written as follows:

$$\text{Assets} = \text{Liabilities} + \text{Equity}$$

This equality is called the **accounting equation.** At May 31, 2000, **Nike**'s assets of $5,856.9 equal its liabilities of $2,720.9 plus its equity of $3,136.0 (in millions):

$$\text{Assets} = \text{Liabilities} + \text{Equity}$$
$$\$5,856.9 = \$2,720.9 + \$3,136.0$$

The accounting equation works for all organizations at all times. It is an important part of accounting. We will return to and use the accounting equation in our analysis of transactions throughout the book.

Operating

An organization's main purpose is to carry out operating activities. **Operating activities** involve using resources to research, develop, purchase, produce, distribute, and market products and services. They also include management activities such as worker supervision and compliance with laws. Sales are the inflow of assets from selling products and services. Costs and expenses are the outflow of assets to support operating activities. Examples of costs and expenses are salaries, rent, electricity, and supplies. *Strategic management* is the process of determining the right mix of operating activities for the type of organization, its plans, and its market. How well an organization carries out its operating activities determines its success and return.

Exhibit 1.7 summarizes these activities. Planning is part of each activity, and gives the activities meaning and focus. Investing (assets) and financing (liabilities and equity) are set opposite each other to stress their balance. Operating activities are shown below investing and financing activities to emphasize that operating activities are the result of investing and financing.

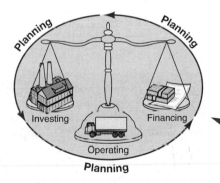

Exhibit 1.7
Activities in Organizations

Infographics reinforce key concepts through visual learning.

Quick Check
7. What are the three basic forms of business organization?
8. What are examples of nonbusiness organizations?
9. What are the three major activities in organizations?

Answers—p. 23

Four basic financial statements report on an organization's activities: balance sheet, income statement, statement of changes in owner's (or shareholders') equity, and statement of cash flows. This section introduces us to each of these statements using **Nike**'s data. We cover details of each statement in later chapters.

Financial Statements

Balance Sheet

A balance sheet reports on investing and financing. It lists amounts for assets, liabilities, and equity at a *point in time*. The balance sheet for **Nike** is shown in Exhibit 1.8. Its accounting (fiscal) year ends on May 31. Nike's numbers are all in millions, meaning we must multiply its numbers by 1 million to get actual amounts. Nike's assets total $5,856.9 and is the amount invested. Its liabilities are $2,720.9, and its equity is $3,136.0—their sum equals total financing.

Exhibit 1.8

Balance Sheet

NIKE Balance Sheet (in millions) May 31, 2000			
Assets	$5,856.9	Liabilities	$2,720.9
		Equity	3,136.0
Total assets	$5,856.9	Total liabilities and equity	$5,856.9

Exhibit 1.9

Income Statement

NIKE Income Statement (in millions) For Year Ended May 31, 2000	
Revenues	$8,995.1
Costs and expenses	8,416.0
Net income	$ 579.1

Income Statement

An income statement reports on operating activities. It lists amounts for sales (revenues) less all costs and expenses over a *period of time*. This yields the "bottom line" net income amount. **Nike**'s income statement is shown in Exhibit 1.9. Net income is $579.1 and is computed as revenues of $8,995.1 less its costs and expenses of $8,416.0 (in millions).

Statement of Changes in Owner's Equity

A statement of changes in owner's equity reports changes in the owner's claim on the business's assets over a *period of time*. This includes changes due to income and any owner contributions and withdrawals. Since **Nike** is a corporation, its owners are called *shareholders*. The statement of changes in shareholders' equity for Nike is shown in Exhibit 1.10. Two major items affecting Nike's equity are its net income of $579.1 and withdrawals (dividends) of $131.5.

Exhibit 1.10

Statement of Changes in Owner's (Shareholders') Equity

NIKE Statement of Changes in Owner's (Shareholders') Equity (in millions) For Year Ended May 31, 2000	
Equity, May 31, 1999	$3,334.6
Add: Net income	579.1
Less: Withdrawals (dividends)	(131.5)
Other changes	(646.2)
Equity, May 31, 2000	$3,136.0

Statement of Cash Flows

The statement of cash flows reports on cash flows for operating, investing, and financing activities over a *period of time*. **Nike**'s statement of cash flows is shown in Exhibit 1.11. Its cash balance increased by $56.2. Of this increase in cash, Nike's operating activities provided $759.9 in cash, its investing activities used $440.0, and its financing activities (including exchange rate changes) used $263.7.

Exhibit 1.11

Statement of Cash Flows

NIKE Statement of Cash Flows (in millions) For Year Ended May 31, 2000	
Cash from operating activities	$759.9
Cash from investing activities	(440.0)
Cash from financing activities	(263.7)
Net increase in cash	$ 56.2

Organizations set up accounting information systems to help them and others make better decisions. Every organization uses some type of information system to report on its activities. Exhibit 1.12 shows that the accounting information system serves many kinds of users including managers, lenders, suppliers, customers, directors, auditors, employees, and current and potential investors.

External Information Users

External users of accounting information are *not* directly involved in running the organization. They include shareholders, lenders, directors, customers, suppliers, regulators, lawyers, brokers, and the press. External users rely on accounting information to make better decisions. For example, lenders are less likely to make bad loans and shareholders bad investments when they know the current and past income of a business.

Users of Accounting Information

 Identify users and uses of accounting.

Internal users

External users

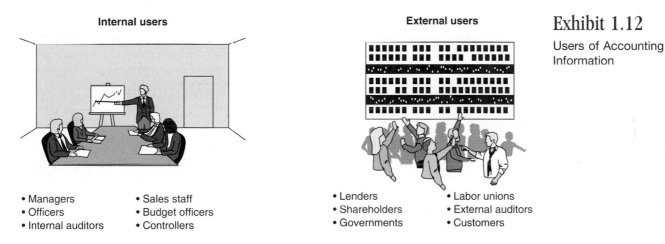

- Managers
- Officers
- Internal auditors
- Sales staff
- Budget officers
- Controllers

- Lenders
- Shareholders
- Governments
- Labor unions
- External auditors
- Customers

Exhibit 1.12

Users of Accounting Information

Financial accounting is the area of accounting aimed at serving external users. Its main objective is to provide financial statements to help users analyze an organization's activities. External users have limited access to an organization's information. Their success depends on financial statements that are reliable, relevant, and comparable. Some governmental and regulatory agencies have the power to require statements in specific forms, but most external users must rely on *general-purpose financial statements*. The phrase *general-purpose* refers to the broad range of purposes for which external users rely on these statements.

Each external user has special information needs depending on the types of decisions to be made. These decisions involve getting answers to key questions, answers that are often available in accounting reports. This section describes several external users and questions they ask.

Point: EDGAR is a database of documents that public companies file electronically with the SEC. Several Web sites offer easy-to-use interfaces (most are free), making it a snap to find most public info on a company—see www.freeedgar.com, www.edgar-online.com, or edgarscan.tc.pw.com.

Lenders (Creditors)

Lenders loan money or other resources to an organization. They include banks, savings and loans, co-ops, and mortgage and finance companies. Lenders look for information to help them assess whether an organization is likely to repay its loans with interest. Financial statements help them answer questions about an organization such as:

- ■ Has it promptly paid past loans?
- ■ What are its current risks?
- ■ Can it repay current loans?
- ■ What is its income outlook?

The questions can also change for short- and long-term lending decisions. The more long-term a loan, the more a lender's questions look like those of an owner.

Shareholders (Owners)

Shareholders have legal control over part or all of a corporation. They are its owners and in many cases are not part of management. Owners are exposed to the greatest return and risk. Risk is high because there is no promise of either repayment or a return on investment. They can lose their entire investment. On the upside, owners have a claim on assets after a business pays its debts. Many businesses do not return income to owners but instead invests it in company growth. Financial statements aim to help answer shareholder (owner) questions such as these:

- What is current and past income?
- Are assets adequate to meet plans?
- Do expenses seem reasonable?
- Do customers pay bills promptly?
- Do loan amounts seem too high?

Real company logos often accompany references to actual financial data.

Shareholders typically elect a board of directors to oversee their interests in an organization. Since directors are responsible to shareholders, their questions are similar.

External Auditors

External (independent) auditors examine financial statements and provide an opinion on whether the statements are prepared according to generally accepted accounting principles. Auditors use financial statements of competing organizations to help assess the reasonableness of a client's statements. **Nike**'s auditor is **PricewaterhouseCoopers LLP.**

Employees

Employees have a special interest in an organization. They are interested in judging the fairness of wages and in assessing future job prospects. Financial statements provide information useful in addressing these interests. They are also used in bargaining for better wages when an organization is successful.

Regulators

Regulators often have legal authority or significant influence over the activities of organizations. The Internal Revenue Service (IRS) and other tax authorities require organizations to use specific reports in computing taxes. These taxes include income, unemployment, sales, and social security. Tax reports usually require special forms and supporting records. Examples of other regulators include utility boards that use accounting information to set utility rates and securities regulators that require special filings for businesses with publicly traded securities.

Other Important External Users

Accounting serves the needs of many other important external users. Voters, legislators, and elected officials use accounting information to monitor and evaluate a government's receipts and expenses. Contributors to nonprofit organizations use accounting information to evaluate the use and impact of their donations. Suppliers use accounting information to judge the soundness of a customer before making sales on credit. Customers use financial reports to assess the staying power of potential suppliers.

Internal Information Users

Internal users of accounting information are individuals directly involved in managing and operating an organization. The internal role of accounting is to provide information to help improve the efficiency and effectiveness of an organization in delivering products and services.

Managerial accounting is the area of accounting aimed at serving the decision-making needs of internal users. It provides internal reports to help internal users improve an organization's activities. Internal reports are not subject to the same rules as external reports because decisions of internal users are not constrained by the need to keep certain information private due to competitive concerns. Costs to prepare internal reports usually represent the only constraint on internal reporting. Internal reports aim to answer questions such as these:

- What are costs per product?
- What service mix is most profitable?
- Are sales sufficient to break even?
- Which activities are most profitable?
- What costs vary with sales?

Information to help answer these questions is important for success.

Exhibit 1.13 shows seven internal operating functions common to most organizations: research and development, purchasing, human resources, production, distribution, marketing, and servicing. Accounting is essential to the operation of each function. Each unit often has its own internal user (manager) who makes decisions. Depending on the type of business, not all of these functions may be necessary (or some may be combined). For example, publishing companies usually do not require separate research and development units, and banks do not require production units. We briefly describe the information needs of each function:

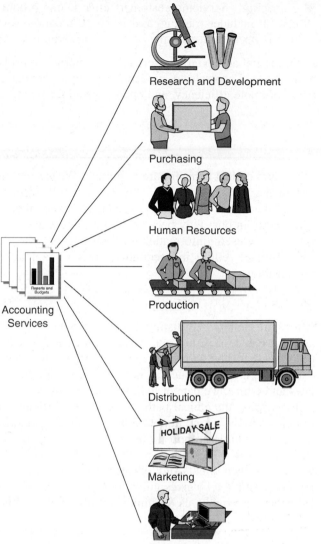

Exhibit 1.13
Internal Operating Functions

Research and Development

Purchasing

Human Resources

Production

Distribution

Marketing

Servicing

Accounting Services

- **Research and development** Research and development seeks to create or improve products and services. Managers need information about current and projected costs and sales.
- **Purchasing** Purchasing involves acquiring and managing materials for operations. Managers need to know what, when, and how much to purchase.
- **Human resources** Human resources management locates, screens, hires, trains, compensates, promotes, and counsels employees. Managers need information about current and potential employees, payroll, benefits, performance, and compensation.
- **Production** Production is the mix of activities to produce products and services. Good production methods depend on information to monitor costs and ensure quality.
- **Distribution** Distribution involves timely and accurate delivery of products and services. Information is often key to quality, low-cost distribution.
- **Marketing** Marketing promotes and advertises products and services. Marketing managers use reports about sales and costs to target consumers, set prices, and monitor consumer needs, tastes, and price concerns.

Point: There are 3 different types of businesses: (1) Services—provide services for profit, (2) Merchandisers—buy products and sell them for profit, and (3) Manufacturers—create products and sell them for profit.

■ **Servicing**   Servicing customers after selling products and services is often key to success. It includes training, assistance, installation, warranties, and maintenance. Information is needed on both the costs and benefits of servicing.

Both internal and external users rely on internal controls to monitor and control these functions. Internal controls are procedures set up to protect assets, ensure reliable accounting reports, promote efficiency, and encourage adherence to company policies.

Ethics and Social Responsibility

C5 Explain why ethics and social responsibility are crucial to accounting.

Ethics and ethical behavior are important. We are reminded of this when we run across stories in the media about cheating, harassment, misconduct, bribery, or when we witness wrongful actions. This section explains ethics and their effect on organizations. We consider ethics early in our study because of their importance to accounting. The goal of accounting is to provide useful information for decisions. For information to be useful, it must be trusted. This demands ethics in accounting. This section also discusses social responsibility for organizations.

Understanding Ethics

Ethics are beliefs that distinguish right from wrong. They are accepted standards of good and bad behavior. Ethics and laws often coincide, with the result that many unethical actions (such as theft and physical violence) are also illegal. Yet other actions are legal but are considered unethical, such as not helping people in need. Because of differences between laws and ethics, we cannot look to laws to always keep people ethical.

Point: AICPAs *Code of Professional Conduct* is available at www.AICPA.org.

Identifying the ethical path is sometimes difficult. The preferred path is a course of action that avoids casting doubt on our decision. For example, accounting users are less likely to trust an auditor's report if the auditor's pay depends on the success of the client. To avoid such concerns, ethics rules are often set. For example, auditors are banned from direct investment in their client. Auditors also cannot accept pay that depends on figures in the client's reports. Exhibit 1.14 gives guidelines for making ethical decisions. A commitment to ethical behavior requires us to think carefully before we act to be certain we are making ethical decisions.

Exhibit 1.14

Guidelines for Ethical Decision Making

Identify ethical concerns

Use personal ethics to recognize an ethical concern.

Analyze options

Consider all good and bad consequences.

Make ethical decision

Choose best option after weighing all consequences.

Organizational Ethics

Organizational ethics are likely learned through example and leadership. Companies such as **McDonald's, Marriott,** and **IBM** work hard to instill ethics in employees, yet we still hear people express concern about what they see as poor ethics in organizations. One survey of executives, educators, and legislators showed that 9 of 10 participants believe organizations are troubled by ethical problems. Yet this survey also revealed that the vast majority of participants believe organizations that are successful over the long run follow high ethical standards. This finding confirms an old saying: *Good ethics are good business*. Ethical practices build trust, which promotes loyalty and long-term relationships with customers, suppliers, and employees. Because of this and the public interest in ethics, many organizations have their own code of ethics. These codes set standards for internal activities and external relationships.

Accounting Ethics

Ethics are crucial in accounting. Providers of accounting information often face ethical choices as they prepare financial reports. Their choices can affect both the use and receipt of money, including taxes owed and the money dispersed to owners. They can affect the price a buyer pays and the wages paid to workers. They can even affect the success of products, services, and divisions. Misleading information can lead to a wrongful closing of a division that harms workers, customers, and suppliers. Accordingly, codes of accounting ethics are set up and enforced. These codes include those of the American Institute of Certified Public Accountants and the Institute of Management Accountants. These codes can help when confronted with ethical dilemmas. For example, organizations often pay managers bonuses based on the amount of income reported. Managers can benefit from applying accounting in ways to increase their pay. This can reduce the money available for employee wages, training programs, and community giving. Ethics codes also can help in dealing with confidential information. For example, auditors have access to an organization's confidential salaries and strategies. Organizations can be harmed if auditors pass this information to others. To prevent this, auditors' ethics codes require them to keep this information confidential. Internal accountants also are not to use confidential information for personal gain.

Social Responsibility

Social responsibility refers to a concern for the impact of actions on society. Organizations are increasingly concerned with their social responsibility. **Reebok** proclaims in its annual report: "We have a deep-felt commitment to operate in a socially responsible way and we stand for human rights throughout the world." Society has increased the pressure on organizations to act responsibly, and they have responded to this challenge.

An organization's social responsibility can include donations to hospitals, colleges, community programs, and law enforcement. It also can include programs to reduce pollution, increase product safety, improve worker conditions, support continuing education, and better use our natural resources. Yet most organizations are more likely to invest in their own social programs. For example, **Nike** invests in its *P.L.A.Y.* (*Participate in the Lives of America's Youth*) program that provides facilities for kids to pursue fitness and fun. **Xerox** offers its workers up to a one-year leave to work for a nonprofit organization. During their leaves, the workers receive full salary and benefits. We are aware of well over 1,000 businesses that offer social programs to their employees to pursue community service activities. These programs are not limited to large companies. For example, many independently owned theaters and sports businesses offer discounts to students and senior citizens. Still others help sponsor events such as the Special Olympics and summer reading programs with the local library.

Did You Know?

Returns on Social Responsibility   Virtue is not always its own reward. Compare the **S&P 500,** which includes companies selling weapons, alcohol, and tobacco, with the **Domini Social Index (DSI),** which covers 400 companies that have especially good records of social responsibility. Notice that returns for companies with socially responsible behavior are at least as high if not higher than those of the S&P 500.

Point: Paul Newman donates all income from sale of his *Newman's Own* products to charity.

Support for social programs by organizations is not universal. Some argue that an organization's interests might be different from those of its workers and customers. It is sometimes argued that an organization should instead increase pay to its workers so that they can contribute to their own community's concerns. While debate about the charitable giving of organizations will continue, social responsibility is part of modern business.

Quick Check

10. Who are the internal and external users of accounting information?

11. Identify seven internal operating functions in organizations.

12. Why are internal controls important?

13. What are the guidelines in helping us make ethical decisions?

14. Why are ethics and social responsibility valuable to organizations?

15. Why are ethics crucial in accounting?

Answers—p. 23

Opportunities in Practice

C6 Identify opportunities in accounting and related fields.

Accounting information affects many aspects of our lives. When we earn money, pay taxes, invest savings, budget earnings, and plan for the future, we are influenced by accounting. Accounting knowledge helps us better perform and compete in society. This section discusses four areas of opportunities in accounting: financial, managerial, taxation, and accounting-related. Exhibit 1.15 lists selected opportunities in each area. These areas employ millions of individuals in accounting or accounting-related careers.

Exhibit 1.15

Opportunities in Practice

Financial Accounting

Financial accounting provides information to decision makers that are external to an organization. This information is normally in the form of general-purpose financial statements. The process of preparing financial statements demands the input of many individuals within and outside accounting. There is also a demand for auditing in financial accounting. An **audit** is a check of an organization's accounting systems and records using various tests. It increases the credibility of financial statements. When an audit is complete, an auditor writes an *audit report* expressing a professional *opinion* about whether the financial statements are fairly presented. It is an opinion because an auditor does not verify every transaction and event. **Nike**'s audit report is in Appendix A.

Managerial Accounting

Managerial accounting provides information to an organization's internal decision makers. Managerial accounting activities generally fall within one of five areas:

1. *General accounting* refers to the recording of transactions, the processing of data, and the preparing of reports for internal use. It is supervised by a chief accounting officer called a *controller*.
2. *Cost accounting* is a process of accumulating the information managers need to identify, measure, and control costs. It involves accounting for the costs of products and services and is useful for evaluating managerial performance.
3. *Budgeting* is the development of formal plans for an organization's future activities. It provides a basis for evaluating actual performance.
4. *Internal auditing* adds credibility to reports that are produced and used within the organization. Internal auditors assess the effectiveness and efficiency of established operating procedures.
5. *Management consulting* helps organizations design and install new accounting and control systems, develop budgeting procedures, and set up employee benefit plans.

Point: Accounting offers many career opportunities that are both challenging and rewarding and that require strong interpersonal and communication skills.

Tax Accounting

Taxes raised by federal, state, and local governments include those based on income reported by taxpayers. *Tax accounting* helps taxpayers comply with the law by preparing tax returns. It also plans future transactions to minimize taxes. The Internal Revenue Service is a major employer of tax services. It is responsible for collecting federal taxes and enforcing tax law.

Point: The Internal Revenue Code is complex. As a result, it is often less costly for small companies to pay accountants to do their tax work than to develop the necessary expertise among their employees.

Accounting Specialization

The majority of accounting professionals work in **private accounting** as shown in Exhibit 1.16. A large company can employ 100 or more accounting professionals, but most have fewer. Another large number of accounting professionals are employed in **public accounting** whose services are available to the public. Many in public accounting are self-employed; others work for public accounting firms whose employees number from few to several thousand. Another large number of accounting professionals work in nonbusiness organizations, with many of these in federal, state, or local government. *Government accountants* perform accounting services for government units, including business regulation and investigation of law violations.

Accounting specialists are highly regarded. Their professional standing often is denoted by a certificate. Certified Public Accountants (CPAs) must meet education and experience requirements, pass the CPA examination, and exhibit ethical character. Most states require a college degree with the equivalent of a major in accounting. The CPA examination covers topics in financial and managerial accounting, taxation, auditing, and business law. Many accounting specialists hold certificates in addition to or instead of the CPA license. Two of the most common are the Certificate in Management Accounting (CMA) and the Certified Internal Auditor (CIA). Holders of these certificates must meet examination, education, and experience requirements similar to those of a CPA. The CMA is awarded by the Institute of Management Accountants and the CIA is granted by the Institute of Internal Auditors. Another prestigious certificate is the Chartered Financial Analyst (CFA) awarded by the Association for Investment Management and

Accounting Jobs by Area

- Private accounting 60%
- Public accounting 25%
- Government accounting 12%
- Accounting education 3%

Exhibit 1.16

Accounting Jobs by Area

Point: Many states accept graduate study in accounting as a substitute for experience in meeting CPA requirements.

Research (AIMR). Employers also look for specialists with designations such as certified bookkeeper (CB), certified payroll professional (CPP), and personal financial specialist (PFS).

Accounting-Related Opportunities

Accounting-related opportunities are vast. Accounting is the common language of modern business communications. It spans professions, continents, and economies. Exhibit 1.15 listed several accounting-related opportunities, including lenders, consultants, analysts, and planners. Less traditional ones include community activist, political consultant, reporter, salesperson, union official, entrepreneur, programmer, and engineer.

Outlook and Compensation

Point: The firm of Ernst & Young gives its interns a vacation at Disney World.

Employers are desperately seeking to hire individuals with accounting knowledge. Beyond the usual accounting work, however, employers want these individuals to help with financial analysis, strategic planning, e-commerce, product feasibility, information technology, and financial management. Demand is so great that many employers are offering signing bonuses along with stock options, profit sharing, and performance bonuses. Benefit packages often include flexible work schedules, telecommuting options, career path options, casual work environments, extended vacation time, and child and elder care. Employers are also offering options to full-time work, including temporary employment and project work.

Point: For updated salary information, check out
www.accountemps.com
www.aicpa.org
www.abbott-langer.com
www.experienceondemand.com
www.mamag.com/strategicfinance

Intense demand for accounting specialists led the American Institute of Certified Public Accountants (AICPA) to send career information to thousands of high schools. Demand for accounting specialists is also boosting salaries. Exhibit 1.17 reports average starting salaries for several accounting positions. Note that for each position, salary variation depends on location, company size, professional designation, expertise, experience, and other factors. For example, salaries for chief financial officers range from under $75,000 to more than $500,000 per year. Likewise, salaries for bookkeepers range from under $28,000 to more than $45,000.

Exhibit 1.17

Accounting Salaries

Title (experience)	2000 Salary	2005 Estimate*
Public Accounting		
Partner	$121,000	$155,000
Manager	66,500	82,000
Senior	45,500	59,000
Staff (1–3 years)	39,000	48,000
Entry (0–1 years)	34,000	43,500
Private Accounting		
CFO/Treasurer	149,000	185,500
Controller	111,000	144,000
Asst. treasurer/Controller	70,000	87,500
Manager	64,000	80,000
Senior	46,000	60,000
Staff (1–3 years)	39,000	49,000
Entry (0–1 years)	33,500	42,500
Bookkeeping		
Full-charge bookkeeper	38,000	47,500
Payroll manager	35,000	44,500
Accounts manager	34,500	44,000
Assistant bookkeeper	30,500	38,500
Accounting clerk	26,500	34,500

* Estimates assume a 5% compounded annual increase over current levels; these estimates are likely low since the National Association of Colleges and Employers reported an 8.8% increase in starting pay of accounting graduates for 2000 alone.

Using The Information (a section at the end of each chapter) introduces and explains important ratios and tools helpful in decision making. It illustrates these using real company data.

Return on Investment   Using the Information

We introduced return on investment in assessing return and risk earlier in the chapter. Return on investment is also useful in evaluating management, analyzing and forecasting profits, and planning activities. **Dell Computer** has its marketing department compute return on investment for *every* mailing. Dell's chief financial officer says it spent over a year teaching its workers how to apply return on investment. This section describes return on investment and how it can help us with financial analysis. **Return on investment (ROI),** also called *return on assets (ROA),* is viewed as an indicator of operating efficiency and is defined in Exhibit 1.18.

 Compute and interpret return on investment.

$$\text{Return on investment} = \frac{\text{Net income}}{\text{Average total assets}}$$

Exhibit 1.18

Return on Investment

Net income is usually taken from the annual income statement.[2] The average total assets figure is usually computed by adding the beginning and ending amounts of total assets for that same period and dividing by 2. To illustrate, let's look at Nike. Nike reports net income of $579.1 million in 2000. At the beginning of 2000, its total assets are $5,247.7 million and at the end of 2000 they total $5,856.9 million. Nike's return on investment for 2000 is:

$$\text{Return on investment} = \frac{\$579.1 \text{ mil.}}{(\$5,247.7 \text{ mil.} + \$5,856.9 \text{ mil.})/2} = 10.4\%$$

5552.3

Is a 10.4% return on investment good or bad for Nike? To help answer this question and others like it, we can compare (benchmark) Nike's return on investment with its prior performance, the returns of similar companies (such as **Reebok, Converse, Skechers,** and **Vans**), and the returns from alternative investments. Nike's return on investment for each of the prior five years is reported in the second column of Exhibit 1.19, which ranges from 7.4% to 17.1%. These returns suggest a recent decline with Nike's efficiency in using its assets. We can also compare Nike to a similar company such as Reebok, whose return on investment is shown in the third column of Exhibit 1.19. In four of the five years shown, Nike's return exceeds Reebok's, and its average return is higher for this period. We can also

	Return on Investment		
Fiscal Year	**Nike**	**Reebok**	**Industry**
2000	10.4%	0.7%	1.4%
1999	8.5	1.4	1.8
1998	7.4	7.7	3.7
1997	17.1	8.1	5.9
1996	15.6	10.0	8.6

Exhibit 1.19

Nike, Reebok, and Industry Returns

[2] For a noncorporation, the owner's effort on its behalf is not a recordable expense. This is because a noncorporation is not legally separate from its owner(s). Therefore, for a noncorporation, we compute a *modified return on investment* ratio that reduces net income by the value of the owner's effort (if any) as follows:

$$\text{Modified return on investment} = \frac{\text{Net income} - \text{Value of owner's effort}}{\text{Average total assets}}$$

> **You Make the Call** concludes each *Using the Information* section with a role-playing scenario to show the usefulness of the ratio.

You Make the Call

Entrepreneur　You own a small winter ski resort that earns a 21% return on its investment. An opportunity to purchase a winter ski equipment manufacturer is offered to you. This manufacturer earns a 19% return on its investment. The industry return for this manufacturer is 14%. Do you purchase this manufacturer?

Answer—p. 23

compare Nike's return to the normal return for manufacturers of athletic footwear. Industry averages are available from services such as **Dun & Bradstreet**'s (D&B) *Industry Norms and Key Ratios* and **Robert Morris Associates**' (RMA) *Annual Statement Studies*. When compared to its competitors, Nike performs well.[3] Another useful analysis is to compare Nike's returns to those of companies outside its industry.

> A **Summary** organized by learning objectives concludes each chapter.

Summary

C1 **Explain the aim and influence of accounting in the information age.** Accounting is an information and measurement system that aims to identify, record, and communicate relevant, reliable, and comparable information about business activities. It helps assess opportunities, products, investments, and social and community responsibilities.

C2 **Identify forms of organization and their characteristics.** Organizations can be classified as either businesses or nonbusinesses. Businesses are organized for profit; nonbusinesses serve us in ways not always measured by profit. Businesses take one of three basic forms: sole proprietorship, partnership, or corporation. These forms of organization have characteristics that hold important implications for legal liability, taxation, continuity, number of owners, and legal status.

C3 **Identify and describe the three major activities in organizations.** Organizations carry out three major activities: financing, investing, and operating. Financing is the means used to pay for resources such as land, buildings, and machines. Investing refers to the buying and selling of resources used in acquiring and selling products and services. Operating activities are those necessary for carrying out the organization's plans.

C4 **Identify users and uses of accounting.** Users of accounting are both internal and external. Some users and uses of accounting include (a) managers in controlling, monitoring, and planning; (b) lenders for measuring the risk and return of loans; (c) shareholders for assessing the return and risk of stock; (d) directors for overseeing management; and (e) employees for judging employment opportunities.

C5 **Explain why ethics and social responsibility are crucial to accounting.** The goal of accounting is to provide useful information for decision making. For information to be useful, it must be trusted. This demands ethics and socially responsible behavior in accounting.

C6 **Identify opportunities in accounting and related fields.** Opportunities in accounting include financial, managerial, and tax accounting. They also include accounting-related fields such as lending, consulting, managing, and planning. Many other opportunities with accounting knowledge also exist.

A1 **Describe income and its two major components.** Income (also called profit or earnings) is the amount a business earns after subtracting all expenses necessary for its sales (Sales − Expenses = Income). Sales (also called revenues) are the amounts earned from selling products and services. Expenses are the costs incurred with generating sales. A loss arises when expenses are more than sales.

A2 **Explain the relation between return and risk.** *Return* refers to income, and *risk* is the uncertainty about the return we hope to make. All business decisions involve risk. The lower the risk of an investment, the lower is its expected return. Higher risk implies higher, but riskier, expected return.

A3 **Explain and interpret the accounting equation.** Investing activities are funded by financing activities. An organization cannot have more or less assets than its financing and, similarly, it cannot have more or less nonowner (liabilities) and owner (equity) financing than its assets. This relation yields the accounting equation: Assets = Liabilities + Equity.

A4 **Compute and interpret return on investment.** Return on investment is computed as net income divided by the average amount invested. For example, if we have an average balance of $100 in a savings account and it earns $5 interest for the year, the return on investment is $5/$100, or 5%.

P1 **Identify and prepare basic financial statements.** Four basic financial statements report on an organization's activities: balance sheet, income statement, statement of changes in owner's equity, and statement of cash flows.

---

[3] The industry ratio, shown in the fourth column of Exhibit 1.19, is the median value computed from 10 competitors, including Fila, Converse, Stride Rite, K-Swiss, Skechers, and Vans among others.

Guidance Answers to **You Make the Call**

Programmer As the computer programmer, you confront a trade-off between return (salary) and risk (dependable employment). The start-up company has an uncertain future and is willing to increase your pay to balance the added risk you take in working for it (it could fail). The established company pays less, but you are reasonably assured of employment. If you or others depend on your salary, the risk of the start-up company might be too high. Yet if you depend less on your salary, the increased pay might be worth the risk.

Entrepreneur You should probably form the business as a corporation if potential lawsuits are of prime concern. The corporate form of organization protects your personal property from lawsuits directed at the business and would place only the corporation's resources at risk. A downside of the corporate form is double taxation—the corporation must pay taxes on its income, and you must

pay taxes on any money distributed to you from the business (even though the corporation already paid taxes on this money). You should also examine the ethical and socially responsible aspects of starting a business in which you anticipate injuries to others. (Chapter 13 describes LLCs as another reasonable form.)

Entrepreneur The 19% return on investment for the manufacturer exceeds the 14% industry return (and many others). This is a positive factor for a potential purchase. Also, the purchase of this manufacturer is an opportunity to spread your risk over two businesses as opposed to one. Still, you should hesitate to purchase a business whose return of 19% is lower than your current resort's return of 21%. You are probably better off directing efforts to increase investment in your resort, assuming you can continue to earn a 21% return.

Guidance Answers to **Quick Checks**

1. Accounting is an information and measurement system that identifies, records, and communicates relevant information to help people make better decisions. These decisions can involve opportunities, products, investments, and social and community activities.

2. Income is what a business earns after paying for all expenses necessary for its sales. Sales are the amounts earned from providing products and services. Expenses are the costs incurred with generating sales.

3. The lower the risk of an investment, the lower is the expected return. Similarly, higher expected return offsets higher risk (*actual* return usually differs from *expected* return). Higher risk implies higher, but riskier, expected returns.

4. Recordkeeping, also called *bookkeeping,* is the recording of financial transactions and events, either manually or electronically. Recordkeeping is essential to data reliability; accounting is this and much more. Accounting includes identifying, measuring, recording, reporting, and analyzing business events and transactions.

5. Many individuals and groups determine accounting rules that reflect society's needs, not those of accountants or any other single constituency. Major participants in setting rules include the Securities and Exchange Commission (SEC) and the Financial Accounting Standards Board (FASB).

6. Technology offers increased accuracy, speed, efficiency, and convenience in accounting.

7. The three basic forms of business organizations are sole proprietorships, partnerships, and corporations.

8. Nonbusiness organizations include airports, libraries, museums, churches, cities, police, colleges, bus lines, utilities, highways, fraternities, shelters, parks, hospitals, and schools.

9. Organizations pursue financing, investing, and operating activities. These three major activities all require planning.

10. External users of accounting include lenders, shareholders, directors, customers, suppliers, regulators, lawyers, brokers, and the press. Internal users of accounting include managers, officers, and other internal decision makers involved with strategic and operating decisions.

11. Internal operating functions include research and development, purchasing, human resources, production, distribution, marketing, and servicing.

12. Internal controls are procedures set up to protect assets, ensure reliable accounting reports, promote efficiency, and encourage adherence to company policies. Internal controls are crucial for relevant and reliable information.

13. Ethical guidelines are threefold: (1) identify ethical concerns using personal ethics, (2) analyze options considering all good and bad consequences, and (3) make ethical decision after weighing all consequences.

14. Ethics and social responsibility often translate into higher profits and a better working environment.

15. For accounting to provide useful information for decisions, it must be trusted. Trust demands ethics in accounting.

Glossary

Accounting an information and measurement system that identifies, records, and communicates relevant information about a company's business activities. (p. 4).

Accounting equation the equality where Assets = Liabilities + Equity. (p. 11).

Assets resources expected to produce current and future benefits. (p. 10).

Audit an analysis and report of an organization's accounting system and its records using various tests. (p. 18).

A **Glossary** of key terms concludes each chapter (a complete glossary is on the book's Web site).

Bonds written promises to repay amounts loaned with interest. (p. 6).

Bookkeeping part of accounting that involves recording transactions and events, either electronically or manually (also called *recordkeeping*). (p. 6).

Business one or more individuals selling products and/or services for profit. (p. 4).

Common stock a corporation's basic ownership share (also called *capital stock*). (p. 9).

Corporation a business that is a separate legal entity under state or federal laws with owners called *shareholders* or *stockholders*. (p. 9).

Earnings (see *income*). (p. 5).

Ethics codes of conduct by which actions are judged as right or wrong, fair or unfair, honest or dishonest. (p. 16).

Expenses the costs incurred to earn sales. (p. 5).

External users persons using accounting information who are not directly involved in running the organization. (p. 13).

Financial accounting area of accounting aimed at serving external users. (p. 13).

Financial Accounting Standards Board (FASB) independent group of seven full-time members who are responsible for setting accounting rules. (p. 7).

Financing activities means organizations use to pay for their resources such as land, buildings, and machinery. (p. 10).

Generally accepted accounting principles (GAAP) rules that specify acceptable accounting practice. (p. 7).

Income (see *net income*). (p. 5).

Information age a time period that emphasizes communication, data, news, facts, access, and commentary. (p. 4).

Internal users persons using accounting information who are directly involved in managing the organization. (p. 14).

Investing activities the buying and selling of resources that an organization controls. (p. 10).

Liabilities creditors' claims on an organization's assets. (p. 11).

Loss arises when expenses are more than sales. (p. 5).

Managerial accounting area of accounting aimed at serving the decision-making needs of internal users. (p. 14).

Net income amount earned after subtracting all expenses necessary for sales (also called *income, profit* or *earnings*). (p. 5).

Operating activities use of assets to carry out an organization's plans in the areas of research, development, purchasing, production, distribution, and marketing. (p. 11).

Owner's equity owner's claim on an organization's assets (also called *equity*). (p. 11).

Partnership a business owned by two or more people that is not organized as a corporation. (p. 8).

Planning term for an organization's ideas, goals, and strategic actions. (p. 10).

Private accounting accounting services provided for an employer other than the government. (p. 19).

Profit (see *income*). (p. 5).

Public accounting accounting services provided to many different clients. (p. 19).

Recordkeeping part of accounting that involves recording transactions and events, either manually or electronically (also called *bookkeeping*). (p. 6).

Return the income from an investment. (p. 5).

Return on investment a ratio serving as an indicator of operating efficiency; defined as net income divided by average total assets. (p. 5).

Revenues amounts earned from selling products or services (also called *sales*). (p. 5).

Risk the amount of uncertainty about an expected return. (p. 5).

Sales amounts earned from selling products or services (also called *revenues*). (p. 5).

Securities and Exchange Commission (SEC) federal agency charged by Congress to set reporting rules for organizations that sell ownership shares to the public. (p. 7).

Shareholders owners of a corporation (also called *stockholders*). (p. 9).

Shares equity of a corporation divided into units (also called *stock*). (p. 9).

Social responsibility being accountable for the impact one's actions might have on society. (p. 17).

Sole proprietorship business owned by one person that is not organized as a corporation (also called *proprietorship*). (p. 8).

Stock (see *shares*). (p. 9).

Stockholders (see *shareholders*). (p. 9).

Questions

1. What is the purpose of accounting in society?
2. What is the relation between accounting and the information superhighway?
3. Identify three businesses that offer services and three businesses that offer products.
4. Explain business income and its computation.
5. Explain return and risk. Discuss the trade-off between them.
6. Why do organizations license and monitor accounting and accounting-related professionals?
7. Technology is increasingly used to process accounting data. Why then do we need to study and understand accounting?
8. Describe the three basic forms of business organization and their characteristics.
9. Identify three types of organizations that can be formed as either profit-oriented businesses, government units, or non-profit establishments.
10. Describe the three major activities in organizations.
11. Explain why investing (assets) and financing (liabilities and equity) totals are always equal.
12. Identify four external users and their uses of accounting information.
13. What are at least three questions business owners might be able to answer by looking at accounting information?
14. Identify at least four managerial accounting tasks performed by both private and government accountants.
15. Describe the internal role of accounting for organizations.

16. What type of accounting information might be useful to those who carry out the marketing activities of a business?

17. What ethical issues might accounting professionals face in dealing with confidential information?

18. Identify three types of services typically offered by accounting professionals.

19. Why is accounting described as a service activity?

20. Identify at least three tasks performed by government accounting professionals.

21. What work do tax accounting professionals perform in addition to preparing tax returns?

22. Define and explain *return on investment* (return on assets).

23. This chapter introduced **Nike**'s financial statements. Nike was initially organized as a partnership. Identify important characteristics of partnerships and their implications.

24. Access the SEC's EDGAR database [**www.sec.gov**] and retrieve **Nike**'s 10-K for fiscal year 2000. Identify Nike's chief financial officer. How many directors does Nike have?

25. Identify the dollar amounts of **Reebok**'s 1999 assets, liabilities, and equity shown in its statements in Appendix A near the end of the book.

26. Access the SEC EDGAR database [**www.sec.gov**] and retrieve **Gap**'s 10-K for year 2000. Identify its audit firm. What responsibility does its independent auditor claim regarding Gap's financial statements?

Quick Study exercises give readers a brief test of key elements.

QUICK STUDY

Identify the meaning of each of the following accounting and business abbreviations: GAAP, SEC, FASB, IOSCO, and AICPA.

QS 1-1
Identifying accounting abbreviations

C1

Accounting provides information about an organization's business transactions and events. Identify at least two examples of both (*a*) business transactions and (*b*) business events.

QS 1-2
Identifying transactions and events

C3

Identify at least three responsibilities in the *executive management* (planning) activity of an organization.

QS 1-3
Identifying planning activities

C3

An important responsibility of many accounting professionals is to design and implement internal control procedures for organizations. Explain the purpose of internal control procedures.

QS 1-4
Explaining internal control

C4

Identify at least three main areas of opportunities for accounting professionals. For each area, identify at least three accounting-related work opportunities in practice.

QS 1-5
Accounting opportunities

C6

Accounting professionals must sometimes choose between two or more acceptable methods of accounting for business transactions and events. Explain why these situations can involve difficult matters of ethical concern.

QS 1-6
Identifying ethical concerns

C5

---

a. Total assets of Keller Financial Co. equal $50,000 and its equity is $20,000. What is the amount of its liabilities?

b. Total assets of Echo Valley Co. equal $25,000 and its liabilities and equity amounts are equal. What is the amount of its liabilities? What is the amount of its equity?

QS 1-7
Applying the accounting equation

A3

QS 1-8

Applying the accounting equation

A3

Use the accounting equation to compute the missing financial statement amounts.

Assets	=	Liabilities	+	Equity
$ 40,000		$ (a)		$10,000
$ (b)		$60,000		$20,000
$110,000		$20,000		$ (c)

QS 1-9

Identifying and computing assets, liabilities, and equity

A3 **GAP**

Use **Gap**'s January 2000 annual report, printed in Appendix A near the end of the book, to answer the following:

a. Identify the dollar amounts of Gap's 2000 (1) assets, (2) liabilities, and (3) equity.

b. Using Gap's amounts from part (a), verify that: Assets = Liabilities + Equity.

QS 1-10

Identifying items in financial statements

P1

Indicate in which financial statement each item would most likely appear: income statement (I), balance sheet (B), statement of changes in owner's equity (OE), or statement of cash flows (CF).

a. Assets   **d.** Liabilities   **g.** Total liabilities and equity

b. Revenues   **e.** Withdrawal   **h.** Cash from operating activities

c. Equity   **f.** Costs and expenses   **i.** Net decrease (or increase) in cash

---

EXERCISES

Exercise 1-1

Distinguishing business organizations

C2

The following describe several different business organizations. Determine whether the description refers to a sole proprietorship, partnership, or corporation.

a. Ownership of Cola Company is divided into 1,000 shares of stock.

b. Trimark is owned by Sarah Gates, who is personally liable for the debts of the business.

c. Jerry Staley and Susan Morris own Financial Services, a financial services provider. Neither Staley nor Morris has personal responsibility for the debts of Financial Services.

d. Nancy Case and Frank Pruitt own Get-It-There, a courier service. Both are personally liable for the debts of the business.

e. WSP Consulting Services does not have separate legal existence apart from the one person who owns it.

f. BioLife Enterprises does not pay taxes and has one owner.

g. Tampa Trade pays its own taxes and has two owners.

Exercise 1-2

Identifying business activities

C3

Match each task to a major type of organization activity: financing activities (F), investing activities (I), or operating activities (O).

a. _____ An owner contributes resources to the business.

b. _____ An organization purchases equipment.

c. _____ An organization advertises a new product.

d. _____ The organization borrows money from a bank.

e. _____ An organization sells some of its assets.

Exercise 1-3

Describing accounting responsibilities

C6

Many accounting professionals work in one of the following three areas:

A. Financial accounting   **B.** Managerial accounting   **C.** Tax accounting

Identify the area of accounting that is most involved in each of the following responsibilities:

_____ **1.** Auditing financial statements.

_____ **2.** Planning transactions to minimize taxes.

_____ **3.** Cost accounting.

_____ **4.** Preparing external financial statements.

_____ **5.** Reviewing reports for SEC compliance.

_____ **6.** Budgeting.

_____ **7.** Internal auditing.

_____ **8.** Investigating violations of tax laws.

Identify at least three external users of accounting information and indicate some questions they might seek to answer through their use of accounting information.

Exercise 1-4

Identifying accounting users and uses

Select the internal operating function from the two choices provided that is most likely to regularly use the information described. The information is likely used in both functions, but it is most relevant to one.

a. Which internal operating function is more likely to use payroll information: marketing or human resources?

b. Which internal operating function is more likely to use sales report information: marketing or research and development?

c. Which internal operating function is more likely to use inventory information: purchasing or human resources?

d. Which internal operating function is more likely to use budget and cost information: production or distribution?

e. Which internal operating function is more likely to use product quality information: human resources or production?

Exercise 1-5

Determining accounting use in internal operating functions

C4

Assume the following role and describe a situation in which ethical considerations play an important part in guiding your action:

a. You are a student in an accounting principles course.

b. You are a manager with responsibility for several employees.

c. You are an accounting professional preparing tax returns for clients.

d. You are an accounting professional with audit clients that are competitors in business.

Exercise 1-6

Identifying ethical concerns

C5

Indicate which term best fits each of the following descriptions:

A. Audit   **C.** Cost accounting   **E.** Ethics   **G.** Budgeting
B. Controller   **D.** GAAP   **F.** General accounting **H.** Tax accounting

_____ **1.** An accounting area that includes planning future transactions to minimize taxes paid.

_____ **2.** A managerial accounting system designed to help managers identify, measure, and control operating costs.

_____ **3.** Principles that determine whether an action is right or wrong.

_____ **4.** An examination of an organization's accounting system and its records that adds credibility to financial statements.

_____ **5.** The task of recording transactions, processing recorded data, and preparing reports and financial statements.

_____ **6.** The chief accounting officer of an organization.

Exercise 1-7

Learning the language of business

C1 – C6

Indicate which term best fits each of the following descriptions:

A. Government accountants   **C.** IRS   **E.** CIA   **G.** Risk   **I.** AICPA
B. Internal auditing   **D.** SEC   **F.** Income   **H.** Public accountants   **J.** CMA

_____ **1.** Process of examining an organization's recordkeeping, assessing whether managers are following established procedures, and appraising the efficiency of operating techniques.

_____ **2.** Amount of uncertainty associated with an expected return.

_____ **3.** Amount a business earns after paying all expenses and costs associated with its sales.

_____ **4.** Federal agency responsible for collecting federal taxes and enforcing tax law.

_____ **5.** Accounting professionals who provide services to many different clients.

_____ **6.** Accounting professionals employed by federal, state, or local branches of government.

Exercise 1-8

Learning the language of business

A1   A2   C4   C6

Exercise 1-9

Using the accounting equation

A3

Answer the following questions. (*Hint:* Use the accounting equation.)

a. Wes Knight's medical supplies business has assets equal to $119,000 and liabilities equal to $47,000 at the end of the year. What is the total equity for Knight's business at the end of the year?

b. At the beginning of the year, Amber Company's assets are $300,000 and its equity is $100,000. During the year, assets increase $80,000 and liabilities increase $50,000. What is the equity at the end of the year?

c. At the beginning of the year, New Navy Company's liabilities equal $70,000. During the year, assets increase by $60,000, and at year-end they equal $190,000. Liabilities decrease $5,000 during the year. What are the beginning and ending amounts of equity?

Exercise 1-10

Using the accounting equation

A3

Determine the amount missing from each accounting equation below.

	Assets	=	Liabilities	+	Equity
a.	?	=	$20,000	+	$45,000
b.	$100,000	=	$34,000	+	?
c.	$154,000	=	?	+	$40,000

Exercise 1-11

Return on investment

A4

Fineva Group reports net income of $30,000 for 2002. At the beginning of 2002, Fineva Group had $110,000 in assets. By the end of 2002, assets had grown to $150,000. What is Fineva Group's return on investment?

A **Problem Set B** located at the end of **Problem Set A** is provided for *each* problem to reinforce the learning process.

PROBLEM SET A

Problem 1-1A

Computing and interpreting return on investment

A4

Coca-Cola and PepsiCo both produce and market beverages that are direct competitors. Key financial figures (in $ millions) for these businesses over the past year follow:

Key Figures	Coca-Cola	PepsiCo
Sales	$19,805	$20,237
Net income	2,431	2,050
Average invested (assets)	21,623	17,551

[handwritten: net income by sales]

Required

Check   (1) PepsiCo return, 11.68%

1. Compute return on investment for (*a*) Coca-Cola and (*b*) PepsiCo.

2. Which company is more successful in its amount of sales to consumers?

3. Which company is more successful in returning net income from its amount invested?

Analysis Component

4. Write a one-paragraph memorandum explaining which company you would invest your money in and why.

Problem 1-2A

Identifying risk and return

A2

All business decisions involve risk and return.

Required

Identify the risk and return in each of the following activities:

1. Investing $2,000 in a 5% savings account.

2. Placing a $2,500 bet on your favorite sports team.

3. Investing $10,000 in Yahoo! stock.

4. Taking out a $7,500 college loan to study accounting.

Quadcomm manufactures, markets, and sells cellular telephones. The average amount invested, or average total assets, in Quadcomm is $250,000. In its most recent year, Quadcomm reported net income of $65,000 on sales of $475,000.

Problem 1-3A

Determining profits, sales, costs, and returns

Required

1. What is Quadcomm's return on investment?
2. Does return on investment seem satisfactory for Quadcomm given that its competitors average a 12% return on investment?
3. What are total expenses for Quadcomm in its most recent year?
4. What is the average total amount of financing (liabilities plus equity) for Quadcomm?

Check   (3) $410,000

A new startup company often engages in the following transactions in its first year of operations. Classify these transactions in one of the three major categories of an organization's business activities.

A. Financing   **B.** Investing   **C.** Operating

_____ **1.** Contributing land to the business.   _____ **5.** Purchasing equipment.

_____ **2.** Purchasing a building.   _____ **6.** Selling and distributing products.

_____ **3.** Purchasing land.   _____ **7.** Conducting advertising.

_____ **4.** Borrowing cash from a bank.   _____ **8.** Paying employee wages.

Problem 1-4A

Describing organizational activities

Identify an organization's three major business activities, including descriptions for each.

Problem 1-5A

Describing organizational activities

The following is selected financial information for Vascro Energy for the year ended December 31, 2002: Revenues, $55,000; costs and expenses, $40,000; net income, $15,000.

Required

Prepare the 2002 annual income statement for Vasero Energy.

Problem 1-6A

Preparing an income statement

P1

The following is selected financial information for Sumoco as of December 31, 2002: Liabilities, $44,000; equity, $46,000; assets, $90,000.

Required

Prepare the balance sheet for Sumoco as of December 31, 2002.

Problem 1-7A

Preparing a balance sheet

P1

The following is selected financial information for ComCast for the year ended December 31, 2002:

Cash used by investing activities	$(2,000)
Net increase in cash	1,200
Cash used by financing activities	(2,800)
Cash from operating activities	6,000

Required

Prepare the 2002 annual statement of cash flows for ComCast.

Problem 1-8A

Preparing a statement of cash flows

P1

The following is selected financial information for Boardwalk for the year ended December 31, 2002:

Equity, Dec. 31, 2002	$14,000	Withdrawals	$1,000
Net income	8,000	Equity, Dec. 31, 2001	7,000

Required

Prepare the 2002 annual statement of changes in owner's equity for Boardwalk.

Problem 1-9A

Preparing a statement of changes in owner's equity

P1

PROBLEM SET B

Problem 1-1B
Computing and interpreting
return on investment

A4

AT&T and GTE produce and market telecommunications products and are competitors. Key financial figures (in $ millions) for these businesses over the past year follow:

Key Figures	AT&T	GTE
Sales	$ 62,391	$25,336
Net income	5,450	4,033
Average invested (assets) . .	130,973	50,832

Required

Check (1) GTE return, 7.9%

1. Compute return on investment for (*a*) AT&T and (*b*) GTE.

2. Which company is more successful in the amount of sales to consumers?

3. Which company is more successful in returning net income from its amount invested?

Analysis Component

4. Write a one-paragraph memorandum explaining which company you would invest your money in.

Problem 1-2B
Identifying risk and return

A2

All business decisions involve risk and return.

Required

Identify the risk and return in each of the following activities:

1. Stashing $500 under your mattress.

2. Placing a $250 bet on a horse running in the Kentucky Derby.

3. Investing $20,000 in Nike stock.

4. Investing $25,000 in U.S. Savings Bonds.

Problem 1-3B
Determining profits, sales,
costs, and returns

A1 **A3** **A4**

Kasper Company manufactures, markets, and sells snowmobile equipment. The average amount invested, or average total assets, in Kasper Company is $3,000,000. In its most recent year, Kasper reported net income of $200,000 on sales of $1,400,000.

Required

1. What is Kasper Company's return on investment?

2. Does return on investment seem satisfactory for Kasper given that its competitors average a 9.5% return on investment?

Check (3) $1,200,000

3. What are the total expenses for Kasper Company in its most recent year?

4. What is the average total amount of financing (liabilities plus equity) for Kasper Company?

Problem 1-4B
Describing organizational
activities

C3

A new start-up company often engages in the following activities during its first year of operations. Classify each of the following activities into one of the three major activities of an organization:

A. Financing   **B.** Investing   **C.** Operating

_____ **1.** Providing services.

_____ **2.** Obtaining a bank loan.

_____ **3.** Purchasing machinery.

_____ **4.** Researching products.

_____ **5.** Supervising workers.

_____ **6.** Contributing savings to the business.

_____ **7.** Renting office space.

_____ **8.** Paying utilities expenses.

Problem 1-5B
Describing organizational
activities

Identify in outline format the three major business activities of an organization. For each activity, identify at least two specific actions normally undertaken by its owners or managers.

The following is selected financial information for Pricenet for the year ended December 31, 2002:

Problem 1-6B
Preparing an income statement

P1

| Revenues .... | $68,000 | Costs and expenses .... | $40,000 | Net income .... | $28,000 |

Required

Use the information provided to prepare the 2002 annual income statement for Pricenet.

The following is selected financial information for MicroUS as of December 31, 2002:

Problem 1-7B
Preparing a balance sheet

P1

| Liabilities .... | $64,000 | Equity .... | $50,000 | Assets .... | $114,000 |

Required

Use the information provided to prepare the balance sheet for MicroUS as of December 31, 2002.

The following is selected financial information of Intertec for the year ended December 31, 2002:

Problem 1-8B
Preparing a statement of cash flows

P1

Cash from investing activities	$1,600
Net increase in cash	400
Cash from financing activities	1,800
Cash used by operating activities	(3,000)

Required

Use this information to prepare the 2002 annual statement of cash flows for Intertec.

The following is selected financial information of CountryUS for the year ended December 31, 2002:

Problem 1-9B
Preparing a statement of changes in owner's equity

P1

Equity, Dec. 31, 2002	$47,000	Withdrawals	$ 7,000
Net income	5,000	Equity, Dec. 31, 2001	49,000

Required

Prepare the 2002 annual statement of changes in owner's equity for CountryUS.

Beyond the Numbers *is a special problem section aimed to refine communication, conceptual analysis, and research skills. It includes many activities helpful in developing an active learning environment.*

Beyond the Numbers

BTN 1-1   Key financial figures for **Nike's** fiscal year ended May 31, 2000, follow:

Reporting in Action

A1 A3 A4

NIKE

Key Figure	In Millions
Financing (liabilities + equity)	$5,856.9
Net income (profit)	579.1
Revenues (sales)	8,995.1

Required

1. What is the total amount of assets invested in Nike?
2. What is Nike's return on investment? Nike's assets at May 31, 1999, equal $5,247.7 (in millions).
3. How much are total expenses for Nike?
4. Does Nike's return on investment seem satisfactory if competitors average a 2% return?

Swoosh Ahead

5. Obtain Nike's annual report(s) (Form 10-K) for fiscal years ending after May 31, 2000, from its Web site (**www.nike.com**) or from the SEC Web site (**www.sec.gov**). Compute Nike's return on investment using this current annual report information. Compare the May 31, 2000, fiscal year-end return on investment to any subsequent years' returns you are able to compute.

Comparative Analysis

A1 A3 A4

NIKE

Reebok

BTN 1-2   Key comparative figures ($ millions) for both **Nike** and **Reebok** follow:

Key Figure	Nike	Reebok
Financing (liabilities + equity)	$5,856.9	$1,564.1
Net income (profit)	579.1	11.0
Revenues (sales)	8,995.1	2,899.9

Required

1. What is the total amount of assets invested in (*a*) Nike and (*b*) Reebok?

2. What is the return on investment for (*a*) Nike and (*b*) Reebok? Nike's beginning-year assets equal $5,247.7 (in millions) and Reebok's beginning-year assets equal $1,684.6 (in millions).

3. How much are expenses for (*a*) Nike and (*b*) Reebok?

4. Is return on investment satisfactory for (*a*) Nike and (*b*) Reebok [assume competitors average a 2% return]?

5. What can you conclude about Nike and Reebok from these computations?

Ethics Challenge

C5

BTN 1-3   Julian Brown works in a public accounting firm and hopes to eventually be a partner. The management of Vianet Company invites Brown to prepare a bid to audit Vianet's financial statements. In discussing the audit's fee, Vianet's management suggests a fee range in which the amount depends on the reported profit of Vianet. The higher its profit, the higher will be the audit fee paid to Brown's firm.

Required

1. Identify the parties potentially affected by this situation.

2. What are the ethical factors in this situation? Explain.

3. Would you recommend that Brown accept this audit fee arrangement? Why or why not?

4. Describe some ethical considerations guiding your recommendation.

Communicating in Practice

A2 C2

BTN 1-4   Refer to this chapter's opening vignette about **JobDirect.** Assume that before establishing the business, Bell and Sutton met with a loan officer of a Pittsburgh bank to discuss a loan.

Required

1. Prepare a one-half-page report outlining the information you would request from Bell and Sutton if you were the loan officer.

2. Indicate whether the information you request and your loan decision are affected by the form of business organization for **JobDirect.**

Taking It to the Net

C1 C2 C4

BTN 1-5   In 1999, the **Worldwide Wrestling Federation** began selling stock to the public. A company's first sale of stock to investors outside the company is termed an *initial public offering* (*IPO*). Access Edgar Online at www.edgar-online.com. Click on the IPO Headlines link. Next Search IPOs by Worldwide Wrestling Federation's ticker symbol WWFE. You should see a link to information regarding WWFE's recent initial public offering. Search links at this page and determine the initial opening stock offering price for the Worldwide Wrestling Federation.

BTN 1-6   Teamwork is important in today's business world. Successful teams schedule convenient meetings, maintain regular communications, and cooperate with and support team members. This assignment aims to establish accounting principles' support teams, initiate discussions, and set meeting times.

Teamwork in Action

Required

1. Form teams and open a team discussion to determine a regular time and place for your team to meet between each scheduled class meeting. Notify your instructor via a memorandum or e-mail message as to when and where your team will hold regularly scheduled meetings.

2. Develop a list of telephone numbers and/or e-mail addresses of your teammates.

BTN 1-7   *Business Week* publishes a ranking of the top 1,000 companies based on several performance measures. This issue is called the **BUSINESS WEEK GLOBAL 1000.** Obtain the July 10, 2000 (or more recent) publication of this issue—this book's Web site maintains free access to this article.

Business Week Activity

Book's Web site provides free and easy access to all articles for every Business Week *Activity.*

Required

1. What are the top 10 companies on the basis of market value?
2. Which companies are ranked in the top 10 in both 1999 and 2000 for market value?
3. How many of the top 10 on market capitalization are not U.S. companies?

BTN 1-8   Shanda Lowry is preparing to launch her new business, Your Boards (YB). YB would be a small retail store located on the Pacific coast that buys and sells skateboards, surfboards, snowboards, and related accessories.

Entrepreneurial Decision

C2   **A3**

e

Required

1. As what organization form should YB be set up? Explain.
2. YB obtains a $25,000 bank loan and Lowry contributes $28,000 of her own assets to the business.
   a. What is YB's total amount of financing?
   b. What is YB's total amount of assets?

Financial Statements and Business Transactions

"I use accounting in all my business decisions," —Chuck Taylor.

Shoes on Trial

e **LOS ANGELES**—Tucked along an oceanside street, **FastForward** could be another trendy sports shop. But its small back lot, where Chuck Taylor runs up grassy mounds, in sand pits, and through mud, makes clear this is something far different. These obstacles are product research tools. FastForward consults on athletic footwear. In just one year, Taylor has become a consultant sought after by sports clubs, schools, and amateur athletes.

FastForward's story is the envy of every entrepreneur. Taylor, 29, loved sports—but hated his shoes. He never had the right shoes for the right conditions. Independent tests of shoe performance were either nonexistent or outdated. So this past year, Taylor had an idea. He went out and purchased 21 pairs of the best off-road training shoes on the market. He ran the shoes through a battery of tests under many different conditions. His results were striking. Many medium-priced, lesser-known shoes performed on par with or better than many big-ticket, big-name shoes. He carried his findings to sports clubs and amateur athletes, and got a welcome reception and payment for his services.

Taylor recently quit his job to devote full time to his new business. "I instantly needed accounting skills to keep track of receipts, bills, everything," says Taylor. "When I applied for a loan, the bank couldn't believe my poor accounting records. But what'd you expect from a sports junkie!"

Taylor eventually shaped up his accounting and got the loan. To boost growth, FastForward is now moving into testing of soccer, track, cross-trainer, adventure, and skateboarding shoes. "We are meeting a market need and satisfying people," says Taylor. And you can count Taylor as one of the satisfied. [Source: Adapted from *Californian*, September 2001; *Sporting Trends*, July 4, 2001.]

Learning Objectives

Conceptual

C1 Identify and explain the content and reporting aims of financial statements.

C2 Describe differences in financial statements across forms of business organization.

C3 Explain the financial reporting environment.

C4 Identify those responsible for setting accounting and auditing principles.

C5 Identify, explain, and apply accounting principles.

Analytical

A1 Analyze business transactions using the accounting equation.

A2 Compute return on equity and use it to analyze company performance.

Procedural

P1 Prepare financial statements from business transactions.

Chapter Preview

Financial statements report on the financial performance and condition of an organization. They are some of the most important products of accounting and are useful to both internal and external decision makers. Chuck Taylor of **FastForward** recognized the importance of accounting reports in running his own business and in applying for a loan. Financial statements are the way businesspeople communicate. Knowledge of their preparation, organization, and analysis is important. In this chapter, we describe the type of information reflected in financial statements. We also discuss the principles and assumptions guiding their preparation. This discussion includes those that regulate and influence accounting. An important goal of this chapter is to illustrate how transactions are reflected in financial statements and how they impact our analysis. Special attention is devoted to a discussion of FastForward, whose first month's transactions are a main focus of our analysis.

Communicating with Financial Statements

In Chapter 1, we discussed how accounting provides information to help people make better decisions. Many organizations report their accounting information to internal and external users in the form of financial statements. These statements are useful in revealing an organization's financial health and performance in a summarized and easy-to-read format. They give an overall view of an organization's financing, investing, and operating activities.

Previewing Financial Statements

C1 Identify and explain the content and reporting aims of financial statements.

Concept 2-1

Point: A statement's heading lists the 3 W's: **W**ho—name of organization, **W**hat—name of statement, **W**hen—statement's point in time or period of time.

The four major **financial statements** are income statement, balance sheet, statement of changes in owner's equity, and statement of cash flows. We begin our study of these statements with a brief description of each.

How these statements are linked in time is illustrated in Exhibit 2.1. A balance sheet reports on an organization's financial position at a *point in time*. The income statement, statement of changes in owner's equity, and statement of cash flows report on financial performance over a *period of time*. The three statements in the middle column of Exhibit 2.1 link balance sheets from the beginning to the end of a reporting period. They explain how the financial position of an organization changes from one point to another.

Preparers and users (including regulatory agencies) determine the length of the reporting period. A one-year, or annual, reporting period is common, as are semiannual, quarterly, and monthly periods. The one-year reporting period is known as the *accounting*, or *fiscal*, *year*. Businesses whose accounting year begins on January 1 and ends on December 31 are known as *calendar-year* companies. Many companies choose a fiscal year ending on a date other than December 31. **Nike** is a *noncalendar-year* company as reflected in the headings of its

Exhibit 2.1

Link between Financial Statements

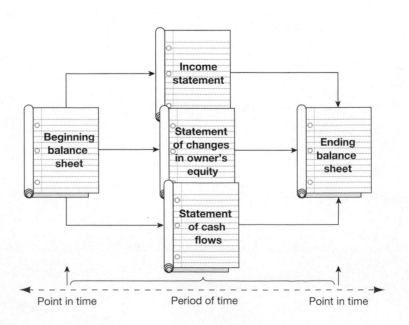

May 31 year-end financial statements in Appendix A. Some companies choose a fiscal year-end when sales and inventory are low. For example, **GAP**'s fiscal year-end is always near February 1, after the busy holiday season.

Income Statement

An **income statement** reports the revenues earned less the expenses incurred by a business over a period of time. **Net income** occurs when revenues exceed expenses. A **net loss,** or simply *loss,* occurs when expenses exceed revenues.

The income statement for FastForward's first month of operations is shown in Exhibit 2.2 (FastForward is a sole proprietorship).[1] An income statement does not simply report net income or net loss. It lists the types and amounts of important revenues and expenses. This is crucial information for users because it helps in understanding and predicting company performance. For example, **Walt Disney** classifies its revenues and expenses in three categories: theme parks, filmed entertainment, and consumer products. **Midway Games** separates its revenues into two groups: company-operated video and home video.

Exhibit 2.2

Income Statement

FASTFORWARD Income Statement For Month Ended December 31, 2001		
Revenues		
Consulting revenue ..	$5,800	
Rental revenue	300	
Total revenues		$6,100
Expenses		
Rent expense	1,000	
Salaries expense	700	
Total expenses		1,700
Net income		$4,400

Revenues

Revenues are inflows of assets in exchange for products and services provided to customers as part of a company's operations. Assets include items such as cash, land, equipment, and buildings. The income statement in Exhibit 2.2 shows that FastForward earned total revenues of $6,100 during December from both consulting and rental revenue.

Expenses

Expenses are outflows or the using up of assets in providing products and services to customers. The income statement in Exhibit 2.2 shows FastForward used $1,000 of its assets in paying for rented store space. FastForward also paid $700 for an employee's salary.

The income statement heading identifies the company, the type of statement, and the time period covered. Knowledge of the time period is important in judging whether a company's performance is satisfactory. In assessing whether FastForward's $4,400 net income is satisfactory, we must remember it earned this amount during a one-month period.

Point: An income statement is also referred to as an *earnings statement, a statement of operations,* or a *P&L* (Profit and Loss) *statement*.

Example: How would the income statement in Exhibit 2.2 change if FastForward paid $3,000 for rent? How would this change impact net income? *Answer:* Total operating expenses increase to $3,700 and net income decreases to $2,400.

You Make the Call

Web Designer You are working as a Web Designer at a local Internet Consulting Company and feel your wages are too low. You decide to ask the owner for a raise. How can you use the company's income statement to help in your request?

Answer—p. 58

Statement of Changes in Owner's Equity

Equity refers to the owner's claim on assets. The **statement of changes in owner's equity** (SCOE) reports on changes in equity over the reporting period. This statement starts with beginning equity and adjusts it for transactions and events that (1) increase it—investments by the owner and net income and (2) decrease it—net loss and owner withdrawals.

Point: While all revenues earned increase equity and expenses incurred decrease equity, the amounts are not reported in detail in the SCOE. Instead, the net effect of revenues and expenses is summarized in net income.

---

[1] For simplicity, FastForward's financial statements in this chapter do not reflect *all* of its December transactions. Its other December transactions are introduced in Chapter 3 and 4.

The statement of changes in owner's equity for FastForward's first month of operations is shown in Exhibit 2.3. This statement describes events that changed owner's equity during the month. It reports Taylor's initial equity investment of $30,000. It also reports $4,400 of net income earned during the month, and Taylor's $600 withdrawal. Taylor's equity balance at the end of the month is $33,800.[2]

Exhibit 2.3
Statement of Changes in Owner's Equity

FASTFORWARD Statement of Changes in Owner's Equity For Month Ended December 31, 2001		
C.Taylor, Capital, December 1, 2001		$ 0
Add: Investments by owner	$30,000	
Net income	4,400	34,400
. . . .		$34,400
Less: Withdrawals by owner		(600)
C.Taylor, Capital, December 31, 2001		$33,800

Balance Sheet

The **balance sheet** (also called the *statement of financial position*) reports the financial position of a company at a point in time, usually at the end of a month, quarter, or year. The balance sheet describes financial position by listing the types and dollar amounts of important assets, liabilities, and equity. Exhibit 2.4 shows the balance sheet for FastForward as of December 31. The balance sheet heading lists the company, the statement, and the date on which assets, liabilities, and equity are identified and measured. The amounts in the balance sheet are measured as of the close of business on that date.

Exhibit 2.4
Balance Sheet

FASTFORWARD Balance Sheet December 31, 2001			
Assets		**Liabilities**	
Cash	$ 4,400	Accounts payable	$ 6,200
Supplies	9,600	Total liabilities	$ 6,200
Equipment	26,000		
		Equity	
		C.Taylor, Capital	$33,800
Total assets	$40,000	Total liabilities and equity	$40,000

Example: How would the balance sheet in Exhibit 2.4 change if FastForward pays off $4,000 of its payable on December 31 using its Cash account? What would be the new amount of total assets? Would the balance sheet still balance? *Answers:* Cash would be $400, accounts payable would be $2,200, total assets (and liabilities) would be $36,000, and the balance sheet would still balance.

The balance sheet for FastForward shows it owns three different assets at the close of business on December 31: cash, supplies, and equipment. The total dollar amount for these assets is $40,000. The balance sheet also shows total liabilities of $6,200. Owner's equity is $33,800. Consistent with the accounting equation, the total amounts on each side of the balance sheet are equal (Assets = Liabilities + Equity). This equality is the reason the statement is named a *balance sheet*. This name also reflects the reporting of asset, liability, and equity *balances* in the statement.

---

[2] The beginning capital balance in the statement of changes in owner's equity is rarely zero. An exception is for the first period of a company's operations. Since FastForward began operations in December, its beginning capital balance for the month of December is zero. The beginning capital balance in January 2002 for FastForward is $33,800 (this is December's ending balance).

Assets

Assets are resources owned or controlled by a company that provide expected future benefits to the company. Assets are of many types. A familiar asset is cash. Another is accounts receivable. An **account receivable** is an asset created by selling products or services on credit. It reflects amounts owed to a company by its credit customers. These customers and other individuals and organizations who owe a company are called its **debtors.** Other common assets include merchandise held for sale, supplies, equipment, buildings, and land. Assets also can include intangible rights such as those granted by a patent, copyright, or license.

Liabilities

Liabilities are obligations of a company that reflect the claims of others against assets. A common characteristic of liabilities is their potential for reducing future assets or requiring future services or products. Liabilities take many forms. An **account payable** is a liability created by buying products or services on credit. It reflects amounts owed to others. A **note payable** is a liability expressed by a written promise to make a future payment at a specific time. Other familiar liabilities are salaries and wages owed to employees and interest payable.

Individuals and organizations that own the right to receive payments from a company are called its **creditors.** One entity's payable is another entity's receivable. If a company fails to pay its obligations, the law gives creditors a right to force the sale of this company's assets to obtain the money to meet creditors' claims. When assets are sold under these conditions, creditors are paid first, but only up to the amount of their claims. Any remaining money, the residual, goes to the owner of the company. Creditors often use a balance sheet to help decide whether to loan money to a company. They compare the amounts of liabilities and assets. A loan is less risky if liabilities are small in comparison to assets because there are more resources than claims on resources.

Equity

Equity is the owner's claim on the assets of a business. It is the owner's *residual interest* in the assets of a business after deducting liabilities. Equity is also called **net assets.** Owner investments and revenues increase owner's equity. It is decreased by owner withdrawals and by expenses. Exhibit 2.5 shows these important relations. Owner investments are assets the owner put into the business. Owner withdrawals are assets the owner takes from the business. These changes in equity are reported in the statement of changes in owner's equity and yield the ending equity balance called *capital*. This ending balance is also reported in the balance sheet.

Point: Review these concepts by preparing your own personal balance sheet.

Statement of Cash Flows

The **statement of cash flows** describes the sources (inflows) and uses (outflows) of cash for a reporting period. It also reports the amount of cash at both the beginning and end of

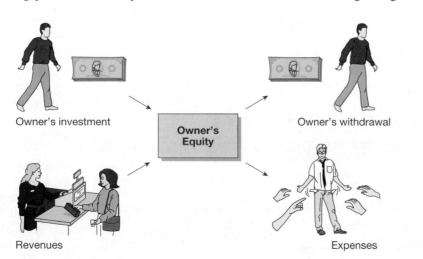

Owner's investment

Revenues

Owner's Equity

Owner's withdrawal

Expenses

Exhibit 2.5

Flows in and out of Owner's Equity

a period. The statement of cash flows is organized according to a company's major activities: operating, investing, and financing. A company must carefully manage cash if it is to survive and prosper.

FastForward's statement of cash flows for December is in Exhibit 2.6. The first section shows that net cash flows from operating activities equal $1,000. This is the result of $6,100 of cash received from customers less $5,100 paid for supplies, rent, and salaries. The second section reports on investing activities and shows a $26,000 cash outflow for buying equipment. The third section reports a $29,400 net cash inflow from financing activities that include an investment and a withdrawal by the owner.

Exhibit 2.6

Statement of Cash Flows

FASTFORWARD		
Statement of Cash Flows		
For Month Ended December 31, 2001		
Cash flows from operating activities:		
Cash received from clients	$ 6,100	
Cash paid for supplies	(3,400)	
Cash paid for rent	(1,000)	
Cash paid to employee	(700)	
Net cash provided by operating activities		$ 1,000
Cash flows from investing activities:		
Purchase of equipment	(26,000)	
Net cash used by investing activities		(26,000)
Cash flows from financing activities:		
Investments by owner	30,000	
Withdrawals by owner	(600)	
Net cash provided by financing activities		29,400
Net increase in cash		$ 4,400
Cash balance, December 1, 2001		0
Cash balance, December 31, 2001		$ 4,400

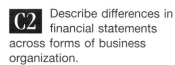 **C2** Describe differences in financial statements across forms of business organization.

Financial Statements and Organizational Form

Chapter 1 described three different forms of business organization: proprietorship, partnership, and corporation. Financial statements for these organizations are very similar. The most visible *difference* is in the equity section of the balance sheet. A proprietorship's balance sheet lists the equity balance beside the owner's name as in Exhibit 2.4. A partnership's balance sheet uses the same approach, unless it has too many owners to fit their names in the available space. For example, if Chuck Taylor is part of an equal partnership with his sister Jane, the equity section would appear as in Exhibit 2.7.

A corporation's balance sheet does not list the names of its shareholders. Instead, equity is divided into **contributed capital** (also called **paid-in capital**) and **retained earnings.** Contributed capital reflects shareholders' investments. Retained earn-

Exhibit 2.7

Equity Section of a Partnership Balance Sheet

FASTFORWARD	
Partial Balance Sheet	
December 31, 2001	
Partners' Equity	
Chuck Taylor, Capital	$16,900
Jane Taylor, Capital	16,900
Total partners' equity	$33,800

ings equals a corporation's accumulated net income (loss) for all prior periods that has not been distributed to shareholders. To illustrate, assume Chuck Taylor had set up FastForward as a corporation in which he was the sole shareholder. If he is issued common stock equal to his $30,000 investment, the equity section of the balance sheet would look like the one in Exhibit 2.8. FastForward earned $4,400 in its first (and only) period, of which $600 is distributed to Taylor, leaving $3,800 in retained earnings.

When an owner of a proprietorship or a partnership takes cash or other assets from a company, the distributions are called **withdrawals.** When an owner of a corporation receives cash or other assets from a company, the distributions are called **dividends.** Withdrawals and dividends are not reported as part of the income statement because they are *not* expenses incurred to generate revenues. Also, when the owner of a proprietorship is its manager, no salary expense is reported on the income statement for this service. The same is true for a partnership. But since a corporation is a separate legal entity, salaries paid to its managers are reported as expenses on its income statement. This different treatment of owners' salaries requires special consideration when analyzing an income statement. We explain one special adjustment for return on equity near the end of this chapter.

The emphasis in the early chapters of this book is on sole proprietorships. This allows us to focus on important measurement and reporting issues in accounting without getting caught up in the complexities of different organizational forms. We do discuss forms of organization and provide examples when appropriate. Chapters 13 and 14 return to this topic and provide details about the financial statements of both partnerships and corporations.

FASTFORWARD Partial Balance Sheet December 31, 2001	
Shareholders' Equity	
Contributed capital:	
Common stock	$30,000
Retained earnings	3,800
Total shareholders' equity	$33,800

Exhibit 2.8
Equity Section of a Corporation Balance Sheet

Global: Global markets present challenges in terminology. For example, U.S. users refer to equity shares as *stock*, while U.K. users refer to inventory as *stock*.

Answer—p. 58

Quick Check

1. What are the four major financial statements?

2. Describe revenues and expenses.

3. Explain assets, liabilities, and equity.

4. What are three differences in financial statements for the three different organizational forms?

Generally Accepted Accounting Principles

We explained in Chapter 1 how financial accounting practice is governed by rules called *generally accepted accounting principles,* or *GAAP.* To use and interpret financial statements effectively, we need to understand these principles. A main purpose of GAAP is to make information in financial statements relevant, reliable, and comparable. *Relevant information* affects the decisions of its users. *Reliable information* is trusted by users. *Comparable information* is helpful in comparing organizations. This section describes the process for setting GAAP and identifies several crucial accounting principles.

Financial Reporting Environment

Accounting principles are developed in response to users' needs. Exhibit 2.9 shows how accounting principles, auditing standards, and various parties interact in the financial reporting environment. Accounting principles are applied in preparing financial statements. Preparers use preferred procedures in accounting for business transactions and events. Audits are performed in accordance with **generally accepted auditing standards (GAAS),** which are the accepted rules for conducting audits of financial statements. Both accounting and auditing help assure users that financial statements include relevant, reliable, and comparable information. An audit report tells whether or not the statements are prepared using

 C3 Explain the financial reporting environment.

Point: An audit does *not* attest to the absolute accuracy of financial statements.

Identify those responsible for setting accounting and auditing principles.

accepted accounting principles. **Ernst and Young** states in its audit report of **Harley-Davidson:** "In our opinion, the consolidated financial statements . . . present fairly, in all material respects . . . in conformity with generally accepted accounting principles."

Setting Accounting Principles

Accounting principles were historically developed through common usage. A principle was acceptable if most professionals permitted it. This history is reflected in the phrase *generally accepted*. As business transactions became more complex, users were less satisfied with the lack of more concrete guidance. Many of these users desired more uniformity in practice. Authority for developing accepted principles was eventually assigned to a select group of professionals.

Exhibit 2.9 shows the primary authoritative sources of GAAP and GAAS. The Financial Accounting Standards Board (FASB) is the primary authoritative source of GAAP. The Board seeks advice from all users and often holds public hearings. Its goal is to improve financial reporting and balance the interests of all users. The FASB communicates its decisions in various publications. Most notable are **Statements of Financial Accounting Standards (SFAS).** These statements set generally accepted standards in the United States and often affect international practices.[3]

Exhibit 2.9

Financial Reporting Environment

Point: The five largest international accounting firms are Arthur Andersen, Deloitte & Touche, Ernst & Young, KPMG Peat Marwick, and PricewaterhouseCoopers.

Global: Both U.S. and the U.K. accounting principles are developed in the private sector. This is likely tied to both countries' legal systems based on English common law, in which professionals tend to make the rules. In contrast, government sets accounting principles in most continental European countries. This is likely tied to their legal systems that tend to be based on codified law.

The FASB draws its authority from two major sources. The first is the Securities and Exchange Commission (SEC), which Congress created to regulate securities markets, including the flow of information from companies to the public. The SEC designates the FASB as its primary authority for setting GAAP. It can overrule the FASB but rarely does so. The second source of authority comes from state boards that license CPAs. State ethics codes

---

[3] Predecessors to the FASB were the Accounting Principles Board (APB) and the Committee on Accounting Procedure (CAP).

require CPAs who audit financial statements to disclose areas where they fail to comply with FASB rules. If CPAs fail to report noncompliance, they can lose their licenses to practice. Also, the AICPA's Code of Professional Conduct states that a member can be expelled for not objecting to financial statements that fail to comply with FASB rules.[4] Authority for generally accepted auditing standards (GAAS) belongs to the *Auditing Standards Board (ASB),* a special committee of the AICPA with unpaid volunteer members.

International Accounting Principles

In today's global economy, companies in different countries increasingly do business with each other. For example, **Coca-Cola** does business with numerous companies located in nearly 200 countries across the world. **Nike** says the following about its global operations: "The Company currently markets its products in approximately 110 countries . . . through independent distributors, licensees, subsidiaries and branch offices . . . Non-U.S. sales accounted for 43 percent of total revenues . . ."

Despite this global economy, most countries continue to maintain a unique set of accounting practices. Consider a Canadian company selling stock to foreign investors. Should it prepare financial statements that comply with Canadian standards or with the standards of another country? Should it prepare different sets of reports to gain access to financial markets in more countries? This is a difficult and pressing problem.

One response has been to create an **International Accounting Standards Committee (IASC).** The IASC issues *International Accounting Standards* that identify preferred accounting practices. By narrowing the range of alternative practices, the IASC hopes to create more harmony among accounting practices

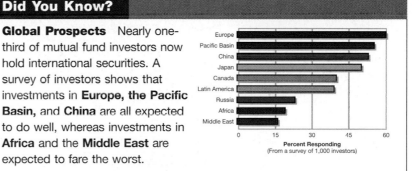

Did You Know?

Global Prospects   Nearly one-third of mutual fund investors now hold international securities. A survey of investors shows that investments in **Europe, the Pacific Basin,** and **China** are all expected to do well, whereas investments in **Africa** and the **Middle East** are expected to fare the worst.

of different countries. If standards are harmonized, one company can use a single set of financial statements in all financial markets. Many countries' standard setters support the IASC, yet it does not have authority to impose its standards on companies. While interest in moving U.S. GAAP toward the IASC's preferred practices is growing, authority to make such changes rests with the FASB and the SEC.

Global: The IASC has its own set of accounting concepts to help guide the setting of international accounting principles.

Global: IASC standards are frequently adopted by newly industrialized countries such as Malaysia and Singapore, and by developing countries such as Nigeria.

Quick Check

5. What organization sets U.S. GAAP? From where does it draw authority?
6. What is GAAS? What organization sets GAAS?
7. How are U.S. companies affected by international accounting standards?

Answers—p. 58

Principles of Accounting

Accounting principles are both general and specific. *General principles* are the basic assumptions, concepts, and guidelines for preparing financial statements. *Specific principles* are detailed rules used in reporting business transactions and events. General principles stem from long-used accounting practices. Specific principles arise more often from the rulings of authoritative groups.

Identify, explain, and apply accounting principles.

---

[4] Many other professional organizations support the FASB, including the American Accounting Association (AAA), Financial Executives Institute (FEI), Institute of Management Accountants (IMA), Association for Investment Management and Research (AIMR), and Securities Industry Association (SIA). They increase the Board's credibility by participating in its process for setting GAAP. Working alongside the FASB is the Governmental Accounting Standards Board (GASB), which identifies special accounting principles to be applied in preparing financial statements for state and local governments.

We need to understand both general and specific principles to effectively use accounting information. Since general principles are especially crucial in using accounting information,

Exhibit 2.10

Building Blocks for the House of GAAP

we emphasize them in the early chapters of this book. The general principles described in this chapter include business entity, objectivity, cost, going-concern, monetary unit, and revenue recognition. General principles described in later chapters include time period, matching, materiality, full disclosure, consistency, and conservatism. General principles are portrayed as building blocks for the *House of GAAP* in Exhibit 2.10. The specific principles are especially important to understanding individual items in financial statements. They are described as we encounter them.

Business Entity Principle

The **business entity principle** means that a business is accounted for separately from its owner(s). It also means we account separately for each business that is controlled by the same owner. The reason for this principle is that separate information about each business is necessary for good decisions. To illustrate, suppose Chuck Taylor, the owner, wants to know how well FastForward is doing. For financial statements to serve his need, FastForward's transactions must be separate from his personal transactions. For example, Taylor's personal expenses (such as entertainment and clothes) must not be subtracted from FastForward's revenues on its income statement because they are not part of its business. A company's statements must reflect only the transactions and events of its *own business*. For reports and decision making to be effective, businesses must apply the entity principle.

Did You Know?

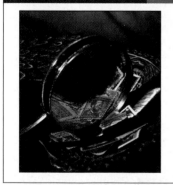

Sham-Barter Transactions Abuse of the objectivity and cost principles brought down executives at **Itex Corp** who bartered assets of little or no value and then reported them at grossly inflated values—recognizing fictitious gains and assets. The barter deals involved difficult-to-value assets such as artwork and stamp collections.

Objectivity Principle

The **objectivity principle** means that financial statement information is supported by independent, unbiased evidence. It demands more than one person's opinion. Information is not reliable if it is based only on what a preparer thinks might be true. A preparer can be too optimistic or pessimistic. An unethical preparer might try to mislead users by misrepresenting the truth. The objectivity principle is intended to make financial statements useful by ensuring they report reliable and verifiable information.

Global: Accounting principles are set by *directives* in the European Union.

Point: The cost principle is also called the *historical cost principle*.

Cost Principle

The **cost principle** means financial statements are based on actual costs incurred in business transactions. Cost is measured on a cash or equal-to-cash basis. This means if cash is given for an asset or service, its cost is measured as the amount of cash paid. If something besides cash is exchanged (such as a car traded for a truck), cost is measured as the cash equal to what is given up or received. The cost principle emphasizes reliability and relevance. It is also consistent with *objectivity* in that information based on cost is considered objective. For example, reporting purchases of assets and services at cost is more objective than reporting a manager's estimate of their current value. To illustrate this principle, suppose FastForward pays $5,000 for equipment. The cost principle requires that this purchase be recorded at a cost of $5,000. It makes no difference if Chuck Taylor thinks this equipment is really worth $7,000.

Going-Concern Principle

The **going-concern principle** means financial statements reflect an assumption that the business will continue operating instead of being closed or sold. This means a balance sheet reports items at cost instead of, say, liquidation values that assume closure. If a company is expected to fail or be liquidated, neither the going-concern principle nor the cost principle is appropriate. Instead, market values are then relevant.

Point: There are exceptions to the cost principle. For example, investments in some securities are reported at market values. We cover this when we study investments.

Monetary Unit Principle

The **monetary unit principle** means we can express transactions and events in monetary, or money, units. Money is the common denominator in business. Expressing transactions and events in monetary units is crucial to the use of financial statements for business communications. Examples of monetary units are the dollar in the United States, Canada, Australia, and Singapore; the pound sterling in the United Kingdom; and the peso in Mexico, the Philippines, and Chile. An *exchange rate* expresses the value of one currency relative to another. Exchange rates change frequently and are tied to many economic and political factors. The following chart lists recent exchange rates in terms of U.S. dollars:

Point: For currency conversion, check out *CNNfn* at cnnfn.com/markets/currencies.

Country	U.S. $ Equivalent	Country	U.S. $ Equivalent
Canada (dollar)	0.68	United Kingdom (pound)	1.50
Taiwan (dollar)	0.03	Mexico (peso)	0.11
Germany (mark)	0.47	Europe (Euro)	0.91

The monetary unit an organization uses in its reports usually depends on the country where it operates, but more companies are expressing financial statements in more than one monetary unit. Exhibit 2.11 shows that **Nintendo** reports its financial statements in *both* yen and dollars.

Example: Cadbury, a leading chocolate producer, recently reported sales of £5,115 million. What is the U.S. $ equivalent of these sales using the exchange rate from the preceding chart? *Answer:* $7,673 million (5,115 × 1.50)

NINTENDO'S FINANCIAL HIGHLIGHTS Year Ended March 31, 1999		
	Yen (¥) in Millions	**U.S. $ in Millions**
Total revenues	¥598,417	$4,946
Net income	85,817	709
Total assets	893,374	7,383
Total equity	700,292	5,788

Exhibit 2.11

Nintendo's Financial Highlights in both Dollars and Yen

Accounting generally assumes a *stable* monetary unit. This means the value of a currency is not expected to change. The more changes in the monetary unit, the more difficult it is to use and interpret financial statements, especially across time.

Quick Check

8. Why is the business entity principle important?

9. How are the objectivity and cost principles related?

Answers—p. 58

Transactions and the Accounting Equation

Point: To apply these concepts, work QS 2-1 or QS 2-2.

Financial statements reflect a company's business activities. We know many of these activities, such as purchases and sales, involve transactions. To understand information in financial statements, we need to know how an accounting system captures relevant data about transactions, classifies and records data, and reports data in financial statements. This section starts us on this important path.

The basic tool of modern accounting systems is the **accounting equation:**

$$\text{Assets} = \text{Liabilities} + \text{Equity}$$

The accounting equation is also called the **balance sheet equation** because of its link to the balance sheet. Like any mathematical equation, the accounting equation can be modified by rearranging terms. Moving liabilities to the left side of the equality, for example, gives us an equation for equity in terms of assets and liabilities:

$$\text{Assets} - \text{Liabilities} = \text{Equity}$$

The accounting equation helps track changes in a company's assets, liabilities, and equity to provide useful information and to help with interpretation.

Transaction Analysis—Part I

A1 Analyze business transactions using the accounting equation.

Concept 2-2

A **business transaction** is an exchange of economic consideration between two parties. Examples of economic consideration include products, services, money, and rights to collect money. A transaction affects one or more components of the accounting equation. Remember that each transaction leaves the equation in balance. Assets *always* equal the sum of liabilities and equity. We show how this equality is preserved by looking at 11 transactions for FastForward in its first month of operations.

Transaction 1: Investment by Owner

On December 1, Chuck Taylor forms an athletic shoe consulting business. He sets it up as a proprietorship. Taylor owns and manages the business. The marketing plan for the business is to focus primarily on consulting with schools, sports clubs, amateur athletes, and others who place orders of athletic shoes with manufacturers. Taylor personally invests $30,000 cash in the new company and deposits it in a bank account opened under the name of **FastForward.** After this transaction, the cash (an asset) and the owner's equity (called *C. Taylor, Capital*) each equal $30,000. The effect of this transaction on FastForward as reflected in the accounting equation follows:

	Assets	=	Liabilities	+	Equity
	Cash	=			C.Taylor, Capital
(1)	+$30,000	=			+$30,000 Investment

This transaction analysis reveals that FastForward has one asset, cash, equal to $30,000. It reveals no liabilities and an owner's equity of $30,000. The source of increase in equity is identified as an owner investment. Notice that the accounting equation is in balance.

Transaction 2: Purchase Supplies for Cash

FastForward uses $2,500 of its cash to buy supplies of brand name athletic shoes for testing over the next few months. This transaction is an exchange of cash, an asset, for another kind of asset, supplies. It merely changes the form of assets from cash to supplies. The decrease in cash is exactly equal to the increase in supplies. These supplies of athletic shoes are assets because of the expected future benefits from the test results of their performance. This transaction is reflected in the accounting equation as follows:

Assets			=	Liabilities	+	Equity
Cash	+	Supplies	=			C.Taylor, Capital
Old Bal. $30,000			=			$30,000
(2) −2,500	+	$2,500				
New Bal. $27,500	+	$2,500	=			$30,000
	$30,000				$30,000	

Transaction 3: Purchase Equipment for Cash

FastForward spends $26,000 to acquire equipment for testing athletic shoes. Like transaction 2, transaction 3 is an exchange of one asset, cash, for another asset, equipment. The equipment is an asset because of the expected future benefits from using it to test athletic shoes. This purchase changes the makeup of assets but does not change the asset total. The equation remains in balance.

Assets					=	Liabilities	+	Equity
Cash	+	Supplies	+	Equipment	=			C.Taylor, Capital
Old Bal. $27,500	+	$2,500			=			$30,000
(3) −26,000				+$26,000				
New Bal. $1,500	+	$2,500	+	$26,000	=			$30,000
	$30,000					$30,000		

Transaction 4: Purchase Supplies on Credit

Taylor decides he needs more supplies of athletic shoes. These supplies total $7,100, but as we see from the accounting equation in transaction 3, FastForward has only $1,500 in cash. Taylor arranges to purchase them on credit from CalTech Supply Company. Thus, FastForward acquires supplies in exchange for a promise to pay for them later. This yields a liability to CalTech Supply of $7,100. The effects of this purchase on the accounting equation are as follows:

Assets					=	Liabilities	+	Equity
Cash	+	Supplies	+	Equipment	=	Accounts Payable	+	C.Taylor, Capital
Old Bal. $1,500	+	$2,500	+	$26,000	=			$30,000
(4)	+	7,100				+$7,100		
New Bal. $1,500	+	$9,600	+	$26,000	=	$7,100	+	$30,000
	$37,100					$37,100		

This purchase increases assets by $7,100 in supplies while liabilities (called *accounts payable*) increase by the same amount.

Transaction 5: Services Rendered for Cash

A main business objective is to increase its owner's wealth. This goal is met when a business produces sufficient *net income*. Net income is reflected in the accounting equation as an increase in equity. FastForward earns revenues by consulting with clients about test results on athletic shoes. FastForward earns net income only if its revenues are greater than

Example: If FastForward pays $500 in cash in transaction 4, how does this cash payment affect the liability to CalTech? What would be FastForward's cash balance? *Answers:* The liability to CalTech would be reduced to $6,600 and the cash balance would be reduced to $1,000.

its expenses incurred in earning them. In one of its first jobs FastForward provides consulting services to an athletic club and immediately collects $4,200 cash. The accounting equation reflects an increase in cash of $4,200 and in equity of $4,200. This increase in equity is identified in the far right column as a revenue because it is earned by providing services. These identifications are useful in later preparing and interpreting both the statement of changes in owner's equity and the income statement.

	Assets			=	Liabilities	+	Equity	
	Cash	+ Supplies	+ Equipment	=	Accounts Payable	+	C.Taylor, Capital	
Old Bal.	$1,500	+ $9,600	+ $26,000	=	$7,100	+	$30,000	
(5)	+ 4,200					+	4,200	Consulting Revenue
New Bal.	$5,700	+ $9,600	+ $26,000	=	$7,100	+	$34,200	
		$41,300				$41,300		

Transactions 6 and 7: Payment of Expenses in Cash

FastForward pays $1,000 rent to the landlord of the building where its store is located. Paying this amount allows FastForward to occupy the space for the month of December. The effects of this payment as reflected in the accounting equation follow as transaction 6. FastForward also pays the biweekly $700 salary of the company's only employee. This is reflected in the accounting equation as transaction 7.

	Assets			=	Liabilities	+	Equity	
	Cash	+ Supplies	+ Equipment	=	Accounts Payable	+	C.Taylor, Capital	
Old Bal.	$5,700	+ $9,600	+ $26,000	=	$7,100	+	$34,200	
(6)	−1,000						− 1,000	Rent Expense
Bal.	$4,700	+ $9,600	+ $26,000	=	$7,100	+	$33,200	
(7)	− 700						− 700	Salary Expense
New Bal.	$4,000	+ $9,600	+ $26,000	=	$7,100	+	$32,500	
		$39,600				$39,600		

Both transactions 6 and 7 are December expenses for FastForward. The costs of both rent and salary are expenses, as opposed to assets, because their benefits are used in December (they have no future benefits after December). These transactions use up an asset (cash) as part of FastForward's operations. The accounting equation shows both transactions reduce cash and equity. The far right column identifies these decreases as expenses.

Summary of Part I Transactions

FastForward has net income when its revenues exceed its expenses. Net income increases equity. If expenses exceed revenues, a net loss occurs and decreases equity. Net income (and loss) is not affected by transactions between a business and its owner. This means Taylor's initial investment of $30,000 is not income to FastForward, although it increased equity. To stress that revenues and expenses yield changes in equity, we have added revenues directly to equity and subtracted expenses directly from equity in this chapter. In practice and in later chapters, information about revenues and expenses is compiled separately during the accounting period. These amounts are then added to or subtracted from equity at the *end* of the period. We describe this process in Chapters 3, 4, and 5.

Point: To apply these concepts, work Exercises 2-1 and 2-3.

Revenue Recognition Principle

We briefly interrupt the analysis of FastForward's transactions to describe the revenue recognition principle. Companies need guidance in deciding when to recognize revenue. *Recognize* means to record a transaction or event for purposes of reporting its effects in financial statements. If revenue is recognized too early, the income statement reports revenue sooner than it should, and the business looks more profitable than it is. If revenue is recognized too late, the income statement shows lower revenue and net income than it should, and the business looks less profitable than it is. In both cases, the income statement does not provide decision makers with the most useful information about company success.

The **revenue recognition principle** provides guidance on when to recognize revenue on the income statement. The recognition principle includes three important guidelines:

1. *Revenue is recognized when earned.* Preparing for services, finding customers, and promoting sales all contribute to revenue. Yet, we usually cannot reliably determine revenue earned until services or products are delivered. This means revenue is usually not recognized until the earnings process is complete. The earnings process is normally complete when services are rendered or the seller transfers ownership of products to the buyer. To illustrate, suppose a customer pays in advance of taking delivery of a product or service. The seller must not recognize revenue because the earnings process is not complete. This practice is called the *sales basis* of revenue recognition.

> ### Did You Know?
>
> Revenues for the New York Yankees baseball team include ticket sales, television and cable broadcasts, radio rights, concessions, and advertising. Revenues from ticket sales are recognized when the Yankees play each game. Advance ticket sales are not revenues; instead, they represent a liability for the Yankees to play a baseball game at a later specified date.

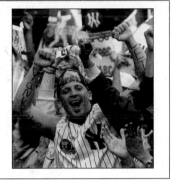

2. *Assets received from selling products and services need not be in cash.* A common non-cash asset received by a seller in a revenue transaction is a customer's promise to pay at a future date. The seller views the customer's promise as an account receivable. These transactions are called *credit sales*. If evidence shows the seller has the right to collect from a customer, this seller recognizes an asset (account receivable) and records revenue. When cash is later collected, no additional revenue is recognized. It merely changes the makeup of assets from a receivable to cash.

Example: When a bookstore sells a textbook on credit is its earnings process complete? *Answer:* The bookstore can record sales for these book sales minus an amount expected for returns.

3. *Revenue recognized is measured by the cash received plus the cash equivalent (market) value of any other assets received.* This means, for example, if a revenue transaction creates an account receivable, the seller recognizes revenue equal to the value of the receivable, which usually is the amount of cash expected to be collected.

Financial statements include an explanation of the revenue recognition method used. **General Motors,** for instance, reports in its annual report that "sales are generally recorded by the Corporation when products are shipped to independent dealers."

Transaction Analysis—Part II

To show how revenue recognition works, let's return to FastForward's transactions.

Transaction 8: Services and Facilities Rendered for Credit

FastForward provides consulting services of $1,600 and rented its test facilities to an amateur sports team for $300. The rental involved allowing team members to try recommended shoes at FastForward's testing grounds. The sports team is billed for the $1,900 total. This transaction results in a new asset, account receivable, from this client. It also yields an increase in equity from the two revenue components identified in the far right column of the accounting equation:

	Cash	+	Accounts Receivable	+	Supplies	+	Equipment	=	Accounts Payable	+	C. Taylor, Capital	
	Assets							=	**Liabilities**	+	**Equity**	
Old Bal.	$4,000	+		+	$9,600	+	$26,000	=	$7,100	+	$32,500	
(8)		+	$1,900							+	1,600	Consulting Revenue
										+	300	Rental Revenue
New Bal.	$4,000	+	$1,900	+	$9,600	+	$26,000	=	$7,100	+	$34,400	
			$41,500								$41,500	

Transaction 9: Receipt of Cash from Accounts Receivable

Point: Note that receipt of cash is not necessarily a revenue.

The client (amateur sports team) pays $1,900 10 days after it is billed for consulting services in transaction 8. This transaction 9 does not change the total amount of assets and does not affect liabilities or equity. It converts the receivable (an asset) to cash (another asset). It does not create new revenue. Revenue was recognized when FastForward rendered the services (transaction 8), not when the cash is now collected. This emphasis on the earnings process instead of cash flows is a goal of the revenue recognition principle and yields useful information to users. The new balances follow:

		Cash	+	Accounts Receivable	+	Supplies	+	Equipment	=	Accounts Payable	+	C. Taylor, Capital
				Assets					=	**Liabilities**	+	**Equity**
Old Bal.		$4,000	+	$1,900	+	$9,600	+	$26,000	=	$7,100	+	$34,400
(9)	+	1,900		−1,900								
New Bal.		$5,900	+	$ 0	+	$9,600	+	$26,000	=	$7,100	+	$34,400
				$41,500							$41,500	

Transaction 10: Payment of Accounts Payable

FastForward pays $900 to CalTech Supply as partial payment for its earlier $7,100 purchase of supplies (transaction 4), leaving $6,200 unpaid. The accounting equation shows this transaction decreases FastForward's cash by $900 and decreases its liability to CalTech Supply by $900. Equity does not change. This event does not create an expense even though cash flows out of FastForward (the expense is recorded when FastForward derives the benefits from these supplies—Chapter 3 will explain this concept in detail).

	Cash	+	Accounts Receivable	+	Supplies	+	Equipment	=	Accounts Payable	+	C. Taylor, Capital
			Assets					=	**Liabilities**	+	**Equity**
Old Bal.	$5,900	+	$ 0	+	$9,600	+	$26,000	=	$7,100	+	$34,400
(10)	− 900								− 900		
New Bal.	$5,000	+	$ 0	+	$9,600	+	$26,000	=	$6,200	+	$34,400
			$40,600							$40,600	

Transaction 11: Withdrawal of Cash by Owner

Taylor withdraws $600 in cash from FastForward for personal living expenses. A proprietorship's distribution of cash, or other assets, to its owner is called a *withdrawal*. Withdrawals (decreases in equity) are not expenses because they are not part of the company's earnings process. Since withdrawals are not expenses, they are not used in computing net income.

	Cash	+	Accounts Receivable	+	Supplies	+	Equipment	=	Accounts Payable	+	C.Taylor, Capital	
Old Bal.	$5,000	+	$ 0	+	$9,600	+	$26,000	=	$6,200	+	$34,400	
(11)	− 600										− 600	Withdrawal
New Bal.	$4,400	+	$ 0	+	$9,600	+	$26,000	=	$6,200	+	$33,800	

Assets = $40,000   Liabilities + Equity = $40,000

Summary of Transactions

FastForward engaged in transactions with five major entities: the owner, its suppliers, an employee, its customers, and the landlord. We identify the transactions by number with the specific entity in Exhibit 2.12. We also summarize in Exhibit 2.13 the effects of these 11 transactions of FastForward using the accounting equation. Three points should be noted. First, the accounting equation remains in balance after each transaction. Second, transactions can be analyzed by their effects on components of the accounting equation. For example, in transactions 2, 3, and 9, one asset increased while another decreased by equal amounts. Third, the equality of effects in the accounting equation is crucial to the double-entry accounting system. We discuss this system in the next chapter.

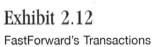

Exhibit 2.12

FastForward's Transactions Grouped by Entities

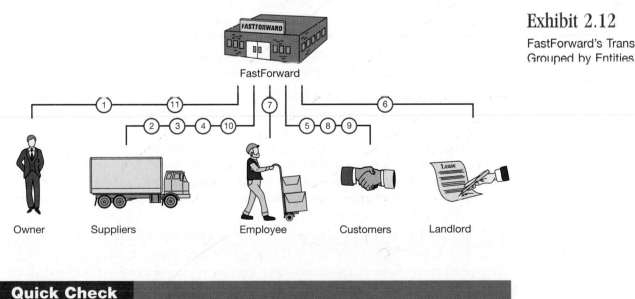

Answer—p. 58

Quick Check

12. Why is the revenue recognition principle important?

13. Identify a transaction decreasing both assets and liabilities.

14. When is the accounting equation in balance, and what does that mean?

Exhibit 2.13

Summary of Transactions
Using the Accounting
Equation

		Assets				= Liabilities +	Equity	
	Cash	+ Accounts Receivable	+ Supplies	+ Equipment	=	Accounts Payable	+ C.Taylor, Capital	
(1)	$30,000						$30,000	Investment
(2)	−2,500		+$2,500					
Bal.	27,500		2,500				30,000	
(3)	−26,000			+$26,000				
Bal.	1,500		2,500	26,000			30,000	
(4)			+7,100			+$7,100		
Bal.	1,500		9,600	26,000		7,100	30,000	
(5)	+4,200						+4,200	Consulting Revenue
Bal.	5,700		9,600	26,000		7,100	34,200	
(6)	−1,000						−1,000	Rent Expense
Bal.	4,700		9,600	26,000		7,100	33,200	
(7)	− 700						− 700	Salary Expense
Bal.	4,000		9,600	26,000		7,100	32,500	
(8)		+$1,900					+1,600	Consulting Revenue
							+ 300	Rental Revenue
Bal.	4,000	1,900	9,600	26,000		7,100	34,400	
(9)	+1,900	−1,900						
Bal.	5,900	0	9,600	26,000		7,100	34,400	
(10)	− 900					− 900		
Bal.	5,000	0	9,600	26,000		6,200	34,400	
(11)	− 600						− 600	Withdrawal
Bal.	$4,400	+ $ 0	+ $9,600	+ $26,000	=	$6,200	+ $33,800	

Financial Statements

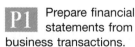

P1 Prepare financial statements from business transactions.

Point: Knowing how financial statements are prepared improves our analysis of them. We develop the skills for analysis of financial statements throughout the book. Chapter 18 focuses on financial statement analysis.

This section shows how the four major financial statements are prepared from business transactions. Recall that the four major financial statements and their purposes are:

1. *Income statement*—describes a company's revenues and expenses along with the resulting net income or loss over a period of time. It explains how equity changes during a period due to earnings activities.

2. *Statement of changes in owner's equity*—explains changes in equity from net income (or loss) and the owner's investments and withdrawals over a period of time.

3. *Statement of cash flows*—identifies cash inflows (receipts) and outflows (payments) over a period of time. It explains how the cash balance on the balance sheet changes from the beginning to the end of a period.

4. *Balance sheet*—describes a company's financial position (types and amounts of assets, liabilities, and equity) at a point in time.

We prepare these financial statements using the first 11 transactions of FastForward.

Income Statement

FastForward's income statement for December is shown at the top of Exhibit 2.15. Information about revenues and expenses is conveniently taken from the equity column of Exhibit 2.13. Revenues are reported first on the income statement. They include consulting revenues of $5,800 from transactions 5 and 8, and rental revenue of $300 from transaction 8. Expenses are reported after revenues. We can list revenues and expenses in different ways. For convenience in this chapter, we list larger amounts first. Rent and salary expenses are from transactions 6 and 7. Expenses reflect the costs to generate the revenues reported. Net income (or loss) is reported at the bottom of the statement and is the amount earned in December. Owner's investments and withdrawals are *not* part of income. Pie charts shown in Exhibit 2.14 are helpful in analyzing the makeup of revenues and expenses.

Revenue sources for FastForward

Expense sources for FastForward

Exhibit 2.14
Pie Chart Analysis

Statement of Changes in Owner's Equity

The statement of changes in owner's equity reports information about how equity changes over the reporting period. This statement shows beginning equity, events that increase it (investments by owner and net income), and events that decrease it (withdrawals and net loss). Ending equity is computed in this statement and is carried over and reported on the balance sheet. FastForward's statement of changes in owner's equity is the second report in Exhibit 2.15. The beginning balance of equity is measured as of the start of business on December 1. It is zero because FastForward did not exist before then. An existing business reports the beginning balance as of the end of the prior reporting period (such as from November 30). FastForward's statement shows that Taylor's initial investment created $30,000 of equity. It also shows the $4,400 of net income earned during the month. This links the income statement to the statement of changes in owner's equity. The statement also reports Taylor's $600 withdrawal and FastForward's $33,800 end-of-month equity balance.

Example: If Taylor purchased $3,000 of additional equipment with personal funds and invested it, how would the financial statement in Exhibit 2.15 change? *Answer:* The statement of changes in owner's equity would show owner's investments of $33,000 and an ending balance of $36,800. The balance sheet would show equipment with a cost of $29,000, total assets of $43,000, equity of $36,800, and total liabilities and equity of $43,000.

Balance Sheet

FastForward's balance sheet is the third report in Exhibit 2.15. This statement refers to FastForward's financial condition at the close of business on December 31. The left side of the balance sheet lists FastForward's assets: cash, supplies, and equipment. The upper right side of the balance sheet shows FastForward owes $6,200 to creditors. All other liabilities (such as a bank loan) would be listed here. The equity section shows an ending balance of $33,800. Note the link between the ending balance of the statement of changes in owner's equity and the equity balance here. (This presentation of the balance sheet is called the *account form*—assets on the left and liabilities and equity on the right. Another presentation is the *report form*—assets on top, followed by liabilities and then equity. Either presentation is acceptable.)

You Make the Call *e*

Entrepreneur You open a wholesale business selling entertainment equipment to retail outlets. You find that most of your customers demand to buy on credit. How can you use the balance sheets of these customers to decide which ones to extend credit to?

Answer—p. 58

Statement of Cash Flows

FastForward's statement of cash flows is the final report in Exhibit 2.15. This statement describes where FastForward's cash came from and where it went during December. It also shows the amount of cash at the beginning of the period and the amount left at the end. This information is important because a company must carefully manage cash if it is to succeed. **Amazon.com** must do a better job of managing its cash flows if it is to prosper.

FASTFORWARD
Income Statement
For Month Ended December 31, 2001

Revenues:		
Consulting revenue ($4,200 + $1,600)	$5,800	
Rental revenue	300	
Total revenues		$6,100
Expenses:		
Rent expense	1,000	
Salaries expense	700	
Total expenses		1,700
Net income		**$4,400** ◀

FASTFORWARD
Statement of Changes in Owner's Equity
For Month Ended December 31, 2001

C.Taylor, Capital, December 1, 2001		$ 0
Plus: Investments by owner	$30,000	
Net income	**4,400** ◀	34,400
		$34,400
Less: Withdrawals by owner		(600)
C.Taylor, Capital, December 31, 2001		**$33,800** ◀

FASTFORWARD
Balance Sheet
December 31, 2001

Assets		Liabilities	
▶ Cash	**$ 4,400**	Accounts payable	$ 6,200
Supplies	9,600	Total liabilities	$ 6,200
Equipment	26,000		
		Equity	
		C.Taylor, Capital.	**$33,800** ◀
Total assets	$40,000	Total liabilities and equity .	$40,000

FASTFORWARD
Statement of Cash Flows
For Month Ended December 31, 2001

Cash flows from operating activities:		
Cash received from clients ($4,200 + $1,900) . .	$ 6,100	
Cash paid for supplies ($2,500 + $900)	(3,400)	
Cash paid for rent	(1,000)	
Cash paid to employee	(700)	
Net cash provided by operating activities		$ 1,000
Cash flows from investing activities:		
Purchase of equipment	(26,000)	
Net cash used by investing activities		(26,000)
Cash flows from financing activities:		
Investments by owner	30,000	
Withdrawals by owner	(600)	
Net cash provided by financing activities		29,400
Net increase in cash		$ 4,400
Cash balance, December 1, 2001		0
▶ Cash balance, December 31, 2001		**$ 4,400**

Exhibit 2.15

Financial Statements and Their Links

Point: Arrow lines show how the statements are linked.

Point: Final totals are double underlined. Negative amounts are often in parentheses.

The first section reports cash flows from *operating activities*. The $6,100 of cash received from clients equals total revenue on the income statement because FastForward collected all revenues in cash. If some credit sales are not collected, or if credit sales from a prior period are collected this period, the amount of cash received from customers will not equal the revenues reported on the income statement for this period. This section also lists cash paid for supplies, rent, and employee salaries. These cash flows are from transactions 2, 6, and 7. We put these amounts in parentheses to indicate they are subtracted. Amounts for rent and salaries equal the expenses on FastForward's income statement because it paid these expenses in cash. The payment for supplies is an operating activity because they are expected to be used up in short-term operations (their benefits are not long term). Net cash provided by operating activities for December is $1,000. If cash paid exceeded cash received, we would call it "cash used by operating activities." Decision makers are especially interested in the operating section of the statement of cash flows as it helps assess how much income is in the form of cash.

The second section of the statement of cash flows describes *investing activities*. Investing activities involve buying and selling assets such as land and equipment that are held for *long term use* in the business. FastForward's only investing activity is the $26,000 purchase of equipment in transaction 3. Decision makers are interested in this section of the statement because it describes how a company is preparing for its future. If it is spending cash on productive assets, it should be able to grow and increase net income. A user is also concerned that a company does not overly spend on productive assets and face a cash shortage. If a company is selling its productive assets, it is downsizing its operations.

The third section shows cash flows related to *financing activities*. Financing activities include *long-term* borrowing and repaying cash from lenders, and the owner's cash investments and withdrawals. The statement of cash flows in Exhibit 2.15 shows FastForward received $30,000 from Chuck Taylor's initial investment in transaction 1. If the business had borrowed cash, that amount would appear here as an increase in cash. The financing section also shows the $600 owner withdrawal in transaction 11. The total effect of financing activities is a $29,400 net inflow of cash. The financing section shows us why FastForward did not run out of cash even though it spent $26,000 on equipment and generated only $1,000 from operating activities: it used the owner's cash investment. Decision makers are interested in the financing section because excessive borrowing can burden a company and reduce its potential for growth.

The final part of the statement of cash flows is the net increase or decrease in cash. It shows FastForward increased its cash balance to $4,400 in December. Because it started with no cash, the ending balance is also $4,400. This ending amount is the link from the statement of cash flows to the balance sheet. We give a more detailed explanation of the statement of cash flows in Chapters 5 and 17.

Point: Investing activities refer to long-term asset investments in the company, *not* to owner investments.

Example: How would the cash flow statement in Exhibit 2.15 change if FastForward had paid $27,000 cash for the equipment and had borrowed $5,000 from a bank to help finance future operations? *Answer:* The investing section would show the $27,000 paid for equipment; the financing section would report the $5,000 loan as additional cash provided; and the net increase in cash and ending cash balance would be increased from $4,400 to $8,400.

Quick Check

15. Explain the link between the income statement and the statement of changes in owner's equity.

16. Describe the link between the balance sheet and the statement of changes in owner's equity.

17. Discuss the three major sections of the statement of cash flows.

Answers—p. 58

A2	Compute return on equity and use it to analyze company performance.

An important reason for recording information about assets, liabilities, equity, and income is to help an owner judge the company's success compared to other business or personal opportunities. One measure of success is the **return on equity** ratio. This ratio is computed by taking net income and dividing it by average equity for the period as shown in Exhibit 2.16.

Exhibit 2.16
Return on Equity

$$\text{Return on equity} = \frac{\text{Net income}}{\text{Average equity}}$$

FastForward's return on equity for the month of December is computed as[5]

$$\frac{\$4,400}{[\$30,000 + \$33,800]/2} = 13.8\%$$

31,900

Taylor's return for December is high compared to many investments, especially for the first month of operations, but we must remember that net income for a proprietorship does not include an expense for the effort exerted by the owner to manage its operations. To consider this, we can compute a **modified return on equity** for proprietorships and partnerships. This modified return on equity reduces net income by the value of the owner's efforts and is computed as shown in Exhibit 2.17.

Exhibit 2.17
Modified Return on Equity

$$\text{Modified return on equity} = \frac{\text{Net income} - \text{Value of owner's efforts}}{\text{Average equity}}$$

Other employment opportunities suggest that Taylor's efforts are valued at $3,800 per month. FastForward's modified return on equity is then computed as

$$\frac{\$4,400 - \$3,800}{[\$30,000 + \$33,800]/2} = 1.9\%$$

600

31,900

This modified return of 1.9% per month is quite different from the 13.8%. Taylor would then compare this return with other opportunities to determine whether it is adequate. Examples of other opportunities are savings accounts, company stock, and different jobs.

Exhibit 2.18
Return on Equity for Selected Industries

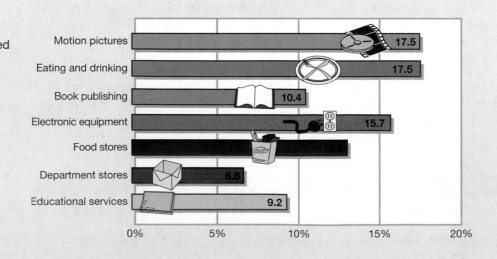

Motion pictures	17.5
Eating and drinking	17.5
Book publishing	10.4
Electronic equipment	15.7
Food stores	
Department stores	6.8
Educational services	9.2

0%   5%   10%   15%   20%

---

[5] A simple average is computed as the sum of the beginning and ending balances divided by 2. For a company's first period of operations, the owner's initial investment is commonly used as the beginning balance.

Taylor likely will continue to operate FastForward because 1.9% per month is more than 20% per year.[6] For further comparison, Exhibit 2.18 shows the return on equity for different industries. FastForward's return exceeds these.

Three additional points are important. First, an evaluation of returns should recognize risk. Risk can differ considerably across investment alternatives. Second, income can vary from month to month. Income variation is related to risk. Third, because of company, business, and economic fluctuations, a better measure of return is obtained by computing it over a longer period such as one year.

You Make the Call

Engineer   You are considering launching a proprietorship to manufacture custom-fit athletic shoes. Your current salary is $2,500 per month. You estimate the new business will yield a net income of $4,500 per month and require an average equity balance of $400,000. Do you pursue this opportunity?

Answer—p. 58

Summary

C1   Identify and explain the content and reporting aims of financial statements. The major financial statements are income statement, balance sheet, statement of changes in owner's equity, and statement of cash flows. An income statement shows a company's profitability, including revenues, expenses, and net income (loss). A balance sheet reports a company's financial position, including assets, liabilities, and equity. A statement of changes in owner's equity explains how equity changes from the beginning to the end of a period, and the statement of cash flows identifies all cash inflows and outflows for the period.

C2   Describe differences in financial statements across forms of business organization. One important difference is in the equity section of the balance sheet. Proprietorship and partnership balance sheets list the equity balance beside the owner's name. Names of a corporation's shareholders are not listed. Another difference is in the way assets are taken. When an owner of a proprietorship or a partnership takes them from the company, they are called *withdrawals*. When owners of a corporation receive assets from the company, they are called *dividends*. Another difference is that no salary expense is recorded when the owner of a proprietorship or partnership is its manager.

C3   Explain the financial reporting environment. Accounting professionals prepare financial statements, independent auditors often examine them and prepare an audit report, and users rely on them to make important decisions. Preparers use GAAP, and auditors are guided by GAAS. Applying both GAAP and GAAS helps ensure that financial statements include relevant, reliable, and comparable information.

C4   Identify those responsible for setting accounting and auditing principles. The FASB is the primary authoritative source of GAAP. The FASB draws its authority from two major sources: the SEC and state boards that license CPAs. Authority for GAAS belongs to the ASB. The SEC is an important source of the ASB's authority.

C5   Identify, explain, and apply accounting principles. Accounting principles aid in producing relevant, reliable, and comparable information. The business entity principle means that a business is accounted for separately from its owner(s). The objectivity principle means independent, objective evidence supports the information. The cost principle means financial statements are based on actual costs incurred. The monetary unit principle assumes transactions can be captured in money terms. The going-concern principle means financial statements assume the business will continue. The revenue recognition principle means revenue is recognized when earned.

A1   Analyze business transactions using the accounting equation. A transaction is an exchange of economic consideration between two parties. Examples include exchanges of products, services, money, and rights to collect money. Business transactions always have at least two effects on one or more components of the accounting equation. The accounting equation is: Assets = Liabilities + Equity. This equation is always in balance.

A2   Compute return on equity and use it to analyze company performance. Return on equity is computed as net income divided by average equity. A modified return on equity for proprietorships and partnerships is computed as net income less the value of the owner's efforts, and then this quantity is divided by average equity.

P1   Prepare financial statements from business transactions. Business transactions can be summarized using the accounting equation from which we can prepare financial statements. The balance sheet uses the ending balances in the accounting equation. The statement of changes in owner's equity and the income statement use data from the Equity column for the period. The statement of cash flows uses data from the Cash column.

---

[6] The annual rate is approximated by taking the 1.9% monthly rate and multiplying by the 12 months in a year, or 22.8%.

Guidance Answers to **You Make the Call**

Web Designer A designer's efforts are reflected in the income statement. The income statement reports information on the revenues and expenses associated with operating activities. If operating activities are successful and you can point to specific contributions such as increased sales or reduced expenses, you are more likely to get a wage increase.

Entrepreneur We can use the accounting equation to help us identify risky customers to whom we would likely not want to extend credit. The accounting equation is: Assets = Liabilities + Equity. A balance sheet provides amounts for each of these key components. The lower equity is relative to liabilities, the less likely you would extend credit. A low equity means the business has little value that does not already have creditor claims to it.

Engineer The modified return on equity is relevant for your decision. This return equals 0.5%, computed as [\$4,500 − \$2,500]/\$400,000. This is about 6% per year, approximated as $0.5\% \times 12$ months. You would not likely quit your current job and salary and take the risk of a new business for an expected return of 6% per year.

Guidance Answers to **Quick Checks**

1. The four major financial statements are income statment, balance sheet, statement of changes in owner's (or shareholders') equity, and statement of cash flows.

2. Revenues are inflows of assets in exchange for products or services provided to customers as part of the main operations of a business. Expenses are outflows or the using up of assets that result from providing products or services to customers.

3. Assets are the resources a business owns or controls that carry expected future benefits. Liabilities are the obligations of a business, representing the claims of others against the assets of a business. Equity is the owner's claim on the assets of the business after deducting liabilities.

4. Note three differences: (*a*) A proprietorship's balance sheet lists the equity balance beside the owner's name. Partnerships do the same unless they have too many owners to list. Names of a corporation's owners are not listed in the balance sheet. (*b*) Distributions of cash or other assets to owners of a proprietorship or partnership are called *withdrawals*. Distributions of cash or other assets to owners of a corporation are called *dividends*. (*c*) When the owner of a proprietorship is also its manager, no salary expense is reported on the income statement. The same is true for a partnership, but salaries paid to a corporation's owners are reported as expenses on its income statement.

5. The FASB is the primary organization that sets GAAP. Its decisions are reflected in *Statements of Financial Accounting Standards*. The FASB draws authority from two main sources: the SEC and state boards that license CPAs.

6. *GAAS* refer to generally accepted auditing standards and are the guidelines for performing audits of financial statements. GAAS are set by the Auditing Standards Board (ASB).

7. U.S. companies are not directly affected by international accounting standards. International standards are put forth as preferred accounting practices. However, stock exchanges and other parties are increasing the pressure to narrow differences in worldwide accounting practices. International accounting standards are playing an important role in that process.

8. Users desire information about the performance of a specific entity. If information is mixed between two or more entities, its usefulness decreases.

9. The objectivity and cost principles are related in that most users consider information based on cost as objective. Information prepared using both principles is considered highly reliable and often relevant.

10. A transaction that changes the makeup of assets would not affect liability and equity accounts. Both transactions 2 and 3 are examples. Each exchanges one asset for another.

11. Earning revenue by performing services, such as in transaction 5, increases equity (and assets). Incurring expenses while servicing clients, such as in transactions 6 and 7, decreases equity (and assets). Other examples include owner investments that increase equity and withdrawals that decrease equity.

12. The revenue recognition principle gives preparers guidelines on when to recognize (record) revenue. This is important; for example, if revenue is recognized too early, the income statement reports revenue sooner than it should and the business looks more profitable than it is.

13. Paying a liability with an asset reduces both asset and liability totals. One example is transaction 10 of FastForward, where a payable is reduced by paying cash.

14. The accounting equation is: Assets = Liabilities + Equity. This equation is always in balance, both before and after every transaction.

15. An income statement presents a company's revenues and expenses along with the resulting net income or loss. A statement of changes in owner's equity shows changes in equity, including that from net income or loss. Both statements report transactions occurring over a period of time.

16. The balance sheet describes a company's financial position (assets, liabilities, and equity) at a point in time. The equity account in the balance sheet is obtained from the statement of changes in owner's equity.

17. Cash flows from operating activities report cash receipts and payments from the primary business the company is engaged in. Cash flows from investing activities involve cash transactions from buying and selling long-term assets. Cash flows from financing activities include long-term cash borrowings and repayments from lenders and the cash investments and withdrawals of the owner.

After several months of planning, Sylvia Workman started a haircutting business, Expressions. The following events occurred during its first month:

a. On August 1, Workman put $3,000 cash into a checking account in the name of Expressions. She also invested $15,000 of equipment that she already owned.

b. On August 2, Workman paid $600 cash for furniture for the shop.

c. On August 3, Workman paid $500 cash to rent space in a strip mall for August.

d. On August 4, Workman purchased some new equipment for the shop that she bought on credit (using a note payable) for $1,200.

e. On August 5, Expressions opened for business. Cash received from services provided in the first week and a half of business (ended August 15) is $825.

f. On August 15, Workman provided haircutting services on account for $100.

g. On August 17, Workman received a $100 check for services previously rendered on account.

h. On August 17, Workman paid $125 to an assistant for working during the grand opening.

i. Cash received from services provided during the second half of August is $930.

j. On August 31, Workman paid a $400 installment on the note payable entered into on August 4.

k. On August 31, Workman withdrew $900 cash for her personal use.

Demonstration Problem

*The **Demonstration Problem** is a review of key chapter materials. The Planning the Solution offers strategies in solving the problem.*

Required

1. Arrange the following asset, liability, and equity titles in a table similar to the one in Exhibit 2.13: Cash, Accounts Receivable, Furniture, Store Equipment, Note Payable, and Sylvia Workman, Capital. Show the effects of each transaction on the equation. Add explanations for each of the changes in equity.

2. Prepare an income statement for August.

3. Prepare a statement of changes in owner's equity for August.

4. Prepare a balance sheet as of August 31.

5. Prepare a statement of cash flows for August.

6. Determine the return on equity ratio for August.

7. Determine the modified return on equity ratio for August, assuming Workman's management efforts were worth $1,000.

Planning the Solution

• Set up a table with the appropriate columns, including a final column for describing the transactions that affect equity.

• Analyze each transaction and show its effects as increases or decreases in the appropriate columns. Be sure the accounting equation remains in balance after each transaction.

• To prepare the income statement, find revenues and expenses in the last column. List those items on the statement, compute the difference, and label the result as *net income* or *net loss*.

• Use information in the explanations column to prepare the statement of changes in owner's equity.

• Use information in the last row of the table to prepare the balance sheet.

• To prepare the statement of cash flows, include all events listed in the Cash column of the table. Classify each cash flow as operating, investing, or financing.

• Calculate return on equity by dividing net income by average equity. Calculate the modified return by subtracting the $1,000 value of Workman's efforts from net income, and then dividing the difference by average equity.

Solution to Demonstration Problem

1.

	Assets				= Liabilities +		Equity	
	Cash	+ Accounts Receivable	+ Furniture	+ Store Equipment	= Note Payable	+ Sylvia Workman, Capital	Explanation of Change
a.	$3,000			$15,000		$18,000	Investment
b.	− 600		+$600				
Bal.	2,400		600	15,000		18,000	
c.	− 500					− 500	Rent Expense
Bal.	1,900		600	15,000		17,500	
d.				+ 1,200	+$1,200		
Bal.	1,900		600	16,200	1,200	17,500	
e.	+ 825					+ 825	Haircutting Services Revenue
Bal.	2,725		600	16,200	1,200	18,325	
f.		+$100				+ 100	Haircutting Services Revenue
Bal.	2,725	100	600	16,200	1,200	18,425	
g.	+ 100	− 100					
Bal.	2,825	0	600	16,200	1,200	18,425	
h.	− 125					− 125	Wages Expense
Bal.	2,700		600	16,200	1,200	18,300	
i.	+ 930					+ 930	Haircutting Services Revenue
Bal.	3,630		600	16,200	1,200	19,230	
j.	− 400				− 400		
Bal.	3,230		600	16,200	800	19,230	
k.	− 900					− 900	Withdrawal
Bal.	$2,330 +		$600 +	$16,200 =	$800 +	$18,330	

2.

EXPRESSIONS
Income Statement
For Month Ended August 31

Revenues:		
Haircutting services revenue		$1,855
Operating expenses:		
Rent expense	$500	
Wages expense	125	
Total operating expenses		625
Net Income		$1,230

3.

EXPRESSIONS Statement of Changes in Owner's Equity For Month Ended August 31		
S. Workman, Capital, August 1		$ 0
Plus: Investments by owner	$18,000	
Net income	1,230	19,230
		$19,230
Less: Withdrawals by owner		(000)
S. Workman, Capital, August 31		$18,330

4.

EXPRESSIONS Balance Sheet August 31			
Assets		**Liabilities**	
Cash	$ 2,330	Note payable	$ 800
Furniture	600	**Equity**	
Store equipment	16,200	S. Workman, Capital	18,330
Total assets	$19,130	Total liabilities and equity	$19,130

5.

EXPRESSIONS Statement of Cash Flows For Month Ended August 31		
Cash flows from operating activities:		
Cash received from customers	$1,855	
Cash paid for rent	(500)	
Cash paid for wages	(125)	
Net cash provided by operating activities		$1,230
Cash flows from investing activities:		
Cash paid for furniture		(600)
Cash flows from financing activities:		
Cash received from owner	3,000	
Cash paid to owner	(900)	
Partial repayment of note payable	(400)	
Net cash provided by financing activities		1,700
Net increase in cash		$2,330
Cash balance, August 1		0
Cash balance, August 31		$2,330

6. Return on equity $= \dfrac{\text{Net income}}{\text{Average equity}} = \dfrac{\$1,230}{(\$18,000 + \$18,330)/2} = \dfrac{\$1,230}{\$18,165} = \underline{\underline{\mathbf{6.77\,\%}}}$

7. Modified return on equity $= \dfrac{\text{Net income} - \text{Owner's efforts}}{\text{Average equity}}$

$= \dfrac{\$1,230 - \$1,000}{(\$18,000 + \$18,330)/2} = \dfrac{\$230}{\$18,165} = \underline{\underline{\mathbf{1.27\,\%}}}$

Glossary

Accounting equation relation between a company's assets, liabilities, and equity; expressed as Assets = Liabilities + Equity; also called *balance sheet equation*. (p. 46).

Account payable liability created by buying goods or services on credit. (p. 39).

Account receivable asset created by selling products or services on credit. (p. 39).

Assets resources a business owns or controls that are expected to provide future benefits to the business. (p. 39).

Balance sheet financial statement that lists the types and dollar amounts of assets, liabilities, and equity at a specific date; also called *statement of financial position*. (p. 38).

Balance sheet equation (see *accounting equation*). (p. 46).

Business entity principle the principle that requires a business to be accounted for separately from its owner(s). (p. 44).

Business transaction an exchange of economic consideration (such as goods, services, money, or rights to collect money) between two parties. (p. 46).

Contributed capital the category of equity created by shareholders' investments; also called *paid-in capital*. (p. 40).

Cost principle the accounting principle that requires financial statement information to be based on actual costs incurred in business transactions. (p. 44).

Creditors individuals or organizations entitled to receive payments from a company. (p. 39).

Debtors individuals or organizations that owe money to a business. (p. 39).

Dividends a corporation's distributions of assets to its owners. (p. 41).

Equity owner's claim on the assets of a business; equals the residual interest in an entity's assets after deducting liabilities; also called *net assets*. (p. 39).

Expenses outflows or the using up of assets as part of operations of a business to generate sales. (p. 37).

Financial statements includes the balance sheet, income statement, statement of changes in owner's equity, and statement of cash flows. (p. 36).

Generally accepted auditing standards (GAAS) rules adopted for conducting audits of financial statements. (p. 41).

Going-concern principle a principle that requires financial statements to reflect the assumption that the business will continue operating; also called *continuing-concern principle*. (p. 45).

Income statement financial statement that subtracts expenses from revenues to yield a net income or loss over a specified period of time. (p. 37).

International Accounting Standards Committee (IASC) a committee that identifies preferred accounting practices and encourages their worldwide acceptance. (p. 43).

Liabilities claims by others that will reduce the future assets of a business or require services or products. (p. 39).

Modified return on equity ratio of net income minus the value of owner's effort divided by average equity. (p. 56).

Monetary unit principle a principle that assumes transactions and events can be expressed in money units. (p. 45).

Net assets (see *equity*). (p. 39).

Net income the excess of revenues over expenses for a period. (p. 37).

Net loss the excess of expenses over revenues for a period (p. 37).

Note payable a liability expressed by a written promise to make a future payment at a specific time. (p. 39).

Objectivity principle a principle that requires financial statement information to be supported by independent, unbiased evidence. (p. 44).

Paid-in capital (see *contributed capital*). (p. 40).

Retained earnings a corporation's accumulated net income and losses that have not been distributed to shareholders. (p. 40).

Return on equity ratio of net income to average equity. (p. 56).

Revenue recognition principle the principle that revenue is recognized when earned. (p. 49).

Revenues inflows of assets received in exchange for goods or services provided to customers as part of operations. (p. 37).

Statement of cash flows a financial statement that lists cash inflows (receipts) and cash outflows (payments) during a period; arranged by operating, investing, and financing. (p. 39).

Statement of changes in owner's equity a report of changes in equity over a period; adjusted for increases (owner investment and net income) and for decreases (withdrawals and net loss). (p. 37).

Statements of Financial Accounting Standards (SFAS) FASB publications that establish U.S. GAAP. (p. 42).

Withdrawal a payment of cash or other assets from a proprietorship or partnership to its owner or owners. (p. 41).

Questions

1. Identify the four main financial statements of a business.
2. What information is reported in an income statement?
3. What do accountants mean by the term *revenue?*
4. Why does the user of an income statement need to know the time period that it covers?
5. Give two examples of expenses a business might incur.
6. Which financial statement is sometimes called the *statement of financial position?*
7. What information is reported in a balance sheet?
8. Define (*a*) assets, (*b*) liabilities, (*c*) equity, and (*d*) net assets.
9. The statement of cash flows reports on what major activities?
10. Contrast the equity sections of the balance sheet for a sole proprietorship, partnership, and corporation.
11. What FASB pronouncements make up generally accepted accounting principles?
12. Identify two categories of accounting principles.
13. What does the objectivity principle require for information reported in financial statements? Why?
14. A business reports its own office stationery on the balance sheet at its $430 cost, although it cannot be sold for more than $10 as scrap paper. Which accounting principle justifies this treatment?

15. Why is the revenue recognition principle needed? What does it require?
16. What events or transactions change owner's equity?
17. To what should a company's return on equity ratio be compared with to determine whether the owner has made a good investment?
18. Refer to the financial statements of **Nike** in Appendix A. To what level of significance are the dollar amounts rounded? What time period does the income statement cover?
19. Review the balance sheet of **Reebok** in Appendix A. What amount of total assets is reported at December 31, 1999? Prove the accounting equation for Reebok at December 31, 1999.
20. Refer to **Gap**'s income statement in Appendix A. How does the name of this statement differ from FastForward's income statement? How does Gap's 2000 net income compare to its previous year?
21. Refer to FastForward's financial statements in the chapter for the month ended December 31, 2001. (*a*) Review the balance sheet and identify the business form Chuck Taylor used to organize his business. (*b*) How much net cash did FastForward generate from the total of its operating, investing, and financing activities in December 2001?

Instructions: In this book's assignments, assume no income taxes unless explicitly mentioned.

Determine the missing amount for each of the following separate cases:

	Assets	=	Liabilities	+	Equity
a.	$ 80,000	=	$ 42,500	+	?
b.	$500,000	=	?	+	$225,000
c.	?	=	$193,000	+	$ 47,000

QUICK STUDY

QS 2-1
Applying the accounting equation

A1

Use the accounting equation in the following separate cases to determine the:
a. Equity in a business that has $195,000 of assets and $23,000 of liabilities.
b. Liabilities of a business having $162,400 of assets and $122,900 of equity.
c. Assets of a business having $32,890 of liabilities and $134,655 of equity.

QS 2-2
Applying the accounting equation

A1

Identify the financial statement(s) where each of the following items appears:
a. Service fees earned
b. Owner cash withdrawals
c. Office equipment
d. Accounts payable
e. Cash repaid on bank loan
f. Utilities expenses
g. Office supplies
h. Cash received from prior period credit sale

QS 2-3
Identifying financial statement items

C1

QS 2-4
Computing return on equity

In a recent year's financial statements, **Boeing Company,** which is the largest aerospace company in the United States, reported the following:

Sales	$57,993 million
Net income	2,309 million
Total assets	36,147 million
Total beginning-of-year equity	12,316 million
Total end-of-year equity	11,462 million

Calculate Boeing's return on equity for that year.

QS 2-5
Identifying accounting principles

Identify which general accounting principle best describes each of the following practices:

a. Le Ann Welch owns both Sailing Passions and Dockside Supplies, both of which are sole proprietorships. In preparing financial statements for Dockside Supplies, Welch makes sure that the expense transactions of Sailing Passions are kept separate from Dockside's statements.

b. In December, 2001, Renew-A-Floor received a customer's order to install carpet in a new house that would not be ready for installation until March 2002. Renew-A-Floor should record the revenue for the order in March 2002, not in December 2001.

c. If $40,000 cash is paid to buy land, the land is reported on the buyer's balance sheet at $40,000.

EXERCISES

Exercise 2-1
Analysis using the accounting equation

Sarah Wells began a new consulting firm on January 5. The accounting equation showed the following balances after each of the company's first five transactions. Analyze the accounting equation for each transaction and describe each of the five transactions with their amounts.

		Assets			=	Liabilities	+	Equity
Trans-action	Cash	+ Accounts Receivable	+ Office Supplies	+ Office Furniture =	Accounts Payable	+	S. Wells, Capital
a.	$20,000	$ 0	$ 0	$ 0	$ 0		$20,000
b.	19,000	0	1,500	0	500		20,000
c.	11,000	0	1,500	8,000	500		20,000
d.	11,000	3,000	1,500	8,000	500		23,000
e.	11,500	3,000	1,500	8,000	500		23,500

Exercise 2-2
Identifying effects of transactions on the accounting equation

The following changes in items of the accounting equation are described in the separate cases *a* through *g*. Provide an example of a transaction that creates the described effects for each case.

a. Decreases an asset and decreases equity.

b. Increases an asset and increases a liability.

c. Decreases a liability and increases a liability.

d. Increases an asset and decreases an asset.

e. Decreases an asset and decreases a liability.

f. Increases a liability and decreases equity.

g. Increases an asset and increases equity.

Exercise 2-3
Identifying effects of transactions on accounting equation

The following table shows the effects of five transactions (*a* through *e*) on the assets, liabilities, and equity of Benton Boutique. Write short descriptions of the probable nature of each transaction.

	Assets						=	Liabilities	+	Equity
	Cash	+	Accounts Receivable	+	Office Supplies	+	Land	=	Accounts Payable	+	C. Benton, Capital
	$10,500				$1,500		$ 9,500				$21,500
a.	− 2,000						+ 2,000				
	8,500				1,500		11,500				21,500
b.					+ 500				+$500		
	8,500				2,000		11,500		500		21,500
c.			+$950								⊢ 050
	8,500		950		2,000		11,500		500		22,450
d.	− 500								− 500		
	8,000		950		2,000		11,500		0		22,450
e.	+ 950		−950								
	$ 8,950	+	$ 0	+	$2,000	+	$11,500	=	$ 0	+	$22,450

A sole proprietorship had the following assets and liabilities at the beginning and end of a recent year:

	Assets	Liabilities
Beginning of the year	$ 60,000	$20,000
End of the year	105,000	36,000

Determine the net income earned or net loss incurred by the business during the year under each of the following separate assumptions:

a. Owner made no investments in the business and withdrew no assets during the year.

b. Owner made no investments in the business during the year but withdrew $1,250 per month to pay personal expenses.

c. Owner withdrew no assets during the year but invested an additional $55,000 cash.

d. Owner withdrew $1,250 per month to pay personal expenses and invested an additional $35,000 cash.

Mary Campion began a professional practice on June 1 and plans to prepare financial statements at the end of each month. During June, Campion completed these transactions:

Exercise 2-5
Identifying effects of transactions on the accounting equation and computing return on equity

a. Invested $60,000 cash along with equipment that had an $8,000 market value.

b. Paid $1,500 cash for rent of office space for the month.

c. Purchased $15,000 of additional equipment on credit.

d. Completed work for a client and immediately collected the $1,000 cash earned.

e. Completed work for a client and sent a bill for $6,000 to be paid within 30 days.

f. Purchased additional equipment for $5,000 cash.

g. Paid an assistant $2,700 cash as wages for the month.

h. Collected $4,000 cash on the amount owed by the client described in transaction *e*.

i. Paid cash for the equipment purchased in transaction *c*.

j. Withdrew $900 cash for personal use.

Required

Create a table like the one in Exhibit 2.13, using the following headings for columns: Cash; Accounts Receivable; Equipment; Accounts Payable; and M. Campion, Capital. Then use additions and subtractions to show the effects of the transactions on individual items of the accounting equation. Show new balances after each transaction. Determine the modified return on equity for Campion assuming that her management efforts during June have a value of $4,000.

Check   Net income, $2,800

Exercise 2-6

Identifying accounting principles

C5 **C3**

Match each of the following numbered descriptions with the principle it best reflects. Indicate your answer by writing the letter for the appropriate principle in the blank space next to each description.

A. General accounting principle
B. Cost principle
C. Business entity principle
D. Revenue recognition principle
E. Specific accounting principle
F. Objectivity principle
G. Going-concern principle

_____ **1.** Usually created by a pronouncement from an authoritative body. _E_

_____ **2.** Requires financial statements to reflect the assumption that the business will continue operating.

_____ **3.** Derived from long-used and generally accepted accounting practices.

_____ **4.** Requires financial statement information to be supported by evidence other than someone's opinion or belief.

_____ **5.** Requires every business to be accounted for separately from its owner or owners.

_____ **6.** Requires revenue to be recorded only when the earnings process is complete.

_____ **7.** Requires information to be based on costs incurred in transactions.

Exercise 2-7

Reporting financial statement items

C1 **P1**

Match each of the following numbered items with the financial statement or statements on which it should be reported. Indicate your answer by writing the letter or letters for the correct statement in the blank space next to each item.

A. Income statement
B. Statement of changes in owner's equity
C. Balance sheet
D. Statement of cash flows

_____ **1.** Office supplies

_____ **2.** Cash received from customers

_____ **3.** Consulting fees earned and received in cash

_____ **4.** Rent expense incurred and paid in cash

_____ **5.** Investments of cash by owner

_____ **6.** Accounts payable

_____ **7.** Cash withdrawals by owner   _out flow_

_____ **8.** Accounts receivable

Exercise 2-8

Preparing a statement of changes in owner's equity

C1 **P1**

Compute the amount of the missing item in each of the following separate cases *a* through *d*:

	(a)	(b)	(c)	(d)
2 Equity, January 1	$ 0	$ 0	$ 0	$ 0
3 Owner's investments during the year	110,000	?	87,000	210,000
4 Owner's withdrawals during the year	?	(47,000)	(10,000)	(55,000)
5 Net income (loss) for the year	22,000	90,000	(4,000)	?
6 Equity, December 31	104,000	85,000	?	110,000

Exercise 2-9

Identifying sections of statement of cash flows

C1

Indicate the section where each of the following cash flows would appear on the statement of cash flows.

A. Cash flow from operating activity
B. Cash flow from investing activity
C. Cash flow from financing activity

_____ **1.** Cash paid for wages

_____ **2.** Cash withdrawal by owner

_____ **3.** Cash purchase of equipment

_____ **4.** Cash paid for advertising

_____ **5.** Cash paid on a payable

_____ **6.** Cash investment by owner

_____ **7.** Cash received from clients

_____ **8.** Cash paid for rent

On October 1, Bernice Haddox organized a new consulting firm called Tech Answers. On October 31, the company's records show the following items and amounts. Use this information to prepare an October income statement for the business.

Cash	$11,000	Owner's withdrawals	$ 2,360
Accounts receivable	14,000	Consulting fees earned	14,000
Office supplies	3,250	Rent expense	3,550
Automobiles	46,000	Salaries expense	7,000
Office equipment	18,000	Telephone expense	760
Accounts payable	8,500	Miscellaneous expenses	580
Owner's investments	84,000		

Exercise 2-10
Preparing an income statement

Check Net income, $2,110

Use the information in Exercise 2-10 to prepare an October statement of changes in owner's equity for Tech Answers.

Exercise 2-11
Preparing a statement of changes in owner's equity

Use the information in Exercise 2-10 (if completed, you can also use your solution to Exercise 2-11) to prepare an October 31 balance sheet for Tech Answers.

Exercise 2-12
Preparing a balance sheet

Use the information in Exercise 2-10 to prepare an October 31 statement of cash flows for Tech Answers. Also assume the following:
- The owner's initial investment consists of $38,000 cash and $46,000 in automobiles.
- The $18,000 equipment purchase is paid in cash.
- The accounts payable balance of $8,500 consists of the $3,250 office supplies purchase and $5,250 in employee salaries yet to be paid.
- The rent, telephone, and miscellaneous expenses are paid in cash.
- No cash has yet been collected for consulting services provided.

Exercise 2-13
Preparing a statement of cash flows

Use information from each of the following separate cases *a* through *d* to calculate the company's return on equity and its modified return on equity:

Exercise 2-14
Calculating return on equity

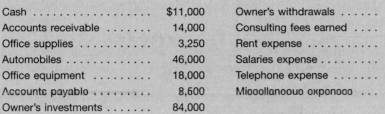

	(a)	(b)	(c)	(d)
Average equity	$100,000	$900,000	$250,000	$633,000
Net income	20,000	210,000	110,000	178,000
Value of owner's efforts	6,000	80,000	54,000	125,000

PROBLEM SET A

Problem 2-1A
Calculating missing information using accounting knowledge

The following financial statement information is known about five separate proprietorships:

	Company A	Company B	Company C	Company D	Company E
December 31, 2001:					
Assets	$55,000	$34,000	$24,000	$60,000	$119,000
Liabilities	24,500	21,500	9,000	40,000	?
December 31, 2002:					
Assets	58,000	40,000	?	85,000	113,000
Liabilities	?	26,500	29,000	24,000	70,000
During year 2002:					
Owner investments	6,000	1,400	9,750	?	6,500
Net income	8,500	?	8,000	14,000	20,000
Owner withdrawals	3,500	2,000	5,875	0	11,000

Required

1. Answer the following questions about Company A:
   a. What is the equity amount on December 31, 2001?
   b. What is the equity amount on December 31, 2002?
   c. What is the amount of liabilities on December 31, 2002?

2. Answer the following questions about Company B:
   a. What is the equity amount on December 31, 2001?
   b. What is the equity amount on December 31, 2002?
   c. What is net income for year 2002?

Check   Co. C, Dec. 31, 2002, Assets, $55,875

3. Calculate the amount of assets for Company C on December 31, 2002.

4. Calculate the amount of owner investments in Company D during year 2002.

5. Calculate the amount of liabilities for Company E on December 31, 2001.

Problem 2-2A
Identifying effects of transactions on financial statements

C1 A1 P1

Identify how each of the following separate transactions affects financial statements. For the balance sheet, identify how each transaction affects total assets, total liabilities, and equity. For the income statement, identify how each transaction affects net income. For the statement of cash flows, identify how each transaction affects cash flows from operating activities, cash flows from financing activities, and cash flows from investing activities. For increases, place a "+" in the column or columns. For decreases, place a "−" in the column or columns. If both an increase and a decrease occur, place a "+/−" in the column or columns. The first transaction is completed as an example.

		Balance Sheet			Income Statement	Statement of Cash Flows		
	Transaction	**Total Assets**	**Total Liab.**	**Equity**	**Net Income**	**Operating Activities**	**Financing Activities**	**Investing Activities**
1	Owner invests cash	+		+			+	
2	Performs services for cash							
3	Pays wages incurred with cash							
4	Pays for services received on credit							
5	Borrows cash by signing note payable							
6	Owner withdraws cash							
7	Buys land by signing note payable							
8	Performs services on credit							
9	Buys office equipment for cash							
10	Collects cash on receivable from (8)							

A new start-up business, Copy This, has the following beginning cash balance and cash flows for the month of December:

Cash balance, December 1	$ 0
Cash withdrawal by owner	600
Cash received from customers	5,000
Cash payment of long-term liabilities	1,200
Cash paid for store supplies	2,800
Cash purchase of equipment	23,000
Cash paid for ront	1,000
Cash paid to employee	570
Cash investment by owner	38,000

Required

Prepare a statement of cash flows for Copy This for the month of December.

Problem 2-3A
Preparing a statement of cash flows

Check   Cash bal., Dec. 31, $13,830

John Elfrink started a new business called Elfrink Enterprises and it completed the following transactions during its first six months of operations:

a. Elfrink invests $50,000 cash and office equipment valued at $25,000 in the business.

b. Paid $200,000 for a building to be used as an office. Elfrink paid $40,000 in cash and signed a note payable promising to pay the balance over the next four years.

c. Purchased office supplies for $5,000 cash.

d. Purchased $27,000 of office equipment on credit.

e. Performed services and billed the client $5,000 to be received later.

f. Paid a local newspaper $800 cash for an advertisement of the new business.

g. Performed services for a client and collected $22,000 cash.

h. Made a $3,000 cash payment on the equipment purchased in transaction *d*.

i. Received $4,000 cash from the client described in transaction *e*.

j. Paid $2,000 cash for the office secretary's wages.

k. Elfrink withdrew $2,400 cash from the company bank account for personal living expenses.

Problem 2-4A
Analyzing effects of transactions and computing return on equity

Required

Preparation Component

1. Create a table like the one in Exhibit 2.13, using the following headings for the columns: Cash; Accounts Receivable; Office Supplies; Office Equipment; Building; Accounts Payable; Note Payable; and J. Elfrink, Capital. Leave space for an Explanation column to the right of the Capital column. Identify revenues and expenses by name in the Explanation column.

2. Use additions and subtractions to show the transactions' effects on individual items of the accounting equation. Show new balances after each transaction. Indicate next to each change in equity whether it was caused by an investment, a revenue, an expense, or a withdrawal.

3. Once you have completed the table, determine the company's net income.

Check   Net income, $24,200

Analysis Component

4. Determine the return on equity for Elfrink Enterprises (use the $75,000 initial investment as the beginning balance of equity). Assuming Elfrink could have earned $5,000 for the period from another job, determine the modified return on equity for the period. State whether you think the business is a good use of Elfrink's money if an alternative investment would have returned 8% for the same period.

JD Simpson started a new business called The Simpson Co. that began operations on May 1. Simpson completed the following transactions during the month:

May 1   Simpson invested $40,000 cash in the business.
 1   Rented a furnished office and paid $2,200 cash for May's rent.
 3   Purchased office equipment for $1,890 on credit.
 5   Paid $750 cash for this month's cleaning services.
 8   Provided consulting services for a client and immediately collected $5,400 cash.

Problem 2-5A
Preparing a balance sheet, an income statement, a statement of changes in owner's equity, and a statement of cash flows

12	Provided $2,500 of consulting services for a client on credit.
15	Paid $750 cash for an assistant's salary for the first half of this month.
20	Received cash payment in full for the services provided on May 12.
22	Provided $3,200 of consulting services on credit.
28	Received full cash payment for the services provided on May 22.
29	Paid cash for the office equipment purchased on May 3.
30	Purchased $80 of advertising in this month's local paper on credit; cash payment is due June 1.
30	Paid $300 cash for this month's telephone bill.
30	Paid $280 cash for this month's utilities.
30	Paid $750 cash for an assistant's salary for the second half of this month.
30	Simpson withdrew $1,400 cash from the business for personal use.

Required

1. Arrange the following asset, liability, and equity titles in a table like Exhibit 2.13: Cash; Accounts Receivable; Office Equipment; Accounts Payable; and JD Simpson, Capital. Include an Explanation column for changes in equity.

2. Show effects of the transactions on the items of the accounting equation by recording increases and decreases in the appropriate columns. Do not determine new account balances after each transaction. Next to each change in equity, state whether it was caused by an investment, a revenue, an expense, or a withdrawal. Determine the final total for each item and verify that the equation is in balance.

Check   Net income, $5,990

3. Prepare an income statement for May, a statement of changes in owner's equity for May, a May 31 balance sheet, and a statement of cash flows for May.

Problem 2-6A
Computing net income, preparing a balance sheet, and calculating return on equity

The accounting records of Sarasota Shipping Services show the following assets and liabilities as of December 31, 2001, and 2002:

	December 31	
	2001	**2002**
Cash	$ 64,300	$ 15,640
Accounts receivable	26,240	19,390
Office supplies	3,160	1,960
Office equipment	148,000	157,000
Trucks	44,000	44,000
Building	0	80,000
Land	0	60,000
Accounts payable	3,500	33,500
Note payable	0	40,000

Late in December 2002, Trey Davis, the owner, purchased a small office building and moved the business from rented quarters to the new building. The building and the land it occupies cost $140,000. The business paid $100,000 cash toward the purchase and a $40,000 note payable was signed for the balance. Davis had to invest $35,000 cash in the business to enable it to pay the $100,000. Davis also withdraws $3,000 cash per month from his proprietorship for personal expenses.

Required

1. Prepare balance sheets for the business as of December 31, 2001, and 2002. (Remember that equity equals the difference between assets and liabilities.)

Check   Net income, $23,290

2. By comparing equity amounts from the balance sheets and using the additional information presented in this problem, prepare a calculation to show how much net income was earned by the business during 2002.

Check   Modified return on equity, 1.1%

3. Calculate the year 2002 return on equity for the business. Also calculate the modified return on equity assuming that Davis's efforts are worth $20,000 for the year.

Curtis Hamilton started a new business and completed these transactions during December:

Dec. 1   Curtis Hamilton transferred $65,000 cash from a personal savings account to a checking account in the name of Hamilton Electric.

1   Rented office space and paid $1,000 cash for the December rent.

3   Purchased electrical equipment from an electrician who was going out of business for $13,000 by paying $4,800 cash and agreeing to pay the balance in six months.

5   Purchased office supplies by paying $800 cash.

6   Completed electrical work and immediately collected $1,200 cash for the work.

8   Purchased $2,530 of office equipment on credit.

15   Completed electrical work on credit in the amount of $5,000.

18   Purchased $350 of office supplies on credit.

20   Paid cash for the office equipment purchased on December 8.

24   Billed a client $900 for electrical work completed; the balance is due in 30 days.

28   Received $5,000 cash for the work completed on December 15.

30   Paid the assistant's salary of $1,400 cash for this month.

30   Paid $540 cash for this month's utility bill.

30   Hamilton withdrew $950 cash from the business for personal use.

Required

Preparation Component

1. Arrange the following asset, liability, and equity titles in a table like Exhibit 2.13: Cash; Accounts Receivable; Office Supplies; Office Equipment; Electrical Equipment; Accounts Payable; and Curtis Hamilton, Capital. Leave space for an Explanation column to the right of Curtis Hamilton, Capital.

2. Use additions and subtractions to show the effects of each transaction on the items in the accounting equation. Show new balances after each transaction. Next to each change in equity, state whether the change was caused by an investment, a revenue, an expense, or a withdrawal.

3. Use the increases and decreases in the last column of the table from part 2 to prepare an income statement and a statement of changes in owner's equity for the month. Also prepare a balance sheet as of the end of the month.

4. Calculate the return on equity for the month, using the $65,000 initial investment as the beginning balance of equity.

Analysis Component

5. Assume the investment transaction on December 1 was $49,000 instead of $65,000 and that Hamilton obtained the $16,000 difference by borrowing it from a bank. Explain the effect of this change on total assets, total liabilities, equity, and return on equity.

The following financial statement information is known about five separate proprietorships:

	Company V	Company W	Company X	Company Y	Company Z
December 31, 2001:					
Assets	$54,000	$80,000	$141,500	$92,500	$144,000
Liabilities	25,000	60,000	68,500	51,500	?
December 31, 2002:					
Assets	59,000	100,000	186,500	?	170,000
Liabilities	36,000	?	65,800	42,000	42,000
During year 2002:					
Owner investments	5,000	20,000	?	48,100	60,000
Net income	?	40,000	18,500	24,000	32,000
Owner withdrawals	5,500	2,000	0	20,000	8,000

Required

1. Answer the following questions about Company V:
   a. What is the amount of equity on December 31, 2001?
   b. What is the amount of equity on December 31, 2002?
   c. What is net income for year 2002?
2. Answer the following questions about Company W:
   a. What is the amount of equity on December 31, 2001?
   b. What is the amount of equity on December 31, 2002?
   c. What is the amount of liabilities on December 31, 2002?
3. Calculate the amount of owner investments in Company X during 2002.
4. Calculate the amount of assets for Company Y on December 31, 2002.
5. Calculate the amount of liabilities for Company Z on December 31, 2001.

Check Co. Y, Dec. 31, 2002
Assets, $135,100

Problem 2-2B
Identifying effects of
transactions on financial
statements

Identify how each of the following separate transactions affects the company's financial statements. For the balance sheet, identify how each transaction affects total assets, total liabilities, and equity. For the income statement, identify how each transaction affects net income. For the statement of cash flows, identify how each transaction affects cash flows from operating activities, cash flows from financing activities, and cash flows from investing activities. For increases, place a "+" in the column or columns. For decreases, place a "−" in the column or columns. If both an increase and a decrease occur, place "+/−" in the column or columns. The first transaction is completed as an example.

		Balance Sheet			Income Stmt.	Statement of Cash Flows		
	Transaction	Total Assets	Total Liab.	Equity	Net Income	Operating Activities	Financing Activities	Investing Activities
1	Owner invests cash	+		+			+	
2	Borrows cash by signing note payable							
3	Pays wages incurred with cash							
4	Performs services for cash							
5	Pays rent incurred with cash							
6	Pays for services received on credit							
7	Buys store equipment for cash							
8	Owner withdraws cash							
9	Performs services on credit							
10	Collects cash on receivable from (9)							

Problem 2-3B
Preparing a statement of
cash flows

A new business, AllNet, has the following cash balance and cash flows for the month of December:

Cash balance, December 1	$ 0
Cash withdrawal by owner	2,000
Cash received from customers	12,400
Cash payment of long-term liabilities	1,500
Cash paid for store supplies	3,200
Cash purchase of equipment	39,000
Cash paid for rent	1,750
Cash paid to employee	2,000
Cash investment by owner	57,000

Check Cash Bal., Dec. 31,
$19,950

Required

Prepare a statement of cash flows for AllNet for the month of December.

Fiona Dare started a new business called Midwest Consulting and it completed the following transactions during its first year of operations:

a. Dare invests $70,000 cash and office equipment valued at $10,000 in the business.

b. Paid $150,000 for a building to use as an office. Dare paid $20,000 in cash and signed a note payable promising to pay the balance over the next ten years.

c. Purchased office equipment for $15,000 cash.

d. Purchased $1,200 of office supplies and $1,700 of office equipment on credit.

e. Paid a local newspaper $500 cash for an announcement of the office's opening.

f. Completed a financial plan on credit and billed the client $2,800 for the service.

g. Designed a financial plan for another client and collected a $4,000 cash fee.

h. Dare withdrew $3,275 cash from the company bank account to pay personal expenses.

i. Received $1,800 cash from the client described in transaction *f*.

j. Made a $700 cash payment on the equipment purchased in transaction *d*.

k. Paid $1,800 cash for the office secretary's wages.

Required

Preparation Component

1. Create a table like the one in Exhibit 2.13, using the following headings for the columns: Cash; Accounts Receivable; Office Supplies; Office Equipment; Building; Accounts Payable; Note Payable; and Fiona Dare, Capital. Leave space for an Explanation column to the right of the Capital column. Identify revenues and expenses by name in the Explanation column.

2. Use additions and subtractions to show the effects of these transactions on individual items of the accounting equation. Show new balances after each transaction. Indicate next to each change in equity whether it was caused by an investment, a revenue, an expense, or a withdrawal.

3. Once you have completed the table, determine the company's net income.

Analysis Component

4. Determine the return on equity for Midwest Consulting (use the $80,000 initial investment as the beginning balance of equity). Assuming that Dare could have earned $3,000 for the period from another job, determine the modified return on equity for the period. State whether you think the business is a good use of Dare's money if an alternative investment would have returned 10% for the same period.

Problem 2-4B
Analyzing effects of transactions and calculating return on equity

Check Net income, $4,500

use excell ?
graded
✓ homework

Ken Stone launched a new business called Ken's Maintenance Co. that began operations on June 1. The following transactions were completed during the month:

June	1	Stone invested $130,000 cash in the business.
	1	Rented a furnished office of a maintenance company that was going out of business and paid $6,000 cash for June's rent.
	4	Purchased tools for $2,400 on credit.
	6	Paid $1,150 cash for advertising the opening of the business.
	8	Completed maintenance services for a customer and immediately collected $850 cash.
	14	Completed $7,500 of maintenance services for First Union Center on credit.
	16	Paid $800 cash for an assistant's salary for the first half of the month.
	20	Received cash payment in full for services completed for First Union Center on June 14.
	21	Completed $7,900 of maintenance services for Skyway Co. on credit.
	24	Completed $675 of maintenance services for Comfort Motel on credit.
	29	Received full cash payment from Skyway Co. for the work completed on June 21.
	29	Made a payment of $2,400 cash for the tools purchased on June 4.
	30	Paid $150 cash for this month's telephone bill.
	30	Paid $890 cash for this month's utilities.
	30	Paid $800 cash for an assistant's salary for the second half of this month.
	30	Stone withdrew $4,000 cash from the business for personal use.

Required

1. Arrange the following asset, liability, and equity titles in a table like Exhibit 2.13: Cash; Accounts Receivable; Tools; Accounts Payable; Ken Stone, Capital. Include an Explanation column for changes in equity.

Problem 2-5B
Preparing a balance sheet, an income statement, a statement of changes in owner's equity, and a statement of cash flows

2. Show the effects of the transactions on the items of the accounting equation by recording increases and decreases in the appropriate columns. Do not determine new account balances after each transaction. Next to each change in equity, state whether it was caused by an investment, a revenue, an expense, or a withdrawal. Determine the final total for each item and verify that the equation is in balance.

Check Ending owner's equity, $133,135

3. Prepare a June income statement, a June statement of changes in owner's equity, a June 30 balance sheet, and a June statement of cash flows.

Problem 2-6B
Calculating net income, preparing a balance sheet, and calculating return on equity

The accounting records of Affleck Co. show the following assets and liabilities as of December 31, 2001, and 2002:

	December 31	
	2001	**2002**
Cash	$20,000	$ 5,000
Accounts receivable	35,000	25,000
Office supplies	8,000	13,500
Office equipment	40,000	40,000
Machinery	28,500	28,500
Building	0	250,000
Land	0	50,000
Accounts payable	4,000	12,000
Note payable	0	250,000

Late in December 2002, Wes Affleck, the owner, purchased a small office building and moved the business to it from rented quarters. The building and the land it occupies cost $300,000. The business paid $50,000 cash toward the purchase and a $250,000 note payable was signed for the balance. Affleck had to invest an additional $15,000 cash to enable it to pay the $50,000. Affleck also withdraws $250 cash per month from his proprietorship for personal use.

Required

1. Prepare balance sheets for the business as of December 31, 2001, and 2002. (Remember that equity equals the difference between assets and liabilities.)

Check Net income, $10,500

2. By comparing equity amounts from the balance sheets and using the additional information presented in the problem, prepare a calculation to show how much net income was earned by the business during 2002.

Check Modified return on equity, –6.85%

3. Calculate the year 2002 return on equity for the business. Also, calculate the modified return on equity assuming that Affleck's efforts are worth $20,000 for the year.

Problem 2-7B
Analyzing transactions, preparing financial statements, and calculating return on equity

Swender Excavating Co., owned by Patrick Swender, began operations in July and completed these transactions during the month:

July 1   Swender invested $80,000 cash in the business.
1   Rented office space and paid $700 cash for the July rent.
1   Purchased excavating equipment for $5,000 by paying $1,000 cash and agreeing to pay the balance in six months.
6   Purchased office supplies by paying $600 cash.
8   Completed work for a customer and immediately collected $7,600 cash for the work.
10   Purchased $2,300 of office equipment on credit.
15   Completed work for a customer on credit in the amount of $8,200.
17   Purchased $3,100 of office supplies on credit.
23   Paid cash for the office equipment purchased on July 10.
25   Billed a customer $5,000 for completed work; the balance is due in 30 days.
28   Received $8,200 cash for the work completed on July 15.
31   Paid an assistant's salary of $1,560 cash for this month.
31   Paid $295 cash for this month's utility bill.
31   Swender withdrew $1,800 cash from the business to pay personal expenses.

Required

Preparation Component

1. Arrange the following asset, liability, and equity titles in a table like Exhibit 2.13: Cash; Accounts Receivable; Office Supplies; Office Equipment; Excavating Equipment; Accounts Payable; and Patrick Swender, Capital. Leave space for an Explanation column to the right of the Patrick Swender, Capital column.

2. Use additions and subtractions to show the effects of each transaction on the items in the accounting equation. Show new balances after each transaction. Next to each change in equity, state whether the change was caused by an investment, a revenue, an expense, or a withdrawal.

3. Use the increases and decreases in the last column of the table from part 2 to prepare an income statement and a statement of changes in owner's equity for the month. Also prepare a balance sheet as of the end of the month.

Check Ending owner's equity, $96,445

4. Calculate return on equity for the month, using the $80,000 initial investment as the beginning balance of equity.

Analysis Component

5. Assume that Swender's $5,000 purchase of excavating equipment on July 1 was financed from his personal investment of another $5,000 cash in the business (instead of the purchase conditions described in the transaction). Explain the effect of this change on total assets, total liabilities, equity, and return on equity.

Beyond the Numbers

BTN 2-1   Refer to **Nike**'s annual report in Appendix A to answer the following questions:

Required

1. Examine Nike's consolidated balance sheet. To what level are its dollar amounts rounded?

2. What is the reporting date of Nike's most recent annual reporting period?

3. What amount of net income did Nike earn for the fiscal year ended May 31, 2000?

4. How much cash (and equivalents) did Nike hold at fiscal year-end May 31, 2000?

5. What was the net amount of cash provided by its operating activities for the fiscal year ended May 31, 2000?

6. Did its investing activities for fiscal year ended May 31, 2000, create a net cash inflow or outflow? What was the amount of this net cash flow?

7. Compare fiscal year 2000's results to 1999's results to determine whether revenues increased or decreased. What was the amount of the increase or decrease?

8. What is the change in net income between fiscal years 2000 and 1999?

9. What amount is reported as total assets at fiscal year-end 2000?

10. Calculate return on equity for fiscal year ended May 31, 2000.

Reporting in Action

C1 A2

NIKE

Swoosh Ahead

11. Obtain Nike's annual report for a fiscal year ending after May 31, 2000, from its Web site [www.nike.com] or the SEC's EDGAR database [www.sec.gov]. Recompute Nike's return on equity with the updated annual report information. Compare the May 31, 2000, fiscal year-end return on equity to any subsequent year's return you are able to calculate. Also compare how Nike's total assets, total revenues, and net income have changed since May 31, 2000.

BTN 2-2   Key comparative figures ($ millions) for both **Nike** and **Reebok** follow:

Key Figures	Nike	Reebok
Beginning equity	$3,334.6	$524.4
Ending equity	3,136.0	528.8
Net income	579.1	11.05

Comparative Analysis

A2

NIKE

Reebok

Required

1. What is the return on equity for (*a*) Nike and (*b*) Reebok?

2. Is return on equity satisfactory for (*a*) Nike and (*b*) Reebok if competitors average a 10% return?

3. Would it be appropriate to calculate the modified return on equity for either Reebok or Nike?

Ethics Challenge

C5

BTN 2-3 Damara Crist is an entry-level accountant for a mail-order company that specializes in supplying skateboards and accessories. At the end of its fiscal period, Damara is advised by a supervisor to include as revenue for the period any orders that have been charged by phone but not yet shipped. Damara is also advised to include as revenue any orders received by mail with checks enclosed that are also pending shipment.

Required

1. Identify the most relevant accounting principle in assessing the supervisor's instructions.

2. What are the ethical factors in this situation?

3. Would you recommend that Damara follow the supervisor's directions?

4. What alternatives might be available to Damara other than following the supervisor's directions?

Communicating in Practice

C1

BTN 2-4 Rochelle Roither is an aspiring entrepreneur and your friend. She is having difficulty understanding the purposes of financial statements and how they fit together across time.

Required

Write a one-page memorandum to Rochelle Roither explaining the purposes of the four major financial statements and how they are linked in time.

Taking It to the Net

C1 **C5**

BTN 2-5 Visit the Edgar database online at www.edgar-online.com. Alphabetically search for **Fogdog Sports** (ticker FOGD). Fogdog Sports is an online retailer of sports clothing and equipment. View Fogdog's March 20, 2000, 10-K405 report filed with the SEC. Using the full filing feature of Edgar, search Fogdog's 10-K until you find the annual income statement that reports results for 1999, 1998, and 1997.

Required

1. What is the net income trend (level and direction) for Fogdog during its most recent 3 years?

2. What expense reported on the income statement provides a clue that Fogdog is an Internet-based company?

Teamwork in Action

C5 **A1**

BTN 2-6 The accounting equation can be used to reveal useful information on changes in a company's assets, liabilities, and equity.

Required

1. Form *learning teams* of four (or more) members. Each team member must select one of the following four categories (each team must have at least one expert in each category): (*a*) assets, (*b*) liabilities, (*c*) equity—investments and withdrawals, and (*d*) equity—revenues and expenses.

2. Form *expert teams* from individuals who have selected the same category in (*1*). Expert teams are to discuss and draft a report that each expert will present to his/her learning team addressing the following:

  a. Description of a transaction, with amounts, that increases its category.

  b. Using the transaction and amounts in (*a*), verify the equality of the accounting equation.

  c. Description of a transaction, with amounts, that decreases its category.

  d. Using the transaction and amounts in (*c*), verify the equality of the accounting equation.

3. Each expert should return to his/her learning team. In rotation, each member presents his/her expert team's report to the learning team. Team discussion is encouraged.

BTN 2-7 *Business Week* periodically publishes a ranking of "Hot Growth Companies." It contains tables of selected accounting measures. Obtain the most recent issue on hot growth companies. (*Note:* May 29, 2000, was one such issue.)

Business Week Activity

A2

Required

1. What company is ranked number 1 using return on equity (also called return on capital)?

2. What is the return on equity (capital) for the number 1 company?

3. Refer to the return on equity (capital) table and consider the relation between return and risk. Identify and discuss common risk characteristics for the top five companies.

BTN 2-8 On weekends, Richard Hepperly is the organizer and member of a rock band. Hepperly is considering pursuing his rock band full-time. To help in this decision, he has made the following annual financial estimates: Average equity investment required, $250,000; Revenues, $310,000; and Expenses, $189,000.

Entrepreneurial Decision

A2

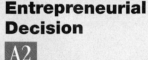

Required

1. Compute an estimated return on equity for R. Hepperly.

2. Compute an estimated modified return on equity for R. Hepperly knowing that he will be giving up $50,000 in annual wages from his current job.

3. Should R. Hepperly pursue his rock band full-time?

Analyzing and Recording Transactions

We explained the value of accounting in the information age. We showed how financial statements, prepared according to accounting principles, communicate useful information. We also analyzed and prepared simple financial statements from transactions.

A Look at This Chapter

This chapter focuses on the accounting process. We describe transactions and source documents as inputs for analysis. We explain analysis and recording of transactions for preparing financial statements. T-accounts, postings, ledgers, and trial balances are shown as useful tools in carrying out these steps.

A Look Ahead

Chapter 4 extends our focus on processing information. We explain the importance of adjusting accounts and the procedures in preparing financial statements.

"The only thing that sets you apart from your competitors is people"— Kristin Knight

Learning Objectives

Explain the steps in processing transactions.

Describe source documents and their purpose.

Describe an account and its use in recording information about transactions.

Describe a ledger and a chart of accounts.

Define debits and credits and explain their role in double-entry accounting.

Analytical

A1 Analyze the impact of transactions on accounts and financial statements.

A2 Compute the debt ratio and describe its use in analyzing company performance.

Procedural

P1 Record transactions in a journal and post entries to a ledger.

P2 Prepare and explain the use of a trial balance.

Creative Assets

e SEATTLE—When 22-year-old Kristin Knight quit her job at Microsoft to pursue her dream of starting a company, she didn't get much encouragement, "Most people thought I was crazy to leave," says Knight.

Crazy like a fox. Knight now runs **Creative Assets**, a company offering its clients access to some of the best freelance talent around [**Creative Assets.com**]. "We represent freelance creative talent in the digital media area and match them up with companies," explains Knight. About two-thirds of her creative people are graphic designers or production artists, and a growing number are writers. Projects typically last from 3 to 9 months. Last year, its revenues exceeded $5 million. This year that figure is expected to hit $20 million. Entrepreneur Magazine recently listed Knight among its "entrepreneurial superstars under 40."

Yet, while a great idea is key, Knight asserts that a successful business depends on accurate accounting information. When Creative Assets added its first branch office, Knight confesses it "didn't have the [accounting] systems in place to support the growth that came with it, especially on the financial side." She adds, "I overlooked the vital role . . . of accounting, technology, and database systems."

Mistakes in the recording and analyzing of business transactions proved costly for the company, but taught Knight a valuable lesson. "It was an expensive . . . lesson, but now I realize the importance of setting up [accounting] systems." Creative Assets continues to astound observers with its rapid growth. But this entrepreneurial venture, like most others, would not have achieved what it has without effective accounting systems. [Sources: *Creative Assets Web Site*, May 2001; *Pugent Sound Business Journal*, March 16, 1998; *Seattle Times*, July 14, 1998]

Chapter Preview

The accounting process is crucial to producing useful financial information. We explained in Chapter 2 how the accounting equation (Assets = Liabilities + Equity) helps us understand and analyze transactions and events. In this chapter we further describe processing transactions and recording their effects in accounts. All accounting systems use procedures similar to those described here. These procedures are important steps leading to financial statements. We begin by describing how source documents provide crucial information about transactions. We then describe accounts and explain their purpose. Debits and credits are introduced and identified as valuable tools in helping us understand and process transactions. This background enables us to describe the process of recording events in a journal and how they are posted to a ledger. We return to transactions of **FastForward,** first introduced in Chapter 2, to illustrate these procedures. We conclude the chapter by describing how to use a company's debt ratio to assess its risk.

Transactions and Documents

C1 Explain the steps in processing transactions.

We explained in Chapter 1 how accounting provides information to help people make better decisions. This information is the result of an accounting process that reflects business transactions and events, analyzes and records their effects, and summarizes and prepares information in reports and financial statements. These reports and statements are used for making investing, lending, and other business decisions. We illustrate the steps in the accounting process in Exhibit 3.1.

Exhibit 3.1

Accounting Process

Transaction or event → Source document → Analysis → Recording and posting → Trial balance → Reporting

Transactions and events are the starting points in the accounting process. Relying on source documents, we analyze transactions and events using the accounting equation to understand how they affect company performance and financial position. These effects are recorded in accounting records, informally referred to as the *accounting books,* or simply the *books.* Additional processing steps such as posting and preparing a trial balance help us summarize and classify the effects of transactions and events. A final step in the accounting process is to provide information in useful reports or financial statements to decision makers. We begin our overview of the accounting process with a discussion of transactions and events. Later sections explain the remaining steps.

Transactions and Events

Business activities can be described in terms of transactions and events. **External transactions** are exchanges of economic consideration between two separate entities. External transactions yield changes in the accounting equation. **Internal transactions** are exchanges within an entity; they can also affect the accounting equation. One example is a company using supplies in its operating activities. As supplies are used, their costs are reported as expenses.

Events are happenings that both affect an entity's financial position and can be reliably measured. These include financial events such as changes in the market value of certain assets and liabilities and natural events such as floods and fires that destroy assets and create losses.

Source Documents

C2 Describe source documents and their purpose.

Companies use various documents when doing business. **Source documents,** or *business papers,* identify and describe transactions and events entering the accounting process. They are the sources of accounting information and can be in either hard copy or electronic form.

Examples are sales tickets, checks, purchase orders, charges to customers, bills from suppliers, employee earnings records, and bank statements.

For example, when we buy an item on credit, the store usually prepares at least two copies of a sales invoice. One copy is given to us. Another gives rise to an entry in the store's information system to record a sale. This copy is often sent electronically. Also, for both cash and credit sales, the item is usually entered into a register that records the amount of each sale. Many registers record this information for each sale on a tape or electronic file locked inside the register. Total sales for a day, or for any time period, can be obtained immediately from these registers. This record can be used as a source document for recording sales in the accounting records. These accounting procedures are also part of an information system designed to ensure that accounting records include all transactions. They also help prevent mistakes and theft. To encourage employees to follow procedures such as these, stores often give discounts or free goods if a customer is not provided a receipt. This is part of good internal control. Both buyers and sellers use sales invoices as source documents. Sellers use them for recording sales and for control. Buyers use them for recording purchases and for monitoring purchasing activity. In both cases, a copy of the invoice is a source document.

Point: To ensure that all sales are rung up on the register, it helps to require customers to have their receipts to exchange or return purchased items.

> ### You Make the Call—Ethics
>
> **Cashier** When you were hired as a cashier, the manager explained the policy of immediately entering each sale. Recently, lunch hour traffic has increased and the assistant manager asks you to avoid delays by taking customers' cash and making change without entering sales. The assistant manager says she will add up cash and enter sales after lunch. She says that in this way, the register will always match the cash amount when the manager arrives at three o'clock. What do you do?

Answer—p. 106

Source documents, especially if obtained from outside the organization, provide objective and reliable evidence about transactions and events and their amounts. Many accounting systems still require manual (pencil and paper) recording and processing of transaction data. These are mostly limited to small businesses. In today's information age, computers assist us in recording and processing data, yet they are only part of the process, and modern technology still demands human insight and understanding of transactions. In our discussion of the steps making up the accounting process, we often refer to a *manual system* for simplicity in presentation, but the fundamental concepts of the manual system are identical to those of a computerized information system.

> ### Quick Check
>
> 1. Describe external and internal transactions.
> 2. Identify examples of accounting source documents.
> 3. Explain the importance of source documents.

Answers—p. 106

Accounts and Double-Entry Accounting

This section explains what an *account* is and its importance to accounting and business. We also describe several crucial elements and tools that support an accounting system. These include ledgers, T-accounts, debits and credits, and double-entry accounting.

The Account

C3 Describe an account and its use in recording information about transactions.

An **account** is a detailed record of increases and decreases in a specific asset, liability, equity, revenue, or expense. Information is taken from an account, then analyzed, summarized, and presented in reports and financial statements. A separate account is kept for each asset, liability, equity, revenue, and expense item important to business decisions. Changes in owner withdrawals and contributions are also kept in separate accounts.

A **ledger** is a record containing all accounts used by a company. This is often in electronic form and is what we mean when we refer to the *books*. While most companies' ledgers contain similar accounts, several accounts are often unique to a company because of its type of operations. Accounts are arranged into three general categories (based on the accounting equation) as shown in Exhibit 3.2.

Exhibit 3.2
Accounts Organized by the Accounting Equation

The remainder of this section describes accounts common to most organizations.

Asset Accounts

Assets are resources owned or controlled by a company that have expected future benefits. Most accounting systems include separate accounts for the assets described here.

Cash

A *Cash* account reflects the cash balance, and increases and decreases in cash are recorded in it. A Cash account includes money and any medium of exchange that a bank accepts for deposit (coins, currency, checks, money orders, and checking account balances).

Accounts Receivable

Products and services are often sold to customers in return for promises to pay in the future. These transactions are often called *credit sales* or *sales on account*. Promises of payment from buyers are called *accounts receivable* to sellers. Accounts receivable are increased by credit sales and are decreased by customer payments. A company needs to know the amount currently due from each customer to send bills. A separate record for each customer's purchases and payments is necessary for this purpose. We describe the system for maintaining these records in Chapters 6 and 10. For now, we use the simpler practice of recording all increases and decreases in receivables in a single account called *Accounts Receivable.* The importance of accounts receivable to a company, like many other accounts, depends on its type of business. For example, **Florida Panthers'** accounts receivable amount to less than 3% of its assets. In comparison, **Nike**'s accounts receivable amount to more than 30% of its assets.

Note Receivable

A **note receivable,** or **promissory note,** is a written promise to pay a definite sum of money on a specified future date(s). A company holding a promissory note signed by another party has an asset that is recorded in a Note (or Notes) Receivable account.

Prepaid Expenses

Prepaid expenses are assets because they represent prepayments of future expenses (*not* current expenses). In the future, when the expenses are incurred, the amounts in prepaid expenses are transferred to expense accounts. Common examples of prepaid expenses include prepaid insurance, prepaid rent, and prepaid services (such as club memberships). Prepaid expenses expire with the passage of time (such as with rent) or through use (such as with prepaid meal tickets). When financial statements are prepared, prepaid expenses are adjusted so that (1) all expired and used prepaid expenses are recorded as regular expenses and (2) all unexpired and unused prepaid expenses are recorded as assets (reflecting future use in future periods). An exception exists for prepaid expenses that will expire or be used before the end of the current accounting period when financial statements will be prepared. In this case, the prepayments *can* be recorded immediately as expenses.

Point: College tuition fees are prepaid expenses. At the beginning of the term, they represent an asset that entitles you to attend class, access college libraries, and so forth. This asset decreases in size (benefits expire) as the term progresses. At term-end, prepaid tuition fees (asset) equal zero and the amount for them is recorded as tuition expenses.

For example, if FastForward pays $1,000 for December rent at the beginning of the month, it can record this prepaid rent as rent expense since its benefit will be fully expired when the statements are prepared on December 31. As another example consider prepaid insurance, one of the most common prepaid expenses. Insurance contracts provide us protection against losses caused by fire, theft, accidents, and other events. An insurance policy often requires the fee, called a *premium,* to be paid in advance. Protection can be purchased for almost any time period, including a month, year, or several years. When an insurance premium is paid in advance, the cost is typically recorded in an asset account called *Prepaid Insurance.* Over time, the expiring portion of the insurance cost is removed from this asset account and reported in expenses on the income statement. Any unexpired portion remains in Prepaid Insurance and is reported on the balance sheet as an asset.

Point: Prepaid expenses that apply to current *and* future periods are assets. These assets are adjusted at the end of each period to reflect only those amounts that have not yet expired, and to record as expenses those amounts that have expired.

Office Supplies

All companies use office supplies such as stationery, computer paper and toner, and pens. These supplies are assets until they are used. When they are used up, their costs are then reported as expenses. The costs of unused supplies are recorded in an *Office Supplies* asset account.

Store Supplies

Many stores keep supplies for circumstances such as wrapping and packaging purchases for customers. These include plastic and paper bags, gift boxes, cartons, and ribbons. The costs of these unused supplies are recorded in a *Store Supplies* asset account. When supplies are used, their costs are transferred from the supplies asset account to the supplies expense account.

Equipment

Most organizations own computers, printers, desks, chairs, and other office equipment. Costs incurred to buy this equipment are recorded in an *Office Equipment* asset account. The costs of assets used in a store such as counters, showcases, forklifts, hoists, and cash registers are recorded in a *Store Equipment* asset account.

Point: Some assets are described as *intangible* because they do not have physical existence or their benefits are highly uncertain. A recent balance sheet for Coca-Cola Company shows $1.96 billion in intangible assets.

Buildings

Buildings owned by an organization can provide space for a store, an office, a warehouse, and a factory. Buildings are assets because they provide expected future benefits. Their costs are recorded in a *Buildings* asset account. When several buildings are owned, separate accounts are sometimes kept for each of them.

Land

A *Land* account records the cost of land owned by a business. The cost of land is separated from the cost of buildings located on the land to provide more useful information in financial statements.

Liability Accounts

Liabilities are obligations to transfer assets or provide products or services to other entities. An organization often has several different liabilities, each represented by a separate account. The more common liability accounts are described here.

Accounts Payable

Purchases of merchandise, supplies, equipment, or services made by an oral or implied promise to pay later create liabilities called *Payables.* Accounting systems keep separate records about purchases from and payments to each creditor. We describe these individual records in Chapter 6. For now, we use the simpler practice of recording all increases and decreases in such payables in a single account called *Accounts Payable.*

Point: Accounts Payable are also called Trade Payables.

Note Payable

When an organization formally recognizes a promise to pay a future amount by signing a **promissory note,** the resulting liability is a **Note Payable.** It is recorded in either a Short-Term

Note Payable account or a Long-Term Note Payable account depending on when it must be repaid. We explain details of short- and long-term classification in Chapter 5.

Unearned Revenue

Chapter 2 explained that the *revenue recognition principle* requires that revenues be reported on the income statement when earned. This principle means that when customers pay in advance for products or services (before revenue is earned), the seller considers this pay as unearned revenues. **Unearned Revenue** is a liability account that is settled in the future when products or services are delivered. Examples of unearned revenue include magazine subscriptions collected in advance by a publisher, sales of gift certificates by stores, and season ticket sales by sports teams. The seller would record these in liability accounts such as Unearned Subscriptions, Unearned Store Sales, and Unearned Ticket Revenue. When products and services are delivered, the earned portion of the unearned revenues is transferred to revenue accounts such as Subscription Fees, Store Sales, and Ticket Sales.[1]

Did You Know?

MLB Accounting The **Cleveland Indians** report *Unearned Revenues* of nearly $50 million that consist of advance ticket sales. When the Indians play their regular season home games, they settle this liability to their customers (fans) and transfer the amount to *Ticket Revenues.*

Accrued Liabilities

Point: Many companies offer warranties on their products and must report a liability by estimating future warranty costs.

Common accrued liabilities include wages payable, taxes payable, and interest payable. Each represents amounts owed that are not yet paid. These are often recorded in separate liability account by the same title. If they are not large in amount, one or more of them may be added and reported as a single amount on the balance sheet. For example, the liabilities section of **Harley-Davidson**'s balance sheet reports accrued liabilities of more than $160 million.

Equity Accounts

Chapter 2, described the four types of transactions that affect owner's equity. They are (1) investments by the owner, (2) withdrawals by the owner, (3) revenues, and (4) expenses. We entered all equity transactions in a single column under the owner's name in Chapter 2. When we later prepared the income statement and the statement of changes in owner's equity, we reviewed the items in that column to properly classify them in financial statements. To better track these items, four separate account categories are used: Owner's Capital, Owner's Withdrawals, Revenues, and Expenses. We show this visually in Exhibit 3.3 by expanding the accounting equation.

Exhibit 3.3

Expanded Accounting Equation

---

[1] In practice, account titles vary. As one example, Subscription Fees is sometimes called Subscription Fees Revenue, Subscription Fees Earned, or Earned Subscription Fees. As another example, Rent Earned is sometimes called Rent Revenue, Rental Revenue, or Earned Rent Revenue. We must use our good judgment when reading financial statements, since titles can differ even within the same industry. For example, product sales are called *revenues* at **Nike** and **K. Swiss**, but *net sales* at **Reebok** and **Converse.** The term *revenues* or *fees* is more commonly used with service businesses, and *net sales* or *sales* with product businesses.

Information in these separate categories is then readily used to prepare financial statements. We describe these four types of accounts in this section.

Owner's Capital

When a person invests in a proprietorship or partnership, the invested amount is recorded in an account identified by the owner's name and the title Capital. An account called *Chuck Taylor, Capital,* is used to record Taylor's investment in FastForward. Any further investments by the owner also are recorded in this capital account.

Owner's Withdrawals

Equity increases when a company earns income. The owner can leave this equity intact or can withdraw assets from the business. When the owner withdraws assets, perhaps to cover personal expenses, the withdrawal decreases both the company's assets and its equity. Owners of proprietorships commonly withdraw weekly or monthly amounts of cash. Owners of proprietorships cannot receive salaries because they are not legally separate from their companies and cannot enter into salary (or any other) contracts with themselves. Withdrawals are neither income to the owners nor expenses of the business. They are simply the opposite of investments by owners. Most accounting systems use an account with the name of the owner and the word *withdrawals* in recording withdrawals by the owner. An account called *Chuck Taylor, Withdrawals,* is used to record Taylor's withdrawals from FastForward.

Point: The Owner's Withdrawals account (also called *Drawing* or *Personal* account) is sometimes referred to as a contra equity account because it reduces the normal balance of equity.

Point: Withdrawals in a partnership are treated similarly to those of a proprietorship.

Revenues and Expenses

Decision makers often want information about revenues earned and expenses incurred for a period. Various revenue and expense accounts are used to report this information. Different companies have different kinds of revenue and expense accounts reflecting their own unique activities. Examples of revenue accounts are Sales, Commissions Earned, Professional Fees Earned, Rent Earned, and Interest Earned. Examples of expense accounts are Advertising Expense, Store Supplies Expense, Office Salaries Expense, Office Supplies Expense, Rent Expense, Utilities Expense, and Insurance Expense. We can get an idea of the variety of revenues and expenses by looking at the *chart of accounts* which follows the index at the back of this book. It lists accounts needed to solve some of the assignments in the book.[2]

> **Did You Know?**
>
> **NBA Accounting**   The **Boston Celtics** report the following major revenue and expense accounts:
>
> | Revenues | Expenses |
> | --- | --- |
> | Basketball ticket sales | Team salaries |
> | TV and radio broadcast fees | Game costs |
> | Advertising revenues | NBA franchise costs |
>
>

Ledger and Chart of Accounts

The actual recording of accounts can differ depending on the system. Computerized systems store accounts in files on electronic storage devices. Manual systems often record accounts on separate pages in a file. The collection of all accounts for an information system is called a *ledger*. If accounts are in files on a

> **Did You Know?**
>
> **Ledger Bytes**   What does technology mean for accounting information processing? Using computing technology, **Sears** shrank its annual financial plan from 100 square-foot flow charts with more than 300 steps to 25 steps on *one* $8^1/_2$-by-11-inch sheet of paper! Technology also allows Sears' execs to analyze budgets and financial plans on their PCs. Sears says it slashed $100 million in recordkeeping costs.

---

[2] Different companies sometimes use different account titles than those in this book's chart of accounts. For example, a company might use Interest Revenue instead of Interest Earned, or Rental Expense instead of Rent Expense. It is important only that an account title describe the item it represents.

Describe a ledger and a chart of accounts.

hard drive, the sum of those files is the ledger. If the accounts are pages in a file, that file is the ledger.

A company's size and diversity of operations affect the number of accounts needed in its accounting system. A small company may get by with as few as 20 or 30 accounts; a large company may need several thousand. The **chart of accounts** is a list of all accounts a company uses. The chart includes an identification number assigned to each account. A small business might use the following numbering system for its accounts:

101–199	Asset accounts
201–299	Liability accounts
301–399	Equity accounts
401–499	Revenue accounts
501–699	Expense accounts

These numbers provide a three-digit code that is useful in recordkeeping. In this case, the first digit assigned to asset accounts is a 1, the first digit assigned to liability accounts is a 2, and so on. The second and third digits also relate to the accounts' subcategories. A partial chart of accounts is shown in Exhibit 3.4 for FastForward.

Exhibit 3.4

Partial Chart of Accounts

Account Number	Account Name	Account Number	Account Name
101	Cash	301	C. Taylor, Capital
106	Accounts receivable	302	C. Taylor, Withdrawals
126	Supplies	403	Consulting revenue
128	Prepaid insurance	406	Rental revenue
167	Equipment	622	Salaries expense
201	Accounts payable	637	Insurance expense
236	Unearned consulting revenue	640	Rent expense
		652	Supplies expense
		690	Utilities expense

Debits and Credits

 Define *debits* and *credits* and explain their role in double-entry accounting.

Point: Think of *debit* and *credit* as accounting directions for left and right.

The left side of an account is called the **debit** side, often abbreviated *Dr.* The right side is called the **credit** side, abbreviated *Cr.*[3] To enter amounts on the left side of an account is to *debit* the account. To enter amounts on the right side is to *credit* the account. We must guard against the error of thinking that the terms *debit* and *credit* mean increase or decrease. Whether a debit is an increase or decrease depends on the account. Similarly, whether a credit is an increase or decrease depends on the account. In each account, however, a debit and a credit have opposite effects. In an account where a debit is an increase, the credit is a decrease; in an account where a debit is a decrease, the credit is an increase. Identifying the account is the key to understanding the effects of debits and credits. The difference between total debits and total credits for an account is the **account balance.** When the sum of debits exceeds the sum of credits, the account has a *debit balance*. It has a *credit balance* when the sum of credits exceeds the sum of debits. When the sum of debits equals the sum of credits, the account has a *zero balance*.

A **T-account** is a helpful tool in analyzing the effects of transactions and events on individual accounts. Its name comes from its shape like the letter **T.** The T-account is shown in Exhibit 3.5.

---

[3] These abbreviations are remnants of 18th-century English recordkeeping practices where the terms *debitor* and *creditor* were used instead of *debit* and *credit*. The abbreviations use the first and last letters of these terms, just as we still do for Saint (St.) and Doctor (Dr.).

The format of a T-account is (1) the account title on top, (2) a left, or debit side, and (3) a right, or credit, side. One side is for recording increases in the account and the other side is for decreases. Whether increases are recorded on the right or the left side depends on the type of account.

Account Title	
(Left side)	(Right side)
Debit	**Credit**

Exhibit 3.5

The T-Account

Point: Debits and credits do not mean favorable or unfavorable. A debit to an asset increases it, as does a debit to an expense. A credit to a liability increases it, as does a credit to a revenue.

To determine the account's balance, we start with the beginning balance and then (1) compute the total increases shown on one side, (2) compute the total decreases shown on the other side, and (3) subtract the sum of the decreases from the sum of the increases. The T-account for FastForward's Cash account, reflecting the transactions from Chapter 2 (Exhibit 2.13), is shown in Exhibit 3.6. The total increases in its Cash account are $36,100, the total decreases are $31,700, and the account balance is $4,400.

Cash			
Investment by owner	30,000	Purchase of supplies	2,500
Consulting services revenue earned	4,200	Purchase of equipment	26,000
Collection of account receivable	1,900	Payment of rent	1,000
		Payment of salary	700
		Payment of note payable	900
		Withdrawal by owner	600
Total increases	**36,100**	Total decreases	**31,700**
Less decreases	**−31,700**		
Balance	**4,400**		

Exhibit 3.6

Computing the Balance for a T-Account

Point: The ending balance is on the side with the largest dollar amount.

Quick Check

4. Identify each of the following accounts as either an asset, liability, or equity: (a) Prepaid Rent, (b) Unearned Fees, (c) Building, (d) Wages Payable, and (e) Office Supplies.

5. What is an account? What is a ledger?

6. What determines the number and types of accounts a company uses?

7. Does *debit* always mean increase and *credit* always mean decrease?

Answers—p. 106

Double-Entry Accounting

Double-entry accounting requires that each transaction affect, and be recorded in, at least two accounts. It also means the *total amount debited must equal the total amount credited* for each transaction. Accordingly, the sum of the debits for all entries must equal the sum of the credits for all entries, and the sum of debit account balances in the ledger must equal the sum of credit account balances.

The system for recording debits and credits follows from the usual accounting equation—see Exhibit 3.7. Assets are on the left side of this equation. Liabilities and equity are on the right side. Two points are important here. First, like any simple mathematical relation, net increases or decreases on one side have equal net effects on the other side. For example, a net increase in assets must be accompanied by an identical net increase in the liabilities and equity side. Also recall that some transactions affect only one side of the equation, meaning that two or more accounts on one side are affected, but their net effect on this one side is zero. Second, we treat the left side as the *normal balance* side for assets, and the right side as the *normal balance* for liabilities and equity. This matches their layout in the accounting equation.

"Total debits equal total credits for each entry."

Point: Luca Pacioli is considered a pioneer in accounting and the first to devise double-entry accounting.

Exhibit 3.7

Debits and Credits in the Accounting Equation

Three important rules for recording transactions in a double-entry accounting system follow from Exhibit 3.7:

1. Increases in assets are debits to asset accounts. Decreases in assets are credits to asset accounts.
2. Increases in liabilities are credits to liability accounts. Decreases in liabilities are debits to liability accounts.
3. Increases in equity are credits to equity accounts. Decreases in equity are debits to equity accounts.

We showed in Chapter 2 how equity increases from owner's investments and revenues and how it decreases from expenses and withdrawals. These important equity relations are conveyed by expanding the accounting equation to include debits and credits in double-entry form as shown in Exhibit 3.8.

Exhibit 3.8

Debit and Credit Effects for Component Accounts

Point: Consider mnemonic aids: *DAWE*–Debit Assets, Withdrawals, Expenses. *CRIL*–Credit Revenues, Investments, Liabilities.

Increases (credits) to capital or revenues *increase* owner's equity; increases (debits) to withdrawals or expenses *decrease* owner's equity. These relations are reflected in the following important rules:

1. Investments are credited to owner's capital because they increase equity.
2. Withdrawals are debited to owner's withdrawals because they decrease equity.
3. Revenues are credited to revenue accounts because they increase equity.
4. Expenses are debited to expense accounts because they decrease equity.

Our understanding of these diagrams and rules is especially helpful in analyzing and recording transactions. It also helps us prepare, analyze, and interpret financial statements.

You Make the Call

Marketing Manager   You are a marketing manager and you want to know your company's revenues for this period. Financial statements are not yet available. Where do you search for this information? Would source documents or the ledger be more useful?

Answer—p. 106

Processing Transactions

P1 Record transactions in a journal and post entries to a ledger.

Processing transactions is a crucial part of accounting. The four main steps of this process are depicted in Exhibit 3.9. Steps 1 and 2—involving transaction analysis and double-entry accounting—were introduced in the prior section. This section extends that discussion and focuses on steps 3 and 4 of the accounting process. Step 3 is to record each transaction in a journal. A **journal** gives us a complete record of each transaction in one place. It also shows debits and credits for each transaction. The process of recording transactions in a journal is called **journalizing.** Step 4 is to transfer (or **post**) entries from the journal to the ledger. The process of transferring journal entry information to the ledger is called **posting.** This section describes both journalizing and posting transactions.

Journalizing Transactions

The process of journalizing transactions requires an understanding of a journal. While companies can use various journals, every company uses a **general journal,** which shows the debits and credits of each transaction. It can be used to record any transaction. A general journal entry includes the following information about each transaction: (1) date of transaction, (2) titles of affected accounts, (3) dollar amount of each debit and credit, and (4) explanation of the transaction. Exhibit 3.10 shows how the first two transactions of FastForward are recorded in a general journal. This process is similar for manual and computerized systems. Computerized journals are often designed to look like a manual journal page as in Exhibit 3.10. Computerized systems typically include error-checking routines that ensure debits equal credits for each entry. Shortcuts often allow recordkeepers to enter account numbers instead of names and to enter account names and numbers with pull-down menus.

Recording entries in a general journal follow standard procedures. It is helpful to refer to the entries in Exhibit 3.10 when reviewing these steps.

1. Date the transaction: Enter the year at the top of the first column and the month on the first line of the journal entry. Enter the day of the transaction in the second column on the first line of each entry.
2. Enter titles of accounts debited. Account titles are taken from the chart of accounts and are aligned with the left margin of the Account Titles and Explanation column. Enter debit amounts in the Debit column on the same line as the accounts debited.
3. Enter titles of accounts credited. Account titles are taken from the chart of accounts and are indented from the left margin of the Account Titles and Explanation column to distinguish them from debited accounts. Enter credit amounts in the Credit column on the same line as the accounts credited.
4. Enter a brief explanation of the transaction on the line below the entry (it often references a source document). This explanation is indented about half as far as the credited account titles to avoid confusing it with accounts. We italicize explanations.
5. Skip a line between each journal entry for clarity.

The **posting reference (PR) column** is left blank when a transaction is initially recorded. Individual account numbers are later entered into the PR column when entries are posted to the ledger.

Balance Column Account

T-accounts are simple and direct means to show how the accounting process works. Accounting systems in practice need more structure and use **balance column accounts** as in Exhibit 3.11.

Exhibit 3.9

Steps in Processing Transactions

Step 1: Analyze transactions and source documents.

Step 2: Apply double-entry accounting.

Step 3: Record journal entry.

General Journal		
Dec. 1 Cash	30,000	
Taylor, Capital		30,000
Dec. 2 Supplies	2,500	
Cash		2,500

Step 4: Post entry to ledger.

Exhibit 3.10

General Journal					Page 1
Date		**Account Titles and Explanation**	**PR**	**Debit**	**Credit**
2001 Dec.	1	Cash		30,000	
		C.Taylor, Capital			30,000
		Investment by owner.			
	2	Supplies		2,500	
		Cash			2,500
		Purchased store supplies for cash.			

Partial General Journal for FastForward

Concept 3-2

Exhibit 3.11

Cash Account in Balance
Column Format

Cash						Account No. 101
Date		Explanation	PR	Debit	Credit	Balance
2001 Dec	1		G1	30,000		30,000
	2		G1		2,500	27,500
	3		G1		26,000	1,500
	10		G1	4,200		5,700

The balance column account format is similar to a T-account in having columns for debits and credits. It is different by including transaction date and explanation columns. It also has a column with the balance of the account after each entry is recorded. For example, FastForward's Cash account in Exhibit 3.11 is debited on December 1 for the $30,000 investment by Taylor, yielding a $30,000 debit balance. The account is credited on December 2 for $2,500, yielding a $27,500 debit balance. On December 3, it is credited again, this time for $26,000, and its debit balance is reduced to $1,500. The Cash account is debited for $4,200 on December 10, and its debit balance increases to $5,700.

Point: A journal is often referred to as the *book of original entry*.

When a balance column account is used, the heading of the Balance column does not show whether it is a debit or credit balance. An account is assumed to have a *normal balance*. The normal balance of each account (asset, liability, equity, revenue, or expense) refers to the left or right (debit or credit) side where *increases* are recorded. Exhibit 3.12 shows normal balances for accounts.

Exhibit 3.12

Normal Balances for Accounts

Assets		=	Liabilities		+	Owner's Capital		−	Owner's Withdrawals		+	Revenues		−	Expenses	
Dr. for increases	Cr. for decreases		Dr. for decreases	Cr. for increases		Dr. for decreases	Cr. for increases		Dr. for increases	Cr. for decreases		Dr. for decreases	Cr. for increases		Dr. for increases	Cr. for decreases
+	−		−	+		−	+		+	−		−	+		+	−
Normal				**Normal**			**Normal**		**Normal**				**Normal**		**Normal**	

Point: The ledger is referred to as the *book of final entry* because financial statements are prepared from it.

Unusual events can sometimes temporarily give an account an abnormal balance. An *abnormal balance* refers to a balance on the side where decreases are recorded. For example, a customer might mistakenly overpay a bill. This gives that customer's account receivable an abnormal (credit) balance. An abnormal balance is often identified by circling it or by entering it in red or some other unusual color. Computerized systems often provide a code beside a balance such as *dr.* or *cr.* to identify its balance. A zero balance for an account is usually shown by writing zeros or a dash in the Balance column. This practice avoids confusion between a zero balance and one omitted in error.

Posting Journal Entries

Step 4 of processing transactions is to post journal entries to ledger accounts (see Exhibit 3.9). To ensure that the ledger is up to date, entries are posted as soon as possible. This might be daily, weekly, or when time permits. All entries must be posted to the ledger by the end of a reporting period. This is necessary so account balances are current when financial statements are prepared. When entries are posted to the ledger, the debits in journal entries are copied into ledger accounts as debits, and credits are copied into ledger accounts as credits. The usual process is to post debits first and then credits. Exhibit 3.13 shows the four steps to post a journal entry. First, identify the ledger account that is debited in the entry. In the ledger, enter the date of the entry, the journal and page in the PR column[4], the debit amount from the journal, and the new balance of the ledger account. Second, enter the ledger account number in the PR column of the journal next to the entry. Next, repeat these two steps for credit entries and amounts.

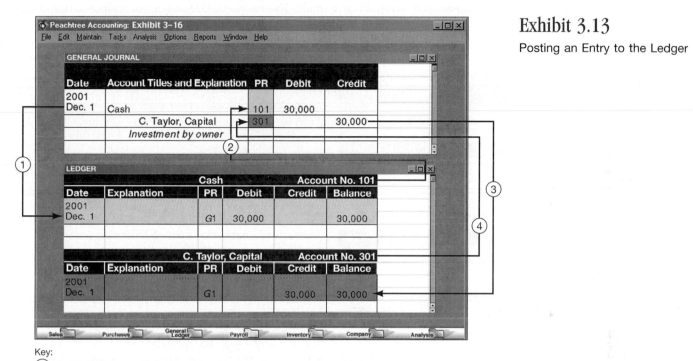

Exhibit 3.13

Posting an Entry to the Ledger

Key:

(1) Identify debit account in Ledger: enter date, journal page, amount, and balance.

(2) Enter the debit account number from the Ledger in the PR column of the journal.

(3) Identify credit account in Ledger: enter date, journal page, amount, and balance.

(4) Enter the credit account number from the Ledger in the PR column of the journal.

The posting process creates a link between the ledger and the journal entry. This link is a useful cross-reference for tracing an amount from one record to another. It also shows the stage of completion in the posting process. This permits you to easily start and stop the posting process. Computerized systems require no added effort to post journal entries to the ledger. These systems automatically transfer debit and credit entries from the journal to the ledger. Many systems have programs testing the reasonableness of a journal entry and the account balance when recorded. For example, the payroll program might alert a preparer to hourly wage rates exceeding $500.

Point: Explanations are typically only included in ledger accounts for unusual transactions or events.

---

[4] The letter *G* shows it came from the General Journal. Other journals are identified by their own letters. We discuss other journals in Chapter 8.

Analyzing Transactions

A1 Analyze the impact of transactions on accounts and financial statements.

Concept 3-1

FASTforward

We return to the activities of **FastForward** to show how double-entry accounting is useful in analyzing and processing transactions. We analyze each of FastForward's transactions in four stages. First, we review the transaction and any source documents. Second, we analyze the transaction using the accounting equation. Third, we use double-entry accounting to record the transaction, in both the required journal entry form and the optional T-account form (the T-accounts can be viewed as simple ledger accounts). Fourth, we show how each transaction affects (links to) the financial statements. Exhibit 3.15 (on page 99) eventually summarizes these links.

We should study each transaction thoroughly before proceeding to the next transaction. The first 11 transactions are familiar to us from Chapter 2. We expand our analysis of these transactions and consider five other FastForward December transactions (numbered 12 through 16) that were omitted from Chapter 2.

1. Investment by Owner

Cash		101
(1)	30,000	

C.Taylor, Capital		301
	(1)	30,000

Transaction: Chuck Taylor invests $30,000 cash in FastForward on December 1.

Analysis:

	Assets	=	Liabilities	+	Equity
	+30,000	=	0	+	30,000

Double entry:

(1)	Cash	101	30,000	
	C.Taylor, Capital	301		30,000

Statements affected:[5] BS, SCF, and SCOE

2. Purchase Supplies for Cash

Supplies		126
(2)	2,500	

Cash		101
(1)	30,000	(2)	2,500

Transaction: FastForward pays $2,500 cash for supplies.

Analysis:

	Assets	=	Liabilities	+	Equity
	+2,500	=	0	+	0
	−2,500				

Changes the composition of assets but not their total.

Double entry:

(2)	Supplies	126	2,500	
	Cash	101		2,500

Statements affected: BS and SCF

3. Purchase Equipment for Cash

Equipment		167
(3)	26,000	

Cash		101
(1)	30,000	(2)	2,500
		(3)	26,000

Transaction: FastForward pays $26,000 cash for equipment.

Analysis:

	Assets	=	Liabilities	+	Equity
	+26,000	=	0	+	0
	−26,000				

Changes the composition of assets but not their total.

Double entry:

(3)	Equipment	167	26,000	
	Cash	101		26,000

Statements affected: BS and SCF

4. Purchase Supplies on Credit

Supplies		126
(2)	2,500	
(4)	7,100	

Accounts Payable		201
	(4)	7,100

Transaction: FastForward purchases $7,100 of supplies on credit.

Analysis:

	Assets	=	Liabilities	+	Equity
	+7,100	=	+7,100	+	0

Double entry:

(4)	Supplies	126	7,100	
	Accounts Payable	201		7,100

Statements affected: BS

---

[5] We use abbreviations for the statements: income statement (IS), balance sheet (BS), statement of cash flows (SCF), and statement of changes in owner's equity (SCOE).

5. Provide Services for Cash

Cash			101
(1)	30,000	(2)	2,500
(5)	4,200	(3)	26,000

Consulting Revenue			403
		(5)	4,200

Transaction: FastForward provides consulting services and immediately collects $4,200 cash.

Analysis:

	Assets	=	Liabilities	+	Equity
	+4,200	=	0	+	4,200

Double entry:

(5)	Cash	101	4,200	
	Consulting Revenue	403		4,200

Statements affected: BS, IS, SCF, and SCOE

6. Payment of Expense in Cash

Rent Expense			640
(6)	1,000		

Cash			101
(1)	30,000	(2)	2,500
(5)	4,200	(3)	26,000
		(6)	1,000

Transaction: FastForward pays $1,000 cash for December rent.

Analysis:

	Assets	=	Liabilities	+	Equity
	−1,000	=	0	+	−1,000

Double entry:

(6)	Rent Expense	640	1,000	
	Cash	101		1,000

Statements affected: BS, IS, SCF, and SCOE

7. Payment of Expense in Cash

Salaries Expense			622
(7)	700		

Cash			101
(1)	30,000	(2)	2,500
(5)	4,200	(3)	26,000
		(6)	1,000
		(7)	700

Transaction: FastForward pays $700 cash in employee wages.

Analysis:

	Assets	=	Liabilities	+	Equity
	−700	=	0	+	−700

Double entry:

(7)	Salaries Expense	622	700	
	Cash	101		700

Statements affected: BS, IS, SCF, and SCOE

Point: *Salary* usually refers to compensation for an employee who receives a fixed amount for a given time period, whereas *wages* usually refers to compensation based on time worked.

8. Provide Consulting and Rental Services on Credit

Accounts Receivable			106
(8)	1,900		

Consulting Revenue			403
		(5)	4,200
		(8)	1,600

Rental Revenue			406
		(8)	300

Transaction: FastForward provides consulting services of $1,600 and rents its test facilities for $300. The customer is billed $1,900 for these services.

Analysis:

	Assets	−	Liabilities	+	Equity
	+1,900	=	0	+	{ +1,600
					{ + 300

Double entry:

(8)	Accounts Receivable	106	1,900	
	Consulting Revenue	403		1,600
	Rental Revenue	406		300

Statements affected: BS, IS, and SCOE

Point: Transaction 8 is a **compound journal entry.** A compound journal entry affects three or more accounts.

9. Receipt of Cash on Account

Cash			101
(1)	30,000	(2)	2,500
(5)	4,200	(3)	26,000
(9)	1,900	(6)	1,000
		(7)	700

Accounts Receivable			106
(8)	1,900	(9)	1,900

Transaction: FastForward receives $1,900 cash from the client billed in transaction 8.

Analysis:

	Assets	=	Liabilities	+	Equity
	+1,900 }	=	0	+	0
	−1,900 }				

Double entry:

(9)	Cash	101	1,900	
	Accounts Receivable	106		1,900

Statements affected: BS and SCF

Point: The *revenue recognition principle* requires revenue to be recognized when earned, which is when the company provides products or services to a customer. This is not necessarily the same time that the customer pays. A customer can pay before or after the product or service is provided.

10. Partial Payment of Accounts Payable

Accounts Payable 201		
(10) 900	(4)	7,100

Cash		101
(1) 30,000	(2)	2,500
(5) 4,200	(3)	26,000
(9) 1,900	(6)	1,000
	(7)	700
	(10)	900

Transaction: FastForward pays CalTech Supply $900 cash toward the payable of transaction 4.

Analysis:

	Assets	=	Liabilities	+	Equity
	−900	=	−900	+	0

Double entry:

(10)	Accounts Payable	201	900	
	Cash	101		900

Statements affected: BS and SCF

11. Withdrawal of Cash by Owner

C.Taylor, Withdrawals		302
(11) 600		

Cash		101
(1) 30,000	(2)	2,500
(5) 4,200	(3)	26,000
(9) 1,900	(6)	1,000
	(7)	700
	(10)	900
	(11)	600

Transaction: Chuck Taylor withdraws $600 cash from FastForward for personal expenses.

Analysis:

	Assets	=	Liabilities	+	Equity
	−600	=	0	+	−600

Double entry:

(11)	C.Taylor, Withdrawals	302	600	
	Cash	101		600

Statements affected: BS, SCF, and SCOE

12. Receipt of Cash for Future Services

Cash		101
(1) 30,000	(2)	2,500
(5) 4,200	(3)	26,000
(9) 1,900	(6)	1,000
(12) 3,000	(7)	700
	(10)	900
	(11)	600

Unearned Consulting Revenue		236
	(12)	3,000

Transaction: FastForward receives $3,000 cash in advance of providing consulting services to a customer.

Analysis:

	Assets	=	Liabilities	+	Equity
	+3,000	=	+3,000	+	0

Accepting $3,000 cash obligates FastForward to perform future services and is a liability. No revenue is earned until services are provided.

Double entry:

(12)	Cash	101	3,000	
	Unearned Consulting Revenue	236		3,000

Statements affected: BS and SCF

13. Pay Cash for Future Insurance Coverage

Prepaid Insurance 128		
(13) 2,400		

Cash		101
(1) 30,000	(2)	2,500
(5) 4,200	(3)	26,000
(9) 1,900	(6)	1,000
(12) 3,000	(7)	700
	(10)	900
	(11)	600
	(13)	2,400

Transaction: FastForward pays $2,400 cash (premium) for a 2-year insurance policy. Coverage begins on December 1.

Analysis:

	Assets	=	Liabilities	+	Equity
	+2,400				
	−2,400	=	0	+	0

Changes the composition of assets from cash to prepaid insurance. Expense is incurred as insurance coverage expires.

Double entry:

(13)	Prepaid Insurance	128	2,400	
	Cash	101		2,400

Statements affected: BS and SCF

14. Purchase Supplies for Cash

Supplies	126	
(2)	2,500	
(4)	7,100	
(14)	**120**	

Cash	101		
(1)	30,000	(2)	2,500
(5)	4,200	(3)	26,000
(9)	1,900	(6)	1,000
(12)	3,000	(7)	700
		(10)	900
		(11)	600
		(13)	2,400
		(14)	**120**

Transaction: FastForward pays $120 cash for supplies.

Analysis:

Assets	=	Liabilities	+	Equity
+120	=	0	+	0
−120				

Double entry:

(14)	Supplies	126	120	
	Cash	101		120

Statements affected: BS and SCF

15. Payment of Expense in Cash

Utilities Expense	690	
(15)	230	

Cash	101		
(1)	30,000	(2)	2,500
(5)	4,200	(3)	26,000
(9)	1,900	(6)	1,000
(12)	3,000	(7)	700
		(10)	900
		(11)	600
		(13)	2,400
		(14)	120
		(15)	**230**

Transaction: FastForward pays $230 cash for December utilities.

Analysis:

Assets	=	Liabilities	+	Equity
−230	=	0	+	−230

Double entry:

(15)	Utilities Expense	690	230	
	Cash	101		230

Statements affected: BS, IS, SCF, and SCOE

16. Payment of Expense in Cash

Salaries Expense	622	
(7)	700	
(16)	**700**	

Cash	101		
(1)	30,000	(2)	2,500
(5)	4,200	(3)	26,000
(9)	1,900	(6)	1,000
(12)	3,000	(7)	700
		(10)	900
		(11)	600
		(13)	2,400
		(14)	120
		(15)	230
		(16)	**700**

Transaction: FastForward pays $700 cash in employee wages.

Analysis:

Assets	=	Liabilities	+	Equity
−700	=	0	+	−700

Double entry:

(16)	Salaries Expense	622	700	
	Cash	101		700

Statements affected: BS, IS, SCE, and SCOE

Point: We could merge transactions 14–16 into one *compound entry.*

Point: Some small businesses use an outside recordkeeping service to make entries once each month.

Accounting Equation Analysis

Point: Technology does not provide the judgment required to analyze most business transactions. Analysis requires the expertise of skilled and ethical professionals.

Exhibit 3.14 shows the accounts of FastForward after all 16 transactions have been recorded and the balances computed. The accounts are grouped into three major columns corresponding to the accounting equation: assets, liabilities, and equity. Note several important points. First, as with each transaction, the totals for the three columns must obey the accounting equation. Specifically, assets equal $42,070 ($3,950 + $0 + $9,720 + $2,400 + $26,000); liabilities equal $9,200 ($6,200 + $3,000); and equity equals $32,870 ($30,000 − $600 + $5,800 + $300 − $1,400 − $1,000 − $230). These numbers obey the accounting equation: $42,070 = $9,200 + $32,870. Second, the capital, withdrawals, revenue, and expense accounts reflect the transactions that change equity. Their balances make up the statement of changes in owner's equity. Third, the revenue and expense account balances will be summarized and reported in the income statement. Fourth, components of the cash account make up the elements reported in the statement of cash flows.

Exhibit 3.14

Ledger for FastForward
(in T-account Form)

Assets				=	Liabilities			+	Equity		

Cash 101

(1)	30,000	(2)	2,500
(5)	4,200	(3)	26,000
(9)	1,900	(6)	1,000
(12)	3,000	(7)	700
		(10)	900
		(11)	600
		(13)	2,400
		(14)	120
		(15)	230
		(16)	700
Balance	3,950		

Accounts Receivable 106

| (8) | 1,900 | (9) | 1,900 |
| Balance | 0 | | |

Supplies 126

(2)	2,500	
(4)	7,100	
(14)	120	
Balance	9,720	

Prepaid Insurance 128

| (13) | 2,400 | |

Equipment 167

| (3) | 26,000 | |

Accounts Payable 201

| (10) | 900 | (4) | 7,100 |
| | | Balance | 6,200 |

Unearned Consulting Revenue 236

| | (12) | 3,000 |

C. Taylor, Capital 301

| | (1) | 30,000 |

C. Taylor, Withdrawals 302

| (11) | 600 | |

Consulting Revenue 403

	(5)	4,200
	(8)	1,600
	Balance	5,800

Rental Revenue 406

| | (8) | 300 |

Salaries Expense 622

(7)	700	
(16)	700	
Balance	1,400	

Rent Expense 640

| (6) | 1,000 | |

Utilities Expense 690

| (15) | 230 | |

Accounts in this white area reflect those reported on the income statement.

$42,070	=	$9,200	+	$32,870

Financial Statement Links

Exhibit 3.15 extends the analysis and summarizes how **FastForward**'s transactions impact all financial statements. Some transactions such as purchasing supplies on credit (No. 4) impact only one statement. Others such as receiving cash for services performed (No. 5) impact all of the statements. We should review this exhibit and understand how transactions link to financial statements. We return to explain the details of these links in Chapter 4, including the adjusting and closing processes.

Quick Check

8. What types of transactions increase equity? What types decrease equity?

9. Why are accounting systems called *double entry?*

10. For each transaction, double-entry accounting requires: (a) Debits to asset accounts must create credits to liability or equity accounts, (b) A debit to a liability account must create a credit to an asset account, or (c) Total debits must equal total credits.

11. An owner invests $15,000 cash and equipment having a market value of $23,000 in a proprietorship. Prepare the journal entry to record this owner's investment.

12. Explain what a compound journal entry is.

13. Why are posting reference numbers entered in the journal when entries are posted to ledger accounts?

Answers—p. 106

Double-entry accounting requires the sum of debit account balances to equal the sum of credit account balances. A trial balance is used to verify this. A **trial balance** is a list of accounts and their balances at a point in time. Account balances are reported in the debit or credit column of a trial balance. Exhibit 3.16 shows the trial balance for FastForward after its 16 entries have been posted to the ledger.

Trial Balance

P2 Prepare and explain the use of a trial balance.

Preparing a Trial Balance

Preparing a trial balance involves three steps:

1. List each account title and its amount (from the ledger) in the trial balance.[6]
2. Compute the total of debit balances and the total of credit balances.
3. Verify (*prove*) total debit balances equal total credit balances.

The total of debit balances equals the total of credit balances for the trial balance in Exhibit 3.16. If these two totals were not equal, then one or more errors exist. However, equality of these two totals does not guarantee that no errors were made.

Point: The ordering of accounts in a trial balance typically follows their identification number from the chart of accounts.

Point: A trial balance is *not* a financial statement but a mechanism for checking equality of debits and credits in the ledger. Financial statements do not have debit and credit columns.

Using a Trial Balance

One or more errors exist when a trial balance does not balance (when its columns are not equal). When errors exist, they often occur in one of the following steps in the accounting process: (1) preparing journal entries, (2) posting entries to the ledger, (3) computing account balances, (4) entering account balances on the trial balance, or (5) totaling the trial balance columns. When a trial balance does balance, the accounts are likely free of the kinds of errors that create unequal debits and credits, yet errors can still exist. One example is when a debit or credit of a correct amount is made to a wrong account. This can occur when either journalizing or posting. This error would produce incorrect balances in two accounts, but the trial balance would balance. Another error is to record equal debits and credits of an incorrect amount. This error produces incorrect balances in two accounts, but again the

---

[6] If an account has a zero balance, it can be listed in the trial balance with a zero in its normal balance column.

		Balance Sheet (BS)									
Transactions		**Assets**					**=**	**Liabilities**		**+**	**Equity**
No.	**Description**	**Cash**	**+ Accts. Rec.**	**+ Prepaid Insur.**	**+ Supplies**	**+ Equip.**	**= Accts. Pay.**	**+ Unearned Revenue**		**+ Taylor Capital**
1	Owner investment	30,000					=			+	30,000
2	Purch. supp.	(2,500)			2,500		=			+	
3	Purch. equip.	(26,000)				26,000	=			+	
4	Credit purch.				7,100		=	7,100		+	
5	Services for cash	4,200					=			+	4,200
6	Rent exp.	(1,000)					=			+	(1,000)
7	Salary exp.	(700)					=			+	(700)
8	Services for credit		1,900				=			+	1,600 300
9	Cash rec'd. on Acct. Rec.	1,900	(1,900)				=			+	
10	Payment of Acct. Pay.	(900)					=	(900)		+	
11	Owner Withdrawal	(600)					=			+	(600)
12	Cash for future service	3,000					=		3,000	+	
13	Payment of future insur.	(2,400)		2,400			=			+	
14	Purch. supp.	(120)			120		=			+	
15	Utility exp.	(230)					=			+	(230)
16	Salary exp.	(700)					=			+	(700)
	Totals	3,950	0	2,400	9,720	26,000	= 6,200	3,000		+	32,870

Example: If a credit to Unearned Consulting Revenue were incorrectly posted from the journal as a credit to the Consulting Revenue ledger account, would the ledger still balance? Would the financial statements be correct? *Answers:* The ledger would still balance, but the financial statements would be incorrect. Liabilities would be understated, equity would be overstated, and net income would be overstated as a result of overstated revenues.

debits and credits are equal. These examples show that when a trial balance does balance, it does not prove that all entries have been recorded and posted correctly.

Searching for Errors

If the trial balance does not balance, the error (or errors) must be found and corrected before preparing financial statements. Searching for the error is more efficient if we check the journalizing, posting, and trial balance preparation process in *reverse order*. While methods vary, we suggest the following sequence of steps. Step 1 is to verify that the trial balance columns are correctly added. If step 1 fails to find the error, then step 2 is to verify that account balances are accurately entered from the ledger. Step 3 is to see whether a debit (or credit) balance is mistakenly listed in the trial balance as a credit (or debit). A clue to this kind of error is when the difference between total debits and total credits in the trial balance equals twice the amount of the incorrect account balance. If the error is still undiscovered, Step 4 is to recompute each account balance in the ledger. Step 5 is to verify that each journal entry is properly posted to ledger accounts. Step 6 is to verify that the original journal entry has equal debits and credits. At this point, all errors should be uncovered.[7]

---

[7] *Transposition* occurs when two digits are switched, or transposed, within a number. If transposition is the only error, it yields a difference between the two trial balance totals that is evenly divisible by 9. For example, assume that a $691 debit in an entry is incorrectly posted to the ledger as $619. Total credits in the trial balance are then larger than total debits by $72 ($691 − $619). The $72 error is *evenly* divisible by 9 (72/9 = 8). The first digit

Income Statement (IS)			Statement of Cash Flows (SCF)				Transactions	
Rev. –	Exp. =	Net Inc.	Oper. Cash Flow +	Inv. Cash Flow +	Fin. Cash Flow =	Net Cash Flow	No.	Description
	– =				30,000 =	30,000	1	Owner investment
	– =		(2,500)		=	(2,500)	2	Purch. supp.
	– =			(26,000)	=	(26,000)	3	Purch. equip.
	– =				=		4	Credit purch.
4,200 –	=	4,200	4,200		=	4,200	5	Services for cash
	– 1,000 =	(1,000)	(1,000)		=	(1,000)	6	Rent exp.
	– 700 =	(700)	(700)		=	(700)	7	Salary exp.
1,600 –	=	1,600					8	Services for credit
300 –	=	300						
	– =		1,900		=	1,900	9	Cash rec'd on Acct. Rec.
	– =		(900)		=	(900)	10	Payment of Acct. Pay.
	– –				(600) –	(600)	11	Owner Withdrawal
	– =		3,000		=	3,000	12	Cash for future service
	– =		(2,400)		=	(2,400)	13	Payment of future insur.
	– =		(120)		=	(120)	14	Purch. supp.
	– 230 =	(230)	(230)		=	(230)	15	Utilities exp.
	– 700 =	(700)	(700)		=	(700)	16	Salary exp.
6,100 –	2,630 =	3,470	550 +	(26,000) +	29,400 =	3,950		Totals

Exhibit 3.15

Financial Statement Links to Transactions

Exhibit 3.16

Trial Balance

Peachtree Accounting: Exercise 3-18

File Edit Maintain Tasks Analysis Options Reports Window Help

FAST FORWARD
Trial Balance
December 31, 2001

	Debit	Credit
Cash	$ 3,950	
Accounts Receivable	0	
Supplies	9,720	
Prepaid insurance	2,400	
Equipment	26,000	
Accounts payable		$ 6,200
Unearned consulting revenue		3,000
C. Taylor, Capital		30,000
C. Taylor, Withdrawals	600	
Consulting revenue		5,800
Rental revenue		300
Salaries expense	1,400	
Rent expense	1,000	
Utilities expense	230	
Totals	$ 45,300	$ 45,300

Sales   Purchases   General Ledger   Payroll   Inventory   Company   Analysis

of the quotient (in our example it is 8) equals the difference between the digits of the two transposed numbers (the 9 and the 1). The number of digits in the quotient also tells the location of the transposition, starting from the right. The quotient in our example had only one digit (8), so it tells us the transposition is in the first digit. Consider another example where a transposition error involves posting $961 instead of the correct $691. The difference in these numbers in $270, and its quotient is 30 (270/9). The quotient has two digits, so it tells us to check the second digit from the right for a transposition of two numbers that have a difference of 3.

Correcting Errors

Point: IRS requires companies to keep records that can be audited.

If errors are discovered in either the journal or the ledger, they must be corrected. Our approach to correcting errors depends on the type of error and when it is discovered.

In one case, if an error in a journal entry is discovered before the error is posted, it can be corrected in a manual system by drawing a line through the incorrect information. The correct information is written above it to create a record of change for the auditor. Many computerized systems allow the operator to replace the incorrect information directly. If a correct amount in the journal is posted incorrectly to the ledger, we can correct it the same way.

Another case occurs when an error in a journal entry is not discovered until after it has been posted. We usually do not strike through both erroneous entries in the journal and ledger. Instead, the usual practice is to correct the error in the original journal entry by creating *another* journal entry. This *correcting entry* removes the amount from the wrong account and records it to the correct account. As an example, suppose we recorded a purchase of office supplies in the journal with an incorrect debit to Office Equipment:

Assets = Liabilities + Equity
+1,600
−1,600

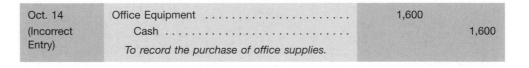

Oct. 14	Office Equipment	1,600	
(Incorrect	Cash		1,600
Entry)	*To record the purchase of office supplies.*		

We then post this incorrect entry to the ledger. The Office Supplies ledger account balance is understated by $1,600, and the Office Equipment ledger account balance is overstated by $1,600. When we discover the error three days later, we make the following correcting entry:

Assets = Liabilities + Equity
+1,600
−1,600

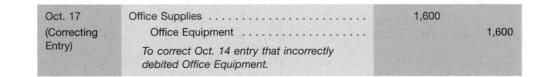

Oct. 17	Office Supplies	1,600	
(Correcting	Office Equipment		1,600
Entry)	*To correct Oct. 14 entry that incorrectly debited Office Equipment.*		

The credit in the correcting entry removes the error from the first entry. The debit correctly records the office supplies. The explanation reports exactly what happened. Computerized systems often use similar correcting entries. The exact procedure depends on the system used and management policy. Nearly all systems include controls to show when and where a correction is made.

Presentation Issues

Point: There are no exact rules for writing journal entry explanations. An explanation should be short yet describe why an entry is made.

Dollar signs are not used in journals and ledgers. They do appear in financial statements and other reports such as trial balances. The usual practice is to put a dollar sign beside the first amount in each column of numbers, and beside the first amount appearing after a ruled line. The financial statements in Exhibit 2.15 demonstrate this. Another practice is to put dollar signs beside only the first and last numbers in a column. **Nike**'s financial statements in Appendix A show this. When amounts are entered in a journal, ledger, or trial balance, commas are optional to indicate thousands, millions, and so forth. However, commas are always used in financial statements. Companies also commonly round amounts to the nearest dollar, or even to a higher level. Nike is typical of many companies in that it rounds its financial statement amounts to the nearest one-tenth of a million. This decision is based on the perceived impact of rounding for users' business decisions.

Point: To *foot* a column of numbers is to add them.

Quick Check

14. Describe a chart of accounts.

15. Where are dollar signs typically entered in financial statements?

16. If a $4,000 debit to Equipment in a journal entry is incorrectly posted to the ledger as a $4,000 credit, and the ledger account has a resulting debit balance of $20,000, what is the effect of this error on the trial balance column totals?

Answers—p. 106

Debt Ratio

Using the Information

Accounting records are designed to provide useful information to users of financial statements. One important objective for many users is gathering information to help them assess a company's risk of failing to pay its debts when they are due. This section describes the debt ratio and how it can help in this task.

A2 Compute the debt ratio and describe its use in analyzing company performance.

Most companies finance a portion of their assets with liabilities and the remaining portion with equity. A company that finances a relatively large portion of its assets with liabilities is said to have a high degree of *financial leverage*. Higher financial leverage involves greater risk because liabilities must be repaid and often require regular interest payments (equity financing does not). The risk that a company might not be able to meet required payments is higher if it has more liabilities (is more highly leveraged).

One way to assess the risk associated with a company's use of liabilities is to compute and analyze the debt ratio. The **debt ratio** reflects the relation between a company's liabilities and its assets and is defined in Exhibit 3.17.

$$\text{Debt ratio} = \frac{\text{Total liabilities}}{\text{Total assets}}$$

Exhibit 3.17

Debt Ratio

To see how we apply the debt ratio, let's look at **Stride Rite**'s liabilities and assets—it makes Keds, Pro-Keds, and other footwear. Exhibit 3.18 computes and reports the debt ratio for Stride Rite at the end of each of the past five years.

	1999	1998	1997	1996	1995
Total liabilities (in mil.)	$ 96	$ 91	$102	$103	$ 99
Total assets (in mil.)	$346	$335	$344	$364	$367
Debt ratio	**.277**	**.272**	**.297**	**.283**	**.270**
Industry debt ratio*	.46	.52	.59	.64	.47

* Industry debt ratio is the median value from ten competitors.

Exhibit 3.18

Computation and Analysis of Debt Ratio

Note that Stride Rite's debt ratio is stable over recent years, ranging from a low of .270 to a high of .297. This ratio is low for Stride Rite and most other companies as evidenced by comparisons with its industry ratio. Stride Rite also reports that it carries no long-term debt, which is also unusual. This analysis implies a low risk from financial leverage for Stride Rite. Still, evaluating a company's debt ratio depends on several factors, such as the nature of its operations, its ability to generate cash flows, its

You Make the Call

Investor   You consider buying stock in **Converse**. As part of your analysis, you compute its debt ratio for 1997, 1998, and 1999: 1.20, 1.35, and 1.74, respectively.* Based on the debt ratio, is Converse a low-risk investment? Has the risk of buying Converse stock changed over this period?

*Converse's equity balance is negative for these years because of losses.

Answer—p. 106

industry, and its economic conditions. Saying that a specific debt ratio is good or bad for a company is not possible. Instead, we need to compare performance over time and across companies both inside and outside the industry. In simplest terms, we need to compare the company's return on the money it has borrowed to the rate it is paying creditors. If the company's return is higher, it is successfully borrowing money to make more money. We must be aware that company returns change over time due to many factors. Accordingly, a company's success with making money from borrowed money can quickly turn unprofitable if its own return declines.

Demonstration Problem

(*Note: This demonstration problem is based on the same facts as the demonstration problem at the end of Chapter 2.*) The following events occurred during the first month of Sylvia Workman's new haircutting business called Expressions:

a. On August 1, Workman put $3,000 cash into a checking account in the name of Expressions. She also invested $15,000 of equipment that she already owned.

b. On August 2, Workman paid $600 cash for furniture for the shop.

c. On August 3, Workman paid $500 cash to rent space in a strip mall for August.

d. On August 4, Workman purchased some new equipment for the shop that she bought on credit (using a note payable) for $1,200.

e. On August 5, Expressions opened for business. Cash receipts from haircutting services provided in the first week and a half of business (ended August 15) are $825.

f. On August 15, Workman provided haircutting services on account for $100.

g. On August 17, Workman received a $100 check for services previously rendered on account.

h. On August 17, Workman paid $125 cash to an assistant for working during the grand opening.

i. Cash received from services provided during the second half of August is $930.

j. On August 31, Workman paid a $400 cash installment on the note payable from part (*d*).

k. On August 31, Workman withdrew $900 cash for her personal use.

Required

1. Prepare general journal entries for the preceding transactions.

2. Open the following accounts (account numbers are in parentheses): Cash (101); Accounts Receivable (102); Furniture (161); Store Equipment (165); Note Payable (240); Sylvia Workman, Capital (301); Sylvia Workman, Withdrawals (302); Haircutting Services Revenue (403); Wages Expense (623); and Rent Expense (640).

3. Post the journal entries from (1) to the ledger accounts from part (2).

4. Prepare a trial balance as of August 31.

Extended Analysis

5. In the coming months, Expressions will experience an even greater variety of business transactions. Identify which accounts are debited and which are credited for the following transactions. (*Hint:* You may have to use some accounts not listed in part (2).)

   a. Purchase supplies with cash.

   b. Pay cash for future insurance coverage.

   c. Receive cash for services to be provided in the future.

   d. Purchase supplies on account.

Planning the Solution

- Analyze each transaction to identify the accounts affected and the amount of each effect.
- Use the debit and credit rules to prepare a journal entry for each transaction.
- Post each debit and each credit in journal entries to their ledger accounts and cross-reference each amount in the Posting Reference columns of the journal and ledger.
- Calculate each account balance and list the accounts with their balances on a trial balance.
- Verify that total debits in the trial balance equal total credits.
- Analyze the future transactions to identify the accounts affected and apply debit and credit rules.

Solution to Demonstration Problem

1. General journal entries:

Date	Account Titles and Explanations	PR	Debit	Credit
Aug. 1	Cash	101	3,000	
	Store Equipment	165	15,000	
	Sylvia Workman, Capital	301		18,000
	Owner's initial investment.			
2	Furniture	161	600	
	Cash	101		600
	Purchased furniture for cash.			
3	Rent Expense	640	500	
	Cash	101		500
	Paid rent for August.			
4	Store Equipment	165	1,200	
	Note Payable	240		1,200
	Purchased additional equipment on credit.			
15	Cash	101	825	
	Haircutting Services Revenue	403		825
	Cash receipts from 10 days of operations.			
15	Accounts Receivable	102	100	
	Haircutting Services Revenue	403		100
	To record revenue for services provided on account.			
17	Cash	101	100	
	Accounts Receivable	102		100
	To record cash received as payment on account.			
17	Wages Expense	623	125	
	Cash	101		125
	Paid wages to assistant.			
31	Cash	101	930	
	Haircutting Services Revenue	403		930
	Cash receipts from second half of August.			
31	Note Payable	240	400	
	Cash	101		400
	Paid an installment on the note payable.			
31	Sylvia Workman, Withdrawals	302	900	
	Cash	101		900
	Owner withdrew cash from the business.			

2. & 3. Open ledger accounts and post journal entries from (1):

		Cash			Account No. 101	
Date		Explanation	PR	Debit	Credit	Balance
Aug.	1		G1	3,000		3,000
	2		G1		600	2,400
	3		G1		500	1,900
	15		G1	825		2,725
	17		G1	100		2,825
	17		G1		125	2,700
	31		G1	930		3,630
	31		G1		400	3,230
	31		G1		900	2,330

Accounts Receivable   Account No. 102

Date		Explanation	PR	Debit	Credit	Balance
Aug.	15		G1	100		100
	17		G1		100	0

Furniture   Account No. 161

Date		Explanation	PR	Debit	Credit	Balance
Aug.	2		G1	600		600

Store Equipment   Account No. 165

Date		Explanation	PR	Debit	Credit	Balance
Aug.	1		G1	15,000		15,000
	4		G1	1,200		16,200

Note Payable   Account No. 240

Date		Explanation	PR	Debit	Credit	Balance
Aug.	4		G1		1,200	1,200
	31		G1	400		800

Sylvia Workman, Capital   Account No. 301

Date		Explanation	PR	Debit	Credit	Balance
Aug.	1		G1		18,000	18,000

Sylvia Workman, Withdrawals   Account No. 302

Date		Explanation	PR	Debit	Credit	Balance
Aug.	31		G1	900		900

Haircutting Services Revenue   Account No. 403

Date		Explanation	PR	Debit	Credit	Balance
Aug.	15		G1		825	825
	15		G1		100	925
	31		G1		930	1,855

Wages Expense   Account No. 623

Date		Explanation	PR	Debit	Credit	Balance
Aug.	17		G1	125		125

Rent Expense   Account No. 640

Date		Explanation	PR	Debit	Credit	Balance
Aug.	3		G1	500		500

4. Prepare trial balance from ledger:

EXPRESSIONS Trial Balance August 31	Debit	Credit
Cash	$ 2,330	
Accounts receivable	0	
Furniture	600	
Store equipment	16,200	
Note payable		$ 800
Sylvia Workman, Capital		18,000
Sylvia Workman, Withdrawals	900	
Haircutting services revenue		1,855
Wages expense	125	
Rent expense	500	
Totals	$20,655	$20,655

5a. Supplies debited
     Cash credited

5b. Prepaid Insurance debited
     Cash credited

5c. Cash debited
     Unearned Services Revenue credited

5d. Supplies debited
     Accounts Payable credited

Summary

C1 **Explain the steps in processing transactions.** The accounting process captures business transactions and events, analyzes and records their effects, and summarizes and prepares information useful in making decisions. Transactions and events are the starting points in the accounting process. Source documents help in their analysis. The effects of transactions and events are recorded in journals. Posting along with a trial balance helps summarize and classify these effects.

C2 **Describe source documents and their purpose.** Source documents identify and describe transactions and events. Examples are sales tickets, checks, purchase orders, bills, and bank statements. Source documents provide objective and reliable evidence, making information more useful.

C3 **Describe an account and its use in recording information about transactions.** An account is a detailed record of increases and decreases in a specific asset, liability, equity, revenue, or expense item. Information is taken from accounts and then analyzed, summarized, and presented in reports and financial statements for decision makers to use.

C4 **Describe a ledger and a chart of accounts.** A ledger is a record containing all accounts used by a company and their balances. This is referred to as the *books*. The chart of accounts is a list of all accounts and usually includes an identification number assigned to each account.

C5 **Define debits and credits and explain their role in double-entry accounting.** *Debit* refers to left, and *credit* refers to right. Debits increase assets, withdrawals, and expenses, while credits decrease them. Credits increase liabilities, capital, and revenues; debits decrease them. Double-entry accounting means each transaction affects at least two accounts and has at least one debit and one credit. The system for recording debits and credits follows from the accounting equation. The left side of an account is the normal balance for assets and expenses, and the right side is the normal balance for liabilities, equity, and revenues.

A1 **Analyze the impact of transactions on accounts and financial statements.** We analyze transactions using concepts of double-entry accounting. This analysis is performed by determining a transaction's effects on accounts. These effects are recorded in journals and posted to ledgers.

A2 **Compute the debt ratio and describe its use in analyzing company performance.** A company's debt ratio is computed as total liabilities divided by total assets. It tells us how much of the assets are financed by creditor (nonowner) financing. The higher this ratio, the more risk a company faces because liabilities must be repaid at specific dates.

P1 **Record transactions in a journal and post entries to a ledger.** Transactions are recorded in a journal. Each entry in a journal is posted to the accounts in the ledger. This provides information for accounts that is used to produce financial statements. Balance column accounts are widely used and include columns for debits, credits, and the account balance.

P2 **Prepare and explain the use of a trial balance.** A trial balance is a list of accounts from the ledger showing their debit or credit balances in separate columns. The trial balance is a convenient summary of the ledger's contents and is useful in preparing financial statements and in revealing errors.

Guidance Answers to You Make the Call

Cashier   The advantages to the process proposed by the assistant manager include improved customer service, fewer delays, and less work for you. However, you should have serious concerns about internal control and the potential for fraud. In particular, the assistant manager could steal cash and simply enter fewer sales to match the remaining cash. You should reject her suggestion without the manager's approval. Moreover, you should have an ethical concern about the assistant manager's suggestion to ignore store policy.

Marketing Manager   You direct your search to the accounting information system. Source documents contain all revenue information you desire but you must go through all documents, identify

revenues, and compute the total. The ledger also contains the information you desire and is a preferred source because it keeps a running balance of each account and directly answers your question.

Investor   The debt ratio suggests the stock of **Converse** is of higher risk than normal and that this risk is rising. Industry ratios reported in Exhibit 3.18 further support this conclusion. The debt ratio for Converse is now more than triple the industry norm of 0.46. Also, a debt ratio larger than 1.0 indicates negative equity. Excessive cumulative losses for Converse led to its negative equity.

Guidance Answers to Quick Checks

1. External transactions are exchanges of economic consideration between an organization and some other entity. Internal transactions are exchanges within an organization, for example, a company using equipment in its operations.

2. Examples of source documents are sales tickets, checks, purchase orders, charges to customers, bills from suppliers, employee earnings records, and bank statements.

3. Source documents serve many purposes, including record-keeping and internal control. Source documents, especially if obtained from outside the organization, provide objective and reliable evidence about transactions and their amounts.

4.

Assets	Liabilities	Equity
a,c,e	b,d	—

5. An account is a record in an accounting system that records and stores the increases and decreases in a specific asset, liability, equity, revenue, or expense. A ledger is a collection of all the accounts of a company.

6. A company's size and diversity affect the number of accounts in its accounting system. The types of accounts used depend on information the company needs to both effectively operate and report its activities in financial statements.

7. No. Debit and credit both can mean increase or decrease. The particular meaning in a circumstance depends on the *type of account*. For example, a debit increases the balance of asset and expense accounts, but it decreases the balance of liability, equity, and revenue accounts.

8. Equity is increased by revenues and by an owner's investments. Equity is decreased by expenses and by withdrawals.

9. The name *double entry* is used because all transactions affect at least two accounts. There must be at least one debit in one account and at least one credit in another account.

10. Answer is (*c*).

11.
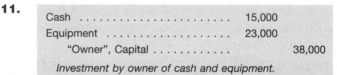

Cash	15,000	
Equipment	23,000	
"Owner", Capital		38,000
Investment by owner of cash and equipment.		

12. A compound journal entry affects three or more accounts.

13. Posting reference numbers are entered in the journal when posting to the ledger as a cross-reference that allows the recordkeeper or auditor to trace debits and credits from one record to another. They also create a "marker" in case the posting process is interrupted.

14. A chart of accounts is a list of all of a company's accounts and their identification numbers.

15. At a minimum, dollar signs are placed beside the first and last numbers in a column. It is also common to place dollar signs beside any amount that appears after a ruled line to indicate that an addition or subtraction has occurred.

16. The Equipment account balance is incorrectly reported at $20,000—it should be $28,000. The effect of this error understates the trial balance's Debit column total by $8,000. This results in an $8,000 difference between the two columns' totals.

Glossary

Account a record within an accounting system where increases and decreases in a specific asset, liability, equity, revenue, or expense are entered and stored. (p. 81).

Account balance the difference between total debits and total credits (including the beginning balance) for an account. (p. 86).

Balance column account an account with debit and credit columns for recording entries and another column for showing the balance of the account after each entry. (p. 89).

Chart of accounts a list of accounts used by a company; includes an identification number for each account. (p. 86).

Compound journal entry a journal entry that affects at least three accounts. (p. 93).

Credit recorded on the right side; an entry that decreases asset and expense accounts, and increases liability, equity, and revenue accounts; abbreviated Cr. (p. 86).

Debit recorded on the left side; an entry that increases asset and expense accounts, and decreases liability, equity, and revenue accounts; abbreviated Dr. (p. 86).

Debt ratio the ratio of total liabilities to total assets; used to reflect risk associated with a company's debts. (p. 101).

Double-entry accounting an accounting system in which each transaction affects at least two accounts and has at least one debit and one credit. (p. 87).

Events happenings that both affect an organization's financial position and can be reliably measured. (p. 80).

External transactions exchanges of economic consideration between one entity and another entity. (p. 80).

General journal a record of the debits and credits of transactions and events. (p. 89).

Internal transactions activities within an organization that can affect the accounting equation. (p. 80).

Journal a record where transactions are recorded before they are posted to ledger accounts; also called *book of original entry*. (p. 88).

Journalizing process of recording transactions in a journal. (p. 89).

Ledger record containing all accounts (with amounts) for a business. (p. 81).

Note payable written promise to pay a definite sum of money on demand or on a specific future date(s); also called *promissory note*. (p. 83).

Posting process of transferring journal entry information to the ledger. (p. 89).

Posting reference (PR) column a column in journals where individual account num-

bers are entered when entries are posted to ledger accounts. (p. 89).

Promissory note see *note payable* or *note receivable*. (p. 82).

Source documents the source of information for accounting entries and can be in either paper or electronic form; also called *business papers*. (p. 80).

T-account an account form used as a tool to show the effects of transactions and events on individual accounts. (p. 86).

Trial balance list of accounts and their balances at a point in time; total debit balances equal total credit balances. (p. 97).

Unearned revenue a liability created when customers pay in advance for products or services; earned when the products or services are delivered in the future. (p. 84).

Questions

1. What is the difference between a note payable and an account payable?
2. Provide the names of two (a) asset accounts, (b) liability accounts, and (c) equity accounts.
3. Discuss the steps in processing business transactions.
4. Are debits or credits listed first in general journal entries? Are the debits or the credits indented?
5. What kinds of transactions can be recorded in a general journal?
6. Should a transaction be recorded first in a journal or the ledger? Why?
7. If assets are valuable resources and asset accounts have debit balances, why do expense accounts have debit balances?

8. Why does the recordkeeper prepare a trial balance?
9. Review the **Nike** balance sheet in Appendix A. Identify three accounts on the balance sheet that carry debit balances and three accounts on the balance sheet that carry credit balances.
10. Review the **Reebok** balance sheet in Appendix A. Identify three different liability accounts that include the word *payable* in the account title.
11. Locate **Gap**'s income statement in Appendix A. What is the name of its revenue account?
12. If a wrong amount is journalized and posted to the accounts, how should the error be corrected?

Indicate whether a debit or credit *decreases* the normal balance of each of the following accounts:

a. Office Supplies
b. Repair Services Revenue
c. Interest Payable
d. Accounts Receivable
e. Salaries Expense
f. Owner, Capital
g. Prepaid Insurance
h. Buildings
i. Interest Revenue
j. Owner, Withdrawals

QUICK STUDY

QS 3-1

Linking debit or credit with normal balance   **C5**

Identify whether a debit or credit yields the indicated change for each of the following accounts:

a. To increase Store Equipment
b. To increase Owner, Withdrawals
c. To decrease Cash
d. To increase Utilities Expense
e. To increase Fees Earned
f. To decrease Unearned Revenue   *decrease*
g. To decrease Prepaid Insurance   *liability*
h. To increase Notes Payable   *liability*
i. To decrease Accounts Receivable
j. To increase Owner, Capital

QS 3-2

Analyzing debit or credit by account   **C5**

QS 3-3

Identifying source documents

C2

Select items from the following list that are likely to serve as source documents:

a. Bank statement   **e.** Telephone bill

b. Sales ticket   **f.** Invoice from supplier

c. Income statement   **g.** Owner's withdrawals account

d. Trial balance   **h.** Balance sheet

QS 3-4

Classifying accounts in financial statements

A1

Indicate the financial statement on which each of the following accounts appears. Use IS for income statement, SCOE for statement of changes in owner's equity, and BS for balance sheet:

a. Office Supplies *(Asset)* BS   **f.** Equipment   BS

b. Services Revenue IS   **g.** Prepaid Insurance BS

c. Interest Payable BS   **h.** Buildings   BS

d. Accounts Receivable BS   **i.** Interest Revenue   IS   *not listed*

e. Salaries Expense   IS   **j.** Owner, Withdrawals SCOE

QS 3-5

Identifying a posting error

P2

A trial balance has total debits of $20,000 and total credits of $24,500. Which one of the following errors would create this imbalance? Explain.

a. A $2,250 debit to Rent Expense in a journal entry is incorrectly posted to the ledger as a $2,250 credit, leaving the Rent Expense account with a $3,000 debit balance.

b. A $4,500 debit to Salaries Expense in a journal entry is incorrectly posted to the ledger as a $4,500 credit, leaving the Salaries Expense account with a $750 debit balance.

c. A $2,250 credit to Consulting Fees Earned in a journal entry is incorrectly posted to the ledger as a $2,250 debit, leaving the Consulting Fees Earned account with a $6,300 credit balance.

QS 3-6

Preparing journal entries

P1

Prepare journal entries for each of the following selected transactions:

a. On January 13, Bella Woods opens a landscaping business called Showcase Yards by investing $70,000 cash along with equipment having a $30,000 value.

b. On January 21, Showcase Yards purchases office supplies on credit for $280.

c. On January 29, Showcase Yards receives $7,800 cash for performing landscaping services.

EXERCISES

Exercise 3-1

Analyzing effects of transactions on accounts

A1

Lori Fitterling recently notified a client that it would have to pay a $62,000 fee for services. Unfortunately, the client did not have enough cash to pay the entire bill. Fitterling agreed to accept the following items in full payment: (1) $10,000 cash, (2) computer equipment worth $80,000, and (3) assumed responsibility for a $28,000 note payable related to the computer equipment. The entry Fitterling makes to record this transaction includes which one or more of the following items?

a. $28,000 increase in a liability account.   **d.** $62,000 increase in L. Fitterling, Capital account.

b. $10,000 increase in the Cash account.   **e.** $62,000 increase in a revenue account.

c. $10,000 increase in a revenue account.

Exercise 3-2

Recording effects of transactions in T-accounts

A1

Open the following T-accounts: Cash; Accounts Receivable; Office Supplies; Office Equipment; Accounts Payable; Robert Dejonge, Capital; Robert Dejonge, Withdrawals; Fees Earned; and Rent Expense. Record the transactions of Dejonge Company by recording the debit and credit entries directly in T-accounts. Use the letters beside each transaction to identify entries. Determine the ending balance of each T-account.

a. Robert Dejonge invested $13,325 cash in the business.

b. Purchased office supplies for $475 cash.

c. Purchased $6,235 of office equipment on credit.

d. Received $2,000 cash as fees for services provided to a customer.

e. Paid cash to settle the payable for the office equipment purchased in transaction *c*.

f. Billed a customer $3,300 as fees for services provided.

g. Paid the monthly rent with $775 cash.

h. Collected $2,300 cash toward the account receivable created in transaction *f*.

i. Robert Dejonge withdrew $800 cash from the business for personal use.

After recording the transactions of Exercise 3-2 in T-accounts and calculating the balance of each account, prepare a trial balance. Use May 31, 2002, as its date.

Exercise 3-3
Preparing a trial balance

Complete the following table by (1) identifying the type of account as an asset, liability, equity, revenue, or expense, (2) entering *debit* (*Dr.*) or *credit* (*Cr.*) to identify the kind of entry that would increase or decrease the account balance, and (3) identifying the normal balance of the account.

Exercise 3-4
Identifying increases, decreases, and normal balances of accounts

	Account	Type of Account	Increase (Dr. or Cr.)	Decrease (Dr. or Cr.)	Normal Balance
a.	Unearned revenue				
b.	Accounts payable				
c.	Postage expense				
d.	Prepaid insurance				
e.	Land				
f.	P. Maben, Capital				
g.	Accounts receivable				
h.	P. Maben, Withdrawals				
i.	Cash				
j.	Equipment				
k.	Fees earned				
l.	Wages expense				

Seven transactions *a* through *g* are posted to the following T-accounts. Provide a short description of each transaction. Include the amounts in your descriptions.

Exercise 3-5
Describing transactions from T-accounts

Cash			
(a)	6,000	(b)	4,800
(e)	4,500	(c)	900
		(f)	1,600
		(g)	820

Automobiles	
(a)	12,000

Accounts Payable			
(f)	1,600	(d)	10,000

Office Supplies	
(c)	900
(d)	300

David Joy, Capital			
		(a)	25,600

Prepaid Insurance	
(b)	4,800

Delivery Services Revenue			
		(e)	4,500

Equipment	
(a)	7,600
(d)	9,700

Gas and Oil Expense	
(g)	820

Use information from the T-accounts in Exercise 3-5 to prepare general journal entries for the seven transaction *a* through *g*.

Exercise 3-6
Preparing general journal entries

Exercise 3-7

Analyzing account entries and balances

A1

Use the information in each of the following separate cases to calculate the unknown amount:

1. During October, Rightlane Company had $102,500 of cash receipts and $103,150 of cash disbursements. The October 31 Cash balance was $18,600. Determine how much cash the company had at the close of business on September 30.

2. On September 30, Rightlane had a $102,500 balance in Accounts Receivable. During October, the company collected $102,890 from its credit customers. The October 31 balance in Accounts Receivable was $89,000. Determine the amount of sales on account that occurred in October.

3. Rightlane had $152,000 of accounts payable on September 30 and $132,500 on October 31. Total purchases on account during October were $281,000. Determine how much cash was paid on accounts payable during October.

Exercise 3-8

Preparing general journal entries

A1 **P1**

Prepare general journal entries for the following transactions of a new business called Click and Shoot.

Aug. 1   Hannah Hicks, the owner, invested $6,500 cash and $33,500 of photography equipment.
        1   Paid $2,100 cash for an insurance policy covering the next two years.
        5   Purchased office supplies for $880 cash.
       20   Received $3,331 cash in photography fees earned.
       31   Paid $675 cash for August utilities.

Exercise 3-9

Preparing T-accounts and the trial balance

P2

Use the information provided in Exercise 3-8 to prepare an August 31 trial balance for Click and Shoot. Open these T-accounts: Cash; Office Supplies; Prepaid Insurance; Photography Equipment; Hannah Hicks, Capital; Photography Fees Earned; and Utilities Expense. Post the general journal entries to the T-accounts, and prepare a trial balance.

Exercise 3-10

Analyzing and journalizing revenue transactions

A1 **P1**

Examine the following transactions and identify those that create revenues for Stout Services, a sole proprietorship owned by David Stout. Prepare general journal entries to record those transactions and explain why the other transactions did not create revenues.

a. David Stout invests $39,350 cash in the business.

b. Provided $2,300 of services on credit.

c. Provided services to a client and received $875 cash.

d. Received $10,200 cash from a client in payment for services to be provided next year.

e. Received $3,500 cash from a client in partial payment of an account receivable.

f. Borrowed $120,000 cash from the bank by signing a promissory note.

Exercise 3-11

Analyzing and journalizing expense transactions

A1 **P1**

Examine the following transactions and identify those that create expenses for Stout Services. Prepare general journal entries to record those transactions and explain why the other transactions did not create expenses.

a. Paid $12,200 cash for office supplies purchased 13 months previously.

b. Paid $1,233 cash for the two-week salary of the receptionist.

c. Paid $39,200 cash for equipment.

d. Paid utility bill with $870 cash.

e. Owner withdrew $4,500 cash from the business for personal use.

Exercise 3-12

Preparing a corrected trial balance

P2

On January 1, Megan Taylor started a new business called The Right Stuff. Because she lacked accounting knowledge, Taylor made a number of mistakes in preparing the year-end trial balance shown here.

An analysis of the situation reveals the following:

a. The sum of the debits in the Cash ledger account is $38,125 and the sum of its credits is $31,490.

b. A $425 payment from a credit customer is posted to Cash but is not posted to Accounts Receivable.

THE RIGHT STUFF
Trial Balance
December 31, 2002

	Debit	Credit
Cash	$ 5,500	
Accounts receivable . .		$ 7,900
Office supplies	2,650	
Office equipment	20,500	
Accounts payable . . .		9,465
Megan Taylor, Capital .	16,745	
Services revenue		22,350
Wages expense		6,000
Rent expense		4,800
Advertising expense . .		1,400
Totals	$45,395	$51,985

c. A credit purchase of office supplies for $500 is completely unrecorded.

d. A transposition error occurred in copying the balance of the Services Revenue account to the trial balance. The correct amount is $23,250.

e. Errors are also made in assigning account balances (all with normal balances) to the Debit and Credit columns of the trial balance and in computing totals of the columns.

Use this information to prepare a correct trial balance.

Posting errors are identified in the following table. In column (1), enter the amount of the difference between the two (debit and credit) trial balance columns due to the error. In column (2), identify the trial balance column (debit or credit) with the larger amount if they are not equal. In column (3), identify the account(s) affected by the error. In column (4), indicate the amount by which the account(s) in column (3) is (are) under- or overstated. Answers for the first error are given.

Exercise 3-13

Identifying effects of posting errors on the trial balance

	Description of Posting Error	(1) Difference between Debit and Credit Columns	(2) Column with the Larger Total	(3) Identify Account(s) Incorrectly Stated	(4) Amount that Account(s) is Over- or Understated
a.	$3,600 debit to Rent Expense is posted as a $1,340 debit.	$2,260	Credit	Rent Expense	Rent Expense understated $2,260
b.	$6,500 credit to Cash is posted twice as two credits to Cash.				
c.	$10,900 debit to the owner's withdrawals account is debited to owner's capital.				
d.	$2,050 debit to Prepaid Insurance is posted as a debit to Insurance Expense.				
e.	$38,000 debit to Machinery is posted as a debit to Accounts Payable.				
f.	$5,850 credit to Services Revenue is posted as a $585 credit.				
g.	$1,390 debit to Store Supplies is not posted.				

---

1. Calculate the debt ratio for each of the following six separate cases:

Exercise 3-14

Computing and interpreting the debt ratio

Case	Assets	Liabilities	Equity
Company 1	$ 90,500	$ 12,000	$ 78,500
Company 2	64,000	47,000	17,000
Company 3	32,500	26,500	6,000
Company 4	147,000	56,000	91,000
Company 5	92,000	31,000	61,000
Company 6	104,500	51,500	53,000

2. Of the six cases, which business relies most heavily on creditor (non-owner) financing?

3. Of the six cases, which business relies most heavily on equity (owner) financing?

4. Which two companies indicate the greatest risk?

Exercise 3-15

Analyzing a trial balance error

You are told the column totals in a trial balance are not equal. After careful analysis, you discover only one error. Specifically, the balance of the Office Equipment account has a debit balance of $37,100 on the trial balance. However, you find that a correctly journalized credit purchase of a computer for $18,950 is posted from the journal to the ledger with an $18,950 debit to Office Equipment and another $18,950 debit to Accounts Payable. Answer each of the following questions and compute the dollar amount of any misstatement:

a. Is the debit column total of the trial balance overstated, understated, or correctly stated?

b. Is the credit column total of the trial balance overstated, understated, or correctly stated?

c. Is the balance of the Office Equipment account overstated, understated, or correctly stated in the trial balance?

d. Is the balance of the Accounts Payable account overstated, understated, or correctly stated in the trial balance?

e. If the debit column total of the trial balance is $360,000 before correcting the error, what is the total of the credit column before correction?

PROBLEM SET A

Problem 3-1A

Preparing and posting general journal entries; preparing a trial balance

Check Cash Bal., $59,465

Roberto Ricci opens a computer consulting business called Financial Consultants and completes the following transactions in April:

April 1	Ricci invests $80,000 cash along with office equipment valued at $26,000.
1	Prepaid $9,000 cash for three months' rent for office space. (*Hint:* Debit Prepaid Rent for $9,000.)
2	Made credit purchases of office equipment for $8,000 and office supplies for $3,600.
6	Completed services for a client and immediately received $4,000 cash.
9	Completed a $6,000 project for a client, who will pay within 30 days.
10	Paid the account payable created on April 2 in cash.
19	Paid $2,400 cash for the premium on a 12-month insurance policy.
22	Received $4,400 cash as partial payment for the work completed on April 9.
25	Completed work for another client for $2,890 on credit.
30	Ricci withdrew $5,500 cash from the business for personal use.
30	Purchased $600 of additional office supplies on credit.
30	Paid $435 cash for this month's utility bill.

Required

1. Prepare general journal entries to record these transactions (use account titles listed in part 2).

2. Open the following ledger accounts (use the balance column format): Cash (101); Accounts Receivable (106); Office Supplies (124); Prepaid Insurance (128); Prepaid Rent (131); Office Equipment (163); Accounts Payable (201); Roberto Ricci, Capital (301); Roberto Ricci, Withdrawals (302); Services Revenue (403); and Utilities Expense (690). Post journal entries from part *1* to the ledger accounts and enter the balance after each posting.

3. Prepare a trial balance as of the end of this month's operations.

Problem 3-2A

Recording transactions in T-accounts; preparing a trial balance

Business transactions completed by Steven Woolery during the month of September are as follows:

a. Steven Woolery invested $60,000 cash along with office equipment valued at $25,000 in a new sole proprietorship named SW Consulting.

b. Purchased land and a small office building. The land is worth $40,000, and the building is worth $160,000. The purchase price is paid with $30,000 cash and a long-term note payable for $170,000.

c. Purchased $2,000 of office supplies on credit.

d. Steven Woolery invested his personal automobile in the business. The automobile has a value of $16,500 and is to be used exclusively in the business.

e. Purchased $5,600 of additional office equipment on credit.

f. Paid $1,800 cash salary to an assistant.

g. Provided services to a client and collected $8,000 cash.

h. Paid $635 cash for this month's utilities.

i. Paid cash to settle the account payable created in transaction *c.*

j. Purchased $30,000 of new office equipment by paying $20,300 cash and trading in old equipment with a recorded net cost of $9,700.

k. Completed $6,250 of services for a client. This amount is to be received within 30 days.

l. Paid $1,800 cash salary to an assistant.

m. Received $4,000 cash on the receivable created in transaction *k.*

n. Woolery withdrew $2,800 cash from the business for personal use.

Required

1. Open the following T-accounts: Cash; Accounts Receivable; Office Supplies; Automobiles; Office Equipment; Building; Land; Accounts Payable; Long-Term Notes Payable; Steven Woolery, Capital; Steven Woolery, Withdrawals; Fees Earned; Salaries Expense; and Utilities Expense.

2. Record the preceding transactions by entering debits and credits directly in T-accounts. Use the transaction letters to identify each debit and credit entry.

3. Determine the balance of each account and prepare a trial balance as of September 30.

Check Trial balance totals, $291,350

Shelton Engineering, a sole proprietorship, completed the following transactions in the month of June.

a. Sandra Shelton, the owner, invested $100,000 cash, office equipment with a value of $5,000, and $60,000 of drafting equipment to launch the business.

b. Purchased land for an office. The land is worth $49,000, and is paid with $6,300 cash and a long-term note payable for $42,700.

c. Purchased a portable building with $55,000 cash and moved it onto the business's land.

d. Paid $3,000 cash for the premium on a two-year insurance policy.

e. Completed and delivered a set of plans for a client and collected $6,200 cash.

f. Purchased additional drafting equipment for $20,000. Paid $9,500 cash and signed a long-term note payable for the $10,500 balance.

g. Completed $14,000 of engineering services for a client. This amount is to be received in 30 days.

h. Purchased $1,150 of additional office equipment on credit.

i. Completed engineering services for $22,000 on credit.

j. Received a bill for rent of equipment that was used on a recently completed job. The $1,333 rent must be paid within 30 days.

k. Collected $7,000 cash from the client described in transaction *g.*

l. Paid $1,200 cash wages to a drafting assistant.

m. Paid cash to settle the account payable created in transaction *h.*

n. Paid $925 cash for some repairs to an item of drafting equipment.

o. Sandra Shelton withdrew $9,480 cash from the business for personal use.

p. Paid $1,200 cash wages to a drafting assistant.

q. Paid $2,500 cash for advertisements in the local newspaper during June.

Problem 3-3A

Recording transactions in T-accounts, preparing a trial balance, and computing a debt ratio

Required

1. Open the following T-accounts: Cash; Accounts Receivable; Prepaid Insurance; Office Equipment; Drafting Equipment; Building; Land; Accounts Payable; Long-Term Notes Payable; Sandra Shelton, Capital; Sandra Shelton, Withdrawals; Engineering Fees Earned; Wages Expense; Equipment Rental Expense; Advertising Expense; and Repairs Expense.

2. Record the transactions by entering debits and credits directly in T-accounts. Use the transaction letters to identify each debit and credit. Prepare a trial balance as of June 30.

Check Trial balance totals, $261,733

3. Calculate the company's debt ratio. Use $245,095 as the total assets. Are the company's assets financed more by debt or equity?

Problem 3-4A

Preparing and posting general journal entries; preparing a trial balance

Stuart Birch opens a Web consulting business called Show-Me-the-Money Consultants and completes the following transactions in March:

March 1   Birch invested $150,000 cash along with $22,000 of office equipment.
       1   Prepaid $6,000 cash for three months' rent for an office. (*Hint:* Debit Prepaid Rent for $6,000.)
       2   Made credit purchases of office equipment for $3,000 and office supplies for $1,200.
       6   Completed services for a client and immediately received $4,000 cash.
       9   Completed a $7,500 project for a client, who will pay within 30 days.
      10   Paid cash to settle the account payable created on March 2.
      19   Paid $5,000 cash for the premium on a 12-month insurance policy.
      22   Received $3,500 cash as partial payment for the work completed on March 9.
      25   Completed work for another client for $3,820 on credit.
      31   Birch withdrew $5,100 cash from the business for personal use.
      31   Purchased $600 of additional office supplies on credit.
      31   Paid $500 cash for this month's utility bill.

Required

1. Prepare general journal entries to record these transactions (use the account titles listed in part 2).

2. Open the following accounts (use the balance column format): Cash (101); Accounts Receivable (106); Office Supplies (124); Prepaid Insurance (128); Prepaid Rent (131); Office Equipment (163); Accounts Payable (201); Stuart Birch, Capital (301); Stuart Birch, Withdrawals (302); Services Revenue (403); and Utilities Expense (690). Post journal entries to the accounts and enter the balance after each posting.

Check   Cash bal. $136,700

3. Prepare a trial balance as of the end of this month's operations.

Problem 3-5A

Classifying accounts in financial statements

Loretta Pacey operates a surveying company. For the first few months of the company's life (through February 28), the accounting records were maintained by an outside accounting service. According to those records, the L. Pacey, Capital account balance is $65,000 as of February 28. To save on expenses, Pacey decides to keep the records herself. She manages to record March's transactions properly, but she has problems classifying accounts in financial statements. Her versions of the balance sheet and income statement follow. Using the information contained in these financial statements, prepare revised statements, including a statement of changes in owner's equity for the month of March.

	PACEY SURVEYING	
	Income Statement	
	For Month Ended March 31, 2002	
Revenue		
Investments by owner	$4,000	
Unearned surveying fees	8,000	
Total revenues		$12,000
Expenses		
Rent expense	4,100	
Telephone expense	700	
Surveying equipment	6,400	
Advertising expense	4,200	
Utilities expense	400	
Insurance expense	1,000	
Withdrawals by owner	3,000	
Total expenses		19,800
Net income (loss)		$(7,800)

PACEY SURVEYING
Balance Sheet
March 31, 2002

Assets			Liabilities		
Cash	$ 4,900		Accounts payable	$ 3,400	
Accounts receivable	3,700		Surveying fees earned	20,000	
Prepaid insurance	2,800		Short-term notes payable	55,400	
Prepaid rent	3,200		Total liabilities	$ 78,800	
Office supplies	400				
Buildings	71,000				
Land	46,000		**Equity**		
Salaries expense	4,000		Loretta Pacey, Capital	$ 57,200	
Total assets	$136,000		Total liabilities and equity	$136,000	

Check L. Pacey, Capital, March 31, 2002, $71,600

Mark Bauman started a business called Bauman Movers and began operations in June. He correctly recorded the following journal entries during June:

Problem 3-6A

Interpreting journals; posting; correcting a trial balance

A1   P1   P2

June 1	Cash	50,000	
	Trucks	34,000	
	Mark Bauman, Capital		84,000
2	Office Supplies	1,393	
	Cash		1,393
4	Moving Equipment	11,500	
	Accounts Payable		11,500
8	Cash	1,000	
	Accounts Receivable	12,000	
	Moving Fees Earned		13,000
12	Cash	2,200	
	Moving Fees Earned		2,200
15	Prepaid Insurance	3,400	
	Cash		3,400
21	Cash	12,000	
	Accounts Receivable		12,000
23	Accounts Payable	11,500	
	Cash		11,500
25	Office Equipment	17,800	
	Mark Bauman, Capital		17,800
29	Office Supplies	3,105	
	Accounts Payable		3,105
30	Mark Bauman, Withdrawals	5,913	
	Cash		5,913
30	Wages Expense	7,384	
	Cash		7,384

Based on these entries, Bauman prepared the trial balance shown on the top of the next page.

Preparation Component

1. Bauman remembers something about trial balances and realizes that he has at least one error. To help him find the error(s), set up the following balance column accounts and post his entries to them: Cash (101); Accounts Receivable (106); Office Supplies (124); Prepaid Insurance (128); Trucks (153); Office Equipment (163); Moving Equipment (167); Accounts Payable (201); Mark Bauman, Capital (301); Mark Bauman, Withdrawals (302); Moving Fees Earned (401); and Wages Expense (623).

Check Trial balance totals,
$120,105

BAUMAN MOVERS Trial Balance For Month Ended June 30, 2002		
	Debit	Credit
Cash	$ 35,610	
Accounts receivable	0	
Office supplies	4,489	
Prepaid insurance	3,400	
Trucks	34,000	
Office equipment	17,800	
Moving equipment		$ 11,500
Accounts payable		14,605
Mark Bauman, Capital		101,800
Mark Bauman, Withdrawals	591	
Moving fees earned		15,200
Wages expense	7,384	
Totals	$ 111,706	$ 143,105

Analysis Components

2. Although Bauman's journal entries are correct, he forgot to provide explanations. Analyze each entry and present a reasonable explanation of what happened for each one.

3. Prepare a correct trial balance and describe the errors that Bauman made.

Problem 3-7A

Analyzing account balances and reconstructing transactions

Juan Mayetta started an engineering firm called Mayetta Engineering. He began operations and completed seven transactions in May, which included his initial investment of $18,000 cash. After these transactions, the ledger included the following accounts with normal balances:

Cash	$37,641
Office supplies	890
Prepaid insurance	4,600
Office equipment	12,900
Accounts payable	12,900
Juan Mayetta, Capital	18,000
Juan Mayetta, Withdrawals	3,329
Engineering fees earned	36,000
Rent expense	7,540

Required

Preparation Component

Check Trial balance totals,
$66,900

1. Prepare a trial balance for this business at the end of May.

Analysis Components

2. Analyze the accounts and their balances and prepare a list that describes each of the seven most likely transactions and their amounts.

3. Prepare a schedule of cash received and cash paid showing how the seven transactions in part (*2*) yield the $37,641 ending Cash balance.

PROBLEM SET B

Problem 3-1B

Preparing and posting general journal entries; preparing a trial balance

Lummus Management Services opens for business and completes these transactions in September:

Sept. 1   Rhonda Lummus, the owner, invests $38,000 cash along with office equipment valued at $15,000.

2   Prepaid $9,000 cash for three months' rent for office space. (*Hint:* Debit Prepaid Rent for $9,000.)

4   Made credit purchases of office equipment for $8,000 and office supplies for $2,400.

8   Completed work for a client and immediately received $3,280 cash.

12   Completed a $15,400 project for a client, who will pay within 30 days.

13   Paid the account payable created on September 4 in cash.

19   Paid $1,900 cash for the premium on an 18-month insurance policy.

22   Received $7,700 cash as partial payment for the work completed on September 12.

24   Completed work for another client for $2,100 on credit.

28   Rhonda Lummus withdrew $5,300 cash from the business for personal use.

29   Purchased $550 of additional office supplies on credit.

30   Paid $860 cash for this month's utility bill.

Required

1. Prepare general journal entries to record these transactions (use account titles listed in part *2*).

2. Open the following ledger accounts (use the balance column format): Cash (101); Accounts Receivable (106); Office Supplies (124); Prepaid Insurance (128); Prepaid Rent (131); Office Equipment (163); Accounts Payable (201); Rhonda Lummus, Capital (301); Rhonda Lummus, Withdrawals (302); Service Fees Earned (401); and Utilities Expense (690). Post journal entries from part *1* to the ledger accounts and enter the balance after each posting.

Check   Cash Bal., $21,520

3. Prepare a trial balance as of the end of this month's operations.

North Consulting completed the following transactions during June:

a. Nick North, the sole proprietor, invested $35,000 cash along with office equipment valued at $11,000 in the new business.

b. Purchased land and a small office building. The land is worth $7,500, and the building is worth $40,000. The purchase price is paid with $15,000 cash and a long-term note payable for $32,500.

c. Purchased $500 of office supplies on credit.

d. Nick North invested his personal automobile in the business. The automobile has a value of $8,000 and is to be used exclusively in the business.

e. Purchased $1,200 of additional office equipment on credit.

f. Paid $1,000 cash salary to an assistant.

g. Provided services to a client and collected $3,200 cash.

h. Paid $540 cash for this month's utilities.

i. Paid cash to settle the account payable created in transaction *c*.

j. Purchased $5,000 of new office equipment by paying $3,400 cash and trading in old equipment with a recorded net cost of $1,600.

k. Completed $4,200 of services for a client. This amount is to be received within 30 days.

l. Paid $1,000 cash salary to an assistant.

m. Received $2,200 cash on the receivable created in transaction *k*.

n. North withdrew $1,100 cash from the business for personal use.

Problem 3-2B
Recording transactions in T-accounts; preparing a trial balance

Required

1. Open the following T-accounts: Cash; Accounts Receivable; Office Supplies; Automobiles; Office Equipment; Building; Land; Accounts Payable; Long-Term Notes Payable; Nick North, Capital; Nick North, Withdrawals; Fees Earned; Salaries Expense; and Utilities Expense.

2. Record the preceding transactions by entering debits and credits directly in T-accounts. Use the transaction letters to identify each debit and credit entry.

3. Determine the balance of each account and prepare a trial balance as of June 30.

Check   Trial balance totals, $95,100

At the beginning of April, Brooke Wilson launched a custom computer programming company called Softways. The company had the following transactions during April:

a. Brooke Wilson invested $65,000 cash, office equipment with a value of $5,750, and $30,000 of computer equipment.

b. Purchased land for an office. The land is worth $22,000 and is paid for with $5,000 cash and a long-term note payable for $17,000.

c. Purchased a portable building with $34,500 cash and moved it onto the business's land.

d. Paid $5,000 cash for the premium on a two-year insurance policy.

e. Provided services to a client and collected $4,600 cash.

f. Purchased additional computer equipment for $4,500. Paid $800 cash and signed a long-term note payable for the $3,700 balance.

g. Completed $4,250 of services for a client. This amount is to be received within 30 days.

h. Purchased $950 of additional office equipment on credit.

Problem 3-3B
Recording transactions in T-accounts; preparing a trial balance; computing a debt ratio

i. Completed client services for $10,200 on credit.

j. Received a bill for rent of a computer testing device that was used on a recently completed job. The $580 rent must be paid within 30 days.

k. Collected $5,100 cash from the client described in transaction *i*.

l. Paid $1,800 cash wages to an assistant.

m. Paid cash to settle the account payable created in transaction *h*.

n. Paid $608 cash for some repairs to an item of computer equipment.

o. Brooke Wilson withdrew $6,230 cash from the business for personal use.

p. Paid $1,800 cash wages to an assistant.

q. Paid $750 cash for advertisements in the local newspaper during April.

Required

1. Open the following T-accounts: Cash; Accounts Receivable; Prepaid Insurance; Office Equipment; Computer Equipment; Building; Land; Accounts Payable; Long-Term Notes Payable; Brooke Wilson, Capital; Brooke Wilson, Withdrawals; Fees Earned; Wages Expense; Computer Rental Expense; Advertising Expense; and Repairs Expense.

Check Trial balance totals, $141,080

2. Record the transactions by entering debits and credits directly in T-accounts. Use the transaction letters to identify each debit and credit. Prepare a trial balance as of April 30.

3. Calculate the company's debt ratio. Use $129,312 as its total assets. Are the company's assets financed more by debt or equity?

Problem 3-4B

Preparing and posting general journal entries; preparing a trial balance

A1 P1 P2

Shaw Management Services opens for business and completes these transactions in November:

Nov.	1	Ken Shaw, the owner, invested $30,000 cash along with $15,000 of office equipment.
	2	Prepaid $4,500 cash for three months' rent for an office (*Hint:* Debit Prepaid Rent for $4,500.)
	4	Made credit purchases of office equipment for $2,500 and of office supplies for $600.
	8	Completed work for a client and immediately received $3,400 cash.
	12	Completed a $10,200 project for a client, who will pay within 30 days.
	13	Paid cash to settle the account payable created on November 4.
	19	Paid $1,800 cash for the premium on a 24-month insurance policy.
	22	Received $5,200 cash as partial payment for the work completed on November 12.
	24	Completed work for another client for $1,750 on credit.
	28	Ken Shaw withdrew $5,300 cash from the business for personal use.
	29	Purchased $249 of additional office supplies on credit.
	30	Paid $831 cash for this month's utility bill.

Required

1. Prepare general journal entries to record these transactions (use account titles listed in part 2).

2. Open the following accounts (use the balance column format): Cash (101); Accounts Receivable (106); Office Supplies (124); Prepaid Insurance (128); Prepaid Rent (131); Office Equipment (163); Accounts Payable (201); Ken Shaw, Capital (301); Ken Shaw, Withdrawals (302); Services Revenue (403); and Utilities Expense (690). Post journal entries to the accounts and enter the balance after each posting.

Check Cash bal., $23,069

3. Prepare a trial balance as of the end of this month's operations.

Problem 3-5B

Classifying accounts in financial statements

A1

Christina Savery operates a computer programming company specializing in html programming and Web site construction. For the first few months of the company's life (through April 30), the accounting records were maintained by an outside accounting service. According to those records, C. Savery, Capital account balance is $13,500 as of April 30. To save on expenses, Savery decides to keep the records herself. She manages to record May's transactions properly, but she has problems classifying accounts in financial statements. Her versions of the balance sheet and income statement follow. Using the information contained in these financial statements, prepare revised statements, including a statement of changes in owner's equity for the month of May.

R2D2 CONSULTING
Income Statement
May 31

Revenue		
Investments by owner	$5,000	
Unearned programming fees	7,000	
Total revenues		$12,000
Expenses		
Rent expense	3,100	
Telephone expense	800	
Office equipment	6,500	
Advertising expense	2,200	
Utilities expense	580	
Insurance expense	900	
Withdrawals by owner	6,555	
Total expenses		19,635
Net income (loss)		$(7,635)

R2D2 CONSULTING
Balance Sheet
For Month Ended May 31

Assets		Liabilities	
Cash	$ 5,900	Accounts payable	$ 2,000
Accounts receivable	3,600	Programming fees earned	40,000
Prepaid insurance	1,800	Short-term notes payable	3,135
Prepaid rent	5,100	Total liabilities	$45,135
Office supplies	600		
Computer equipment	30,000	**Equity**	
Salaries expense	4,000	Christina Savery, Capital	5,865
Total assets	$51,000	Total liabilities and equity	$51,000

Check   Savery, Capital, May 31, $40,365

Chuck Naylor started a business called All Board on April 1 and completed several transactions in April. The following are the journal entries that he correctly recorded during April:

Problem 3-6B
Interpreting journals; posting; correcting a trial balance

April 1	Cash	12,000	
	Store Equipment	8,000	
	Chuck Naylor, Capital		20,000
2	Prepaid Insurance	600	
	Cash		600
6	Accounts Receivable	2,000	
	Fees Earned		2,000
9	Office Supplies	400	
	Office Equipment	4,100	
	Accounts Payable		4,500
11	Cash	1,100	
	Fees Earned		1,100
14	Accounts Payable	200	
	Office Supplies		200
20	Cash	1,750	
	Accounts Receivable		1,750
21	Accounts Payable	4,300	
	Cash		4,300
23	Automobile	9,000	
	Chuck Naylor, Capital		9,000
28	Chuck Naylor, Withdrawals	800	
	Cash		800
29	Salaries Expense	1,200	
	Cash		1,200
30	Office Supplies	490	
	Accounts Payable		490

Based on these entries, Naylor prepared this trial balance:

ALL BOARD Trial Balance For Month Ended April 30		
	Debit	Credit
Cash	$ 7,590	
Accounts receivable	400	
Office supplies	960	
Prepaid insurance	6,000	
Automobiles	9,000	
Office equipment		$ 4,100
Store equipment		8,000
Accounts payable		940
Chuck Naylor, Capital		29,000
Chuck Naylor, Withdrawals		800
Fees earned		3,100
Salaries expense	1,300	
Totals	$ 25,250	$ 45,940

Required

Preparation Component

1. Naylor remembers something about trial balances and realizes that he has at least one error. To help him find the error(s), set up the following balance column accounts and post his entries to them: Cash (101); Accounts Receivable (106); Office Supplies (124); Prepaid Insurance (128); Automobiles (151); Office Equipment (163); Store Equipment (165); Accounts Payable (201); Chuck Naylor, Capital (301); Chuck Naylor, Withdrawals (302); Fees Earned (401); and Salaries Expense (622).

Analysis Component

2. Although Naylor's journal entries are correct, he forgot to provide explanations. Analyze each entry and present a reasonable explanation of what happened for each one.

Check   Trial balance total, $32,590

3. Prepare a correct trial balance and describe the errors that Naylor made.

Problem 3-7B

Analyzing account balances and reconstructing transactions

Cassandra Todd started a Web consulting firm called Todd Solutions. She began operations and completed seven transactions in April that resulted in the following accounts, which all have normal balances:

Cash	$19,982
Office supplies	760
Prepaid rent	1,800
Office equipment	12,250
Accounts payable	12,250
Cassandra Todd, Capital	15,000
Cassandra Todd, Withdrawals	5,200
Consulting fees earned	20,400
Operating expenses	7,658

Required

Preparation Component

Check   Trial balance total, $47,650

1. Prepare a trial balance for this business at the end of April.

Analysis Component

2. Analyze the accounts and their balances and prepare a list that describes each of the seven most likely transactions and their amounts.

3. Present a schedule that shows how the seven transactions in part (2) yield the $19,982 Cash balance.

(This comprehensive problem starts in this chapter and continues in Chapters 4 and 5. Because of its length, it is most readily solved if you use the Working Papers that accompany this textbook.)

SERIAL PROBLEM

Sierra Systems

On October 1, 2002, Sela Solstise launched a computer services company called **Sierra Systems,** which is organized as a sole proprietorship and provides consulting services, computer system installations, and custom program development. Solstise adopts the calendar year for reporting purposes and expects to prepare the company's first set of financial statements on December 31, 2002. The initial chart of accounts for its accounting system includes these items:

Account	No.	Account	No.
Cash	101	Sela Solstise, Capital	301
Accounts Receivable	106	Sela Solstise, Withdrawals	302
Computer Supplies	126	Computer Services Revenue	403
Prepaid Insurance	128	Wages Expense	623
Prepaid Rent	131	Advertising Expense	655
Office Equipment	163	Mileage Expense	676
Computer Equipment	167	Miscellaneous Expenses	677
Accounts Payable	201	Repairs Expense, Computer	684

Required

1. Prepare journal entries to record each of the following transactions for Sierra Systems.

Oct. 1   Sela Solstise invested $55,000 cash, a $20,000 computer system, and $8,000 of office equipment in the business.
2   Paid $3,300 cash for four months' rent. (*Hint:* Debit Prepaid Rent for $3,300.)
3   Purchased computer supplies on credit for $1,420 from Appier Office Products.
5   Paid $2,220 cash for one year's premium on a property and liability insurance policy. (*Hint:* Debit Prepaid Insurance for $2,220.)
6   Billed Prime Leasing $4,800 for services performed in installing a new Web server.
8   Paid cash for the computer supplies purchased from Appier Office Products on Oct. 3.
10   Hired Suzie Smith as a part-time assistant for $125 per day, as needed.
12   Billed Prime Leasing another $1,400 for services performed.
15   Received $4,800 cash from Prime Leasing on its account.
17   Paid $805 cash to repair computer equipment damaged when moving it.
20   Paid $1,940 cash for an advertisement in the local newspaper.
22   Received $1,400 cash from Prime Leasing on its account.
28   Billed Dade Company $5,208 for services performed.
31   Paid Suzie Smith's wages in cash for seven days' work.
31   Solstise withdrew $3,600 cash from the business for personal use.
Nov. 1   Reimbursed Solstise in cash for business automobile mileage allowance (Solstise logged 1,000 miles at $0.32 per mile).
2   Received $4,633 cash from Elan Corporation for computer services performed.
5   Purchased computer supplies for $1,125 cash from Appier Office Products.
8   Billed Foster Co. $5,668 for services performed.
13   Received notification from Antonio's Engineering Co. that Sierra's bid of $3,950 for an upcoming project is accepted.
18   Received $2,208 cash from Dade Company as partial payment of the bill dated October 28.
22   Donated $250 cash to the United Way in the company's name.
24   Completed work for Antonio's Engineering Co. and sent it a bill for $3,950.
25   Sent another bill to Dade Company for the past-due amount of $3,000.
28   Reimbursed Solstise in cash for business automobile mileage (1,200 miles at $0.32 per mile).
30   Paid Suzie Smith's wages in cash for 14 days' work.
30   Solstise withdrew $2,000 cash from the business for personal use.

2. Open balance column ledger accounts and post the journal entries from part *1* to them.

Beyond the Numbers

Reporting in Action

C3 **A2**

NIKE

BTN 3-1 Refer to **Nike**'s financial statements in Appendix A to answer the following questions.

Required

1. How many revenue categories does Nike report on its consolidated statement of income?
2. What current assets are reported on Nike's consolidated balance sheet?
3. What current liabilities are reported on its balance sheet?
4. For the year ended May 31, 2000, how much cash is paid in dividends?
5. What is Nike's debt ratio at May 31, 2000? (*Hint:* Use Liabilities = Assets − Shareholders' Equity.) How does this compare to its ratio at May, 31 1999?

Swoosh Ahead

6. Assess Nike's annual report for a fiscal year ending after May 31, 2000, from its Web site [www.nike.com] or through the SEC's EDGAR database [www.sec.gov]. Recompute Nike's debt ratio with the updated annual report information. Compare the May 31, 2000, fiscal year-end debt ratio to any subsequent year's debt ratio that you are able to calculate.

Comparative Analysis

A2

NIKE

Reebok

BTN 3-2 Key comparative figures ($ millions) for both **Nike** and **Reebok** follow:

Key Figures	Nike	Reebok
Total liabilities	$2,720.9	$1,035.3
Total equity	3,136.0	528.8

Required

Use the information in the preceding table to answer the following questions:
1. What are total assets for (*a*) Nike and (*b*) Reebok?
2. What is the debt ratio for (*a*) Nike and (*b*) Reebok?
3. Which of the two companies has the higher degree of financial leverage? What does this imply?

Ethics Challenge

C2

BTN 3-3 Review the *You Make the Call—Ethics* case from the first part of this chapter involving the cashier. The guidance answer suggests that you should not comply with the assistant manager's request.

Required

Propose and evaluate two other courses of action you might consider, and explain why.

Communicating in Practice

A2

BTN 3-4 The class should be divided into teams. Each team is to select an industry, and each team member is to select a different company in that industry. Each team member is to acquire the annual report of the company selected. Annual reports can be obtained in many ways, including accessing the SEC's EDGAR database [www.sec.gov].

Required

1. Each team member should use the annual report to compute the debt ratio.
2. Communicate with teammates via a meeting, e-mail, or telephone. The team must prepare a single memorandum reporting (*a*) the meaning of the debt ratio, (*b*) how different companies compare to each other, and (*c*) the industry norm. Identify any conclusions or consensus of opinion reached during the team's discussion. The memo is to be copied and distributed to the instructor and all classmates.

BTN 3-5 Access EDGAR online [**www.edgar-online.com**] and locate the 10-K report of Amazon.com (ticker AMZN) filed on March 29, 2000. Review its cash flow statements reported for fiscal years ended 1997, 1998, and 1999 to answer the following questions:

1. What are the amounts of its net losses reported for each of these three years?
2. Does Amazon's operations provide cash or use cash for each of these three years?
3. If Amazon has a net loss and a use of cash provided by operations in 1999, how is it possible that the cash balance at December 31, 1999, shows an increase relative to the balance at January 1, 1999?

Taking It to the Net

BTN 3-6 The expanded accounting equation consisting of assets, liabilities, owner's capital, owner's withdrawals, revenues, and expenses can give us useful information on changes in a company's financial position.

Required

1. Form *learning teams* of six (or more) members. Each team member must select one of the six components and each team must have at least one expert on each component: (*a*) assets, (*b*) liabilities, (*c*) owner's capital, (*d*) owner's withdrawals, (*e*) revenues, and (*f*) expenses.
2. Form *expert teams* of individuals who selected the same component in (*1*). Expert teams are to draft a report that each expert will present to his/her learning team addressing the following:
   a. Identify for its component the (i) increase and decrease side of the account and (ii) normal balance side of the account.
   b. Describe a transaction, with amounts, that increases its component.
   c. Using the transaction and amounts in (*b*), verify the equality of the accounting equation and then explain any effects on the income statement and statement of cash flows.
   d. Describe a transaction, with amounts, that decreases its component.
   e. Using the transaction and amounts in (*d*), verify the equality of the accounting equation and then explain any effects on the income statement and statement of cash flows.
3. Each expert should return to his/her learning team. In rotation, each member presents his/her expert team's report to the learning team. Team discussion is encouraged.

Teamwork in Action

BTN 3-7 Read the article "Can Amazon Make It?" in the July 10, 2000, issue of *Business Week*. You may access this article online at the book's Web site.

Required

1. As of July 2000, why were analysts and investors skeptical about **Amazon**'s future?
2. In the article, how does CEO Jeff Bezos respond to the critics?
3. What five strategies for Amazon's survival does the article suggest?

Business Week Activity

BTN 3-8 Liang Lu is a young entrepreneur who operates Lu Music Services, offering singing lessons and instruction on musical instruments. Lu wishes to expand but needs a loan. The bank requests Lu to prepare a balance sheet and key financial ratios. Lu has not kept formal records but is able to provide the following accounts and their amounts as of December 31, 2002:

Entrepreneurial Decision

Cash	$ 1,800	Accounts Receivable . . .	$4,800	Prepaid Insurance . .	$ 750
Prepaid Rent	4,700	Store Supplies	3,300	Equipment	25,000
Accounts Payable . .	1,100	Unearned Lesson Fees . .	7,800	L. Lu, Capital*	31,450
Annual net income . .	20,000				

* Capital account reflects all revenues, expenses, and withdrawals through Dec. 31, 2002.

Required

1. Prepare a balance sheet as of December 31, 2002, for Lu Music Services.
2. Compute Lu's debt ratio, return on equity (from Chapter 2), and return on assets (from Chapter 1). Assume average equity and average assets equal their respective ending balances.
3. Do you think the prospects of a $15,000 bank loan are good? Why or why not?

Accrual Accounting and Financial Statements

"I think you have to go with your gut and stay on course"—Katrina Garnett

A Look Back

Chapter 3 explained the analysis and recording of transactions. We showed how to work with source documents, T-accounts, double-entry accounting, ledgers, postings, and trial balances.

A Look at This Chapter

This chapter explains the timing of reports and the need to adjust accounts. Adjusting accounts is important for recognizing revenues and expenses in the proper period. We also describe the adjusted trial balance and

A Look Ahead

Chapter 5 highlights the completion of the accounting cycle. We explain the important final steps in the accounting process. These include closing procedures, the post-closing trial balance, and reversing entries.

Learning Objectives

Conceptual

C1 Explain the importance of periodic reporting and the time period principle.

C2 Describe the purpose of adjusting accounts at the end of a period.

C3 Explain accrual accounting and how it makes financial statements more useful.

C4 Identify the types of adjustments and their purpose.

Analytical

A1 Explain how accounting adjustments link to financial statements.

A2 Compute profit margin and describe its use in analyzing company performance.

Procedural

P1 Prepare and explain adjusting entries.

P2 Explain and prepare an adjusted trial balance.

P3 Prepare financial statements from an adjusted trial balance.

CrossWorlds of Accounting

e BURLINGAME, CA—Although ads for her company show her in black eveningwear, Australian-born Katrina Garnett is much more than a pretty face. "In Silicon Valley, the first question you get as a woman is 'How technical are you?'" says Garnett. With degrees in both business and engineering and experience in product management, she certainly meets the threshold. But Garnett is not your stereotypical nerd from Silicon Valley. Her captivating charm and keen business sense set her apart. Her two-year-old company, **CrossWorlds** (**CrossWorlds.com**) has set itself apart in making *Fortune*'s list of *Cool Companies*.

CrossWorlds pioneers new software known as *processware*. Processware integrates the business activities of a company, including its accounting processes. However, getting quality output from processware requires quality accounting data recorded from business transactions. It also requires the user to understand the accounting process.

Unfortunately, "integration [of business and accounting processes] has been a runaway expense" for most companies, explains Garnett. CrossWorlds offers a new way to control those expenses. The secret of CrossWorlds' success is its innovative software that links business transactions, accounting reports, and decision making. For integration to work, however, decision makers must understand the concept of accounting adjustments, the system of accounting entries and reports, and the difference between accrual and cash numbers.

CrossWorlds' processware has attracted the attention of such clients as Hewlett-Packard and digital TV provider PRIMESTAR. Its sales are expected to approach $20 million this year. The total processware market is about $2 billion per year and growing. "It's an open opportunity for everyone," says Garnett. This means "being aggressive and pursuing it and networking like a fiend." But success with processware (and business) requires an understanding of accounting processes and reports—without it you don't stand a chance. [Sources: *Entrepreneur*, November 12, 1998; *CrossWorlds Web Site*, May, 2001; *Sydney Morning Herald*, May 26, 1998.]

Chapter Preview

Financial statements reflect revenues when earned and expenses when incurred. This is known as *accrual accounting*. Accrual accounting requires several steps. We described many of these steps in Chapter 3. We showed how companies use accounting systems to collect information about *external* transactions and events. We also explained how journals, ledgers, and other procedures are useful in preparing financial statements. This chapter describes the accounting process for producing useful information involving *internal* transactions and events. An important part of this process is adjusting the account balances, which are then reported in financial statements. Adjusting accounts is necessary so that financial statements at the end of a reporting period reflect the effects of all transactions. We also define and explain a company's profit margin.

Timing and Reporting

Regular, or periodic, reporting is an important part of the accounting process. This section describes the impact on the accounting process of the point in time or the period of time that a report refers to.

The Accounting Period

The value of information is often linked to its timeliness. Useful information must reach decision makers frequently and promptly. To provide timely information, accounting systems prepare reports at regular intervals. This results in an accounting process impacted by the

"Nike releases its earnings per share of . . ."

time period (or periodicity) principle. The **time period principle** assumes that an organization's activities can be divided into specific time periods such as a month, a three-month quarter, or a year as shown in Exhibit 4.1. Time periods covered by statements are called **accounting,** or *reporting,* **periods.** Most organizations use a year as their primary accounting period. Reports covering a one-year period are known as **annual financial statements.** Many organizations also prepare **interim financial statements** covering one, three, or six months of activity.

Exhibit 4.1

Accounting Periods

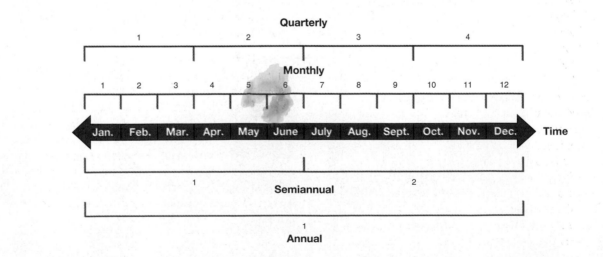

The annual reporting period is not always a calendar year ending on December 31. An organization can adopt a **fiscal year** consisting of any 12 consecutive months. It is also acceptable to adopt an annual reporting period of 52 weeks. For example, **GAP**'s fiscal year consistently ends the final week of January or the first week of February each year.

Companies with little seasonal variation in sales during the year often choose the calendar year as their fiscal year. For example, the financial statements of **Alcoa** reflect a fiscal year that ends on December 31. Companies experiencing seasonal variations in sales often choose a fiscal year corresponding to their natural business year. The **natural business year** ends when sales activities are at their lowest point during the year. The natural business year for retailers ends around January 31, after the holiday season. Examples of these companies include **Wal-Mart**, **Kmart**, **Dell**, and **FUBU**. Most start their annual accounting periods on or near February 1.

Purpose of Adjusting

The usual accounting process is to record external transactions and events (with outside parties) during an accounting period. After external transactions have been recorded, several accounts in the ledger need adjustments before their balances appear in financial statements. This need arises because internal transactions and events remain unrecorded.

An example is the cost of certain assets that expire as time passes. The Prepaid Insurance account of **FastForward** is one of these. FastForward's trial balance (in Exhibit 3.16) shows Prepaid Insurance (asset) with a balance of $2,400. This amount is the premium for *two years* of insurance benefits beginning on December 1. By December 31, one month's coverage is used up. Because these benefits cost an average of $100 per month ($2,400/24 months), the Prepaid Insurance account balance must be reduced by one month's cost. The December income statement must report a $100 cost as insurance expense. Moreover, at December 31, the Prepaid Insurance asset account is adjusted to a balance of $2,300. This adjusted balance reflects the remaining 23 months of insurance benefits.

Another example is FastForward's $9,720 balance in Supplies. This balance includes the costs of all supplies that FastForward purchased in December. At December 31, many of these supplies have been used up. The costs of supplies used must be reported as an expense on the December income statement. Also, the Supplies asset account balance must be adjusted to include the costs of only the remaining unused supplies. Other accounts also require adjustments to prepare financial statements. We explain in the next section how this adjusting process is carried out.

C2 Describe the purpose of adjusting accounts at the end of a period.

Concept 4-1

Point: Many companies record adjusting entries only at the end of each year because of the time and cost necessary. For interim financial statements, adjustments sometimes are omitted.

Recognizing Revenues and Expenses

We use the time period principle to divide a company's activities into specific time periods, but not all activities are complete when financial statements are prepared. This means we must make some adjustments in reporting to avoid misleading decision makers.

We rely on two principles in the adjusting process: revenue recognition and matching. Chapter 2 explained that the *revenue recognition principle* requires that revenue be recorded when earned, not before and not after. Most companies earn revenue when they provide services and products to customers. If FastForward provides consulting to a client in December, the revenue is earned in December. This means it must be reported on the December income statement, even if the client paid for the services in a month other than December. A major goal of the adjusting process is to have revenue recognized (reported) in the time period when it is earned.

The **matching principle** aims to record expenses in the same accounting period as the revenues that are earned as a result of these expenses. This matching of costs (expenses) with benefits (revenues) is a major part of the adjusting process. One example is FastForward, which earns monthly revenues while operating in rented store space. The earning of revenues required rented space. The matching principle tells us that rent must be reported on the income statement for December, even if rent is paid in a month either before or after December. This ensures that rent expense for December is matched with December's revenues.

Point: IBM's revenues from services to customers is recorded when services are performed. Its revenues from product sales are recorded when products are shipped.

Did You Know?

Doing Accounting Time **Centennial Technology**, like many companies, recognizes revenue when it ships products. What is not common is that Centennial's CEO shipped products to the warehouses of friends and reported it as revenue. In another case, **Informix**, a database software maker, records revenue when products are passed to distributors. It admits now that there were "errors in the way revenues had been recorded," and its CEO is in jail. These and other risky revenue recognition practices are often revealed by a large increase in the accounts receivable to sales ratio.

Global: Some countries allow *income smoothing*. This means balance sheet reserves can be set up by reducing income in good years and drawing down those reserves in bad years to increase income.

C3 Explain accrual accounting and how it makes financial statements more useful.

Point: Cash basis accounting is generally used for tax returns.

Matching expenses with revenues often requires us to predict certain events. When we use financial statements, we must understand that they require estimates. This means they include measures that are not precise. **Walt Disney**'s annual report explains that its film and television production costs from shows such as *Dinosaur* and *The Kid* are matched to revenues based on a ratio of current revenues from the show divided by its predicted total revenues.

Accrual Basis versus Cash Basis

Accrual basis accounting uses the adjusting process to recognize revenues when earned and to match expenses with revenues. This means that the economic effects of revenues and expenses are recorded when earned or incurred, not when cash is received or paid.

Cash basis accounting means that revenues are recognized when cash is received and expenses are recorded when cash is paid. For example, if a business provides services in December but does not receive cash from clients until January, then cash basis accounting reports this revenue in January. This means that cash basis net income for a period is the difference between cash receipts and cash payments (disbursements). Cash basis accounting for the income statement, balance sheet, and statement of changes in owner's equity is not consistent with accepted accounting principles. It is commonly held that accrual accounting better indicates business performance than information about cash receipts and payments. Accrual accounting also increases the *comparability* of financial statements from one period to another. Yet many companies and users of statements still find cash basis accounting useful for several internal reports and business decisions. While accrual basis accounting is generally accepted for external reporting, information about cash flows is also useful and is the reason companies must report a statement of cash flows.

To see the impact of these different accounting systems, let's consider FastForward's Prepaid Insurance account. FastForward paid $2,400 for two years of insurance coverage beginning on December 1, 2001. Accrual accounting says that $100 of insurance expense is reported on December's income statement. Another $1,200 of expense is reported in year 2002, and the remaining $1,100 is reported as expense in the first 11 months of 2003. Exhibit 4.2 illustrates this allocation of insurance cost across these three years.

Exhibit 4.2
Accrual Basis Accounting for Prepaid Insurance

Transaction: Purchase 24 months' insurance beginning December 2001

Insurance Expense 2001			
Jan $0	Feb $0	Mar $0	Apr $0
May $0	June $0	July $0	Aug $0
Sept $0	Oct $0	Nov $0	Dec $100

Insurance Expense 2002			
Jan $100	Feb $100	Mar $100	Apr $100
May $100	June $100	July $100	Aug $100
Sept $100	Oct $100	Nov $100	Dec $100

Insurance Expense 2003			
Jan $100	Feb $100	Mar $100	Apr $100
May $100	June $100	July $100	Aug $100
Sept $100	Oct $100	Nov $100	Dec $0

Exhibit 4.3
Cash Basis Accounting for Prepaid Insurance

A cash basis income statement for December 2001 reports insurance expense of $2,400 as shown in Exhibit 4.3. The cash basis income statements for years 2002 and 2003 report no insurance expense from this policy.

Transaction: Purchase 24 months' insurance beginning December 2001

Insurance Expense 2001			
Jan $0	Feb $0	Mar $0	Apr $0
May $0	June $0	July $0	Aug $0
Sept $0	Oct $0	Nov $0	Dec $2,400

Insurance Expense 2002			
Jan $0	Feb $0	Mar $0	Apr $0
May $0	June $0	July $0	Aug $0
Sept $0	Oct $0	Nov $0	Dec $0

Insurance Expense 2003			
Jan $0	Feb $0	Mar $0	Apr $0
May $0	June $0	July $0	Aug $0
Sept $0	Oct $0	Nov $0	Dec $0

The accrual basis balance sheet reports the remaining unexpired premium as a Prepaid Insurance asset. The cash basis never reports this asset. The cash basis information is less useful for most business decisions because reported income for 2001–2003 fails to match the cost of insurance with the insurance benefits received for those years.

Quick Check

1. Describe a company's annual reporting period.
2. Why do companies prepare interim financial statements?
3. What accounting principles most directly drive the adjusting process?
4. Is cash basis accounting consistent with the matching principle? Why or why not?
5. If your company pays a $4,800 premium on April 1, 2002, for two years' insurance coverage, how much insurance expense is reported in 2003 using cash basis accounting?

Answers—p. 147

Adjusting Accounts

The process of adjusting accounts involves analyzing each account balance, and the transactions and events that affect it, to determine any needed adjustments. An **adjusting entry** is recorded to bring an asset or liability account balance to its proper amount when an adjustment is needed. This entry also updates the related expense or revenue account. This section explains why adjusting entries are needed to provide useful information. It also shows the mechanics of adjusting entries and their links to financial statements.

C4 Identify the types of adjustments and their purpose.

Framework for Adjustments

Adjustments are necessary for transactions and events that extend over more than one period. It is helpful to group adjustments by the timing of cash receipt or cash payment in relation to the recognition of the related revenues or expenses. Exhibit 4.4 identifies four types of adjustments that involve both expenses and revenues.

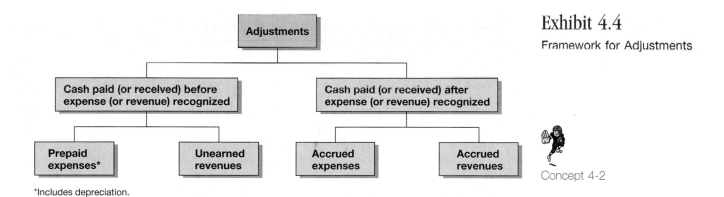

*Includes depreciation.

Exhibit 4.4

Framework for Adjustments

Concept 4-2

Both prepaid expenses (including depreciation) and unearned revenues reflect transactions when cash is paid or received *before* a related expense or revenue is recognized. (Prepaids are also called *deferrals* because the recognition of an expense (or revenue) is *deferred* until after the related cash is paid (or received).) Accrued expenses and accrued revenues reflect transactions when cash is paid or received *after* a related expense or revenue is recognized. Adjusting entries are necessary for each of these so that revenues, expenses, assets, and liabilities are correctly reported. It is helpful to remember that each adjusting entry affects one or more income statement accounts *and* one or more balance sheet accounts. An adjusting entry *never* involves the Cash account.

Point: Source documents provide information for daily transactions, and in many businesses the recordkeepers record them. Adjustments often require more knowledge and are usually handled by more senior accounting professionals.

Prepare and explain
adjusting entries.

"Here is the first 24 months'
insurance in advance."

Adjusting Prepaid Expenses

Prepaid expenses refer to items *paid for* in advance of receiving their benefits. Prepaid expenses are assets. When these assets are used, their costs become expenses. Adjusting entries for prepaids involve increasing (debiting) expenses and decreasing (crediting) assets as shown in the T-accounts of Exhibit 4.5. Adjustments are made to reflect transactions and events that impact the amount of prepaid expenses (including passage of time). To illustrate the accounting for prepaid expenses, this section focuses on prepaid insurance, supplies, and depreciation.

Prepaid Insurance

We illustrate prepaid insurance using **FastForward**'s payment of $2,400 for 24 months of insurance benefits beginning on December 1, 2001. With the passage of time, the benefits of the insurance gradually expire and a portion of the Prepaid Insurance asset becomes expense. For instance, one month's insurance coverage

Exhibit 4.5

Adjusting for Prepaid
Expenses

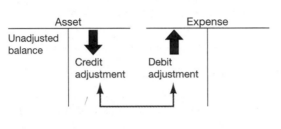

expires by December 31, 2001. This expense is $100, or 1/24 of $2,400. Our adjusting entry to record this expense and reduce the asset follows:

Assets = Liabilities + Equity
−100   −100

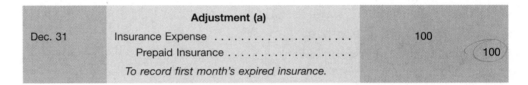

	Adjustment (a)		
Dec. 31	Insurance Expense	100	
	Prepaid Insurance		100
	To record first month's expired insurance.		

Posting this adjusting entry affects the accounts as shown in Exhibit 4.6.

Exhibit 4.6

Insurance Accounts after
Adjusting for Prepaids

Prepaid Insurance			128
Dec. 26	2,400	Dec. 31	100
Balance	2,300		

Insurance Expense		637
Dec. 31	100	

After adjusting and posting, the $100 balance in Insurance Expense and the $2,300 balance in Prepaid Insurance are ready for reporting in financial statements. *Not* making the adjustment on or before December 31 would (1) understate expenses by $100 and overstate net income by $100 for the December income statement and (2) overstate both Prepaid Insurance (assets) and equity (because of net income) by $100 in the December 31 balance sheet. It is also evident from Exhibit 4.2 that year 2002's adjustments must transfer a total of $1,200 from Prepaid Insurance to Insurance Expense, and year 2003's adjustments must transfer the remaining $1,100 to Insurance Expense.

Point: An alternative method to record prepaids is to initially debit expense for the total amount. The adjusted financial statement information is identical under either method. We discuss this alternative in the appendix to this chapter.

Supplies

Supplies are another prepaid expense often requiring adjustment. FastForward purchased $9,720 of supplies in December and used some of them during that month. Use of supplies creates expenses equal to their cost. Daily usage of supplies is not recorded in FastForward's accounts because this information is not needed. Also, making only one adjusting entry when financial statements are prepared can reduce recordkeeping costs. Because the income statement is for December, the cost of supplies used during December must be recognized as an expense. FastForward computes (takes inventory of) its remaining unused supplies. The amount of these remaining supplies is then deducted from the total unadjusted amount of supplies to obtain the amount used. FastForward has $8,670 of supplies remaining of the $9,720 total supplies in December. The $1,050 difference between these two amounts is the cost of the supplies used. This amount is December's supplies expense. Our adjusting entry to record this expense and reduce the Supplies asset account follows:

Point: Some assets, liabilities, revenues, and expenses are so small in amount they do not affect analyses of financial statements. For example, office supplies are sometimes immaterial and immediately recorded as expenses. Management still sets up controls over their use.

	Adjustment (b)		
Dec. 31	Supplies Expense	1,050	
	Supplies		1,050
	To record supplies used.		

Assets = Liabilities + Equity
−1,050   1,050

Posting this adjusting entry affects the accounts as shown in Exhibit 4.7. The balance of the Supplies account is $8,670 after posting—equaling the cost of remaining supplies. *Not* making the adjustment on or before December 31 would (1) understate expenses by $1,050 and overstate net income by $1,050 for the December income statement and (2) overstate both Supplies and equity (because of net income) by $1,050 in the December 31 balance sheet.

Supplies		126	Dec. 31	1,050
Dec. 2	2,500			
6	7,100			
26	120			
Balance	8,670			

Supplies Expense		652
Dec. 31	1,050	

Exhibit 4.7

Supplies Accounts after Adjusting for Prepaids

Other Prepaid Expenses

Other prepaid expenses, such as Prepaid Rent, are accounted for exactly as Insurance and Supplies are. We should also note that some prepaid expenses are both paid for and fully used up within a single accounting period. One example is when a company pays monthly rent on the first day of each month. This payment creates a prepaid expense on the first day of each month that fully expires by the end of the month. In these special cases, we can record the cash paid with a debit to the expense account instead of an asset account. This practice is described more completely later in the chapter.

You Make the Call

Appraiser A small publishing company signs a well-known athlete to write a book. The company pays the athlete $500,000 to sign, plus future book royalties. A note to the company's financial statement says "prepaid expenses include $500,000 in author signing fees to be matched against future expected sales." Is this accounting for the signing bonus acceptable? How does it affect your appraisal?

Answer—p. 147

Adjusting for Depreciation

A special category of prepaid expenses is that of plant and equipment. **Plant and equipment** refers to long-term tangible assets used to produce and sell products and services. These assets are expected to provide benefits for more than one period. Examples of plant and equipment are buildings, machines, vehicles, and fixtures. All plant and equipment assets, with a general exception for land, eventually wear out or decline in usefulness. The costs of these assets are deferred but are gradually reported as expenses in the income statement over the assets' useful lives (benefit periods). **Depreciation** is the process of allocating the cost of these assets over their expected useful lives. Depreciation expense is recorded with an adjusting entry similar to that for other prepaid expenses.

Recall **FastForward** purchased equipment for $26,000 in early December to use in earning revenue. This equipment's cost must be depreciated. Chuck Taylor expects this

Point: Depreciation does not necessarily measure the decline in market value.

Point: We use straight-line depreciation in the early chapters of the book when necessary to explain accounting for plant and equipment.

equipment to have a useful life (benefit period) of four years. He expects to sell the equipment for about $8,000 at the end of four years. This means the *net* cost of this equipment over its useful life is $18,000 ($26,000 − $8,000). We can use several methods to allocate this $18,000 net cost to expense. FastForward uses a method called *straight-line depreciation*. (Depreciation methods are explained in Chapter 11, but we briefly describe the straight-line method to help explain the adjusting process). **Straight-line depreciation** allocates equal amounts of an asset's net cost to depreciation during its useful life. Dividing the $18,000 net cost by the 48 months in the asset's useful life gives an average monthly cost of $375 ($18,000/48). Our adjusting entry to record monthly depreciation expense follows:

Assets = Liabilities + Equity
−375   −375

	Adjustment (c)		
Dec. 31	Depreciation Expense	375	
	Accumulated Depreciation—Equipment . . .		375
	To record monthly equipment depreciation.		

Posting this adjusting entry affects the accounts as shown in Exhibit 4.8. After posting the adjustment, the Equipment account ($26,000) less its Accumulated Depreciation ($375) account equals the $25,625 net cost of the 47 remaining months in the benefit period. The $375 balance in the Depreciation Expense account is reported in the December income statement. *Not* making the adjustment at December 31 would (1) understate expenses by $375 and overstate net income by $375 for the December income statement and (2) overstate both assets and equity (because of income) by $375 in the December 31 balance sheet.

Exhibit 4.8

Accounts after Depreciation Adjustments

Equipment		167
Dec. 3	26,000	

Contra

Accumulated Depreciation – Equipment		168
	Dec. 31	375

Depreciation Expense – Equipment		612
Dec. 31	375	

Decreases in an asset account are commonly recorded with a credit to the account, but this procedure is *not* followed when recording depreciation. Instead, depreciation is recorded in a separate contra account. A **contra account** is an account linked with another account and having an opposite normal balance. It is reported as a subtraction from the other account's balance. For instance, FastForward's contra account of Accumulated Depreciation—Equipment is subtracted from the Equipment account in the balance sheet (see Exhibit 4.22).

You Make the Call   *e*

Entrepreneur   You are preparing an offer to purchase a family-run restaurant. The depreciation schedule for the restaurant's building and equipment shows costs of $175,000 and accumulated depreciation of $155,000. This leaves a net for building and equipment of $20,000. Is this information useful in deciding on a purchase offer?

Answer—p. 147

Use of a contra account allows balance sheet readers to know both the full cost of an asset and the total amount of depreciation charged to expense. By knowing both these amounts, decision makers can better assess a company's capacity and its need to replace an asset. For example, FastForward's balance sheet shows both the $26,000 original cost of equipment and the $375 balance in the accumulated depreciation contra account. This information reveals that the equipment is close to new. If FastForward reports equipment only at its net amount of $25,625, users cannot assess the equipment's age or its need for replacement.

Point: The cost principle requires an asset to be initially recorded at original cost. Depreciation causes the asset's book value to decline over time.

The title of this contra account, *Accumulated Depreciation,* indicates that the account includes total depreciation expense for all prior periods for which the asset was used. For instance, FastForward's Equipment and Accumulated Depreciation accounts appear as shown in Exhibit 4.9 on February 28, 2002, after three months of adjusting entries.

Equipment	167			Accumulated Depreciation — Equipment	168
Dec. 3 26,000				Dec. 31	375
				Jan. 31	375
				Feb. 28	375
				Balance	**1,125**

Exhibit 4.9

Accounts after Three Months of Depreciation Adjustments

These account balances would be reported in the assets section of the February 28 balance sheet as shown in Exhibit 4.10. The net amount is called *book value*. **Book value** equals the asset's original costs less its accumulated depreciation.

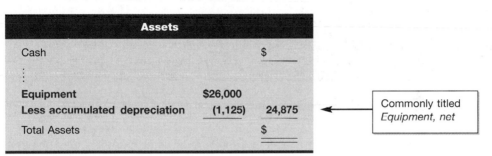

Assets		
Cash		$ ____
⋮		
Equipment	**$26,000**	
Less accumulated depreciation	**(1,125)**	**24,875**
Total Assets		$ ____

Commonly titled *Equipment, net*

Exhibit 4.10

Equipment and Accumulated Depreciation in the February 28th Balance Sheet

Adjusting Unearned Revenues

Unearned revenues refer to cash *received* in advance of providing products and services. Unearned revenues, also known as *deferred revenues,* are liabilities. When cash is accepted, an obligation to provide products or services is accepted. As products or services are provided, the unearned revenues become *earned* revenues. Adjusting entries for unearned revenues involve increasing (crediting) revenues and decreasing (debiting) unearned revenues as shown in Exhibit 4.11. These adjustments reflect transactions and events that impact unearned revenues (including passage of time).

Point: *To defer* is to postpone. We postpone reporting amounts received as revenues until they are earned.

An example of unearned revenues is from **The New York Times**, which reports unexpired (unearned) subscriptions of more than $80 million: "Proceeds from subscriptions . . . are deferred at the time of sale and are included in . . . income on a pro rata basis over the terms of the subscription." Unearned revenues are more than 10% of total current liabilities for the Times. Another example comes from the **Boston Celtics**. When the Celtics receive cash from advance ticket sales and broadcast fees, they record it in an unearned revenue account called *Deferred Game Revenues*. The Celtics recognize this unearned revenue with adjusting entries on a game-by-game basis. Because the NBA regular season begins in October and ends in April, revenue recognition is mainly limited to this period. For a recent season, the Celtics' quarterly revenues (in millions) were $0 for July–September; $25 for October–December; $40 for January–March; and $11 for April–June.

Exhibit 4.11

Adjusting for Unearned Revenues

Liability — Revenue

Unadjusted balance

Debit adjustment — Credit adjustment

FastForward also has unearned revenues. It agreed on December 26 to provide consulting services to a client for a fixed fee of $3,000 for 60 days. On that same day, this client

paid the 60 days' fees in advance, covering the period December 27 to February 24. The entry to record the cash received in advance is

Assets = Liabilities + Equity
+3,000   +3,000

Dec. 26	Cash	3,000	
	Unearned Consulting Revenue		3,000
	Received advance payment for services over the next 60 days.		

This advance payment increases cash and creates an obligation to do consulting work over the next 60 days. As time passes, FastForward will earn this payment through consulting. By December 31, it has provided five days' service and earns one-twelfth of the $3,000 unearned revenue. This amounts to $250 ($3,000 × 5/60). The *revenue recognition principle* implies that $250 of unearned revenue must be reported as revenue on the December income statement. The adjusting entry to reduce the liability account and recognize earned revenue is

Assets = Liabilities + Equity
           −250   +250

	Adjustment (d)		
Dec. 31	Unearned Consulting Revenue	250	
	Consulting Revenue		250
	To record earned revenue that was received in advance ($3,000 × 5/60).		

After posting the adjusting entry, the accounts appear as in Exhibit 4.12. The adjusting entry transfers $250 from unearned revenue (a liability account) to a revenue account. *Not* making the adjustment (1) understates revenue and net income by $250 in the December income statement and (2) overstates unearned revenue and understates equity by $250 on the December 31 balance sheet.

Exhibit 4.12

Revenue Accounts after Adjusting for Prepaids

Unearned Consulting Revenue		236				
Dec. 31		250	Dec. 26	3,000		
			Balance	2,750		

Consulting Revenue		403	
		Dec. 10	4,200
		12	1,600
		31	**250**
		Balance	6,050

Adjusting Accrued Expenses

Accrued expenses refer to costs that are incurred in a period but are both unpaid and unrecorded. Accrued expenses must be reported on the income statement of the period when incurred. Adjusting entries for recording accrued expenses involves increasing (debiting) expenses and increasing (crediting) liabilities as shown in Exhibit 4.13. This adjustment recognizes expenses incurred in a period but not yet paid. Common examples of accrued expenses are salaries, interest, rent, and taxes. We use salaries and interest to show how to adjust accounts for accrued expenses.

Exhibit 4.13

Adjusting for Accrued Expenses

Accrued Salaries Expense

FastForward's employee earns $70 per day, or $350 for a five-day workweek beginning on Monday and ending on Friday. This employee is paid every two weeks on Friday. On December 12 and 26, the wages are paid, recorded in the journal, and posted to the ledger.

However, the calendar in Exhibit 4.14 shows three working days after the December 26 pay-day (29, 30, and 31). This means the employee has earned three days' salary by the close of business on Wednesday, December 31, yet this salary cost is not paid or recorded.

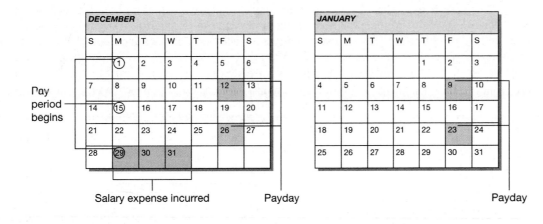

Salary expense incurred   Payday   Payday

Exhibit 4.14

Salary Accrual and Paydays

The financial statements would be incomplete if FastForward fails to report the added expense and liability to the employee for unpaid salary from December 29–31. The adjusting entry to account for accrued salaries is

Adjustment (e)		
Dec. 31	Salaries Expense	210	
	Salaries Payable		210
	To record three days' accrued salary (3 × $70).		

Point: Assume: (1) the last payday for the year is December 19, (2) the next payday is January 2, and (3) December 25 is a paid holiday. Record the December 31 adjusting entry. *Answer:* We must accrue pay for eight working days instead of three:

Salaries Expense . . . 560
   Salaries Payable 560

Assets = Liabilities + Equity
             +210   −210

After the adjusting entry is posted, the expense and liability accounts appear as shown in Exhibit 4.15:

Salaries Expense	622			Salaries Payable	209	
Dec. 12	700				Dec. 31	210
26	700					
31	210					
Balance	1,610					

Exhibit 4.15

Salary Accounts after Accrual Adjustments

This means that $1,610 of salaries expense is reported on the income statement and a $210 salaries payable (liability) is reported in the balance sheet. *Not* making the adjustment (1) understates Salaries Expense and overstates net income by $210 in the December income statement and (2) understates Salaries Payable (liabilities) and overstates equity by $210 on the December 31 balance sheet.

Point: An employer records salaries expense and vacation pay liability when employees earn vacation pay.

Accrued Interest Expense

Companies commonly have accrued interest expense on notes payable and other long-term liabilities at the end of a period. Interest expense is incurred with the passage of time. Unless interest is paid on the last day of an accounting period, we need to adjust accounts for interest expense incurred but not yet paid. This means we must accrue interest cost from the most recent payment date up to the end of the period. (The formula for computing accrued interest is: *Payable amount owed × Annual interest rate × Fraction of year since last payment date.*) The adjusting entry is similar to the one for accruing unpaid salary, with a debit to Interest Expense and a credit to Interest Payable (liability).

Adjusting Accrued Revenues

Accrued revenues refer to revenues earned in a period that are both unrecorded and not yet received in cash (or other assets). Accrued revenues are earned revenues that must be reported on the income statement. An example is a technician who bills customers only when the job is done. If one-third of a job is complete by the end of a period, then the technician must record one-third of the expected billing as revenue in that period—even though there is no billing or collection. The adjusting entries for accrued revenues increase (debit) assets and increase (credit) revenues as shown in Exhibit 4.16. Accrued revenues commonly arise from services, products, interest, and rent. We use service fees and interest to show how to adjust accounts for accrued revenues.

Exhibit 4.16

Adjusting for Accrued Revenues

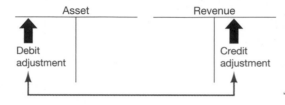

Accrued Services Revenue

Accrued revenues are not recorded until adjusting entries are made at the end of the accounting period. These accrued revenues are earned but unrecorded because either the buyer has not yet paid for them or the seller has not yet billed the buyer.

FastForward provides an example. In the second week of December, it agreed to provide 30 days of consulting services to a local sports club for a fixed fee of $2,700. The terms of the initial agreement call for FastForward to provide services from December 12, 2001, through January 10, 2002, or 30 days of service. The club agrees to pay FastForward $2,700 on January 10, 2002, when the service period is complete. At December 31, 2001, 20 days of services have already been provided. Since the contracted services are not yet entirely provided, FastForward has neither billed the club yet nor recorded the services already provided. Still, FastForward has earned two-thirds of the 30-day fee, or $1,800 ($2,700 × 20/30). The *revenue recognition principle* implies we must report the $1,800 on the December income statement because it was earned in December. The balance sheet also must report that the club owes FastForward $1,800. The year-end adjusting entry to account for accrued services revenue is

Assets = Liabilities + Equity
+1,800   +1,800

	Adjustment (f)		
Dec. 31	Accounts Receivable	1,800	
	Consulting Revenue		1,800
	To record 20 days' accrued revenue.		

The debit to accounts receivable reflects the amount the club owes FastForward for consulting services already provided. After the adjusting entry is posted, the affected accounts appear as shown in Exhibit 4.17.

Exhibit 4.17

Receivable and Revenue Accounts after Accrual Adjustments

Accounts Receivable			**106**
Dec. 12	1,900	Dec. 22	1,900
31	**1,800**		
Balance	1,800		

Consulting Revenue			**403**
		Dec. 10	4,200
		12	1,600
		31	250
		31	**1,800**
		Balance	7,850

Point: What is the adjusting entry if the 30-day consulting period began on December 22? *Answer:* One-third of the fee is earned:
Accounts Receivable . . . 900
    Consulting Revenue . . . 900

Accounts receivable are reported on the balance sheet at $1,800, and $7,850 of consulting revenue is reported on the income statement. *Not* making the adjustment would understate (1) both Consulting Revenue and net income by $1,800 in the December income statement and (b) both Accounts Receivable (assets) and equity by $1,800 on the December 31 balance sheet.

Accrued Interest Revenue

In addition to the accrued interest expense we described earlier, interest can yield an accrued revenue when a debtor owes money (or other assets) to a company. If a company is holding notes or accounts receivable that produce interest revenue, we must adjust the accounts to record any earned and yet uncollected interest revenue. The adjusting entry is similar to the one for accruing services revenue. Specifically, we debit Interest Receivable (asset) and credit Interest Revenue.

Links to Financial Statements

The process of adjusting accounts is intended to bring an asset or liability account balance to its correct amount. The adjusting entry also updates a related expense or revenue account. These adjustments are necessary for transactions and events that extend over more than one period. Adjusting entries are posted like any other entry.

Exhibit 4.18 lists the four types of transactions requiring adjustment. Adjusting entries are necessary for each. Understanding this exhibit is important to understanding the adjusting process and its importance to financial statements. Remember that each adjusting entry affects one or more income statement accounts *and* one or more balance sheet accounts. An adjusting entry never affects cash.

Exhibit 4.19 summarizes the adjusting entries of FastForward on December 31. The post-

You Make the Call

Loan Officer   You are the loan officer when the owner of an electronics store applies for a business loan. The store's financial statements reveal large increases in current year's revenues and profits. Analysis shows these increases are due to a promotion that lets consumers buy now and pay nothing until January 1 of next year. The store records these sales as accrued revenue. Does your analysis raise any concerns?

Answer—p. 147

You Make the Call—Ethics

Financial Officer   At year-end, the president instructs you, the financial officer, to not record accrued expenses until next year because they will not be paid until then. The president also asks about a recent purchase order from a major customer that requires merchandise to be delivered two weeks after the year-end. The president points out that the order has been received, that your company is ready to make delivery, and that you are to record this sale in the current year. Your company would report a net income instead of a net loss if you carry out these orders. What do you do?

Answer—p. 147

A1   Explain how accounting adjustments link to financial statements.

	Before Adjusting		
Category	**Balance Sheet**	**Income Statement**	**Adjusting Entry**
Prepaid expense	Asset overstated	Expense understated	Dr. Expense Cr. Asset*
Unearned revenues	Liability overstated	Revenue understated	Dr. Liability Cr. Revenue
Accrued expenses	Liability understated	Expense understated	Dr. Expense Cr. Liability
Accrued revenues	Asset understated	Revenue understated	Dr. Asset Cr. Revenue

Exhibit 4.18

Summary of Adjustments and Financial Statement Links

* For depreciation, the credit is to Accumulated Depreciation (contra asset).

ing of each adjusting entry to ledger accounts was shown when we described each transaction and is not repeated here. Adjusting entries are often set apart from other journal entries with the caption Adjusting Entries as shown.

Exhibit 4.19
Journalizing Adjusting Entries

GENERAL JOURNAL					Page #
Date	**Account Titles and Explanation**	**PR**	**Debit**	**Credit**
2001	*Adjusting Entries*				
(a) Dec. 31	Insurance Expense		100	
	Prepaid Insurance			100
	To record expired insurance.			
(b) 31	Supplies Expense		1,050	
	Supplies			1,050
	To record supplies used.			
(c) 31	Depreciation Expense—Equipment		375	
	Accumulated Depreciation—Equipment			375
	To record monthly depreciation on equipment.			
(d) 31	Unearned Consulting Revenue		250	
	Consulting Revenue			250
	To record earned revenue received in advance.			
(e) 31	Salaries Expense		210	
	Salaries Payable			210
	To record three days' accrued salary.			
(f) 31	Accounts Receivable		1,800	
	Consulting Revenue			1,800
	To record 20 days' accrued revenue.			

Quick Check

6. If you omit an adjusting entry for accrued revenues of $200 at year-end, what is this error's effect on the year-end income statement and balance sheet?

7. What is a contra account? Explain.

8. What is an accrued expense? Give an example.

9. Describe how an unearned revenue arises. Give an example.

Answers—p. 147

Adjusted Trial Balance

 P2 Explain and prepare an adjusted trial balance.

An **unadjusted trial balance** is a list of accounts and balances prepared *before* adjustments are recorded. An **adjusted trial balance** is a list of accounts and balances prepared *after* adjusting entries have been recorded and posted to the ledger. Exhibit 4.20 shows both the unadjusted and the adjusted trial balances for **FastForward** at December 31, 2001. Several new accounts arise from the adjusting entries. The order of accounts in the trial balance is usually set up to match the order in the chart of accounts.

Exhibit 4.20 shows all the accounts, their adjustments, and their final adjusted balances. Each adjustment is identified by a letter in parentheses that links it to an adjusting entry shown earlier (see Exhibit 4.19 for a summary). Each amount in the Adjusted Trial Balance columns is computed by taking that account's amount from the Unadjusted Trial Balance columns and adding or subtracting its adjustment(s). To illustrate, Supplies has a $9,720 Dr. balance in the unadjusted columns. Subtracting the $1,050 Cr. amount shown in the adjustments columns yields an adjusted $8,670 Dr. balance for Supplies. An account can have more than one adjustment, such as for Consulting Revenue. Also, some accounts might not require adjusting, such as Accounts Payable for this period.

Accrual Reversals in Future Periods

The adjusting entries for both accrued expenses and accrued revenues foretell cash transactions in future periods. For example, accrued expenses at the end of one accounting period usually result in cash *payments* in the *next* period. Also, accrued revenues at the end of one

Exhibit 4.20

Unadjusted and Adjusted Trial Balances

FASTFORWARD
Trial Balance
December 31, 2001

	Unadjusted Trial Balance		Adjustments		Adjusted Trial Balance	
	Dr.	Cr.	Dr.	Cr.	Dr.	Cr.
Cash	$ 3,950				$ 3,950	
Accounts receivable	0		(f) 1,800		1,800	
Supplies	9,720			(b) 1,050	8,670	
Prepaid insurance	2,400			(a) 100	2,300	
Equipment	26,000				26,000	
Accumulated depreciation—Equip.		$ 0		(c) 375		$ 375
Accounts payable		6,200				6,200
Salaries payable		0		(e) 210		210
Unearned consulting revenue		3,000	(d) 250			2,750
Chuck Taylor, Capital		30,000				30,000
Chuck Taylor, Withdrawals	600				600	
Consulting revenue		5,800		(d) 250		7,850
				(f) 1,800		
Rental revenue		300				300
Depreciation expense—Equip.	0		(c) 375		375	
Salaries expense	1,400		(e) 210		1,610	
Insurance expense	0		(a) 100		100	
Rent expense	1,000				1,000	
Supplies expense	0		(b) 1,050		1,050	
Utilities expense	230				230	
Totals	$ 45,300	$ 45,300	$ 3,785	$ 3,785	$ 47,685	$ 47,685

accounting period usually result in cash *receipts* in the *next* period. This section explains how we account for these cash payments and cash receipts in future periods.

Paying Accrued Expenses

Recall that FastForward recorded accrued salaries with this adjusting entry:

(e) Dec. 31	Salaries Expense	210	
	Salaries Payable		210
	To record three days' accrued salary (3 × $70).		

Assets = Liabilities + Equity
        +210   −210

On Friday, January 9, the first payday of the next period, the following entry settles the accrued liability (salaries payable) and records additional salaries expense for seven days of work in January:

Jan. 9	Salaries Payable (3 days at $70)	210	
	Salaries Expense (7 days at $70)	490	
	Cash		700
	Paid two weeks' salary including three days accrued in December.		

Assets = Liabilities + Equity
−700   −210   −490

The first debit in the January 9 entry records the payment of the liability for the three days' salary accrued on December 31. The second debit records the salary for January's first seven working days (including the New Year's Day holiday) as an expense of the new accounting period. The credit records the total amount of cash paid to the employee.

Receiving Accrued Revenues

Recall that **FastForward** made the following adjusting entry to record 20 days' accrued revenue earned from its consulting contract:

(f) Dec. 31	Accounts Receivable	1,800	
	Consulting Revenue		1,800
	To record 20 days' accrued revenue.		

Assets = Liabilities + Equity
+1,800   +1,800

When FastForward receives the first month's fee on January 10, it makes the following entry to remove the accrued asset (accounts receivable) and recognize the additional revenue earned in January:

Assets = Liabilities + Equity
+2,700   +900
−1,800

Jan. 10	Cash	2,700	
	Accounts Receivable		1,800
	Consulting Revenue		900
	Received cash for accrued asset and recorded earned consulting revenue.		

The debit reflects the cash received. The first credit reflects the removal of the receivable, and the second credit records the revenue earned in January.

Preparing Financial Statements

P3 Prepare financial statements from an adjusted trial balance.

Exhibit 4.21

Preparing the Income Statement and Statement of Changes in Owner's Equity from the Adjusted Trial Balance

We can prepare financial statements directly from information in the *adjusted* trial balance. An adjusted trial balance (see the right-most columns in Exhibit 4.20) includes all balances appearing in financial statements. A trial balance summarizes information in the ledger by listing accounts and their balances, and is easier to work from than the entire ledger when preparing financial statements.

Exhibit 4.21 shows how **FastForward**'s revenue and expense balances are transferred from the adjusted trial balance to (1) the income statement and (2) the statement of changes in owner's equity. Notice that we use the net income and withdrawals account to prepare the statement of changes in owner's equity.

Exhibit 4.22 shows how FastForward's asset and liability balances on the adjusted trial balance are transferred to the balance sheet. The ending owner's equity is determined on the statement of changes in owner's equity and is transferred to the balance sheet. The balance sheet in Exhibit 4.22 is in report form. The **report form balance sheet** lists assets, liabilities, and

From Exhibit 4.20

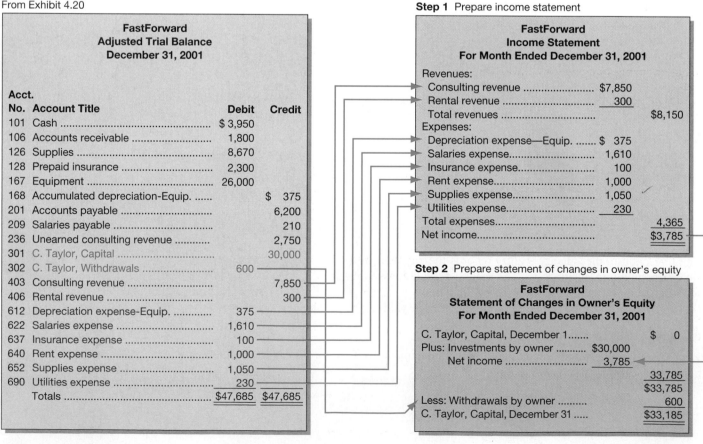

FastForward
Adjusted Trial Balance
December 31, 2001

Acct. No.	Account Title	Debit	Credit
101	Cash	$ 3,950	
106	Accounts receivable	1,800	
126	Supplies	8,670	
128	Prepaid insurance	2,300	
167	Equipment	26,000	
168	Accumulated depreciation-Equip.		$ 375
201	Accounts payable		6,200
209	Salaries payable		210
236	Unearned consulting revenue		2,750
301	C. Taylor, Capital		30,000
302	C. Taylor, Withdrawals	600	
403	Consulting revenue		7,850
406	Rental revenue		300
612	Depreciation expense-Equip.	375	
622	Salaries expense	1,610	
637	Insurance expense	100	
640	Rent expense	1,000	
652	Supplies expense	1,050	
690	Utilities expense	230	
	Totals	$47,685	$47,685

Step 1 Prepare income statement

FastForward
Income Statement
For Month Ended December 31, 2001

Revenues:		
Consulting revenue	$7,850	
Rental revenue	300	
Total revenues		$8,150
Expenses:		
Depreciation expense—Equip.	$ 375	
Salaries expense............................	1,610	
Insurance expense..........................	100	
Rent expense.................................	1,000	
Supplies expense...........................	1,050	
Utilities expense.............................	230	
Total expenses...............................		4,365
Net income....................................		$3,785

Step 2 Prepare statement of changes in owner's equity

FastForward
Statement of Changes in Owner's Equity
For Month Ended December 31, 2001

C. Taylor, Capital, December 1.......		$ 0
Plus: Investments by owner	$30,000	
Net income	3,785	
		33,785
		$33,785
Less: Withdrawals by owner		600
C. Taylor, Capital, December 31		$33,185

From Exhibit 4.20

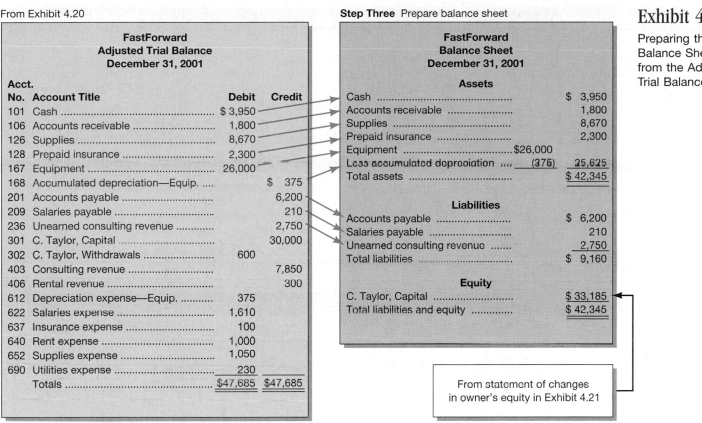

Step Three Prepare balance sheet

Exhibit 4.22

Preparing the Balance Sheet from the Adjusted Trial Balance

equity in vertical order. **Nike** uses a report form. The **account form balance sheet** lists assets on the left and liabilities and equity on the right side. Its name comes from its link to the accounting equation, Assets − Liabilities + Equity. The balance sheet in Exhibit 2.15 is in account form. Both forms are widely used and are considered equally helpful to users.

We usually prepare financial statements in the following order: income statement, statement of changes in owner's equity, and balance sheet. This order makes sense since the balance sheet uses information from the statement of changes in owner's equity, which in turn uses information from the income statement. We describe the preparation of the statement of cash flows in Chapters 5 and 17.

Quick Check

10. Music-Mart records $1,000 of accrued salaries on December 31. Five days later, on January 5 (the next payday), salaries of $7,000 are paid. What is the January 5 entry?

11. Jordan Air has the following information in its unadjusted and adjusted trial balances:

	Unadjusted		Adjusted	
	Debit	Credit	Debit	Credit
Prepaid insurance	$6,200		$5,900	
Salaries payable		$ 0		$1,400

What are the adjusting entries that Jordan Air likely recorded?

12. What accounts are taken from the adjusted trial balance to prepare an income statement?

13. In preparing financial statements from an adjusted trial balance, what statement is usually prepared second?

Answers—p. 147–8

Using the Information   **Profit Margin**

A2 Compute profit margin and describe its use in analyzing company performance.

Business decision makers want financial statements to reflect relevant information about a company's financial performance and condition. A useful measure of a company's operating results is the ratio of its net income to net sales (revenues). This ratio is called **profit margin,** or *return on sales*, and is computed as shown in Exhibit 4.23.

Exhibit 4.23

Profit Margin

$$\text{Profit margin} = \frac{\text{Net income}}{\text{Net sales}}$$

This ratio is interpreted as reflecting the percent of profit in each dollar of sales. To illustrate how we compute and use profit margin, let's look at the results of **Ben & Jerry's Homemade Ice Cream** in Exhibit 4.24. Profit margin is one measure we can use to help evaluate Ben & Jerry's performance during the past four years.

Exhibit 4.24

Ben & Jerry's Profit Margin

	1999	1998	1997	1996
Net income (in mil.)	$ 3.4	$ 6.2	$ 3.9	$ 3.9
Net sales (in mil.)	$237.0	$209.2	$174.2	$167.2
Profit margin	1.4%	3.0%	2.2%	2.3%
Industry profit margin	2.2%	1.6%	2.0%	2.1%

Ben & Jerry's average profit margin is 2.2% over this period. Year 1999 especially stands out as poor. This is mainly due to special charges tied to the discontinuance of a manufacturing plant. The profit margin is expected to increase in subsequent years. Also note the steady increase in Ben & Jerry's sales, from less than $170 million in 1996 to more than $237 million in 1999. This analysis can also benefit from a comparison of profit margins across competitors (see last row of Exhibit 4.24). Ben & Jerry's is a relatively small competitor in the super-premium ice cream industry, but its historical profit margins tend to be at or better than those of its competitors. Still, competition from larger super-premium companies keeps Ben & Jerry's from enjoying a higher margin, and played a part in its recent purchase by **Unilever**.

It is important when we evaluate the profit margin of a sole proprietorship that we modify the profit margin ratio by subtracting the value of the owner's efforts from net income. To illustrate this for **FastForward**, assume that other job opportunities indicate that the efforts of Chuck Taylor, the owner, are worth $3,500 per month. FastForward's profit margin for December 2001 is then computed as shown in Exhibit 4.25.

Point: Because sole proprietorships and partnerships are not separate legal entities, salaries to owners are not expenses. This leads to their use of the modified profit margin.

Exhibit 4.25

Modified Profit Margin

$$\text{Modified profit margin} = \frac{\text{Net income} - \text{Value of owner's efforts}}{\text{Net sales}}$$
$$= \frac{(\$3,785 - \$3,500)}{\$8,150} = 3.5\%$$

Demonstration Problem

The following information relates to Fanning's Electronics on December 31, 2002. The company, which uses the calendar year as its annual reporting period, initially records prepaid and unearned items in balance sheet accounts (assets and liabilities, respectively).

a. The company's weekly payroll is 8,750, paid every Friday for a five-day workweek. December 31, 2002, falls on a Monday, but the employees will not be paid their wages until Friday, January 4, 2003.

b. Eighteen months earlier, on July 1, 2001, the company purchased equipment that cost $20,000 and had no salvage value. Its useful life is predicted to be five years.

c. On October 1, 2002, the company agreed to work on a new housing development. For installing alarm systems in 24 new homes, the company is paid $120,000 in advance on October 1. That amount was credited to the Unearned Services Revenue account. Between October 1 and December 31, work on 20 homes was completed.

d. On September 1, 2002, the company purchased a 12-month insurance policy for $1,800. The transaction was recorded with an $1,800 debit to Prepaid Insurance.

e. On December 29, 2002, the company performed a $7,000 service that has not been billed as of December 31, 2002.

Required

1. Prepare adjusting entries needed on December 31, 2002, to record the previously unrecorded effects of these transactions and events.

2. Prepare T-accounts for accounts affected by adjusting entries. Post adjusting entries to T-accounts. Determine the adjusted balances for the Unearned Revenue and the Prepaid Insurance accounts.

3. Complete the following table describing the amounts and effects of your adjusting entries on the year 2002 income statement and the December 31, 2002, balance sheet. Use up (down) arrows to indicate an increase (decrease) in the Effect columns.

Entry	Amount in the Entry	Effect on Net Income	Effect on Total Assets	Effect on Total Liabilities	Effect on Equity

Planning the Solution

- Analyze information for each situation to determine which accounts need to be updated with an adjustment.
- Calculate the amount of each adjustment and prepare the necessary journal entries.
- Show the amount entered by each adjustment in the designated accounts, determine the adjusted balance, and then determine the balance sheet classification that the account falls within.
- Determine each entry's effect on net income for the year and on total assets, total liabilities, and equity at the end of the year.

Solution to Demonstration Problem

1. Adjusting journal entries.

(a) Dec. 31	Wages Expense	1,750	
	Wages Payable		1,750
	To accrue wages for the last day of the year ($8,750 × 1/5).		
(b) Dec. 31	Depreciation Expense—Equipment	4,000	
	Accumulated Depreciation—Equipment ...		4,000
	To record depreciation expense for the year ($20,000/5 years = $4,000 per year).		
(c) Dec. 31	Unearned Services Revenue	100,000	
	Services Revenue		100,000
	To recognize services revenue earned ($120,000 × 20/24).		
(d) Dec. 31	Insurance Expense	600	
	Prepaid Insurance		600
	To adjust for expired portion of insurance ($1,800 × 4/12).		
(e) Dec. 31	Accounts Receivable	7,000	
	Services Revenue		7,000
	To record services revenue earned.		

2. T-accounts for adjusting journal entries *a* through *e*.

Wages Expense	
(*a*) 1,750	

Wages Payable	
	(*a*) 1,750

Depreciation Expense — Equipment	
(*b*) 4,000	

Accumulated Depreciation — Equipment	
	(*b*) 4,000

Unearned Revenue	
	Beg. Bal. 120,000
(*c*) 100,000	
	End Bal. 20,000

Services Revenue	
	(*c*) 100,000
	(*e*) 7,000
	Adj. Bal. 107,000

Insurance Expense	
(*d*) 600	

Prepaid Insurance	
Beg. Bal 1,800	
	(*d*) 600
End. Bal. 1,200	

Accounts Receivable	
(*e*) 7,000	

3. Financial statement effects of adjusting journal entries.

Entry	Amount in the Entry	Effect on Net Income	Effect on Total Assets	Effect on Total Liabilities	Effect on Equity
a	$ 1,750	$ 1,750 ↓	No effect	$ 1,750 ↑	$ 1,750 ↓
b	4,000	4,000 ↓	$4,000 ↓	No effect	4,000 ↓
c	100,000	100,000 ↑	No effect	$100,000 ↓	100,000 ↑
d	600	600 ↓	$ 600 ↓	No effect	600 ↓
e	7,000	7,000 ↑	$7,000 ↑	No effect	7,000 ↑

APPENDIX

4A Alternative Accounting for Prepaids

This section explains an alternative in accounting for prepaid expenses and for unearned (prepaid) revenues.

Recording Prepaid Expenses in Expense Accounts

 P4 Identify and explain an alternative in accounting for prepaids.

An alternative method is to record *all* prepaid expenses with debits to expense accounts. If any prepaids remain unused or unexpired at the end of an accounting period, then adjusting entries must transfer the cost of the unused portions from expense accounts to prepaid expense (asset) accounts. This alternative method is acceptable. The financial statements are identical under either method, but the adjusting entries are different. To illustrate the accounting differences between these two methods, let's look at **FastForward**'s cash payment of December 26 for 24 months of insurance coverage beginning on December 1. FastForward recorded that payment with a debit to an asset account, but it could have recorded a debit to an expense account. These alternatives are shown in Exhibit 4A.1.

		Payment Recorded as Asset	Payment Recorded as Expense
	Cash	2,400	
Dec. 26	Insurance Expense		2,400
	Cash		2,400

Exhibit 4A.1

Alternative Initial Entries for Prepaid Expenses

At the end of its accounting period on December 31, insurance protection for one month has expired. This means $100 ($2,400/24) of the insurance coverage expires and becomes an expense for December. The adjusting entry depends on how the original payment was recorded. This is shown in Exhibit 4A.2.

		Payment Recorded as Asset	Payment Recorded as Expense
Dec. 31	Insurance Expense	100	
	Prepaid Insurance		100
Dec. 31	Prepaid Insurance		2,300
	Insurance Expense		2,300

Exhibit 4A.2

Adjusting Entry for Prepaid Expenses for the Two Alternatives

When these entries are posted to the accounts in the ledger, we can see that these two methods give identical results. The December 31 adjusted account balances in Exhibit 4A.3 show Prepaid Insurance of $2,300 and Insurance Expense of $100 for both methods.

Payment Recorded as Asset

Prepaid Insurance			128
Dec. 26	2,400	Dec. 31	100
Balance	2,300		

Insurance Expense			637
Dec. 31	100		

Payment Recorded as Expense

Prepaid Insurance			128
Dec. 31	2,300		

Insurance Expense			637
Dec. 26	2,400	Dec. 31	2,300
Balance	100		

Exhibit 4A.3

Account Balances under Two Alternatives for Recording Prepaid Expenses

Recording Unearned Revenues in Revenue Accounts

As with prepaid expenses, an alternative method is to record *all* unearned revenues with credits to revenue accounts. If any revenues are unearned at the end of an accounting period, then adjusting entries must transfer the unearned portions from revenue accounts to unearned revenue (liability) accounts. This alternative method is acceptable. While the adjusting entries are different for these two alternatives, the financial statements are identical. To illustrate the accounting differences between these two methods, let's look at FastForward's December 26 receipt of $3,000 for consulting services covering the period December 27 to February 24. FastForward recorded this transaction with a credit to a liability account. The alternative is to record it with a credit to a revenue account as shown in Exhibit 4A.4.

		Receipt Recorded as Liability	Receipt Recorded as Revenue
Dec. 26	Cash	3,000	
	Unearned Consulting Revenue	3,000	
Dec. 26	Cash		3,000
	Consulting Revenue		3,000

Exhibit 4A.4

Alternative Initial Entries for Unearned Revenues

By the end of its accounting period on December 31, FastForward has earned $250 of this revenue. This means $250 of the liability has been satisfied. Depending on how the initial receipt is recorded, the adjusting entry is as shown in Exhibit 4A.5.

Exhibit 4A.5

Adjusting Entry for Unearned Revenues for the Two Alternatives

			Receipt Recorded as Liability	Receipt Recorded as Revenue
Dec. 31	Unearned Consulting Revenue	....	250	
	Consulting Revenue	....		250
Dec. 31	Consulting Revenue	....		2,750
	Unearned Consulting Revenue	....		2,750

After adjusting entries are posted, the two alternatives give identical results. The December 31 adjusted account balances in Exhibit 4A.6 show unearned consulting revenue of $2,750 and consulting revenue of $250 for both methods.

Exhibit 4A.6

Account Balances under Two Alternatives for Recording Unearned Revenues

Receipt Recorded as Liability

Unearned Consulting Revenue 236			
Dec. 31	250	Dec. 26	3,000
		Balance	2,750

Consulting Revenue 403			
		Dec. 31	250

Receipt Recorded as Revenue

Unearned Consulting Revenue 236			
		Dec. 31	2,750

Consulting Revenue 403			
Dec. 31	2,750	Dec. 26	3,000
		Balance	250

Summary

C1 **Explain the importance of periodic reporting and the time period principle.** The value of information is often linked to its timeliness. To provide timely information, accounting systems prepare periodic reports at regular intervals. The time period principle assumes that an organization's activities can be divided into specific time periods for periodic reporting.

C2 **Describe the purpose of adjusting accounts at the end of a period.** After recording external transactions and events, several accounts often need adjusting for correct balances in financial statements. This need arises because internal transactions and events remain unrecorded. The purpose of adjusting accounts at the end of a period is to properly recognize revenues earned and expenses incurred for the period.

C3 **Explain accrual accounting and how it enhances financial statements.** Accrual accounting recognizes revenue when earned and expenses when incurred—not necessarily when cash inflows and outflows occur. This information is valuable in assessing a company's financial position and performance.

C4 **Identify the types of adjustments and their purpose.** Adjustments can be grouped according to the timing of cash receipts and payments relative to when they are recognized as revenues or expenses as follows: prepaid expenses, unearned revenues, accrued expenses, and accrued revenues. Adjusting entries are necessary so that revenues, expenses, assets, and liabilities are correctly reported.

A1 **Explain how accounting adjustments link to financial statements.** Accounting adjustments bring an asset or liability account balance to its correct amount. They also update related expense or revenue accounts. Every adjusting entry affects one or more income statement accounts *and* one or more balance sheet accounts. An adjusting entry never affects cash.

A2 **Compute profit margin and describe its use in analyzing company performance.** *Profit margin* is defined as the reporting period's net income divided by net sales for the same period. Profit margin reflects on a company's earnings activities by showing how much profit is in each dollar of sales.

P1 **Prepare and explain adjusting entries.** *Prepaid expenses* refer to items paid for in advance of receiving their benefits. Prepaid expenses are assets. Adjusting entries for prepaids involve increasing (debiting) expenses and decreasing (crediting) assets. *Unearned* (or *prepaid*) *revenues* refer to cash received in advance of providing products and services. Unearned revenues are liabilities. Adjusting entries for unearned revenues involves increasing (crediting) revenues and decreasing (debiting) unearned revenues. *Accrued expenses* refer to costs incurred in a period that are both unpaid and unrecorded. Adjusting entries for recording accrued expenses involves increasing (debiting) expenses and increasing (crediting) liabilities. *Accrued revenues* refer to revenues earned in a period that are both unrecorded and not yet received in cash. Adjusting entries for recording accrued revenues involves increasing (debiting) assets and increasing (crediting) revenues.

P2 **Explain and prepare an adjusted trial balance.** An adjusted trial balance is a list of accounts and balances prepared after recording and posting adjusting entries. Financial statements are often prepared from the adjusted trial balance.

P3 **Prepare financial statements from an adjusted trial balance.** Revenue and expense balances are transferred to the income statement and statement of changes in owner's equity. Asset, liability, and equity balances are transferred to the balance sheet. We usually prepare statements in the following order.

income statement, statement of changes in owner's equity, balance sheet, and statement of cash flows.

P4 **Identify and explain alternatives in accounting for prepaids.** Charging all prepaid expenses to expense accounts when they are purchased is acceptable. When this is done, adjusting entries must transfer any unexpired amounts from expense accounts to asset accounts. Crediting all unearned revenues to revenue accounts when cash is received is also acceptable. In this case, the adjusting entries must transfer any unearned amounts from revenue accounts to unearned revenue accounts.

Guidance Answers to **You Make the Call**

Appraiser Prepaid expenses are items paid for in advance of receiving their benefits. They are assets and are expensed as they are used up. The publishing company's treatment of the signing bonus is acceptable provided future book sales can at least match the $500,000 expense. As an appraiser, you are concerned about the risk of future book sales. The riskier the likelihood of future book sales is, the more likely your analysis is to treat the $500,000, or a portion of it, as an expense, not a prepaid expense (asset).

Entrepreneur Depreciation is a process of cost allocation, not asset valuation. Knowing the depreciation schedule is not especially useful in your estimation of what the building and equipment are currently worth. Your own assessment of the age, quality, and usefulness of the building and equipment is more important.

Loan Officer Your concern in lending to this store arises from analysis of current-year sales. While increased revenues and profits

are fine, your concern is with the collectibility of these promotional sales. If the owner sold products to customers with poor records of paying bills, then probable collectibility of these sales is low. Your analysis must assess this possibility and recognize any expected losses.

Financial Officer Omitting accrued expenses and recognizing revenue early can mislead financial statement users (including managers, owners, and lenders). One action is to request a second meeting with the president so you can explain that accruing expenses when incurred and recognizing revenue when earned are required practices. You should also mention the ethical implications of not complying with accepted practice. If the president persists, you might discuss the situation with legal counsel and any auditors involved. Your ethical action might cost you this job, but the potential pitfalls for falsification of statements, reputation loss, personal integrity, and other costs are too great.

Guidance Answers to **Quick Checks**

1. An annual reporting (or accounting) period covers one year and refers to the preparation of annual financial statements. The annual reporting period is not always a calendar year that ends on December 31. An organization can adopt a fiscal year consisting of any consecutive 12 months or 52 weeks.

2. Interim (less than one year) financial statements are prepared to provide decision makers information frequently and promptly.

3. The revenue recognition principle and the matching principle lead most directly to the adjusting process.

4. No. Cash basis accounting is not consistent with the matching principle because it reports expenses when paid, not in the period when revenue is earned as a result of those expenses.

5. No expense is reported in 2003. Under cash basis accounting the entire $4,800 is reported as expense in April 2002 when the premium is paid.

6. If the accrued revenues adjustment of $200 is not made, then both revenues and net income are understated by $200 on the

current year's income statement, and both assets and equity are understated by $200 on the balance sheet.

7. A contra account is an account that is subtracted from the balance of a related account. Use of a contra account provides more information than simply reporting a net amount.

8. An accrued expense is a cost incurred in a period that is both unpaid and unrecorded prior to adjusting entries. One example is salaries earned but not yet paid at period-end.

9. An unearned revenue arises when a firm receives cash (or other assets) from a customer before providing the services or products to the customer. A magazine subscription paid in advance is one example, season ticket sales is another.

10.

Salaries Payable	1,000	
Salaries Expense	6,000	
Cash		7,000

Paid salary including accrual from December.

11. The probable adjusting entries of Jordan Air are

Insurance Expense   300
    Prepaid Insurance   300
    To record insurance expired.

Salaries Expense   1,400
    Salaries Payable   1,400
    To record accrued salaries.

12. Revenue accounts and expense accounts.

13. Statement of changes in owner's equity.

Glossary

Account form balance sheet balance sheet that lists assets on the left side and liabilities and equity on the right. (p. 141).

Accounting period length of time covered by financial statements; also called *reporting period*. (p. 126).

Accrual basis accounting accounting system that recognizes revenues when earned and expenses when incurred; the basis for GAAP. (p. 128).

Accrued expenses costs incurred in a period that are both unpaid and unrecorded; adjusting entries for recording accrued expenses involve increasing (debiting) expenses and increasing (crediting) liabilities. (p. 134).

Accrued revenues revenues earned in a period that are both unrecorded and not yet received in cash (or other assets); adjusting entries for recording accrued revenues involve increasing (debiting) assets and increasing (crediting) revenues. (p. 136).

Adjusted trial balance list of accounts and balances prepared after adjustments are recorded and posted. (p. 138).

Adjusting entry journal entry at the end of an accounting period to bring an asset or liability account to its proper amount and update the related expense or revenue account. (p. 129).

Annual financial statements financial statements covering a one-year period; often based on a calendar year, but any consecutive 12-month (or 52-week) period is acceptable. (p. 126).

Book value equals the asset's original costs less its accumulated depreciation. (p. 133).

Cash basis accounting accounting system that recognizes revenues when cash is received and records expenses when cash is paid. (p. 128).

Contra account account linked with another account and having an opposite normal balance; reported as a subtraction from the other account's balance. (p. 132).

Depreciation expense created by allocating the cost of plant and equipment to periods in which they are used; represents the expense of using the asset. (p. 131).

Fiscal year consecutive 12 months (or 52 weeks) chosen as the organization's annual accounting period. (p. 126).

Interim financial statements financial statements covering periods of less than one year; usually based on one-, three-, or six-month periods. (p. 126).

Matching principle requires expenses to be reported in the same period as the revenues that were earned as a result of the expenses. (p. 127).

Natural business year 12-month period that ends when a company's sales activities are at their lowest point. (p. 127).

Plant and equipment tangible long-lived assets used to produce or sell products and services; also called *fixed assets*. (p. 131).

Prepaid expenses items paid for in advance of receiving their benefits; classified as assets. (p. 130).

Profit margin ratio of a company's net income to its net sales; the percent of profit in each dollar of revenue. (p. 142).

Report form balance sheet balance sheet that lists accounts vertically in the order of assets, liabilities, and equity. (p. 140).

Straight-line depreciation method allocates equal amounts of an asset's cost (less any salvage value) to depreciation expense during its useful life. (p. 132).

Time period principle assumes an organization's activities can be divided into specific time periods such as months, quarters, or years. (p. 126).

Unadjusted trial balance list of accounts and balances prepared before adjustments are recorded and posted. (p. 138).

Unearned revenues cash (or other assets) received in advance of providing products or services; a liability. (p. 133).

[Superscript letter ^A denotes assignments based on Appendix 4A.]

Questions

1. What is the difference between the cash and accrual bases of accounting?

2. Why is the accrual basis of accounting generally preferred over the cash basis?

3. What type of business is most likely to select a fiscal year that corresponds to the natural business year instead of the calendar year?

4. Where is a prepaid expense reported in the financial statements?

5. What type of asset(s) requires adjusting entries to record depreciation?

6. What contra account is used when recording and reporting the effects of depreciation? Why is it used?

7. Where is unearned revenue reported in financial statements?

8. What is an accrued revenue? Give an example.

9. Why does a sole proprietorship require special procedures in calculating the profit margin?

10.ᴬ If a company initially records prepaid expenses with debits to expense accounts, what type of account is debited in the adjusting entries for prepaid expenses?

11. Review the balance sheet of **Nike** in Appendix A. Identify two asset accounts that require adjustment before annual financial statements can be prepared.

What would be the effect on the income statement if these two asset accounts were not adjusted?

12. Review the balance sheet of **Reebok** in Appendix A. In addition to prepaid expenses and property and equipment, identify two accounts (either assets or liabilities) requiring adjusting entries.

13. Refer to **Gap**'s balance sheet in Appendix A. Identify three types of property and equipment that it must depreciate.

---

a. On July 1, 2002, McCay Company paid $1,200 for six months of insurance coverage. No adjustments have been made to the Prepaid Insurance account and it is now December 31, 2002. Prepare the journal entry to show the expiration of the insurance as of December 31, 2002.

b. Taylor Company has a supplies balance of $500 on January 1, 2002. During 2002, it purchased $2,000 of supplies. As of December 31, 2002, a supplies inventory shows $800 of supplies available. Prepare the adjusting journal entry to correctly state the balance of the Supplies account and Supplies Expense account as of December 31, 2002.

QUICK STUDY

QS 4-1
Adjusting prepaid expenses

P1

---

a. Decker Company purchases $20,000 of equipment on January 1, 2002. The equipment is expected to last five years and be worth $2,000 at the end of that time. Prepare the entry to record one year's depreciation expense for Decker's equipment as of December 31, 2002.

b. Decker Company purchases $10,000 of land on January 1, 2002. The land is expected to last indefinitely. What depreciation adjustment, if any, should Decker Company make with respect to the Land account as of December 31, 2002?

QS 4-2
Adjusting for depreciation

P1

---

a. William Nelson has a client that paid $10,000 cash in advance for legal fee. He will work on this client's case over a four-month period. William receives the cash advance on October 1, 2002, and records it by debiting Cash and crediting Unearned Revenue for $10,000. It is now December 31, 2002, and William has worked as planned on the client's case. What adjusting entry should William make to account for the work performed from October 1 through December 31, 2002?

b. Patty Tidwell has started a new publication called *Contest News*. Her subscribers pay $24 to receive 12 issues of the magazine. With every new subscriber, Patty debits Cash and credits Unearned Subscription Revenue for the amounts received. Patty has 100 subscribers as of July 1, 2002. She sends *Contest News* to each subscriber every month from July through December. Assuming no changes in subscribers, prepare the journal entry that Patty must make as of December 31, 2002, to adjust the Subscription Revenue account and the Unearned Subscription Revenue account.

QS 4-3
Adjusting for unearned revenues

P1

Robin Fischer employs three college students every summer in her coffee shop. The students work the five weekdays and are paid on Friday one week after their pay period ends. (For example, a student who works Monday through Friday, June 1 through June 5, is paid for that work on Friday, June 12.) Robin adjusts her books monthly, if needed, to show salaries earned but unpaid at month-end. All three students work the last week of July—Friday is August 1. If each student earns $100 per day, what adjusting entry must Robin make to correctly record salaries expense for July?

QS 4-4
Accruing salary

P2

Classify the following adjusting entries as involving prepaid expenses (PE), depreciation (D), unearned revenues (UR), accrued expenses (AE), or accrued revenues (AR).

a. _____ Entry to show revenue earned that was previously received as cash in advance.

b. _____ Entry to record annual depreciation expense.

c. _____ Entry to show wages expense incurred but not yet paid (nor recorded).

d. _____ Entry to show revenue earned but not yet billed (nor recorded).

e. _____ Entry to show expiration of prepaid insurance.

QS 4-5
Identifying accounting adjustments

C4

QS 4-6

Recording and analyzing adjusting entries

A1

Adjusting entries affect at least one balance sheet account and at least one income statement account. For the following entries, identify the account to be debited and the account to be credited. Indicate which of the accounts is the income statement account and which is the balance sheet account.

a. Entry to record revenue earned that was previously received as cash in advance.

b. Entry to record annual depreciation expense.

c. Entry to record wages expense incurred but not yet paid (nor recorded).

d. Entry to record revenue earned but not yet billed (nor recorded).

e. Entry to record expiration of prepaid insurance.

QS 4-7

Using accrual and cash accounting **C3**

In its first year of operations, Heyer Co. earned $42,000 in revenues and received $37,000 cash from customers. The company incurred expenses of $25,500 but had not paid $5,250 of them at year-end. In addition, Heyer prepaid $6,750 cash for expenses that would be incurred the next year. Calculate the first year's net income under both the cash basis and the accrual basis of accounting.

QS 4-8

Preparing adjusting entries

C4

During the year, Stone Co. records prepayments of expenses in asset accounts and receipts of unearned revenues in liability accounts. At the end of its annual accounting period, the company must make three adjusting entries: (1) accrue salaries expense, (2) adjust the Unearned Services Revenue account to recognize earned revenue, and (3) record the earning of services revenue for which cash will be received the following period. For each of these adjusting entries (1), (2), and (3), use the letters assigned to the following accounts to indicate the account to be debited and the account to be credited.

a. Accounts Receivable

b. Prepaid Salaries

c. Cash

d. Salaries Payable

e. Unearned Services Revenue

f. Salaries Expense

g. Services Revenue

QS 4-9

Determining effects of adjusting entries

C4 **A1**

In making adjusting entries at the end of its accounting period, Malson Consulting Agency failed to record $1,600 of insurance premiums that had expired. This cost had been initially debited to the Prepaid Insurance account. The company also failed to record accrued salaries payable of $1,000. As a result of these two oversights, the financial statements for the reporting period will [choose one] (1) understate assets by $1,600; (2) understate expenses by $2,600; (3) understate net income by $1,000; or (4) overstate liabilities by $1,000.

QS 4-10

Interpreting adjusting entries

C4

The following information is taken from Case Company's unadjusted and adjusted trial balances:

	Unadjusted		Adjusted	
	Debit	**Credit**	**Debit**	**Credit**
Prepaid insurance	$4,100		$3,700	
Interest payable		$ 0		$800

Given this information, which of the following items must be included among its adjusting entries?

a. A $400 credit to Prepaid Insurance and an $800 debit to Interest Payable.

b. A $400 debit to Insurance Expense and an $800 debit to Interest Payable.

c. A $400 debit to Insurance Expense and an $800 debit to Interest Expense.

QS 4-11

Analyzing profit margin **A2**

Hao Company had net income of $48,152 and net sales of $425,000 for the year ended December 31, 2002. Calculate Hao's profit margin. Interpret the profit margin calculation.

QS 4-12[A]

Preparing adjusting entries

C4 **P4**

Bergez Consulting Company initially records prepaid and unearned items in income statement accounts. Given Bergez Consulting Company's accounting practices, which of the following applies to the preparation of adjusting entries at the end of the company's first accounting period?

a. Earned but unbilled (and unrecorded) consulting fees will be recorded with a debit to Unearned Consulting Fees and a credit to Consulting Fees Earned.

b. Unpaid salaries will be recorded with a debit to Prepaid Salaries and a credit to Salaries Expense.

c. The cost of unused office supplies will be recorded with a debit to Supplies Expense and a credit to Office Supplies.

d. Unearned fees (on which cash was received in advance earlier in the period) will be recorded with a debit to Consulting Fees Earned and a credit to Unearned Consulting Fees.

EXERCISES

For each of the following separate cases, prepare adjusting entries required for financial statements for the year (or date) ended December 31, 2002. (Assume prepaid expenses are initially recorded in asset accounts and that fees collected in advance of work are initially recorded as liabilities.)

Exercise 4-1
Preparing adjusting entries

a. One-third of the work related to $15,000 cash received in advance is performed this period.

b. Wages of $8,000 are earned by workers but not paid as of December 31, 2002.

c. Depreciation on the company's equipment for 2002 is $18,534.

d. The Office Supplies account had a $240 debit balance on January 1, 2002. During the year, $5,239 of office supplies are purchased. A physical count of supplies at December 31, 2002, shows $487 of supplies available.

e. The Prepaid Insurance account had a $4,000 balance on January 1, 2002. An analysis of the company's insurance policies shows that $1,200 of unexpired insurance benefits remain at December 31, 2002.

f. The company has earned _{revenue} (but not recorded) $1,000 of interest from investments in CDs as of December 31, 2002. The interest earned will be received on January 10, 2003.

g. The company has a bank loan and has incurred (but not recorded) interest expenses of $2,500 as of December 31, 2002. The company must pay the interest on January 2, 2003.

Prepare adjusting journal entries for the year ended December 31, 2002, for each of these independent situations. Assume prepaid expenses are initially recorded in asset accounts. Also assume fees collected in advance of work are initially recorded as liabilities.

Exercise 4-2
Preparing adjusting entries

a. Depreciation on the company's equipment for 2002 is computed to be $18,000.

b. The Prepaid Insurance account had a $6,000 debit balance at December 31, 2002, before adjusting for the costs of any expired coverage. An analysis of the company's insurance policies showed that $1,100 of unexpired insurance remained in effect.

c. The Office Supplies account had a $700 debit balance on January 1, 2002; $3,480 of office supplies were purchased during the year; and the December 31, 2002, physical count showed $298 of supplies available.

d. One-half of the work related to $15,000 cash received in advance was performed this period.

e. The Prepaid Insurance account had a $6,800 debit balance at December 31, 2002 before adjusting for the costs of any expired coverage. An analysis of the company's insurance policies showed that $5,800 of coverage had expired.

f. Wages of $3,200 have been earned by workers but not paid as of December 31, 2002.

Asset Management has five part-time employees, each of whom earns $250 per day. They are normally paid on Fridays for work completed Monday through Friday of the same week. They were paid in full on Friday, December 28, 2002. The next week, the five employees worked only four days because New Year's Day was an unpaid holiday. Show the adjusting entry that would be recorded on Monday, December 31, 2002, and the journal entry that would be made to record paying the employees' wages on Friday, January 4, 2003.

Exercise 4-3
Adjusting and paying accrued wages

In the blank space beside each adjusting entry, enter the letter of the explanation *a* through *f* that most closely describes the entry:

a. To record this period's depreciation expense.

b. To record accrued salaries expense.

c. To record this period's use of a prepaid expense.

d. To record accrued interest income.

e. To record accrued interest expense.

f. To record the earning of previously unearned income.

Exercise 4-4
Classifying adjusting entry

___ **1.**	Salaries Expense	13,280	
	Salaries Payable		13,280
___ **2.**	Interest Expense	2,208	
	Interest Payable		2,208
___ **3.**	Insurance Expense	3,180	
	Prepaid Insurance		3,180
___ **4.**	Unearned Professional Fees	19,250	
	Professional Fees Earned		19,250
___ **5.**	Interest Receivable	3,300	
	Interest Revenue		3,300
___ **6.**	Depreciation Expense	38,217	
	Accumulated Depreciation		38,217

Exercise 4-5

Determining cost flows
through accounts

Determine the missing amounts in each of these four separate situations *a* through *d*:

	a	b	c	d
Supplies available—January 1	$ 400	$1,200	$1,260	?
Supplies purchased during the year	2,800	6,500	?	$3,000
Supplies available—December 31	650	?	1,350	700
Supplies expense for the year	?	1,200	8,400	4,588

Exercise 4-6

Adjusting and paying
accrued expenses

The following three situations require adjusting journal entries to prepare financial statements as of April 30. For each situation, present both the adjusting entry and the entry to record the payment of the accrued liability during May.

a. On April 1, the company retained an attorney at a flat monthly fee of $3,500. This amount is payable on the 12th of the following month.

b. An $800,000 note payable requires 1.0% interest to be paid every 30 days. The interest was last paid on April 20 and the next payment is due on May 20.

c. Total weekly salaries expense for all employees is $10,000. This amount is paid at the end of the day on Friday of each 5-day workweek. April 30 falls on Tuesday of this year, which means that the employees had worked two days since the last payday. The next payday is May 3.

Exercise 4-7

Determining assets and
expenses for accrual and cash
accounting

On March 1, 2001, a company paid an $18,000 premium on a three-year insurance policy for coverage beginning on that date. Refer to that policy and fill in the blanks in the following table:

	Balance Sheet Asset under the		Insurance Expense under the		
	Accrual Basis	Cash Basis		Accrual Basis	Cash Basis
Dec. 31, 2001	$_____	$_____	2001	$_____	$_____
Dec. 31, 2002	_____	_____	2002	_____	_____
Dec. 31, 2003	_____	_____	2003	_____	_____
Dec. 31, 2004	_____	_____	2004	_____	_____
			Total	$_____	$_____

Exercise 4-8

Computing and interpreting
profit margin

Use the following information to compute profit margin for each separate company *a* through *e*:

	Net Income	Net Sales		Net Income	Net Sales
a.	$ 4,390	$ 44,830	**d.**	$65,234	$1,458,999
b.	97,644	398,954	**e.**	80,158	435,925
c.	111,385	257,082			

Which of the five companies is the most profitable according to the profit margin ratio? Interpret that company's profit margin ratio.

Following are two income statements for Clark Co. for the year ended December 31. The left column is prepared before any adjusting entries are recorded, and the right column includes the effects of adjusting entries. The company records cash receipts and disbursements related to unearned and prepaid items in balance sheet accounts. Analyze the statements and prepare the eight adjusting entries that must have been recorded. (*Note:* 30% of the $7,000 adjustment for Fees Earned has been earned but not billed, and the other 70% has been earned by performing services that were paid for in advance.)

Exercise 4-9
Analyzing and preparing adjusting entries

CLARK CO. Income Statements For Year Ended December 31	Before Adjustments	After Adjustments
Revenues		
Fees earned	$18,000	$25,000
Commissions earned	36,500	36,500
Total revenues	$54,500	$61,500
Expenses		
Depreciation expense—Computers	0	1,600
Depreciation expense—Office furniture	0	1,850
Salaries expense	13,500	15,750
Insurance expense	0	1,400
Rent expense	3,800	3,800
Office supplies expense	0	580
Advertising expense	2,500	2,500
Utilities expense	1,245	1,335
Total expenses	$21,045	$28,815
Net income	$33,455	$32,685

Tri-Mark Construction began operations on December 1. In setting up its accounting procedures, the company decided to debit expense accounts when it prepays its expenses and to credit revenue accounts when customers pay for services in advance. Prepare journal entries for (a) through (d) and the adjusting entries as of December 31 for items (e) through (g).

a. Supplies are purchased on December 1 for $2,000 cash.

b. The company prepaid its insurance premiums for $1,540 cash on December 2.

c. On December 15, the company receives an advance payment of $13,000 cash from a customer for remodeling work.

d. On December 28, the company receives $3,700 cash from another customer for remodeling work to be performed in January.

e. A physical count on December 31, indicates that Tri-Mark has $1,840 of supplies available.

f. An analysis of the insurance policies in effect on December 31 shows that $340 of insurance coverage had expired.

g. As of December 31, only one project has been completed. The $5,570 fee for this project had been received in advance.

Exercise 4-10^A
Adjusting for prepaids recorded as expense and unearned revenues recorded as revenue

Globus Company experienced the following events and transactions during July:

July	1	Received $3,000 cash in advance of performing work for Nicole Renker.
	6	Received $7,500 cash in advance of performing work for Lisa Gardner.
	12	Completed the job for Nicole Renker.
	18	Received $8,500 cash in advance of performing work for Drew Hanson.
	27	Completed the job for Lisa Gardner.
	31	None of the work for Drew Hanson has been performed.

Exercise 4-11^A
Recording and reporting revenues received in advance
P4

a. Prepare journal entries (including any adjusting entry as of the end of the month) to record these events using the procedure of initially crediting the Unearned Fees account when payment is received from a customer in advance of performing services.

b. Prepare journal entries (including any adjusting entry as of the end of the month) to record these events using the procedure of initially crediting the Fees Earned account when payment is received from a customer in advance of performing services.

c. Under each method, determine the amount of earned fees reported on the income statement for July and the amount of unearned fees reported on the balance sheet as of July 31.

PROBLEM SET A

Problem 4-1A

Identifying adjusting entries with explanations

 C4   P1

For each of the following entries, enter the letter of the explanation that most closely describes it in the space beside each entry. (You can use letters more than once.)

a. To record receipt of unearned revenue.
b. To record this period's earning of prior unearned revenue.
c. To record payment of an accrued expense.
d. To record receipt of an accrued revenue.
e. To record an accrued expense.

f. To record an accrued revenue.
g. To record this period's use of a prepaid expense.
h. To record payment of a prepaid expense.
i. To record this period's depreciation expense.

G	1.	Rent Expense	2,000	
		Prepaid Rent		2,000
E	2.	Interest Expense	1,000	
		Interest Payable		1,000
I	3.	Depreciation Expense	4,000	
		Accumulated Depreciation		4,000
B	4.	Unearned Professional Fees	3,000	
		Professional Fees Earned		3,000
G	5.	Insurance Expense	4,200	
		Prepaid Insurance		4,200
C	6.	Salaries Payable	1,400	
		Cash		1,400
H	7.	Prepaid Rent	4,500	
		Cash		4,500
E	8.	Salaries Expense	6,000	
		Salaries Payable		6,000
F	9.	Interest Receivable	5,000	
		Interest Revenue		5,000
D	10.	Cash	9,000	
		Accounts Receivable		9,000
A	11.	Cash	7,500	
		Unearned Professional Fees		7,500
D	12.	Cash	2,000	
		Interest Receivable		2,000

(handwritten notes in left margin: "receiving i? not accrued"; "payable i? accrued")

Problem 4-2A

Preparing adjusting and subsequent journal entries

A1   P1

Feinman Co. follows the practice of recording prepaid expenses and unearned revenues in balance sheet accounts. Feinman's annual accounting period ends on December 31, 2003. The following information concerns the adjusting entries to be recorded as of that date:

a. The Office Supplies account started the year with a $4,000 balance. During 2003, the company purchased supplies for $13,400, which was added to the Office Supplies account. The inventory of supplies available at December 31 totaled $2,554.

b. An analysis of the company's insurance policies provided these facts:

Policy	Date of Purchase	Years of Coverage	Cost
A	April 1, 2002	2	$14,400
B	April 1, 2003	3	12,960
C	August 1, 2003	1	2,400

The total premium for each policy was paid in full (for all years) at the purchase date, and the Prepaid Insurance account was debited for the full cost.

c. The company has 14 employees who earn a total of $1,960 in salaries every working day. They are paid each Monday for their work in the five-day workweek ending on the previous Friday. December 31, 2003, falls on Tuesday, and all 14 employees worked the first two days of that week. Because New Year's Day is a paid holiday, they will be paid salaries for five full days on Monday, January 6, 2004.

d. The company purchased a building on January 1, 2003. It cost $960,000 and is expected to have a $45,000 salvage value at the end of its predicted 30-year life.

e. Since the company is not large enough to occupy the entire building, it rented some space to a tenant at $3,000 per month, starting on November 1, 2003. The rent was paid on time on November 1, and the amount received was credited to the Rent Earned account. However, the tenant has not paid the December rent. The company has worked out an agreement with the tenant, who has promised to pay both December and January rent in full on January 15. The tenant has agreed not to fall behind again.

f. On November 1, the company rented space to another tenant for $2,800 per month. The tenant paid five months' rent in advance on that date. The payment was recorded with a credit to the Unearned Rent account.

Required

1. Use the information to prepare adjusting entries as of December 31, 2003.

2. Prepare journal entries to record the first subsequent cash transaction for both parts (c) and (e).

Check Insurance expense, $11,440

Thomas Technical Institute, a school owned by Joshua Thomas, provides training to individuals who pay tuition directly to the school. The school also offers training to groups in off-site locations. The school's unadjusted trial balance as of December 31, 2002, follows. Thomas Technical Institute initially records prepaid expenses and unearned revenues in balance sheet accounts. Items that require adjusting entries on December 31, 2002, are described after the trial balance.

Problem 4-3A

Making adjusting entries, preparing financial statements, and calculating profit margin

P1 P3 A1 A2

S

THOMAS TECHNICAL INSTITUTE Unadjusted Trial Balance December 31, 2002		
Cash	$ 34,000	
Accounts receivable	0	
Teaching supplies	8,000	
Prepaid insurance	12,000	
Prepaid rent	3,000	
Professional library	35,000	
Accumulated depreciation—Professional library		$ 10,000
Equipment	80,000	
Accumulated depreciation—Equipment		15,000
Accounts payable		26,000
Salaries payable		0
Unearned training fees		12,500
J. Thomas, Capital		70,000
J. Thomas, Withdrawals	30,000	
Tuition fees earned		123,900
Training fees earned		40,000
Depreciation expense—Professional library	0	
Depreciation expense—Equipment	0	
Salaries expense	50,000	
Insurance expense	0	
Rent expense	33,000	
Teaching supplies expense	0	
Advertising expense	6,000	
Utilities expense	6,400	
Totals	$ 297,400	$ 297,400

Additional Items

a. An analysis of the company's insurance policies shows that $2,400 of coverage has expired.

b. An inventory shows that teaching supplies costing $2,800 are available at year-end.

c. Annual depreciation on the equipment is $13,200.

12,500

d. Annual depreciation on the professional library is $7,200.

e. On November 1, the company agreed to do a special six-month course for a client. The contract calls for a monthly fee of $2,500, and the client paid the first five months' fees in advance. When the cash was received, the Unearned Training Fees account was credited. The fee for the sixth month will be recorded when it is collected in 2003.

2.5

f. On October 15, the school agreed to teach a four-month class for an individual for $3,000 tuition per month payable at the end of the class. The services are being provided as agreed, and no payment has been received. (*Hint:* The class began on October 15.)

g. The school's two employees are paid weekly. As of the end of the year, two days' wages have accrued at the rate of $100 per day for each employee.

h. The balance in the Prepaid Rent account represents rent for December.

Required

1. Prepare T-accounts with the balances from the unadjusted trial balance.

2. Prepare adjusting journal entries for items (a) through (h) and post them to the T-accounts. Assume adjusting entries are made only at year-end.

3. Update balances in the T-accounts for the adjusting entries and prepare an adjusted trial balance.

Check Ending owner's equity, $89,600

4. Prepare Thomas Technical Institute's income statement and statement of changes in owner's equity for the year 2002 and prepare its balance sheet as of December 31, 2002.

5. Calculate the company's profit margin for the year. The owner does not work in the company.

Problem 4-4A

Interpreting unadjusted and adjusted trial balances, preparing financial statements, and calculating profit margin

A six-column table for JLK Company follows. The first two columns contain the unadjusted trial balance for the company as of July 31, 2002. The last two columns contain the adjusted trial balance as of the same date.

	Unadjusted Trial Balance		Adjustments		Adjusted Trial Balance	
Cash	$ 34,000				$ 34,000	
Accounts receivable	14,000				22,000	
Office supplies	16,000				2,000	
Prepaid insurance	8,540				2,960	
Office equipment	84,000				84,000	
Accum. depreciation—Office equip.		$ 14,000				$ 20,000
Accounts payable		9,100				10,000
Interest payable		0				1,000
Salaries payable		0				7,000
Unearned consulting fees		18,000				15,000
Long-term notes payable		52,000				52,000
J.L. Kane, Capital		40,000				40,000
J.L. Kane, Withdrawals	5,000				5,000	
Consulting fees earned		123,240				134,240
Depreciation expense—Office equip.	0				6,000	
Salaries expense	67,000				74,000	
Interest expense	1,200				2,200	
Insurance expense	0				5,580	
Rent expense	14,500				14,500	
Office supplies expense	0				14,000	
Advertising expense	12,100				13,000	
Totals	$256,340	$256,340			$279,240	$279,240

Required

Preparation Component

1. Prepare the company's income statement and its statement of changes in owner's equity for the year ended July 31, 2002.

2. Prepare the company's balance sheet as of July 31, 2002.

3. Calculate the company's profit margin for the year ended July 31, 2002.

Check Profit margin, 3.7%

Analysis Component

4. Analyze the differences between the unadjusted and adjusted trial balances to determine the adjustments that must have been made. Show the results of your analysis by inserting amounts from this company's adjusting journal entries in the table's two middle columns. Label each adjustment with a letter and provide a short description of it.

The adjusted trial balance for Callahay Company as of December 31, 2002, follows:

Problem 4-5A

Preparing financial statements from the adjusted trial balance and calculating profit margin

	Debit	Credit
Cash.	$ 30,000	
Accounts receivable.	52,000	
Interest receivable	18,000	
Notes receivable (due in 90 days)	168,000	
Office supplies.	16,000	
Automobiles	168,000	
Accumulated depreciation—Automobiles.		$ 50,000
Equipment.	138,000	
Accumulated depreciation—Equipment.		18,000
Land.	78,000	
Accounts payable		96,000
Interest payable.		20,000
Salaries payable.		19,000
Unearned fees.		30,000
Long-term notes payable		138,000
J. Callahay, Capital.		255,800
J. Callahay, Withdrawals.	46,000	
Fees earned		484,000
Interest earned.		24,000
Depreciation expense—Automobiles	26,000	
Depreciation expense—Equipment	18,000	
Salaries expense	188,000	
Wages expense.	40,000	
Interest expense	32,000	
Office supplies expense	34,000	
Advertising expense.	58,000	
Repairs expense—Automobiles.	24,800	
Totals	$1,134,800	$1,134,800

Required

1. Use the information in the adjusted trial balance to prepare (a) the income statement for the year ended December 31, 2002; (b) the statement of changes in owner's equity for the year ended December 31, 2002; and (c) the balance sheet as of December 31, 2002.

Check Total assets, $600,000

2. Assume that J. Callahay's services to the business are valued at $40,000 for the year. Calculate the modified profit margin for year 2002.

Problem 4-6A

Computing accrual income
from cash income

The records for Turf's Up Landscape Co. are kept on the cash basis instead of the accrual basis. The company is now applying for a loan and the bank wants to know what its net income for year 2002 is under the accrual basis. Its income statement for year 2002 under the cash basis follows:

TURF'S UP LANDSCAPE CO. Income Statement (Cash Basis) For Year Ended December 31, 2002	
Revenues	$625,000
Expenses	440,000
Net income	$185,000

Additional information was gathered to help convert the income statement to the accrual basis:

Hint

Cash inflows 2002
+ Accrued revenues 2002
+ Unearned revenues 2001
– Accrued revenues 2001
– Unearned revenues 2002
Accrual revenues 2002

	As of 12/31/2001	As of 12/31/2002
Accrued revenues	$13,000	$17,500
Unearned revenues	67,000	22,000
Accrued expenses	15,700	10,000
Prepaid expenses	28,000	21,700

All prepaid expenses from the beginning of the year have been used or expired, all unearned revenues from the beginning of the year have been earned, and all accrued expenses and accrued revenues from the beginning of the year have been paid or collected.

Required

Check Net income, $233,900

Prepare the accrual basis income statement for year 2002. Provide schedules that explain how you converted from cash revenues and cash expenses to accrual revenues and accrual expenses.

Problem 4-7A[A]

Recording prepaid expenses
and unearned revenues

P1 P4

Quisp Co. had the following transactions in the last two months of its year ended December 31:

Nov. 1   Paid $1,800 cash for future newspaper advertising.
      1   Paid $2,460 cash for 12 months of insurance through October 31 of the following year.
     30   Received $3,600 cash for future services to be provided to a customer.
Dec. 1   Paid $3,000 cash for a consultant's services to be received over the next three months.
     15   Received $7,950 cash for future services to be provided to a customer.
     31   Of the advertising paid for on November 1, $1,200 worth is yet to be used.
     31   A portion of the insurance paid for on November 1 has expired.
     31   Services worth $1,500 are not yet provided to the customer who paid on November 30.
     31   One-third of the consulting services paid for on December 1 have been received.
     31   The company has performed $3,300 of services that the customer paid for on December 15.

Required

Preparation Component

1. Prepare entries for these transactions under the method that records prepaid expenses as assets and records unearned revenues as liabilities. Also prepare adjusting entries at the end of the year.

2. Prepare entries for these transactions under the method that records prepaid expenses as expenses and records unearned revenues as revenues. Also prepare adjusting entries at the end of the year.

Analysis Component

3. Explain why the alternative sets of entries in requirements (1) and (2) do not result in different financial statement amounts.

PROBLEM SET B

Problem 4-1B

Identifying adjusting
entries with
explanations

For each of the following entries, enter the letter of the explanation that most closely describes it in the space beside each entry. (You can use letters more than once.)

a. To record receipt of accrued revenue.

b. To record payment of an accrued expense.

c. To record payment of a prepaid expense.

d. To record this period's depreciation expense.

e. To record this period's earning of prior un-earned revenue.

f. To record this period's use of a prepaid expense.

g. To record an accrued revenue.

h. To record receipt of unearned revenue.

i. To record an accrued expense.

_____	**1.**	Unearned Professional Fees	6,000	
		Professional Fees Earned		6,000
_____	**2.**	Interest Receivable	3,500	
		Interest Revenue		3,500
_____	**3.**	Salaries Payable	9,000	
		Cash		9,000
_____	**4.**	Depreciation Expense	8,000	
		Accumulated Depreciation		8,000
_____	**5.**	Cash	9,000	
		Unearned Professional Fees		9,000
_____	**6.**	Insurance Expense	4,000	
		Prepaid Insurance		4,000
_____	**7.**	Interest Expense	5,000	
		Interest Payable		5,000
_____	**8.**	Cash	1,500	
		Accounts Receivable		1,500
_____	**9.**	Salaries Expense	7,000	
		Salaries Payable		7,000
_____	**10.**	Cash	1,000	
		Interest Receivable		1,000
_____	**11.**	Prepaid Rent	3,000	
		Cash		3,000
_____	**12.**	Rent Expense	7,500	
		Prepaid Rent		7,500

Problem 4-2B
Preparing adjusting and subsequent journal entries

Sanuk Co. follows the practice of recording prepaid expenses and unearned revenues in balance sheet accounts. Sanuk's annual accounting period ends on October 31, 2003. The following information concerns the adjusting entries that need to be recorded as of that date:

a. The Office Supplies account started the fiscal year with a $600 balance. During the fiscal year, the company purchased supplies for $4,570, which was added to the Office Supplies account. The supplies available at October 31 totaled $800.

b. An analysis of the company's insurance policies provided these facts:

Policy	Date of Purchase	Years of Coverage	Cost
A	April 1, 2002	2	$6,000
B	April 1, 2003	3	7,200
C	August 1, 2003	1	1,320

The total premium for each policy was paid in full (for all years) at the purchase date, and the Prepaid Insurance account was debited for the full cost.

c. The company has five employees who earn a total of $1,000 for every work day. They are paid each Monday for their work in the five-day workweek ending on the previous Friday. October 31, 2003, falls on Monday, and all five employees worked the first day of that week. They will be paid salaries for five full days on Monday, November 7, 2003.

d. The company purchased a building on November 1, 2002, that cost $175,000 and is expected to have a $40,000 salvage value at the end of its predicted 25-year life.

e. Since the company is not large enough to occupy the entire building, it rented some space to a tenant at $1,000 per month, starting on September 1, 2003. The rent was paid on time on September 1, and the amount received was credited to the Rent Earned account. However, the October rent has not been paid. The company has worked out an agreement with the tenant, who has promised to pay both October and November rent in full on November 15. The tenant has agreed not to fall behind again.

f. On September 1, the company rented space to another tenant for $725 per month. The tenant paid five months' rent in advance on that date. The payment was recorded with a credit to the Unearned Rent account.

Required

Check   Insurance expense, $4,730

1. Use the information to prepare adjusting entries as of October 31, 2003.

2. Prepare journal entries to record the first subsequent cash transaction for both parts (c) and (e).

Problem 4-3B
Preparing adjusting entries, preparing financial statements, and calculating profit margin

Following is the unadjusted trial balance for Triangle Institute as of December 31, 2002, which initially records prepaid expenses and unearned revenues in balance sheet accounts. The institute provides one-on-one training to individuals who pay tuition directly to the business and offers extension training to groups in off-site locations. Shown after the trial balance are items that require adjusting entries as of December 31, 2002.

	File Edit View Insert Format Tools Data Window Help					
	TRIANGLE INSTITUTE **Unadjusted Trial Balance** **December 31, 2002**					
	A	B	C	D	E	F
2	Cash	$ 60,000				
3	Accounts receivable	0				
4	Teaching supplies	70,000				
5	Prepaid insurance	19,000				
6	Prepaid rent	3,800				
7	Professional library	12,000				
8	Accumulated depreciation—Professional library		$ 2,500			
9	Equipment	40,000				
10	Accumulated depreciation—Equipment		20,000			
11	Accounts payable		11,200			
12	Salaries payable		0			
13	Unearned training fees		28,600			
14	Julie Stevens, Capital		69,500			
15	Julie Stevens, Withdrawals	18,000				
16	Tuition fees earned		129,200			
17	Training fees earned		68,000			
18	Depreciation expense—Professional library	0				
19	Depreciation expense—Equipment	0				
20	Salaries expense	44,200				
21	Insurance expense	0				
22	Rent expense	29,600				
23	Teaching supplies expense	0				
24	Advertising expense	19,000				
25	Utilities expense	13,400				
26	Totals	$ 329,000	$ 329,000			

Additional Items

a. An analysis of the institute's insurance policies shows that $9,500 of coverage has expired.

b. An inventory shows that teaching supplies costing $20,000 are available at the end of the year.

c. Annual depreciation on the equipment is $5,000.

d. Annual depreciation on the professional library is $2,400.

e. On November 1, the institute agreed to do a special four-month course for a client. The contract calls for a $5,600 monthly fee, and the client paid the first two months' fees in advance. When the cash was received, the Unearned Training Fees account was credited. The last two months' fees will be recorded when collected in 2003.

f. On October 15, the institute agreed to teach a four-month class to an individual for $2,300 tuition per month payable at the end of the class. The class started on October 15, but no payment has been received.

g. The institute's only employee is paid weekly. As of the end of the year, three days' wages have accrued at the rate of $150 per day.

h. The balance in the Prepaid Rent account represents rent for December.

Required

1. Prepare T-accounts with the balances from the unadjusted trial balance.

2. Prepare adjusting journal entries for items (a) through (h) and post them to the T-accounts.

3. Update balances in the T-accounts for the adjusting entries and prepare an adjusted trial balance.

4. Prepare Triangle Institute's income statement and the statement of changes in owner's equity for the year 2002, and prepare its balance sheet as of December 31, 2002.

Check   Ending owner's equity, $88,300

5. Compute the company's profit margin for the year. The owner does not work for the company.

A six-column table for Daxu Consulting Company follows. The first two columns contain the unadjusted trial balance for the company as of December 31, 2002, and the last two columns contain the adjusted trial balance as of the same date.

Problem 4-4B
Interpreting unadjusted and adjusted trial balances, preparing financial statements, and calculating profit margin

	Unadjusted Trial Balance		Adjustments		Adjusted Trial Balance	
Cash	$ 45,000				$ 45,000	
Accounts receivable	60,000				66,660	
Office supplies	40,000				17,000	
Prepaid insurance	8,200				3,600	
Office equipment	120,000				120,000	
Accumulated depreciation—Office equip.		$ 20,000				$ 30,000
Accounts payable		26,000				32,000
Interest payable		0				2,150
Salaries payable		0				16,000
Unearned consulting fees		40,000				27,800
Long-term notes payable		75,000				75,000
Daxu Chen, Capital		80,200				80,200
Daxu Chen, Withdrawals	20,000				20,000	
Consulting fees earned		234,600				253,460
Depreciation expense—Office equip.	0				10,000	
Salaries expense	112,000				128,000	
Interest expense	8,600				10,750	
Insurance expense	0				4,600	
Rent expense	20,000				20,000	
Office supplies expense	0				23,000	
Advertising expense	42,000				48,000	
Totals	$475,800	$475,800			$516,610	$516,610

Required

Preparation Component

1. Prepare this company's income statement and its statement of changes in owner's equity for the year ended December 31, 2002.

2. Prepare the company's balance sheet as of December 31, 2002.

3. Calculate the company's modified profit margin for the year ended December 31, 2002, assuming the value of the owner's services to the business during the year is $30,000.

Check   Modified profit margin, −8.2%

Analysis Component

4. Analyze the differences between the unadjusted and adjusted trial balances to determine the adjustments that must have been made. Show the results of your analysis by inserting amounts from this company's adjusting journal entries in the table's two middle columns. Label each adjustment with a letter and provide a short description of it.

Problem 4-5B

Preparing financial statements from the adjusted trial balance and calculating profit margin

The adjusted trial balance for Lightning Courier as of December 31, 2002, follows:

	Debit	Credit
Cash	$ 58,000	
Accounts receivable	120,000	
Interest receivable	7,000	
Notes receivable (due in 90 days)	210,000	
Office supplies	22,000	
Trucks	134,000	
Accumulated depreciation—Trucks		$ 58,000
Equipment	270,000	
Accumulated depreciation—Equipment		200,000
Land	100,000	
Accounts payable.		134,000
Interest payable		20,000
Salaries payable.		28,000
Unearned delivery fees		120,000
Long-term notes payable		200,000
J. Hallam, Capital.		125,000
J. Hallam, Withdrawals	50,000	
Delivery fees earned		611,800
Interest earned		34,000
Depreciation expense—Trucks	29,000	
Depreciation expense—Equipment	48,000	
Salaries expense	74,000	
Wages expense	300,000	
Interest expense.	15,000	
Office supplies expense	31,000	
Advertising expense	27,200	
Repairs expense—Trucks	35,600	
Totals	$1,530,800	$1,530,800

Required

Check   Total assets, $663,000

1. Use the information in the adjusted trial balance to prepare (a) the income statement for the year ended December 31, 2002, (b) the statement of changes in owner's equity for the year ended December 31, 2002, and (c) the balance sheet as of December 31, 2002.

2. Assume the services of the owner to the business during year 2002 are valued at $30,000. Calculate the modified profit margin for year 2002.

Problem 4-6B

Computing accrual income from cash income

C3

The records for Web Products are kept on the cash basis instead of the accrual basis. The company is now applying for a loan and the bank wants to know what its net income for year 2002 is under the accrual basis. Its income statement for year 2002 under the cash basis follows:

WEB PRODUCTS **Income Statement (Cash Basis)** **For Year Ended December 31, 2002**	
Revenues	$185,000
Expenses	86,000
Net income	$ 99,000

Additional information was gathered to help convert the income statement to the accrual basis:

	As of 12/31/2001	As of 12/31/2002
Accrued revenues	$13,100	$ 5,600
Unearned revenues	9,050	9,800
Accrued expenses	6,800	13,400
Prepaid expenses	8,300	5,300

Hint
Cash outflows 2002
+ Accrued expenses 2002
+ Prepaid expenses 2001
− Accrued expenses 2001
− Prepaid expenses 2002
Accrual expenses 2002

All prepaid expenses from the beginning of the year are used or expired, all unearned revenues from the beginning of the year are earned, and all accrued expenses and accrued revenues from the beginning of the year are paid or collected.

Required

Prepare the accrual basis income statement for year 2002. Provide schedules that explain how you converted from cash revenues and cash expenses to accrual revenues and accrual expenses.

Check Net income, $81,150

Quake Company had the following transactions in the last two months of its fiscal year ended May 31:

Apr. 1 Paid $2,450 cash for future consulting services.
　　 1 Paid $3,600 cash for 12 months of insurance through March 31 of the following year.
　　30 Received $8,500 cash for future services to be provided to a customer.
May 1 Paid $4,450 cash for future newspaper advertising.
　　23 Received $10,450 cash for future services to be provided to a customer.
　　31 Of the consulting services paid for on April 1, $2,000 worth has been received.
　　31 A portion of the insurance paid for on April 1 has expired. No adjustment was made in April to Prepaid Insurance.
　　31 Services worth $4,600 are not yet provided to the customer who paid on April 30.
　　31 Of the advertising paid for on May 1, $2,050 worth is not yet used.
　　31 The company has performed $5,500 of services that the customer paid for on May 23.

Problem 4-7B[A]

Recording prepaid expenses and unearned revenues

Required

Preparation Component

1. Prepare entries for these transactions under the method that records prepaid expenses and unearned revenues in balance sheet accounts. Also prepare adjusting entries at the end of the year.

2. Prepare entries for these transactions under the method that records prepaid expenses and unearned revenues in income statement accounts. Also prepare adjusting entries at the end of the year.

Analysis Component

3. Explain why the alternative sets of entries in parts (1) and (2) do not result in different financial statement amounts.

---

*(This serial problem involving **Sierra Systems** was introduced in Chapter 3 and continues in Chapters 5 and 6. If the Chapter 3 segment has not been completed, the assignment can begin at this point. You need to use the facts for the serial problem at the end of Chapter 3. Because of its length, this problem is best solved if you use the Working Papers that accompany this book.)*

SERIAL PROBLEM

Sierra Systems

After the success of its first two months, Sela Solstise decides to continue operating Sierra Systems. (Transactions that occurred in these first two months are described in Chapter 3.) On December 1, Solstise adds these new accounts to its chart of accounts:

Account	No.
Accumulated Depreciation—Office equipment	164
Accumulated Depreciation—Computer equipment	168
Wages Payable	210
Unearned Computer Services Revenue	236
Depreciation Expense—Office equipment	612

[continued on next page]

[continued from previous page]

Account	No.
Depreciation Expense—Computer equipment	613
Insurance Expense	637
Rent Expense	640
Computer Supplies Expense	652
Income Summary	901

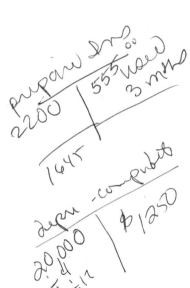

Sierra Systems had the following transactions and events in December 2002:

Dec. 2   Paid $1,025 cash to Hilldale Mall for Sierra Systems' share of mall advertising costs.
    3   Paid $500 cash to repair the company's computer.
    4   Received $3,950 cash from Antonio's Engineering Co. for the receivable from November.
   10   Paid Suzie Smith cash for six days of work at the rate of $125 per day.
   14   Notified by Antonio's Engineering Co. that Sierra's bid of $7,000 on a proposed project has been accepted. Antonio's paid an advance of $1,500 cash.
   15   Purchased $1,100 of computer supplies on credit from Appier Office Products.
   16   Sent a reminder to Foster Co. to pay the fee for services recorded on November 8.
   20   Completed project for Elan Corporation and received $5,625 cash.
22–26   Took the week off for the holidays.
   28   Received $3,000 cash from Foster Co. on its receivable.
   29   Reimbursed Solstise's business automobile mileage (600 miles at $0.32 per mile).
   31   Solstise withdrew $1,500 cash from the business.

The following additional facts are collected for use in making adjusting entries prior to preparing financial statements for the company's first three months:

a. The December 31 inventory of computer supplies is $580.
b. Three months have passed since the annual insurance premium was paid.
c. As of December 31, Suzie Smith has not been paid for four days of work at $125 per day.
d. The company's computer is expected to have a four-year life with no salvage value.
e. The office equipment is expected to have a five-year life with no salvage value.
f. Prepaid rent for three of the four months has expired.

Required

1. Prepare journal entries to record each of the December transactions and events for Sierra Systems. Post entries to the accounts in the ledger.
2. Prepare all necessary adjusting entries. Post these entries to the accounts in the ledger.
3. Prepare an adjusted trial balance as of December 31, 2002.
4. Prepare an income statement for the three months ended December 31, 2002.
5. Prepare a statement of changes in owner's equity for the three months ended December 31, 2002.
6. Prepare a balance sheet as of December 31, 2002.

Check Adjusted trial balance totals, $119,034

Beyond the Numbers

Reporting in Action

C4   A1   A2

NIKE

BTN 4-1   Refer to the financial statements for **Nike** in Appendix A to answer the following questions:
1. What are the major items making up Nike's prepaid expenses listed in its balance sheet?
2. When does Nike recognize its prepaid advertising costs as expenses?
3. What is Nike's profit margin for 2000 and 1999?

Swoosh Ahead

4. Access Nike's annual report for fiscal years ending after May 31, 2000, at its Web site [**www.nike.com**] or the SEC's EDGAR database [**www.sec.gov**]. Compare the May 31, 2000, fiscal year profit margin to any subsequent year's profit margin that you are able to calculate. Also compare the change in Nike's net amount of property, plant, and equipment since May 31, 2000.

BTN 4-2 Key comparative figures ($ millions) for both **Nike** and **Reebok** follow:

Key Figures	Nike		Reebok	
	Current Year	Prior Year	Current Year	Prior Year
Net income ..	$ 579	$ 451	$ 11	$ 24
Net sales ...	8,995	8,777	2,900	3,225

Comparative Analysis

A2

NIKE

Reebok

Required

1. Compute profit margins for (a) Nike and (b) Reebok for the two years of data shown.
2. Which company is more successful on the basis of profit margin?
3. Is it appropriate to calculate the modified profit margin for Nike and/or Reebok?

BTN 4-3 Jackie Houston works for Seitzer Co. She and Bob Welch, her manager, are preparing adjusting entries for annual financial statements. Jackie computes depreciation and records it as

Ethics Challenge

A1

Depreciation Expense—Equipment	123,000	
Accumulated Depreciation—Equipment		123,000

Bob agrees with her computation but says the credit entry should be directly to the Equipment account. He argues that while accumulated depreciation is technically correct, "it is less hassle not to use a contra account and just credit the Equipment account directly. And besides, the balance sheet shows the same amount for total assets under either method."

Required

1. How should depreciation be recorded? Do you support Jackie or Bob?
2. Evaluate the strengths and weaknesses of Bob's reasons for preferring his method.
3. Indicate whether the situation Jackie faces is an ethical problem.

BTN 4-4 Failure to properly apply accounting principles can influence reported profits as well as the success or failure of a business. Read the article, "Anatomy of the Kurzweil Fraud," in the September 1996 issue of *Business Week*. Write a summary that includes the following:

Communicating in Practice

C1 C2 A1

1. Identification of the specific accounting principle that this article discusses and an explanation of what this principle requires and prohibits.
2. A description of the accounting practice for Kurzweil that the article questions.
3. Identification of stakeholders and possible consequences of the questioned accounting practice.
4. An explanation of how this article relates to the material in the chapter.

BTN 4-5 Access the **Cannondale** promotional Web site at **www.cannondale.com.**
1. What is the primary product that Cannondale sells?
2. Review its 10-K, the annual report required by the SEC. You can access this from the Edgar system [**www.sec.gov**]. You must scroll down the form to find the statements.
3. What is Cannondale's fiscal year-end?
4. What are Cannondale's net sales for the annual period ended July 3, 1999?
5. What is Cannondale's net income for the annual period ended July 3, 1999?
6. Compute Cannondale's profit margin ratio for the annual period ended July 3, 1999.
7. Do you think its decision to use a year-end of late June or early July relates to its natural business year?

Taking It to the Net

C1 A2

Teamwork in Action

C2 A1 P1

BTN 4-6   Five types of adjustments are described in the chapter: (1) prepaid expenses, (2) depreciation (part of prepaid), (3) unearned revenues, (4) accrued expenses, and (5) accrued revenues.

Required

1. Form *learning teams* of five (or more) members. Each team member must select one of the five adjustments as an area of expertise (each team must have at least one expert in each area).
2. Form *expert teams* from the individuals who have selected the same area of expertise. Expert teams are to discuss and write a report that each expert will present to his/her learning team addressing the following:
   a. Description of the adjustment and why it's necessary.
   b. Example of a transaction or event, with dates and amounts, that requires adjustment.
   c. Adjusting entry(ies) for the example in requirement (b).
   d. Status of the affected account(s) before and after the adjustment in requirement (c).
   e. Effects on financial statements of not making the adjustment.
3. Each expert should return to his/her learning team. In rotation, each member should present his/her expert team's report to the learning team. Team discussion is encouraged.

Business Week Activity

A2

BTN 4-7   Read the article, "Gaping Holes at the Gap," in the April 24, 2000, issue of *Business Week*.

Required

1. Identify the three different chains owned by **Gap**.
2. What are some of the challenges facing its CEO?
3. Is the sales trend for the **Old Navy** stores positive or negative? What factors are driving the trend you identified?
4. Do the new stores opened in 2000 grow faster or slower than the new stores opened in 1999?
5. Who are Gap's retail competitors cited in the article?

Entrepreneurial Decision

C3

e

BTN 4-8   Robin Drucker operates a collection agency. For a 50% commission, she collects on accounts receivables from her clients' customers who are delinquent in their payments. For example, a company turns over a $100 accounts receivable to Robin. If she can collect the $100 from the customer, then she keeps $50 and remits the other $50 to her client. Robin has more than 100 clients. As her client list has grown, manually accounting for her business activities is becoming increasingly challenging.

Required

1. Why would a company hire a collection agency to pursue its accounts?
2. Robin is trying to decide whether to buy preprogrammed collection software from a major vendor in her industry or hire a programmer to write specialized software tailored exactly to her needs. Identify advantages and disadvantages of packaged versus proprietary software.

5

Completing the Accounting Cycle

A Look Back

Chapter 4 explained the timing of reports. We described why adjusting accounts is important for recognizing revenues and expenses in the proper period. We explained how to prepare an adjusted trial balance and use it in preparing financial statements.

A Look at This Chapter

This chapter emphasizes the final steps in the accounting process and reviews the entire accounting cycle. We explain the closing process, including accounting procedures and the use of a post-closing trial balance. We show how a work sheet aids in preparing financial statements. A classified balance sheet and its use in analyzing information are explained.

A Look Ahead

Chapter 6 looks at accounting for merchandising activities. We describe the sale and purchase of merchandise and their implications for preparing and analyzing financial statements.

Learning Objectives

Explain why temporary accounts are closed each period.

Identify steps in the accounting cycle.

Explain and prepare a classified balance sheet.

Analytical

A1 Compute the current ratio and describe what it reveals about a company's financial condition.

Procedural

P1 Describe and prepare closing entries.

P2 Explain and prepare a post-closing trial balance.

P3 Prepare a work sheet and explain its usefulness.

Red Hat Trick

e DURHAM, NC–Bill Gates, watch your back. Here comes Bob Young. In just four years, the former newsletter publisher has made his company, **Red Hat [RedHat.com]**, the hot name in the growing Linux movement. Linux is *open source* software, meaning it's developed and refined by thousands of individuals in a desire to advance accounting and information services. And, best of all, its free. But unlike Windows or Macintosh systems, Linux doesn't hide computing from the user. That means friendly interfaces and prompts are typically absent. Enter Red Hat. It pastes friendly, easy-to-use interfaces on Linux accounting and other software. While abhorrent to Linux geeks, such improvements are great for entrepreneurs. Especially, according to Young, those interested in "higher-quality, better-priced" accounting software–extending from accounting transaction analysis and recording to financial statement preparation and e-commerce applications.

Still, Young claims he is not out to compete with mighty Microsoft. Instead, he says Red Hat reflects "a revolution" in the accounting software model in favor of users. But you would never guess it from the attention he is getting from the software giant. In confidential memos, Microsoft researchers warned Chairman Bill Gates that Red Hat poses a serious threat. Microsoft lawyers even hoisted a copy of Red Hat's latest release during Microsoft's antitrust trial as proof that it faces plenty of competition. Young does, however, concede a battle between proprietary and open source accounting software. "It is a David and Goliath battle," says Young. "But we are Goliath and Microsoft is David."

Make no mistake, Red Hat is red-hot these days. Young's unwavering brand evangelism, delivered with an aw-shucks twang, and savvy marketing maneuvers has made his company's trademark red fedora synonymous with Linux. As evidence of success, Young's net worth is now reported to exceed $2 billion. Moreover, his company's revenues are projected to exceed $50 million this year. While many challenges remain, many are betting that Red Hat will stay red hot. [Sources: *Business Week*, 10 January 2000, *Linux World*, 24 March 2000 and 25 May 1999; *Red Hat Web site*, May 2001]

Financial statement preparation is a major purpose of accounting. Many of the important steps leading to financial statements were explained in earlier chapters. We described how transactions and events are analyzed, journalized, and posted. We also described important adjustments that are often necessary to properly reflect both revenues when earned and expenses when incurred. This chapter describes the final steps in the accounting process. It explains the closing process that readies revenue, expense, and withdrawal accounts for the next reporting period and updates the capital account. A work sheet is shown as a useful tool in preparing financial statements. We explain how accounts are classified on a balance sheet to increase their usefulness to decision makers. We also describe the current ratio and explain how it is used to assess a company's ability to pay its liabilities in the near future.

Closing Process

C1 Explain why temporary accounts are closed each period.

The **closing process** is an important step at the end of an accounting period *after* financial statements have been completed. It prepares accounts for recording the transactions and the events of the *next* period. In the closing process we must (1) Identify accounts for closing, (2) Record and post the closing entries, (3) Prepare a post-closing trial balance. The purpose of the closing process is twofold. First, it resets revenue, expense, and withdrawal account balances to zero at the end of each period. This is done so that these accounts can properly measure income and withdrawal amounts for the next period. Second, it helps in summarizing a period's revenues and expenses. This section explains the closing process.

Temporary and Permanent Accounts

Temporary Accounts

Revenues
Expenses
Withdrawals
Income Summary

Permanent Accounts

Assets
Liabilities
Capital

Temporary (or *nominal*) **accounts** accumulate data related to one accounting period. They include all income statement accounts, withdrawal accounts, and Income Summary. They are temporary because the accounts are opened at the beginning of a period, used to record events for that period, and then closed at the end of the period. *The closing process applies only to temporary accounts.* **Permanent** (or *real*) **accounts** report on activities related to one or more future accounting periods. They carry their ending balances into the next period and include all balance sheet accounts. Asset, liability, and capital accounts are not closed as long as a company continues to own the assets, owe the liabilities, and have equity.

Recording Closing Entries

P1 Describe and prepare closing entries.

Concept 5-1

To record and post **closing entries** is to transfer the end-of-period balances in revenue, expense, and withdrawal accounts to the permanent owner's capital account. Closing entries are necessary at the end of each period after financial statements are prepared because

- Revenue, expense, and withdrawal accounts must begin each period with zero balances.
- The owner's capital account must reflect (1) increases from revenues and (2) decreases from both expenses and withdrawals.

An income statement aims to report revenues earned and expenses incurred for a specific accounting period. It is prepared from information recorded in revenue and expense accounts. The statement of changes in owner's equity aims to report changes in the owner's capital account for a specific period. It uses information on revenues and expense along with amounts in the withdrawals account. Because revenue, expense, and withdrawal accounts accumulate information for only one period, they must start each period with zero balances.

Point: To understand the closing process, it can help to focus on its *outcomes—updating* the capital account balance to its proper ending balance, and getting *temporary accounts* to show *zero balances* for purposes of accumulating data for the next period.

To close revenue and expense accounts, we transfer their balances first to an account called *Income Summary.* **Income Summary** is a temporary account that contains a credit for the sum of all revenues and a debit for the sum of all expenses. Its balance equals net income or net loss and is transferred to the owner's capital account. We then transfer the withdrawals account balance to the owner's capital account. After these closing entries are posted, the revenue, expense, Income Summary, and withdrawals accounts have zero balances. These accounts are then said to be *closed* or *cleared*. This process is illustrated in Exhibit 5.1.

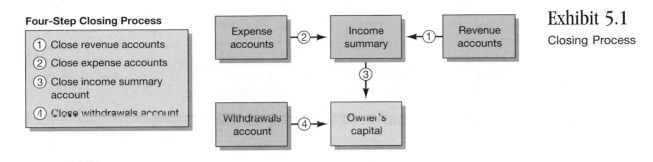

Four-Step Closing Process

① Close revenue accounts

② Close expense accounts

③ Close income summary account

④ Close withdrawals account

Exhibit 5.1

Closing Process

Exhibit 5.2 uses the adjusted account balances of **FastForward** from Exhibit 4.20 (repeated on the left side of Exhibit 5.3) to show the four steps necessary to close its revenue, expense, Income Summary, and withdrawals accounts. We explain each of these four steps.

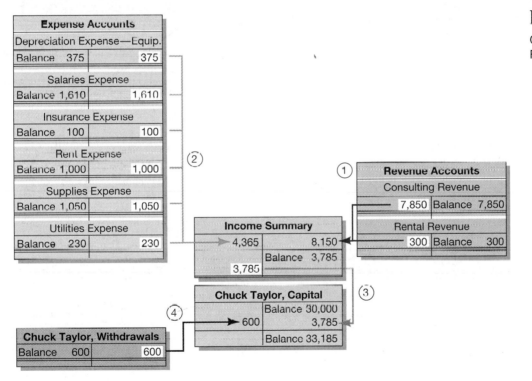

Exhibit 5.2

Closing Entries for FastForward

Step 1: Close Credit Balances in Revenue Accounts to Income Summary

The first closing entry transfers credit balances in revenue accounts to the Income Summary account. We bring accounts with credit balances to zero by debiting them. For FastForward, this journal entry is

Dec. 31	Consulting Revenue	7,850	
	Rental Revenue	300	
	Income Summary		8,150
	To close revenue accounts.		

This entry closes revenue accounts and leaves them with zero balances. They are now ready to record revenues for the next period. The Income Summary account is created and used *only* for the closing process. The current $8,150 credit balance in Income Summary equals total revenues for the period.

Step 2: Close Debit Balances in Expense Accounts to Income Summary

The second closing entry transfers debit balances in expense accounts to the Income Summary account. We bring expense accounts' debit balances to zero by crediting them. With a balance of zero, these accounts are ready to accumulate a record of expenses for the next period. This second closing entry for FastForward is

Dec. 31	Income Summary	4,365	
	Depreciation Expense—Equipment		375
	Salaries Expense		1,610
	Insurance Expense		100
	Rent Expense		1,000
	Supplies Expense		1,050
	Utilities Expense		230
	To close expense accounts.		

Exhibit 5.2 shows that posting this entry gives each expense account a zero balance. The entry also makes the balance of Income Summary equal to December's net income of $3,785. All debit and credit balances related to expense and revenue accounts are now collected in the Income Summary account.

Step 3: Close Income Summary to Owner's Capital

The third closing entry transfers the balance of the Income Summary account to the owner's capital account. This entry closes the Income Summary account and adds the company's net income to the owner's capital account:

Dec. 31	Income Summary	3,785	
	Chuck Taylor, Capital		3,785
	To close the Income Summary account.		

Point: The Income Summary is used only for closing entries.

The Income Summary account has a zero balance after posting this entry. It continues to have a zero balance until the closing process occurs at the end of the next period. The owner's capital account has now been increased by the amount of net income. Increases to owner's capital from net income are credits.

Step 4: Close Withdrawals Account to Owner's Capital

The fourth closing entry transfers any debit balance in the withdrawals account to the owner's capital account. This entry for FastForward is

Dec. 31	Chuck Taylor, Capital	600	
	Chuck Taylor, Withdrawals		600
	To close the withdrawals account.		

This entry gives the withdrawals account a zero balance, and the account is ready to accumulate next period's withdrawals. This entry also reduces the capital account balance to the $33,185 amount reported on the balance sheet in Exhibit 4.22.

Sources of Closing Entry Information

We select the accounts and amounts needing to be closed by identifying individual revenue, expense, and withdrawals accounts in the ledger. If we prepare an adjusted trial balance after the adjusting process, the information for closing entries is readily taken from it. This is illustrated in Exhibit 5.3 where we show how to prepare closing entries using only the adjusted trial balance.

Exhibit 5.3

Preparing Closing Entries from an Adjusted Trial Balance

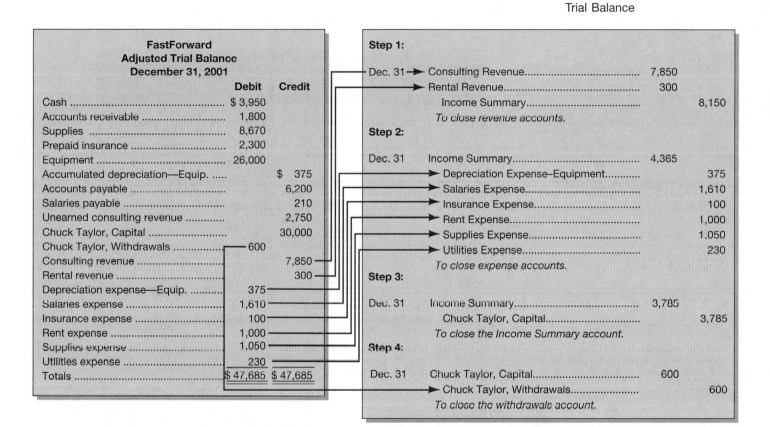

FastForward
Adjusted Trial Balance
December 31, 2001

	Debit	Credit
Cash	$ 3,950	
Accounts receivable	1,800	
Supplies	8,670	
Prepaid insurance	2,300	
Equipment	26,000	
Accumulated depreciation—Equip.		$ 375
Accounts payable		6,200
Salaries payable		210
Unearned consulting revenue		2,750
Chuck Taylor, Capital		30,000
Chuck Taylor, Withdrawals	600	
Consulting revenue		7,850
Rental revenue		300
Depreciation expense—Equip.	375	
Salaries expense	1,610	
Insurance expense	100	
Rent expense	1,000	
Supplies expense	1,050	
Utilities expense	230	
Totals	$ 47,685	$ 47,685

Step 1:

Dec. 31	Consulting Revenue	7,850	
	Rental Revenue	300	
	Income Summary		8,150
	To close revenue accounts.		

Step 2:

Dec. 31	Income Summary	4,365	
	Depreciation Expense–Equipment		375
	Salaries Expense		1,610
	Insurance Expense		100
	Rent Expense		1,000
	Supplies Expense		1,050
	Utilities Expense		230
	To close expense accounts.		

Step 3:

Dec. 31	Income Summary	3,785	
	Chuck Taylor, Capital		3,785
	To close the Income Summary account.		

Step 4:

Dec. 31	Chuck Taylor, Capital	600	
	Chuck Taylor, Withdrawals		600
	To close the withdrawals account.		

A company is usually not able to make all adjusting and closing entries on the last day of each period. Information about some transactions and events that require adjusting is not always available until several days or even weeks later. This means some adjusting and closing entries are recorded later than, but dated as of, the last day of the period. One example is a company that receives a utility bill on January 14 for costs incurred for the month of December. When it receives the bill, the company records the expense and the payable as of December 31. Other examples include long-distance phone usage and costs of many Web billings. The December income statement reflects these additional expenses incurred, and

Did You Know?

Virtual Financial Statements

Leading-edge companies venturing into the information age are seeing changes in the accounting process. Quantum leaps in computing technology are increasing the importance of accounting analysis and interpretation. We are moving toward what Clark Johnson, chief financial officer of **Johnson & Johnson**, calls the "virtual financial statement." This means we can get up-to-date financials with a click of a mouse.

the December 31 balance sheet includes these payables, although the amounts were not actually known on December 31.[1]

Post-Closing Trial Balance

 Explain and prepare a post-closing trial balance.

A **post-closing trial balance** is a list of permanent accounts and their balances from the ledger after all closing entries have been journalized and posted. It lists the balances for all accounts not closed. These accounts are a company's assets, liabilities, and equity, and they are identical to those in the balance sheet. The aim of a post-closing trial balance is to verify that (1) total debits equal total credits for permanent accounts and (2) all temporary accounts have zero balances. **FastForward**'s post-closing trial balance is shown in Exhibit 5.4. The post-closing trial balance is the last step in the accounting process. Like the unadjusted and adjusted trial balances, the post-closing trial balance does not necessarily tell us that all transactions are recorded or the ledger is correct.

Exhibit 5.4

Post-Closing Trial Balance

FASTFORWARD Post-Closing Trial Balance December 31, 2001		
	Debit	**Credit**
Cash	$ 3,950	
Accounts receivable	1,800	
Supplies	8,670	
Prepaid insurance	2,300	
Equipment	26,000	
Accumulated depreciation—Equipment		$ 375
Accounts payable		6,200
Salaries payable		210
Unearned consulting revenue		2,750
C. Taylor, Capital		33,185
Totals	**$42,720**	**$42,720**

Exhibit 5.5 shows the entire ledger of FastForward as of December 31 after adjusting and closing entries are posted. Note the temporary accounts (revenues, expenses, and withdrawals) have balances equal to zero.

Quick Check

1. What are the four major steps in preparing closing entries?

2. Why are revenue and expense accounts called *temporary*? Are there other temporary accounts?

3. What accounts are listed on the post-closing trial balance?

Answers—p. 191

Work Sheet as a Tool

Accountants use various analyses and internal documents when organizing information for reports to internal and external decision makers. Internal documents are important and are often called **working papers.** One widely used working paper is the **work sheet** which is a useful tool for preparers in working with accounting information. It is usually not available to external decision makers.

---

[1] The closing process has focused on proprietorships. It is identical for partnerships with the exception that each owner has separate capital and withdrawals accounts (for steps 3 and 4). The closing process for a corporation is identical with the exception that it uses a Retained Earnings account instead of a capital account (for step 3) and a withdrawals account (for step 4).

Exhibit 5.5

Ledger after the Closing Process for FastForward

General Ledger

Asset Accounts

Cash   Acct. No. 101

Date	Explan.	PR	Debit	Credit	Balance
2001					
Dec. 1		G1	30,000		30,000
2		G1		2,500	27,500
3		G1		26,000	1,500
10		G1	4,200		5,700
12		G1		1,000	4,700
12		G1		700	4,000
22		G1	1,900		5,900
24		G1		900	5,000
24		G1		600	4,400
26		G1	3,000		7,400
26		G1		2,400	5,000
26		G1		120	4,880
26		G1		230	4,650
26		G1		700	3,950

Accounts Receivable   Acct. No. 106

Date	Explan.	PR	Debit	Credit	Balance
2001					
Dec.12		G1	1,900		1,900
22		G1		1,900	0
31	Adj.	G1	1,800		1,800

Supplies   Acct. No. 126

Date	Explan.	PR	Debit	Credit	Balance
2001					
Dec. 2		G1	2,500		2,500
6		G1	7,100		9,600
26		G1	120		9,720
31	Adj.	G1		1,050	8,670

Prepaid Insurance   Acct. No. 128

Date	Explan.	PR	Debit	Credit	Balance
2001					
Dec. 26		G1	2,400		2,400
31	Adj.	G1		100	2,300

Equipment   Acct. No. 167

Date	Explan.	PR	Debit	Credit	Balance
2001					
Dec. 3		G1	26,000		26,000

Accumulated Depreciation— Equipment   Acct. No. 168

Date	Explan.	PR	Debit	Credit	Balance
2001					
Dec. 31	Adj.	G1		375	375

Liability and Equity Accounts

Accounts Payable   Acct. No. 201

Date	Explan.	PR	Debit	Credit	Balance
2001					
Dec. 6		G1		7,100	7,100
24		G1	900		6,200

Salaries Payable   Acct. No. 209

Date	Explan.	PR	Debit	Credit	Balance
2001					
Dec. 31	Adj.	G1		210	210

Unearned Consulting Revenue   Acct. No. 236

Date	Explan.	PR	Debit	Credit	Balance
2001					
Dec. 26		G1		3,000	3,000
31	Adj.	G1	250		2,750

C. Taylor, Capital   Acct. No. 301

Date	Explan.	PR	Debit	Credit	Balance
2001					
Dec. 1		G1		30,000	30,000
31	Closing	G1		3,785	33,785
31	Closing	G1	600		33,185

C. Taylor, Withdrawals   Acct. No. 302

Date	Explan.	PR	Debit	Credit	Balance
2001					
Dec. 24		G1	600		600
31	Closing	G1		600	0

Revenue and Expense Accounts (including Income Summary)

Consulting Revenue   Acct. No. 403

Date	Explan.	PR	Debit	Credit	Balance
2001					
Dec.10		G1		4,200	4,200
12		G1		1,600	5,800
31	Adj.	G1		250	6,050
31	Adj.	G1		1,800	7,850
31	Closing	G1	7,850		0

Rental Revenue   Acct. No. 406

Date	Explan.	PR	Debit	Credit	Balance
2001					
Dec.12		G1		300	300
31	Closing	G1	300		0

Depreciation Expense— Equipment   Acct. No. 612

Date	Explan.	PR	Debit	Credit	Balance
2001					
Dec.31	Adj.	G1	375		375
31	Closing	G1		375	0

Salaries Expense   Acct. No. 622

Date	Explan.	PR	Debit	Credit	Balance
2001					
Dec.12		G1	700		700
26		G1	700		1,400
31	Adj.	G1	210		1,610
31	Closing	G1		1,610	0

Insurance Expense   Acct. No. 637

Date	Explan.	PR	Debit	Credit	Balance
2001					
Dec.31	Adj.	G1	100		100
31	Closing	G1		100	0

Rent Expense   Acct. No. 640

Date	Explan.	PR	Debit	Credit	Balance
2001					
Dec.12		G1	1,000		1,000
31	Closing	G1		1,000	0

Supplies Expense   Acct. No. 652

Date	Explan.	PR	Debit	Credit	Balance
2001					
Dec. 31	Adj.	G1	1,050		1,050
31	Closing	G1		1,050	0

Utilities Expense   Acct. No. 690

Date	Explan.	PR	Debit	Credit	Balance
2001					
Dec. 26		G1	230		230
31	Closing	G1		230	0

Income Summary   Acct. No. 901

Date	Explan.	PR	Debit	Credit	Balance
2001					
Dec. 31	Closing	G1		8,150	8,150
31	Closing	G1	4,365		3,785
31	Closing	G1	3,785		0

Benefits of a Work Sheet

P3 Prepare a work sheet and explain its usefulness.

A work sheet is *not* a required financial report, yet using a manual or electronic work sheet has several potential benefits: (1) Reduces errors when working with systems involving many accounts and adjustments, (2) Links accounts and adjustments to their impacts in financial statements, (3) Assists in planning and organizing an audit of financial statements—it can be used to reflect any adjustments necessary, (4) Is useful in preparing interim (monthly or quarterly) financial statements when the journalizing and posting of adjusting entries are postponed until the year-end, (5) Is helpful in showing the effects of proposed or "what if" transactions.

Did You Know?

Silicon Accounting   An electronic work sheet using spreadsheet software such as **Excel** allows us to easily change numbers, assess the impact of alternative strategies, and quickly prepare financial statements at lower cost. It can also decrease the time devoted to the accounting process and increase the time for analysis and interpretation.

Using a Work Sheet

Point: A work sheet sometimes has two separate columns for the balance sheet and two separate columns for the statement of changes in owner's equity.

When a work sheet is used to prepare financial statements, it is constructed at the end of a period before the adjusting process. The work sheet includes a listing of the accounts, their balances and adjustments, and their sorting into financial statement columns. Exhibit 5.6 shows the form of a work sheet and the five steps in preparing it. The work sheet provides two columns each for the unadjusted trial balance, the adjustments, the adjusted trial balance, the income statement, and the balance sheet (including the statement of changes in owner's equity).

Exhibit 5.6

Form and Preparation of a Work Sheet

To describe and interpret the work sheet, we use the information from **FastForward**. Preparing the work sheet has five important steps. Each step, 1 through 5, is color-coded and explained with reference to Exhibits 5.7 and 5.8.[2]

---

[2] The *Ready Slides* PowerPoint presentation mimics this acetate overlay.

① Step 1. Enter Unadjusted Trial Balance

Refer to Exhibit 5.7. The first step in preparing a work sheet is to list the title of every account that is expected to appear on the company's financial statements.[3] The unadjusted balance for each account in the ledger is recorded in the appropriate Debit or Credit column of the unadjusted trial balance. The totals of these two columns must be equal. Exhibit 5.7 shows FastForward's work sheet after completing this first step. The unadjusted trial balance reflects the account balances after the December transactions are recorded but *before any adjusting entries are journalized and posted.* Sometimes blank lines are left on the work sheet based on past experience to indicate where lines will be needed for adjustments to certain accounts. Exhibit 5.7 shows Consulting Revenue as one example. An alternative is to squeeze adjustments on one line or to combine the effects of two or more adjustments in one amount.

② Step 2. Enter Adjustments

Refer to Exhibit 5.8a (turn over first transparency). The second step in preparing a work sheet is to enter adjustments in the Adjustments columns, as shown in Exhibit 5.8a. The adjustments shown are the same ones we discussed in Exhibit 4.20. An identifying letter links the debit and credit of each adjusting entry. This is called *keying* the adjustments. After preparing a work sheet, we still must enter adjusting entries in the journal and post them to the ledger.

Point: A recordkeeper often can complete the procedural task of journalizing and posting adjusting entries by using a work sheet and the guidance that *keying* provides.

③ Step 3. Prepare Adjusted Trial Balance

Refer to Exhibit 5.8b (turn over second transparency). The adjusted trial balance is prepared by combining the adjustments with the unadjusted balances for each account. As an example, the Prepaid Insurance account has a $2,400 debit balance in the Unadjusted Trial Balance columns. This $2,400 debit is combined with the $100 credit in the Adjustments columns to give Prepaid Insurance a $2,300 debit in the Adjusted Trial Balance columns. The totals of the Adjusted Trial Balance columns confirm the equality of debits and credits.

Point: To avoid omitting the transfer of an account balance, start with the first line (cash) and continue in account order.

④ Step 4. Sort Adjusted Trial Balance Amounts to Financial Statements

Refer to Exhibit 5.8c (turn over third transparency). This step involves sorting account balances in the adjusted trial balance to their proper financial statement columns. Expenses go to the Income Statement Debit column and revenues to the Income Statement Credit column. Assets and withdrawals go to the Balance Sheet & Statement of Changes in Owner's Equity Debit column. Liabilities and owner's capital go to the Balance Sheet & Statement of Changes in Owner's Equity Credit column.

⑤ Step 5. Total Statement Columns, Compute Income or Loss, and Balance Columns

Refer to Exhibit 5.8d (turn over fourth transparency). Each financial statement column (from Step 4) is totaled. The difference between the totals of the Income Statement columns is net income or net loss. This occurs because revenues are entered in the Credit column and expenses in the Debit column. If the Credit total exceeds the Debit total, there is net income. If the Debit total exceeds the Credit total, there is a net loss. For FastForward, the Credit total exceeds the Debit total, giving a $3,785 net income.

The net income from the Income Statement columns is then entered in the Balance Sheet & Statement of Changes in Owner's Equity Credit column. Adding net income to the last Credit column implies it is to be added to owner's capital. If a loss occurs, it is added to the Debit column. This implies it is to be subtracted from owner's capital. The ending balance of owner's capital does not appear in the last two columns as a single amount, but it is computed as the owner's capital account balance *plus* net income (or minus net loss) and

(continued on p. 180)

---

[3] This includes all accounts in the ledger plus any new ones from adjusting entries. Most adjusting entries—including expenses from salaries, supplies, depreciation, and insurance—are predictable and recurring. In the unusual case when an account is not predicted, we can add a new line for such an account following the *Totals* line for the adjusted trial balance.

Exhibit 5.7

Work Sheet with Unadjusted Trial Balance

File Edit View Insert Format Tools Data Window Help

Exhibit 5-7

No.	Account	Unadjusted Trial Balance Dr.	Unadjusted Trial Balance Cr.	Adjustments Dr.	Adjustments Cr.	Adjusted Trial Balance Dr.	Adjusted Trial Balance Cr.	Income Statement Dr.	Income Statement Cr.	Balance Sheet & Statement of Changes in Owner's Equity Dr.	Balance Sheet & Statement of Changes in Owner's Equity Cr.
	FastForward										
	Work Sheet										
	For Month Ended December 31, 2001										
101	Cash	3,950									
106	Accounts receivable	0									
126	Supplies	9,720									
128	Prepaid insurance	2,400									
167	Equipment	26,000									
168	Accumulated depreciation—Equip.		0								
201	Accounts payable		6,200								
209	Salaries payable		0								
236	Unearned consulting revenue		3,000								
301	Chuck Taylor, Capital		30,000								
302	Chuck Taylor, Withdrawals	600									
403	Consulting revenue		5,800								
406	Rental revenue		300								
612	Depreciation expense—Equip.	0									
622	Salaries expense	1,400									
637	Insurance expense	0									
640	Rent expense	1,000									
652	Supplies expense	0									
690	Utilities expense	230									
	Totals	45,300	45,300								

Sheet1 / Sheet2 / Sheet3

List all accounts from the ledger and those expected to arise from adjusting entries.

A worksheet collects and summarizes information used to prepare adjusting entries, financial statements, and closing entries.

Enter all amounts available from ledger accounts. Column totals must be equal.

FASTFORWARD
Income Statement
For Month Ended December 31, 2001

Revenues		
Consulting revenue	$ 7,850	
Rental revenue	300	
Total revenues		$ 8,150
Expenses		
Depreciation expense—Equip.	375	
Salaries expense	1,610	
Insurance expense	100	
Rent expense	1,000	
Supplies expense	1,050	
Utilities expense	230	
Total expenses		4,365
Net income		$ 3,785

FASTFORWARD
Statement of Changes in Owner's Equity
For Month Ended December 31, 2001

C. Taylor, Capital, December 1		$ 0
Add: Investment by owner	$30,000	
Net income	3,785	33,785
		$33,785
Less: Withdrawals by owner		600
C. Taylor, Capital, December 31		$33,185

FASTFORWARD
Balance Sheet
December 31, 2001

Assets		
Cash		$ 3,950
Accounts receivable		1,800
Supplies		8,670
Prepaid insurance		2,300
Equipment	$26,000	
Accumulated depreciation—Equip.	(375)	25,625
Total assets		$42,345
Liabilities		
Accounts payable		$ 6,200
Salaries payable		210
Unearned consulting revenue		2,750
Total liabilities		$ 9,160
Equity		
C. Taylor, Capital		$33,185
Total liabilities and equity		$42,345

Exhibit 5.9

Financial Statements Prepared from the Work Sheet

minus the withdrawals account balance. When net income or net loss is added to the proper Balance Sheet & Statement of Changes in Owner's Equity column, the totals of the last two columns must balance. If they do not, one or more errors have been made. The error can be mathematical or involve sorting one or more amounts to incorrect columns. A balance in the last two columns is not proof of no errors.

Entering adjustments in the Adjustments columns of a work sheet does not adjust the ledger accounts. Adjusting entries still must be entered in the general journal and posted to ledger accounts. The Adjustments columns provide the information for these entries. The adjustments in Exhibit 5.8a match the adjusting entries we described in Exhibit 4.19. Also, all items in the Income Statement columns must be closed to Income Summary. The resulting net income or loss shown in the Income Summary, along with the withdrawals account from the right-most Debit column, must be closed to owner's capital.

You Make the Call

e

Entrepreneur   You make a printout of the electronic work sheet used to prepare financial statements. There is no depreciation adjustment, yet you own a large amount of equipment. Does the lack of depreciation adjustment concern you?

Answer—p. 190

Work Sheet Application and Analysis

A work sheet does not substitute for financial statements; it is a tool we can use at the end of an accounting period to help organize data and prepare financial statements. FastForward's financial statements are shown in Exhibit 5.9. Its income statement amounts are taken from the Income Statement columns of the work sheet. Similarly, amounts for its balance sheet and its statement of changes in owner's equity are taken from the Balance Sheet & Statement of Changes in Owner's Equity columns of the work sheet. FastForward's statement of cash flows is prepared from the Cash account and supporting documents.

Work sheets are also useful in analyzing the effects of proposed, or what-if, transactions. This is done by entering financial statement amounts in the Unadjusted (what-if) columns. Proposed transactions are then entered in the Adjustments columns. We then compute "adjusted" amounts from these proposed transactions. The extended amounts in the financial statement columns show the effects of these proposed transactions. These financial statement columns yield **pro forma financial statements** because they show the statements *as if* the proposed transactions occurred.

Quick Check

4. Where do we get the amounts to enter in the Unadjusted Trial Balance columns of a work sheet?

5. What are the advantages of using a work sheet to help prepare adjusting entries?

6. What are the overall benefits of a work sheet?

Answers—p. 191

Statement of Cash Flows

The statement of cash flows is usually the final statement prepared. All of **FastForward**'s cash receipts and cash payments are recorded in its Cash account in the ledger. This Cash account holds information about cash flows from operating, investing, and financing activities and is shown in Exhibit 5.10. It reports individual cash transactions that are keyed to the transactions numbered (1) through (16) from Chapter 3.

To prepare the statement of cash flows, we must determine whether a cash flow reflects an operating, investing, or financing activity. We then report amounts in their proper category on the statement of cash flows. FastForward's statement of cash flows is shown in Exhibit 5.11.

Analysis of the Cash account provides a direct means to prepare the statement of cash flows, but this method has two limitations. First, companies often have so many individual cash receipts and disbursements that it is difficult to review them all. Second, the Cash account often does not contain a description of each cash transaction. Chapter 17 explains how to prepare the statement of cash flows when facing these limitations.

Global: Both U.S. and international standards require that cash flows be classified as operating, investing, or financing.

Cash				
Investment by owner (1)	30,000	Purchase of supplies (2)	2,500	
Consulting revenue (5)	4,200	Purchase of equipment (3)	26,000	
Collection of account receivable (9) ..	1,900	Payment of rent (6)	1,000	
Receipts for future services (12)	3,000	Payment of salary (7)	700	
		Payment of account payable (10)	900	
		Withdrawal by owner (11)	600	
		Payment of insurance (13)	2,400	
		Purchase of supplies (14)	120	
		Payment of utilities (15)	230	
		Payment of salary (16)	700	
Balance	**3,950**			

Exhibit 5.10
Cash Account of FastForward

FASTFORWARD Statement of Cash Flows For Month Ended December 31, 2001		
Cash flows from operating activities		
Cash received from clients (5 + 9 + 12)	$ 9,100	
Cash paid for supplies (2 + 10 + 14)	(3,520)	
Cash paid for rent (6)	(1,000)	
Cash paid for insurance (13)	(2,400)	
Cash paid for utilities (15)	(230)	
Cash paid to employee (7 + 16)	(1,400)	
Net cash provided by operating activities		$ 550
Cash flows from investing activities		
Purchase of equipment (3)	(26,000)	
Net cash used by investing activities		(26,000)
Cash flows from financing activities		
Investment by owner (1)	30,000	
Withdrawal by owner (11)	(600)	
Net cash provided by financing activities		29,400
Net increase in cash		$ 3,950
Cash balance, December 1		0
Cash balance, December 31		$ 3,950

*Transaction numbers from Exhibit 5.10 are shown in parentheses.

Exhibit 5.11
Statement of Cash Flows*

Reviewing the Accounting Cycle

The **accounting cycle** refers to the steps in preparing financial statements. It is called a *cycle* because the steps are repeated each reporting period. Exhibit 5.12 shows the 10 steps in the cycle. They are shown in order, beginning with analyzing transactions and ending with a post-closing trial balance or reversing entries. Steps 1 through 3 usually occur regularly as a company enters into transactions. Steps 4 through 9 are done at the end of a period. Reversing entries in step 10 are optional and are explained in Appendix 5A. Detailed descriptions of these steps are in Chapters 3, 4, and 5.

Identify steps in the accounting cycle.

Did You Know?

Data Speedway Five years ago **Sun Microsystems** took almost a month to prepare statements after its year-end. Today, it takes only 24 hours to deliver preliminary figures to key decision makers. What is Sun's secret? Transactions are entered into a network of computers so everyone can share and quickly manage data. This frees its accounting professionals for a more active role in managing and strategizing.

Exhibit 5.12

Steps in the
Accounting Cycle*

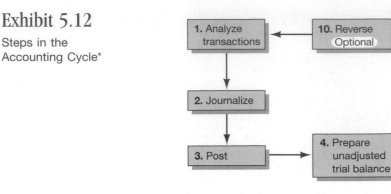

Explanations

Step	Explanation
1. Analyze transaction	Analyze transactions to prepare for journalizing.
2. Journalize	Record accounts, including debits and credits, in a journal.
3. Post	Transfer debits and credits from the journal to the ledger.
4. Prepare unadjusted trial balance	Summarize unadjusted ledger accounts and amounts.
5. Adjust	Record adjustments to bring account balances up to date; journalize and post adjusting entries.
6. Prepare adjusted trial balance	Summarize adjusted ledger accounts and amounts.
7. Prepare statements	Use adjusted trial balance to prepare statements.
8. Close	Journalize and post entries to close temporary accounts and update the owner's capital account.
9. Prepare post-closing trial balance	Test clerical accuracy of the closing procedures.
10. Reverse (optional)	Reverse certain adjustments in the next period—optional step; see Appendix 5A.

*Steps 4, 6, and 9 can be done on a work sheet. A work sheet is useful in planning adjustments, but adjustments (step 5) must always be journalized and posted.

Classified Balance Sheet

C3   Explain and prepare a classified balance sheet.

Our discussion to this point has been limited to unclassified financial statements. But companies also prepare classified financial statements. This section focuses on a classified balance sheet. Chapter 6 describes a classified income statement. An **unclassified balance sheet** is one whose items are broadly grouped into assets, liabilities, and equity. One example is FastForward's balance sheet in Exhibit. 5.9. A **classified balance sheet** organizes assets and liabilities into important subgroups. The information in a balance sheet is more useful to decision makers if assets and liabilities are classified into subgroups. One example is information to distinguish liabilities that are due soon from those not due for several years. This information helps us better assess a company's ability to meet liabilities when they come due.

Exhibit 5.13

Typical Categories in a
Classified Balance Sheet

Assets	Liabilities and Equity
Current assets	Current liabilities
Noncurrent assets	Noncurrent liabilities
Long-term investments	Equity
Plant assets	
Intangible assets	

Concept 5-2

Classification Structure

A classified balance sheet has no required layout. At the very least, it usually contains the categories in Exhibit 5.13. One of the more important classifications is the separation between current and noncurrent items for both assets and liabilities. Current items are those expected to come due (either collected or owed) within the longer of (a) one year or (b) the company's operating cycle. An operating cycle is the length of time between (1) purchases of services or products from suppliers and (2) cash receipts from the sale of services or products to customers. The length of a company's operating cycle depends on its activities. Exhibit 5.14 shows key points in the operating cycle for both a service company and a merchandising company. For a service company, the **operating cycle** is the normal time between (1) paying employees who perform the services and (2)

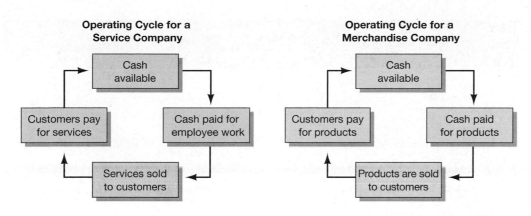

Operating Cycle for a Service Company

Cash available → Cash paid for employee work → Services sold to customers → Customers pay for services → Cash available

Operating Cycle for a Merchandise Company

Cash available → Cash paid for products → Products are sold to customers → Customers pay for products → Cash available

Exhibit 5.14

Operating Cycles for a Service Company and a Merchandise Company

receiving cash from customers. For a merchandiser selling products, the operating cycle is the normal time between (1) paying suppliers for merchandise and (2) receiving cash from customers.

Most operating cycles are less than one year. This means most companies use a one-year period in deciding which assets and liabilities are current. Other companies have an operating cycle longer than one year. For instance, producers of certain beverages (wine) and products (ginseng) that require aging for several years have operating cycles longer than one year. These companies use their multiyear operating cycles in deciding which balance sheet items are current or noncurrent.

A balance sheet usually lists current assets before noncurrent assets and current liabilities before noncurrent liabilities. This consistency in presentation allows users to quickly identify current assets that are most easily converted to cash and current liabilities that are shortly coming due. Items in the current group are usually listed in the order of how quickly they will be converted to, or paid in, cash.

The balance sheet for **Music Components** is shown in Exhibit 5.15. It shows the more typical categories. Its assets are classified as either current or noncurrent. Its noncurrent assets include three main categories: investments, plant assets, and intangible assets. Its liabilities are classified as either current or long term. Not all companies use the same categories of assets and liabilities for their balance sheets. **K2**'s balance sheet lists only three asset classes: current assets; property, plant and equipment; and other assets.

> **Point:** Current is also called *short term*, and noncurrent is also called *long term*.

Classification Categories

This section describes the most common categories in a classified balance sheet.

Current Assets

Current assets are cash and other resources that are expected to be sold, collected, or used within the longer of one year or the company's operating cycle. Examples are cash, short-term investments, accounts receivable, short-term notes receivable, goods for sale (called *merchandise* or *inventory*), and prepaid expenses. A company's prepaid expenses are usually small in amount compared to many other assets and are often combined and shown as a single item. The prepaid expenses in Exhibit 5.15 likely include items such as prepaid insurance, prepaid rent, office supplies, and store supplies. Prepaid expenses are usually listed last because they will not be converted to cash (instead, they are used).

> **Point:** Short-term investments maturing within three months are combined with cash on both the balance sheet and cash flow statement. This combination is called *cash and cash equivalents.*

Long-Term Investments

A second major balance sheet classification is **long-term** (or *noncurrent*) **investments.** Notes receivable and investments in stocks and bonds are long-term assets when they are expected to be held for more than the longer of one year or the operating cycle. We further explain the differences between short- and long-term investments later in the book.

> **Global:** In the U.K. and many countries influenced by U.K. reporting, noncurrent assets are listed first and current assets are listed last.

Exhibit 5.15

Typical Example of a
Classified Balance Sheet

MUSIC COMPONENTS Balance Sheet January 31, 2002			
Assets			
Current assets			
Cash		$ 6,500	
Short-term investments		2,100	
Accounts receivable		4,400	
Merchandise inventory		27,500	
Prepaid expenses		2,400	
Total current assets			$ 42,900
Long-term investments			
Notes receivable		1,500	
Disney common stock		18,000	
Land held for future expansion		48,000	
Total investments			67,500
Plant assets			
Store equipment	$ 33,200		
Less accumulated depreciation	8,000	25,200	
Buildings	170,000		
Less accumulated depreciation	45,000	125,000	
Land		73,200	
Total plant assets			223,400
Intangible assets			10,000
Total assets			$343,800
Liabilities			
Current liabilities			
Accounts payable		$15,300	
Wages payable		3,200	
Notes payable		3,000	
Current portion of long-term liabilities		7,500	
Total current liabilities			$ 29,000
Long-term liabilities (net of current portion)			150,000
Total liabilities			$179,000
Equity			
D. Bowie, Capital			164,800
Total liabilities and equity			$343,800

Point: Plant assets are also called **fixed assets** and **property, plant and equipment.**

Plant Assets

Plant assets are tangible long-lived assets used to help produce or sell products and services. Examples are equipment, vehicles, buildings, and land. Items in this category are both *long lived* and *used to produce* or *sell products and services*. For example, land held for future expansion is *not* a plant asset because it is not used to produce or sell products and services. The order of listing plant assets is usually from most liquid to least liquid such as equipment and machinery to buildings and land.

Intangible Assets

Intangible assets are long-term resources used to produce or sell products and services. They usually lack physical form and have uncertain benefits. Examples are patents, trademarks, copyrights, franchises, and goodwill. Their value comes from the privileges or rights granted to or held by the owner. **Outboard Marine** reports intangible assets of $79.3 million, which is nearly 10 percent of its total assets. Its intangibles include trademarks, patents, and its dealer network.

Current Liabilities

Current liabilities are obligations due to be paid or settled within the longer of one year or the operating cycle. They are usually settled by paying out current assets such as cash. Current liabilities often include accounts payable, notes payable, wages payable, taxes payable, interest payable, and unearned revenues. Also, any portion of a long-term liability due to be paid within the longer of one year or the operating cycle is a current liability—Exhibit 5.15 shows an example. Unearned revenues are current liabilities when they will be settled by delivering products or services within the longer of the year or the operating cycle. Although practice varies, current liabilities are often reported in the order of those to be settled first.

Long-Term Liabilities

Long-term liabilities are obligations *not* due within the longer of one year or the operating cycle. Notes payable, mortgages payable, bonds payable, and lease obligations are common long-term liabilities. If a company has both short- and long-term items in one of these accounts, they are commonly separated into two accounts in the ledger.

Equity

Owner's equity is the owner's claim on a proprietorship's assets. It is reported in the equity section with an owner's capital account. For a partnership, the equity section reports a capital account for each partner. For a corporation, the equity section is divided into two main subsections, capital stock and retained earnings. Chapter 2 described these alternative organization forms and their implications for financial reporting.

> **Point:** Companies sometimes have intangible assets but because of materiality or cost principles, they are not reported.

> **Point:** Many financial ratios are distorted if accounts are not classified correctly. We must be especially careful when analyzing accounts whose balances are separated into short and long term.

> **Point** Many companies report two or more categories of long-term liabilities. See the balance sheets in Appendix A for examples.

Quick Check

7. Identify which of the following assets are classified as (1) current assets or (2) plant assets: (a) land used in operations, (b) office supplies, (c) receivables from customers due in 10 months, (d) insurance protection for the next nine months, (e) trucks used to provide services to customers, (f) trademarks.

8. Cite two examples of assets classified as investments on the balance sheet.

9. Explain the operating cycle for a service company.

Answers—p. 191

Current Ratio   **Using the Information**

An important use of financial statements is to aid in assessing a company's ability to pay its debts in the near future. This type of analysis affects decisions by suppliers when allowing a company to buy on credit. It also affects decisions by creditors when lending money to a company, including loan terms such as interest rate, due date, and collateral requirements. It can also affect a manager's decisions about using cash to pay existing debts when they come due. The **current ratio** is an important measure of a company's ability to pay its short-term obligations. It is defined in Exhibit 5.16 as current assets divided by current liabilities:

$$\text{Current ratio} = \frac{\text{Current assets}}{\text{Current liabilities}}$$

Using financial information from **Ben & Jerry**'s, we compute its current ratios for a recent four-year period. The results are shown in Exhibit 5.17.

> **A1** Compute the current ratio and describe what it reveals about a company's financial condition.

Exhibit 5.16

Current Ratio

Exhibit 5.17

Ben & Jerry's Current Ratio

($ in Millions)	1999	1998	1997	1996
Total current assets	$87.3	$82.3	$80.1	$68.1
Total current liabilities	$44.5	$33.9	$28.7	$18.1
Current ratio	**2.0**	**2.4**	**2.8**	**3.8**
Industry current ratio	1.8	2.1	2.3	2.2

Ben & Jerry's current ratio dipped to 2.0 in 1999 compared to higher ratios for prior years. Still, the current ratio for all of these years suggests that its short-term obligations can be covered with its short-term assets. If the ratio moved closer to 1, Ben & Jerry's would expect to face more challenges in covering liabilities. If the ratio were *less* than 1, Ben & Jerry's current liabilities would exceed its current assets, and it would likely face problems in covering current liabilities. However, in this case, Ben & Jerry's current ratio implies that its ability to pay short-term obligations is good.

You Make the Call

Analyst You are analyzing the financial condition of a fitness club to assess its ability to meet upcoming loan payments. You compute its current ratio as 1.2. You also find that a major portion of accounts receivable is due from one client who has not made any payments in the past 12 months. Removing this receivable from current assets drops the current ratio to 0.7. What do you conclude?

Answer—p. 191

Demonstration Problem

Following is the partial work sheet of Midtown Repair Company at December 31, 2002:

	Adjusted Trial Balance		Income Statement		Balance Sheet and Statement of Changes in Owner's Equity	
	Debit	**Credit**	**Debit**	**Credit**	**Debit**	**Credit**
Cash	95,600					
Notes receivable	50,000					
Prepaid insurance	16,000					
Prepaid rent	4,000					
Equipment	170,000					
Accumulated depreciation—Equipment		57,000				
Accounts payable		52,000				
Long-term notes payable		63,000				
C. Trout, Capital		178,500				
C. Trout, Withdrawals	30,000					
Repair services revenue		180,800				
Interest earned		7,500				
Depreciation expense—Equipment	28,500					
Wages expense	85,000					
Rent expense	48,000					
Insurance expense	6,000					
Interest expense	5,700					
Totals	538,800	538,800				

Required

1. Complete the work sheet by extending the adjusted trial balance totals to the appropriate financial statement columns.

2. Prepare closing entries for Midtown Repair Company.

3. Set up the Income Summary and the C. Trout, Capital account in the general ledger and post the closing entries to these accounts.

4. Determine the balance of the C. Trout, Capital account to be reported on the December 31, 2002 balance sheet.

Planning the Solution

- Extend the adjusted trial balance account balances to the appropriate financial statement columns.
- Prepare entries to close the revenue accounts to Income Summary, to close the expense accounts to Income Summary, to close Income Summary to the capital account, and to close the withdrawals account to the capital account.
- Post the first and second closing entries to the Income Summary account. Examine the balance of income summary and verify that it agrees with the net income shown on the work sheet.
- Post the third and fourth closing entries to the capital account.

Solution to Demonstration Problem

1. Completing the work sheet:

	Adjusted Trial Balance		Income Statement		Balance Sheet and Statement of Changes in Owner's Equity	
	Debit	**Credit**	**Debit**	**Credit**	**Debit**	**Credit**
Cash	95,600				95,600	
Notes receivable	50,000				50,000	
Prepaid insurance	16,000				16,000	
Prepaid rent	4,000				4,000	
Equipment	170,000				170,000	
Accumulated depreciation—Equipment		57,000				57,000
Accounts payable		52,000				52,000
Long-term notes payable		63,000				63,000
C. Trout, Capital		178,500				178,500
C. Trout, Withdrawals	30,000				30,000	
Repair services revenue		180,800		180,800		
Interest earned		7,500		7,500		
Depreciation expense—Equipment	28,500		28,500			
Wages expense	85,000		85,000			
Rent expense	48,000		48,000			
Insurance expense	6,000		6,000			
Interest expense	5,700		5,700			
Totals	538,800	538,800	173,200	188,300	365,600	350,500
Net Income			15,100			15,100
Totals			188,300	188,300	365,600	365,600

2. Closing entries:

Dec. 31	Repair Services Revenue	180,800	
	Interest Earned	7,500	
	Income Summary		188,300
	To close revenue accounts.		

[continued on next page]

[continued from previous page]

Dec. 31	Income Summary	173,200	
	Depreciation Expense—Equipment		28,500
	Wages Expense		85,000
	Rent Expense		48,000
	Insurance Expense		6,000
	Interest Expense		5,700
	To close expense accounts.		
Dec. 31	Income Summary	15,100	
	C. Trout, Capital		15,100
	To close the Income Summary account.		
Dec. 31	C. Trout, Capital	30,000	
	C. Trout, Withdrawals		30,000
	To close the withdrawals account.		

3. Set up the Income Summary and the capital ledger accounts and post the closing entries.

Income Summary						Account No. 901
Date	**Explanation**	**PR**	**Debit**	**Credit**	**Balance**	
2002						
Jan. 1	Beginning balance				0	
Dec. 31	Close revenue accounts			188,300	188,300	
31	Close expense accounts		173,200		15,100	
31	Close income summary		15,100		0	

C. Trout, Capital						Account No. 301
Date	**Explanation**	**PR**	**Debit**	**Credit**	**Balance**	
2002						
Jan. 1	Beginning balance				178,500	
Dec. 31	Close Income Summary			15,100	193,600	
31	Close C. Trout, Withdrawals		30,000		163,600	

4. The final capital balance of $163,600 [from part (3)] will be reported on the December 31, 2002 balance sheet. The final capital balance reflects the increase due to the net income earned during the year and the decrease for the owner's withdrawals during the year.

APPENDIX

5A   Reversing Entries

This appendix describes the use of reversing entries in accounting.

Reversing Entries

Point: As a general rule, adjusting entries that create new asset or liability accounts are likely candidates for reversing.

Reversing entries are optional. They are linked to accrued assets and liabilities that were created by adjusting entries at the end of a reporting period. The purpose of reversing entries is to simplify a company's recordkeeping. Exhibit 5A.1 shows how reversing entries work for **FastForward**. The top of the exhibit shows the adjusting entry FastForward recorded on December 31 for its employee's earned but unpaid salary. The entry recorded three days' salary of $210, which increased December's total salary expense to $1,610. The entry also recognized a liability of $210. The expense is reported on December's income statement. The expense account is then closed. The ledger on January 1, 2002, shows a $210 liability and a zero balance in the Salaries Expense account. At this point, the choice is made between using or not using reversing entries.

Accounting *without* Reversing Entries

The path down the left side of Exhibit 5A.1 is described in detail in Chapter 4. To summarize here, when the next payday occurs on January 9, we record payment with a compound entry that debits both the expense and liability accounts and credits Cash. Posting that entry creates a $490 balance in

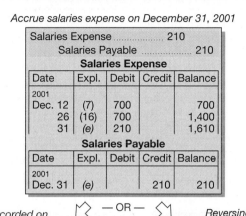

Exhibit 5A.1

Reversing Entries for Accrued Expenses

Accrue salaries expense on December 31, 2001

Salaries Expense 210
    Salaries Payable 210

Salaries Expense

Date	Expl.	Debit	Credit	Balance
2001				
Dec. 12	(7)	700		700
26	(16)	700		1,400
31	(e)	210		1,610

Salaries Payable

Date	Expl.	Debit	Credit	Balance
2001				
Dec. 31	(e)		210	210

— OR —

No reversing entry recorded on January 1, 2002

NO ENTRY

Salaries Expense

Date	Expl.	Debit	Credit	Balance
2002				

Salaries Payable

Date	Expl.	Debit	Credit	Balance
2001				
Dec. 31	(e)		210	210
2002				

Reversing entry recorded on January 1, 2002

Salaries Payable 210
    Salaries Expense 210

Salaries Expense*

Date	Expl.	Debit	Credit	Balance
2002				
Jan. 1			210	(210)

Salaries Payable

Date	Expl.	Debit	Credit	Balance
2001				
Dec. 31	(e)		210	210
2002				
Jan. 1		210		0

Pay the accrued and current salaries on January 9, the first payday in 2002

Salaries Expense 490
Salaries Payable 210
    Cash 700

Salaries Expense

Date	Expl.	Debit	Credit	Balance
2002				
Jan. 9		490		490

Salaries Payable

Date	Expl.	Debit	Credit	Balance
2001				
Dec. 31	(e)		210	210
2002				
Jan. 9		210		0

Salaries Expense 700
    Cash 700

Salaries Expense*

Date	Expl.	Debit	Credit	Balance
2002				
Jan. 1			210	(210)
Jan. 9		700		490

Salaries Payable

Date	Expl.	Debit	Credit	Balance
2001				
Dec. 31	(e)		210	210
2002				
Jan. 1		210		0

Under both approaches, the expense and liability accounts have identical balances after the cash payment on January 9.

Salaries Expense $490
Salaries Payable .... $ 0

*Circled numbers in the *Balance* column indicate abnormal balances.

the expense account and reduces the liability account balance to zero because the debt has been settled. The disadvantage of this approach is the slightly more complex entry required on January 9. Paying the accrued liability means that this entry differs from the routine entries made on all other paydays. To construct the proper entry on January 9, we must recall the effect of the December 31 adjusting entry. Reversing entries overcome this disadvantage.

Accounting *with* Reversing Entries

Prepare reversing entries and explain their purpose.

The right side of Exhibit 5A.1 shows how a reversing entry on January 1 overcomes the disadvantage of the January 9 entry when not using reversing entries. A reversing entry is the exact opposite of an adjusting entry. For FastForward, the Salaries Payable liability account is debited for $210, meaning that this account now has a zero balance after the entry is posted. The Salaries Payable account temporarily understates the liability, but this is not a problem since financial statements are not prepared before the liability is settled on January 9. The credit to the Salaries Expense account is unusual because it gives the account an *abnormal credit balance*. We highlight an abnormal balance by circling it. Because of the reversing entry, the January 9 entry to record payment is straightforward. This entry debits the Salaries Expense account and credits Cash for the full $700 paid. It is the same as all other entries made to record 10 day's salary for the employee. Notice that after the payment entry is posted, the Salaries Expense account has a $490 balance that reflects seven days' salary of $70 per day, (see the lower right side of Exhibit 5A.1). The zero balance in the Salaries Payable account is now correct.

The lower section of Exhibit 5A.1 shows that the expense and liability accounts have exactly the same balances whether reversing entries are used or not. This means both approaches yield identical results.

Summary

C1 **Explain why temporary accounts are closed each period.** Temporary accounts are closed at the end of each accounting period for two main reasons. First, the closing process updates the owner's capital account to include the effects of all transactions and events recorded for the period. Second, it prepares revenue, expense, and withdrawals accounts for the next reporting period by giving them zero balances.

C2 **Identify steps in the accounting cycle.** The accounting cycle consists of 10 steps: (1) analyze transactions, (2) journalize, (3) post, (4) prepare an unadjusted trial balance, (5) adjust accounts, (6) prepare an adjusted trial balance, (7) prepare statements, (8) close, (9) prepare a post-closing trial balance, and (10) prepare (optional) reversing entries.

C3 **Explain and prepare a classified balance sheet.** Classified balance sheets usually report assets and liabilities in two categories: current and noncurrent. Noncurrent assets often include long-term investments, plant and equipment, and intangible assets. Owner's equity for proprietorships and partners' equity for partnerships report the capital account balances. A corporation separates equity into contributed capital and retained earnings.

A1 **Compute the current ratio and describe what it reveals about a company's financial condition.** A company's current ratio is defined as current assets divided by current liabilities. We use it to evaluate a company's ability to pay its current liabilities out of current assets.

P1 **Describe and prepare closing entries.** Closing entries involve four steps: (1) close credit balances in revenue accounts to income summary, (2) close debit balances in expense accounts to income summary, (3) close income summary to owner's capital, and (4) close withdrawals account to owner's capital.

P2 **Explain and prepare a post-closing trial balance.** A post-closing trial balance is a list of permanent accounts and their balances after all closing entries have been journalized and posted. Its purpose is to verify that (1) total debits equal total credits for permanent accounts and (2) all temporary accounts have zero balances.

P3 **Prepare a work sheet and explain its usefulness.** A work sheet can be a useful tool in preparing and analyzing financial statements. It is helpful at the end of a period in preparing adjusting entries, an adjusted trial balance, and financial statements. A work sheet often contains five pairs of columns: Unadjusted Trial Balance, Adjustments, Adjusted Trial Balance, Income Statement, and Balance Sheet and Statement of Changes in Owner's Equity.

P4 **Prepare reversing entries and explain their purpose.** Reversing entries are an optional step. They are applied to accrued assets and liabilities. The purpose of reversing entries is to simplify subsequent journal entries. Financial statements are unaffected by the choice to use or not use reversing entries.

Guidance Answers to **You Make the Call**

Entrepreneur Yes, you are concerned about the absence of a depreciation adjustment. Equipment does depreciate, and financial statements must recognize this occurrence. Its absence suggests an error or a misrepresentation.

Analyst A current ratio of 1.2 suggests that current assets are sufficient to cover current liabilities—but it implies a minimal buffer in case of errors in measuring current assets or liabilities. Removing tardy receivables reduces the current ratio to 0.7. Your assessment is that the club will have difficulty meeting its loan payments.

Guidance Answers to **Quick Checks**

1. The four major steps in preparing closing entries are to close (1) credit balances in revenue accounts to Income Summary, (2) debit balances in expense accounts to Income Summary, (3) Income Summary to owner's capital, and (4) any withdrawals account to owner's capital.

2. Revenue and expense accounts are called *temporary* because they are opened and closed each period. The Income Summary and owner's withdrawals accounts are also temporary.

3. Permanent accounts make up the post-closing trial balance. These accounts are asset, liability, and equity accounts.

4. Amounts in the Unadjusted Trial Balance columns are taken from account balances in the ledger. The balances for new accounts expected to arise from adjusted entries can be left blank or set at zero.

5. A work sheet offers the advantage of listing on one page all necessary information to make adjusting entries.

6. A worksheet can help in (a) avoiding errors, (b) linking transactions and events to their effects in financial statements, (c) showing adjustments for audit purposes, (d) preparing interim financial statements, and (e) showing effects from proposed, or what-if, transactions.

7. Current assets: (b), (c), (d). Plant assets: (a), (e). Item (f) is an intangible asset.

8. Investment in common stock, investment in bonds, land held for future expansion.

9. For a service company, the operating cycle is the usual time between (1) paying employees who do the services and (2) receiving cash from customers for services provided.

Glossary

Accounting cycle recurring steps performed each accounting period, starting with analyzing transactions and continuing through the post-closing trial balance (or reversing entries). (p. 181).

Classified balance sheet balance sheet that presents assets and liabilities in relevant subgroups. (p. 182).

Closing entries entries recorded at the end of each accounting period to transfer end-of-period balances in revenue, expense, and withdrawals accounts to the owner's capital account (p. 170).

Closing process necessary steps to prepare the accounts for recording the transactions of the next period. (p. 170).

Current assets cash or other assets that are expected to be sold, collected, or used within the longer of one year or the company's operating cycle. (p. 183).

Current liabilities obligations due to be paid or settled within the longer of one year or the operating cycle. (p. 185).

Current ratio ratio used to evaluate a company's ability to pay its short-term obligations, calculated by dividing current assets by current liabilities. (p. 185).

Income Summary temporary account used only in the closing process to which the balances of revenue and expense accounts are transferred; its balance is transferred to the owner's capital account. (p. 170).

Intangible assets long-term assets (resources) used to produce or sell products or services; they usually lack physical form and their benefits are uncertain. (p. 184).

Long-term investments assets such as notes receivable and investments in stocks and bonds that are held for more than the longer of one year or the operating cycle. (p. 183).

Long-term liabilities obligations that are not due to be paid within the longer of one year or the operating cycle. (p. 185).

Nominal accounts (*see temporary account*). (p. 170).

Operating cycle normal time between paying cash for merchandise or employee services and receiving cash from customers. (p. 182).

Owner's equity owner's claim on a company's assets. (p. 185).

Permanent accounts accounts used to report activities related to one or more future periods; balance sheet accounts whose balances are not closed; also called *real accounts*. (p. 170).

Plant assets tangible long-lived assets used to produce or sell products or services; also called *property, plant and equipment* or *fixed assets*. (p. 184).

Post-closing trial balance list of permanent accounts and their balances from the ledger after all closing entries are journalized and posted. (p. 174).

Pro forma financial statements statements that show the effects of proposed transactions as if they had occurred. (p. 180).

Real accounts (*see permanent account*). (p. 170).

Reversing entries optional entries recorded at the beginning of a new period that prepare the accounts for the usual journal entries as if adjusting entries had not occurred. (p. 188).

Temporary accounts accounts used to record revenues, expenses, and withdrawals; they are closed at the end of each period; also called *nominal accounts*. (p. 170).

Unclassified balance sheet balance sheet that broadly groups assets, liabilities, and equity accounts. (p. 182).

Working papers analyses and other informal reports prepared by accountants when organizing information for formal reports and financial statements. (p. 174).

Work sheet spreadsheet used to draft an unadjusted trial balance, adjusting entries, adjusted trial balance, and financial statements; an optional step in the accounting process. (p. 174).

[Superscript letter ^{A} denotes assignments based on Appendix 5A.]

Questions

1. What accounts are affected by closing entries? What accounts are not affected?
2. What two purposes are accomplished by recording closing entries?
3. What are the basic four closing entries?
4. What is the purpose of the Income Summary account?
5. Explain whether an error has occurred if a post-closing trial balance includes the account Depreciation Expense—Building.
6. What tasks are aided by a work sheet?
7. Why are the debit and credit entries in the Adjustments columns of the work sheet identified with letters?
8. What is a company's operating cycle?
9. What classes of assets and liabilities are shown on a typical classified balance sheet?

10. How is unearned revenue classified on the balance sheet?
11. What are the characteristics of plant assets?
12.^{A} How do reversing entries simplify a company's recordkeeping?
13.^{A} If a company accrued unpaid salaries expense of $500 at the end of a fiscal year, what reversing entry could be made? When would it be made?
14. Refer to the balance sheet for **Nike** in Appendix A. What percent of Nike's long-term debt is coming due before May 31, 2001?
15. Refer to **Reebok**'s balance sheet in Appendix A. Identify the accounts listed as current liabilities.
16. Refer to **Gap**'s financial statements in Appendix A. What journal entry was likely recorded as of Jan. 29, 2000, to close the company's Income Summary account?

QUICK STUDY

QS 5-1
Identifying the accounting cycle **C2**

List the following steps of the accounting cycle in their proper order:

a. Preparing the post-closing trial balance.
b. Posting the journal entries.
c. Journalizing and posting adjusting entries.
d. Preparing the adjusted trial balance.
e. Journalizing and posting closing entries.
f. Analyzing transactions and events.
g. Preparing the financial statements.
h. Preparing the unadjusted trial balance.
l. Journalizing transactions and events.

QS 5-2
Determining effects of closing entries

C1

Argosy Company began the current period with a $15,000 balance in the Dane Argosy, Capital account. At the end of the period, the company's adjusted account balances include the following temporary accounts with normal balances:

Service fees earned	$36,000	Interest revenue	$4,500
Salaries expense	20,000	Dane Argosy, Withdrawals	7,000
Depreciation expense	5,000	Utilities expense	3,300

After closing revenue and expense accounts, what will be the balance of the Income Summary account? After all closing entries are journalized and posted, what will be the balance of the Dane Argosy Capital account?

QS 5-3
Computing current ratio

A1

Compute Neon Company's current ratio using the following information:

Accounts receivable	$16,000	Long-term notes payable	$21,000
Accounts payable	11,000	Office supplies	2,800
Buildings	43,000	Prepaid insurance	3,500
Cash	7,000	Unearned services revenue	5,000

QS 5-4
Classifying balance sheet items **C3**

The following are common categories on a classified balance sheet:

A. Current assets
B. Long-term investments
C. Plant assets
D. Intangible assets
E. Current liabilities
F. Long-term liabilities

For each of the following items, select the letter that identifies the balance sheet category where the item typically would appear.

_____ **1.** Trademarks   _____ **5.** Cash

_____ **2.** Accounts receivable   _____ **6.** Wages payable

_____ **3.** Land not currently used in operations _____ **7.** Store equipment

_____ **4.** Notes payable (due in three years)   _____ **8.** Accounts payable

---

The following information is taken from the work sheet for Hafka Company as of December 31, 2002. Using this information, determine the amount for S. Hafka, Capital, that should be reported on its December 31, 2002, balance sheet.

QS 5-5

Interpreting a work sheet

P3

	Income Statement		Balance Sheet and Statement of Changes in Owner's Equity	
	Dr.	Cr.	Dr.	Cr.
S. Hafka, Capital				72,000
S. Hafka, Withdrawals			39,000	
Totals	122,000	181,000		

In preparing a work sheet, indicate the financial statement debit column to which a normal balance in the following accounts should be extended. Use IS for the Income Statement Debit column and BS for the Balance Sheet and Statement of Changes in Owner's Equity Debit column.

QS 5-6

Applying a work sheet

P3

_____ **a.** Insurance expense   _____ **d.** Depreciation expense—Equipment

_____ **b.** Equipment   _____ **e.** Prepaid rent

_____ **c.** Owner, Withdrawals   _____ **f.** Accounts receivable

---

On December 31, 2002, Yates Co. prepared an adjusting entry for $7,600 of earned but unrecorded management fees. On January 16, 2003, Yates received $25,500 of management fees, which included the accrued fees earned in 2002. Assuming the company uses reversing entries, prepare the reversing entry and the January 16, 2003, entry.

QS 5-7[A]

Reversing entries

P4

Use information from the following T-accounts to prepare closing journal entries and post them to the T-accounts.

EXERCISES

Exercise 5-1

Preparing and posting closing entries

P1

M. Mallon, Capital		
	Dec. 31	42,000

Rent Expense		
Dec. 31	9,600	

M. Mallon, Withdrawals		
Dec. 31	25,000	

Salaries Expense		
Dec. 31	21,000	

Income Summary		

Insurance Expense		
Dec. 31	4,500	

Services Revenue		
	Dec. 31	74,000

Depreciation Expense		
Dec. 31	17,000	

Exercise 5-2

Preparing
closing entries

The following adjusted trial balance contains the accounts and balances of Clover Company as of December 31, 2002, the end of its fiscal year:

No.	Account Title	Debit	Credit
101	Cash	$19,000	
126	Supplies	13,000	
128	Prepaid insurance	3,000	
167	Equipment	24,000	
168	Accumulated depreciation—Equipment		$ 7,500
301	R. Showers, Capital		47,600
302	R. Showers, Withdrawals	7,000	
404	Services revenue		44,000
612	Depreciation expense—Equipment	3,000	
622	Salaries expense	22,000	
637	Insurance expense	2,500	
640	Rent expense	3,400	
652	Supplies expense	2,200	
	Totals	$99,100	$99,100

Prepare closing entries for Clover Company.

Exercise 5-3

Preparing closing entries and
a post-closing trial balance

The adjusted trial balance for Schwepker Marketing Co. follows. Prepare a table with two columns under each of the following headings: Adjusted Trial Balance, Closing Entries, and Post-Closing Trial Balance. Complete the table by providing four closing entries and the post-closing trial balance.

No.	Account Title	Debit	Credit
101	Cash	$ 9,200	
106	Accounts receivable	25,000	
153	Equipment	42,000	
154	Accumulated depreciation—Equipment		$ 17,500
193	Franchise	31,000	
201	Accounts payable		15,000
209	Salaries payable		4,200
233	Unearned fees		3,600
301	C. Schwepker, Capital		68,500
302	C. Schwepker, Withdrawals	15,400	
401	Marketing fees earned		80,000
611	Depreciation expense—Equipment	12,000	
622	Salaries expense	32,500	
640	Rent expense	13,000	
677	Miscellaneous expenses	8,700	
901	Income summary		
	Totals	$188,800	$188,800

The following balances of Retained Earnings and the temporary accounts are from the adjusted trial balance of Rider, Inc.:

Account Title	Debit	Credit
Retained earnings		$34,600
Services revenue		33,000
Interest earned		6,300
Salaries expense	$26,400	
Insurance expense	4,800	
Rental expense	7,400	
Supplies expense	4,100	
Depreciation expense—Trucks	11,600	

Prepare the closing entries, and then determine the amount of retained earnings to be reported on the company's balance sheet.

Exercise 5-4
Preparing closing entries for a corporation

P1

Use the following adjusted trial balance of Webb Trucking Company to prepare a classified balance sheet as of December 31, 2002.

Account Title	Debit	Credit
Cash	$ 8,000	
Accounts receivable	17,500	
Office supplies	3,000	
Trucks	172,000	
Accumulated depreciation—Trucks		$ 36,000
Land	85,000	
Accounts payable		12,000
Interest payable		4,000
Long-term notes payable		53,000
K. Webb, Capital		175,000
K. Webb, Withdrawals	20,000	
Trucking fees earned		130,000
Depreciation expense—Trucks	23,500	
Salaries expense	61,000	
Office supplies expense	8,000	
Repairs expense—Trucks	12,000	
Total	$410,000	$410,000

Exercise 5-5
Preparing a classified balance sheet

C3

Use the information in the adjusted trial balance reported in Exercise 5-5 to compute the current ratio as of the balance sheet date.

Exercise 5-6
Computing current ratio

Calculate the current ratio in each of the following separate cases:

	Current Assets	Current Liabilities
Case 1	$ 79,000	$ 32,000
Case 2	105,000	76,000
Case 3	45,000	49,000
Case 4	85,500	81,600
Case 5	61,000	100,000

Exercise 5-7
Computing current ratio

Exercise 5-8

Preparing a 10-column worksheet

The following unadjusted trial balance contains the accounts and balances of the Dalton Delivery Company as of December 31, 2002. Use the following information about the company's adjustments to complete a 10-column worksheet for Dalton Delivery.

a. Unrecorded depreciation on the trucks at the end of the year is $40,000.

b. The total amount of incurred but unpaid interest at year-end is $6,000.

c. The cost of unused office supplies still available at the end of the year is $2,000.

	Account Title	Debit	Credit
2	Cash	$ 15,000	
3	Accounts receivable	34,000	
4	Office supplies	5,000	
5	Trucks	350,000	
6	Accumulated depreciation—Trucks		$ 80,000
7	Land	160,000	
8	Accounts payable		24,000
9	Interest payable		5,000
10	Long-term notes payable		100,000
11	V. Dalton, Capital		312,000
12	V. Dalton, Withdrawals	40,000	
13	Delivery fees earned		263,000
14	Depreciation expense—Trucks	40,000	
15	Salaries expense	110,000	
16	Office supplies expense	15,000	
17	Interest expense	5,000	
18	Repairs expense, trucks	10,000	
19	Total	$784,000	$784,000

Exercise 5-9

Preparing adjusting entries from work sheet

Use the following information from the Adjustments columns of a 10-column work sheet to prepare the necessary adjusting journal entries:

		Adjustments	
No.	Account Title	Debit	Credit
109	Interest receivable	(d) $ 880	
124	Office supplies		(b) $ 1,750
128	Prepaid insurance		(a) 900
164	Accumulated depreciation—Office equipment		(c) 2,200
209	Salaries payable		(e) 560
409	Interest revenue		(d) 880
612	Depreciation expense—Office equipment	(c) 2,200	
620	Office salaries expense	(e) 560	
636	Insurance expense, office equipment	(a) 332	
637	Insurance expense, store equipment	(a) 568	
650	Office supplies expense	(b) 1,750	
	Totals	$ 6,290	$ 6,290

Exercise 5-10

Extending adjusted account balances on a work sheet

These 16 accounts are from the Adjusted Trial Balance columns of a company's 10-column work sheet. In the blank space beside each account, write the letter of the appropriate financial statement column (A, B, C, or D) to which a normal account balance is extended.

A. Debit column for the Income Statement columns.

B. Credit column for the Income Statement columns.

C. Debit column for the Balance Sheet and Statement of Changes in Owner's Equity columns.

D. Credit column for the Balance Sheet and Statement of Changes in Owner's Equity columns.

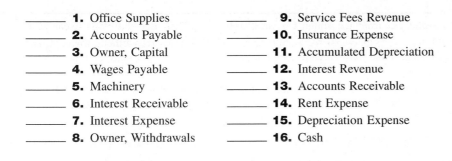

_____	**1.** Office Supplies		_____	**9.** Service Fees Revenue
_____	**2.** Accounts Payable		_____	**10.** Insurance Expense
_____	**3.** Owner, Capital		_____	**11.** Accumulated Depreciation
_____	**4.** Wages Payable		_____	**12.** Interest Revenue
_____	**5.** Machinery		_____	**13.** Accounts Receivable
_____	**6.** Interest Receivable		_____	**14.** Rent Expense
_____	**7.** Interest Expense		_____	**15.** Depreciation Expense
_____	**8.** Owner, Withdrawals		_____	**16.** Cash

The Adjusted Trial Balance columns of a 10-column work sheet for Tara Company follow. Complete the work sheet by extending the account balances into the appropriate financial statement columns and by entering the amount of net income for the reporting period.

Exercise 5-11

Extending accounts in a work sheet

P3

No.	Account Title	Debit	Credit
101	Cash	$ 7,000	
106	Accounts receivable	27,200	
153	Trucks	42,000	
154	Accumulated depreciation—Trucks		$ 17,500
183	Land	32,000	
201	Accounts payable		15,000
209	Salaries payable		4,200
233	Unearned fees		3,600
301	T. Snow, Capital		65,500
302	T. Snow, Withdrawals	15,400	
401	Plumbing fees earned		84,000
611	Depreciation expense—Trucks	6,500	
622	Salaries expense	38,000	
640	Rent expense	13,000	
677	Miscellaneous expenses	8,700	
	Totals	$189,800	$189,800

These partially completed Income Statement columns from a 10-column work sheet are for Red Sail Rental Co. Use the information to determine the amount that should be entered on the net income line of the work sheet. In addition, prepare closing entries for Red Sail Rental. The owner, LeAnn Welch, did not make any withdrawals.

Exercise 5-12

Completing the income statement columns and preparing closing entries

Account Title	Debit	Credit
Rent earned		120,000
Salaries expense	46,300	
Insurance expense	7,400	
Dock rental expense	16,000	
Boat supplies expense	4,200	
Depreciation expense—Boats	20,500	
Totals		
Net income		
Totals		

Exercise 5-13[A]

Preparing reversing entries

P4

The following two events occurred for Totten Co. on October 31, 2002, the end of its fiscal year:

a. Totten rents a building from its owner for $2,800 per month. By a prearrangement, the company delayed paying October's rent until November 5. On this date, the company paid the rent for both October and November.

b. Totten rents space in a building it owns to a tenant for $850 per month. By prearrangement, the tenant delayed paying the October rent until November 8. On this date, the tenant paid the rent for both October and November.

Required

1. Prepare adjusting entries that Totten must record for these events as of October 31.

2. Assuming Totten does *not* use reversing entries, prepare journal entries to record Totten's payment of rent on November 5 and the collection of rent on November 8 from Totten's tenant.

3. Assuming that Totten uses reversing entries, prepare reversing entries on November 1 and the journal entries to record Totten's payment of rent on November 5 and the collection of rent on November 8 from Totten's tenant.

Exercise 5-14[A]

Preparing reversing entries

P4

Hinson Company records prepaid assets and unearned revenues in balance sheet accounts. The following information was used to prepare adjusting entries for Hinson Company as of August 31, the end of the company's fiscal year:

a. The company has earned $6,000 of unrecorded service fees.

b. The expired portion of prepaid insurance is $2,800.

c. Earned $2,000 of the total balance of the Unearned Service Fees account balance.

d. Depreciation expense for office equipment is $2,100.

e. Employees have earned but have not been paid salaries of $2,570.

Prepare necessary reversing entries assuming that Hinson uses reversing entries in its accounting system.

PROBLEM SET A

Problem 5-1A

Applying the accounting cycle

C2   P1   P2

S

On April 1, 2002, Jennifer Stafford created a new travel agency, Ambassador Travel. The following transactions occurred during the company's first month:

April	1	Stafford invested $30,000 cash and computer equipment worth $20,000.
	2	Rented furnished office space by paying $1,800 cash for the first month's rent.
	3	Purchased $1,000 of office supplies for cash.
	10	Paid $2,400 cash for the premium on a one-year insurance policy. Coverage began on April 10.
	14	Paid $1,600 cash for two weeks' salaries to employees.
	24	Collected $8,000 cash on commissions from airlines on tickets obtained for customers.
	28	Paid another $1,600 cash for two weeks' salaries.
	29	Paid this month's $750 telephone bill in cash.
	30	Paid $350 cash to repair the company's computer.
	30	Stafford withdrew $1,500 cash from the business for personal use.

The company's chart of accounts included the following:

101 Cash	405 Commissions Earned
106 Accounts Receivable	612 Depreciation Expense—Computer Equip.
124 Office Supplies	622 Salaries Expense
128 Prepaid Insurance	637 Insurance Expense
167 Computer Equipment	640 Rent Expense
168 Accumulated Depreciation—Computer Equip.	650 Office Supplies Expense
209 Salaries Payable	684 Repairs Expense
301 J. Stafford, Capital	688 Telephone Expense
302 J. Stafford, Withdrawals	901 Income Summary

Required

1. Use the balance column format to set up each account listed in its chart of accounts.

2. Prepare journal entries to record the transactions for April and post them to the accounts. The company records prepaid and unearned items in balance sheet accounts.

3. Prepare an unadjusted trial balance as of April 30.

4. Use the following information to journalize and post adjusting entries for the month:

   a. Two-thirds of one month's insurance coverage has expired.

   b. There are $600 of office supplies available at the end of the month.

   c. Depreciation on the computer equipment is $500.

   d. The employees earned $420 of unpaid and unrecorded salaries.

   e. The company earned $1,750 of commissions that are not yet billed.

5. Prepare the income statement and the statement of changes in owner's equity for April, and the balance sheet at April 30, 2002.

Check   Ending capital balance, $50,697; insurance expense, $133

6. Prepare journal entries to close the temporary accounts and post the entries to the accounts.

7. Prepare a post-closing trial balance.

Sedona Repairs' adjusted trial balance on December 31, 2002, follows:

Problem 5-2A

Preparing closing entries, financial statements, and current ratio

No.	Account Title	Debit	Credit
	SEDONA REPAIRS		
	Adjusted Trial Balance		
	December 31, 2002		
101	Cash	$ 14,000	
124	Office supplies	1,300	
128	Prepaid insurance	2,050	
167	Equipment	50,000	
168	Accumulated depreciation—Equipment		$ 5,000
201	Accounts payable		14,000
210	Wages payable		600
301	K. Brown, Capital		33,000
302	K. Brown, Withdrawals	16,000	
401	Repair fees earned		90,950
612	Depreciation expense—Equipment	5,000	
623	Wages expense	37,500	
637	Insurance expense	800	
640	Rent expense	10,600	
650	Office supplies expense	3,600	
690	Utilities expense	2,700	
	Totals	$143,550	$143,550

Required

Preparation Component

1. Prepare an income statement and a statement of changes in owner's equity for the year 2002, and a classified balance sheet at December 31, 2002. There are no owner investments in 2002.

Check   Ending capital balance, $47,750

2. Enter the adjusted trial balance in the first two columns of a six-column table. Use columns three and four for closing entries and the last two columns for a post-closing trial balance. Insert an Income Summary account as the last item in the trial balance.

3. Enter closing entries in the six-column table and prepare journal entries for them.

4. Determine the company's current ratio.

Analysis Component

5. Assume for Sedona Repairs that:

   a. None of the $800 insurance expense expired during the year. Instead, assume it is a prepayment of future insurance protection.

   b. There are no earned and unpaid wages at the end of the year.

   Describe the financial statement changes that would result from these two assumptions.

Problem 5-3A

Preparing closing entries, financial statements, and ratios

The adjusted trial balance for Sharp Construction as of December 31, 2002, follows:

No.	Account Title	Debit	Credit
	SHARP CONSTRUCTION		
	Adjusted Trial Balance		
	December 31, 2002		
101	Cash	$ 5,000	
104	Short-term investments	23,000	
126	Supplies	8,100	
128	Prepaid insurance	7,000	
167	Equipment	40,000	
168	Accumulated depreciation—Equipment		$ 20,000
173	Building	150,000	
174	Accumulated depreciation—Building		50,000
183	Land	55,000	
201	Accounts payable		16,500
203	Interest payable		2,500
208	Rent payable		3,500
210	Wages payable		2,500
213	Property taxes payable		900
233	Unearned professional fees		7,500
251	Long-term notes payable		67,000
301	J. Sharp, Capital		126,400
302	J. Sharp, Withdrawals	13,000	
401	Professional fees earned		97,000
406	Rent earned		14,000
407	Dividends earned		2,000
409	Interest earned		2,100
606	Depreciation expense—Building	11,000	
612	Depreciation expense—Equipment	6,000	
623	Wages expense	32,000	
633	Interest expense	5,100	
637	Insurance expense	10,000	
640	Rent expense	13,400	
652	Supplies expense	7,400	
682	Postage expense	4,200	
683	Property taxes expense	5,000	
684	Repairs expense	8,900	
688	Telephone expense	3,200	
690	Utilities expense	4,600	
	Totals	$411,900	$411,900

Analysis reveals that Sharp Construction is required to make a $7,000 payment on its long-term note payable during 2003. J. Sharp invested $5,000 cash during year 2002 (the December 31, 2001, balance of the J. Sharp, Capital account was $121,400).

Required

1. Prepare the income statement and the statement of changes in owner's equity for year 2002, and the classified balance sheet at December 31, 2002.
2. Prepare the necessary closing entries at the end of the year 2002.

3. Use the information in the financial statements to calculate these ratios:

   a. Return on equity.

   b. Modified return on equity, assuming the owner's efforts are valued at $4,000 for the year.

   c. Debt ratio.

   d. Profit margin ratio (use total revenues as the denominator).

   e. Current ratio.

This unadjusted trial balance is for Adams Construction Co. as of the end of its 2002 fiscal year. The June 30, 2001, balance of the owner's capital account was $53,660, and the owner invested $35,000 cash in the company during the 2002 fiscal year.

Problem 5-4A

Preparing work sheet, journal entries, financial statements, and current ratio

File Edit View Insert Format Tools Data Window Help

No.	Account Title	Debit	Credit
	ADAMS CONSTRUCTION CO.		
	Unadjusted Trial Balance		
	June 30, 2002		
101	Cash	$ 18,500	
126	Supplies	9,900	
128	Prepaid insurance	7,200	
167	Equipment	132,000	
168	Accumulated depreciation—Equipment		$ 26,250
201	Accounts payable		8,800
203	Interest payable		0
208	Rent payable		0
210	Wages payable		0
213	Property taxes payable		0
251	Long-term notes payable		25,000
301	S. Adams, Capital		88,660
302	S. Adams, Withdrawals	33,000	
401	Construction fees earned		132,100
612	Depreciation expense—Equipment	0	
623	Wages expense	46,860	
633	Interest expense	2,750	
637	Insurance expense	0	
640	Rent expense	12,000	
652	Supplies expense	0	
683	Property taxes expense	7,800	
684	Repairs expense	2,910	
690	Utilities expense	5,890	
	Totals	$ 278,810	$ 278,810

Required

Preparation Component

1. Prepare a 10-column work sheet for fiscal year 2002, starting with the unadjusted trial balance and including adjustments based on these additional facts:

   a. The supplies available at the end of fiscal year 2002 had a cost of $3,300.

   b. The cost of expired insurance for the fiscal year is $3,800.

   c. Annual depreciation on equipment is $8,400.

   d. The June utilities expense of $650 is not included in the unadjusted trial balance because the bill arrived after the trial balance was prepared. The $650 amount owed needs to be recorded.

   e. The company's employees have earned $1,800 of accrued wages at fiscal year-end.

   f. The lease for the office requires the company to pay total rent for the year ended June 30 equal to 10% of the company's annual revenues. Rent has been estimated and is being paid to the building owner with monthly payments of $1,000. If the annual rent owed exceeds the total monthly estimated payments, the company must pay the excess before July 31. If the total owed is less than the amount previously paid, the building owner will refund the difference by July 31.

   g. Additional property taxes of $1,000 have been assessed but have not been paid or recorded in the accounts.

   h. The long-term note payable bears interest at 1% per month, which the company is required to pay by the 10th of the following month. The balance of the Interest Expense account equals the amount paid for the first 11 months of the past fiscal year. The interest for June has not yet been paid or recorded. In addition, the company is required to make a $5,000 payment toward the note payable on August 31, 2002.

2. Use the work sheet to enter the adjusting and closing entries; then journalize them.

3. Prepare the income statement and the statement of changes in owner's equity for the year ended June 30, and the classified balance sheet at June 30. Calculate the company's current ratio.

Check Total assets, $122,550; current liabilities, $16,710

Analysis Component

4. Analyze the following separate errors and describe how each would affect the 10-column work sheet. Explain whether the error is likely to be discovered in completing the work sheet and, if not, the effect of the error on the financial statements.

    a. Assume that the adjustment for supplies used had credited Supplies for $3,300 and debited the same amount to Supplies Expense.

    b. When the adjusted trial balance in the work sheet is completed, the $18,500 cash balance is incorrectly entered in the Credit column.

Problem 5-5A

Determining balance sheet classifications

In the blank space beside each numbered balance sheet item, enter the letter of its balance sheet classification. If the item should not appear on the balance sheet, enter a *Z* in the blank.

A. Current assets   **D.** Intangible assets   **G.** Owner's equity

B. Long-term investments   **E.** Current liabilities   **H.** Stockholders' equity

C. Plant assets   **F.** Long-term liabilities

_____ **1.** Accumulated depreciation— Trucks

_____ **2.** Cash

_____ **3.** Buildings

_____ **4.** Retained earnings

_____ **5.** Office equipment

_____ **6.** Land (used in operations)

_____ **7.** Repairs expense

_____ **8.** Prepaid property taxes

_____ **9.** Current portion of long-term note payable

_____ **10.** Long-term investment in IBM stock

_____ **11.** Depreciation expense—Trucks

_____ **12.** T. Duncan, Capital

_____ **13.** Interest receivable

_____ **14.** T. Duncan, Withdrawals

_____ **15.** Automobiles

_____ **16.** Notes payable (due in 3 years)

_____ **17.** Accounts payable

_____ **18.** Prepaid insurance

_____ **19.** Common stock

_____ **20.** Unearned services revenue

Problem 5-6A^A

Making adjusting, reversing, and subsequent entries

P3   P4

This six-column table for Bullseye Ranges includes the unadjusted trial balance as of December 31, 2002.

	BULLSEYE RANGES December 31, 2002					
Account Title	**Unadjusted Trial Balance**		**Adjustments**		**Adjusted Trial Balance**	
	Dr.	**Cr.**	**Dr.**	**Cr.**	**Dr.**	**Cr.**
Cash	$ 14,000					
Accounts receivable	0					
Supplies	6,500					
Equipment	135,000					
Accumulated depreciation— Equipment		$ 30,000				
Interest payable		0				
Salaries payable		0				
Unearned membership fees		15,000				
Notes payable		75,000				
T. Allen, Capital		50,250				
T. Allen, Withdrawals	21,125					
Membership fees earned		42,000				
Depreciation expense— Equipment	0					
Salaries expense	30,000					
Interest expense	5,625					
Supplies expense	0					
Totals	$212,250	$212,250				

Required

1. Complete the six-column table by entering adjustments that reflect the following information:

   a. As of December 31, 2002, employees had earned $1,200 of unpaid and unrecorded salaries. The next payday is January 4, and the total amount of salaries to be paid is $1,500.

   b. The cost of supplies available at December 31, 2002, is $3,000.

   c. The note payable requires an interest payment to be made every three months. The amount of unrecorded accrued interest at December 31, 2002, is $1,875, and the next payment is due on January 15. This payment will be $2,250.

   d. Analysis of the unearned membership fees shows $5,800 remaining unearned at December 31, 2002.

   e. In addition to the membership fees included in the revenue account balance, the company has earned another $9,300 in fees for year 2002 that will be collected on January 21, 2003. The company is also expected to collect $10,000 on the same day for additional fees earned during January 2003.

   f. Depreciation expense for the year is $15,000.

2. Prepare journal entries for the adjustments entered in the six-column table for part *1*.

3. Prepare journal entries to reverse the effects of the adjusting entries that involve accruals.

4. Prepare journal entries to record the cash payments and collections described for January.

Check Adjusted trial balance totals, $239,625

On July 1, 2002, Lucinda Fogle created a new self-storage business, SafeStore Co. The following transactions occurred during the company's first month:

July	1	Fogle invested $30,000 cash and buildings worth $150,000.
	2	Rented equipment by paying $2,000 rent for the first month.
	5	Purchased $2,400 of office supplies for cash.
	10	Paid $7,200 for the premium on a one-year insurance policy. Coverage begins on July 10.
	14	Paid an employee $1,000 for two weeks' salary.
	24	Collected $9,800 of storage fees from customers.
	28	Paid another $1,000 for two weeks' salary.
	29	Paid the month's $400 telephone bill.
	30	Paid $950 cash to repair a leaking roof.
	31	Fogle withdrew $2,000 cash from the business for personal use.

The company's chart of accounts included the following accounts.

PROBLEM SET B

Problem 5-1B
Applying the accounting cycle

101	Cash	401	Storage Fees Earned
106	Accounts Receivable	606	Depreciation Expense—Buildings
124	Office Supplies	622	Salaries Expense
128	Prepaid Insurance	637	Insurance Expense
173	Buildings	640	Rent Expense
174	Accumulated Depreciation—Buildings	650	Office Supplies Expense
209	Salaries Payable	684	Repairs Expense
301	Lucinda Fogle, Capital	688	Telephone Expense
302	Lucinda Fogle, Withdrawals	901	Income Summary

Required

1. Use the balance column format to set up each account listed in its chart of accounts.

2. Prepare journal entries to record the transactions for July and post them to the accounts. Record prepaid and unearned items in balance sheet accounts.

3. Prepare an unadjusted trial balance as of July 31.

4. Use the following information to journalize and post adjusting entries for the month:

   a. Two-thirds of one month's insurance coverage has expired.

   b. There are $1,525 of office supplies available at the end of the month.

   c. Depreciation on the buildings is $1,500.

   d. The employee earned $100 of unpaid and unrecorded salary.

   e. The company earned $1,150 of storage fees that are not yet billed.

5. Prepare the income statement and the statement of changes in owner's equity for July, and the balance sheet at July 31, 2002.

6. Prepare journal entries to close the temporary accounts and post the entries to the accounts.

7. Prepare a post-closing trial balance.

Problem 5-2B

Preparing closing entries, financial statements, and current ratio

C3 **A1** **P1**

Easy Stride Shoes' adjusted trial balance on December 31, 2002, follows:

EASY STRIDE SHOES Adjusted Trial Balance December 31, 2002			
No.	**Account Title**	**Debit**	**Credit**
101	Cash	$ 14,450	
125	Store supplies	5,140	
128	Prepaid insurance	1,200	
167	Equipment	31,000	
168	Accumulated depreciation—Equipment		$ 8,000
201	Accounts payable		1,500
210	Wages payable		2,700
301	Paul Holt, Capital		35,650
302	Paul Holt, Withdrawals	15,000	
401	Repair fees earned		54,700
612	Depreciation expense—Equipment	2,000	
623	Wages expense	26,400	
637	Insurance expense	600	
640	Rent expense	3,600	
651	Store supplies expense	1,200	
690	Utilities expense	1,960	
	Totals	$102,550	$102,550

Required

Preparation Component

1. Prepare an income statement and a statement of changes in owner's equity for the year 2002, and a classified balance sheet at December 31, 2002. There are no owner investments in 2002.

2. Enter the adjusted trial balance in the first two columns of a six-column table. Use the middle two columns for closing entries and the last two columns for a post-closing trial balance. Insert an Income Summary account as the last item in the trial balance.

3. Enter closing entries in the six-column table and prepare journal entries for them.

4. Determine the company's current ratio.

Analysis Component

5. Assume for Easy Stride that:

a. None of the $600 insurance expense expired during the year. Instead, assume it is a prepayment of future insurance protection.

b. There are no earned and unpaid wages at the end of the year.

Describe the financial statement changes that would result from these two assumptions.

The adjusted trial balance for Giovanni Co. as of December 31, 2002, follows:

Problem 5-3B

Preparing closing entries, financial statements, and ratios

GIOVANNI CO. Adjusted Trial Balance December 31, 2002			
No.	**Account Title**	**Debit**	**Credit**
101	Cash	$ 7,400	
104	Short-term investments	11,200	
126	Supplies	4,600	
128	Prepaid insurance	1,000	
167	Equipment	24,000	
168	Accumulated depreciation—Equipment		$ 4,000
173	Building	100,000	
174	Accumulated depreciation—Building		10,000
183	Land	30,500	
201	Accounts payable		3,500
203	Interest payable		1,750
208	Rent payable		400
210	Wages payable		1,280
213	Property taxes payable		3,330
233	Unearned professional fees		750
251	Long-term notes payable		40,000
301	Joe Giovanni, Capital		92,800
302	Joe Giovanni, Withdrawals	8,000	
401	Professional fees earned		59,600
406	Rent earned		4,500
407	Dividends earned		1,000
409	Interest earned		1,320
606	Depreciation expense—Building	2,000	
612	Depreciation expense—Equipment	1,000	
623	Wages expense	18,500	
633	Interest expense	1,550	
637	Insurance expense	1,525	
640	Rent expense	3,600	
652	Supplies expense	1,000	
682	Postage expense	410	
683	Property taxes expense	4,825	
684	Repairs expense	679	
688	Telephone expense	521	
690	Utilities expense	1,920	
	Totals	$224,230	$224,230

Analysis reveals that Giovanni Company is required to make an $8,400 payment on its long-term note payable during 2003. J. Giovanni invested $40,000 cash during year 2002 (the December 31, 2001, balance of the J. Giovanni, Capital account was $52,800).

Required

1. Prepare the income statement and the statement of changes in owner's equity for year 2002, and the classified balance sheet at December 31, 2002.

Check   Total assets, $164,700

2. Prepare the necessary closing entries at the end of the year 2002.

3. Use the information in the financial statements to calculate these ratios:

   a. Return on equity.

   b. Modified return on equity, assuming the owner's efforts are valued at $15,000 for the year.

    c. Debt ratio.

    d. Profit margin ratio (use total revenues as the denominator).

    e. Current ratio.

Problem 5-4B

Preparing work sheet, journal entries, financial statements, and current ratio

This unadjusted trial balance is for Smash Demolition Company as of the end of its April 30, 2002, fiscal year. The April 30, 2001, balance of the owner's capital account was $46,900, and the owner invested $40,000 cash in the company during the 2002 fiscal year.

SMASH DEMOLITION COMPANY Unadjusted Trial Balance April 30, 2002			
No.	**Account Title**	**Debit**	**Credit**
101	Cash	$ 7,000	
126	Supplies	16,000	
128	Prepaid insurance	12,600	
167	Equipment	200,000	
168	Accumulated depreciation—Equipment		$ 14,000
201	Accounts payable		6,800
203	Interest payable		0
208	Rent payable		0
210	Wages payable		0
213	Property taxes payable		0
251	Long-term notes payable		30,000
301	J. Bonair, Capital		86,900
302	J. Bonair, Withdrawals	12,000	
401	Demolition fees earned		187,000
612	Depreciation expense—Equipment	0	
623	Wages expense	41,400	
633	Interest expense	3,300	
637	Insurance expense	0	
640	Rent expense	13,200	
652	Supplies expense	0	
683	Property taxes expense	9,700	
684	Repairs expense	4,700	
690	Utilities expense	4,800	
	Totals	$ 324,700	$ 324,700

Required

Preparation Component

1. Prepare a 10-column work sheet for fiscal year 2002, starting with the unadjusted trial balance and including these additional facts:

    a. The supplies available at the end of fiscal year 2002 had a cost of $7,900.

    b. The cost of expired insurance for the fiscal year is $10,600.

    c. Annual depreciation on equipment is $7,000.

    d. The April utilities expense of $800 is not included in the unadjusted trial balance because the bill arrived after the trial balance was prepared. The $800 amount owed needs to be recorded.

    e. The company's employees have earned $2,000 of accrued wages at fiscal year-end.

    f. The lease for the office requires the company to pay total rent for each fiscal year equal to 8% of the company's annual revenues. Rent has been estimated and is being paid to the building owner with monthly payments of $1,100. If the annual rent owed exceeds the total monthly estimated payments, the company must pay the excess before May 31. If the total owed is less than the amount previously paid, the building owner will refund the difference by May 31.

    g. Additional property taxes of $550 have been assessed but have not been paid or recorded in the accounts.

    h. The long-term note payable bears interest at 1% per month, which the company is required to pay by the 10th of the following month. The balance of the Interest Expense account equals the amount paid for the first 11 months of the year. The interest for April has not yet been paid or recorded. In addition, the company is required to make a $10,000 payment toward the note payable on June 30, 2002.

2. Use the work sheet to enter the adjusting and closing entries; then journalize them.

Check Total assets, $195,900; rent expense, $14,960

3. Prepare the income statement and the statement of changes in owner's equity for the year ended April 30, and the classified balance sheet at April 30. Calculate the company's current ratio.

Analysis Component

4. Analyze the following separate errors and describe how each would affect the 10-column work sheet. Explain whether the error is likely to be discovered in completing the work sheet and, if not, the effect of the error on the financial statements.

a. The adjustment for expiration of the insurance coverage had credited the Prepaid Insurance account for $2,000 and debited the same amount to the Insurance Expense account.

b. When the adjusted trial balance in the work sheet is completed, the $4,700 Repairs Expense account balance is extended to the Debit column for the balance sheet.

In the blank space beside each numbered balance sheet item, enter the letter of its balance sheet classification. If the item should not appear on the balance sheet, enter a Z in the blank.

Problem 5-5B
Determining balance sheet classifications

C3

A. Current assets   **D.** Intangible assets   **G.** Owner's equity
B. Long-term investments **E.** Current liabilities   **H.** Stockholders' equity
C. Plant assets   **F.** Long-term liabilities

_____ **1.** Buildings
_____ **2.** Prepaid insurance
_____ **3.** Current portion of long-term note payable
_____ **4.** Interest receivable
_____ **5.** Short-term investments
_____ **6.** Land (used in operations)
_____ **7.** Copyrights
_____ **8.** Owner, Withdrawals
_____ **9.** Depreciation expense—Trucks
_____ **10.** Long-term investment in Ford stock

_____ **11.** Office supplies
_____ **12.** Owner, Capital
_____ **13.** Common stock
_____ **14.** Notes receivable (due in 120 days)
_____ **15.** Accumulated depreciation—Trucks
_____ **16.** Salaries payable
_____ **17.** Commissions earned
_____ **18.** Retained earnings
_____ **19.** Office equipment
_____ **20.** Notes payable (due in 5 years)

This six-column table for Rent-A-Way Co. includes the unadjusted trial balance as of December 31, 2002:

Problem 5-6B[A]
Making adjusting, reversing, and subsequent entries

P3 **P4**

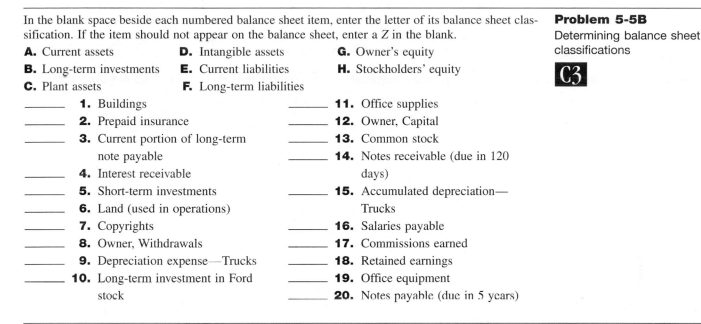

	Unadjusted Trial Balance		Adjustments		Adjusted Trial Balance	
Account Title	Dr.	Cr.	Dr.	Cr.	Dr.	Cr.
Cash	$ 10,000					
Accounts receivable	0					
Supplies	7,600					
Machinery	50,000					
Accumulated depreciation—Machinery		$ 20,000				
Interest payable		0				
Salaries payable		0				
Unearned rental fees		7,200				
Notes payable		30,000				
Gary Clay, Capital		14,200				
Gary Clay, Withdrawals	9,500					
Rental fees earned		32,450				
Depreciation expense—Machinery	0					
Salaries expense	24,500					
Interest expense	2,250					
Supplies expense	0					
Totals	$103,850	$103,850				

RENT-A-WAY CO.
December 31, 2002

Required

1. Complete the six-column table by entering adjustments that reflect the following information:

   a. As of December 31, 2002, employees had earned $400 of unpaid and unrecorded wages. The next payday is January 4, and the total wages to be paid are $1,200.

   b. The cost of supplies available at December 31, 2002, is $3,540.

   c. The note payable requires an interest payment to be made every three months. The amount of unrecorded accrued interest at December 31, 2002, is $800, and the next payment is due on January 15. This payment will be $900.

   d. Analysis of the unearned rental fees shows that $3,200 remains unearned at December 31, 2002.

   e. In addition to the machinery rental fees included in the revenue account balance, the company has earned another $2,450 in fees for year 2002 that will be collected on January 21, 2003. The company is also expected to collect $5,400 on the same day for additional fees earned during January 2003.

   f. Depreciation expense for the year is $3,800.

Check Adjusted trial balance totals, $111,300

2. Prepare journal entries for the adjustments entered in the six-column table for part *1*.

3. Prepare journal entries to reverse the effects of the adjusting entries that involve accruals.

4. Prepare journal entries to record the cash payments and collections described for January.

SERIAL PROBLEM

Sierra Systems

P1 P2

 PeachTree

Check Post-closing trial balance totals, $94,898

[The first two segments of this serial problem were in Chapters 3 and 4, and the final segment is in Chapter 6. If the Chapter 3 and 4 segments have not been completed, the assignment can begin at this point. It is recommended you use the Working Papers that accompany this book because they reflect the account balances that resulted from posting the entries required in Chapters 3 and 4.] The transactions of Sierra Systems for October through December 2002 have been recorded for the serial problem segments in Chapters 3 and 4, as well as the year-end adjusting entries.

Required

1. Record and post the necessary closing entries for Sierra Systems.

2. Prepare a post-closing trial balance.

do statements before closing

Beyond the Numbers

Reporting in Action

P1

NIKE

BTN 5-1   Refer to **Nike**'s financial statements in Appendix A to answer the following:

Required

1. For the fiscal year ended May 31, 2000, what amount will be credited to Income Summary to summarize Nike's revenues earned?

2. For the fiscal year ended May 31, 2000, what amount will be debited to Income Summary to summarize Nike's expenses incurred?

3. For the fiscal year ended May 31, 2000, what will be the balance of the Income Summary account before it is closed?

4. In its statement of cash flows for the year ended May 31, 2000, what amount of cash is paid in dividends to common and preferred stockholders?

Swoosh Ahead

5. Access Nike's annual report for fiscal years ending after May 31, 2000, at its Web site [**www.nike.com**] or the SEC's EDGAR database [**www.sec.gov**]. How has the amount of net income closed to Income Summary changed in the fiscal years ending after May 31, 2000? How has the amount of cash paid as dividends changed in the fiscal years ending after May 31, 2000?

BTN 5-2 Key figures ($ millions) for the recent two years of both **Nike** and **Reebok** follow:

Key Figures	Nike		Reebok	
	Current Year	Prior Year	Current Year	Prior Year
Current assets	$3,596	$3,265	$1,243	$1,363
Current liabilities	2,140	1,447	624	543

Required

1. Compute the current ratio for both years and both companies.
2. Which has the better ability to pay short-term obligations according to the current ratio?
3. Analyze and comment on each company's current ratios for the past two years.
4. How do Nike's and Reebok's current ratios compare to their industry average ratio of about 1.6?

BTN 5-3 On January 20, 2002, Jennifer Nelson, the accountant for Newby Enterprises, is feeling pressure to complete the annual financial statements. The company president has said he needs up-to-date financial statements to share with the bank on January 21 at a dinner meeting that has been called to discuss Newby's obtaining loan financing for a special building project. Jennifer knows that she will not be able to gather all the needed information in the next 24 hours to prepare the entire set of adjusting entries that must be posted before the financial statements accurately portray the company's performance and financial position for the fiscal period ended December 31, 2001. Jennifer ultimately decides to estimate several expense accruals at the last minute. When deciding on estimates for the expenses, she uses low estimates because she does not want to make the financial statements look worse than they are. Jennifer finishes the financial statements before the deadline and gives them to the president without mentioning that several accounts use estimated balances.

Required

1. Identify several courses of action that Jennifer could have taken instead of the one she took.
2. If you were in Jennifer's situation, what would you have done? Briefly justify your response.

BTN 5-4 Assume that one of your classmates said that the *going-concern principle* states that a company's books should be ongoing and therefore not closed until that business is terminated. This classmate does not understand the objective of the closing process or the meaning of the going-concern principle. Write a one-half page memo to this classmate explaining the concept of the closing process by drawing analogies between (1) a scoreboard for an athletic event and the revenue and expense accounts of a business or (2) a sports team's record book and the capital account. (*Hint:* Think about what would happen if the scoreboard is not cleared before the start of a new game.) Your memo should also clarify the meaning of the going-concern principle.

BTN 5-5 Access **edgar-online.com** and view the April 28, 2000, filing of the 10-K405 report of Dillards, Inc. (Ticker: DDS).

Required

1. Locate Dillards' balance sheet within the 10-K405 report. Compute its current ratio for the years ending January 29, 2000, and January 30, 1999.
2. Analyze and comment on Dillard's current ratio.

Teamwork in Action

P1

BTN 5–6 The unadjusted trial balance and information for the accounting adjustments of Noseworthy Investigators follow. Each team member involved in this project is to assume one of the four responsibilities listed. After completing each of these responsibilities, the team should work together to prove the accounting equation utilizing information from teammates (1 and 4). If your equation does not balance, you are to work as a team to resolve the error. The team's goal is to complete the task as quickly and accurately as possible.

Unadjusted Trial Balance		
Account Title	**Debit**	**Credit**
Cash	$15,000	
Supplies	11,000	
Prepaid insurance	2,000	
Equipment	24,000	
Accumulated depreciation—Equipment		$ 6,000
Accounts payable		2,000
D. Noseworthy, Capital		31,000
D. Noseworthy, Withdrawals	5,000	
Investigation fees earned		32,000
Rent expense	14,000	
Totals	$71,000	$71,000

Additional Year-End Information

a. Insurance that expired in the current period amounts to $1,200.
b. Equipment depreciation for the period is $3,000.
c. Unused supplies total $4,000 at period-end.
d. Services in the amount of $500 have been provided but have not been billed or collected.

Responsibilities for Individual Team Members

1. Determine the accounts and adjusted balances to be extended to the balance sheet columns of the work sheet for Noseworthy. Also determine total assets and total liabilities.
2. Determine the adjusted revenue account balance and prepare the entry to close this account.
3. Determine the adjusted account balances for expenses and prepare the entry to close these accounts.
4. Prepare T-accounts for both D. Noseworthy, Capital (reflecting the unadjusted trial balance amount) and Income Summary. Prepare the third and fourth closing entries. Ask teammates assigned to parts (2) and (3) for the postings for Income Summary. Obtain amounts to complete the third closing entry and post both the third and fourth closing entries. Provide the team with the ending capital account balance.
5. The entire team should prove the accounting equation using post-closing balances.

Business Week Activity

C3

BTN 5-7 Read "Computer Learning Centers: School for Scandal?" in the May 4, 1998, issue of *Business Week*.

Required

1. What type of school is CLC?
2. What three revenue accounting issues does the article discuss?
3. Discuss the effects of each of the revenue accounting issues on CLC's financial statements.

BTN 5-8 Identify the entrepreneur of a small business, preferably one you have an interest in. Some possibilities are a musician, singer, consultant, or artist. Call the entrepreneur to set up a time to briefly visit, either in person or over the phone, to answer the following questions.

Entrepreneurial Decision

Required

1. Is the entrepreneur satisfied with his/her accounting for the business? Explain.
2. What is (are) the most difficult aspect(s) of accounting for this business?
3. Does the entrepreneur use accounting software or spreadsheets? If yes, what type?
4. What suggestions for accounting would the entrepreneur offer a person launching a new business?

6

Accounting for Merchandising Activities

A Look Back

Chapter 5 focused on the final steps of the accounting process. We described the closing process, and showed how to prepare financial statements from accounting records.

A Look at This Chapter

This chapter emphasizes merchandising activities. We explain how reporting merchandising activities differs from reporting service activities. Both the perpetual and periodic inventory systems are described. We also analyze and record merchandise purchases and sales transactions and explain the adjustments and closing process for merchandisers.

A Look Ahead

Chapter 7 extends our analysis of merchandising activities and focuses on the valuation of inventory. Topics include the items in inventory, costs assigned, costing methods used, and inventory estimation techniques.

"We constantly seek the input of our retailers and the buying public"— Mark Donovan

Part Two

Casual Success

e HOBOKEN, NJ—Paola Buendia was studying English and Mark Donovan was preparing for a career in business when they met at college. Buendia and Donovan became best friends and were soon married. Following graduation, they both landed good jobs. But something was missing. "I needed a creative outlet," says Buendia. "I started designing things I'd always wanted—pretty simple, basic things, and lots of hats, because I'd always worn them." Then Donovan got involved. With just $5,000, they launched a clothing company, **Wooden Ships of Hoboken** (**WoodenShips.com**).

Inspired by their travels to Indonesia and the corporate trend toward casual clothing, they targeted women's casual wear. Working out of their apartment for the first year and a half, they sold clothing outdoors off a blanket at concerts, street fairs, and other events. Soon afterward, they began supplying retailers. A crucial part of their business success is tracking merchandising activities. Buendia says they spend a lot of time "figuring out how to supply customers." This includes setting prices and making policies for discounts, allowances, and returns on both sales and purchases.

Managing their inventory is equally crucial, "We constantly seek the input of our retailers and the buying public," Donovan says. Buendia adds that Wooden Ships's Web site allows "us to establish an open line of communication with our ultimate consumer . . . and receive direct feedback on styles, colors and other consumer preferences." This information helps them keep the right type and amount of merchandise to avoid the costs of both out-of-stock items and excess inventory.

Buendia and Donovan still enjoy attending a concert or strolling through a street fair. But to their delight, their business no longer depends on selling at such events. Their annual sales are soon expected to top $15 million, with sales to more than 1,800 boutiques. Not bad for a company that began as a creative whim. [Sources: *Entrepreneur*, November 12, 1998; *Wooden Ships Web Site*, May 2001; *Sunday Star-Ledger*, 1998; *Hudson Current*, August–September 1998.]

Learning Objectives

Conceptual

C1 Describe merchandising activities and identify business examples.

C2 Identify and explain the components of income for a merchandising company.

C3 Identify and explain the inventory asset of a merchandising company.

C4 Describe both perpetual and periodic inventory systems.

C5 Analyze and interpret cost flows and operating activities of a merchandising company.

Analytical

A1 Analyze and interpret accruals and cash flows for merchandising activities.

A2 Compute the acid-test ratio and explain its use to assess liquidity.

A3 Compute the gross margin ratio and explain its use to assess profitability.

Procedural

P1 Analyze and record transactions for merchandise purchases using a perpetual system.

P2 Analyze and record transactions for sales of merchandise using a perpetual system.

P3 Prepare adjustments and close accounts for a merchandising company.

P4 Define and prepare multiple-step and single-step income statements.

Merchandising activities are a major part of modern business. Consumers expect a wealth of products, discount prices, inventory on demand, and high quality. This chapter introduces the business and accounting practices used by companies engaged in merchandising activities. These companies buy products and then resell them to customers. We show how financial statements reflect these merchandising activities and explain the new financial statement elements created by merchandising activities. We analyze and record merchandise purchases and sales. We also explain adjustments and the closing process for merchandising companies.

Merchandising Activities

C1 Describe merchandising activities and identify business examples.

Previous chapters emphasized the accounting and reporting activities of service companies such as **JobDirect**, **Creative Assets**, and **CrossWorlds**. In return for services provided to its customers, a service company receives commissions, fares, or fees as revenue. Its net income is the difference between its revenues and the expenses incurred in providing those services.

A merchandising company's activities differ from those of a service company. A **merchandiser** earns net income by buying and selling merchandise. **Merchandise** consists of products, also called *goods,* that a company acquires to resell to customers. Merchandisers are often identified as either wholesalers or retailers. A **wholesaler** is an *intermediary* that buys products from manufacturers or other wholesalers and sells them to retailers or other wholesalers. Wholesalers provide promotion, market information, and financial assistance to retailers. They also provide a sales force, reduced inventory costs, less risk, and market information to manufacturers. Wholesalers include companies such as **Fleming**, **SuperValu**, **McKesson**, and **Sysco**. Another type of intermediary is a **retailer** that buys products from manufacturers or wholesalers and sells them to consumers. Examples of retailers include **Gap**, **Oakley**, **CompUSA**, **Wal-Mart**, and **MusicLand**. Many retailers such as **Best Buy** sell both products and services.

Reporting Financial Performance

C2 Identify and explain the components of income for a merchandising company.

Net income to a merchandiser implies that revenue from selling merchandise exceeds both the cost of merchandise sold to customers and the cost of other expenses for the period (see Exhibit 6.1). The usual accounting term for revenues from selling merchandise is *sales,* and the term used for the cost of buying and preparing the merchandise is *cost of goods sold.*[1] A merchandiser's expenses are often called *operating expenses.*

Exhibit 6.1

Computing Income for a Merchandising Company versus a Service Company

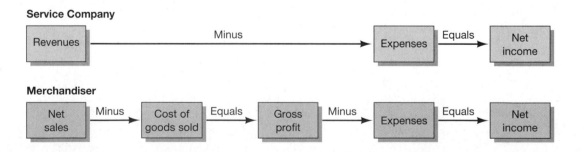

Point: Analysis of gross profit is important to effective business decisions. We describe such analysis later in this chapter.

The condensed income statement for Z-Mart in Exhibit 6.2 shows important components of net income. This statement shows Z-Mart acquired products at a cost of $230,400 and sold them to customers for $314,700. This yields an $84,300 gross profit. **Gross profit,** also called **gross margin,** equals net sales less cost of goods sold. Gross profit is important to merchandisers' profitability. Changes in gross profit often greatly impact a merchandiser's

---

[1] Many service companies use the term *sales* in their income statements to describe revenues. **Marriott** is one example. Cost of goods sold is also called *cost of sales* and is reported as an operating expense.

operations since gross profit must cover all other expenses plus yield a return for the owner. Z-Mart, for instance, used its gross profit to cover $71,400 of other expenses. This left $12,900 in net income.

Reporting Financial Condition

A merchandising company's balance sheet includes a current asset called *merchandise inventory,* an item not on a service company's balance sheet. **Merchandise inventory** refers to products a company owns to sell to customers. Exhibit 6.3 shows the classified balance sheet for Z-Mart, including merchandise inventory of $21,000. The cost of this asset includes the cost incurred to buy the goods, ship them to the store, and make them ready for sale. Many companies simply refer to merchandise inventory as *inventory.*

Z-MART Condensed Income Statement For Year Ended December 31, 2002	
Net sales	$314,700
Cost of goods sold	(230,400)
Gross profit	$ 84,300
Operating expenses	(71,400)
Net income	$ 12,900

Exhibit 6.2

Condensed Income Statement for a Merchandiser

C3 Identify and explain the inventory asset of a merchandising company.

Z-MART Balance Sheet December 31, 2002		
Assets		
Current assets		
Cash		$ 8,200
Accounts receivable		11,200
Merchandise inventory		**21,000**
Prepaid expenses		1,100
Total current assets		$41,500
Plant assets		
Office equipment	$ 4,200	
Less accumulated depreciation	1,400	2,800
Store equipment	30,000	
Less accumulated depreciation	6,000	24,000
Total plant assets		26,800
Total assets		$68,300
Liabilities		
Current liabilities		
Accounts payable		$ 6,000
Salaries payable		800
Total current liabilities		$ 6,800
Long-term note payable		10,000
Equity		
K. Marty, Capital		$51,500
Total liabilities and equity		$68,300

Exhibit 6.3

Classified Balance Sheet for a Merchandiser

Operating Cycle

A merchandising company's operating cycle begins by purchasing merchandise and ends by collecting cash from selling the merchandise. An example is a merchandiser who buys products at wholesale and distributes and sells them to consumers at retail. The length of an operating cycle differs across the types of businesses. Department stores such as **The Limited** and **Dayton Hudson** commonly have operating cycles from three to five months.

Operating cycles for grocery merchants such as **Kroger** and **Safeway** usually range from three to eight weeks.

Exhibit 6.4 illustrates an operating cycle for a merchandiser with (1) cash sales and (2) credit sales. The cash sales cycle moves from (a) merchandise purchases to (b) inventory for sale to (c) cash sales. The credit sales cycle moves from (a) merchandise purchases to (b) inventory for sale to (c) credit sales to (d) accounts receivable to (e) cash. Credit sales delay the receipt of cash until the receivable is paid by the customer. Companies try to shorten their operating cycles because assets tied up in inventory or receivables are not productive.

Exhibit 6.4

Operating Cycle of a Merchandiser*

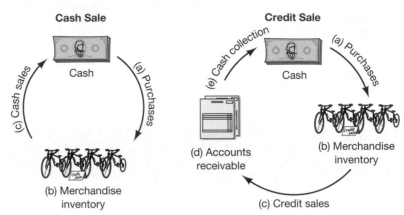

* This exhibit assumes cash purchases. Credit purchases would involve inserting (a) credit purchases, (b) accounts payable, and (c) cash payment in the cycle.

Inventory Systems

We explained that a merchandising company's income statement includes an item called *cost of goods sold* and its balance sheet includes a current asset called *inventory*. **Cost of goods sold** is the cost of merchandise sold to customers during a period. It is often the largest single deduction on a merchandiser's income statement. **Inventory** refers to products a company owns and expects to sell in its normal operations. Inventory items are part of merchandising activities captured in Exhibit 6.5. This exhibit shows that a company's merchandise available for sale is a combination of what it begins with (beginning inventory) and what it purchases (net cost of purchases). The merchandise available is either sold (cost of goods sold) or kept for future sales (ending inventory).

Exhibit 6.5

Merchandising Cost Flow

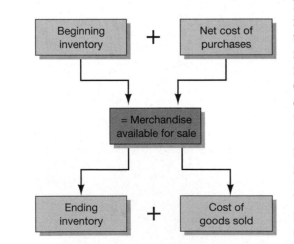

Two alternative inventory accounting systems can be used to collect information about cost of goods sold and cost of inventory available: *periodic system* or *perpetual system*.

Periodic Inventory System

C4 Describe both perpetual and periodic inventory systems.

A **periodic inventory system** requires updating the inventory account only at the *end of a period* to reflect the quantity and cost of goods both available and sold. It does not require continual updating of the inventory account. The cost of merchandise is recorded in a temporary *Purchases* account. When a company sells merchandise, it records revenue but not the cost of the merchandise sold. Instead, when it prepares financial statements, the company takes a *physical count of inventory* by counting the quantities of merchandise available. The cost of merchandise available is computed by linking the quantities counted to the purchase records that show each item's original cost. The cost of merchandise available is then used to compute cost of goods sold. The inventory account is then adjusted to reflect the amount computed from the physical count of inventory. Companies such as hardware, drug, and department stores that sell large quantities of low-value items historically used periodic systems. Without today's computers and scanners, it was not feasible for accounting systems to track numerous, low-cost items such as pens, toothpaste, candy bars, socks, and magazines through inventory and into customers' hands.

Perpetual Inventory System

A **perpetual inventory system** keeps a continual record of the amount of inventory available. A perpetual system accumulates the net cost of merchandise purchases in the inventory account and subtracts the cost of each sale from the same inventory account. When a company sells an item, it records its cost in the *Cost of Goods Sold* account. With a perpetual system we can learn the cost of merchandise available at any time by looking at the balance of the inventory account. We can also learn the current balance of cost of goods sold anytime during a period by looking in the Cost of Goods Sold account.

Point: Growth of super stores such as Price Club and Costco is fed by the efficient use of perpetual inventory techniques and technology.

Before advancements in computing technology, a perpetual system was often limited to businesses making a small number of daily sales such as automobile dealers and major appliance stores. Because transactions were relatively few, a perpetual system was feasible. In today's information age, with widespread use of computing technology, the use of a perpetual system has dramatically increased. A perpetual inventory system gives users more timely information. Accordingly, this chapter emphasizes a perpetual system. However, we analyze and record merchandising transactions using *both* periodic and perpetual inventory systems in the appendix to this chapter.

Did You Know?

Perpetual Info   Technology and perpetual inventory systems are taking the guesswork out of purchasing, slashing inventory cycles, keeping popular items in stock, and cutting return rates. These advances "totally changed the industry from a push industry to a pull industry," says the chairman of **Western Merchandisers**, a supplier of more than 1,000 **Wal-Marts**. A recent study says grocers can cut prices by 11% or more with similar changes.

Quick Check

1. Describe a merchandiser's cost of goods sold.
2. What is gross profit for a merchandising company?
3. Explain why use of the perpetual inventory system has dramatically increased.

Answers   p. 244

With a perpetual inventory system, the cost of merchandise bought for resale is recorded in the Merchandise Inventory asset account. To illustrate, Z-Mart records a $1,200 cash purchase of merchandise on November 2 with this entry:

Nov. 2	Merchandise Inventory	1,200	
	Cash		1,200
	Purchased merchandise for cash.		

Merchandise Purchases

Assets = Liabilities + Equity
+1,200
−1,200

The invoice for this merchandise is shown in Exhibit 6.6. The buyer usually receives the original, and the seller keeps a copy. This *source document* serves as the purchase invoice of Z-Mart (buyer) and the sales invoice for Trex (seller). The amount recorded for merchandise inventory includes its purchase cost, shipping fees, taxes, and any other costs necessary to make it ready for sale.

To compute the total cost of merchandise purchases, we must adjust the invoice cost for (1) any discounts a supplier gives a purchaser, (2) any returns and allowances for unsatisfactory items received from a supplier, and (3) any required freight costs paid by a purchaser. This section explains how these items affect the recorded cost of merchandise purchases.

 P1   Analyze and record transactions for merchandise purchases using a perpetual system.

Concept 6-1

Exhibit 6.6

Invoice

W9797 Cherry Rd.
Antigo, WI 54409

Sold to

Firm Name	Z-Mart ③
Attention of	Tom Novak, Purchasing Agent
Address	10 Michigan Street
Chicago	Illinois	60521
City	State	Zip

Invoice	
Date	Number
11/2/02	4657-2

P.O. Date 10/30/02	Salesperson #141	Terms 2/10, n/30	Freight FOB Destination	Ship Via FedEx
Model No.	Description		Quantity	Price	Amount
CH015	Challenger X7		1	490	490
SD099	Speed Demon		1	710	710

See reverse for terms of sale and returns.

	SubTotal	1,200
	Ship. Chg.	—
	Tax	—
	Total	1,200

Key: ① Seller   ② Invoice date   ③ Purchaser   ④ Order date   ⑤ Credit terms
⑥ Freight terms   ⑦ Goods   ⑧ Total invoice amount

Trade Discounts

Point: The Merchandise Inventory account reflects the cost of goods available for resale.

When a manufacturer or wholesaler prepares a catalog of items it has for sale, it usually gives each item a **list price,** also called a *catalog price.* List price usually is not the item's intended selling price. Instead, its intended selling price equals list price minus a given percent called a **trade discount.**

The amount of trade discount usually depends on whether a buyer is a wholesaler, retailer, or final consumer. A wholesaler buying in large quantities is often granted a larger discount than a retailer buying in smaller quantities. Manufacturers and wholesalers commonly use trade discounts to change selling prices without republishing their catalogs. When a seller wants to change selling prices, it can notify its customers merely by sending them a new table of trade discounts that they can apply to catalog prices.

A buyer does *not* enter list prices and trade discounts in its accounts. Instead, a buyer records the net amount of list price minus trade discount. For example, in the November 2 purchase of merchandise by Z-Mart, the merchandise was listed in the seller's catalog at $2,000 and Z-Mart received a 40% trade discount. This means that Z-Mart's purchase price is $1,200, computed as $2,000 − (40% × $2,000).

Purchase Discounts

Point: Since both the buyer and seller know the invoice date, this date is useful in determining the end of the credit period. Alternatively, the date shipped or received is not known by both parties.

The purchase of goods on credit requires a clear statement of expected amounts and dates of future payments to avoid misunderstandings. **Credit terms** for a purchase include the amounts and timing of payments from a buyer to a seller. Credit terms usually reflect an industry's practices. In some industries, purchasers expect terms requiring payment within 10 days after the end of the month when purchases occur. These credit terms are entered on sales invoices as "n/10 EOM." The **EOM** refers to *end of month.* In other industries, invoices are often due and payable within 30 calendar days after the invoice date. These credit terms are entered as "n/30," expressed as *net 30.* The 30-day period in this case is called the **credit period.** Exhibit 6.7 portrays credit terms.

Exhibit 6.7

Credit Terms

*Discount refers to either purchase or sales discounts.

Sellers often grant a **cash discount** when the credit period is long and buyers pay within a certain period. A buyer views a cash discount as a **purchase discount.** A seller views a cash discount as a **sales discount.** If cash discounts for early payment exist, they are described as credit terms on the invoice. For example, credit terms of "2/10, n/60" imply that a 60-day credit period occurs before full payment is due. The seller allows the buyer to deduct 2% of the invoice amount if payment is made within 10 days of the invoice date. Sellers do this to encourage early payment. The reduced payment can be made during the **discount period.**

To illustrate how a buyer accounts for a purchase discount, let's assume that Z-Mart's purchase of merchandise for $1,200 is on credit with terms of 2/10, n/30. Z-Mart's entry to record this credit purchase is[2]

(a) Nov. 2	Merchandise Inventory	1,200	
	Accounts Payable		1,200
	Purchased merchandise on credit, invoice dated Nov. 2, terms 2/10, n/30.		

Assets = Liabilities + Equity
+1,200   +1,200

If Z-Mart takes advantage of the discount and pays the amount due on November 12, the entry to record payment is

(b) Nov. 12	Accounts Payable	1,200	
	Merchandise Inventory		24
	Cash		1,176
	Paid for the $1,200 purchase of Nov. 2 less the discount of $24(2% × $1,200).		

Assets = Liabilities + Equity
−24   −1,200
−1,176

Z-Mart's Merchandise Inventory account after this entry reflects the net cost of merchandise purchased. Its Accounts Payable account shows a zero balance, meaning the debt is satisfied. Both accounts, in T-account form, follow here:

Merchandise Inventory				Accounts Payable			
Nov. 2	1,200	Nov. 12	24	Nov. 12	1,200	Nov. 2	1,200
Balance	1,176					Balance	0

Managing Discounts

A buyer's failure to pay within a discount period is often expensive. In the preceding example, if Z-Mart does not pay within the 10-day discount period, it can delay payment by 20 more days. This delay costs Z-Mart an added 2% to the cost of merchandise. Most buyers

---

[2] Appendix 6A repeats journal entries *a* through *f* using a periodic inventory system.

You Make the Call

Entrepreneur You purchase a batch of products on terms of 3/10, n/90, but your company has limited cash and you must borrow funds at an 11% annual rate if you are to pay within the discount period. Do you take advantage of the purchase discount?

Answer—p. 243

Did You Know?

Clout! Merchandising companies are unleashing a barrage of demands on suppliers. These include special discounts for new stores, payment of fines for shipping errors, and free samples. One merchandiser warned **Totes** it would impose a $30,000 fine for errors in bar-coding on products Totes shipped. Merchandisers' goals are to slash inventories, shorten lead times, and eliminate error.

try to take advantage of a purchase discount because of the usually high interest rate implied from not taking it. We can approximate the annual rate of interest attached to not paying within the discount period. For Z-Mart's terms of 2/10, n/30, missing the 2% discount for an additional 20 days is equal to an annual interest rate of 36.5%. This is computed as (365 days/20 additional days) × 2% discount rate.[3]

Most companies set up a system to pay invoices with favorable discounts within the discount period. Careful cash management means that no invoice is paid until the last day of a discount period. One technique to achieve this goal is to file each invoice so that it automatically comes up for payment on the last day of its discount period. A simple filing system uses up to 31 folders, one for each day in a month. After an invoice is recorded, it is placed in the folder matching the last day of its discount period. If the last day of an invoice's discount period is November 12, it is filed in folder 12. This and other invoices in the same folder are removed and paid on November 12.

Purchase Returns and Allowances

Purchase returns refer to merchandise a purchaser receives but then returns to the supplier. A *purchase allowance* is a reduction in the cost of defective or unacceptable merchandise that a purchaser receives from a supplier. Purchasers often keep defective but still marketable merchandise if the supplier grants an acceptable allowance.

The purchaser usually informs the supplier in writing of any returns and allowances, often with a **debit memorandum,** a document the purchaser issues to inform the supplier of a debit made to the supplier's account, including the reason for the return or allowance. Exhibit 6.8 shows a debit memorandum prepared by Z-Mart requesting an allowance from Trex for the defective *SpeedDemon* mountain bike. The November 15 entry by Z-Mart to update the Merchandise Inventory account to reflect the purchase allowance requested in the debit memorandum is

Assets = Liabilities + Equity
−300   −300

(c) Nov. 15	Accounts Payable	300	
	Merchandise Inventory		300
	Allowance for defective merchandise.		

Exhibit 6.8

Debit Memorandum

Case: Z-Mart (buyer) proposes $300 allowance for defective merchandise from Trex (seller)

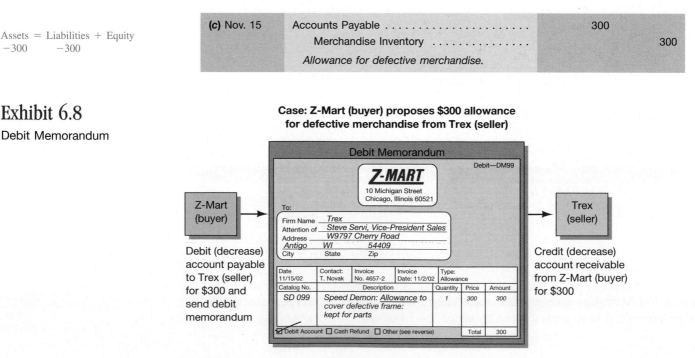

<hr>

[3] The implied interest rate formula is: (365 days ÷ [Credit period − Discount period]) × Cash discount rate.

If this had been a return, then the total recorded cost of the defective merchandise would have been entered.[4] Z-Mart's agreement with this supplier says the cost of returned and defective merchandise is offset against Z-Mart's next purchase or its current account payable balance. Some agreements with suppliers involve refunding the cost to a buyer. When cash is refunded, the Cash account is debited for $300 instead of Accounts Payable.

Discounts and Returns

When goods are returned within the discount period, a buyer can take the discount on only the remaining balance of the invoice. As an example, suppose Z-Mart purchases $1,000 of merchandise offered with a 2% cash discount. Two days later, Z-Mart returns $100 of goods before paying the invoice. When Z-Mart later pays within the discount period, it can take the 2% discount only on the $900 remaining balance. The discount is $18 (2% × $900), and the cash payment is $882 ($900 − $18).

> **You Make the Call—Ethics**
>
> **Credit Manager**   As the new credit manager, you are being trained by the outgoing manager. She explains that the system prepares checks for amounts net of favorable cash discounts, and the checks are dated the last day of the discount period. She also tells you that checks are not mailed until five days later, adding that "the company gets free use of cash for an extra five days, and our department looks better. When a supplier complains, we blame the computer system and the mailroom." Do you continue this payment policy?
>
> Answer—p. 243

Transportation Costs

Depending on terms negotiated with suppliers, a merchandiser is sometimes responsible for paying shipping costs on purchases, often called *transportation-in* or *freight-in* costs. Z-Mart's $1,200 purchase on November 2 is on terms of FOB destination. This means Z-Mart is not responsible for paying transportation costs. When a merchandiser is responsible for paying transportation costs, they are sometimes made to an independent carrier but other times are made directly to the seller. Transportation costs are often included on the invoice when owed to the seller, whereas transportation costs owed to an independent carrier usually are not included on the invoice. The cost principle requires transportation costs be included as part of the cost of purchased merchandise. This means a separate entry is necessary when they are *not* listed on the invoice. For example, Z-Mart's entry to record a $75 freight charge from an independent carrier for merchandise purchased FOB shipping point would be

Example: Suppose Z-Mart pays for $1,000 of merchandise acquired within the discount period and receives a 2% discount. Later, when Z-Mart returns $100 of the original $1,000 merchandise, what amount of cash refund does it receive? How are the return and cash receipt recorded? *Answers:* Cash refund = Net paid for $100 of goods = 98% × $100 − $98. The entry to record this is
Cash 98
   Merchandise Inventory .   98

(d) Nov. 24	Merchandise Inventory	75	
	Cash		75
	Paid freight charges on purchased merchandise.		

Assets − Liabilities + Equity
+75
−75

   Transportation-in costs differ from the costs of shipping goods to customers. Transportation-in costs are included in the cost of merchandise inventory, but the costs of shipping goods to customers are not. The costs of shipping goods to customers are recorded in a delivery expense account when the merchandiser (seller in this case) is responsible for these costs. Delivery expense, also called *freight-out* or *transportation-out*, is reported as a selling expense in the income statement.

Point: When CompUSA purchases merchandise and then distributes it among its stores, the cost of shipping merchandise to the stores is included in the costs of the store inventories according to the cost principle.

Transfer of Ownership

The buyer and seller must agree on who is responsible for paying any freight costs and who bears the risk of loss during transit for merchandising transactions. This is essentially the same as asking at what point ownership transfers from the seller to the buyer. The point of transfer is called the **FOB** (*free on board*) point. The point when ownership transfers from the seller to the buyer determines who pays transportation costs (and other incidental costs of transit such as insurance).

---

[4] *Recorded cost* is the cost reported in the account minus any discounts.

buyer pays

Exhibit 6.9 identifies two alternative points of transfer. The first is FOB shipping point. *FOB shipping point,* also called *FOB factory,* means the buyer accepts ownership at the seller's place of business. The buyer is then responsible for paying shipping costs and bearing the risk of damage or loss when goods are in transit. The goods are part of the buyer's inventory when they are in transit since ownership has transferred to the buyer. **Midway Games** is a leader in entertainment software and uses FOB shipping point. Midway has released many popular games including Mortal Kombat, Cruis'n USA, Cruis'n World, NBA Jam, Joust, Defender, and Pacman.

Exhibit 6.9

Identifying Transfer of Ownership

FOB shipping point (buyer pays)   Carrier   FOB destination (seller pays)

	Ownership Transfers when Goods Passed to	Transportation Costs Paid by
FOB shipping point	Carrier	Buyer
FOB destination	Buyer	Seller

seller pays

The second means of transfer is *FOB destination,* which means ownership of the goods transfers to the buyer at the buyer's place of business. The seller is responsible for paying shipping charges and bears the risk of damage or loss in transit. The seller does not record revenue from this sale until the goods arrive at the destination because this transaction is not complete before that point. **Compaq Computer** at one time shipped its products FOB shipping point, but it found delivery companies to be unreliable in picking up shipments at scheduled times, causing backups and missing deliveries. This resulted in unhappy consumers. Compaq then changed its agreements to FOB destination, took control of shipping, and eliminated its problems.

In some situations, the party not responsible for shipping costs pays the carrier. In these cases, the party paying these costs either bills the party responsbile or, more commonly, adjusts its account payable or account receivable with the other party. For example, a buyer paying a carrier when terms are FOB destination can decrease its account payable to the seller by the amount of shipping cost. Similarly, a seller who pays a carrier when terms are FOB shipping point can increase its account receivable from the buyer by the amount of shipping cost.

Recording Purchases Information

We explained that purchase discounts, purchase returns and allowances, and transportation-in are included in computing the total cost of merchandise inventory. Purchases are initially recorded as debits to Merchandise Inventory. Any later purchase discounts, returns, and allowances are credited (decreases) to Merchandise Inventory. Transportation-in is debited (added) to Merchandise Inventory. Z-Mart's itemized costs of merchandise purchases for year 2002 are in Exhibit 6.10. The Merchandise Inventory account reflects the net cost of purchased merchandise according to the *cost principle.* Recall that the Merchandise Inventory account is updated after each transaction that affects the cost of goods either purchased or sold. These timely updates of the Merchandise Inventory account reflect a perpetual inventory system.

Exhibit 6.10

Itemized Costs of Merchandise Purchases

Z-MART Itemized Costs of Merchandise Purchases For Year Ended December 31, 2002	
Invoice cost of merchandise purchases	$235,800
Less: Purchase discounts received	(4,200)
Purchase returns and allowances	(1,500)
Add: Costs of transportation-in	2,300
Total cost of merchandise purchases	**$232,400**

The accounting system described here does not provide separate records for total purchases, total purchase discounts, total purchase returns and allowances, and total transportation-in. Managers usually need this information, however, to evaluate and control each of these cost elements. Nearly all companies collect this information in supplementary records. **Supplementary records,** also called *supplemental records,* refer to information outside the usual accounting records and ledger accounts.

Point: Some companies have separate accounts for purchase discounts, returns and allowances, and transportation-in. Balances of these accounts are then transferred to Merchandise Inventory at the end of each period. This is a hybrid system of perpetual and periodic. That is, Merchandise Inventory is updated on a perpetual basis but only for purchases and cost of goods sold.

Quick Check

4. How long are the credit and discount periods when credit terms are 2/10, n/60?
5. Identify items subtracted from the *list* amount and not recorded when computing purchase price: (a) freight-in; (b) trade discount; (c) purchase discount; (d) purchase return.
6. Explain the meaning of *FOB*. What does *FOB destination* mean?

Answers—p. 244

Merchandise Sales

We explained that companies buying merchandise for resale need to account for purchases, purchase discounts, and purchase returns and allowances. Merchandising companies also must account for sales, sales discounts, sales returns and allowances, and cost of goods sold. A merchandising company such as Z-Mart reports these items in the gross profit section of its income statement as shown in Exhibit 6.11.

Exhibit 6.11

Gross Profit Section of Income Statement

Z-MART Computation of Gross Profit For Year Ended December 31, 2002		
Sales		$321,000
Less: Sales discounts	$4,300	
Sales returns and allowances	2,000	6,300
Net sales		$314,700
Cost of goods sold		(230,400)
Gross profit		**$ 84,300**

Concept 6-2

This section explains how information in this computation is derived from transactions involving sales, sales discounts, and sales returns and allowances.

Sales Transactions

Each sales transaction for a seller of merchandise involves two parts. One part is the revenue received in the form of an asset from a customer. The second part is the recognition

 P2 Analyze and record transactions for sales of merchandise using a perpetual system.

of the cost of merchandise sold to a customer. Accounting for a sales transaction means capturing information about both parts. Moreover, sales transactions of merchandisers usually include both sales for cash and sales on credit. Whether a sale is for cash or on credit, it requires two entries: one for revenue and one for cost. To illustrate, Z-Mart sold $2,400 of merchandise on credit on November 3. The revenue part of this transaction is recorded as

Assets = Liabilities + Equity
+2,400   +2400

(e) Nov. 3	Accounts Receivable	2,400	
	Sales		2,400
	Sold merchandise on credit.		

This entry reflects an increase in Z-Mart's assets in the form of an account receivable. It also shows the revenue (Sales) from the credit sale.[5] If the sale is for cash, the debit is to Cash instead of Accounts Receivable. The cost of the merchandise Z-Mart sold on November 3 is $1,600. (In Chapter 7 we explain the computation of the cost of merchandise.) The entry to record the cost part of this sales transaction (under a perpetual inventory system) is

Assets = Liabilities + Equity
−1,600   −1,600

(e) Nov. 3	Cost of Goods Sold	1,600	
	Merchandise Inventory		1,600
	To record the cost of Nov. 3 sale.		

Since the cost part is recorded each time a sale occurs, the Merchandise Inventory account will reflect the cost of the remaining merchandise available for sale.

Sales Discounts

Selling goods on credit demands that the amounts and dates of future payments be made clear to avoid misunderstandings. We explained earlier in this chapter that credit terms often include a discount to encourage early payment. Companies granting cash discounts to customers refer to these as *sales discounts*. Sales discounts can benefit a seller by decreasing the delay in receiving cash. Prompt payments also reduce future efforts and costs of billing customers.

At the time of a credit sale, a seller does not know whether a customer will pay within the discount period and take advantage of a cash discount. This means the seller usually does not record a sales discount until a customer actually pays within the discount period. To illustrate, Z-Mart completes a credit sale for $1,000 on November 12, subject to terms of 2/10, n/60. The entry to record the revenue part of this sale is

Assets = Liabilities + Equity
+1,000   +1,000

Nov. 12	Accounts Receivable	1,000	
	Sales		1,000
	Sold merchandise under terms of 2/10, n/60.		

This entry records the receivable and the revenue as if the customer will pay the full amount. The customer has two options, however. One is to wait 60 days until January 11 and pay the full $1,000. In this case, Z-Mart records the payment as

Assets = Liabilities + Equity
+1,000
−1,000

Jan. 11	Cash	1,000	
	Accounts Receivable		1,000
	Received payment for Nov. 12 sale.		

The customer's second option is to pay $980 within a 10-day period running through November 22. If the customer pays on or before November 22, Z-Mart records the payment as

[5] We describe in Chapter 10 the accounting for sales to customers who use third-party credit cards such as those issued by banks and other organizations.

Nov. 22	Cash	980	
	Sales Discounts	20	
	Accounts Receivable		1,000
	Received payment for Nov. 12 sale less the discount.		

Assets = Liabilities + Equity
+980   −20
−1,000

Sales Discounts is a contra-revenue account. Management monitors Sales Discounts to assess the effectiveness and cost of its discount program. The Sales Discounts account is deducted from the Sales account when computing a company's net sales (see Exhibit 6.11). Information about sales discounts is seldom reported on income statements distributed to external users.

> **Did You Know?**
>
> **Discount Targeting   Catalina Supermarkets** uses bar codes, software, and the Web to help execs keep tabs on who buys what foods, how often, and at what price. Its high-profit customer rate is up because most discounts and services, such as coupons and free delivery, are given almost exclusively to its best customers.

Sales Returns and Allowances

Sales returns refer to merchandise that customers return to the seller after a sale. Many companies allow customers to return merchandise for a full refund. *Sales allowances* refer to reductions in the selling price of merchandise sold to customers. This can occur with damaged merchandise that a customer is willing to purchase with a decrease in selling price. Sales returns and allowances involve dissatisfied customers and the possibility of lost future sales, and managers need information about returns and allowances to monitor these problems. Many accounting systems record returns and allowances in a separate contra-revenue account.

To illustrate, recall Z-Mart's sale of merchandise on November 3 for $2,400 that had cost $1,600. Assume that the customer returns part of the merchandise on November 6, and the returned items sell for $800 and cost $600. The revenue part of this transaction must reflect the decrease in sales from the customer's return of merchandise:

(f) Nov. 6	Sales Returns and Allowances	800	
	Accounts Receivable		800
	Customer returns merchandise of Nov. 3 sale.		

Assets = Liabilities + Equity
−800   −800

Managers monitor the Sales Returns and Allowances contra account for quality purposes. Published income statements usually omit this detail and show only net sales.

If merchandise returned to Z-Mart is not defective and can be resold to another customer, Z-Mart returns these goods to its inventory. The entry necessary to restore the cost of these goods to the Merchandise Inventory account is

> **Did You Know?**
>
> **MegaReturns   Book merchandisers** such as **Barnes & Noble** and **Borders Books** can return unsold books to publishers at purchase price. Publishers say returns of new hardcover books run between 35% and 50%. This compares with 15% to 25% ten years ago.
>
>

Nov. 6	Merchandise Inventory	600	
	Cost of Goods Sold		600
	Returned goods to inventory.		

Assets = Liabilities + Equity
+600   +600

But if the merchandise returned is defective, the seller may discard it. In this case, the cost of returned merchandise is not restored to the Merchandise Inventory account but is left in the Cost of Goods Sold account.[6]

---

[6] When managers want to monitor the cost of defective merchandise, a better method is to remove the cost from (credit) Cost of Goods Sold and charge it to (debit) a Loss from Defective Merchandise account.

Another possibility is that $800 of the merchandise Z-Mart sold on November 3 is defective but the customer decides to keep it because Z-Mart offers a $500 price reduction. The entry Z-Mart must make in this case is to record the allowance and decrease expected assets:

Assets = Liabilities + Equity
−500   −500

Nov. 6	Sales Returns and Allowances	500	
	Accounts Receivable		500
	To record sales allowance of Nov. 3 sale.		

The seller usually prepares a credit memorandum to confirm a customer's return or allowance. A **credit memorandum** informs a customer of a credit to its Account Receivable account from a sales return or allowance. Z-Mart's credit memorandum issued to the customer for the $500 sales allowance on November 6 is shown in Exhibit 6.12.

Exhibit 6.12

Credit Memorandum

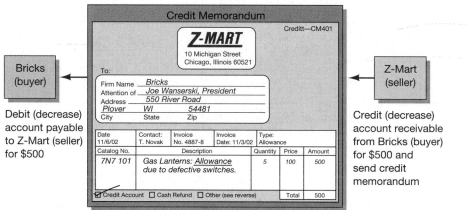

Case: Z-Mart (seller) approves $500
sales allowance to Bricks (buyer)

Quick Check

7. Why are sales discounts and sales returns and allowances recorded in contra-revenue accounts instead of directly in the Sales account?

8. Under what conditions are two entries necessary to record a sales return?

9. When merchandise is sold on credit and the seller notifies the buyer of a price reduction, does the seller send a credit memorandum or a debit memorandum?

Answers—p. 244

Additional Merchandising Issues

This section explains merchandising activities' effect on other accounting processes. We address cost and price adjustments, preparation of adjusting and closing entries, and relations between important accounts.

Cost and Price Adjustments

Buyers and sellers sometimes need to adjust the amount owed between them. Such adjustments can occur when purchased merchandise does not meet specifications, unordered goods are received, quantities different than were ordered and billed are received, or errors occur in billing. The buyer can sometimes adjust the balance without negotiation. For example, when a seller makes an error on an invoice and the buyer discovers it, the buyer can make an adjustment and notify the seller by sending a debit or a credit memorandum. Sometimes adjustments can be made only after negotiations between the buyer and seller, for example, when a buyer claims that some merchandise does not meet specifications. In this case, the amount of allowance given by the seller is usually arrived at only after discussion.

Adjusting Entries

Most adjusting entries are the same for merchandising companies and service companies. In all cases, the adjustments are limited to prepaid expenses (including depreciation), accrued expenses, unearned revenues, and accrued revenues. However, a merchandising company using a perpetual inventory system is usually required to make a special adjustment to update the Merchandise Inventory account to reflect any loss of merchandise. Companies can lose merchandise in several ways, including theft and deterioration. **Shrinkage** is the term used to refer to the loss of inventory.

P3 Prepare adjustments and close accounts for a merchandising company.

While a perpetual inventory system tracks all goods as they move in and out of the company, it is unable to directly measure shrinkage. Instead, we compute shrinkage by comparing a physical count of inventory with recorded quantities. A physical count is usually performed at least once annually to verify the Merchandise Inventory account. Most companies record any necessary adjustment due to shrinkage by charging it to Cost of Goods Sold if shrinkage is not abnormally large.

Did You Know?
Wanted for Shrinkage   Shrinkage can be a sizable cost for many merchandisers. Recent annual losses due to shrinkage are

MusicLand	$22 Million
Sports Authority	9 Million

Companies often invest considerable resources to reduce shrinkage.

To illustrate, Z-Mart's Merchandise Inventory account at the end of year 2002 has a balance of $21,250. A physical count of inventory reveals only $21,000 of inventory available.

Point: Two-thirds of shoplifting losses are thefts by employees.

Z-MART Adjusted Trial Balance December 31, 2002	Debit	Credit
Cash	$ 8,200	
Accounts receivable	11,200	
Merchandise inventory	**21,000**	
Office supplies	550	
Store supplies	250	
Prepaid insurance	300	
Office equipment	4,200	
Accumulated depreciation—Office equipment		$ 1,400
Store equipment	30,000	
Accumulated depreciation—Store equipment		6,000
Accounts payable		16,000
Salaries payable		800
K. Marty, Capital		42,600
K. Marty, Withdrawals	4,000	
Sales		**321,000**
Sales discounts	**4,300**	
Sales returns and allowances	**2,000**	
Cost of goods sold	**230,400**	
Depreciation expense—Store equipment	3,000	
Depreciation expense—Office equipment	700	
Office salaries expense	25,300	
Sales salaries expense	18,500	
Insurance expense	600	
Rent expense, office space	900	
Rent expense, selling space	8,100	
Office supplies expense	1,800	
Store supplies expense	1,200	
Advertising expense	11,300	
Totals	$387,800	$387,800

Exhibit 6.13

Adjusted Trial Balance for a Merchandiser

The adjusting entry to record this $250 shrinkage is

Assets = Liabilities + Equity
−250   −250

Dec. 31	Cost of Goods Sold	250	
	Merchandise Inventory		250
	To adjust for $250 shrinkage revealed by a physical count of inventory.		

Closing Entries

Closing entries are similar for merchandising companies and service companies using a perpetual system. One difference is that we must close additional temporary accounts that arise from merchandising activities. We use Z-Mart's adjusted trial balance in Exhibit 6.13 to show its four-step closing process in Exhibit 6.14.

Exhibit 6.14

Closing Entries for a Merchandiser

Step 1: Close Credit Balances in Temporary Accounts to Income Summary.

Z-Mart has one temporary account with a credit balance; it is closed with this entry:

Dec. 31	**Sales**	**321,000**	
	Income Summary		321,000
	To close credit balances in temporary accounts.		

Step 2: Close Debit Balances in Temporary Accounts to Income Summary.

The second entry closes temporary accounts having debit balances such as Cost of Goods Sold, Sales Discounts, and Sales Returns and Allowances and is shown here:

Dec. 31	Income Summary	308,100	
	Sales Discounts		**4,300**
	Sales Returns and Allowances		**2,000**
	Cost of Goods Sold		**230,400**
	Depreciation Expense—Store Equipment . . .		3,000
	Depreciation Expense—Office Equipment . .		700
	Office Salaries Expense		25,300
	Sales Salaries Expense		18,500
	Insurance Expense		600
	Rent Expense—Office Space		900
	Rent Expense—Selling Space		8,100
	Office Supplies Expense		1,800
	Store Supplies Expense		1,200
	Advertising Expense		11,300
	To close debit balances in temporary accounts.		

Step 3: Close Income Summary to Owner's Capital.

The third closing entry is exactly the same for a merchandising company and a service company. It updates the owner's capital account for income or loss and is shown here:

Dec. 31	Income Summary	12,900	
	K. Marty, Capital		12,900
	To close the Income Summary account.		

The $12,900 amount in the entry is net income reported on the income statement in Exhibit 6.2.

Step 4: Close Withdrawals Account to Owner's Capital.

The fourth closing entry is exactly the same for a merchandising company and a service company. It closes the withdrawals account and adjusts the owner's capital account balance to the amount shown on the balance sheet. This entry for Z-Mart is

Dec. 31	K. Marty, Capital	4,000	
	K. Marty, Withdrawals		4,000
	To close the withdrawals accounts.		

When these entries are posted, all temporary accounts are set to zero and are ready to record events for next year. Also, the capital account now is updated to reflect all prior transactions.

Z-Mart's trial balance includes several accounts unique to merchandising companies: Merchandise Inventory, Sales (of goods), Sales Discounts, Sales Returns and Allowances, and Cost of Goods Sold. Their existence in the ledger means the first two closing entries for a merchandiser are slightly different from the ones described in Chapter 5 for a service company. These differences are bolded in the closing entries of Exhibit 6.14.

Merchandising Cost Flows

Exhibit 6.15 shows the relations between inventory, merchandise purchases, and cost of goods sold across periods. We already explained that the net cost of purchases reflects trade discounts, purchase discounts, and purchase returns and allowances. These items constituting the cost of purchases are recorded in the Merchandise Inventory account under a perpetual system. When each sale occurs, the cost of items sold is transferred from Merchandise Inventory to the Cost of Goods Sold account. Cost of goods sold is reported on the income statement. The ending balance in Merchandise Inventory is reported on the balance sheet.

 Analyze and interpret cost flows and operating activities of a merchandising company.

The Merchandise Inventory account balance at the end of one period is the amount of beginning inventory for the next period. The cost of each purchase is added to the Merchandise Inventory account, and the cost of each sale is transferred from Merchandise Inventory to Cost of Goods Sold. At the end of the period, the Merchandise Inventory balance is reported on the balance sheet.

Exhibit 6.15

Merchandising Cost Flow Across Periods*

Merchandising Cost Accounts

To explain how merchandising transactions affect the Merchandise Inventory and Cost of Goods Sold accounts, we summarize Z-Mart's merchandising activities for year 2002 using T-accounts in Exhibit 6.16. Most amounts are summary representations of several entries made during the year.

We explained that the perpetual inventory accounting system does not include separate accounts for purchases, purchase discounts, purchase returns and allowances, and transportation-in. But Z-Mart, like most companies, keeps supplementary records of these items. These supplementary records are used to accumulate the information in Exhibit 6.16. Z-Mart also keeps a separate record for the cost of merchandise returned by customers and restored in inventory.

The Cost of Goods Sold ending balance of $230,400 is the amount reported on the income statement in Exhibit 6.2. The Merchandise Inventory ending balance of $21,000 is the amount reported as a current asset on the balance sheet in Exhibit 6.3. These amounts also appear on Z-Mart's adjusted trial balance in Exhibit 6.13.

* Cost of goods sold is reported on the income statement. Ending inventory is reported on the balance sheet. One period's ending inventory is the next period's beginning inventory.

Quick Check

10. When a merchandiser uses a perpetual inventory system, why is it sometimes necessary to adjust the Merchandise Inventory balance with an adjusting entry?

11. What temporary accounts do you expect to find in a merchandising business but not in a service business?

12. Describe the closing entries normally made by a merchandising company.

Answers—p. 244

Exhibit 6.16

Merchandising Transactions Reflected in T-Accounts

Merchandise Inventory			
Jan. 1, balance	19,000		
Purchases of merchandise	235,800	Purchase discounts received	4,200
Merchandise returned by customers and restored to inventory	1,400	Purchase returns and allowances	1,500
Transportation-in costs	2,300	Cost of sales to customers	231,550
Dec. 31, unadjusted balance	21,250		
		Dec. 31, shrinkage	250
Dec. 31, adjusted balance	21,000		

Cost of Goods Sold			
Cost of sales	231,550	Merchandise returned by customers and restored to inventory	1,400
Inventory shrinkage adjusting entry	250		
Dec. 31, balance (before closing)	230,400		

Income Statement Formats

P4 Define and prepare multiple-step and single-step income statements.

Generally accepted accounting principles do not require companies to use any one format for financial statements, and we see many different formats in practice. The main part of this section describes two common income statement formats using Z-Mart's data: multiple step and single step. The final part of this section compares accrual and cash flow measures of gross profit.

Multiple-Step Income Statement

A **multiple-step income statement** contains more detail than simply a list of revenues and expenses. Exhibit 6.17 shows a multiple-step income statement for Z-Mart. This format shows detailed computations of net sales and other costs and expenses, and reports subtotals for various classes of items. Z-Mart's sales section is the same as shown earlier in the chapter. The cost of goods sold section draws on Exhibit 6.16. The difference between net sales and cost of goods sold is Z-Mart's gross profit. Further, its operating expenses are classified into two categories. **Selling expenses** include the expenses of promoting sales by displaying and advertising merchandise, making sales, and delivering goods to customers. **General and administrative expenses** support a company's overall operations and include expenses related to accounting, human resource management, and financial management. Also, expenses are often allocated between categories when they contribute to more than one activity. Exhibit 6.17 shows that Z-Mart allocates rent expense of $9,000 from its store building between two categories: $8,100 to selling expense and $900 to general and administrative expense.

Single-Step Income Statement

A **single-step income statement** is another widely used format, and is shown in Exhibit 6.18 for Z-Mart. It includes cost of goods sold as an operating expense and shows only one subtotal for total expenses. Operating expenses are grouped into very few categories. For example, **Reebok**'s income statement in Appendix A shows a single line item titled *Selling, general and administrative expenses*. Its annual report does, however, include management's discussion and analysis on various details of these expenses. Many companies use formats that combine features of both the single- and multiple-step statements. As long as income statement items are shown sensibly, management can choose the format it wants.[7] Similar options are available for the statement of changes in owner's equity and statement of cash flows.

Point: Many companies report interest expense and interest income in a separate category after income from operations and before subtracting income taxes expense. As one example, see Gap's income statement in Appendix A.

---

[7] In later chapters, we describe some items, such as extraordinary gains and losses, that must be shown in certain locations on the income statement.

Z-MART
Income Statement
For Year Ended December 31, 2002

Sales			$321,000
Less: Sales discounts		$ 4,300	
Sales returns and allowances		2,000	6,300
Net sales			$314,700
Cost of goods sold			230,400
Gross profit			$ 84,300
Operating expenses			
Selling expenses			
Depreciation expense—Store equipment	$ 3,000		
Sales salaries expense	18,500		
Rent expense, selling space	8,100		
Store supplies expense	1,200		
Advertising expense	11,300		
Total selling expenses		42,100	
General and administrative expenses			
Depreciation expense—Office equipment	700		
Office salaries expense	25,300		
Insurance expense	600		
Rent expense, office space	900		
Office supplies expense	1,800		
Total general and administrative expenses		29,300	
Total operating expenses			71,400
Net income			$ 12,900

Exhibit 6.17

Multiple-Step Income Statement

Z-MART
Income Statement
For Year Ended December 31, 2002

Net sales		$314,700
Cost of goods sold	$230,400	
Selling expenses	42,100	
General and administrative expenses	29,300	
Total expenses		301,800
Net income		$ 12,900

Exhibit 6.18

Single-Step Income Statement

Merchandising Cash Flows

Another aspect of merchandising activities relates to their cash flow impacts. Merchandising sales and costs reported in the income statement usually differ from their cash receipts and payments for a specific period. This is because an income statement is prepared using accrual accounting, not cash flows. Recognition of sales earned rarely equals cash received from customers. Also, recognition of cost of goods sold incurred rarely equals cash paid to suppliers for a given period.

We use Z-Mart's data in Exhibit 6.19 to illustrate this point. Z-Mart's net sales in the income statement total $314,700, yet cash receipts from customers are only $309,200 (shown on the right side of Exhibit 6.19). This difference reflects a $5,500 *increase* in the Accounts Receivable balance during this period for Z-Mart.

A1 Analyze and interpret accruals and cash flows for merchandising activities.

Exhibit 6.19

Analysis of Merchandising
Cash Flows

Z-MART For Year Ended December 31, 2002			
Income Statement		**Statement of Cash Flows**	
Net sales	$314,700	Receipts from customers	$309,200
Cost of goods sold	230,400	Payments to suppliers	240,900
Gross profit	$ 84,300	Net cash flows from customers and suppliers . .	$ 68,300

An increase in accounts receivable means both a delay in receipt of cash from customers and that cash received from customers this period is less than net sales. To see this, recall that net sales and cash received are the same if all net sales are cash sales. But when some or all net sales are credit sales, the amounts for net sales and cash likely differ. Since Accounts Receivable increased during the period, we know cash received is less than net sales. But if Accounts Receivable had decreased, then cash received would be greater than net sales.

We apply similar analysis to cost of goods sold. Z-Mart's cost of goods sold reported in its income statement totals $230,400, but cash paid to suppliers is $240,900. The difference between cost of goods sold and cash paid to suppliers reflects *two* items: (1) change in inventory and (2) change in accounts payable.

Buying and selling merchandise is the most important activity for a merchandiser such as Z-Mart. We need to analyze both accrual measures and cash flows of this activity for signs of opportunities or problems. Z-Mart is trying to expand its sales by extending credit to more customers. However, extending credit to customers who do not pay their bills can backfire. For effective decision making, we must always analyze important differences in accrual and cash flow figures and assess their future implications. We analyze the relation between accrual and cash flows in more detail in Chapter 17.

Did You Know?

Entrepreneur Incubators Hundreds of entrepreneur incubators provide startups a space plus services for a fee. Services typically include management advice, office support, and financial, legal, and technical help. Entrepreneurs usually leave an incubator after two to three years. Nearly 90% of entrepreneurs that "hatch" from incubators are still in business six years later, which is more than double the usual success rate.

Using the Information   Acid-Test and Gross Margin

Companies with merchandising activities have at least two major differences from service companies. First, merchandise inventory often makes up a large part of a merchandiser's assets, especially current assets. Second, merchandising activities result in cost of goods sold, which is often the largest cost for these companies. Companies with merchandising activities alter our ratio analysis. This is especially the case with the current ratio and the profit margin ratio (see Chapters 4 and 5). This section describes adjustments to these ratios to help us analyze merchandising companies.

Acid-Test Ratio

 Compute the acid-test ratio and explain its use to assess liquidity.

For many merchandising companies, inventory makes up a large portion of current assets. This means a large part of current assets is not readily available for paying liabilities. This happens because inventory must be sold and any resulting accounts receivable must be collected before cash is available. Information about current assets is important since we use it to assess a company's ability to pay its current liabilities. We explained in Chapter 5 that the current ratio, defined as current assets divided by current liabilities, is useful in assessing a company's ability to pay current liabilities. Since it is sometimes unreasonable to assume that inventories are a source of payment for current liabilities, we look to another measure.

One measure to help us assess a company's ability to pay its current liabilities (called *liquidity*) is the acid-test ratio. It differs from the current ratio by excluding less liquid current assets such as inventory. The less liquid assets or liabilities are those that will take longer to be converted to or paid in cash. The **acid-test ratio,** also called *quick ratio,* is defined as *quick assets* (cash, short-term investments, and current receivables) divided by current liabilities—see Exhibit 6.20. This is similar to the current ratio except that the numerator omits inventory and prepaid expenses.

$$\text{Acid-test ratio} = \frac{\text{Cash and equivalents} + \text{Short-term investments} + \text{Short-term receivables}}{\text{Current liabilities}}$$

Exhibit 6.20

Acid-Test (Quick) Ratio

Exhibit 6.21 shows both the acid-test and current ratios of **JCPenney** for 1998 through 2000. Penney's acid-test ratio recently declined. While the industry acid-test ratio also declined, it did not decrease to the extent that Penney's ratio did. Penney's current ratio suggests its short-term obligations can be covered with short-term assets. Still, the acid-test ratio raises some concern. An acid-test ratio less than 1.0 means that Penney's current liabilities exceed its quick assets. A rule of thumb is that the acid-test ratio should have a value of at least 1.0 to conclude that a company is unlikely to face liquidity problems in the near future. A value less than 1.0 suggests a liquidity problem unless a company can generate enough cash from sales or if its accounts payable are not due until late in the next period. Similarly, a value greater than 1.0 can hide a liquidity problem if payables are due shortly and receivables will not be collected until late in the next period. Our analysis of Penney emphasizes that one ratio is seldom enough to reach a conclusion as to strength or weakness. The power of a ratio is often its ability to identify areas for detailed analysis.

Point: Successful use of a just-in-time inventory system can narrow the gap between the acid-test ratio and the current ratio.

You Make the Call

Supplier A retail store requests to purchase supplies on credit from your company. You have no prior experience with this store. The store's current ratio is 2.1, its acid-test ratio is 0.5, and inventory makes up most of its current assets. Do you extend credit to this store?

Answer—p. 244

($ in millions)	2000	1999	1998
Total quick assets	$2,371	$ 4,779	$ 5,179
Total current assets	$8,472	$11,007	$11,484
Total current liabilities	$4,465	$ 5,912	$ 6,137
Acid-test ratio	**0.53**	**0.81**	**0.84**
Current ratio	**1.90**	**1.86**	**1.87**
Industry acid-test ratio	0.7	0.8	1.0
Industry current ratio	3.0	3.1	3.5

Exhibit 6.21

JCPenney's Acid-Test and Current Ratios

Gross Margin Ratio

Cost of goods sold makes up much of the costs of merchandising companies. This means that success for merchandising companies often depends on the relation between sales and cost of goods sold. Without sufficient gross profit, a merchandising company will likely fail. To help understand this important relation, users often compute the gross margin ratio. It differs from the profit margin ratio in that it excludes all costs except cost of goods sold. The **gross margin ratio** is defined as *gross margin* (net sales minus cost of goods sold) divided by net sales—see Exhibit 6.22.

A3 Compute the gross margin ratio and explain its use to assess profitability.

$$\text{Gross margin ratio} = \frac{\text{Net sales} - \text{Cost of goods sold}}{\text{Net sales}}$$

Exhibit 6.22

Gross Margin Ratio

Exhibit 6.23 shows the gross margin ratio of **JCPenney** for 1998–2000. The ratio reflects the gross margin in each dollar of sales. In the case of JCPenney, each $1 of sales

Exhibit 6.23

JCPenney's Gross
Margin Ratio

($ in millions)	2000	1999	1998
Gross margin	$ 9,136	$ 8,819	$ 9,116
Net sales	$32,510	$30,461	$30,410
Gross margin ratio	28.1%	29.0%	30.0%

You Make the Call

Financial Officer Your merchandising company has a 36% gross margin ratio and a 17% net profit margin ratio. Industry averages are 44% for gross margin and 16% for net profit margin. Do these results concern you?

Answer—p. 244

in 2000 yielded about 28¢ in gross margin to cover all other expenses and still produce a profit. This 28¢ margin is down from 29¢ in 1999 and from 30¢ in 1998. This decline is an important (and negative) development. Success for merchandisers such as JCPenney depends on maintaining an adequate gross margin. Data in this exhibit reveal that Penney's net sales increase over this period while its gross margin ratio decreases.

Demonstration Problem

Use the following adjusted trial balance and additional information to complete the requirements:

KC ANTIQUES
Adjusted Trial Balance
December 31, 2002

	Debit	Credit
Cash	$ 20,000	
Merchandise inventory	60,000	
Store supplies	1,500	
Equipment	45,600	
Accumulated depreciation—Equipment		$ 16,600
Accounts payable		9,000
Salaries payable		2,000
Kyle Carter, Capital		79,000
Kyle Carter, Withdrawals	10,000	
Sales		343,250
Sales discounts	5,000	
Sales returns and allowances	6,000	
Cost of goods sold	159,900	
Depreciation expense—Store equipment	4,100	
Depreciation expense—Office equipment	1,600	
Sales salaries expense	30,000	
Office salaries expense	34,000	
Insurance expense	11,000	
Rent expense (70% is store, 30% is office)	24,000	
Store supplies expense	5,750	
Advertising expense	31,400	
Totals	$449,850	$449,850

KC Antiques' *supplementary records* for 2002 reveal the following itemized costs for merchandising activities:

Invoice cost of merchandise purchases	$150,000
Purchase discounts received	2,500
Purchase returns and allowances	2,700
Cost of transportation-in	5,000

Required

1. Use the supplementary records to compute the total cost of merchandise purchases for 2002.
2. Prepare a 2002 multiple-step income statement. Inventory at December 31, 2001 is $70,100.
3. Prepare a single-step income statement for 2002.
4. Prepare closing entries for KC Antiques at December 31, 2002.
5. Compute the acid-test ratio and the gross margin ratio. Explain the meaning of each ratio and interpret them for KC Antiques.

Planning the Solution

- Compute the total cost of merchandise purchases for 2002.
- To prepare the multiple-step statement, first compute net sales. Then, to compute cost of goods sold, add the net cost of merchandise purchases for the year to beginning inventory and subtract the cost of ending inventory. Subtract cost of goods sold from net sales to get gross profit. Then classify operating expenses as selling expenses or general and administrative expenses.
- To prepare the single-step income statement, begin with net sales. Then list and subtract the operating expenses.
- The first closing entry debits all temporary accounts with credit balances and opens the Income Summary account. The second closing entry credits all temporary accounts with debit balances. The third entry closes the Income Summary account to the owner's capital account, and the fourth closing entry closes the withdrawals account to the capital account.
- Identify the quick assets on the adjusted trial balance. Compute the acid-test ratio by dividing quick assets by the amount of current liabilities. Compute the gross margin ratio by dividing the gross profit from requirement (2) by net sales.

Solution to Demonstration Problem

1.

Invoice cost of merchandise purchases	$150,000
Less: Purchases discounts received	(2,500)
Purchase returns and allowances	(2,700)
Add: Cost of transportation-in	5,000
Total cost of merchandise purchases	$149,800

2. Multiple-step income statement

KC ANTIQUES
Income Statement
Year Ended December 31, 2002

Sales		$343,250
Less: Sales discounts	$ 5,000	
Sales returns and allowances	6,000	11,000
Net sales		$332,250
Cost of goods sold'		159,900
Gross profit		$172,350
Operating expenses		
Selling expenses		
Depreciation expense—Store equipment	$ 4,100	
Sales salaries expense	30,000	
Rent expense—Selling space	16,800	
Store supplies expense	5,750	
Advertising expense	31,400	
Total selling expenses	88,050	

[continued on next page]

[continued from previous page]

General and administrative expenses:

Depreciation expense—Office equipment	$ 1,600		
Office salaries expense	34,000		
Insurance expense	11,000		
Rent expense—Office space	7,200		
Total general and administrative expenses		53,800	
Total operating expenses			141,850
Net income			$ 30,500

* Cost of goods sold computation:

Merchandise inventory, December 31, 2001	$ 70,100
Total cost of merchandise purchases (from part 1)	149,800
Goods available for sale	$219,900
Merchandise inventory, December 31, 2002	60,000
Cost of goods sold	$159,900

3. Single-step income statement

KC ANTIQUES
Income Statement
For Year Ended December 31, 2002

Net sales		$332,250
Cost of goods sold	$159,900	
Selling expenses	88,050	
General and administrative expenses	53,800	301,750
Net income		$ 30,500

4.

Dec. 31	Sales	343,250	
	Income Summary		343,250
	To close credit balances in temporary accounts.		
Dec. 31	Income Summary	312,750	
	Sales Discounts		5,000
	Sales Returns and Allowances		6,000
	Cost of Goods Sold		159,900
	Depreciation Expense—Store Equipment . .		4,100
	Depreciation Expense—Office Equipment . .		1,600
	Sales Salaries Expense		30,000
	Office Salaries Expense		34,000
	Insurance Expense		11,000
	Rent Expense		24,000
	Store Supplies Expense		5,750
	Advertising Expense		31,400
	To close debit balances in temporary accounts.		
Dec. 31	Income Summary	30,500	
	Kyle Carter, Capital		30,500
	To close the Income Summary account.		
Dec. 31	Kyle Carter, Capital	10,000	
	Kyle Carter, Withdrawals		10,000
	To close the withdrawals account.		

5. Acid test ratio = Cash/(Accounts payable + Salaries payable)

= $20,000/($9,000 + $2,000) = $20,000/$11,000 = 1.82

Gross margin ratio = Gross profit/Net sales = $172,350/$332,250 = 0.52

KC Antiques has a healthy acid-test ratio of 1.82. This means it has more than $1.80 in liquid assets to satisfy each $1.00 in current liabilities. (With this ratio, neither supplies nor inventory are considered liquid assets readily convertible into cash for use in satisfying short-term obligations.) The gross margin of 0.52 shows that KC Antiques spends 48¢ ($1.00 − $0.52) of every dollar of net sales on the costs of acquiring the merchandise it sells. This leaves 52¢ of every dollar of net sales to cover other expenses incurred in the business and to provide a profit.

Comparing Periodic and Perpetual Inventory Systems

6A

Recall that under a perpetual system, the Merchandise Inventory account is updated after each purchase and each sale. The Cost of Goods Sold account also is updated after each sale so that during the period its account balance reflects the period's total cost of goods sold to date. Under a periodic inventory system, the Merchandise Inventory account is updated only once each accounting period. This update occurs at the *end* of the period. During the period, the Merchandise Inventory balance remains unchanged. It reflects the beginning inventory balance until it is updated at the end of the period. Similarly, in a periodic inventory system, cost of goods sold is not recorded as each sale occurs. Instead, the total cost of goods sold during the period is computed at the end of the period.

Under a perpetual system, each purchase, purchase return and allowance, purchase discount, and transportation-in transaction is recorded in the Merchandise Inventory account. Under a periodic system, a separate temporary account is set up for *each* of these items. At period-end, each of these temporary accounts is closed and the Merchandise Inventory account is updated. To illustrate the differences, we use parallel columns to show journal entries for the most common transactions using both periodic and perpetual inventory systems (codes (*a*) through (*f*) link these transactions to those in the chapter, and we drop explanations for simplicity).

Recording Merchandise Transactions

P5 Record and compare merchandising transactions using both periodic and perpetual inventory systems.

Purchases

The periodic system uses a temporary *Purchases* account that accumulates the cost of all purchase transactions during the period. Z-Mart purchases merchandise for $1,200 on credit with terms of 2/10, n/30. Z-Mart's entry to record this credit purchase is

(*a*)

Periodic			Perpetual		
Purchases	1,200		Merchandise Inventory	1,200	
Accounts Payable . .		1,200	Accounts Payable		1,200

Purchase Discounts

The periodic system uses a temporary *Purchase Discounts* account that accumulates discounts taken on purchase transactions during the period. If payment in (*a*) is delayed until after the discount period expires, the entry under both methods is to debit Accounts Payable and credit Cash for $1,200 each. However, when Z-Mart pays the supplier for the previous purchase in (*a*) within the discount period, the required payment is $1,176 ($1,200 × 98%) and is recorded as

(b)

Periodic			Perpetual		
Accounts Payable	1,200		Accounts Payable	1,200	
Purchase Discounts .		24	Merchandise Inventory .		24
Cash		1,176	Cash		1,176

Purchase Returns and Allowances

Z-Mart returns merchandise purchased on November 2 because of defects. In the periodic system, the temporary *Purchase Returns and Allowances* account accumulates the cost of all returns and allowances during a period. If the recorded cost (including discounts) of the defective merchandise is $300, Z-Mart records the return with this entry:

(c)

Periodic			Perpetual		
Accounts Payable	300		Accounts Payable	300	
Purchase Returns and Allowances . .		300	Merchandise Inventory .		300

Transportation-In

Z-Mart paid a $75 freight charge to haul merchandise to its store. In the periodic system, this cost is charged to a temporary *Transportation-In* account.

(d)

Periodic			Perpetual		
Transportation-In	75		Merchandise Inventory	75	
Cash		75	Cash		75

Sales

Under the periodic system, the cost of goods sold is not recorded at the time of sale. (We later show how to compute total cost of goods sold at the end of a period.) Z-Mart sold $2,400 of merchandise on credit, and its cost of this merchandise is $1,600:

(e)

Periodic			Perpetual		
Accounts Receivable . . .	2,400		Accounts Receivable	2,400	
Sales		2,400	Sales		2,400
			Cost of Goods Sold	1,600	
			Merchandise Inventory .		1,600

Sales Returns

A customer returns part of the merchandise from the previous transaction in (*e*), where returned items sell for $800 and cost $600. (*Recall:* The periodic system records only the revenue effect, not the cost effect, for sales transactions.) Z-Mart restores the merchandise to inventory and records the return as

(f)

Periodic			Perpetual		
Sales Returns and Allowances	800		Sales Returns and Allowances	800	
Accounts Receivable		800	Accounts Receivable . .		800
			Merchandise Inventory	600	
			Cost of Goods Sold . . .		600

Adjusting and Closing Entries

The periodic and perpetual inventory systems have slight differences in adjusting and closing entries. Z-Mart's adjusted trial balances (except for shrinkage) under each system are shown in Exhibit 6A.1.

The Merchandise Inventory balance is $19,000 under the periodic system and $21,250 under the perpetual system. Because the periodic system does not revise the Merchandise Inventory balance during the period, the $19,000 amount is the beginning inventory. However, the $21,250 balance un-

Exhibit 6A.1

Comparison of Adjusted Trial
Balances (absent shrinkage)—
Periodic and Perpetual

Z-MART
Adjusted Trial Balance (Periodic System)
December 31, 2002

	Debit	Credit
Cash	$ 8,200	
Accounts receivable	11,200	
Merchandise inventory	19,000	
Office supplies	550	
Store supplies	250	
Prepaid insurance	300	
Office equipment	4,200	
Accum. depreciation—Office eq.		$ 1,400
Store equipment	30,000	
Accum. depreciation—Store eq.		6,000
Accounts payable		16,000
Salaries payable		800
K. Marty, Capital		42,600
K. Marty, Withdrawals	4,000	
Sales		321,000
Sales discounts	4,300	
Sales returns and allowances	2,000	
Purchases	235,800	
Purchase discounts		4,200
Purchase returns and allowances		1,500
Transportation-in	2,300	
Depreciation expense—Store eq.	3,000	
Depreciation expense—Office eq.	700	
Office salaries expense	25,300	
Sales salaries expense	18,500	
Insurance expense	600	
Rent expense—Office space	900	
Rent expense—Selling space	8,100	
Office supplies expense	1,800	
Store supplies expense	1,200	
Advertising expense	11,300	
Totals	$393,500	$393,500

Z-MART
Adjusted Trial Balance (Perpetual System)
December 31, 2002

	Debit	Credit
Cash	$ 8,200	
Accounts receivable	11,200	
Merchandise inventory	21,250	
Office supplies	550	
Store supplies	250	
Prepaid insurance	300	
Office equipment	4,200	
Accum. depreciation—Office eq.		$ 1,400
Store equipment	30,000	
Accum. depreciation—Store eq.		6,000
Accounts payable		16,000
Salaries payable		800
K. Marty, Capital		42,600
K. Marty, Withdrawals	4,000	
Sales		321,000
Sales discounts	4,300	
Sales returns and allowances	2,000	
Cost of goods sold	230,150	
Depreciation expense—Store eq.	3,000	
Depreciation expense—Office eq.	700	
Office salaries expense	25,300	
Sales salaries expense	18,500	
Insurance expense	600	
Rent expense—Office space	900	
Rent expense—Selling space	8,100	
Office supplies expense	1,800	
Store supplies expense	1,200	
Advertising expense	11,300	
Totals	$387,800	$387,800

der the perpetual system is the recorded ending inventory before adjusting for any inventory shrinkage. A physical count of inventory taken at the end of the period reveals $21,000 of merchandise available. We know then that inventory shrinkage is $21,250 − $21,000 = $250.

The adjusting entry for shrinkage and the closing entries for the two systems are shown in Exhibit 6A.2. The periodic system does not require an adjusting entry to record inventory shrinkage. Instead, it puts the ending inventory of $21,000 in the Merchandise Inventory account (which is net of shrinkage) in the first closing entry and removes the $19,000 beginning inventory balance from the account in the second closing entry.

Exhibit 6A.2

Comparison of Adjusting and
Closing Entries—Periodic and
Perpetual

Periodic		
Adjusting Entry—Shrinkage		
None		

Perpetual		
Adjusting Entry—Shrinkage		
Cost of Goods Sold	250	
Merchandise Inventory		250

Closing Entries		
(1) Sales	321,000	
Merchandise Inventory	**21,000**	
Purchase Discounts	**4,200**	
Purchase Returns and Allowances . . .	**1,500**	
Income Summary		347,700
(2) Income Summary	334,800	
Sales Discounts		4,300
Sales Returns and Allowances		2,000
Merchandise Inventory		**19,000**
Purchases		**235,800**
Transportation-In		**2,300**
Depreciation Expense—Store eq. . . .		3,000
Depreciation Expense—Office eq. . .		700
Office Salaries Expense		25,300
Sales Salaries Expense		18,500
Insurance Expense		600
Rent Expense—Office space		900
Rent Expense—Selling space		8,100
Office Supplies Expense		1,800
Store Supplies Expense		1,200
Advertising Expense		11,300
(3) Income Summary	12,900	
K. Marty, Capital		12,900
(4) K. Marty, Capital	4,000	
K. Marty, Withdrawals		4,000

Closing Entries		
(1) Sales	321,000	
Income Summary		321,000
(2) Income Summary	308,100	
Sales Discounts		4,300
Sales Returns and Allowances		2,000
Cost of Goods Sold		**230,400**
Depreciation Expense—Store eq. . . .		3,000
Depreciation Expense—Office eq. . .		700
Office Salaries Expense		25,300
Sales Salaries Expense		18,500
Insurance Expense		600
Rent Expense—Office space		900
Rent Expense—Selling space		8,100
Office Supplies Expense		1,800
Store Supplies Expense		1,200
Advertising Expense		11,300
(3) Income Summary	12,900	
K. Marty, Capital		12,900
(4) K. Marty, Capital	4,000	
K. Marty, Withdrawals		4,000

By updating Merchandise Inventory and closing Purchases, Purchase Discounts, Purchase Returns and Allowances, and Transportation-In, the periodic system transfers the cost of goods sold amount to Income Summary. Review the periodic side of Exhibit 6A.2 and notice that the colored items affect Income Summary as follows:

Credited to Income Summary in the first closing entry	
Merchandise inventory (ending)	$ 21,000
Purchase discounts	4,200
Purchase returns and allowances	1,500
Debited to Income Summary in the second closing entry	
Merchandise inventory (beginning)	(19,000)
Purchases	(235,800)
Transportation-in	(2,300)
Net effect on Income Summary	**$(230,400)**

This $230,400 effect on Income Summary is the cost of goods sold amount. This figure is confirmed as follows:

Beginning inventory		$ 19,000
Purchases	$235,800	
Less purchase discounts	(4,200)	
Less purchase returns and allowances	(1,500)	
Plus transportation-in	2,300	
Net cost of goods purchased		232,400
Cost of goods available for sale		$251,400
Less ending inventory		(21,000)
Cost of goods sold		**$230,400**

This shows that the periodic system transfers cost of goods sold to the Income Summary account but without using a Cost of Goods Sold account. Also, the periodic system does not separately measure shrinkage. Instead, it computes cost of goods available for sale, subtracts the cost of ending inventory, and defines the difference as cost of goods sold. This difference includes shrinkage.

Exhibit 6A.3 shows the work sheet that we could prepare in developing financial statements. It slightly differs from the work sheet in Chapter 5—the differences are bolded. The adjustments in the work sheet reflect the following economic events: (a) Expiration of $600 of prepaid insurance. (b) Use of $1,200 of store supplies. (c) Use of $1,800 of office supplies. (d) Depreciation of $3,000 for store

Work Sheet for a Merchandiser

Exhibit 6A.3

Work Sheet for Merchandiser
(using a perpetual system)

No.	Account	Unadjusted Trial Balance Dr.	Cr.	Adjustments Dr.	Cr.	Adjusted Trial Balance Dr.	Cr.	Income Statement Dr.	Cr.	Balance Sheet and Statement of Changes in Owner's Equity Dr.	Cr.
101	Cash	8,200				8,200				8,200	
106	Accounts receivable	11,200				11,200				11,200	
119	**Merchandise Inventory**	21,250			(g) 250	21,000				21,000	
124	Office supplies	2,350			(c) 1,800	550				550	
125	Store supplies	1,450			(b) 1,200	250				250	
128	Prepaid insurance	900			(a) 600	300				300	
163	Office equipment	4,200				4,200				4,200	
164	Accum. depr.—office equip.		700		(e) 700		1,400				1,400
165	Store equipment	30,000				30,000				30,000	
166	Accum. depr.—office equip.		3,000		(d) 3,000		6,000				6,000
201	Accounts payable		16,000				16,000				16,000
209	Salaries payable				(f) 800		800				800
301	K. Marty, Capital		42,600				42,600				42,600
302	K. Marty, Withdrawals	4,000				4,000				4,000	
413	**Sales**		321,000				321,000		321,000		
414	**Sales returns and allowances**	2,000				2,000		2,000			
415	**Sales discounts**	4,300				4,300		4,300			
502	**Cost of goods sold**	230,150		(g) 250		230,400		230,400			
612	Depr. expense—store equip.			(d) 3,000		3,000		3,000			
613	Depr. expense—office equip.			(e) 700		700		700			
620	Office salaries expense	25,000		(f) 300		25,300		25,300			
621	Sales salaries expense	18,000		(f) 500		18,500		18,500			
637	Insurance expense			(a) 600		600		600			
641	Rent expense, office space	900				900		900			
642	Rent expense, selling space	8,100				8,100		8,100			
650	Office supplies expense			(c) 1,800		1,800		1,800			
651	Store supplies expense			(b) 1,200		1,200		1,200			
655	Advertising expense	11,300				11,300		11,300			
	Totals	383,300	383,300	8,350	8,350	387,800	387,800	308,100	321,000	79,700	66,800
	Net income							12,900			12,900
	Totals							321,000	321,000	79,700	79,700

equipment. (*e*) Depreciation of $700 for office equipment. (*f*) Accrual of $300 of unpaid office salaries and $500 of unpaid store salaries. (*g*) Inventory shrinkage of $250. Once the adjusted amounts are extended into the financial statement columns, the information is used to develop financial statements.

Adjusting Entry Method—Periodic System

In our discussion of the periodic system, the change in the Merchandise Inventory account is recorded as part of the closing process. This *closing entry method* is common. An alternative method, called the *adjusting entry method,* also is used. The *adjusting entry method* records the change in the Merchandise Inventory account with adjusting entries. Under this method, the first two closing entries (see Exhibit 6A.2) do not include the Merchandise Inventory account.

Adjusting Entries

Under the adjusting entry method of the periodic system, Z-Mart removes the beginning balance from the Merchandise Inventory account by recording this adjusting entry at the end of the period:

Dec. 31	Income Summary	19,000	
	Merchandise Inventory		19,000
	To remove the beginning balance from the		
	Merchandise Inventory account.		

A second adjusting entry inserts the ending balance in the inventory account:

Dec. 31	Merchandise Inventory	21,000	
	Income Summary		21,000
	To insert the ending balance in the		
	Merchandise Inventory account.		

After these entries are posted, the Merchandise Inventory account appears as follows:

Merchandise Inventory			
Beg. balance	19,000		
		Adjustment	19,000
Adjustment	21,000		
End. balance	21,000		

Closing Entries

If the adjusting entry method for inventory is used, the closing entries do not include the Merchandise Inventory account. In particular, entries (1) and (2) in Exhibit 6A.2 are the same except for removing the Merchandise Inventory account and its balance from both entries (including its amount from Income Summary). Entry (3) to close Income Summary is unchanged. The adjusting entry method took four entries instead of two to get net income of $12,900 into Income Summary.

Quick Check

13. What account is used in a perpetual inventory system but not in a periodic system?

14. Which of the following accounts are temporary accounts under a periodic system? (a) Merchandise Inventory; (b) Purchases; (c) Transportation-In.

15. How is cost of goods sold computed under a periodic inventory system?

16. Do reported amounts of ending inventory and net income differ if the adjusting entry method of recording the change in inventory is used instead of the closing entry method?

Answer—p. 244

Summary

C1 Describe merchandising activities and identify business examples. Operations of merchandisers involve buying products and reselling them. Examples of merchandisers include **Wal-Mart**, **Home Depot**, **The Limited**, and **Barnes & Noble**.

C2 Identify and explain the components of income for a merchandising company. A merchandiser's costs on an income statement include an amount for cost of goods sold. Gross profit, or gross margin, equals sales minus cost of goods sold.

C3 Identify and explain the inventory asset of a merchandising company. The current asset section of a merchandising company's balance sheet includes *merchandise inventory*, which refers to the products a merchandiser sells and are available for sale at the balance sheet date.

C4 Describe both perpetual and periodic inventory systems. A perpetual inventory system continuously tracks the cost of goods available for sale and the cost of goods sold. A periodic system accumulates the cost of goods purchased during the period and does not compute the amount of inventory or the cost of goods sold until the end of a period.

C5 Analyze and interpret cost flows and operating activities of a merchandising company. Costs of merchandise purchases flow into Merchandise Inventory and from there to Cost of Goods Sold on the income statement. Any remaining Merchandise Inventory is reported as a current asset on the balance sheet.

A1 Analyze and interpret accruals and cash flows for merchandising activities. Merchandising sales and costs of sales reported in the income statement usually differ from their corresponding cash receipts and cash payments. Cash received from customers equals net sales less the increase (or plus the decrease) in Accounts Receivable during the period. Cash paid to suppliers equals cost of goods sold less the increase (or plus the decrease) in Accounts Payable and less the decrease (or plus the increase) in Inventory during the period.

A2 Compute the acid-test ratio and explain its use to assess liquidity. The acid-test ratio is computed as quick assets (cash, short-term investments, and current receivables) divided by current liabilities. It indicates a company's ability to pay its current liabilities with its existing quick assets. A ratio equal to or greater than 1.0 is often adequate.

A3 Compute the gross margin ratio and explain its use to assess profitability. The gross margin ratio is computed as gross margin (net sales minus cost of goods sold) divided by net sales. It indicates a company's profitability before considering operating expenses.

P1 Analyze and record transactions for merchandise purchases using a perpetual system. For a perpetual inventory system, purchases of inventory (net of trade discounts) are added (debited) to the Merchandise Inventory account. Purchase discounts and purchase returns and allowances are subtracted (credited) from Merchandise Inventory, and transportation-in costs are added (debited) to Merchandise Inventory.

P2 Analyze and record transactions for sales of merchandise using a perpetual system. A merchandiser records sales at list price less any trade discounts. The cost of items sold is transferred from Merchandise Inventory to Cost of Goods Sold. Refunds or credits given to customers for unsatisfactory merchandise are recorded (debited) in Sales Returns and Allowances, a contra account to Sales. If merchandise is returned and restored to inventory, the cost of this merchandise is removed from Cost of Goods Sold and transferred back to Merchandise Inventory. When cash discounts from the sales price are offered and customers pay within the discount period, the seller records (debits) Sales Discounts, a contra account to Sales.

P3 Prepare adjustments and close accounts for a merchandising company. With a perpetual system, it is often necessary to make an adjustment for inventory shrinkage. This is computed by comparing a physical count of inventory with the Merchandise Inventory balance. Shrinkage is normally charged to Cost of Goods Sold. Temporary accounts closed to Income Summary for a merchandiser include Sales, Sales Discounts, Sales Returns and Allowances, and Cost of Goods Sold.

P4 Define and prepare multiple-step and single-step income statements. Multiple-step income statements include greater detail for sales and expenses than do single-step income statements. They also show details of net sales and report expenses in categories reflecting different activities.

P5 Record and compare merchandising transactions using both periodic and perpetual inventory systems. Transactions involving the sale and purchase of merchandise are recorded and analyzed under both the periodic and perpetual inventory systems. Adjusting and closing entries for both inventory systems are illustrated and explained.

Guidance Answers to **You Make the Call**

Entrepreneur For terms of 3/10, n/90, missing the 3% discount for an additional 80 days equals an annual interest rate of 13.69% computed as (365 days ÷ 80 days) × 3%. Since you can borrow funds at 11% (assuming no other processing costs), it is better to borrow and pay within the discount period. You save 2.69% (13.69% − 11%) in interest costs by paying early.

Credit Manager—Ethics Your decision here is whether to comply with prior policy or to create a new policy and not abuse

discounts offered by suppliers. Your first step should be to meet with your superior to find out if the late payment policy is the actual policy and, if so, its rationale. If it is the policy to pay late, you must apply your own sense of ethics. One point of view is that the late payment policy is unethical. A deliberate plan to make late payments means the company lies when it pretends to make purchases within the credit terms. The potential is that your company can lose its ability to get future credit. Another view is that the late payment policy is acceptable. In some markets, attempts to take discounts through late payments are accepted as a continued phase of "price negotiation." Also, your company's suppliers can respond by billing your company for the discounts not accepted because of late payments. However, this is a dubious viewpoint, especially since the prior manager proposes you explain late payments as computer or mail problems and given that some suppliers have complained.

Supplier A current ratio of 2.1 suggests sufficient current assets to cover current liabilities. An acid-test ratio of 0.5 suggests, however, that quick assets can cover only about one-half of current liabilities. This implies the store depends on profits from sales of inventory to pay current liabilities. If sales of inventory decline or profit margins decrease, the likelihood that this store will default

on its payments increases. Your decision is probably not to extend credit to the store. If you do extend credit, you are likely to closely monitor the store's financial condition.

Financial Officer Your company's net profit margin is about equal to the industry average and suggests typical industry performance. However, gross margin reveals that your company is paying far more in cost of goods sold or receiving far less in sales price than competitors. Your attention must be directed to finding the problem with cost of goods sold, sales, or both. One positive note is that your company's expenses make up 19% of sales (36% − 17%). This favorably compares with competitors' expenses that make up 28% of sales (44% − 16%).

Guidance Answers to **Quick Checks**

1. Cost of goods sold is the cost of merchandise purchased from a supplier that is sold to customers during a specific period.

2. Gross profit (or gross margin) is the difference between net sales and cost of goods sold.

3. Widespread use of computing and related technology has dramatically increased the use of the perpetual inventory system.

4. Under credit terms of 2/10, n/60, the credit period is 60 days and the discount period is 10 days.

5. (b)

6. *FOB* means free on board. It is used in identifying the point when ownership transfers from seller to buyer. *FOB destination* means the seller transfers ownership of goods to the buyer when they arrive at the buyer's place of business. It also means the seller is responsible for paying shipping charges and bears the risk of damage or loss during shipment.

7. Recording sales discounts and sales returns and allowances separately from sales gives useful information to managers for internal monitoring and decision making.

8. When a customer returns merchandise *and* the seller restores the merchandise to inventory, two entries are necessary. One entry records the decrease in revenue and credits the cus-

tomer's account. The second entry debits inventory and reduces cost of goods sold.

9. Credit memorandum.—seller credits accounts receivable from buyer.

10. Merchandise Inventory may need adjusting to reflect shrinkage.

11. Sales (of goods), Sales Discounts, Sales Returns and Allowances, and Cost of Goods Sold.

12. Four closing entries: (1) close credit balances in temporary accounts to Income Summary, (2) close debit balances in temporary accounts to Income Summary, (3) close Income Summary to owner's capital, and (4) close withdrawals account to owner's capital.

13. Cost of Goods Sold.

14. (b) Purchases and (c) Transportation-In.

15. Under a periodic inventory system, the cost of goods sold is determined at the end of an accounting period by adding the net cost of goods purchased to the beginning inventory and subtracting the ending inventory.

16. Both methods report the same ending inventory and net income.

Glossary

Acid-test ratio ratio used to assess a company's ability to settle its current debts with its most liquid assets; defined as quick assets (cash, short-term investments, and current receivables) over current liabilities. (p. 233).

Cash discount reduction in the price of merchandise granted by a seller to a buyer when payment is made within the *discount period.* (p. 219).

Cost of goods sold cost of inventory sold to customers during a period. (p. 216)

Credit memorandum notification that the sender has credited the recipient's account kept by the sender. (p. 226).

Credit period time period that can pass before a customer's payment is due. (p. 218).

Credit terms description of the amounts and timing of payments that a buyer agrees to make in the future. (p. 218).

Debit memorandum notification that the sender has debited the recipient's account kept by the sender. (p. 220).

Discount period time period in which a cash discount is available and the buyer can make a reduced payment. (p. 219).

EOM abbreviation for *end of month;* used to describe credit terms for some transactions. (p. 218).

FOB abbreviation for *free on board;* the point when ownership of goods passes to the buyer; *FOB shipping point* (or *factory*) means the buyer pays shipping costs and accepts ownership of goods at the seller's place of business; *FOB destination* means the seller pays shipping costs and accepts ownership of goods at the buyer's place of business. (p. 221).

General and administrative expenses expenses that support the operating activities of a business. (p. 230).

Gross margin (see gross profit). (p. 214).

Gross margin ratio gross margin (sales minus cost of goods sold) divided by sales; also called *gross profit ratio*. (p. 233).

Gross profit net sales minus cost of goods sold; also called *gross margin*. (p. 214).

Inventory merchandise a company owns and expects to sell in its normal operations. (p. 216).

List price catalog price of an item before any trade discount is deducted. (p. 218).

Merchandise (see *merchandise inventory*). (p. 214).

Merchandise inventory products that a company owns and expects to sell to customers; also called *merchandise*. (p. 215).

Merchandiser entity that earns net income by buying and selling merchandise. (p. 214).

Multiple-step income statement income statement format that shows subtotals between sales and net income and details of net sales and expenses. (p. 230).

Periodic inventory system method that records the cost of inventory purchased but does not track the quantity available or sold to customers; records are updated at the end of each period to reflect the physical count of goods available. (p. 216).

Perpetual inventory system method that maintains continuous records of the cost of inventory available and the cost of goods sold. (p. 217).

Purchase discount term used by a purchaser to describe a cash discount granted to the purchaser for paying within the discount period. (p. 219).

Retailer intermediary that buys products from manufacturers or wholesalers and sells them to consumers. (p. 214).

Sales discount term used by a seller to describe a cash discount granted to buyers who pay within the discount period. (p. 219).

Selling expenses expenses of promoting sales, such as displaying and advertising merchandise, making sales, and delivering goods to customers. (p. 230).

Shrinkage inventory losses that occur as a result of theft or deterioration. (p. 227).

Single-step income statement income statement format that includes cost of goods sold as an expense and shows only one subtotal for total expenses. (p. 230).

Supplementary records information outside the usual accounting records; also called *supplemental records*. (p. 223).

Trade discount reduction below a list or catalog price that can vary for wholesalers, retailers, and consumers. (p. 218).

Wholesaler intermediary that buys products from manufacturers or other wholesalers and sells them to retailers or other wholesalers. (p. 214).

[The superscript letter ^A denotes assignments based on Appendix 6A.]

Questions

1. In comparing the accounts of a merchandising company with those of a service company, what additional accounts would the merchandising company likely use, assuming it employs a perpetual inventory system?

2. What items appear in financial statements of merchandising companies but not in the statements of service companies?

3. Explain how a business can earn a positive gross profit on its sales and still have a net loss.

4. Why do companies offer a cash discount?

5. How does a company that uses a perpetual inventory system determine the amount of inventory shrinkage?

6. Distinguish between cash discounts and trade discounts. Is the amount of a trade discount on purchased merchandise recorded in the accounts?

7. What is the difference between a sales discount and a purchase discount?

8. Why would a company's manager be concerned about the quantity of its purchase returns if its suppliers allow unlimited returns?

9. Does the sender of a debit memorandum record a debit or a credit in the recipient's account? Which (debit or credit) does the recipient record?

10. What is the difference between single-step and multiple-step income statement formats?

11. Refer to the income statement for **Nike** in Appendix A. What term is used instead of cost of goods sold? Does the company present a detailed calculation of its cost of goods sold?

12. Refer to the balance sheet for **Reebok** in Appendix A. What does Reebok call its inventory account? What alternate name could it use?

13. Refer to the income statement of **Gap** in Appendix A. Does its income statement report a gross profit figure?

14. Companies need to be skillful in negotiating purchase contracts with suppliers. What type of shipping terms should a purchaser attempt to negotiate to minimize freight-in costs?

Prepare journal entries to record each of the following transactions of a merchandising company. Show any supporting calculations. Assume a perpetual inventory system.

Mar. 5   Purchased 600 units of product with a list price of $10 per unit. The purchaser is granted a trade discount of 20%; terms of the sale are 2/10, n/60.

Mar. 7   Returned 25 defective units from the March 5 purchase and received full credit.

Mar. 15 Paid the amount due from the March 5 purchase, less the return on March 7.

QUICK STUDY

QS 6-1
Recording purchases
—perpetual system **P1**

QS 6-2
Recording sales—
perpetual system
P2

Prepare journal entries to record each of the following transactions of a merchandising company. Show any supporting calculations. Assume a perpetual inventory system.

Apr. 1   Sold merchandise for $3,000, granting the customer terms of 2/10, EOM. The cost of the merchandise is $1,800.

Apr. 4   The customer in the April 1 sale returned merchandise and received credit for $600. The merchandise, which had cost $360, is returned to inventory.

Apr. 11   Received payment for the amount due from the April 1 sale less the return on April 4.

QS 6-3[A]
Contrasting periodic and
perpetual systems
C4

Identify whether each description best applies to a periodic or a perpetual inventory system.

a. Provides more timely information to managers.

b. Requires an adjusting entry to record inventory shrinkage.

c. Markedly increased in frequency and popularity in business within the past decade.

d. Records cost of goods sold each time a sales transaction occurs.

QS 6-4
Computing and analyzing
gross margin
C2 A3

Compute net sales, gross profit, and the gross margin ratio for each situation (a) through (d):

	a	b	c	d
Sales	$150,000	$550,000	$38,700	$255,700
Sales discounts	5,200	17,500	600	4,200
Sales returns and allowances	20,000	6,000	5,300	900
Cost of goods sold	79,600	329,700	24,300	128,900

Interpret the gross margin ratio for situation (a).

QS 6-5
Acid-test ratio
A2

Use the following information on current assets and current liabilities to compute and interpret the acid-test ratio. Also explain what the acid-test ratio of a company measures.

Cash	$1,500
Accounts receivable	2,800
Inventory	6,000
Prepaid expenses	700
Accounts payable	5,750
Other current liabilities	850

QS 6-6
Contrasting liquidity
ratios   **A2**

Identify similarities and differences between the acid-test ratio and the current ratio. Compare and describe how the two ratios reflect a company's ability to meet its current obligations.

QS 6-7
Accounting for shrinkage—
perpetual system
P3

Bemis Company's ledger on July 31, its fiscal year-end, includes the following accounts that have normal balances:

Merchandise inventory	$ 37,800	Sales returns and allowances ..	$ 6,500
T. Bemis, Capital	118,300	Cost of goods sold	105,000
T. Bemis, Withdrawals	7,000	Depreciation expense	10,300
Sales	160,200	Salaries expense	32,500
Sales discounts	4,700	Miscellaneous expenses	5,000

A physical count of its July 31 year-end inventory discloses that the cost of the merchandise available for sale is $35,900. Prepare the entry to record any inventory shrinkage.

QS 6-8   **P3**
Closing entries

Refer to QS 6-7 and prepare journal entries to close the balances in temporary accounts. Remember to consider the entry that is made to solve QS 6-7.

Prepare journal entries to record the following transactions for a retail store. Assume a perpetual inventory system.

Apr. 2   Purchased merchandise from Blass Company under the following terms: $4,600 invoice price, 2/15, n/60 credit terms, FOB shipping point.
     3   Paid $300 for shipping charges on the April 2 purchase.
     4   Returned to Blass Company unacceptable merchandise that had an invoice price of $600.
    17   Sent a check to Blass Company for the April 2 purchase, net of the discount and the returned merchandise.
    18   Purchased merchandise from Flow Corp. under the following terms: $8,500 invoice price, 2/10, n/30 credit terms, FOB destination.
    21   After negotiations, received from Flow an $1,100 allowance on the April 18 purchase.
    28   Sent a check to Flow paying for the April 18 purchase, net of the discount and allowance.

EXERCISES

Exercise 6-1
Recording entries for merchandise purchases

Insert the letter for each term in the blank space beside the definition that it most closely matches:

A. Cash discount   **E.** FOB shipping point   **H.** Purchase discount
B. Credit period   **F.** Gross profit   **I.** Sales discount
C. Discount period   **G.** Merchandise inventory   **J.** Trade discount
D. FOB destination   ~seller pays freight

_____ **1.** Ownership of goods is transferred at the seller's place of business.
_____ **2.** Reduction below list or catalog price that is negotiated in setting the price of goods.
_____ **3.** Seller's description of a cash discount granted to customers in return for early payment.
_____ **4.** Time period that can pass before a customer's payment is due.
_____ **5.** Goods a company owns and expects to sell to its customers.
_____ **6.** Ownership of goods is transferred at the buyer's place of business.
_____ **7.** Time period in which a cash discount is available.
_____ **8.** Difference between net sales and the cost of goods sold.
_____ **9.** Reduction in a receivable or payable that is granted if it is paid within the discount period.
_____ **10.** Purchaser's description of a cash discount received from a supplier of goods.

Exercise 6-2
Applying merchandising terms

Sundance Company purchased merchandise for resale from Phoenix with an invoice price of $24,000 and credit terms of 3/10, n/60. The merchandise had cost Phoenix $16,000. Sundance paid within the discount period. Assume that both buyer and seller use a perpetual inventory system.

Required

1. Prepare entries that the buyer should record for the purchase and cash payment.
2. Prepare entries that the seller should record for the sale and cash collection.
3. Assume that the buyer borrowed enough cash to pay the balance on the last day of the discount period at an annual interest rate of 8% and paid it back on the last day of the credit period. Compute how much the buyer saved by following this strategy. (Use a 365-day year.)

Exercise 6-3
Analyzing and recording merchandise transactions—both buyer and seller

---

On May 11, Recovery Co. accepts delivery of $40,000 of merchandise it purchases for resale from Hoak Corporation. With the merchandise is an invoice dated May 11, with terms of 3/10, n/90, FOB factory. The cost of the goods for Hoak is $30,000. When the goods are delivered, Recovery pays $345 to Express Shipping Service for delivery charges on the merchandise. On May 12, Recovery returns $1,400 of goods to Hoak, who receives them one day later and restores them to inventory. The returned goods had cost Hoak $800. On May 20, Recovery mails a check to Hoak Corporation for the amount owed. Hoak receives it the following day.

Required

1. Prepare journal entries that Recovery Co. records for these transactions. Recovery uses a perpetual inventory system.
2. Prepare journal entries that Hoak Corporation records for these transactions. Hoak uses a perpetual inventory system.

Exercise 6-4
Analyzing and recording merchandise transactions—both buyer and seller

Exercise 6-5

Calculating expenses and
cost of goods sold

 X

Monk Company's ledger and supplementary records at the end of the period reveal the following:

Sales	$380,000
Sales discounts	6,500
Sales returns	15,000
Merchandise inventory (beginning of period)	31,000
Invoice cost of merchandise purchases	176,000
Purchase discounts received	4,600
Purchase returns and allowances	5,000
Costs of transportation-in	12,000
Gross profit	155,000
Net income	65,000

Required

Compute (1) total operating expenses, (2) cost of goods sold, and (3) merchandise inventory (end of
period). (*Hint:* Review Exhibits 6.10 and 6.11.)

Exercise 6-6ᴬ ✓

Determining components of
cost of goods sold

C5

Using the data provided from the general ledger and supplementary records, determine each of the
missing numbers in the separate situations (a), (b), and (c):

	a	b	c
Invoice cost of merchandise purchases	$94,000	$40,000	$32,500
Purchase discounts received	5,000	?	800
Purchase returns and allowances	2,000	2,500	1,200
Costs of transportation-in	?	4,500	5,000
Merchandise inventory (beginning of period)	9,000	?	10,000
Total cost of merchandise purchases	91,400	40,500	?
Merchandise inventory (end of period)	5,400	8,500	?
Cost of goods sold	?	42,600	35,130

Exercise 6-7

Recording sales returns and
allowances

P2

A1 Parts is organized on May 1, 2002, and made its first purchase of merchandise on May 3. The
purchase is for 2,000 units at a price of $10 per unit. On May 5, A1 Parts sold 600 of the units
for $14 per unit to Dean Co. Terms of the sale are 2/10, n/60. Prepare entries for A1 Parts to
record the May 5 sale and each of the following separate transactions using a perpetual inventory
system.

a. On May 7, Dean returns 200 units because they did not fit the customer's needs. A1 Parts restores
the units to its inventory.

b. On May 8, Dean discovers that 200 units are damaged but of some use and, therefore, keeps the
units. A1 Parts sends Dean a credit memorandum for $600 to compensate for the damage.

c. On May 15, Dean returns 20 defective units and A1 Parts concludes that these units cannot be
resold. As a result, A1 Parts discards them.

Exercise 6-8

Recording purchase
returns and allowances

Refer to Exercise 6-7 and prepare the appropriate journal entries for Dean Co. to record the purchase
and each of the three separate transactions. Dean is a retailer that uses a perpetual inventory system
and purchases these units for resale.

Fill in the blanks in the following separate income statements *a* through *e*. Identify any negative amount by putting it in parentheses.

Exercise 6-9ᴬ
Calculating revenues, expenses, and income

	a	b	c	d	e
Sales	$62,000	$43,500	$46,000	$?	$25,600
Cost of goods sold					
Merchandise inventory (beginning)	8,000	17,050	7,500	8,000	4,560
Total cost of merchandise purchases	38,000	?	?	32,000	6,600
Merchandise inventory (ending)	?	(2,700)	(9,000)	(6,600)	?
Cost of goods sold	$34,050	$15,900	$?	$?	$ 6,600
Gross profit	$?	$?	$ 3,750	$45,600	$?
Expenses	10,000	10,650	12,150	3,600	6,000
Net income (loss)	$?	$16,950	$(8,400)	$42,000	$?

Briefly explain why a company's manager wants the accounting system to record customers' returns of unsatisfactory goods in the Sales Returns and Allowances account instead of the Sales account. In addition, explain whether this information would be useful for external decision makers.

Exercise 6-10
Sales returns
and allowances

A retail company recently completed a physical count of ending merchandise inventory to use in preparing adjusting entries. In determining the cost of the counted inventory, company employees failed to consider that $3,000 of incoming goods had been shipped by a supplier on December 31 under an FOB shipping point agreement. These goods had been recorded in Merchandise Inventory as a purchase, but they were not included in the physical count because they were in transit. Explain how this overlooked fact affects the company's financial statements and the following ratios: return on equity, debt ratio, current ratio, profit margin ratio, and acid-test ratio.

Exercise 6-11
Interpreting physical count error as shrinkage

The following supplementary records summarize Duncan Company's merchandising activities for year 2002. Set up T-accounts for Merchandise Inventory and Cost of Goods Sold. Then record the summarized activities in the T-accounts and compute account balances. (*Hint:* See Exhibit 6.16.)

Exercise 6-12
Recording effects of merchandising activities

Cost of merchandise sold to customers in sales transactions	$196,000
Merchandise inventory, December 31, 2001	25,000
Invoice cost of merchandise purchases	192,500
Shrinkage determined on December 31, 2002	800
Cost of transportation-in	2,900
Cost of merchandise returned by customers and restored to inventory	2,100
Purchase discounts received	1,700
Purchase returns and allowances	4,000

Calculate the current and acid-test ratios for each of the following separate cases:

Exercise 6-13
Computing and analyzing acid-test and current ratios

	Case X	Case Y	Case Z
Cash	$ 900	$ 810	$1,000
Short-term investments	0	0	600
Receivables	0	1,090	700
Inventory	3,000	1,100	4,100
Prepaid expenses	1,300	500	900
Total current assets	$5,200	$3,500	$7,300
Current liabilities	$2,200	$1,200	$3,750

Which company case is in the best position to meet short-term obligations? Explain your choice.

Exercise 6-14
Determining profitability and merchandising cash flows

A1

A company reports the following balances and activities at year-end:

Net sales	$1,010,000
Cost of goods sold	565,000
Increase in accounts receivable for the period	45,000
Cash payments to suppliers of goods	515,000

Required

1. Calculate gross profit.

2. Calculate cash received from customers.

3. Calculate cash flows from customers less cash flows paid to suppliers.

Exercise 6-15[A]
Preparing adjusting and closing entries for a merchandiser

P3

The following list includes some permanent accounts and all of the temporary accounts from the December 31, 2002, unadjusted trial balance of Davis Sales, a business owned by Julie Davis. Use these account balances along with the additional information to journalize adjusting and closing entries. Davis Sales uses a perpetual inventory system.

	Debit	Credit
Merchandise inventory	$ 30,000	
Prepaid selling expenses	5,500	
Julie Davis, Withdrawals	2,200	
Sales		$529,000
Sales returns and allowances	17,500	
Sales discounts	5,000	
Cost of goods sold	212,000	
Sales salaries expense	48,000	
Utilities expense	15,000	
Selling expenses	36,000	
Administrative expenses	105,000	

Additional Information

Accrued sales salaries amount to $1,700. Prepaid selling expenses of $3,000 have expired. A physical count of merchandise inventory discloses $28,450 of goods available.

Exercise 6-16[A]
Preparing journal entries to contrast the periodic and perpetual systems

P1 **P2** **P5**

Journalize the following merchandising transactions for Texas Systems assuming it uses a (a) periodic system and (b) perpetual system.

1. On November 1, Texas Systems purchases merchandise for $1,500 on credit with terms of 2/5, n/30, FOB shipping point.

2. On November 5, Texas Systems pays cash for the November 1 purchase.

3. On November 7, Texas Systems discovers and returns $200 of defective merchandise purchased on November 1 for a cash refund.

4. On November 10, Texas Systems pays $90 cash for transportation costs with the November 1 purchase.

5. On November 13, Texas Systems sells merchandise for $1,600 on credit. The cost of the merchandise is $800.

6. On November 16, the customer returns merchandise from the November 13 transaction. The returned items sell for $300 and cost $150.

PROBLEM SET A

Problem 6-1A
Preparing journal entries for merchandising activities (perpetual system)

Prepare journal entries to record the following perpetual system merchandising transactions of Heflin Company. (Use a separate account for each receivable and payable; for example, record the purchase on August 1 in Accounts Payable—Chapman Co.)

Aug. 1   Purchased merchandise from Chapman Company for $7,500 under credit terms of 1/10, n/30, FOB destination.

    4   At Chapman's request, Heflin paid $200 cash for freight charges on the August 1 purchase, reducing the amount owed to Chapman.

    5   Sold merchandise to Griffin Corp. for $5,200 under credit terms of 2/10, n/60, FOB destination. The merchandise had cost $4,000.

8   Purchased merchandise from Follmer Corporation for $5,400 under credit terms of 1/10, n/45, FOB shipping point. The invoice showed that at Heflin's request, Follmer paid the $140 shipping charges and added that amount to the bill.

9   Paid $125 cash for shipping charges related to the August 5 sale to Griffin Corp.

10 Griffin returned merchandise from the August 5 sale that had cost $400 and been sold for $600. The merchandise was restored to inventory.

12 After negotiations with Follmer Corporation concerning problems with the merchandise purchased on August 8, Heflin received a credit memorandum from Follmer granting a price reduction of $700.

15 Received balance due from Griffin Corp. for the August 5 sale less the return on August 10.

18 Paid the amount due Follmer Corporation for the August 8 purchase less the price reduction granted.

        Check Aug. 18, Cr. Cash, $4,793

19 Sold merchandise to Trigger for $4,800 under credit terms of 1/10, n/30, FOB shipping point. The merchandise had cost $2,400.

22 Trigger requested a price reduction on the August 19 sale because the merchandise did not meet specifications. Sent Trigger a credit memorandum for $500 to resolve the issue.

29 Received Trigger's cash payment for the amount due from the August 19 purchase.

30 Paid Chapman Company the amount due from the August 1 purchase.

Prepare journal entries to record the following perpetual system merchandising transactions of Beltran Company. (Use a separate account for each receivable and payable; for example, record the purchase on July 1 in Accounts Payable—White Co.)

July 1 Purchased merchandise from White Company for $6,000 under credit terms of 1/15, n/30, FOB shipping point.

2   Sold merchandise to Terry Co. for $900 under credit terms of 2/10, n/60, FOB shipping point. The merchandise had cost $500.

3   Paid $125 cash for freight charges on the purchase of July 1.

8   Sold merchandise that cost $1,300 for $1,700 cash.

9   Purchased merchandise from Kane Co. for $2,200 under credit terms of 2/15, n/60, FOB destination.

11 Received a $200 credit memorandum from the return of merchandise purchased on July 9.

12 Received the balance due from Terry Co. for the credit sale dated July 2, net of the discount.

16 Paid the balance due to White Company within the discount period.

19 Sold merchandise that cost $800 to Jolie Co. for $1,200 under credit terms of 2/15, n/60, FOB shipping point.

21 Issued a $150 credit memorandum to Jolie Co. for an allowance on goods sold on July 19.

22 Received a debit memorandum from Jolie Co. for an error that overstated the total sales invoice by $50.

24 Paid Kane Co. the balance due after deducting the discount.

30 Received the balance due from Jolie Co. for the credit sale dated July 19, net of discount.

31 Sold merchandise that cost $4,800 to Terry Co. for $7,000 under credit terms of 2/10, n/60, FOB shipping point.

Problem 6-2A

Preparing journal entries for merchandising activities (perpetual system)

        Check July 30, Dr. Cash, $980

The following unadjusted trial balance is prepared at fiscal year-end for Tioga Company:

Problem 6-3A

Preparing adjusting entries and income statements, and computing gross margin, acid-test, and current ratios

TIOGA COMPANY Unadjusted Trial Balance January 31, 2002	Debit	Credit
Cash	$ 5,200	
Merchandise inventory	12,500	
Store supplies	5,800	
Prepaid insurance	2,400	
Store equipment	42,900	
Accumulated depreciation—Store equipment		$ 15,250
Accounts payable		10,000
Laura Izon, Capital		36,200
Laura Izon, Withdrawals	4,200	
Sales		111,950
Sales discounts	2,000	
Sales returns and allowances	2,200	
Cost of goods sold	38,400	
Depreciation expense—Store equipment	0	
Salaries expense	33,000	
Insurance expense	0	
Rent expense	15,000	
Store supplies expense	0	
Advertising expense	9,800	
Totals	$ 173,400	$ 173,400

Rent and salaries expenses are equally divided between selling activities and the general and administrative activities. Tioga Company uses a perpetual inventory system.

Required

1. Prepare adjusting journal entries for the following:

    a. Store supplies available at fiscal year-end amount to $1,750.

    b. Expired insurance, an administrative expense, for the fiscal year is $1,400.

    c. Depreciation expense on store equipment, a selling expense, is $1,525 for the fiscal year.

    d. To estimate shrinkage, a physical count of ending merchandise inventory is taken. It shows $10,900 of goods are available for sale.

2. Prepare a multiple-step income statement for fiscal year 2002.

3. Prepare a single-step income statement for fiscal year 2002.

4. Compute the company's current ratio, acid-test ratio, and gross margin ratio as of January 31, 2002.

Check   (3) Total expenses, $104,775

Problem 6-4A

Computing and formatting an income statement

Big Star Company's adjusted trial balance on August 31, 2002, its fiscal year-end, follows:

	Debit	Credit
Merchandise inventory	$ 41,000	
Other assets	130,400	
Liabilities		$ 25,000
S. Stone, Capital		110,550
S. Stone, Withdrawals	14,000	
Sales		225,600
Sales discounts	2,250	
Sales returns and allowances	12,000	
Cost of goods sold	74,500	
Sales salaries expense	32,000	
Rent expense, selling space	8,000	
Store supplies expense	1,500	
Advertising expense	13,000	
Office salaries expense	28,500	
Rent expense, office space	3,600	
Office supplies expense	400	
Totals	$361,150	$361,150

On August 31, 2001, merchandise inventory amounted to $26,000. Supplementary records of merchandising activities for the year ended August 31, 2002, reveal the following itemized costs:

Invoice cost of merchandise purchases	$92,000
Purchase discounts received	2,000
Purchase returns and allowances	4,500
Costs of transportation-in	4,000

Required

1. Compute the company's net sales for the year.

2. Compute the company's total cost of merchandise purchased for the year.

3. Prepare a multiple-step income statement that lists the company's net sales, cost of goods sold, and gross profit, as well as the components and amounts of selling expenses and general and administrative expenses.

Check   (4) Total expenses, $161,500

4. Prepare a single-step income statement that lists these costs: cost of goods sold, selling expenses, and general and administrative expenses.

5. Accounts receivable decreased during the period by $30,000. Compute cash received from customers.

Use the data for Big Star Company in Problem 6-4A to complete the following requirements:

Required

Preparation Component

1. Prepare closing entries under the perpetual system as of August 31, 2002.

Analysis Component

2. The company makes all purchases on credit, and its suppliers uniformly offer a 3% sales discount. Does it appear that the company's cash management system is accomplishing the goal of taking all available discounts? Explain.

3. In prior years, the company experienced a 4% return and allowance rate on its sales, which means approximately 4% of its gross sales were eventually returned outright or caused the company to grant allowances to customers. How do this year's results compare to prior years' results?

Problem 6-5A
Preparing closing entries and interpreting information about discounts and returns

Check (1) $49,850 Dr. to close Income Summary

Prepare journal entries to record the following perpetual system merchandising transactions of Whitecap Company. (Use a separate account for each receivable and payable; for example, record the purchase on July 3 in Accounts Payable—MAP Corp.)

July 3 Purchased merchandise from MAP Corp. for $15,000 under credit terms of 1/10, n/30, FOB destination.

4 At MAP's request, Whitecap paid $150 cash for freight charges on the July 3 purchase, reducing the amount owed to MAP.

7 Sold merchandise to Bergez Co. for $11,500 under credit terms of 2/10, n/60, FOB destination. The merchandise had cost $7,750.

10 Purchased merchandise from McFarland Corporation for $14,250 under credit terms of 1/10, n/45, FOB shipping point. The invoice showed that at Whitecap's request, McFarland paid the $500 shipping charges and added that amount to the bill.

11 Paid $300 cash for shipping charges related to the July 7 sale to Bergez Co.

12 Bergez returned merchandise from the July 7 sale that had cost $1,450 and been sold for $1,850. The merchandise was restored to inventory.

14 After negotiations with McFarland Corporation concerning problems with the merchandise purchased on July 10, Whitecap received a credit memorandum from McFarland granting a price reduction of $2,000.

17 Received balance due from Bergez Co. for the July 7 sale less the return on July 12.

20 Paid the amount due McFarland Corporation for the July 10 purchase less the price reduction granted.

21 Sold merchandise to Harden for $11,000 under credit terms of 1/10, n/30, FOB shipping point. The merchandise had cost $7,000.

24 Harden requested a price reduction on the July 21 sale because the merchandise did not meet specifications. Sent Harden a credit memorandum for $1,300 to resolve the issue.

31 Received Harden's cash payment for the amount due from the July 21 purchase.

31 Paid MAP Corp. the amount due from the July 3 purchase.

PROBLEM SET B

Problem 6-1B
Preparing journal entries for merchandising activities (perpetual system)

Check July 20, Cr. Cash, $12,627.5

Prepare journal entries to record the following perpetual system merchandising transactions of Chang Company. (Use a separate account for each receivable and payable; for example, record the purchase on May 2 in Accounts Payable—McManus Co.)

May 2 Purchased merchandise from McManus Co. for $10,000 under credit terms of 1/15, n/30, FOB shipping point.

4 Sold merchandise to Four Winds Co. for $11,000 under credit terms of 2/10, n/60, FOB shipping point. The merchandise had cost $5,600.

5 Paid $250 cash for freight charges on the purchase of May 2.

9 Sold merchandise that cost $2,000 for $2,500 cash.

10 Purchased merchandise from Alvarez Co. for $3,650 under credit terms of 2/15, n/60, FOB destination.

12 Received a $400 credit memorandum from the return of merchandise purchased on May 10.

14 Received the balance due from Four Winds Co. for the credit sale dated May 4, net of the discount.

17 Paid the balance due to McManus Co. within the discount period.

Problem 6-2B
Preparing journal entries for merchandising activities (perpetual system)

20   Sold merchandise that cost $1,450 to Wickham Co. for $2,800 under credit terms of 2/15, n/60, FOB shipping point.

22   Issued a $325 credit memorandum to Wickham Co. for an allowance on goods sold from May 20.

23   Received a debit memorandum from Wickham Co. for an error that overstated the total invoice by $75.

25   Paid Alvarez Co. the balance due after deducting the discount.

Check   May 30, Dr. Cash, $2,352

30   Received the balance due from Wickham Co. for the credit sale dated May 20, net of discount.

31   Sold merchandise that cost $3,600 to Four Winds Co. for $7,200 under credit terms of 2/10, n/60, FOB shipping point.

Problem 6-3B

Preparing adjusting entries and income statements, and computing gross margin, acid-test, and current ratios

The following unadjusted trial balance is prepared at fiscal year-end for Durable Products Co.:

DURABLE PRODUCTS COMPANY Unadjusted Trial Balance October 31, 2002	Debit	Credit
Cash	$ 7,400	
Merchandise inventory	24,000	
Store supplies	9,700	
Prepaid insurance	5,600	
Store equipment	84,800	
Accumulated depreciation—Store equipment		$ 32,000
Accounts payable		18,000
Jan Bargen, Capital		50,400
Jan Bargen, Withdrawals	7,400	
Sales		227,100
Sales discounts	1,000	
Sales returns and allowances	5,000	
Cost of goods sold	75,800	
Depreciation expense—Store equipment	0	
Salaries expense	63,000	
Insurance expense	0	
Rent expense	26,000	
Store supplies expense	0	
Advertising expense	17,800	
Totals	$ 327,500	$ 327,500

Rent and salaries expenses are equally divided between selling activities and the general and administrative activities. Durable Products Company uses a perpetual inventory system.

Required

1. Prepare adjusting journal entries for the following:

   a. Store supplies available at fiscal year-end amount to $3,700.

   b. Expired insurance, an administrative expense, for the fiscal year is $2,800.

   c. Depreciation expense on store equipment, a selling expense, is $3,000 for the fiscal year.

   d. To estimate shrinkage, a physical count of ending merchandise inventory is taken. It shows $21,300 of goods are available for sale.

2. Prepare a multiple-step income statement for fiscal year 2002.

Check   (3) Total expenses, $197,100

3. Prepare a single-step income statement for fiscal year 2002.

4. Compute the company's current ratio, acid-test ratio, and gross margin ratio as of October 31, 2002.

Problem 6-4B

Computing and formatting an income statement

P4 A1

Ryan Company's adjusted trial balance on March 31, 2002, its fiscal year-end, follows:

	Debit	Credit
Merchandise inventory.	$ 56,500	
Other assets.	202,600	
Liabilities		$ 42,500
Cook Ryan, Capital.		175,425
Cook Ryan, Withdrawals	14,000	

[continued on next page]

[continued from previous page]

	Debit	Credit
Sales		332,650
Sales discounts	5,875	
Sales returns and allowances.	20,000	
Cost of goods sold	115,600	
Sales salaries expense	44,500	
Rent expense—Selling space	16,000	
Store supplies expense	3,850	
Advertising expense	26,000	
Office salaries expense	10,750	
Rent expense—Office space	3,800	
Office supplies expense.	1,100	
Totals.	$550,575	$550,575

On March 31, 2001, merchandise inventory amounted to $37,500. Supplementary records of merchandising activities for the year ended March 31, 2002, reveal the following itemized costs:

Invoice cost of merchandise purchases	$138,500
Purchase discounts received	2,950
Purchase returns and allowances	6,700
Costs of transportation-in	5,750

Required

1. Calculate the company's net sales for the year.
2. Calculate the company's total cost of merchandise purchased for the year.
3. Prepare a multiple-step income statement that lists the company's net sales, cost of goods sold, and gross profit, as well as the components and amounts of selling expenses and general and administrative expenses.
4. Prepare a single-step income statement that lists these costs: cost of goods sold, selling expenses, and general and administrative expenses.
5. Accounts receivable increased by $50,000 during the period. Calculate cash received from customers.

Check (4) Total expenses, $251,600

Use the data for Ryan Company in Problem 6-4B to complete the following requirements:

Required

Preparation Component

1. Prepare closing entries under the perpetual system as of March 31, 2002.

Analysis Component

2. The company makes all purchases on credit, and its suppliers uniformly offer a 3% sales discount. Does it appear that the company's cash management system is accomplishing the goal of taking all available discounts? Explain.
3. In prior years, the company experienced a 4% return and allowance rate on its sales, which means approximately 4% of its gross sales were eventually returned outright or caused the company to grant allowances to customers. How do this year's results compare to prior years' results?

Problem 6-5B
Preparing closing entries and interpreting information about discounts and returns

Check (1) $55,175 Dr. to close Income Summary

(The first three segments of this comprehensive problem were presented in Chapters 3, 4, and 5. If those segments have not been completed, the assignment can begin at this point. You should use the Working Papers that accompany this text because they reflect the account balances that resulted from posting the entries required in Chapters 3, 4, and 5.)

SERIAL PROBLEM

Sierra Systems

Earlier segments of this problem have described how Sela Solstise created Sierra Systems on October 1, 2002. The company has been successful, and its list of customers has grown. To accommodate the growth, the accounting system is modified to set up separate accounts for each customer. The following list of customers includes the account number used for each account and any balance as of December 31, 2002. Solstise decided to add a fourth digit with a decimal point to the 106 account number that had been used for the single Accounts Receivable account. This modification allows the company to continue using the existing chart of accounts.

Customer Account	No.	Balance
Antonio's Engineering Co.	106.1	$ 0
Alexander Services	106.2	0
Prime Leasing	106.3	0
Dade Co.	106.4	3,000
Elan Corporation	106.5	0
Foster Co.	106.6	2,668
Olathe Co.	106.7	0
Taos, Inc.	106.8	0
Imagine, Inc.	106.9	0

In response to requests from customers, Solstise has decided to begin selling computer software. The company also will extend credit terms of 1/10, n/30 to all customers who purchase this merchandise. No cash discount will be available on consulting fees. The following additional accounts are added to the general ledger to allow the system to account for the company's new merchandising activities:

Account	No.
Merchandise Inventory	119
Sales.	413
Sales Returns and Allowances	414
Sales Discounts	415
Cost of Goods Sold	502

Sierra Systems does not use reversing entries and, therefore, all revenue and expense accounts have zero balances as of January 1, 2003. Its transactions for January through March follow:

Jan. 4   Paid cash to Suzie Smith for five days' work at the rate of $125 per day. Four of the five days are unpaid days of work from the prior year.

5   Sela Solstise invested an additional $25,000 cash in the business.

7   Purchased $5,800 of merchandise from Jersey Corp. with terms of 1/10, n/30, FOB shipping point.

9   Received $2,668 cash from Foster Co. as final payment on its account.

11   Completed a five-day project for Antonio's Engineering Co. and billed it $5,500, which is the total price of $7,000 less the advance payment of $1,500.

13   Sold merchandise with a retail value of $5,200 and a cost of $3,560 to Elan Corporation with terms of 1/10, n/30, FOB shipping point.

15   Paid $600 cash for freight charges on the merchandise purchased on January 7.

16   Received $4,000 cash from Olathe Co. for computer services provided.

17   Paid Jersey Corp. for the purchase on January 7, net of the discount.

20   Elan Corporation returned $500 of defective merchandise from its purchase on January 13. The returned merchandise, which had a $320 cost, is discarded.

22   Received the balance due from Elan Corporation, net of both the discount and the credit for the returned merchandise.

24   Returned defective merchandise to Jersey Corp. and accepted credit against future purchases. Its cost, net of the discount, was $496.

26   Purchased $9,000 of merchandise from Jersey Corp. with terms of 1/10, n/30, FOB destination.

26   Sold merchandise with a $4,640 cost for $5,800 on credit to Taos, Inc.

29   Received a $496 credit memorandum from Jersey Corp. concerning the merchandise returned on January 24.

31   Paid cash to Suzie Smith for 10 days' work at $125 per day.

Feb. 1   Paid $2,475 cash to Hilldale Mall for another three months' rent in advance.

  3   Paid Jersey Corp. for the balance due, net of the cash discount, less the $496 amount in the credit memorandum.

  5   Paid $600 cash to the local newspaper for an advertising insert in today's paper.

  11 Received the balance due from Antonio's Engineering Co. for fees billed on January 11.

  15 Sela Solstise withdrew $4,800 cash.

  23 Sold merchandise with a $2,660 cost for $3,220 on credit to Olathe Co.

  26 Paid cash to Suzie Smith for eight days' work at $125 per day.

  27 Reimbursed Sela Solstise for business automobile mileage (600 miles at $0.32 per mile).

Mar. 8   Purchased $2,730 of computer supplies from Appier Office Products on credit.

  9   Received the balance due from Olathe Co. for merchandise sold on February 23.

  11 Paid $960 cash to repair the company's computer.

  16 Received $5,260 cash from Imagine, Inc., for computing services provided.

  19 Paid the full amount due to Appier Office Products, including amounts created on December 15 and March 8.

  24 Billed Prime Leasing for $8,900 of computing services provided.

  25 Sold merchandise with a $2,002 cost for $2,800 on credit to Alexander Services.

  30 Sold merchandise with a $1,100 cost for $2,220 on credit to Dade Company.

  31 Reimbursed Sela Solstise for business automobile mileage (400 miles at $0.32 per mile).

The following additional facts are available for preparing adjustments on March 31 prior to financial statement preparation:

a. The March 31 inventory of computer supplies totals $2,005.

b. Three more months have passed since the company purchased its annual insurance policy at a $2,220 cost.

c. Suzie Smith has not been paid for seven days of work.

d. Three months have passed since any prepaid rent has been transferred to expense. The monthly rent is $825.

e. Depreciation on the computer equipment for January 1 through March 31 is $1,250.

f. Depreciation on the office equipment for January 1 through March 31 is $400.

g. The March 31 amount of merchandise inventory totals $704.

Required

1. Prepare journal entries to record each of the January through March transactions.

2. Post the journal entries to the accounts in the company's general ledger. (Begin with the post-closing adjusted balances as of December 31, 2002.)

3. Prepare a partial work sheet consisting of the first six columns (similar to the one shown in Exhibit 6A.3) that includes the unadjusted trial balance, the March 31 adjustments (a) through (g), and the adjusted trial balance. Do not prepare closing entries and do not journalize the adjusting entries or post them to the ledger.

4. Prepare an income statement for the three months ended March 31, 2003. Use a single-step format. List all expenses without differentiating between selling expenses and general and administrative expenses.

5. Prepare a statement of changes in owner's equity for the three months ended March 31, 2003.

6. Prepare a balance sheet as of March 31, 2003.

Beyond the Numbers

BTN 6-1   Refer to **Nike**'s financial statements in Appendix A.

Required

1. Assume that the amounts reported for inventories and cost of sales reflect items purchased in a form ready for resale. Compute the net cost of goods purchased for the fiscal year ended May 31, 2000.

2. Compute the current and acid-test ratios as of May 31, 2000, and May 31, 1999. Comment on the ratio results.

Reporting in Action

A2   C5

NIKE

Swoosh Ahead

3. Access Nike's annual report for fiscal years ending after May 31, 2000, from its Web site [**www.nike.com**] or the SEC's EDGAR database [**www.sec.gov**]. Recompute the current and acid-test ratios for fiscal years ending after May 31, 2000.

Comparative Analysis

A3

Reebok

NIKE

BTN 6-2   Key comparative figures ($ millions) for both **Nike** and **Reebok** follow:

Key Figures	Nike Current Year	Nike Prior Year	Reebok Current Year	Reebok Prior Year
Revenues (net sales)	$8,995.1	$8,776.9	$2,899.9	$3,224.6
Cost of sales	5,403.8	5,493.5	1,783.9	2,037.5

Required

1. Compute the dollar amount of gross margin and the gross margin ratio for the two years shown for both companies.

2. Which company earns more in gross margin for each dollar of net sales?

3. Did the gross margin ratios improve or decline for these companies?

Ethics Challenge

P2

BTN 6-3   Helen Gaines is a student who plans to attend approximately four professional events a year at her college. Each event requires a new dress and accessories that necessitate a financial outlay of $100–$200 per event. After incurring a major hit to her savings for the first event in her freshman year, Helen developed a different approach. She buys the dress on credit the week before the event, wears it to the event, and returns it the next week to the store for a full refund on her charge card.

Required

1. Comment on the ethics exhibited by Helen and possible consequences of her actions.

2. How does the merchandising company account for the dresses that Helen returns?

Communicating in Practice

C4 **C5** **P3**

BTN 6-4   You are the accountant for **Music and More**, a retailer that sells goods for home entertainment needs. The business owner, Mr. U. Paah, recently reviewed the annual financial statements you prepared and sent you an e-mail stating that he thinks you overstated net income. He explains that although he has invested a great deal in security, he is sure shoplifting and other forms of inventory shrinkage have occurred, but he does not see any deduction for shrinkage on the income statement. The store uses a perpetual inventory system.

Required

Prepare a brief memorandum that responds to the owner's concerns in paper or e-mail format. If the response is made via e-mail, assume that your instructor is the owner instead of Mr. U. Paah.

Taking It to the Net **C1**

BTN 6-5   Access **www.edgar-online.com** and obtain the June 2, 2000, 10-K report filed by **eToys.com Inc.** (ticker ETYS). Construct a three-year trend of gross margin ratios for eToys using the net sales and cost of goods sold data on eToys' income statement. Analyze and comment on the trend.

Teamwork in Action

C2 **C5** **A3**

BTN 6-6   **World Brands'** ledger and supplementary records at the end of its current period reveal the following:

Sales	$430,000	Merchandise inventory (beginning of period)	$ 49,000
Sales returns	18,000	Invoice cost of merchandise purchases	180,000
Sales discounts	6,600	Purchase discounts received	4,500
Cost of transportation-in	11,000	Purchase returns and allowances	5,500
Operating expenses	20,000	Merchandise inventory (end of period)	42,000

Required

1. *Each* member of the team is to assume responsibility for computing *one* of the following items. You are not to duplicate your teammates' work. Get any necessary amounts to compute your item from the appropriate teammate. Each member is to explain his/her computation to the team in preparation for reporting to the class.

Point: In teams of four, assign the same student (a) and (e). Rotate teams for reporting on a different computation and the analysis in (3).

    a. Net sales   **d.** Gross profit

    b. Total cost of merchandise purchases   **e.** Net income

    c. Cost of goods sold

2. Check your net income with the instructor. If correct, proceed to step (3).

3. Assume that a physical inventory finds that actual ending inventory is $38,000. Discuss how this affects previously computed amounts in step (1).

BTN 6-7 Read the article, "You Can Survive Online Shopping" in the December 6, 1999, issue of *Business Week*.

Business Week Activity

P4

Required

1. How does the 1999 projected dollar volume of online November and December shopping compare to the 1998 figure?

2. Return policies for e-merchants vary widely. Discuss the variety of return policies implemented by online retailers.

3. What account title would you recommend an online retailer use to record goods returned that were purchased online? Would you record these returns in a separate account from goods that were purchased in a store and returned (assuming the retailer operates a "bricks-and-mortar" storefront as well as online retailing)? Explain your answer.

BTN 6-8 Steve Miller is an entrepreneur who buys and sells new and used musical instruments to small retail outlets that offer musical instruments and training to customers. He recently completed his first year of operations. His income statement follows:

Entrepreneurial Decision

C1 C5 P4

e

MUSICAL INSTRUMENTS Income Statement For Year Ended January 31, 2002	
Net Sales	$ 250,000
Cost of sales	(175,000)
Expenses	(20,000)
Net income	$ 55,000

To increase income, Miller is proposing to offer sales discounts of 3/10, n/30, and to ship all merchandise FOB shipping point. He presently offers no discounts and ships merchandise FOB destination. The discounts are predicted to increase net sales by 14%; the ratio of cost of sales to net sales is expected to remain unchanged. Since delivery expenses are zero under this proposal, the expenses are predicted to increase by only 10%.

Required

1. Prepare a forecasted income statement for the year ended January 31, 2003, based on Miller's proposal.

2. Do you recommend that Miller implement his proposal given your analysis in part *1*?

3. Identify any concerns you might express to Miller regarding his proposal.

7

Merchandise Inventories and Cost of Sales

A Look Back

Chapter 6 focused on merchandising activities and how they are reported. Both the perpetual and periodic inventory systems were described. We also analyzed and recorded merchandise purchases and sales and explained adjustments and the closing process for merchandising companies.

A Look at This Chapter

This chapter emphasizes accounting for inventory. We describe the methods available for assigning costs to inventory and explain the items and costs making up merchandise inventory. We also analyze the effects of inventory on both financial and tax reporting, and we discuss other methods of estimating and measuring inventory.

A Look Ahead

Chapter 8 emphasizes accounting information systems. We describe fundamental system principles, the system's components, use of special journals and subsidiary ledgers, and technology-based systems. We also discuss segment reports and how to analyze these data.

"Never give up . . . no one believed in us."
—Daymond John.

Learning Objectives

FUBU The Collection

e   NEW YORK—It all began when 22-year-old waiter Daymond John and a friend bought a stocking cap from a street vendor. "It was about $20," recalls John. "And we said to ourselves, 'We can make this, we can sew it at home' because I knew how to sew a little bit from watching my mother hem my pants." The first day John hit the streets, he sold 40 hats and earned himself $800. He was hooked and quickly drew up ideas for shirts and sweatshirts. After enlisting the help of three childhood friends—Carl Brown, J. Alexander Martin, and Keith Perrin—John took a $100,000 mortgage on his home in Queens. He turned one-half of the home into a mini-factory and a new clothing company, dubbed **FUBU**, was born [**www.FUBU.com**].

Within a few short months the "team" had sold hats and T-shirts worth $10,000—FUBU was taking off. Within another 12 months, FUBU had $300,000 worth of orders for hats, shirts, and jeans. But a lack of cash flow and inventory management almost brought FUBU down. "I decided it's either do or die right now," recalls John. "And nobody else really cared about what we were doing or actually believed in us." To ensure inventory to meet the backlog of orders, John bought 10 more sewing machines and hired 4 more employees. "It was a very hard struggle," John says, but he was determined to keep FUBU afloat and overcome inventory problems. He installed better cost management and inventory oversight. The company got a further boost when hometown celebrity, rapper LL Cool J, wore FUBU's clothes in his music videos. FUBU was once again heading for the stars.

Today, just a few short years after its meager beginnings, FUBU The Collection is carried in more than 5,000 stores in the United States alone. They're also sold internationally in Australia, France, Germany, and Japan. Annual sales now top $350 million. From suburban teens to soul and pop musicians, FUBU's authentic quality and street credibility continue to attract new customers. [Sources: *Entrepreneur*, 12 November 1998; *FUBU Web Site*, May 2001; *CNNfn Web Site*, August 10, 1998.]

Chapter Preview

Merchandising companies' activities include purchasing and reselling of merchandise. We explained accounting for merchandisers in the last chapter, including the perpetual and periodic inventory systems. In this chapter, we extend the study and analysis of inventory by identifying the items composing it. We also explain the methods used to assign costs to merchandise inventory *and* cost of goods sold. The assigned costs are not always historical cost. Many retailers, wholesalers, and other merchandising companies that purchase products for resale use the principles and methods we describe. These principles and methods affect reported amounts of income, assets, equity, revenues, and expenses. Understanding fundamental concepts of inventory accounting increases our ability to analyze and interpret financial statements. An understanding of these topics also helps people to run their own businesses.

Assigning Costs to Inventory

P1 Compute inventory in a perpetual system using the methods of specific identification, FIFO, LIFO, and weighted average.

Concept 7-1

Point: Inventories are a major current asset for most wholesalers, retailers, and manufacturers. Accounting for inventories is key to determining cost of goods sold on the income statement.

Accounting for inventory affects both the balance sheet and the income statement. A major goal in accounting for inventory is to match relevant costs against revenues. This is important to properly compute income. We use the *matching principle* to decide how much of the cost of the goods available for sale is deducted from sales and how much is carried forward as inventory and matched against future sales. Management must make this decision and several others when accounting for inventory. These decisions include selecting the

- Costing method (specific identification, FIFO, LIFO, or weighted average).
- Inventory system (perpetual or periodic).
- Items included and their costs.
- Use of market values or other estimates.

Decisions on these points affect the reported amounts for inventory, cost of goods sold, gross profit, income, current assets, and other accounts. This chapter discusses all of these important issues and their reporting effects.

One of the most important decisions in accounting for inventory is determining the per unit costs assigned to inventory items. When all units are purchased at the same unit cost, this process is simple. When identical items are purchased at different costs, however, a question arises as to which amounts to record in cost of goods sold when sales occur and which amounts to identify as remaining in inventory. We must record cost of goods sold and reductions in inventory to reflect these sales. How we assign these costs to inventory and cost of goods sold affects the financial statements.

Four methods are commonly used to assign costs to inventory and cost of goods sold: (1) specific identification, (2) first-in, first-out, (3) last-in, first-out, and (4) weighted average. Each method assumes a particular pattern for how costs flow through inventory. Each of these four methods is acceptable whether or not the actual physical flow of goods follows the cost flow assumption.[1] Exhibit 7.1 shows the frequency in the use of these methods.

We use information from **Trekking**, a sporting goods store, to describe the four methods. Among its many products, Trekking carries one type of mountain bike whose sales are directed at biking clubs. Its customers usually purchase in amounts of 10 or more bikes. We use data from Trekking's August 2002 transactions in mountain bikes. Its mountain bike (unit) inventory at the beginning of August and its purchases during August are shown in Exhibit 7.2.

Exhibit 7.1

Frequency in Use of Inventory Methods

LIFO 35%   FIFO 42%

Weighted Average 19%   Other* 4%

*Includes specific identification.

---

[1] Physical flow of goods depends on the type of product and the way it is stored. Perishable goods such as fresh fruit demand that a business attempt to sell them in a first-in, first-out physical flow pattern. Other products such as lanterns or grills can often be sold in a last-in, first-out physical flow pattern. Physical flow and cost flow need not be the same.

Aug. 1	Beginning inventory	10 units @ $ 91 = $ 910
Aug. 3	Purchases	15 units @ $106 = 1,590
Aug. 17	Purchases	20 units @ $115 = 2,300
Aug. 28	Purchases	10 units @ $119 = 1,190
	Totals	**55 units** **$5,990**

Exhibit 7.2

Cost of Goods Available for Sale

Trekking had two large sales of mountain bikes to two different biking clubs in August as shown in Exhibit 7.3. It ends August with 12 bikes remaining in inventory.

Aug. 14	Sales	20 units @ $130 = $2,600
Aug. 31	Sales	23 units @ $150 = 3,450
	Totals	**43 units** **$6,050**

Exhibit 7.3

Retail Sales of Goods

Trekking uses the perpetual inventory system. We explained in Chapter 6 that use of the perpetual inventory system is increasing as a result of advances in information and computing technology. Widespread use of electronic scanners and product bar codes encourages a perpetual inventory system. **(In Appendix 7A, we describe the assignment of costs to inventory using a periodic system.)** Regardless of what inventory method or system is used, cost of goods available for sale is allocated between cost of goods sold and ending inventory.

> **Point:** Cost of goods sold plus ending inventory equals cost of goods available for sale.

Trekking's use of a perpetual inventory system means that its merchandise inventory account is continually updated to reflect purchases and sales. As described in Chapter 6, the important accounting aspects of a perpetual system are:

- Each purchase of merchandise for resale increases (debits) inventory.
- Each sale of merchandise decreases (credits) inventory and increases (debits) costs of goods sold.
- Necessary costs of merchandise such as transportation-in increase (debit) inventory, and cost reductions such as purchase discounts and purchase returns and allowances decrease (credit) inventory.

> **Point:** Three key variables determine the dollar value of ending inventory: (1) inventory quantity, (2) costs of inventory, and (3) cost flow assumption.

Except for any inventory shrinkage, the balance in the Merchandise Inventory account reflects the cost of merchandise available for sale at all times.

Specific Identification

When each item in inventory can be directly identified with a specific purchase and its invoice, we can use **specific identification** (also called *specific invoice inventory pricing*) to assign costs. We also need sales records that identify exactly which items were sold and when. Trekking's internal documents reveal that 6 of the 12 unsold units were from the August 28 purchase and 6 were from the August 17 purchase. We use this information and the specific identification method to assign costs to the 12 units in ending inventory and to the 43 units sold as shown in Exhibit 7.4. Notice that each unit, whether sold or in inventory, has its own specific cost attached to it.

When using specific identification, Trekking's cost of goods sold reported on the income statement is **$4,586**, the sum of $2,000 and $2,586 from the third column of Exhibit 7.4. Trekking's ending inventory reported on the balance sheet is **$1,404**, which is the final inventory balance from the fourth column of Exhibit 7.4. *The assignment of costs to the goods sold and to inventory using specific identification is the same for both the perpetual and periodic systems.*

> **Point:** Companies with expensive, custom-made inventory often use specific identification.

Exhibit 7.4

Specific Identification
Computations

Date	Purchases	Cost of Goods Sold	Inventory Balance
Aug. 1	Beginning balance		10 @ $ 91 = $ 910
Aug. 3	15 @ $106 = $1,590		10 @ $ 91 ⎱ = $2,500 15 @ $106 ⎰
Aug. 14		8 @ $ 91 = $ 728 ⎱ = $2,000* 12 @ $106 = $1,272 ⎰	2 @ $ 91 ⎱ = $ 500 3 @ $106 ⎰
Aug. 17	20 @ $115 = $2,300		2 @ $ 91 ⎱ 3 @ $106 ⎬ = $2,800 20 @ $115 ⎰
Aug. 28	10 @ $119 = $1,190		2 @ $ 91 ⎱ 3 @ $106 ⎬ 20 @ $115 ⎬ = $3,990 10 @ $119 ⎰
Aug. 31		2 @ $ 91 = $ 182 ⎱ 3 @ $106 = $ 318 ⎬ = $2,586* 14 @ $115 = $1,610 ⎬ 4 @ $119 = $ 476 ⎰	6 @ $115 ⎱ = $1,404 6 @ $119 ⎰

* Identification of the specific items sold (and their costs) is obtained from internal documents that track each unit from its purchase to its sale.

First-In, First-Out

Point: Purchases data (column) are identical across all methods. These data are taken from Exhibit 7.2.

The **first-in, first-out (FIFO)** method of assigning costs to both inventory and cost of goods sold assumes that inventory items are sold in the order acquired. When sales occur, the costs of the earliest units acquired are charged to cost of goods sold. This leaves the costs from the most recent purchases in ending inventory. Use of FIFO for computing the costs of inventory and goods sold is shown in Exhibit 7.5.

Exhibit 7.5

FIFO Computations—
Perpetual System

For the 20 units sold on Aug. 14, the first 10 sold are assigned the earliest cost of $91. The next 10 sold are assigned the next earliest cost of $106.

For the 23 units sold on Aug. 31, the first 5 sold are assigned the earliest available cost of $106 (from Aug. 3 purchase). The next 18 sold are assigned the next earliest cost of $115 (from Aug. 17).

Date	Purchases	Cost of Goods Sold	Inventory Balance
Aug. 1	Beginning balance		10 @ $ 91 = $ 910
Aug. 3	15 @ $106 = $1,590		10 @ $ 91 ⎱ = $2,500 15 @ $106 ⎰
Aug. 14		10 @ $ 91 = $ 910 ⎱ = $1,970 10 @ $106 = $1,060 ⎰	5 @ $106 = $ 530
Aug. 17	20 @ $115 = $2,300		5 @ $106 ⎱ = $2,830 20 @ $115 ⎰
Aug. 28	10 @ $119 = $1,190		5 @ $106 ⎱ 20 @ $115 ⎬ = $4,020 10 @ $119 ⎰
Aug. 31		5 @ $106 = $ 530 ⎱ = $2,600 18 @ $115 = $2,070 ⎰	2 @ $115 ⎱ = $1,420 10 @ $119 ⎰

Point: Under FIFO, a unit sold is assigned the earliest (oldest) cost from inventory. This leaves the most recent costs in ending inventory.

Trekking's cost of goods sold reported on the income statement (reflecting the 43 units sold) is **$4,570** ($1,970 + $2,600), and its ending inventory reported on the balance sheet (reflecting the 12 units unsold) is **$1,420**. *The assignment of costs to the goods sold and to inventory using FIFO is the same for both the perpetual and periodic systems.*

Last-In, First-Out

The **last-in, first-out (LIFO)** method of assigning costs assumes that the most recent purchases are sold first. These more recent costs are charged to the goods sold, and the costs of the earliest purchases are assigned to inventory. As with other methods, LIFO is acceptable even when the physical flow of goods does not follow a last-in, first-out pattern. One appeal of LIFO is that by assigning costs from the most recent purchases to cost of goods sold, LIFO comes closest to matching current replacement costs with revenues (compared to FIFO or weighted average). While costs for the most recent purchases are not exactly replacement costs, they usually are close approximations. Exhibit 7.6 shows how LIFO assigns the costs of mountain bikes to the 12 units in inventory and to the 43 units in cost of goods sold.

Point: Under LIFO, a unit sold is assigned the most recent (latest) cost from inventory. This leaves the oldest costs in inventory.

Exhibit 7.6

LIFO Computations—Perpetual System

Date	Purchases	Cost of Goods Sold	Inventory Balance
Aug. 1	Beginning balance		10 @ $ 91 = $ 910
Aug. 3	15 @ $106 = $1,590		10 @ $ 91 15 @ $106 } = $2,500
Aug. 14		15 @ $106 = $1,590 5 @ $ 91 = $ 455 } = $2,045	5 @ $ 91 = $ 455
Aug. 17	20 @ $115 = $2,300		5 @ $ 91 20 @ $115 } = $2,755
Aug. 28	10 @ $119 = $1,190		5 @ $ 91 20 @ $115 10 @ $119 } = $3,945
Aug. 31		10 @ $119 = $1,190 13 @ $115 = $1,495 } = $2,685	5 @ $ 91 7 @ $115 } = $1,260

> For the 20 units sold on Aug. 14, the first 15 sold are assigned the most recent cost of $106. The next 5 sold are assigned the next most recent cost of $91.

> For the 23 units sold on Aug. 31, the first 10 sold are assigned the most recent cost of $119. The next 13 sold are assigned the next most recent cost of $115.

Trekking's cost of goods sold reported on the income statement is **$4,730** ($2,045 + $2,685), and its ending inventory reported on the balance sheet is **$1,260**. The assignment of costs to cost of goods sold and to inventory using LIFO usually gives different results, depending on whether a perpetual or periodic system is used. This is so because LIFO under a perpetual system assigns the most recent costs to goods sold at the time of each sale, whereas the periodic system waits to assign costs until the end of a period.

Global: LIFO is mainly used in the U.S. In some countries such as Australia, Ireland, and the United Kingdom, the use of LIFO is rare.

Weighted Average

The **weighted average** (also called **average cost**) method of assigning cost requires that we compute the weighted average cost per unit of inventory at the time of each sale. Weighted average cost per unit at the time of each sale equals the cost of goods available for sale divided by the units available. The results using weighted average for Trekking are shown in Exhibit 7.7.

Trekking's cost of goods sold reported on the income statement (reflecting the 43 units sold) is **$4,622** ($2,000 + $2,622), and its ending inventory reported on the balance sheet (reflecting the 12 units unsold) is **$1,368**. The assignment of costs to cost of goods sold and to inventory using weighted average usually gives different results, depending on whether a perpetual or periodic system is used. This is so because weighted average under a perpetual system recomputes the per unit cost at the time of each sale, whereas under the periodic system, the per unit cost is computed only at the end of a period.

Point: Under weighted average, a unit sold is assigned the average cost of all items currently available for sale.

Inventory Costing and Technology

A perpetual inventory system can be kept in either electronic or manual form. Using a manual form can make a perpetual inventory system too costly for businesses, especially those with many purchases and sales and with many units in inventory. Advances in information

Point: Inventory costing methods need not follow the physical flow of inventory.

Exhibit 7.7
Weighted Average
Computations—
Perpetual System

Date	Purchases	Cost of Goods Sold	Inventory Balance
Aug. 1	Beginning balance		10 @ $ 91 = $ 910
Aug. 3	15 @ $106 = $1,590		10 @ $ 91 15 @ $106 } = $2,500 (or $100 per unit)[a]
Aug. 14		20 @ $100 = **$2,000**	5 @ $100 = $ 500 (or $100 per unit)[b]
Aug. 17	20 @ $115 = $2,300		5 @ $100 20 @ $115 } = $2,800 (or $112 per unit)[c]
Aug. 28	10 @ $119 = $1,190		5 @ $100 20 @ $115 10 @ $119 } = $3,990 (or $114 per unit)[d]
Aug. 31		23 @ $114 = **$2,622**	12 @ $114 = **$1,368** (or $114 per unit)[e]

[a] $100 per unit = [$2,500 inventory balance ÷ 25 units in inventory].

[b] $100 per unit = [$ 500 inventory balance ÷ 5 units in inventory].

[c] $112 per unit = [$2,800 inventory balance ÷ 25 units in inventory].

[d] $114 per unit = [$3,990 inventory balance ÷ 35 units in inventory].

[e] $114 per unit = [$1,368 inventory balance ÷ 12 units in inventory].

and computing technology have greatly reduced the cost of a perpetual inventory system. Many companies are now asking whether they can afford *not* to have a perpetual inventory system because timely access to inventory information has become a strategy to gain a competitive advantage. Scanned sales data, for instance, can reveal crucial information on buying patterns. It can also help companies target promotional and advertising activities. These and other applications have greatly increased the use of the perpetual inventory system.

Did You Know?

Battle of Inventory   The Pentagon is applying accounting skills to shrink inventories and speed deliveries. Use of bar codes, laser cards, radio tags, and accounting databases to track supplies speeds delivery from factory to foxhole. "We'll have piles of information instead of piles of stock," says Colonel M.D. Russ.

Inventory Analysis and Effects

This section analyzes and compares the alternative inventory costing methods. We also analyze the tax effects of inventory methods, examine managers' preferences for an inventory method, and consider the effects of inventory errors.

Financial Reporting

A1 Analyze the effects of inventory methods for both financial and tax reporting.

When purchase prices do not change, each inventory costing method assigns the same cost amounts to inventory and to cost of goods sold. When purchase prices are different, however, the methods are likely to assign different cost amounts. We show these differences in Exhibit 7.8 using Trekking's segment income statement for its mountain bike operations. The different inventory costing methods show different results for net income. Because Trekking's purchase prices rose in August, FIFO assigned the least amount to cost of goods sold. This led to the highest gross profit and the highest net income. In contrast, LIFO assigned the highest amount to cost of goods sold. This yielded the lowest gross profit and the lowest net income. As expected, amounts from using the weighted average method fell between FIFO and LIFO.[2] The amounts from using specific identification depend on which units are actually sold.

---

[2] The weighted average amount can be outside the FIFO or LIFO amounts if prices do not steadily increase or decrease but exhibit a cyclical pattern.

TREKKING COMPANY
Segment Income Statement—Mountain Bikes
For Month Ended August 31

	Specific Identification	FIFO	LIFO	Weighted Average
Sales	$6,050	$6,050	$6,050	$6,050
Cost of goods sold	4,586	4,570	4,730	4,622
Gross profit	$1,464	$1,480	$1,320	$1,428
Operating expenses	450	450	450	450
Income before taxes	$1,014	$1,030	$ 870	$ 978
Income tax expense (30%)	304	309	261	293
Net income	$ 710	$ 721	$ 609	$ 685

Exhibit 7.8

Income Statement Effects of Inventory Costing Methods

All four inventory costing methods are acceptable in practice. Each method offers certain advantages. One advantage of specific identification is that it exactly matches costs and revenues. This is important when each unit has unique features affecting its cost. An advantage of weighted average is that it tends to smooth out changes in costs. An advantage of FIFO is that it assigns an amount to inventory on the balance sheet that closely approximates current replacement cost. An advantage of LIFO is it assigns the most recent costs incurred to cost of goods sold and likely better matches current costs with revenues on the income statement.

The choice of an inventory costing method can greatly impact amounts on financial statements. **Mobil**, for instance, recently changed its inventory method and reported in a news release that this change "will reduce ... year-to-date, net income by $680 million." Companies must disclose the inventory method used in their financial statements or notes.

Global: Swiss standards require no disclosures related to inventory.

It is important to understand inventory costing for analysis of financial statements. Some companies' financial statements help in our analysis by reporting what the difference would be if another costing method were used. **Kmart**, for instance, reports in a recent annual report that ($ millions): "Inventories valued on LIFO were $360, $407 and $457 lower than amounts that would have been reported using the first-in, first-out (FIFO) method at year end ... [for the most recent 3 years], respectively."

You Make the Call

Financial Planner One of your clients asks if the inventory account of a company using FIFO needs any "adjustments" for analysis purposes in light of recent inflation. What is your advice? Does your advice depend on changes in the costs of these inventories?

Answer—p. 286

Tax Reporting

Trekking's segment income statement in Exhibit 7.8 reflects the company's formation as a corporation because its income statement includes income tax expense (at a rate of 30%). Because inventory costs affect net income, they have potential tax effects for corporations. Trekking gains a temporary tax advantage by using LIFO. This advantage occurs because LIFO assigns a larger dollar amount to cost of goods sold when purchase prices are increasing as in the case of Trekking. This means less income is reported when LIFO is used and purchase prices are rising. This in turn results in the smallest income tax expense.

Global: Countries allowing LIFO for tax reporting include Germany, Belgium, Japan, Taiwan, and South Korea.

The Internal Revenue Service (IRS) identifies several acceptable methods for inventory costing in reporting taxable income for corporations. It is important to know that companies can and often do use different costing methods for financial reporting and tax reporting. *The only exception is when LIFO is used for tax*

Did You Know?

Entrepreneurial Giving Many entrepreneurs donate 10% or more of their pretax income to charities. Consultants cite evidence that socially conscious behavior brings tangible financial rewards. A recent survey found 76% of respondents saying they'd switch from their current store to one with a good cause if price and quality are equal.

purposes; in this case, the IRS requires it be used in financial statements. Since costs tend to rise, LIFO usually gives a lower taxable income and a tax advantage. Many companies use LIFO for this reason, yet managers often have incentives to report higher net income for reasons such as bonus plans, job security, and reputation. FIFO is sometimes preferred in these cases because it tends to report a higher income when prices are rising.

Consistency in Reporting

Inventory costing methods can affect amounts on financial statements, and some managers might be inclined to choose a method most consistent with their hoped-for results each period. One objective might be to pick the method giving the most favorable financial statement amounts. Managers might also be inclined to pick the method giving them the highest bonus since many management bonus plans are based on net income. If managers were allowed to pick the method each period, users of financial statements would have more difficulty comparing a company's financial statements from one period to the next. If income increased, for instance, a user would need to decide whether it resulted from successful operations or from an accounting method change. The consistency principle is used to avoid this problem.

The **consistency principle** requires a company to use the same accounting methods period after period so that financial statements are comparable across periods. The consistency principle applies to all accounting methods. When a company must choose between alternative methods, consistency requires that the company continue to use the selected method period after period. Users of financial statements can then make comparisons of a company's statements across periods because of the assumption that a company uses the same methods across periods.

Global: LIFO is acceptable under international accounting standards.

The consistency principle does *not* require a company to use one method exclusively. It can use different methods to value different categories of inventory. **Harley-Davidson**, for instance, reports the following: "Inventories located in the United States are valued using the last-in, first-out (LIFO) method. Other inventories . . . are valued at the lower of cost or market using the first-in, first-out (FIFO) method." Also, the consistency principle does not imply that a company can never change from one accounting method to another. Instead it means that a company must argue that the method it is changing to will improve its financial reporting. When an alternative method will improve its reporting, a change is acceptable. The *full-disclosure principle* requires that the notes to the statements report this type of change, its justification, and its effect on net income.

You Make the Call—Ethics

Inventory Manager Your compensation as inventory manager includes a bonus plan based on gross profit. Your superior asks your opinion on changing the inventory costing method from FIFO to LIFO. Since costs are expected to continue to rise, your superior predicts that LIFO would match higher current costs against sales, thereby lowering taxable income (and gross profit). This proposed change will likely reduce your bonus. What do you recommend?

Answer—p. 286

Errors in Reporting Inventory

A2 Analyze the effects of inventory errors on current and future financial statements.

Concept 7-2

Companies must take care in both computing and taking a physical count of inventory. An inventory error causes misstatements in cost of goods sold, gross profit, net income, current assets, and equity. It also causes misstatements in the next period's statements because ending inventory of one period is the beginning inventory of the next. An error carried forward causes misstatements in the next period's cost of goods sold, gross profit, and net income. Such misstatements can reduce the usefulness of financial statements.

Income Statement Effects

The income statement effects of an inventory error are evident by reviewing the components of cost of goods sold as shown in Exhibit 7.9—this relation applies to any method under both the perpetual and periodic systems. The effect of an inventory error on cost of goods sold is determined by computing it with the incorrect component amount and comparing it to cost of goods sold when using the correct component amount.

Exhibit 7.9

Cost of Goods Sold Components

We can see, for example, that understating ending inventory in a physical count overstates cost of goods sold. An overstatement in cost of goods sold yields an understatement in net income. We can do the same analysis with overstating ending inventory and for an error in beginning inventory. Exhibit 7.10 shows the effects of inventory errors on the current period's income statement amounts.

Inventory Error	Cost of Goods Sold	Net Income
Understate ending inventory	Overstated	Understated
Understate beginning inventory	Understated	Overstated
Overstate ending inventory*	Understated	Overstated
Overstate beginning inventory*	Overstated	Understated

*These errors are unlikely under a perpetual system because they suggest more inventory than is recorded. Accordingly, management will normally follow up and discover and correct these errors before they impact any accounts.

Exhibit 7.10

Effects of Inventory Errors on This Period's Income Statement

Notice that inventory errors yield opposite effects in cost of goods sold and net income. Inventory errors also carry over to the next period, yielding a reverse effect.

To show these effects, we consider an inventory error for a company with $100,000 in sales for years 2001, 2002, and 2003. If this company maintains a steady $20,000 inventory level during this period and makes $60,000 in purchases in each of these years, its cost of goods sold is $60,000 and its gross profit is $40,000 each year. But what if this company errs in computing its 2001 ending inventory and reports $16,000 instead of the correct amount of $20,000? The effects of this error are shown in Exhibit 7.11. The $4,000 understatement of the year 2001 ending inventory causes a $4,000 overstatement in year 2001 cost of goods sold and a $4,000 understatement in both gross profit and net income for year 2001. Since year 2001 ending inventory becomes year 2002 beginning inventory, this error causes an understatement in 2002 cost of goods sold and a $4,000 overstatement in both gross profit and net income for year 2002. Notice that an inventory error in one period does not affect the third period, year 2003.

If year 2001 ending inventory had been overstated, it would have yielded opposite results. That is, the 2001 net income would have been overstated and the 2002 income understated. An inventory error is said to be *self-correcting* because it always yields an

Example: If year 2001 ending inventory in Exhibit 7.11 is overstated by $3,000, what is the effect on cost of goods sold, gross profit, assets, and equity? *Answer:* Cost of goods sold is understated by $3,000 in 2001 and overstated by $3,000 in 2002. Gross profit and net income are overstated in 2001 and understated in 2002. Assets and equity are overstated in 2001.

	Income Statements				
	2001		**2002**		**2003**
Sales		$100,000		$100,000	$100,000
Cost of goods sold					
Beginning inventory	$20,000		→**$16,000***	→$20,000	
Cost of goods purchased	60,000		60,000	60,000	
Goods available for sale .	$80,000		$76,000	$80,000	
Ending inventory.	**16,000***		20,000	20,000	
Cost of goods sold.		**64,000†**	**56,000†**		60,000
Gross profit.		$ 36,000	$ 44,000		$ 40,000
Operating expenses.		10,000	10,000		10,000
Net income		$ 26,000	$ 34,000		$ 30,000

Exhibit 7.11

Effects of Inventory Errors on Three Periods' Income Statements

* Correct amount is $20,000.   † Correct amount is $60,000.

offsetting error in the next period. This does not make inventory errors less serious. Managers, lenders, owners, and other users make important decisions analysis of changes in net income and cost of goods sold. Therefore, inventory errors must be avoided.

Balance Sheet Effects

Balance sheet effects of an inventory error are evident by considering the components of the accounting equation: Assets = Liabilities + Equity. For example, understating ending inventory understates both current and total assets. An understatement in ending inventory also yields an understatement in equity because of the understatement in net income. Exhibit 7.12 shows the effects of inventory errors on the current period's balance sheet amounts.

Exhibit 7.12

Effects of Inventory Errors on This Period's Balance Sheet

Inventory Error	Assets	Equity
Understate ending inventory	Understated	Understated
Overstate ending inventory	Overstated	Overstated

Errors in *beginning* inventory do not yield misstatements in the end-of-period balance sheet, but they do affect the current period's income statement.

Quick Check

1. Describe one advantage for each of the inventory costing methods: specific identification, FIFO, LIFO, and weighted average.
2. When costs are rising, does LIFO or FIFO report higher net income?
3. When costs are rising, what effect does LIFO have on a balance sheet compared to FIFO?
4. A company takes a physical count of inventory at the end of 2002 and finds that ending inventory is overstated by $10,000. Would this error cause cost of goods sold to be overstated or understated in 2002? In year 2003? If so, by how much?

Answers—pp. 286–287

Inventory Items and Costs

This section identifies the items and costs making up merchandise inventory. This identification is important given the major impact of inventory in financial statements. We also describe the importance of and the method used in taking a physical count of inventory.

Items in Merchandise Inventory

C1 Identify the items making up merchandise inventory.

Merchandise inventory includes all goods that a company owns and holds for sale. This rule holds regardless of where the goods are located when inventory is counted. We must simply see that all items are counted and computations are correct. Certain inventory items require special attention, including goods in transit, goods on consignment, and goods that are damaged or obsolete.

Goods in Transit

Point: Ownership of merchandise held for resale determines whether it is included in inventory. This is consistent with the definition of assets in Chapter 1.

Does a purchaser's inventory include goods in transit from a supplier? The answer is that if ownership has passed to the purchaser, they are included in the purchaser's inventory. Chapter 6 explained how we determine this by reviewing the shipping terms—*FOB destination* or *FOB shipping point*. If the purchaser is responsible for paying freight, ownership passes when goods are loaded on the transport vehicle. If the supplier is responsible for paying freight, owenership passes when goods arrive at their destination.

Goods on Consignment

Goods on consignment are goods shipped by the owner, called the **consignor,** to another party, the **consignee.** A consignee sells goods for the owner. The consignor owns consigned goods and reports them in its inventory. **Score Board**, **Tri Star**, and **Upper Deck**, for instance, pay sports celebrities such as Tiger Woods and Ken Griffey, Jr., to sign memorabilia. These autographed items (footballs, baseballs, jerseys, photos) are offered to shopping networks on consignment and are sold through catalogs and dealers. The consignor must report these items in its inventory until sold.

Goods Damaged or Obsolete

Damaged goods and obsolete (or deteriorated) goods are not counted in inventory if they are unsalable. If these goods are salable at a reduced price, they are included in inventory at a conservative estimate of their **net realizable value.** Net realizable value is sales price minus the cost of making the sale. The period when damage or obsolescence (or deterioration) occurs is the period when the loss in value is reported.

Costs of Merchandise Inventory

Merchandise inventory includes costs of expenditures necessary, directly or indirectly, to bring an item to a salable condition and location. This means the cost of an inventory item includes its invoice price minus any discount, and plus any added or incidental costs necessary to put it in a place and condition for sale.

> **Did You Know?**
>
> **Inventory Online** Warehouse clerks can quickly record inventory by scanning bar codes. Thanks to **Motorola**, a wireless portable computer with a two-way radio allows clerks to send and receive data instantly. It gives managers immediate access to up-to-date information on inventory and location.

Added or incidental costs can include import duties, transportation-in, storage, insurance, and costs incurred in an aging process (for example, aging wine and cheese).

 C2 Identify the costs of merchandise inventory.

Accounting principles imply that incidental costs are assigned to the units purchased. The purpose is to properly match all inventory costs against revenue in the period when inventory is sold. Some companies use the *materiality principle* or the *cost-to-benefit constraint* to avoid assigning incidental costs of acquiring merchandise to inventory. These companies argue either that incidental costs are immaterial or that the effort in assigning these costs to inventory outweighs the benefit. Such companies often value inventory using invoice prices only. When this is done, the incidental costs are allocated to cost of goods sold in the period when they are incurred.

> **Did You Know?**
>
> **Express Lane Shopping** Bar codes and readers are common tools for retailers. More retailers are adding bar code readers on shopping carts for customers to swipe the product over the reader, automatically charging it to a credit card. There is no need to stand in a checkout line. Customers simply pass through a gate that verifies that everything in the cart has been scanned.

Physical Count of Merchandise Inventory

The Inventory account under a perpetual system is always up to date, but events can cause the Inventory account balance to be different from the actual inventory available. Such events include theft, loss, damage, and errors. In response, nearly all companies take a *physical count of inventory* at least once each year, sometimes called *taking an inventory.* This often occurs at the end of a fiscal year or when inventory amounts are low. This physical count is used to adjust the Inventory account balance to the actual inventory available.

Concept 7-2

We determine a dollar amount for the physical count of inventory available by (1) counting the units of each product on hand, (2) multiplying the count for each product by its cost per unit, and (3) adding the costs for all products. When taking a count, items are less likely to be counted more than once or omitted by using prenumbered inventory tickets. We show a typical inventory ticket in Exhibit 7.13.

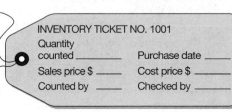

INVENTORY TICKET NO. 1001
Quantity
counted _____   Purchase date _____
Sales price $ _____   Cost price $ _____
Counted by _____   Checked by _____

Exhibit 7.13

Inventory Ticket

The process of a physical count of inventory is fairly standard. Before beginning it, we prepare at least one inventory ticket for each product on hand. These tickets are issued to employees doing the count. An employee counts the quantity of a product and obtains information on its purchase date, selling price, and cost. This information is sometimes included with the products but often must be obtained from accounting records or invoices. Once the necessary information has been collected, the employee records it on the inventory ticket and signs the form. The inventory ticket is then attached to the counted inventory. Another employee often recounts and rechecks information on the ticket, signs it, and returns it to the manager. To ensure that no ticket is lost or missed, internal control procedures verify that all prenumbered tickets are returned. The unit and cost data on inventory tickets are aggregated by multiplying the number of units for each product by its unit cost. This gives us the dollar amount for each product in inventory. The sum total of all product costs is the amount reported for inventory on the balance sheet.

Subsidiary Inventory Records

The Merchandise Inventory account is a controlling account for the subsidiary merchandise inventory ledger. The subsidiary ledger contains a separate record for each product, and it can be in electronic or paper form. Subsidiary inventory records assist managers in planning and controlling inventory. A typical subsidiary ledger is shown in Exhibit 7.14. This record shows both the number of units and costs for each purchase and sale of the item, along with the updated balance after each purchase and sale. The record also identifies the item, its catalog number, and its location (at the top). This ledger reveals by its computations that a FIFO cost flow assumption is being used for sports bags.

Exhibit 7.14

Subsidiary Inventory Record

Item: Leather Sports Bags							Location code: W18C2		
Catalog No.: LSB-117							Units: Maximum 25 Minimum 5		
	Purchases			Cost of Goods Sold			Inventory Balance		
Date	Units	Cost	Total	Units	Cost	Total	Units	Cost	Total
Aug. 1							10	$100	$1,000
Aug. 12				4	$100	$ 400	6	100	600
Aug. 18	20	$110	$2,200				6 / 20	100} / 110}	2,800
Aug. 30				6 / 2	100 / 110	600 / 220	18	110	1,980
Totals	20		$2,220	12		$1,220			

Quick Check

5. What accounting principle most guides the allocation of cost of goods available for sale between ending inventory and cost of goods sold?

6. If **Nike** sells goods to **Target** with terms FOB shipping point, does Nike or Target report these goods in its inventory while they are in transit?

7. An art gallery purchases a painting for $11,400 on terms FOB shipping point. Additional costs in obtaining and offering the artwork for sale include $130 for transportation-in, $150 for import duties, $100 for insurance during shipment, $180 for advertising, $400 for framing, and $800 for office salaries. For computing inventory, what cost is assigned to the painting?

Answers—p. 287

This section describes other methods to value inventory. Knowledge of these methods is important for understanding and analyzing financial statements.

Lower of Cost or Market

We explained how to assign costs to ending inventory and cost of goods sold using one of four costing methods (FIFO, LIFO, weighted average, or specific identification). The cost of inventory, however, is not necessarily the amount always reported on a balance sheet. *Accounting principles require that inventory be reported at the market value (cost) of replacing inventory when market value is lower than cost.* Merchandise inventory is then said to be reported on the balance sheet at the **lower of cost or market (LCM).**

Computing the Lower of Cost or Market

Market in the term LCM is defined as the current market value (cost) of replacing inventory. It is the current cost of purchasing the same inventory items in the usual manner. A decline in market cost reflects a loss of value in inventory because the recorded cost of inventory is higher than the current market cost. When this occurs, a loss is recognized. This is done by recognizing the decline in merchandise inventory from recorded cost to market cost at the end of the current period.

LCM is applied in one of three ways: (1) to each individual item separately, (2) to major categories of items, or (3) to the entire inventory. The less similar the items that make up inventory, the more likely companies are to apply LCM to individual items. Advances in technology further encourage the individual item approach.

To illustrate, we apply LCM to the ending inventory of a motorsports retailer. Inventory data for this retailer and LCM computations are shown in Exhibit 7.15.

Other Inventory Valuations

P2 Compute the lower of cost or market amount of inventory.

Global: In Canada, the Netherlands, and the United Kingdom, the *market* in LCM is defined as "net realizable value" (selling price less costs to complete and sell).

Inventory Items	Units on Hand	Per Unit Cost	Per Unit Market	Total Cost	Total Market	LCM Applied to Items	LCM Applied to Categories	LCM Applied to Whole
Cycles								
Roadster 20		$8,000	$7,000	$160,000	$140,000	$140,000		
Sprint 10		5,000	6,000	50,000	60,000	50,000		
Category subtotal				210,000	200,000		$200,000	
Off-Road								
Trax-4 8		5,000	6,500	40,000	52,000	40,000		
Blazer 5		9,000	7,000	45,000	35,000	35,000		
Category subtotal				85,000	87,000		85,000	
Totals				$295,000	$287,000	**$265,000**	**$285,000**	**$287,000**

Exhibit 7.15

Lower of Cost or Market Computations

When LCM is applied to the *entire* inventory, the market cost is $287,000. Since this market cost is $8,000 lower than the $295,000 recorded cost, it is the amount reported for inventory on the balance sheet. When LCM is applied to the major *categories* of inventory, the market is $285,000. When LCM is applied to individual *items* of inventory, the market cost is $265,000. Since market is again less than the $295,000 recorded cost, market cost is the amount reported for inventory. Any one of these three applications of LCM is acceptable. **Best Buy** follows this method and reports that its "merchandise inventories are recorded at the lower of average cost or market."

The *direct method* is a common way to record inventory at LCM—it substitutes market value (when lower) for cost in the inventory account. Using LCM applied on the entire inventory from Exhibit 7.15, we make the following entry: Cost of Goods Sold, Dr. $8,000; Merchandise Inventory, Cr. $8,000. The Merchandise Inventory account balance is now $287,000, computed as $295,000 minus $8,000.

Conservatism Principle

Accounting rules require recording inventory down to market when market is less than cost, but inventory usually cannot be written up to market when market exceeds cost. If recording inventory down to market is acceptable, why are we not allowed to record inventory up to market? One reason is a concern that the gain from a market increase is not realized until a sales transaction verifies the gain. However, this problem also applies when market is less than cost. The second and primary reason is the **conservatism principle,** which requires the use of the less optimistic amount when more than one estimate of the amount to be received or paid in the future exists and these estimates are about equally likely. LCM is justified with reference to conservatism.

Retail Inventory Method

P3 Apply both the retail inventory and gross profit methods to estimate inventory.

Many companies prepare financial statements on a quarterly or monthly basis, called **interim statements** because they are prepared between the traditional annual statements. The cost of goods sold information needed to prepare interim statements is readily available if a perpetual inventory system is used but requires a physical inventory if the periodic system is used. To avoid the time-consuming and expensive process of taking a physical inventory each month or quarter, some companies use the **retail inventory method** to estimate cost of goods sold and ending inventory. Some companies even use the retail inventory method to prepare the annual statements. **Home Depot**, for instance, says in its recent annual report: "Inventories are stated at the lower of cost (first-in, first-out) or market, as determined by the retail inventory method." Other reasons to estimate inventory are for audit purposes and when inventory is destroyed or damaged.

Computing the Retail Inventory Estimate

The retail inventory method uses a three-step process to estimate ending inventory. We need to know the amount of inventory a company had at the beginning of the period in both *cost*

Exhibit 7.16

Inventory Estimation Using Retail Inventory Method

and *retail* amounts. We already explained how to compute the cost of inventory. The retail amount of inventory refers to its dollar amount measured using selling prices of inventory items. We also need to know the net amount of goods purchased (minus returns, allowances, and discounts) in the period, both at cost and at retail. The amount of net sales at retail is also needed. The process is shown in Exhibit 7.16.

The reasoning behind the retail inventory method is if we can get a good estimate of the cost to retail ratio, we can multiply ending inventory at retail by this ratio to estimate ending inventory at cost. We show in Exhibit 7.17 how these steps are applied to estimate ending inventory for a typical company.

First, we find that $100,000 of goods (at retail selling prices) were available for sale. We see that $70,000 of these goods were sold, leaving $30,000 (retail value) of unsold merchandise in ending inventory. Second, the cost of these goods is 60% of the $100,000 retail

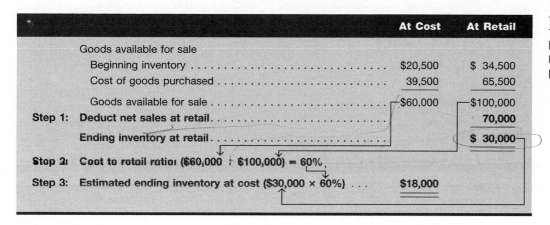

	At Cost	At Retail
Goods available for sale		
Beginning inventory	$20,500	$ 34,500
Cost of goods purchased	39,500	65,500
Goods available for sale	$60,000	$100,000
Step 1: Deduct net sales at retail		70,000
Ending inventory at retail		$ 30,000
Step 2: Cost to retail ratio ($60,000 ÷ $100,000) = 60%		
Step 3: Estimated ending inventory at cost ($30,000 × 60%)	$18,000	

Exhibit 7.17

Estimated Ending Inventory Using the Retail Inventory Method

value. Third, since cost for these goods is 60% of retail, the estimated cost of ending inventory is $18,000.

Estimating Physical Inventory at Cost

Items for sale by retailers usually carry price tags listing selling prices. When a retailer takes a physical inventory, it commonly totals inventory using selling prices of items available. It can then reduce the dollar total of this inventory to a cost basis by applying the cost to retail ratio—use of the cost to retail ratio eliminates the need to look up invoice prices of items. To illustrate, assume the company in Exhibit 7.17 estimates its inventory by the retail method and takes a physical inventory using selling prices. If the retail value of this physical inventory is $29,600, we can compute the cost of this inventory by applying its cost to retail ratio as follows: **$29,600 × 60% = $17,760.** The $17,760 cost figure for ending physical inventory is an acceptable number for annual financial statements and for tax reporting.

Estimating Inventory Shortage at Cost

The inventory estimate in Exhibit 7.17 estimates the amount of goods available at the end of the period (at cost). Since it is computed by deducting sales from goods available for sale (at retail), it does not reveal any shrinkage due to breakage, loss, or theft. We can estimate the amount of shrinkage by comparing the inventory computed in Exhibit 7.17 with the amount from taking a physical inventory. In Exhibit 7.17, for example, at retail we estimated ending inventory as $30,000, but a physical inventory revealed only $29,600 of inventory. The company has an inventory shortage (at retail) of $400, computed as $30,000 − $29,600. The inventory shortage (at cost) is $240, computed as $400 × 60%.

Gross Profit Method

The **gross profit method** estimates the cost of ending inventory by applying the gross profit ratio to net sales (at retail). This type of estimate often is needed when inventory is destroyed, lost, or stolen. These cases require an inventory estimate so a company can file a claim with its insurer. Users also apply this method to see whether inventory amounts from a physical count are reasonable. This method uses the historical relation between cost of goods sold and net sales to estimate the proportion of cost of goods sold making up current sales. This cost of goods sold estimate is then subtracted from cost of goods available for sale to estimate the ending inventory at cost. These two steps are shown in Exhibit 7.18.

Step 1 Net Sales at Retail × 1.0 − Gross Profit Ratio = Estimated Cost of Goods Sold

Step 2 Goods Available for Sale at Cost − Estimated Cost of Goods Sold = Estimated Ending Inventory at Cost

Exhibit 7.18

Ending Inventory Estimated Using the Gross Profit Method

Point: A fire or other catastrophe can result in an insurance claim for lost inventory or income. Backup procedures for financial data and off-site storage of data help ensure coverage for such losses.

We need certain accounting data to apply the gross profit method: the gross profit ratio, beginning inventory (at cost), the net cost of goods purchased, and net sales (at retail). To illustrate, assume that a company's inventory is destroyed by fire in March 2002. This company's normal gross profit ratio is 30% of net sales. When the fire occurs, the company's accounts show the following balances for January through March:

Sales	$31,500
Sales returns	1,500
Inventory, January 1, 2002	12,000
Cost of goods purchased	20,500

Point: Reliability of the gross profit method depends on a good estimate of the gross profit ratio.

We can use the gross profit method to estimate this company's inventory loss. Note that whatever portion of each dollar of net sales is gross profit, the remaining portion is cost of goods sold. If this company's gross profit ratio is 30%, then 30% of each net sales dollar is gross profit and 70% is cost of goods sold. We show in Exhibit 7.19 how this 70% is used to estimate lost inventory of $11,500.

Exhibit 7.19

Estimated Inventory Using the Gross Profit Method

Goods available for sale		
Inventory, January 1, 2002		$12,000
Cost of goods purchased		20,500
Goods available for sale (at cost)		32,500
Net sales at retail ($31,500 − $1,500)		$30,000
Step 1:	**Estimated cost of goods sold ($30,000 × 70%)**	**(21,000)** ← × 0.70
Step 2:	**Estimated March inventory at cost**	**$11,500**

To help understand Exhibit 7.19, think of subtracting ending inventory from goods available for sale to get the cost of goods sold. In Exhibit 7.19 we estimate ending inventory by subtracting cost of goods sold from the goods available for sale.

Quick Check

8. A company's ending inventory includes the following items:

Product	Units	Unit Cost	Unit Market Value
A	20	$ 6	$ 5
B	40	9	8
C	10	12	15

Use LCM applied separately to individual items to compute the amount for inventory.

9. The following data pertain to a company's inventory during its most recent year:

	Cost	Retail
Beginning inventory	$324,000	$530,000
Cost of goods purchased	195,000	335,000
Net sales		320,000

Using the retail method, estimate the cost of ending inventory.

This section describes how we use information about inventory to assess a company's short-term liquidity (ability to pay) and its management of inventory. Two measures useful for these assessments are presented.

A3 Assess inventory management using both inventory turnover and days' sales in inventory.

Inventory Turnover

We described in earlier chapters two important ratios useful in evaluating a company's short-term liquidity: current ratio and acid-test ratio. A merchandiser's ability to pay its short-term obligations also depends on how quickly it sells its merchandise inventory. **Inventory turnover,** also called *merchandise inventory turnover,* is one ratio used to assess this. It is computed as shown in Exhibit 7.20.

$$\text{Inventory turnover} = \frac{\text{Cost of goods sold}}{\text{Average inventory}}$$

Exhibit 7.20

Inventory Turnover

This ratio reveals how many *times* a company turns over its inventory during a period. Average inventory is usually computed by adding beginning and ending inventory amounts and dividing the total by two. If a company's inventory greatly varies within a year, it is often better to average inventory amounts from the end of each quarter or month.

Users apply inventory turnover to help analyze short-term liquidity and to assess whether management is doing a good job controlling the amount of inventory available. A low ratio compared to that of competitors suggests inefficient use of assets. The company may be holding more inventory than it needs to support its sales volume. Similarly, a very high ratio compared to that of competitors suggests inventory might be too low. This can cause lost sales because customers must back order merchandise. Inventory turnover has no simple rule except to say *a high ratio is preferable provided inventory is adequate to meet demand.*

We know the inventory costing methods such as FIFO, LIFO, and weighted average affect reported amounts of inventory and cost of goods sold. The inventory costing method also affects computation of inventory turnover. This means that we must take care when we compare turnover ratios across companies that use different costing methods.

Did You Know?

Dell-ocity   From its roots in a college dorm room, **Dell** now sells 50 million dollars' worth of computers each day from its Web site. "The Internet," says Michael Dell, "is the ultimate direct model." Web sales now account for nearly one-half of the total PC business. The speed of Web technology has allowed Dell to slash inventories. Dell's operating cycle is less than 15 hours and its days' sales in inventory is 3 days. Michael Dell asserts "Speed is everything in this business."

Days' Sales in Inventory

To better interpret inventory turnover, many users measure the adequacy of inventory to meet sales demand. **Days' sales in inventory,** also called *days' stock on hand,* is a ratio that reveals how much inventory is available in terms of the number of days' sales. It can be interpreted as the number of days one can sell from inventory if no new items are purchased. This ratio is often viewed as a measure of the buffer against out-of-stock inventory and is useful in evaluating liquidity of inventory. Days' sales in inventory is computed as shown in Exhibit 7.21.

$$\text{Days' sales in inventory} = \frac{\text{Ending inventory}}{\text{Cost of goods sold}} \times 365$$

Exhibit 7.21

Days' Sales in Inventory

Days' sales in inventory focuses on ending inventory and it estimates how many days it will take to convert inventory at the end of a period into accounts receivable or cash. Notice that days' sales in inventory focuses on *ending* inventory whereas inventory turnover focuses on *average* inventory.

Analysis of Inventory Management

Inventory management is a major emphasis for most merchandisers. They must both plan and control inventory purchases and sales. **Toys "R" Us** is one of those merchandisers. Its merchandise inventory at January 29, 2000, is $2,027 million. This inventory constitutes 70% of it current assets and 24% of its total assets. We apply the analysis tools in this section to Toys "R" Us as shown in Exhibit 7.22.

Exhibit 7.22

Inventory Turnover and Days' Sales in Inventory for Toys "R" Us

($ in millions)	Jan. 29, 2000	Jan. 30, 1999	Jan. 31, 1998
Cost of goods sold	$8,321	$8,191	$7,710
Ending merchandise inventory	$2,027	$1,902	$2,464
Inventory turnover	**4.24** times	**3.75** times	**3.30** times
Industry inventory turnover	3.01 times	2.88 times	2.76 times
Days' sales in inventory	**88.9** days	**84.8** days	**116.6** days
Industry days' sales in inventory	121.3 days	126.7 days	129.7 days

The 2000 inventory turnover of 4.24 for **Toys "R" Us** is computed as $8,321 ÷ [($2,027 + $1,902) ÷ 2]. This means Toys "R" Us turns over its inventory 4.24 times per year, or once every 86 days (365 days ÷ 4.24). We prefer inventory turnover to be high provided inventory is not out of stock and the company is not losing customers. The 2000 days' sales in inventory of 88.9 for Toys "R" Us helps us assess this likelihood and is computed as ($2,027 ÷ $8,321) × 365. This tells us Toys "R" Us is carrying 88.9 days of sales in its inventory. This inventory buffer seems more than adequate. Toys "R" Us might benefit from further management efforts to increase inventory turnover.

You Make the Call

e

Entrepreneur   Analysis of your retail store yields an inventory turnover of 5.0 and a days' sales in inventory of 73 days. The industry norm for inventory turnover is 4.4 and for days' sales in inventory is 74 days. Where do you direct your initial review of inventory management?

Answer—p. 286

Demonstration Problem

Mozart Company uses a perpetual inventory system for its one product. Its beginning inventory and purchases during year 2002 follow:

Date			Units	Unit Cost
Jan.	1	Inventory	400	$14
March	10	Purchase	200	15
May	9	Purchase	300	16
Sept.	22	Purchase	250	20
Nov.	28	Purchase	100	21

At December 31, 2002, 550 units are in inventory. Sales in year 2002 are as follows:

Jan. 15	200 units at $30
April 1	200 units at $30
Nov. 1	300 units at $35

Additional unit cost tracking data for use in applying specific identification: (1) January 15 sale— 200 units @ $14, (2) April 1 sale—200 units @ $15, and (3) November 1 sale—200 units @ $14 and 100 units @ $20.

Required

1. Calculate the cost of goods available for sale.

2. Apply the four different methods of inventory costing (FIFO, LIFO, weighted average, and specific identification) to calculate ending inventory and cost of goods sold under each method.

3. In preparing financial statements for year 2002, the accountant was instructed to use FIFO but failed to do so and computed cost of goods sold according to LIFO. Determine the impact on year 2002's income from the error. Also determine the effect of this error on year 2003's income. Assume no income taxes.

4. Management wants a report that shows how changing from FIFO to another method would change net income. Prepare a schedule showing (1) the cost of goods sold amount under each of the four methods, (2) the amount by which each cost of goods sold total is different from the FIFO cost of goods sold, and (3) the effect on net income if another method is used instead of FIFO.

Planning the Solution

• Make a schedule showing the calculation of cost of goods available for sale. Multiply the units of beginning inventory and each purchase by the appropriate unit costs to determine the total cost of goods available for sale.

• Prepare a perpetual FIFO schedule showing the composition of beginning inventory and how the composition of inventory changes after each purchase of inventory and after each sale (see Exhibit 7.5).

• Prepare a perpetual LIFO schedule showing the composition of beginning inventory and how the composition of inventory changes after each purchase of inventory and after each sale (see Exhibit 7.6).

• Make a schedule of purchases and sales recalculating the average cost of inventory after each purchase to arrive at the weighted average cost of ending inventory. Total the average costs associated with each sale to determine cost of goods sold (see Exhibit 7.7).

• Prepare a schedule showing the computation of cost of goods sold and ending inventory using the specific identification method. Use the information provided to determine which specific units are sold and which specific units remain in inventory (see Exhibit 7.4).

• Compare the ending year 2002 inventory amounts under FIFO and LIFO to determine the misstatement of year 2002 income that results from using LIFO. The errors for year 2002 and 2003 are equal in amount but opposite in effect.

• Create a schedule showing cost of goods sold under each method and how net income would differ from FIFO net income if an alternate method is adopted.

Solution to Demonstration Problem

1. Cost of goods available for sale (this amount is the same for all methods):

Date			Units	Unit Cost	Total Cost
Jan.	1	Inventory	400	$14	$ 5,600
March 10		Purchase	200	15	3,000
May	9	Purchase	300	16	4,800
Sept.	22	Purchase	250	20	5,000
Nov.	28	Purchase	100	21	2,100
Total cost of goods available for sale					$20,500

2a. FIFO perpetual method:

Date	Purchases	Cost of Goods Sold	Inventory Balance	
Jan. 1	Beginning balance		400 @ $14	= $ 5,600
Jan. 15		200 @ $14 = $2,800	200 @ $14	= $ 2,800
Mar. 10	200 @ $15 = $3,000		200 @ $14 ⎫ 200 @ $15 ⎭	= $ 5,800
April 1		200 @ $14 = $2,800	200 @ $15	= $ 3,000
May 9	300 @ $16 = $4,800		200 @ $15 ⎫ 300 @ $16 ⎭	= $ 7,800
Sept. 22	250 @ $20 = $5,000		200 @ $15 ⎫ 300 @ $16 ⎬ 250 @ $20 ⎭	= $12,800
Nov. 1		200 @ $15 = $3,000 100 @ $16 = $1,600	200 @ $16 ⎫ 250 @ $20 ⎭	= $ 8,200
Nov. 28	100 @ $21 = $2,100		200 @ $16 ⎫ 250 @ $20 ⎬ 100 @ $21 ⎭	= **$10,300**
Total cost of goods sold		**$10,200**		

Note to students: **In a classroom situation,** once we compute cost of goods available for sale, we can compute the amount for either cost of goods sold or ending inventory—it is a matter of preference. **In practice,** the costs of items sold are identified as sales are made and immediately transferred from the inventory account to the cost of goods sold account. This transfer makes calculating either account balance at the end of a period unnecessary. The previous solution showing the line-by-line approach illustrates actual application in practice. The following alternate solutions illustrate that, once the concepts are understood, other solution approaches are available.

Alternate FIFO Perpetual Solution

[FIFO Alternate No. 1: Computing cost of goods sold first]

Cost of goods available for sale (from part 1)		$20,500
Cost of goods sold		
Jan. 15 Sold (200 @ $14)	$ 2,800	
April 1 Sold (200 @ $14)	2,800	
Nov. 1 Sold (200 @ $15 and 100 @ $16)	4,600	**10,200**
Ending inventory		**$10,300**

[FIFO Alternate No. 2: Computing ending inventory first]

Cost of goods available for sale (from part 1)		$20,500
Ending inventory*		
Nov. 28 Purchase (100 @ $21)	$2,100	
Sept. 22 Purchase (250 @ $20)	5,000	
May 9 Purchase (200 @ $16)	3,200	
Ending inventory		**10,300**
Cost of goods sold		**$10,200**

* Since FIFO assumes that earlier costs relate to items sold, we determine ending inventory by assigning the most recent costs.

2b. LIFO perpetual method:

Date	Purchases	Cost of Goods Sold	Inventory Balance
Jan. 1	Beginning balance		400 @ $14 = $ 5,600
Jan. 15		200 @ $14 = $2,800	200 @ $14 = $ 2,800
Mar. 10	200 @ $15 = $3,000		200 @ $14 ⎫ = $ 5,800 200 @ $15 ⎭
April 1		200 @ $15 = $3,000	200 @ $14 = $ 2,800
May 9	300 @ $16 = $4,800		200 @ $14 ⎫ = $ 7,600 300 @ $16 ⎭
Sept. 22	250 @ $20 = $5,000		200 @ $14 ⎫ 300 @ $16 ⎬ = $12,600 250 @ $20 ⎭
Nov. 1		250 @ $20 = $5,000 50 @ $16 = $ 800	200 @ $14 ⎫ = $ 6,800 250 @ $16 ⎭
Nov. 28	100 @ $21 = $2,100		200 @ $14 ⎫ 250 @ $16 ⎬ = $ 8,900 100 @ $21 ⎭
Total cost of goods sold		**$11,600**	

Alternate LIFO Perpetual Solution

[LIFO Alternate No. 1: Computing cost of goods sold first]

Cost of goods available for sale (from part 1)		$20,500
Cost of goods sold with LIFO perpetual		
Jan. 15 200 units @ $14	$2,800	
April 1 200 units @ $15	3,000	
Nov. 1 ⎰ 250 units @ $20	5,000	
⎱ 50 units @ $16	800	
Cost of goods sold		**11,600**
Ending inventory		**$ 8,900**

[LIFO Alternate No. 2: Computing ending inventory first]

Cost of goods available for sale (from part 1)		$20,500
Ending inventory		
Jan. 1 Inventory (200 @ $14)	$2,800	
May 9 Purchase (250 @ $16)	4,000	
Nov. 28 Purchase (100 @ $21)	2,100	
Ending inventory		**8,900**
Cost of goods sold		**$11,600**

2c. Weighted average perpetual method:

Date	Purchases	Cost of Goods Sold	Inventory Balance
Jan. 1	Beginning balance		400 @ $14 = $ 5,600
Jan. 15		200 @ $14 = $2,800	200 @ $14 = $ 2,800
Mar. 10	200 @ $15 = $3,000		200 @ $14 ⎱ = $ 5,800 200 @ $15 ⎰ (avg. cost is $14.5)
April 1		200 @ $14.5 = $2,900	200 @ $14.5 = $ 2,900
May 9	300 @ $16 = $4,800		200 @ $14.5 ⎱ = $ 7,700 300 @ $16 ⎰ (avg. cost is $15.4)
Sept. 22	250 @ $20 = $5,000		200 @ $14.5 ⎱ 300 @ $16 ⎬ = $12,700 250 @ $20 ⎰ (avg. cost is $16.93)
Nov. 1		300 @ $16.93 = $5,079	450 @ $16.93 = $7,618.5
Nov. 28	100 @ $21 = $2,100		450 @ $16.93 ⎱ = **$9,718.5** 100 @ $21 ⎰
Total cost of goods sold*		**$10,779**	

* The cost of goods sold ($10,779) plus ending inventory ($9,718.5) is $2.5 less than the cost of goods available for sale ($20,500) due to rounding.

2d. Specific identification method:

Date	Purchases	Cost of Goods Sold	Inventory Balance
Jan. 1	Beginning balance		400 @ $14 = $ 5,600
Jan. 15		200 @ $14 = $2,800	200 @ $14 = $ 2,800
Mar. 10	200 @ $15 = $3,000		200 @ $14 ⎱ = $ 5,800 200 @ $15 ⎰
April 1		200 @ $15 = $3,000	200 @ $14 = $ 2,800
May 9	300 @ $16 = $4,800		200 @ $14 ⎱ = $ 7,600 300 @ $16 ⎰
Sept. 22	250 @ $20 = $5,000		200 @ $14 ⎱ 300 @ $16 ⎬ = $12,600 250 @ $20 ⎰
Nov. 1		200 @ $14 = $2,800 100 @ $20 = $2,000	300 @ $16 ⎱ = $ 7,800 150 @ $20 ⎰
Nov. 28	100 @ $21 = $2,100		300 @ $16 ⎱ 150 @ $20 ⎬ = **$ 9,900** 100 @ $21 ⎰
Total cost of goods sold		**$10,600**	

[Specific Identification Alternate No. 1: Computing cost of goods sold first]

Cost of goods available for sale (from part 1)		$20,500
Cost of goods sold		
Jan. 1 Purchase (400 @ $14)	$5,600	
March 10 Purchase (200 @ $15)	3,000	
Nov. 28 Purchase (100 @ $20)	2,000	
Total cost of goods sold		**10,600**
Ending inventory		**$ 9,900**

[Specific Identification Alternate No. 2: Computing ending inventory first]

Cost of goods available for sale (from part 1)		$20,500
Ending inventory		
May 9 Purchase (300 @ $16)	$4,800	
Sept. 22 Purchase (150 @ $20)	3,000	
Nov. 28 Purchase (100 @ $21)	2,100	
Total ending inventory		**9,900**
Cost of goods sold		**$10,600**

3. Mistakenly using LIFO when FIFO should have been used overstates cost of goods sold in year 2002 by $1,400, which is the difference between the FIFO and LIFO amounts of ending inventory. It understates income in 2002 by $1,400. In year 2003, income is overstated by $1,400 because of the understatement in beginning inventory.

4. Analysis of the effects of alternative inventory methods:

	Cost of Goods Sold	Difference from FIFO Cost of Goods Sold	Effect on Net Income if Adopted Instead of FIFO
FIFO	$10,200	—	—
LIFO	11,600	+$1,400	$1,400 lower
Weighted average	10,779	+ 579	579 lower
Specific identification	10,600	+ 400	400 lower

APPENDIX

Assigning Costs to Inventory— Periodic System

7A

The aim of the periodic system and the perpetual system is the same: to assign costs to inventory and cost of goods sold. The same four methods are used to assign costs under the periodic system—specific identification; first-in, first-out; last-in, first-out; and weighted average. We use information from **Trekking** to describe how we assign costs using these four methods with a periodic system. Data for sales and purchases are reported in the chapter (see Exhibits 7.2 and 7.3).

P4 Compute inventory in a periodic system using the methods of specific identification, FIFO, LIFO, and weighted average.

Recall that we explained the accounting transactions under a periodic system in Appendix 6A. These are the important accounting aspects of a periodic system:

- Each purchase of merchandise for resale increases (debit) the Purchases account.
- Cost of merchandise sold is *not* recorded at the time of each sale. A physical count of inventory at the end of the period is used to compute cost of goods sold and inventory amounts.
- Necessary costs of merchandise such as transportation-in and cost reductions such as purchase discounts and purchase returns and allowances are recorded in *separate* accounts.

Specific Identification

The amount of costs assigned to inventory and cost of goods sold is the same under the perpetual and periodic systems when using specific identification. This is so because specific identification precisely tracks (identifies) which units are in inventory and which have been sold.

First-In, First-Out

The first-in, first-out (FIFO) method of assigning cost to both inventory and cost of goods sold using the periodic system is shown in Exhibit 7A.1.

Exhibit 7A.1

FIFO Computations—
Periodic System

Total cost of 55 units available for sale		$5,990
Less ending inventory priced using FIFO		
10 units from August 28 purchase at $119 each	$1,190	
2 units from August 17 purchase at $115 each	230	
Ending inventory		**1,420**
Cost of goods sold		**$4,570**

Trekking's ending inventory reported on the balance sheet is **$1,420**, and its cost of goods sold reported on the income statement is **$4,570**. These amounts are the same as those computed using the perpetual system. This always occurs because the most recent purchases are in ending inventory under both systems.

Last-In, First-Out

The last-in, first-out (LIFO) method of assigning costs to the 12 remaining units in inventory (and to the 43 units in cost of goods sold) using the periodic system is shown in Exhibit 7A.2.

Exhibit 7A.2

LIFO Computations—
Periodic System

Total cost of 55 units available for sale		$5,990
Less ending inventory priced using LIFO		
10 units in beginning inventory at $ 91 each	$ 910	
2 units from August 3 purchase at $106 each	212	
Ending inventory		**1,122**
Cost of goods sold		**$4,868**

Trekking's ending inventory reported on the balance sheet is **$1,122**, and its cost of goods sold reported on the income statement is **$4,868**. When LIFO is used with the periodic system, cost of goods sold is assigned costs from the most recent purchases for the period. With a perpetual system, cost of goods sold is assigned costs from the most recent purchases at the point of *each sale*.

Weighted Average

The weighted average method of assigning cost involves three important steps. The first two steps are shown in Exhibit 7A.3. First, multiply the per unit cost for beginning inventory and each particular purchase by the corresponding number of units. Second, add these amounts and divide by the total number of units available for sale to find the weighted average cost per unit.

Step 1:	10 units @ $ 91 =	$ 910
	15 units @ $106 =	1,590
	20 units @ $115 =	2,300
	10 units @ $119 =	1,190
	55	**$5,990**
Step 2:	$5,990/55 units = **$108.91** weighted average cost per unit	

Exhibit 7A.3

Weighted Average Cost
per Unit

Example: In Exhibit 7A.3, if 5 more
units had been purchased at $120
each, what would be the weighted
average cost per unit?
Answer: $109.83 ($6,590/60)

The third step is to use the weighted average cost per unit to assign costs to inventory and to the units sold as shown in Exhibit 7A.4.

Step 3:	Total cost of 55 units available for sale	$5,990
	Less **ending inventory** priced on a weighted average	
	cost basis: 12 units at $108.91 each (from Exhibit 7A.3)	1,307
	Cost of goods sold	**$4,683**

Exhibit 7A.4

Weighted Average
Computations—Periodic

Trekking's ending inventory reported on the balance sheet is **$1,307**, and its cost of goods sold reported on the income statement is **$4,683** when using the weighted average method.

Quick Check

10. A company reports the following beginning inventory and purchases, and it ends the period with 30 units in inventory

Beginning Inventory	100 units at $10 cost per unit
Purchase 1	40 units at $12 cost per unit
Purchase 2	20 units at $14 cost per unit

a. Compute ending inventory using the FIFO periodic system.
b. Compute cost of goods sold using the LIFO periodic system.

Answers—p. 287

Summary

C1 **Identify the items making up merchandise inventory.** Merchandise inventory comprises goods owned by a company and held for resale. Three special cases merit our attention. Goods in transit are reported in inventory of the company that holds ownership rights. Goods on consignment are reported in the consignor's inventory. Goods damaged or obsolete are reported in inventory at their net realizable value.

C2 **Identify the costs of merchandise inventory.** Costs of merchandise inventory comprise expenditures necessary, directly or indirectly, to bring an item to a salable condition and location. This includes its invoice cost minus any discount plus any added or incidental costs necessary to put it in a place and condition for sale.

A1 **Analyze the effects of inventory methods for both financial and tax reporting.** When purchase costs are rising or falling, the inventory costing methods are likely to assign different costs to inventory. Specific identification exactly matches costs and revenues. Weighted average smooths out cost changes. FIFO assigns an amount to inventory closely approximating current replacement cost. LIFO assigns the most recent costs incurred to cost of goods sold and likely better matches current costs with revenues.

A2 **Analyze the effects of inventory errors on current and future financial statements.** An error in the amount of ending inventory affects assets (inventory), net income (cost of goods sold), and equity for that period. Since ending inventory is next period's beginning inventory, an error in ending inventory affects next period's cost of goods sold and net income. Financial statement effects of errors in one period are offset in the next.

A3   **Assess inventory management using both inventory turnover and days' sales in inventory.** We prefer a high inventory turnover provided inventory is not out of stock and customers are not turned away. We use days' sales in inventory to assess the likelihood of inventory being out of stock. We prefer a small number of days' sales in inventory if we can serve customer needs and provide a buffer for uncertainties. Each of these ratios helps assess inventory management and evaluate a company's short-term liquidity.

P1   **Compute inventory in a perpetual system using the methods of specific identification, FIFO, LIFO, and weighted average.** Costs are assigned to the cost of goods sold account *each time* a sale occurs in a perpetual system. Specific identification assigns a cost to each item sold by referring to its actual cost (for example, its net invoice cost). Weighted average assigns a cost to items sold by dividing the current balance in the inventory account by the total items available for sale to determine cost per unit. We then multiply the number of units sold by this cost per unit to get the cost of each sale. FIFO assigns cost to items sold assuming that the earliest units purchased are the first units sold. LIFO assigns cost to items sold assuming that the most recent units purchased are the first units sold.

P2   **Compute the lower of cost or market amount of inventory.** Inventory is reported at market value when market is *lower* than cost, called the *lower of cost or market amount of*

inventory. Market is typically measured as replacement cost. Lower of cost or market can be applied separately to each item, to major categories of items, or to the entire inventory.

P3   **Apply both the retail inventory and gross profit methods to estimate inventory.** The retail inventory method involves three computations: (1) goods available at retail minus net sales at retail equals ending inventory at retail, (2) goods available at cost divided by goods available at retail equals the cost to retail ratio, and (3) ending inventory at retail multiplied by the cost to retail ratio equals estimated ending inventory at cost. The gross profit method involves two computations: (1) net sales at retail multiplied by 1 minus the gross profit ratio equals estimated cost of goods sold, and (2) goods available at cost minus estimated cost of goods sold equals estimated ending inventory at cost.

P4   **Compute inventory in a periodic system using the methods of specific identification, FIFO, LIFO, and weighted average.** Periodic inventory systems allocate the cost of goods available for sale between cost of goods sold and ending inventory *at the end of a period.* Specific identification and FIFO give identical results whether the periodic or perpetual system is used. LIFO assigns costs to cost of goods sold assuming the last units purchased for the period are the first units sold. The weighted average cost per unit is computed by dividing the total cost of beginning inventory and net purchases for the period by the total number of units available. Then, multiply cost per unit by the number of units sold to give cost of goods sold.

Guidance Answers to **You Make the Call**

Financial Planner   The FIFO method implies the oldest costs are the first ones assigned to cost of goods sold. This leaves the most recent costs in ending inventory. You report this to your client and note that in most cases, the ending inventory of a company using FIFO is reported at or near its market replacement cost. This means your client need not in most cases adjust the reported value of inventory. Your answer changes only if there are major increases in replacement cost compared to the cost of recent purchases reported in inventory. When major increases in costs occur, your client might wish to adjust inventory (for internal reports) for the difference between the reported cost of inventory and its market replacement cost. (*Note:* Decreases in costs of purchases are recognized under the lower of cost or market adjustment.)

Inventory Manager   Your recommendation is difficult. On one hand, it seems your company can save (or at least postpone) taxes by switching to LIFO, but the switch is likely to reduce bonus money

that you think you have earned and deserve. Since the U.S. tax code requires companies that use LIFO for tax reporting also to use it for financial reporting, your options are even further constrained. Your best decision is to tell your superior about the tax savings with LIFO. You also should discuss your bonus plan and how this is likely to hurt you unfairly. You might propose to compute inventory under the LIFO method for reporting purposes but use the FIFO method for your bonus calculations. Another solution is to revise the bonus plan to reflect the company's use of the LIFO method.

Entrepreneur   Your inventory turnover is markedly higher than the norm, whereas days' sales in inventory approximates the norm. Since your turnover is already 14% better than average, you are probably best served by directing attention to days' sales in inventory. You should see whether you can reduce the level of inventory while maintaining service to customers. Given your higher turnover, you should be able to hold less inventory.

Guidance Answers to **Quick Checks**

1. Specific identification exactly matches costs and revenues. Weighted average tends to smooth out price changes. FIFO assigns an amount to inventory that closely approximates current replacement cost. LIFO assigns the most recent costs in-

curred to cost of goods sold and likely better matches current costs with revenues.

2. FIFO—it gives a lower cost of goods sold, a higher gross profit, and a higher net income when prices are rising.

3. LIFO gives a lower inventory figure on the balance sheet as compared to FIFO when costs are rising. FIFO's inventory amount approximates current replacement costs.
4. Cost of goods sold is understated by $10,000 in 2002 and overstated by $10,000 in year 2003.
5. The matching principle.
6. **Target** reports these goods in its inventory.
7. Total cost assigned to the painting is $12,180, computed as $11,400 + $130 + $150 + $100 + $400.
8. The reported LCM inventory amount in $540, computed as $[(20 \times \$5) + (40 \times \$8) + (10 \times \$12)]$.
9. Estimated ending inventory (at cost) is $327,000. It is computed as follows:

Step 1: $(\$530,000 + \$335,000) - \$320,000 = \$545,000$

Step 2: $\dfrac{\$324,000 + \$195,000}{\$530,000 + \$335,000} = 60\%$

Step 3: $\$545,000 \times 60\% = \$327,000$

10. **a.** FIFO periodic inventory = $(20 \times \$14) + (10 \times \$12)$ = $400.

b. LIFO periodic cost of goods sold = $(20 \times \$14) + (40 \times \$12) + (70 \times \$10)$ = $1,460.

Glossary

Average cost (see *weighted average cost*.) (p. 265)

Conservatism principle principle that seeks to select the less optimistic estimate when two estimates are about equally likely. (p. 274)

Consignee one who receives and holds goods owned by another for purposes of selling the goods for the owner. (p. 271)

Consignor owner of goods who ships them to another party who will then sell them for the owner. (p. 271)

Consistency principle principle encouraging use of the same accounting methods over time so that financial statements are comparable across periods. (p. 268)

Days' sales in inventory estimate of days needed to convert inventory into receivables or cash; equals ending inventory divided by cost of goods sold and then multiplied by 365; also called *days' stock on hand*. (p. 277)

First-in, first-out (FIFO) method to assign cost to inventory that assumes items are sold in the order acquired, the earliest items purchased are the first items sold. (p. 264)

Gross profit method procedure to estimate inventory when the past gross profit rate is used to estimate cost of goods sold, which is then subtracted from the cost of goods available for sale. (p. 275)

Interim statements financial statements for periods of less than one year. (p. 274)

Inventory turnover number of times a company's average inventory is sold during a period; computed by dividing cost of goods sold by average inventory; also called *merchandise turnover*. (p. 277)

Last-in, first-out (LIFO) method to assign cost to inventory that assumes costs for the most recent items purchased are sold first and charged to cost of goods sold. (p. 265)

Lower of cost or market (LCM) method required to report inventory at market when market is lower than cost; market value is the current replacement cost. (p. 273)

Net realizable value expected selling price of an item minus the cost of making the sale. (p. 271)

Retail inventory method method to estimate ending inventory based on the ratio of the amount of goods for sale at cost to the amount of goods for sale at retail. (p. 274)

Specific identification method to assign cost to inventory when the purchase cost of each item in inventory is identified and used to compute cost of inventory. (p. 263)

Weighted average method to assign cost to inventory that assumes the unit costs of items are weighted by the number of units of each in inventory. The total is then divided by the total number of units available for sale to find the average unit cost of inventory and of the units sold. (p. 265)

[The superscript letter ^{A} denotes assignments based on Appendix 7A.]

Questions

1. Describe the flow of costs for the following methods when applied to inventory: (a) FIFO and (b) LIFO.
2. Where is merchandise inventory disclosed in the financial statements?
3. Why are incidental costs sometimes ignored in inventory costing? Under what principle is this permitted?
4. If costs are falling, will the LIFO or the FIFO method of inventory valuation result in the lower cost of goods sold?
5. What effect does the full-disclosure principle have if a company changes from one acceptable accounting method to another?
6. Can a company change its inventory method each accounting period? Explain.
7. Does the accounting principle of consistency preclude any changes from one accounting method to another?
8. If inventory errors are said to correct themselves, why be concerned when such errors are made?

9. Explain the phrase *inventory errors correct themselves.*

10. What is the meaning of *market* as it is used in determining the lower of cost or market for inventory?

11. What guidance does the principle of conservatism provide?

12. When preparing interim financial statements, what two methods can companies utilize to estimate cost of goods sold and ending inventory?

13. What factors contribute to (or cause) inventory shrinkage?

14. Refer to **Nike**'s financial statements in Appendix A. On May 31, 2000, what percent of current assets are represented by inventory? **NIKE**

15. Refer to **Reebok**'s financial statements in Appendix A. Calculate Reebok's cost of goods available for sale for the year ended December 31, 1999. **Reebok**

16. What percent of **Gap**'s current assets are inventory as of January 29, 2000, and January 30, 1999? **GAP**

17.[A] What accounts are used in a periodic inventory system but not in a perpetual inventory system?

QUICK STUDY

QS 7-1
Assigning costs to inventory

P1

Stein Row starts a merchandising business on December 1 and enters into three inventory purchases:

December 7	10 units @	$7
December 14	20 units @	$8
December 21	15 units @	$10

Stein sells 15 units for $25 each on December 15. Eight of the sold units are from the December 7 purchase and seven are from the December 14 purchase. Stein uses a perpetual inventory system. Determine the December 31 costs assigned to ending inventory when costs are assigned based on (a) FIFO, (b) LIFO, (c) weighted average, and (d) specific identification.

QS 7-2
Inventory costs

C2

A car dealer acquires a used car for $14,000, terms FOB shipping point. Additional costs in obtaining and offering the car for sale include $500 for transportation-in, $900 for import duties, $300 for insurance during shipment, $150 for advertising, and $1,250 for sales staff salaries. For computing inventory, what cost is assigned to the used car?

QS 7-3
Inventory ownership

C1

1. At year-end, Damon Co. had shipped $750 of merchandise FOB destination to Wagner Co. Which company should include the $750 of merchandise in transit as part of its inventory at year-end?

2. Damon Company has shipped $600 of goods to Wagner. Wagner has arranged to sell the goods for Damon. Identify the consignor and the consignee. Which company should include any unsold goods as part of its inventory?

QS 7-4
Inventory ownership

C1

Hobby Crafts, a distributor of handmade gifts, operates out of owner Tina Larsen's house. At the end of the current period, Tina reports she has 1,300 units (products) in her basement, 20 of which were damaged by water and cannot be sold. She also has another 350 units in her van, ready to deliver on a customer order, terms FOB destination, and another 80 units out on consignment to a friend who owns a stationery store. How many units should Tina include in her company's end-of-period inventory?

QS 7-5
Cost of goods available for sale

P1

A company has beginning inventory of 10 units at $60 each. Every week for four weeks it purchases an additional 10 units at respective costs of $61, $62, $65, and $70 per unit for weeks one through four. Calculate the cost of goods available for sale and the units available for sale.

QS 7-6
Contrasting inventory costing methods

A1

Identify the inventory costing method best described by each of the following separate statements. Assume a period of increasing costs.

1. The preferred method when each unit of product has unique features that affect cost.

2. Matches recent costs against net sales.

3. Provides a tax advantage (deferral) to a corporation.

4. Understates the market value of inventory on the balance sheet.

5. Results in a balance sheet inventory amount similar to replacement cost.

Bixby & Son, antique dealers, purchased the contents of an estate for $38,500. Terms of the purchase were FOB shipping point, and the cost of transporting the goods to Bixby & Son's warehouse was $1,100. Bixby & Son insured the shipment at a cost of $250. Prior to putting the goods up for sale, they cleaned and refurbished the goods at a cost of $800. Determine the cost of the inventory acquired from the estate.

QS 7-7
Inventory costs

A company had the following beginning inventory and purchases for January. On January 26, 355 units were sold. What is the cost of the 160 units that remain in ending inventory, assuming (a) FIFO, (b) LIFO, and (c) weighted average? (Round unit costs to the nearest cent.)

	Units	Unit Cost
Beginning inventory on January 1	320	$3.00
Purchase on January 9	85	3.20
Purchase on January 25	110	3.35

QS 7-8
Inventory costing methods
P1

Tiffany Trading Co. has the following products in its ending inventory:

Product	Quantity	Cost	Market
Mountain bikes	11	$600	$550
Skateboards	13	350	425
Gliders	26	800	700

Compute lower of cost or market for inventory (a) as a whole and (b) applied separately to each product.

QS 7-9
Applying LCM to inventories
P2

Dell Department Store's inventory is destroyed by a fire on September 5, 2002. The following data for year 2002 are available from the accounting records:

Jan. 1 inventory	$190,000
Jan. 1 through Sept. 5 purchases (net)	$352,000
Jan. 1 through Sept. 5 sales (net)	$685,000
Year 2002 estimated gross profit rate	44%

Estimate the cost of the inventory destroyed by the fire.

QS 7-10
Estimating inventories
P3

In taking a physical inventory at the end of year 2002, Summit Company erroneously forgot to count certain units. Explain how this error affects the following: (a) 2002 cost of goods sold, (b) 2002 gross profit, (c) 2002 net income, (d) 2003 net income, (e) the combined two-year income, and (f) income for years after 2003.

QS 7-11[A]
Inventory errors
A2

Mercantile Company begins the year with $150,000 of goods in inventory. At year-end, the amount in inventory has increased to $180,000. Cost of goods sold for the year is $1,200,000. Compute Mercantile's inventory turnover and days' sales in inventory.

QS 7-12
Analyzing inventory

Foor Corporation purchased its salable product in the current year as follows:

Jan. 1	Beginning inventory . .	140 units @ $6.00 = $ 840
Mar. 7	Purchase	300 units @ $5.60 = 1,680
July 28	Purchase	550 units @ $5.00 = 2,750
Oct. 3	Purchase	350 units @ $4.60 = 1,610
Dec. 19	Purchase	50 units @ $4.10 = 205
	Total	1,390 units $7,085

EXERCISES

Exercise 7-1
Inventory costing methods—perpetual
P1

Foor Corporation resold its product at $15 per unit on the following dates:

Jan. 10	100 units
Mar. 15	225 units
Oct. 5	700 units
Total	1,025 units

Foor uses a perpetual inventory system. Ending inventory consists of 365 units, 315 from the July 28 purchase and 50 from the December 19 purchase. Determine the cost assigned to ending inventory and to cost of goods sold using (a) specific identification, (b) weighted average, (c) FIFO, and (d) LIFO.

Exercise 7-2

Income effects of inventory methods

Use the data in Exercise 7-1 to prepare comparative income statements for Foor Corporation (calendar year-end 2002) similar to those shown in Exhibit 7.8 for the four inventory methods. Assume operating expenses are $1,250. The applicable income tax rate is 30%.

1. Which method yields the highest net income?

2. Does net income using weighted average fall between that using FIFO and LIFO?

3. If costs are rising instead of falling, which method yields the highest net income?

Exercise 7-3

Inventory costing methods (perpetual)—FIFO and LIFO

Ulsh Company purchased its salable product in the current year as follows:

Jan. 1	Beginning inventory	200 units @ $10 =	$ 2,000
Mar. 14	Purchase	350 units @ $15 =	5,250
July 30	Purchase	450 units @ $20 =	9,000
Oct. 26	Purchase	700 units @ $25 =	17,500
	Units available	1,700 units	
	Cost of goods available for sale		$33,750

Ulsh Company resold its product at $40 per unit on the following dates:

Jan. 10	100 units
Mar. 15	150 units
Oct. 5	310 units
Total sales	560 units

Ulsh uses a perpetual inventory system. Determine the costs assigned to ending inventory and to cost of goods sold using (a) FIFO and (b) LIFO. Compute the gross margin for each method.

Exercise 7-4

Specific Identification

Refer to the data in Exercise 7-3. Assume that ending inventory is made up of 100 units from the March 14 purchase, 340 units from the July 30 purchase, and all the units of the October 26 purchase. Using the specific identification method, calculate (a) the costs of goods sold and (b) the gross margin.

Exercise 7-5ᴬ

Alternative cost flow assumptions—periodic

Rasure & Roney Company purchased its salable product in the current year as follows:

Jan. 1	Beginning inventory	100 units @ $2.00 =	$ 200
Mar. 7	Purchase	220 units @ $2.25 =	495
July 28	Purchase	540 units @ $2.50 =	1,350
Oct. 3	Purchase	480 units @ $2.80 =	1,344
Dec. 19	Purchase	160 units @ $2.90 =	464
	Total	1,500 units	$3,853

The company uses a periodic inventory system, and its ending inventory consists of 150 units, 50 from each of the last three purchases. Determine the cost assigned to ending inventory and to cost of goods sold using (a) specific identification, (b) weighted average, (c) FIFO, and (d) LIFO. Which method yields the highest net income?

Erikson Gifts purchased its salable product in the current year as follows:

Exercise 7-6[A]
Alternative cost flow
assumptions—periodic

Jan. 1	Beginning inventory	140 units @ $3.00 = $	420
Mar. 7	Purchase	300 units @ $2.80 =	840
July 28	Purchase	400 units @ $2.50 =	1,000
Oct. 3	Purchase	550 units @ $2.30 =	1,265
Dec. 19	Purchase	125 units @ $2.00 =	250
	Total	1,515 units	$3,775

The company uses a periodic inventory system, and its ending inventory consists of 150 units, 50 from each of the last three purchases. Determine the cost assigned to ending inventory and to cost of goods sold using (a) specific identification, (b) weighted average, (c) FIFO, and (d) LIFO. Which method yields the lowest net income?

Legacy Company's ending inventory includes the following items:

Exercise 7-7
Lower of cost or market

Product	Units	Unit Cost	Market Cost per Unit
Helmets	24	$50	$54
Sticks	17	78	72
Skates	38	95	91
Pads	42	36	36

Compute the lower of cost or market for inventory (a) as a whole and (b) applied separately to each product.

Paul Harrison Company had $850,000 of sales in each of three consecutive years 2002–2004, and it purchased merchandise costing $500,000 in each of the years. It also maintained a $250,000 inventory from the beginning to the end of the three-year period. In accounting for inventory, it made an error at the end of year 2002 that caused its year-end 2002 inventory to appear on its statements as $230,000 rather than the correct $250,000.

Exercise 7-8
Analysis of inventory errors

Required

1. Determine the correct amount of the company's gross profit in each of the years 2002–2004.

2. Prepare comparative income statements as in Exhibit 7.11 to show the effect of this error on the company's cost of goods sold and gross profit in years 2002–2004.

On January 1, The Fun Store had $550,000 of inventory at cost. In the first quarter of the year, it purchased $1,690,000 of merchandise, returned $22,200, and paid freight charges of $27,600 on purchased merchandise, terms FOB shipping point. The store's gross profit averages 28%. The store had $2,000,000 of retail sales (net) in the first quarter of the year. Use the gross profit method to estimate its cost of inventory at the end of the first quarter.

Exercise 7-9
Estimating ending inventory—
gross profit method

P3

Exercise 7-10
Estimating ending inventory—retail method

P3

In 2002, Hayden Company had retail sales (net) of $140,000. The following additional information is available from its records at the end of 2002:

	At Cost	At Retail
Beginning inventory	$32,900	$65,200
Cost of goods purchased	58,700	96,600

Use the retail inventory method to estimate Hayden's 2002 ending inventory at cost. (Round the cost to retail ratio to three digits.)

Exercise 7-11
Computing physical inventory at cost—the retail method

P3

Hayden Company of Exercise 7-10 also took a physical inventory using the marked retail prices at the end of 2002. The total of this physical inventory at marked retail prices is $28,200. Compute (a) the amount of this inventory at cost and (b) inventory shrinkage at retail and at cost.

Exercise 7-12
Inventory turnover and days' sales in inventory

A3

Use the following information for Costner Co. to compute inventory turnover for 2003 and 2002 and days' sales in inventory at December 31, 2003 and 2002. (Round answers to one decimal place.)

	2003	2002	2001
Cost of goods sold	$643,825	$426,650	$391,300
Inventory (Dec. 31)	97,400	87,750	92,500

Comment on Costner's efficiency in using its assets to increase sales from 2002 to 2003.

PROBLEM SET A

Problem 7-1A
Alternative cost flows—perpetual

P1

Helton Company's inventory transactions in the fiscal year ended December 31, 2002, follow:

Jan. 1	Beginning inventory	600 units @ $45/unit
Feb. 10	Purchase	350 units @ $42/unit
Mar. 13	Purchase	200 units @ $29/unit
Aug. 21	Purchase	150 units @ $50/unit
Sept. 5	Purchase	545 units @ $48/unit

Helton Company uses a perpetual inventory system. Its inventory had a selling price of $75 per unit, and it entered into the following sales transactions:

Mar. 15	Sales	600 units @ $75/unit
Sept. 10	Sales	100 units @ $75/unit

Required

Preparation Component

1. Compute both cost of goods available for sale and the number of units available for sale.
2. Compute the number of units remaining in ending inventory.

Check   Ending inventory (FIFO), $49,960

3. Compute the cost assigned to ending inventory using (a) FIFO, (b) LIFO, (c) specific identification (*note:* 600 units from beginning inventory and 100 units from the March 13 purchase are sold), and (d) weighted average.
4. Compute the gross profit earned by the company for each of the costing methods in part *3*.

Analysis Component

5. If Helton Company's manager earns a bonus based on a percent of gross profit, which method of inventory costing will the manager likely prefer?

Stokeley Company's prior financial statements report the following:

Problem 7-2A
Analysis of inventory errors

Key Figures	For Year Ended December 31		
	2000	2001	2002
(a) Cost of goods sold	$ 815,000	$ 957,000	$ 780,000
(b) Net income	230,000	285,000	241,000
(c) Total current assets	1,255,000	1,365,000	1,200,000
(d) Equity	1,387,000	1,530,000	1,242,000

Stokeley recently discovered that in making physical counts of inventory, it had made the following errors: Inventory on December 31, 2000, is understated by $56,000, and inventory on December 31, 2001, is overstated by $20,000.

Required

Preparation Component

1. For each key financial statement figure—(a), (b), (c), and (d)—prepare a schedule similar to the following to show the adjustments necessary to correct the reported amounts.

Figure: _____	2000	2001	2002
Reported amount	_____	_____	_____
Adjustments: 12/31/2000 error	_____	_____	_____
12/31/2001 error	_____	_____	_____
Corrected amount	_____	_____	_____

Check   Corrected net income (2002), $261,000

Analysis Component

2. What is the error in total net income for the combined three-year period resulting from the inventory errors? Explain.

3. Explain why the understatement of inventory by $56,000 at the end of 2000 results in an understatement of equity by the same amount in that year.

A physical inventory of Rap Unlimited taken at December 31 reveals the following:

Problem 7-3A
Lower of cost or market

Item	Units on Hand	Per Unit Cost	Per Unit Market
Audio equipment			
Receivers	345	$ 90	$ 98
CD players	260	111	100
Cassette decks	326	86	95
Speakers	204	52	41
Video equipment			
Televisions	480	150	125
VCRs	291	93	84
Video cameras	212	310	322
Car audio equipment			
Cassette radios	185	70	84
CD radios	170	97	105

Required

Calculate the lower of cost or market for the inventory (a) as a whole, (b) by major category, and (c) applied separately to each item.

Check   (b) $280,702

Problem 7-4A
Retail inventory method

P3

The records of Livingston Company provide the following information for the year ended December 31:

	At Cost	At Retail
January 1 beginning inventory	$ 472,450	$ 928,950
Cost of goods purchased	3,376,050	6,381,482
Sales		5,595,800
Sales returns		42,800

Required

1. Use the retail inventory method to estimate the company's year-end inventory. (Round the cost to retail ratio to three digits.)

Check Inventory shortage at cost, $37,100

2. A year-end physical inventory at marked selling prices yields a total inventory of $1,686,900. Prepare a schedule showing the store's loss from shrinkage at cost and at retail.

Problem 7-5A
Gross profit method

P3

Geiger Company wants to prepare interim financial statements for the first quarter. The company wishes to avoid making a physical count of inventory. Geiger's gross profit rate averages 34%. The following information for the first quarter is available from its records:

January 1 beginning inventory	$ 302,580
Cost of goods purchased	941,040
Sales	1,211,160
Sales returns	8,398

Check Estimated ending inventory, $449,797

Required

Use the gross profit method to estimate the company's first quarter ending inventory.

Problem 7-6A[A]
Alternative cost flows—
periodic

P4

G S

Vandenburg Company began year 2002 with 25,000 units of product in its January 1 inventory costing $15 each. It made successive purchases of its product in year 2002 as follows:

Mar. 7	30,000 units @ $18 each
May 25	32,000 units @ $22 each
Aug. 1	22,000 units @ $24 each
Nov. 10	35,000 units @ $27 each

The company uses a periodic inventory system. On December 31, 2002, a physical count reveals that 40,000 units of its product remain in inventory.

Required

Check Cost of goods sold (FIFO): $2,027,000

1. Compute the number and total cost of the units available for sale in year 2002.

2. Compute the amounts assigned to the 2002 ending inventory and cost of goods sold using (a) FIFO, (b) LIFO, and (c) weighted average.

Problem 7-7A[A]
Income comparisons and
cost flows—periodic

A1　P4

New Navy Corp. sold 6,500 units of its product at $50 per unit in year 2002 and incurred operating expenses of $5 per unit in selling the units. It began the year with 700 units in inventory and made successive purchases of its product as follows:

Jan. 1	Beginning inventory	700 units @ $18 per unit
Feb. 20	Purchase	1,600 units @ $19 per unit
May 16	Purchase	800 units @ $20 per unit
Oct. 3	Purchase	500 units @ $21 per unit
Dec. 11	Purchase	3,500 units @ $22 per unit
	Total	7,100 units

Required

Preparation Component

1. Prepare comparative income statements for the company similar to Exhibit 7.8 for the three different inventory costing methods of FIFO, LIFO, and weighted average. Include a detailed cost of goods sold section as part of each statement. The company uses a periodic inventory system, and its income tax rate is 28%.

Check   Net income (LIFO),
$112,896

Analysis Component

2. How would the financial results from using the three alternative inventory costing methods change if New Navy had been experiencing declining costs in its purchases of inventory?

3. What advantages and disadvantages are offered by using (a) LIFO and (b) FIFO? Assume the continuing trend of increasing costs.

Mercado Company's inventory transactions in the fiscal year ended December 31, 2002, follow:

Jan. 1	Beginning inventory	700 units @ $55/unit
Jan. 10	Purchase	550 units @ $56/unit
Feb. 13	Purchase	220 units @ $57/unit
July 21	Purchase	270 units @ $58/unit
Aug. 5	Purchase	445 units @ $59/unit

Mercado Company uses a perpetual inventory system. Its inventory had a selling price of $100 per unit, and it entered into the following sales transactions:

Feb. 15	Sales	530 units @ $100/unit
Aug. 10	Sales	235 units @ $100/unit

PROBLEM SET B

Problem 7-1B
Alternative cost flows—
perpetual

P1

Required

Preparation Component

1. Compute both cost of goods available for sale and the number of units available for sale.

2. Compute the number of units remaining in ending inventory.

3. Compute the cost assigned to ending inventory using (a) FIFO, (b) LIFO, (c) specific identification (*note:* 700 units from beginning inventory and 65 units from the February 13 purchase are sold), and (d) weighted average.

Check   Ending inventory (FIFO),
$81,615

4. Compute the gross profit earned by the company for each of the costing methods in part 3.

Analysis Component

5. If Mercado Company's manager earns a bonus based on a percent of gross profit, which method of inventory costing will the manager likely prefer?

Secado Company's prior financial statements report the following:

	Year Ended December 31		
Key Figures	**2000**	**2001**	**2002**
(a) Cost of goods sold	$207,200	$213,800	$197,060
(b) Net income	175,800	212,270	184,810
(c) Total current assets ...	276,000	277,500	272,950
(d) Equity	314,000	315,000	346,000

Problem 7-2B
Analysis of inventory errors

Secado recently discovered that in making physical counts of inventory, it had made the following errors: Inventory on December 31, 2000, is overstated by $18,000, and inventory on December 31, 2001, is understated by $26,000.

Required

Preparation Component

1. For each key financial statement figure—(a), (b), (c), and (d)—prepare a schedule similar to the following to show the adjustments necessary to correct the reported amounts.

Figure _____	2000	2001	2002
Reported amount	_____	_____	_____
Adjustments: 12/31/2000 error	_____	_____	_____
12/31/2001 error			_____
Corrected amount	_____	_____	_____

Check Correct net income (2002), $158,810

Analysis Component

2. What is the error in total net income for the combined three-year period resulting from the inventory errors? Explain.

3. Explain why the overstatement of inventory by $18,000 at the end of 2000 results in an overstatement of equity by the same amount in that year.

Problem 7-3B
Lower of cost or market

P2

A physical inventory of Office Outlet taken at December 31 reveals the following:

Item	Units on Hand	Per Unit Cost	Per Unit Market
Office furniture:			
Desks	536	$261	$305
Credenzas	395	227	256
Chairs	687	49	43
Bookshelves	421	93	82
Filing cabinets:			
Two-drawer	114	81	70
Four-drawer	298	135	122
Lateral	75	104	118
Office equipment:			
Fax machines	370	168	200
Copiers	475	317	288
Telephones	302	125	117

Required

Check (b) $601,697

Calculate the lower of cost or market for the inventory (a) as a whole, (b) by major category, and (c) applied separately to each item.

Problem 7-4B
Retail inventory method

P3

The records of R. U. MacBeth Co. provide the following information for the year ended December 31:

	At Cost	At Retail
January 1 beginning inventory	$ 91,770	$ 115,610
Cost of goods purchased	502,250	761,830
Sales		782,300
Sales returns		3,460

Required

1. Use the retail inventory method to estimate the company's year-end inventory. (Round the cost to retail ratio to three digits.)

Check Inventory shortage at cost, $12,287

2. A year-end physical inventory at marked selling prices yields a total inventory of $80,450. Prepare a schedule showing the store's loss from shrinkage at cost and at retail.

Problem 7-5B
Gross profit method

P3

Eck Equipment Co. wants to prepare interim financial statements for the first quarter. The company wishes to avoid making a physical count of inventory. Eck's gross profit rate averages 35%. The following information for the first quarter is available from its records:

January 1 beginning inventory	$ 802,880
Cost of goods purchased	2,209,630
Sales	3,760,250
Sales returns	79,300

Required

Use the gross profit method to estimate the company's first quarter ending inventory.

Blue View Co. began year 2002 with 6,500 units of product in its January 1 inventory costing $35 each. It made successive purchases of its product in year 2002 as follows:

Jan. 4	11,500 units @ $33 each
May 18	13,400 units @ $32 each
July 9	11,000 units @ $29 each
Nov. 21	10,500 units @ $20 each

The company uses a periodic inventory system. On December 31, 2002, a physical count reveals that 18,500 units of its product remain in inventory.

Required

1. Compute the number and total cost of the units available for sale in year 2002.
2. Compute the amounts assigned to the 2002 ending inventory and cost of goods sold using (a) FIFO, (b) LIFO, and (c) weighted average.

Problem 7-6B[A]

Alternative cost flows— periodic

McKray Corp. sold 2,000 units of its product at $108 per unit in year 2002 and incurred operating expenses of $14 per unit in selling the units. It began the year with 840 units in inventory and made successive purchases of its product as follows:

Jan. 1	Beginning inventory	840 units @ $58 per unit
April 2	Purchase	600 units @ $59 per unit
June 14	Purchase	500 units @ $61 per unit
Aug. 29	Purchase	700 units @ $64 per unit
Nov. 18	Purchase	900 units @ $65 per unit
	Total	3,540 units

Problem 7-7B[A]

Income comparisons and cost flows—periodic

Required

Preparation Component

1. Prepare comparative income statements similar to Exhibit 7.8 for the three different inventory costing methods of FIFO, LIFO, and weighted average. Include a detailed cost of goods sold section as part of each statement. The company uses a periodic inventory system, and its income tax rate is 30%.

Analysis Component

2. How would the financial results from using the three alternative inventory costing methods change if McKray had been experiencing decreasing prices in its purchases of inventory?
3. What advantages and disadvantages are offered by using (a) LIFO and (b) FIFO? Assume the continuing trend of increasing costs.

Beyond the Numbers

BTN 7-1 Refer to the financial statements of **Nike** in Appendix A to answer the following:

Required

1. What amount of inventories did Nike hold as a current asset on May 31, 2000? On May 31, 1999?
2. Inventories represent what percent of total assets on May 31, 2000? On May 31, 1999?
3. Comment on the relative size of Nike's inventories compared to its other types of assets.
4. What accounting method did Nike use to compute inventory amounts on its balance sheet?
5. Calculate inventory turnover for fiscal year ended May 31, 2000, and days' sales in inventory as of May 31, 2000. (*Note:* Cost of sales is cost of goods sold.)

Reporting in Action

C2 A3

NIKE

Swoosh Ahead

6. Access Nike's annual report for fiscal years ended after May 31, 2000, at its Web site [**www.nike.com**] or the SEC's EDGAR database [**www.sec.gov**]. Answer questions *1* through *5* using the current Nike information.

Comparative Analysis

A3

BTN 7-2   Key comparative figures ($ millions) for both **Nike** and **Reebok** follow:

	Nike			Reebok		
Key Figures	**Current**	**One Year Prior**	**Two Years Prior**	**Current**	**One Year Prior**	**Two Years Prior**
Inventory	$1,446.0	$1,170.6	$1,396.6	$ 414.6	$ 535.1	$ 563.7
Cost of sales . .	5,403.8	5,493.5	6,065.5	1,783.9	2,037.5	2,294.0

Required

1. Calculate inventory turnover for both companies for the most recent two years shown.

2. Calculate days' sales in inventory for both companies for the three years shown.

3. Comment on your findings from parts (1) and (2).

Ethics Challenge

A1

BTN 7-3   U-Golf Corp. is a retail sports store carrying golf apparel and equipment. The store is at the end of its second year of operation and is struggling. Its cost of inventory has increased in the past two years. In the first year of operations, the store assigned inventory costs using LIFO. A loan agreement the store has with its bank, its prime source of financing, requires the store to maintain a certain profit margin and current ratio. The store's owner is currently looking over U-Golf's preliminary annual financial statements. The numbers are not favorable. The only way the store can meet the required financial ratios agreed on with the bank is to change from LIFO to FIFO. The store originally decided on LIFO because of its tax advantages. The owner recalculates ending inventory using FIFO and submits the statements to the loan officer at the bank for the required bank review. The owner thankfully reflects on the available latitude in choosing the inventory costing method.

Required

1. How does U-Golf's use of FIFO improve its net profit margin and current ratio?

2. Is the action by U-Golf's owner ethical? Explain.

Communicating in Practice

A1

BTN 7-4   You are a financial adviser with a client in the wholesale produce business that just completed its first year of operations. Due to weather conditions, the cost of acquiring produce to resell escalated during the later part of this period. Your client, Juana Peabody, mentions that because the business sells perishable goods, she has striven to maintain a FIFO flow of goods. Although sales are good, the increasing cost of inventory has put the business in a tight cash position. Juana has expressed concern regarding the ability of the business to meet income tax obligations.

Point: If an e-mail response is preferred, students need an e-mail address.

Required

Prepare a memorandum or send an e-mail that identifies, explains, and justifies the inventory method you recommend your client Ms. Peabody, adopt. If the response is to be made via e-mail, you can assume that your instructor is your client.

Taking It to the Net

A3

BTN 7-5   Access the March 30, 2000, filing of the 10-K report for **Oakley, Inc.** (Ticker OO), from **www.edgar-online.com**.

Required

1. What product does Oakley sell that is especially popular with college students?

2. What inventory method does Oakley use? (*Hint:* See the notes to its financial statements.)

3. Compute Oakley's gross margin and gross margin ratio for the most current year's data.

4. Compute Oakley's inventory turnover and days' sales in inventory for the most current year's data.

BTN 7-6   Each team member has the responsibility to become an expert on an inventory method. This expertise will be used to facilitate teammates' understanding of the concepts relevant to that method.

1. Each learning team member should select an area for expertise by choosing one of the following inventory methods: specific identification, LIFO, FIFO, or weighted average.

2. Form expert teams made up of students who have selected the same area of expertise. The instructor will identify where each expert team will meet.

3. Using the following data, each expert team must collaborate to develop a presentation that illustrates the relevant concepts and procedures for its inventory method. Each team member must write the presentation in a format that can be shown to the learning team.

Data

Sunmann Corp. uses a perpetual inventory system. It had the following beginning inventory and current year purchases of its product:

Jan.	1	Beginning inventory	50 units @ $10 = $ 500
Jan.	14	Purchase	150 units @ $12 = 1,800
Apr.	30	Purchase	200 units @ $15 = 3,000
Sept.	26	Purchase	300 units @ $20 = 6,000

Sunmann Corp. transacted sales on the following dates at $35 per unit:

Jan. 10	30 units	(specific cost $10)
Feb. 15	100 units	(specific cost $12)
Oct. 5	350 units	(specific cost: 100 @ $15 and 250 @ $20)

Concepts and Procedures to Illustrate in Expert Presentation

a. Identify and compute the costs to assign to the units sold.

b. Identify and compute the costs to assign to the units in ending inventory.

c. How likely is it that this inventory costing method will reflect the actual physical flow of goods? How relevant is that factor in determining whether this is an acceptable method to use?

d. What is the impact of this method versus others in determining net income and income taxes?

e. How closely does ending inventory reflect replacement costs for the units?

4. Re-form learning teams. In rotation, each expert is to present to the team the presentation developed in part (3). Experts are to encourage and respond to questions.

BTN 7-7   Read the article "Yes, Steve, You Fixed It. Congrats! Now What's Act Two?" from the July 31, 2000, issue of *Business Week*.

Required

1. What percent of the U.S. home computer market does Apple have? What is Apple's overall worldwide market share? Has Apple's worldwide market share grown or declined from 1993?

2. How many days' worth of parts are in its computer parts inventory? How were efficiencies in the parts' inventory achieved?

3. Do critics think that the days' parts in inventory figure is reliable? Explain.

BTN 7-8   Brad Eldridge is an entrepreneur and owner of Home Security, which designs, sells, and installs home security equipment. The company consistently maintains an inventory level of $50,000, meaning that its average and ending inventory levels are the same. Its cost of sales is $190,000. To cut costs, Brad proposes to slash inventory to a constant level of $25,000 with no impact on cost of sales.

Required

1. Compute the company's inventory turnover and its days' sales in inventory under (a) current conditions and (b) proposed conditions.

2. Evaluate and comment on the merits of Brad's proposal given your analysis in part (1). Identify any concerns you would express about the proposal.

Teamwork in Action

P1 A1

Point: Step 1 allows four choices or areas for expertise. Larger teams will have some duplication of choice, but the specific identification method should not be duplicated. Expert teams can use the book and consult with instructor.

Business Week Activity

A3

Entrepreneurial Decision

8

Accounting Information Systems

A Look Back

Chapters 6 and 7 focused on merchandising activities and accounting for inventory. We explained both the perpetual and periodic inventory systems, accounting for inventory transactions, and methods for assigning costs to inventory.

A Look at This Chapter

This chapter emphasizes accounting information systems. We describe fundamental system principles, the system's components, use of special journals and subsidiary ledgers, and technology-based systems. We also discuss segment reporting and how to analyze these data.

A Look Ahead

Chapter 9 focuses on internal controls and accounting for cash and cash equivalents. We explain good internal control procedures and their importance for accounting.

"Untapped market—online accounting for small business."—Evan Goldberg.

Learning Objectives

Conceptual

C1 Identify fundamental principles of accounting information systems.

C2 Identify components of accounting information systems.

C3 Explain the goals and uses of special journals.

C4 Describe the use of controlling accounts and subsidiary ledgers.

C5 Explain how technology-based information systems impact accounting.

Analytical

A1 Analyze a company's performance and financial condition by business segments.

Procedural

P1 Journalize and post transactions using special journals.

P2 Prepare and prove the accuracy of subsidiary ledgers.

Do It on the Net

e SAN MATEO, CA—It began with Evan Goldberg's frustration in accounting for his fledgling business. Goldberg was looking for an integrated accounting package that would allow its transaction system to talk to inventory, inventory to talk to payables and receivables, and so on. He also was tired of upgrades and backups. Goldberg's response was to launch **NetLedger** [**NetLedger.com**], a company devoted to an accounting package run entirely on the Web.

NetLedger "eliminates a lot of the hassles" of existing accounting packages for small businesses, says Goldberg. It lets users manage transactions such as receivables, payables, cash disbursements, and cash receipts. It also provides General Ledger capabilities, online sales and order processing, and immediate purchase orders, invoices, and checks. Audit trails exist to track transactions, and security is a top priority. Goldberg says the site features an encryption system more secure than an armored truck. He won't even disclose the location of its data center where customers' electronic "books" are kept.

Goldberg says NetLedger targets companies with fewer than 100 employees. It is a David trying to take on the accounting software giants PeachTree and QuickBooks. Goldberg is hoping NetLedger's price advantage will be the biggest turn-on for customers—less than $5 per month, including a free trial period. The site even lets you convert data directly from QuickBooks.

So far, the 33-year-old Goldberg couldn't be happier. NetLedger is receiving rave reviews, and Larry Ellison, chairman of Oracle, is helping fund Goldberg's start-up. Says Ellison, "NetLedger is creating a new generation of software—one that is never a product but only a service." Goldberg agrees. He adds, "Internet technology has created a new and currently untapped market—online accounting for small business." [Sources: *eWEEK*, August 9, 1999; *NetLedger Web Site*, May 2001; *Business Week*, October 19, 1999]

Accounting for business activities requires collecting and processing information. With increases in the number and complexity of business activities, demands placed on accounting information systems increase. Accounting information systems must meet this challenge in an efficient and effective manner. In this chapter, we learn about fundamental principles guiding information systems, and we study components making up these systems. We also explain procedures that use special journals and subsidiary ledgers to make accounting information systems more efficient. An understanding of the details of accounting reports makes us better decision makers when using financial information, and it improves our ability to analyze and interpret financial statements.

Fundamental System Principles

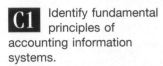

C1 Identify fundamental principles of accounting information systems.

Accounting information systems collect and process data from transactions and events, organize them in useful forms, and communicate results to decision makers. These systems are crucial to effective decision making for both internal and external users of information. With the increasing complexity of business and the growing need for information, accounting information systems are more important than ever.

Today all decision makers need to have a basic knowledge of how accounting information systems work. This knowledge gives decision makers a competitive edge as they gain a better understanding of information constraints, measurement limitations, and potential applications. It allows them to make more informed decisions and to better balance the risks and returns of different strategies. This section explains five basic principles of accounting information systems as shown in Exhibit 8.1.

Exhibit 8.1

System Principles

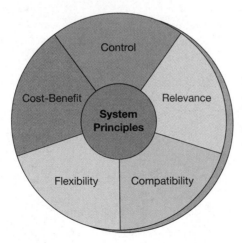

Control Principle

Managers need to control and monitor business activities. To this end, the **control principle** requires an accounting information system to have internal controls. *Internal controls* are methods and procedures allowing managers to control and monitor business activities. They include policies to direct operations toward common goals, procedures to ensure reliable financial reports, safeguards to protect company assets, and methods to achieve compliance with laws and regulations.

Relevance Principle

Decision makers need relevant information to make informed decisions. The **relevance principle** requires that an accounting information system report useful, understandable, timely, and pertinent information for effective decision making. This means that an information system is designed to capture data that make a difference in decisions. To ensure this, all decision makers must be considered when identifying relevant information for disclosure.

Compatibility Principle

Accounting information systems must be consistent with the aims of a company. The **compatibility principle** requires that an accounting information system conform with a company's activities, personnel, and structure. It also must adapt to a company's unique characteristics. The system must not be intrusive but must work in harmony with and be driven by company goals. Most start-up entrepreneurs require only a simple information system. **Nike**, on the other hand, demands both a merchandising and a manufacturing information system able to assemble data from its global operations.

Flexibility Principle

Accounting information systems must be able to adjust to changes. The **flexibility principle** requires that an accounting information system be able to adapt to changes in the company, business environment, and needs of decisions makers. Technological advances, competitive pressures, consumer tastes, regulations, and company activities constantly change. A system must be designed to adapt to these changes.

Cost-Benefit Principle

Accounting information systems must balance costs and benefits. The **cost-benefit principle** requires the benefits from an activity in an accounting information system to outweigh the costs of that activity. The costs and benefits of an activity such as reporting certain information impact the decisions of both external and internal users. Decisions regarding other systems principles (control, relevance, compatibility, and flexibility) are also affected by the cost-benefit principle.

Point: A hacker recently stole 300,000 credit card numbers from online music retailer **CDUniverse.**

Components of Accounting Systems

Accounting information systems consist of people, records, methods, and equipment. The systems are designed to capture information about a company's transactions and to provide output including financial, managerial, and tax reports. All accounting information systems have these same goals, and thus have some basic components. These components apply whether or not a system is heavily computerized, yet the components of computerized systems usually provide more accuracy, speed, efficiency, and convenience.

C2 Identify components of accounting information systems.

The five basic components of an accounting information system are source documents, input devices, information processors, information storage, and output devices. Exhibit 8.2 shows these components as a series of steps, yet we know that much two-way communication occurs between many of these components. We briefly describe each of these key components in this section.

| Source Document | Input Devices | Information Processor | Information Storage | Output Devices |

Exhibit 8.2

Accounting System Components

Source Documents

We described source documents in Chapter 3 and explained their importance for both business transactions and information collection. Source documents provide the basic information processed by an accounting system. Most of us are familiar with source documents such as bank statements and checks received from others. Other examples of source documents include invoices from suppliers, billings to customers, and employee earnings records.

Source documents can be paper based, although they increasingly are taking the form of electronic files and Web communications. A growing number of companies are sending invoices directly from their systems to their customers' and suppliers' systems. The Web is playing a major role in this transformation from paper-based to *paperless* systems.

Accurate source documents are crucial to accounting information systems. Input of faulty or incomplete information seriously impairs the reliability and relevance of the information system. We commonly refer to this as "garbage in, garbage out." Information systems are set up with special attention on control procedures to limit the possibility of entering faulty data in the system.

Input Devices

Input devices capture information from source documents and enable its transfer to the system's information processing component. These

Did You Know?

Scan Links   Scanners are increasingly embedded in cell phones and other handheld devices to gain access to Web sites equipped with bar code readers. The phones scan the bar codes in, say, magazine or newspaper ads and give the user access to sites that market the products or services.

Point: Understanding a manual accounting system is useful in understanding an electronic system.

devices often involve converting data on source documents from written or electronic form to a form usable for the system. Journal entries, both electronic and paper based, are a type of input device. Keyboards, scanners, and modems are some of the most common input devices in practice today. For example, bar code readers capture code numbers and transfer them to the organization's computer for processing. Moreover, a scanner can capture writing samples and other input directly from source documents.

Accounting information systems encourage accuracy by using consistent methods for inputting data. Controls are also used to ensure that only authorized individuals input data to the system. Controls increase the system's reliability and allow false information to be traced back to its source.

Information Processor

An **information processor** is a system that interprets, transforms, and summarizes information for use in analysis and reporting. An important part of an information processor in accounting systems is professional judgment. Accounting principles are never so structured that they limit the need for professional judgment. Other parts of an information processor include journals, ledgers, working papers, and posting procedures. Each assists in transforming raw data to useful information.

Increasingly, computer technology is assisting manual information processors. This assistance is freeing accounting professionals to take on increased analysis, interpretive, and managerial roles. This assistance to information processors includes both computing hardware and software. Web-based application service providers (ASPs) offer another type of information processor.

Information Storage

Point: A financial accounting database can be designed to support a wide range of internal reports for management.

Information storage is the accounting system component that keeps data in a form accessible to information processors. After being input and processed, data are stored for use in future analyses and reports. The database must be accessible to preparers of periodic financial reports. Auditors rely on this database when they audit financial statements and a company's controls. Companies also maintain files of source documents. Technology increasingly assists with information storage. Older systems consisted almost exclusively of paper documents, but most modern systems depend on electronic storage devices. Advances in information storage enable accounting systems to store more detailed data than ever before. This means managers have more data to access and work with in planning and controlling business activities. Information storage can be online, meaning data can be accessed whenever, and from wherever, it is needed. Off-line storage means access often requires assistance and authorization. Information storage is increasingly augmented by Web sources such as SEC databases, benchmarking services, FASB standards, and financial and product markets.

Did You Know?

Geek Chic   Cyberfashion pioneers at **MIT's Media Laboratory** are creating geek chic, a kind of wearable computer. Cyberfashion draws on digital cellular phones, lithium batteries, and miniature monitors. Special thread is woven into clothing to carry low-voltage signals from one part of the system to another, and fabric keyboards are sewn into blue jeans. These creations give new meaning to the term *software*.

Did You Know?

Virtual Output   **Microvision** is developing a screenless computer display. The device, called *virtual retinal display* (VRD), scans rows of pixels directly onto the user's retina by means of a laser, creating images that simulate the experience of viewing a full-size screen. VRDs can also simulate three-dimensional virtual worlds.

Output Devices

Output devices are the means to take information out of an accounting system and make it available to users. Common output devices are printers, monitors, and Web communications. Output devices provide users a variety of items including graphics, analysis reports, bills to customers, checks to suppliers, employee paychecks, financial statements, and internal reports. When requests for output occur, an information processor takes the needed data from a database and prepares the necessary report, which is then sent to an output device.

Information can be output in many forms. For example, one type of output is an electronic fund transfer (EFT) of payroll from the company's bank account to its employees' bank accounts. One output device to accomplish this is an interface that allows a company's accounting system to send payroll data directly to the bank's accounting system. Another EFT output device involves a company recording its payroll data on tape or CD and forwarding it to the bank. The bank then uses this tape or disk to transfer wages earned to employees' accounts.

Quick Check

1. Identify the five primary components of an accounting information system.

2. What is the aim of the information processor component of an accounting system?

3. How are data in the information storage component of an accounting system used?

Answers—p. 331

Special Journals in Accounting

This section describes the underlying records of accounting information systems. Designed correctly, these records support efficiency in processing transactions and events. They are part of all systems in various forms and are increasingly electronically based. But even in technologically advanced systems, a basic understanding of the records we describe in this section aids in using, interpreting, and applying accounting information. It also improves our knowledge of computer-based systems. We must remember that all accounting systems have common purposes and internal workings whether or not they depend on technology.

This section focuses on special journals and subsidiary ledgers that are an important part of accounting systems. We describe how special journals are used to capture transactions, and we explain how subsidiary ledgers are set up to capture details of accounts. This section uses a *perpetual* inventory system, and the special journals are set up using this system. Appendix 8A describes the slight change in special journals required for a *periodic* system. We also include a note at the bottom of each of the special journals under the perpetual system explaining the minor change required if a company uses a periodic system.

C3 Explain the goals and uses of special journals.

Basics of Special Journals

A general journal is an all-purpose journal in which we can record any transaction. Use of a general journal requires that each debit and each credit entered must be individually posted to its respective ledger account. This requires time and effort in posting individual debits and credits, especially for less technologically advanced systems. The costs of posting accounts can be reduced by organizing transactions into common groups through a special journal. A **special journal** is used to record and post transactions of similar type. Most transactions of a merchandiser, for instance, can be categorized as shown in Exhibit 8.3:

Point: Companies can use as many special journals as necessary given their unique business activities.

Sales Journal	Cash Receipts Journal	Purchases Journal	Cash Disbursement Journal	General Journal
For recording credit sales	For recording cash receipts	For recording credit purchases	For recording cash payments	For transactions not in special journals

Exhibit 8.3

Using Special Journals with a General Journal

Point: Each transaction is recorded in only *one* journal.

sales on credit, purchases on credit, cash receipts, and cash disbursements. This section assumes the use of these four special journals along with the general journal.

The general journal continues to be used for transactions not covered by special journals and for adjusting, closing, and correcting entries. We show in the following discussion that special journals are efficient tools in helping journalize and post transactions. This is done, for instance, by accumulating debits and credits of similar transactions, which allows us to post most amounts as column *totals* rather than as individual amounts. The advantage of this system increases as the number of transactions increases. Special journals also allow an efficient division of labor, which can be an effective control procedure.

Subsidiary Ledgers

C4 Describe the use of controlling accounts and subsidiary ledgers.

Concept 8-1

To understand the details of special journals, it is necessary to understand the workings of a **subsidiary ledger,** which is a list of individual accounts with a common characteristic. A subsidiary ledger supports the general ledger with detailed information on specific accounts, which removes unnecessary details from the general ledger. Accounting information systems often include several subsidiary ledgers. Two of the most important involve the amounts due from customers, called *accounts receivable,* and the amounts owed to creditors, called *accounts payable*. These two subsidiary ledgers are known by these titles:

- *Accounts receivable ledger*—stores transaction data of individual customers.
- *Accounts payable ledger*—stores transaction data of individual suppliers.

Individual accounts in subsidiary ledgers are often arranged alphabetically. We describe accounts receivable and accounts payable ledgers in this section. Our discussion of special journals in the next section uses both of these ledgers.

Accounts Receivable Ledger

When we recorded credit sales in prior chapters, we debited (increased) Accounts Receivable. When a company has more than one credit customer, the accounts receivable records must show how much *each* customer purchased, paid, and has yet to pay. This information is collected by keeping a separate account receivable for each credit customer. A separate account for each customer *could* be kept in the general ledger containing the other financial statement accounts, but this is uncommon. Instead, the general ledger usually has a single Accounts Receivable account and a *subsidiary ledger* is set up to keep a separate account for each customer. This subsidiary ledger is called the **accounts receivable ledger** (also called *accounts receivable subsidiary ledger* or *customers ledger*). Like a general ledger, a subsidiary ledger can exist in electronic or paper form. Customer accounts in a subsidiary ledger are kept separate from the Accounts Receivable account in the general ledger.

Exhibit 8.4 shows the relation between the Accounts Receivable account and its related accounts in the subsidiary ledger. After all items are posted, the balance in the Accounts Receivable account must equal the sum of balances in the customers' accounts. The Accounts Receivable account is said to control the accounts receivable ledger and is called a **controlling account.** Since the accounts receivable ledger is a supplementary record controlled by an account in the general ledger, it is called a *subsidiary ledger*.

Accounts Payable Ledger

There are other controlling accounts and subsidiary ledgers. We know, for example, that many companies buy on credit from several suppliers. This means companies must keep a separate account for each supplier by keeping an Accounts Payable controlling account in the general ledger and a separate account for each supplier (creditor) in an **accounts payable ledger** (also called *accounts payable subsidiary ledger* or *creditors ledger*). The concept of a controlling account and its subsidiary ledger as described with accounts receivable also applies to accounts payable.

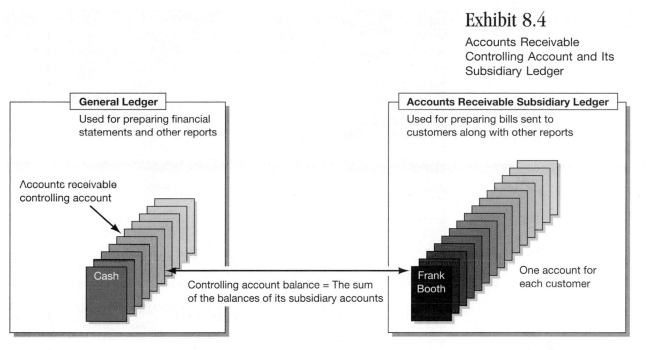

General Ledger

Used for preparing financial
statements and other reports

Accounts receivable
controlling account

Cash

Controlling account balance = The sum
of the balances of its subsidiary accounts

Accounts Receivable Subsidiary Ledger

Used for preparing bills sent to
customers along with other reports

Frank
Booth

One account for
each customer

Other Subsidiary Ledgers

Subsidiary ledgers are common for several other accounts. A company with many classes
of equipment, for example, might keep only one Equipment account in its general ledger,
but its Equipment account would control a subsidiary ledger in which each class of equipment is recorded in a separate account. Similar treatment is common for investments, investments, and any accounts needing separate detailed records. **Polaris** reports detailed sales
information by product line in its annual report. Yet its accounting system most certainly
keeps more detailed sales records. Polaris, for instance, sells hundreds of different products
and must be able to analyze the sales performance of each of them. This detail can be captured by many different general ledger sales accounts but is more likely captured by using
supplementary records that function like subsidiary ledgers. Subsidiary ledgers are applied
in many different ways to ensure that the accounting system captures sufficient details to
support analyses that decision makers need.

Sales Journal

A **sales journal** is used to record sales of inventory on credit. Sales of inventory for cash
are not recorded in a sales journal but in a cash receipts journal. Sales of noninventory assets on credit are recorded in the general journal.

P1 Journalize and post
transactions using
special journals.

Journalizing

Credit sale transactions are recorded with information about each sale entered separately in
a sales journal. This information is often taken from a copy of the sales ticket or invoice
prepared at the time of sale. The top portion of Exhibit 8.5 shows a typical sales journal
from a merchandiser. It has columns for recording the date, customer's name, invoice number, posting reference, and the retail and cost amounts of each credit sale. The sales journal in this exhibit is called a **columnar journal,** which is any journal with more than one
column.

Concept 8-2

Each transaction recorded in the sales journal yields an entry in the Accounts Receivable
Dr., Sales Cr. column. We need only one column for these two accounts. An exception is
when managers need more information about taxes, returns, and other details of transactions. Each transaction in the sales journal also yields an entry in the Cost of Goods Sold
Dr., Inventory Cr. column. This entry reflects the perpetual inventory system of tracking
costs with each sale. To illustrate, on February 2, the company sold merchandise on account

Exhibit 8.5

Sales Journal with Posting*

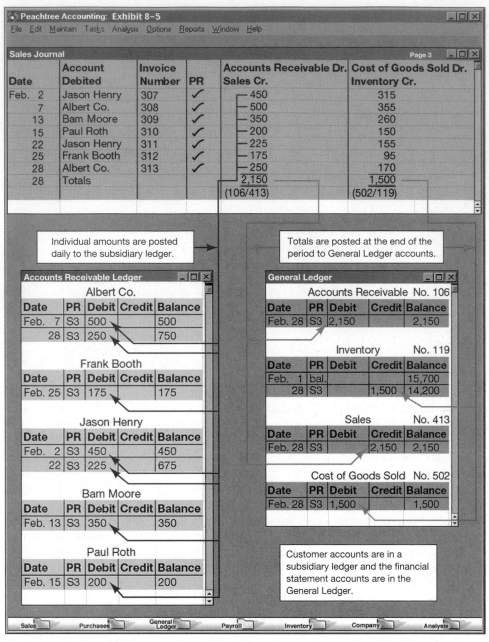

*The Sales Journal in a *periodic* system would exclude the column on the far right titled "Cost of Goods Sold Dr., Inventory Cr." (see Exhibit 8A.1).

to Jason Henry for $450. The invoice number is 307, and the cost of this merchandise is $315. This information is captured on one line in the sales journal. No further explanations or entries are necessary, saving time and effort. Moreover, such a sales journal is consistent with most inventory systems that use bar codes to record both sales and costs with each sale transaction. Note that the Posting Reference (PR) column is not used when entering transactions but is used when posting.

Point: Continuously updated customer accounts provide timely information for customer inquiries on those accounts. Keeping creditor accounts updated provides timely information on current amounts owed.

Posting

A sales journal is posted as reflected in the arrow lines of Exhibit 8.5. Two types of posting can be identified: (1) posting to the general ledger and (2) posting to the subsidiary ledger(s).

Posting to subsidiary ledger. Individual transactions in the sales journal are posted regularly (typically daily) to customer accounts in the accounts receivable ledger. These postings keep customer accounts up to date. This is important for the person granting credit to customers who needs to know the amount owed by credit-seeking customers. If this information in the customer's account is out of date, an incorrect decision can be made. When sales recorded in the sales journal are individually posted to customer accounts in the accounts receivable ledger, check marks are entered in the sales journal's PR column. Check marks are usually used rather than account numbers because customer accounts are not always numbered. Customer accounts usually are arranged alphabetically in the accounts receivable ledger. Note that posting debits to Accounts Receivable twice—once to Accounts Receivable and once to the customer's account—does not violate the accounting equation of debits equal credits. The equality of debits and credits is always maintained in the general ledger. The accounts receivable ledger is a subsidiary record.

Posting to general ledger. The sales journal's dollar amount columns are totaled at the end of each period (the month of February in this case). For the "sales" column, the $2,150 total is debited to Accounts Receivable and credited to Sales in the general ledger (see Exhibit 8.5). The debit records the increase in accounts receivable. The credit records the revenue from sales on account. For the "cost" column, the $1,500 total is debited to Cost of Goods Sold and credited to Inventory in the general ledger (see Exhibit 8.5). When totals are posted to accounts in the general ledger, the account numbers are entered below the column total in the sales journal. For example, we enter (106/413) below the total in the sales column after we post this amount to account number 106 (Accounts Receivable) and account number 413 (Sales). The same rule applies to the cost column total.

A company identifies in the PR column of both ledgers the journal and page number from which an amount is taken. We identify a journal by using an initial. Items posted from the sales journal carry the initial *S* before their journal page numbers in a PR column. Likewise, items from the cash receipts journal carry the initial *R*; items from the cash disbursements journal carry the initial *D*; items from the purchases journal carry the initial *P*; and items from the general journal carry the initial *G*.

Proving the Ledger

Account balances in the general ledger and subsidiary ledgers are proved (or reviewed) for accuracy after posting is complete. We first prepare a trial balance of the general ledger to confirm that debits equal credits (see Chapter 4 for preparing a trial balance). If debits equal credits in the trial balance, the accounts in the general ledger (the controlling accounts) are assumed to be correct. Second, we test the subsidiary ledgers by preparing schedules of individual accounts and amounts. A **schedule of accounts receivable** lists the accounts from the accounts receivable ledger with their balances and the sum of all balances. If this total equals the balance of the Accounts Receivable controlling account, the accounts in the accounts receivable ledger are assumed correct. Exhibit 8.6 shows a schedule of accounts receivable drawn from the accounts receivable ledger of Exhibit 8.5.

P2 Prepare and prove the accuracy of subsidiary ledgers.

Point: In accounting, the word *schedule* generally means a list.

Additional Issues

We consider three additional issues with the sales journal: (1) recording sales taxes, (2) recording sales returns and allowances, and (3) using actual sales invoices as a journal.

Sales taxes

Many cities and states require sellers to collect sales taxes from customers and to periodically send these taxes to the city or state treasurer. When using a columnar sales journal, we can keep a record of taxes collected by adding a Sales Taxes Payable column as shown here:

Schedule of Accounts Receivable February 28	
Frank Booth	$ 175
Jason Henry	675
Bam Moore	350
Paul Roth	200
Albert Co.	750
Total accounts receivable	$2,150

Exhibit 8.6

Schedule of Accounts Receivable

Posting would include crediting the Sales Taxes Payable account for the total of the Sales Taxes Payable column. Individual amounts in the Accounts Receivable column would be posted daily to customer accounts in the accounts receivable ledger. Individual amounts in the Sales Taxes Payable and Sales columns are not posted. A company that collects sales taxes on its cash sales can also use a Sales Taxes Payable column in its cash receipts journal.

Sales returns and allowances

A company with only a few sales returns and allowances can record them in a general journal with an entry such as this:

Assets = Liabilities + Equity
−175   −175

May 17	Sales Returns and Allowances	414	175	
	Accounts Receivable—Ray Ball	106/✓		175
	Customer returned merchandise.			

The debit in this entry is posted to the Sales Returns and Allowances account (no. 414). The credit is posted to both the Accounts Receivable controlling account (no. 106) and to the customer's account. When we enter the account number and the check mark, 106/✓, in the PR column on the credit line, this means both the Accounts Receivable controlling account in the general ledger and the Ray Ball account in the accounts receivable ledger are credited for $175. Both are credited so that the balance of the controlling account in the general ledger equals the sum of the customer account balances in the subsidiary ledger. [*Note:* If the returned goods are not defective and can be resold to another customer, the company would debit (increase) the Inventory account and credit (decrease) the Cost of Goods Sold account. If the returned goods are defective (worthless), the company could simply leave their costs in the Cost of Goods Sold account (see Chapter 6).] A company with a large number of sales returns and allowances can save time by recording them in a special sales returns and allowances journal. More generally, a company will design and use a special journal for any group of similar transactions if it has enough transactions to warrant its use.

Sales invoices as a sales journal

To save costs, some companies avoid using a sales journal for credit sales and instead post each sales invoice amount directly to the customer's account in the subsidiary accounts receivable ledger. Then they put copies of invoices in numerical order in a file. At the end of the period, they total all invoices for that period and make a general journal entry to debit Accounts Receivable and credit Sales for the total amount. The bound invoice copies act as a sales journal. This procedure is called *direct posting of sales invoices*.

Quick Check

4. When special journals are used, where are all cash payments by check recorded?

5. How does a columnar journal save posting time and effort?

6. How do debits and credits remain equal when credit sales are posted twice (once to Accounts Receivable and once to the customer's subsidiary account)?

7. How do we identify the journal from which an amount in a ledger account was posted?

8. How are sales taxes recorded in the context of special journals?

9. What is direct posting of sales invoices?

Cash Receipts Journal

A **cash receipts journal** records all receipts of cash. Exhibit 8.7 shows one common form of the cash receipts journal.

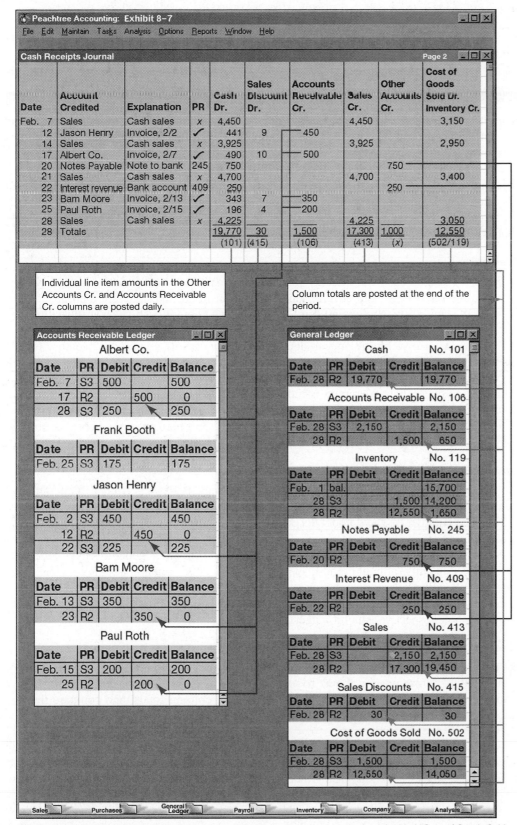

Exhibit 8.7

Cash Receipts Journal with Posting*

*The Cash Receipts Journal in a *periodic* system would exclude the column on the far right titled "Cost of Goods Sold Dr., Inventory Cr." (see Exhibit 8A.2).

Point: Each transaction in the cash receipts journal involves a debit to Cash.

Journalizing and Posting

Cash receipts fall into one of three types: (1) cash from credit customers in payment of their accounts, (2) cash from cash sales, and (3) cash from other sources. The cash receipts journal in Exhibit 8.7 has a separate credit column for each of these three sources. We describe how to journalize transactions for each of these three sources in this section. We then describe how to post them.[1]

Cash from credit customers

Journalizing. To record cash received in payment of a customer's account, the customer's name is first entered in the Account Credited column—see transactions dated February 12, 17, 23, and 25. Then, the amounts debited to both Cash and the Sales Discount (if any) are entered in their respective columns, and the amount credited to the customer's account is entered in the Accounts Receivable Cr. column. The Accounts Receivable Cr. column contains only credits to customer accounts.

Posting. The posting of transactions involving cash from credit customers is twofold. First, individual amounts in the Accounts Receivable Cr. column are posted regularly (daily) to customer accounts in the subsidiary accounts receivable ledger. Second, the $1,500 column total is posted at the end of the period (month) as a credit to the Accounts Receivable controlling account in the general ledger.

Cash sales

Journalizing. When cash sales occur, the debits to Cash are entered in the Cash Debit column and the credits are entered in a separate column titled Sales Cr. The February 7, 14, 21, and 28 transactions are examples of cash sales. (Although cash sales are usually journalized daily (or at point of sale), cash sales are journalized weekly in Exhibit 8.7 for brevity.) Each cash sale also yields an entry to debit Cost of Goods Sold and credit Inventory for the cost of merchandise sold—see the far right column.

Posting. When recording cash sales in the cash receipts journal, we place an *x* in the PR column to indicate that no amount is individually posted from that line of the journal. We post the $17,300 total cash sales for the period in the general ledger as a single amount, taken from the Sales Cr. column. We also post the $12,550 total from the "cost" column to both Cost of Goods Sold and Inventory in the general ledger.

Cash from other sources

Example: Record the sale of machinery at its cost of $100 using a cash receipts journal. *Answer:* Debit the Cash column for $100, and credit the Other Accounts column for $100 (the account credited is Machinery).

Journalizing. Cash from other sources includes money borrowed from a bank, interest received on account, or cash sale of noninventory assets. Examples are the transactions of February 20 and 22. The Other Accounts Cr. column is used for these cash receipt transactions.

Posting. Amounts from these transactions are posted to their general ledger accounts. Postings occur daily, although end-of-period posting of these amounts is acceptable. This journal's PR column is used only for daily postings from the Other Accounts Cr. and the Accounts Receivable Cr. columns. The account numbers in the PR column refer to amounts posted to their respective general ledger accounts.

Footing, Crossfooting, and Posting

To be sure that total debits and credits in a columnar journal are equal, we often crossfoot column totals before posting them. To *foot* a column of numbers is to add it. To *crossfoot* is to add the Debit column totals, then add the Credit column totals, and compare the two sums for equality. Footing and crossfooting of the numbers in Exhibit 8.7 yields the schedule in Exhibit 8.8.

Point: Subsidiary ledgers and their controlling accounts are *in balance* only after all posting is complete.

At the end of the period (month), after crossfooting the journal to confirm that debits equal credits, the total amounts from the columns of the cash receipts journal are posted to their general ledger accounts. The Other Accounts Cr. column total is not posted because

---

[1] An Explanation column is included in the cash receipts journal to identify the source of each cash receipt.

Debit Columns		Credit Columns	
Cash Dr.	$19,770	Accounts Receivable Cr.	$ 1,500
Sales Discounts Dr.	30	Sales Cr.	17,300
		Other Accounts Cr.	1,000
Total	$19,800	Total	$19,800

Exhibit 8.8

Footing and Crossfooting
Journal Totals

the individual amounts are directly posted to their general ledger accounts. We place an *x* below the Other Accounts Cr. column to indicate that this column total is not posted. The account numbers for the column totals that are posted are entered in parentheses below each column. (*Note:* Posting items daily from the Other Accounts Cr. column with a delayed posting of their offsetting items in the Cash column total causes the general ledger to be out of balance during the period. Posting the Cash Dr. column total at the end of the period corrects this imbalance in the general ledger before the trial balance and financial statements are prepared.)

> ## You Make the Call
>
> **Entrepreneur** You want to know how promptly customers are paying their bills. This information can help you decide whether to extend credit and plan your cash payments. Where can you find this information?
>
> Answer—p. 330

Purchases Journal

A **purchases journal** is used to record all purchases on credit. Purchases for cash are recorded in the Cash Disbursements Journal.

Journalizing

The purchases journal in Exhibit 8.9 is a columnar journal in which all credit purchases, including inventory, are recorded. Purchase invoices or other source documents are used to record transactions in the purchases journal. We use the invoice date and terms to compute the date when payment for each purchase is due. The Accounts Payable Cr. column is used to record the amounts owed to each creditor. Inventory purchases are recorded in the Inventory Dr. column. To illustrate, inventory costing $200 is purchased from Ace Manufacturing on February 5. The creditor's name (Ace) is entered in Account column, the invoice date is entered in the Date of Invoice column, and purchase terms are entered in the Terms column. The $200 amount is entered in the Accounts Payable Cr. and the Inventory Dr. columns. When a purchase involves an amount recorded in the Other Accounts Dr. column, we use the Account column to identify the general ledger account debited. For example, the February 28 transaction involves purchases of inventory, office supplies, and store supplies from ITT. The journal has no column for store supplies, so the Other Accounts Dr. column is used. In this case, Store Supplies is entered in the Account column along with the creditor's name (ITT). This purchases journal also includes a separate column for credit purchases of office supplies. A separate column such as this is useful when several transactions involve debits to the same account. Each company uses its own judgment in deciding on the number of separate columns necessary. The Other Accounts Dr. column allows the purchases journal to be used for any purchase transaction on credit.

Point: The number of special journals and the design of each are based on a company's special needs.

Point: Each transaction in the purchases journal involves a credit to Accounts Payable.

Posting

The amounts in the Accounts Payable Cr. column are regularly (daily) posted to individual creditor accounts in the accounts payable subsidiary ledger. Each line of the Account column in Exhibit 8.9 shows the subsidiary ledger account that is posted for amounts in the Accounts Payable Cr. column. Individual amounts in the Other Accounts Dr. column usually are regularly (daily) posted to their general ledger accounts. At the end of the period (month), all column totals except the Other Accounts Dr. column are posted to their general ledger accounts. The balance in the Accounts Payable controlling account must equal the sum of the individual account balances in the accounts payable subsidiary ledger after posting.

Exhibit 8.9

Purchases Journal with Posting*

*Purchases Journal in a *periodic* system replaces "Inventory Dr." with "Purchases Dr." (see Exhibit 8A.3).

Exhibit 8.10

Schedule of Accounts Payable

Schedule of Accounts Payable February 28	
Ace Mfg. Company	$ 300
Horning Supply Company	350
ITT Company	225
Smite Company	300
Wynet & Company.	150
Total accounts payable	$1,325

Proving the Ledger

Account balances in the general ledger and its subsidiary ledgers are proved for accuracy after posting the purchases journal. Similar to proving the ledger for the sales journal, two steps are necessary. First, we prepare a trial balance of the general ledger to confirm debits equal credits. If debits equal credits in the trial balance, the accounts in the general ledger, including the controlling accounts, are assumed to be correct. Second, we prove the subsidiary ledger by preparing a **schedule of accounts payable,** which is a list of accounts from the accounts payable ledger with their balances and the total. If this total equals the balance of the Accounts Payable controlling account, the accounts in the accounts payable ledger are considered correct. Exhibit 8.10 shows a schedule of accounts payable drawn from the accounts payable ledger of Exhibit 8.9.

Cash Disbursements Journal

A **cash disbursements journal,** also called a *cash payments journal,* is used to record all payments of cash. It is set up as a columnar journal because cash payments are made for several different purposes.

Journalizing

The cash disbursements journal shown in Exhibit 8.11 records repetitive cash payments. Note the repetitive credits to the Cash column of this journal. Also note the frequent credits to Inventory (reflecting purchase discounts) and the debits to Accounts Payable. For

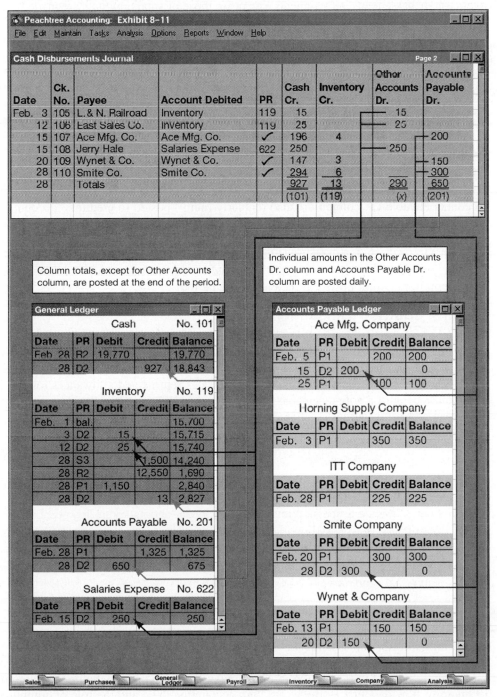

Exhibit 8.11

Cash Disbursements Journal with Posting*

*The Cash Disbursements Journal in a *periodic* system replaces "Inventory Cr." with "Purchases Discounts Cr." (see Exhibit 8A.4).

Point: Each transaction in the cash disbursements journal involves a credit to Cash.

example, on February 15, the company pays Ace on account (credit terms of 2/10, n/30—see February 5 transaction in Exhibit 8.9). Since payment occurs in the discount period, the company pays $196 ($200 invoice less $4 discount). The $4 discount is credited to Inventory. Many companies purchase inventory for cash and, therefore, an Inventory column is not usually included. Instead, the cash purchases of inventory are recorded using the Other Accounts Dr. column and the Cash Cr. column as illustrated in the February 3 and 12 transactions. Generally, the Other Accounts column is used to record cash payments on items for which no column exists. For example, on February 15, the company pays salaries expense of $250. In these cases, the title of the account debited (such as Inventory or Salaries Expense) is entered in the Account Debited column.

The cash disbursements journal has a column titled Ck. No. (check number). For control over cash disbursements, all payments except for those of small amounts are made by check. Checks should be prenumbered and each check's number entered in the journal in numerical order in the column headed Ck. No. This makes it possible to scan the numbers in the column for omitted checks. When a cash disbursements journal has a column for check numbers, it is sometimes called a **check register.**

You Make the Call

Controller You wish to analyze your company's cash payments to suppliers and its purchases discounts. Where might you find this information?

Answer—p. 330

Posting

Individual amounts in the Other Accounts Dr. column of a cash disbursements journal are posted to their general ledger accounts on a regular (daily) basis. Individual amounts in the Accounts Payable Dr. column are also regularly (daily) posted to creditors' accounts in the subsidiary Accounts Payable ledger. At the end of the period (month), we crossfoot column totals and post the Accounts Payable Dr. column total to the Accounts Payable controlling account. Also at the end of the period, the Inventory Cr. column total is posted to the Inventory account, and the Cash Cr. column total is posted to the Cash account. The Other Accounts Dr. column total is not posted at the end of the period.

General Journal Transactions

When special journals are used, we still need a general journal for adjusting, closing, and correcting entries and for any other transactions not recorded in special journals. Examples of these other transactions include purchases returns and allowances, purchases of plant assets by issuing a note payable, sales returns if a sales returns and allowances journal is not used, and receipt of a note receivable from a customer. We described the recording of transactions in a general journal in Chapters 3 and 4.

Quick Check

10. What are the normal recording and posting procedures when using special journals and controlling accounts with their subsidiary ledgers?

11. What is the rule for posting to a subsidiary ledger and its controlling account?

12. How do we prove the accuracy of account balances in the general ledger and subsidiary ledgers after posting?

13. Why does a company need a general journal when using special journals for sales, purchases, cash receipts, and cash disbursements?

Answers—p. 331

Technology-Based Accounting Systems

Accounting information systems are supported with technology, which can range from simple calculators to state-of-the-art advanced electronic systems. Because technology is increasingly important in accounting information systems, we discuss the impact of computer technology, how data processing works with accounting data, and the role of computer networks.

Computer Technology in Accounting

Computer technology can be separated into two categories, hardware and software. **Computer hardware** is the physical equipment in a computerized accounting information system. The physical equipment includes processing units, hard drives, RAM, modems, CD-ROM drives, monitors, workstations, servers, printers, and scanners. **Computer software**

comprises the programs that direct the operations of computer hardware. A program can be written, for instance, to process customers' merchandise orders. Computer technology provides accuracy, speed, efficiency, and convenience in performing accounting tasks.

Widespread use of computer technology has increased the range and power of off-the-shelf programs, which include multipurpose soft-

| C5 | Explain how technology-based information systems impact accounting. |

Did You Know?

Middleware Middleware is software allowing different computer programs in a company or across companies to work together. It allows transfer of purchase orders, invoices, and other electronic documents between accounting systems. It also helps a bank handle a company's electronic payments.

ware applications for a variety of operations. These include familiar word processing programs such as Word® and WordPerfect®, spreadsheet programs such as Excel®, and database management programs. Other off-the-shelf programs meet the needs of specialized users, including accounting programs such as PeachTree® and QuickBooks®. Off-the-shelf programs are designed to be user friendly and menu driven, and many operate more efficiently as *integrated* systems. In an integrated system, actions taken in one part of the system automatically affect related parts. When a credit sale is recorded in an integrated system, for instance, several parts of the system are automatically updated.

Computer technology can dramatically reduce the time and effort devoted to recordkeeping tasks. Less effort spent on recordkeeping tasks means more time for accounting professionals to concentrate on analysis and managerial decision making. These advances have created a greater demand for accounting professionals who understand financial reports and can draw insights and information from mountains of processed data. Accounting

professionals have expertise in determining relevant and reliable information for decision making. They also can assess the effects of transactions and events on a company and its financial statements.

Knowledge of the accounting described in this book enables us to understand and use accounting output. It also enables us to understand the transactions and events driving the output. In this way—and only in this way—can we expect to reap the full benefits of accounting reports. All the reports available can-

Did You Know?

Accounting Tools A new generation of Windows- and Web-based accounting support is available. With the touch of a key, users can create real-time inventory reports showing all payments, charges, and credit limits at any point in the accounting cycle. Many also include "alert signals" notifying the user when, for example, a large order exceeds a customer's credit limit or when purchase orders need to be placed. These tools also support perpetual updating of records.

not help the external or internal user who fails to understand the accounting principles and methods determining the information.

Data Processing in Accounting

Accounting systems differ as to how input is entered and processed. **Online processing** enters and processes data as soon as source documents are available. This means databases are immediately updated. **Batch processing** accumulates source documents for a period of time and then processes them all at once daily, weekly, or monthly. The advantage of online processing is up-to-date databases. This often requires additional costs related to both software and hardware requirements. Companies such as **NetLedger** are making online processing of accounting data a reality for many businesses. The advantage of batch processing is that it requires only periodic updating of databases. Records used to send bills to customers, for instance, might require updating only once a month. The disadvantage of batch processing is the lack of updated databases for management to use when making business decisions.

Computer Networks in Accounting

Networking, or linking computers with each other, can create information advantages. **Computer networks** are links among computers giving different users and different computers access to common databases and programs. Many college computer labs, for instance, are networked. A small computer network is called a *local area network (LAN)*; it links machines with *hard-wire* hookups. Large computer networks extending over long distances often rely on *modem* or *wireless* communication.

Demand for information sometimes requires advanced networks such as the system **Federal Express** uses to track packages and bill customers and the system **Wal-Mart** uses to monitor inventory levels in its stores. These networks include many computers and satellite communications to gather information and to provide ready access to its databases from all locations.

Enterprise Resource Planning Software

Enterprise resource planning (or *ERP*) **software** includes the programs that manage a company's vital operations. They extend from order taking to manufacturing to accounting. When working properly, these integrated programs can speed decision making, slash costs, and give managers control over operations with the click of a mouse. For many managers, ERP software is like a lightbulb illuminating the dark recesses of their company's operations. It allows them to scrutinize business, identify where inventories are piling up, and see what plants are most efficient. The software is designed to link every part of a company's operations. This software allowed **Monsanto** to slash production planning from six weeks to three, trim its inventories, and increase its bargaining power with suppliers. Monsanto estimates that this software saves the company $200 million per year.

ERP has six major suppliers. **SAP** leads the market, with **Oracle** a distant second. SAP software runs the back offices of nearly half of the world's 500 largest companies. It links ordering, inventory, production, purchasing, planning, tracking, and human resources. One transaction or event triggers an immediate chain reaction of events throughout the enterprise. It is making companies more efficient and profitable.

ERP is pushing into cyberspace. Now companies can share data with customers and suppliers. Applesauce maker **Mott**'s is using SAP so that distributors can check the status of orders and place them over the Net, and the

Total ERP Market: About $10 Billion

Other 34% / SAP 33% / Oracle 10% / J.D. Edwards 7% / Peoplesoft 6% / Baan 5% / SSA 5%

Coca-Cola Company uses it to ship soda on time. ERP is also invading small business. For example, **NetLedger**'s accounting services to small and medium businesses are powered by Oracle's system.

Business Segments

The accounting information system is usually more complex when a company is large and operates in more than one business segment. Special journals and subsidiary ledgers also are usually greater in number and more detailed for these companies. A **business segment** is the part of a company that is separately identified by its products or services or by the geographic market it serves. **Nike**, for instance, reports that it operates in four main geographical markets: United States, Europe, Asia/Pacific, and Latin America/Canada. External users of financial statements are especially interested in segment information to better understand a company's business activities.

Information reported about business segments varies in quality and quantity. The full disclosure principle implies that we ought to see detailed financial statements for each important segment. Full disclosure by segments is rare, however, because of difficulties in separating segments and management's reluctance to release information that can harm its competitive position.

Companies offering their shares to the public in U.S. stock exchanges must disclose segment information under certain conditions. Accounting standards apply the definition of segments to industries, international activities, export sales, and major customers. Companies are required to report certain information for these segments, including sales, operating income, identifiable assets, capital expenditures, depreciation, depletion, and amortization. Exhibit 8.12 shows results from a recent survey on the number of companies with different business segments. Companies often have different rates of profitability, risk, and growth for different segments. Evaluating risk and return is a major goal of decision makers, and segment information is useful in this evaluation.

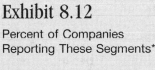

A1 Analyze a company's performance and financial condition by business segments.

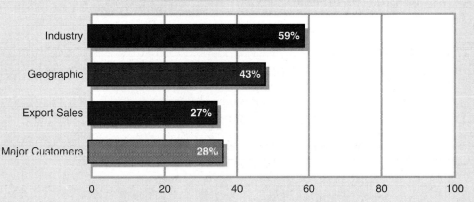

*Total exceeds 100% because companies can report one or more types of segments.

Exhibit 8.12

Percent of Companies Reporting These Segments*

Analysis of a company's segments is aided by a **segment contribution matrix,** which is a table listing one or more important measures (such as sales) by segments. This list usually includes amounts both in dollars and percents and its growth rate. Such analysis helps answer several questions: What is the contribution of one segment versus another? What is the highest growth segment? And which is the lowest? We prepare a segment contribution matrix for **Harley-Davidson**'s sales in Exhibit 8.13.

The second and third columns in Exhibit 8.13 list sales data by geographical segment. These data are drawn from Harley's annual report. We see that its sales are divided into five major segments: U.S., Canada, Germany, Japan, and Other. Columns four and five of Exhibit 8.13 reveal sales contribution *in percent* by segment. Each number is computed by dividing segment sales by total sales. For example, the 1999 sales contribution in percent for the United States is computed as follows: $1,916 ÷ $2,453 = 0.78, or 78%. The results

Point: Segment information can be used in evaluating a company's decision to spin off a segment.

Point: If a company has two segments, and each sells three products in four geographic regions, how many sales accounts are needed to analyze each product in each region? *Answer:* 2 × 3 × 4 = 24 accounts.

Exhibit 8.13

Segment Contribution Matrix for Harley-Davidson

| Sales ($ in 000s) | Sales Contribution (in $ and %) | | | | One-Year Sales Growth Rate |
	1999	1998	1999	1998	
United States	$1,916	$1,567	78%	76%	22%
Canada	80	74	3	4	8
Germany	89	84	4	4	6
Japan	135	102	6	5	32
Other	233	237	9	11	−2
Totals	$2,453	$2,064	100%	100%	19

Point: Software enables us to access electronically stored data and present them in graphical formats such as pie and bar graphs.

show that the United States accounts for nearly 80% of total sales. This shows Harley's sales depend highly on the U.S. market. Analysis of Harley demands special attention to assess future U.S. prospects and the risk of competition in the United States. The far right column of Exhibit 8.13 shows the one-year growth rate in segment sales. A one-year growth rate is computed as follows: (Current period sales ÷ Prior period sales) − 1.0. For example, Harley's one-year growth rate for sales in Japan is computed as follows: ($135 ÷ $102) − 1.0 = 0.32, or 32%. These growth rates reveal that Japan is growing faster than any other segment, followed by the U.S., Canada, and Germany.

We can extend analysis of segment contribution matrixes to other measures such as operating income and assets and to other segments (such as by industry or by Harley vs. Buell motorcycles).

You Make the Call

Banker   A bicycle merchandiser requests a loan from you to expand operations. The owner's financials reveal a solid net income of $220,000, reflecting a 10% increase over the prior year. You ask about any geographic focus. The owner reports that $160,000 of net income is from Cuban operations, reflecting a 60% increase over the prior year. The remaining $60,000 of net income is from U.S. operations, reflecting a 40% decrease. The owner, a Cuban immigrant, tells you of his many business relationships in Cuba. Does this segment information impact your loan decision?

Answer—p. 330

Demonstration Problem— Perpetual System

Pepper Company completes the following transactions and events during March of this year. (Terms of all credit sales are 2/10, n/30.)

Mar. 4   Sold merchandise on credit to Jennifer Nelson, Invoice No. 954, for $16,800 (cost is $12,200).

6   Purchased $1,220 of office supplies on credit from Mack Company. Invoice dated March 3, terms n/30.

6   Sold merchandise on credit to Dennie Hoskins, Invoice No. 955, for $10,200 (cost is $8,100).

11   Received $52,600 of merchandise and an invoice dated March 6, terms 2/10, n/30, from Defore Industries.

12   Borrowed $26,000 cash by giving Commerce Bank a long-term promissory note payable.

14   Received cash payment from Jennifer Nelson for the March 4 sale less the discount.

16   Received a $200 credit memorandum from Defore Industries for unsatisfactory merchandise received on March 11 and returned for credit.

16   Received cash payment from Dennie Hoskins for the March 6 sale less the discount.

18   Purchased $22,850 of store equipment on credit from Schmidt Supply, invoice dated March 15, terms n/30.

20   Sold merchandise on credit to Marjorie Allen, Invoice No. 956, for $5,600 (cost is $3,800).

21   Sent Defore Industries Check No. 516 in payment of its March 6 dated invoice less the returns and the discount.

22   Received $41,625 of merchandise and an invoice dated March 18, terms 2/10, n/30, from Welch Company.

26   Issued a $600 credit memorandum to Marjorie Allen for defective merchandise sold on March 20 and returned for credit.

31   Issued Check No. 517, payable to Payroll, in payment of $15,900 sales salaries for the month. Cashed the check and paid the employees.

31   Cash sales for the month are $134,680 (cost is $67,340). (Cash sales are recorded daily but are recorded only once here to reduce repetitive entries.)

Required

1. Open the following general ledger accounts: Cash (101), Accounts Receivable (106) Inventory (119), Office Supplies (124), Store Equipment (165), Accounts Payable (201), Long-Term Notes Payable (251), Sales (413), Sales Returns and Allowances (414), Sales Discounts (415), Cost of Goods Sold (502), and Sales Salaries Expense (621). Open the following accounts receivable ledger accounts: Marjorie Allen, Dennie Hoskins, and Jennifer Nelson. Open the following accounts payable ledger accounts: Defore Industries, Mack Company, Schmidt Supply, and Welch Company.

2. Enter the transactions using a sales journal, a purchases journal, a cash receipts journal, a cash disbursements journal, and a general journal similar to the ones illustrated in the chapter. Regularly post to the individual customer and creditor accounts. Also, post any amounts that should be posted as individual amounts to general ledger accounts. Foot and crossfoot the journals and make the month-end postings. *Pepper Co. uses the perpetual inventory system.*

3. Prepare a trial balance and prove the accuracy of subsidiary ledgers by preparing schedules of accounts receivable and accounts payable.

Planning the Solution

* Set up the required general ledger, the subsidiary ledger accounts, and the five required journals as illustrated in the chapter.

* Read and analyze each transaction and decide in which special journal (or general journal) the transaction is recorded.

* Record each transaction in the proper journal (and post the appropriate individual amounts).

* Once you have recorded all transactions, total the journal columns. Post from each journal to the appropriate ledger accounts.

* Prepare a trial balance to prove the equality of the debit and credit balances in your general ledger.

* Prepare schedules of accounts receivable and accounts payable. Compare the totals of these schedules to the Accounts Receivable and Accounts Payable controlling account balances, making sure that they agree.

Solution to Demonstration Problem—Perpetual System

		Sales Journal			**Page 2**
Date	**Account Debited**	**Invoice Number**	**PR**	**Accts. Rec. Dr. Sales Cr.**	**Cost of Goods Sold Dr. Inventory Cr.**
Mar. 4	Jennifer Nelson. . . .	954	✓	16,800	12,200
6	Dennie Hoskins. . . .	955	✓	10,200	8,100
20	Marjorie Allen	956	✓	5,600	3,800
31	Totals.			32,600	24,100
				(106/413)	(502/119)

Cash Receipts Journal — Page 3

Date	Account Credited	Explanation	PR	Cash Debit	Sales Discount Debit	Accts. Rec. Credit	Sales Credit	Other Accts. Credit	Cost of Good Sold Dr. Inventory Cr.
Mar. 12	L.T. Notes Payable..	Note to bank	251	26,000				26,000	
14	Jennifer Nelson	Invoice, 3/4	✓	16,464	336	16,800			
16	Dennie Hoskins	Invoice, 3/6	✓	9,996	204	10,200			
31	Sales	Cash sales	x	134,680			134,680		67,340
31	Totals			187,140	540	27,000	134,680	26,000	67,340
				(101)	(415)	(106)	(413)	(x)	(502/119)

Purchases Journal — Page 3

Date	Account	Date of Invoice	Terms	PR	Accts. Payable Credit	Inventory Debit	Office Supplies Debit	Other Accts. Debit
Mar. 6	Office Supplies/Mack Co..............	3/3	n/30	✓	1,220		1,220	
11	Defore Industries..................	3/6	2/10, n/30	✓	52,600	52,600		
18	Store Equipment/Schmidt Supp	3/15	n/30	165/✓	22,850			22,850
22	Welch Company	3/18	2/10, n/30	✓	41,625	41,625		
31	Totals.............................				118,295	94,225	1,220	22,850
					(201)	(119)	(124)	(x)

Cash Disbursements Journal — Page 3

Date	Ck. No.	Payee	Account Debited	PR	Cash Credit	Inventory Credit	Other Accts. Debit	Accts. Payable Debit
Mar. 21	516	Defore Industries	Defore Industries	✓	51,352	1,048		52,400
31	517	Payroll	Sales Salaries Expense	621	15,900		15,900	
31		Totals			67,252	1,048	15,900	52,400
					(101)	(119)	(x)	(201)

General Journal — Page 2

Date				
Mar. 16	Accounts Payable—Defore Industries	201/✓	200	
	Inventory	119		200
	To record credit memorandum received.			
26	Sales Returns and Allowances	414	600	
	Accounts Receivable—Marjorie Allen	106/✓		600
	To record credit memorandum issued.			

Accounts Receivable Ledger

Marjorie Allen

Date	PR	Debit	Credit	Balance
Mar. 20	S2	5,600		5,600
26	G2		600	5,000

Dennie Hoskins

Date	PR	Debit	Credit	Balance
Mar. 6	S2	10,200		10,200
16	R3		10,200	0

Jennifer Nelson

Date	PR	Debit	Credit	Balance
Mar. 4	S2	16,800		16,800
14	R3		10,000	0

Accounts Payable Ledger

Defore Industries

Date	PR	Debit	Credit	Balance
Mar. 11	P3		52,600	52,600
16	G2	200		52,400
21	D3	52,400		0

Mack Company

Date	PR	Debit	Credit	Balance
Mar. 6	P3		1,220	1,220

Schmidt Supply

Date	PR	Debit	Credit	Balance
Mar. 18	P3		22,850	22,850

Welch Company

Date	PR	Debit	Credit	Balance
Mar. 22	P3		41,625	41,625

General Ledger

Cash   Acct. No. 101

Date	PR	Debit	Credit	Balance
Mar. 31	R3	187,140		187,140
31	D4		67,252	119,888

Accounts Receivable   Acct. No. 106

Date	PR	Debit	Credit	Balance
Mar. 26	G2		600	(600)
31	S2	32,600		32,000
31	R3		27,000	5,000

Inventory   Acct. No. 119

Date	PR	Debit	Credit	Balance
Mar. 16	G2		200	(200)
21	D3		1,048	(1,248)
31	P3	94,225		92,977
31	S3		24,100	68,877
31	R3		67,340	1,537

Office Supplies   Acct. No. 124

Date	PR	Debit	Credit	Balance
Mar. 31	P3	1,220		1,220

Store Equipment   Acct. No. 165

Date	PR	Debit	Credit	Balance
Mar. 18	P3	22,850		22,850

Accounts Payable   Acct. No. 201

Date	PR	Debit	Credit	Balance
Mar. 6	G2	200		(200)
31	P3		118,295	118,095
31	D3	52,400		65,695

Long-Term Notes Payable   Acct. No. 251

Date	PR	Debit	Credit	Balance
Mar. 12			26,000	26,000

Sales   Acct. No. 413

Date	PR	Debit	Credit	Balance
Mar. 31	S2		32,600	32,600
31	R3		134,680	167,280

Sales Returns and Allowances   Acct. No. 414

Date	PR	Debit	Credit	Balance
Mar. 26	G2	600		600

Sales Discounts   Acct. No. 415

Date	PR	Debit	Credit	Balance
Mar. 31	R3	540		540

Cost of Good Sold   Acct. No. 502

Date	PR	Debit	Credit	Balance
Mar. 31	R3	67,340		67,340
31	S2	24,100		91,440

Sales Salaries Expense   Acct. No. 621

Date	PR	Debit	Credit	Balance
Mar. 31	D3	15,900		15,900

PEPPER COMPANY Trial Balance March 31		
	Debit	Credit
Cash	$119,888	
Accounts receivable	5,000	
Inventory	1,537	
Office supplies	1,220	
Store equipment	22,850	
Accounts payable		$ 65,695
Long-term notes payable		26,000
Sales		167,280
Sales returns and allowances	600	
Sales discounts	540	
Cost of goods sold	91,440	
Sales salaries expense	15,900	
Totals	$258,975	$258,975

PEPPER COMPANY Schedule of Accounts Receivable March 31	
Marjorie Allen	$5,000
Total accounts receivable	$5,000

PEPPER COMPANY Schedule of Accounts Payable March 31	
Mack Company	$ 1,220
Schmidt Supply	22,850
Welch Company	41,625
Total accounts payable	$65,695

APPENDIX

8A

Special Journals under a Periodic System

P3 Journalize and post transactions using special journals in a periodic inventory system.

This appendix describes special journals under a periodic inventory system. Each journal is slightly impacted. The sales journal and the cash receipts journal both require one less column (namely that of Cost of Goods Sold Dr., Inventory Cr.). The Purchases Journal replaces the Inventory Dr. column with a Purchases Dr. column in a periodic system. The cash disbursements journal replaces the Inventory Cr. column with a Purchases Discounts Cr. column in a periodic system. These changes are illustrated.

Sales Journal

The sales journal using the periodic inventory system is shown in Exhibit 8A.1. The difference in the sales journal between the perpetual and periodic system is the exclusion of the column to record cost of goods sold and inventory amounts for each sale. The periodic system does *not* record the increase in cost of goods sold and the decrease in inventory at the time of sale.

Sales Journal				Page 3
Date	Account Debited	Invoice Number	PR	Accounts Receivable Dr. Sales Cr.
Feb. 2	Jason Henry	307	✓	450
7	Albert Co.	308	✓	500
13	Bam Moore	309	✓	350
15	Paul Roth	310	✓	200
22	Jason Henry	311	✓	225
25	Frank Booth	312	✓	175
28	Albert Co.	313	✓	250
28	Total			2,150
				(106/413)

Exhibit 8A.1

Sales Journal— Periodic System

Cash Receipts Journal

The cash receipts journal under the periodic system is shown in Exhibit 8A.2. Note the absence of the column on the far right side to record debits to Cost of Goods Sold and credits to Inventory for the cost of merchandise sold (that we see under the perpetual system). Consistent with the cash receipts journal shown in the chapter, we show only the weekly (summary) cash sale entries.

Exhibit 8A.2

Cash Receipts Journal— Periodic System

Cash Receipts Journal								Page 2
Date	Account Credited	Explanation	PR	Cash Dr.	Sales Discount Dr.	Accounts Receivable Cr.	Sales Cr.	Other Accounts Cr.
Feb. 7	Sales	Cash Sales	x	4,450			4,450	
12	Jason Henry	Invoice, 2/2	✓	441	9	450		
14	Sales	Cash sales	x	3,925			3,925	
17	Albert Co.	Invoice, 2/7	✓	490	10	500		
20	Notes Payable	Note to bank	245	750				750
21	Sales	Cash sales	x	4,700			4,700	
22	Interest revenue	Bank account	409	250				250
23	Bam Moore	Invoice, 2/13	✓	343	7	350		
25	Paul Roth	Invoice, 2/15	✓	196	4	200		
28	Sales	Cash sales	x	4,225			4,225	
28	Totals			19,770	30	1,500	17,300	1,000
				(101)	(415)	(106)	(413)	(x)

Purchases Journal

The purchases journal under the periodic system is shown in Exhibit 8A.3. This journal under a perpetual system included an Inventory column where the periodic system now has a Purchases column. All else is identical under the two systems.

Exhibit 8A.3

Purchases Journal—
Periodic System

					Accounts Payable Cr.	Purchases Dr.	Office Supplies Dr.	Other Accounts Dr.
Purchases Journal								**Page 1**
Date	**Account**	**Date of Invoice**	**Terms**	**PR**	**Accounts Payable Cr.**	**Purchases Dr.**	**Office Supplies Dr.**	**Other Accounts Dr.**
Feb. 3	Horning Supply Co.	2/2	n/30	✓	350	275	75	
5	Ace Mfg. Co.	2/5	2/10, n/30	✓	200	200		
13	Wynet and Co.	2/10	2/10, n/30	✓	150	150		
20	Smite Co.	2/18	2/10, n/30	✓	300	300		
25	Ace Mfg. Co.	2/24	2/10, n/30	✓	100	100		
28	Store Supplies/ITT Co.	2/28	n/30	125/✓	225	125	25	75
28	Totals				1,325	1,150	100	75
					(201)	(505)	(124)	(x)

Cash Disbursements Journal

The cash disbursements journal under a periodic system is shown in Exhibit 8A.4. This journal under the perpetual system included an Inventory column where the periodic system now has the Purchases Discounts column. All else is identical under the two systems.

Exhibit 8A.4

Cash Disbursements
Journal—Periodic System

						Purchases Discounts Cr.	Other Accounts Dr.	Accounts Payable Dr.
Cash Disbursements Journal								**Page 2**
Date	**Ck. No.**	**Payee**	**Account Debited**	**PR**	**Cash Cr.**	**Purchases Discounts Cr.**	**Other Accounts Dr.**	**Accounts Payable Dr.**
Feb. 3	105	L. and N. Railroad	Purchases	505	15		15	
12	106	East Sales Co.	Purchases	505	25		25	
15	107	Ace Mfg. Co.	Ace Mfg. Co.	✓	196	4		200
15	108	Jerry Hale	Salaries Expense	622	250		250	
20	109	Wynet and Co.	Wynet and Co.	✓	147	3		150
28	110	Smite Co.	Smite Co.	✓	294	6		300
28		Totals			927	13	290	650
					(101)	(507)	(x)	(201)

Demonstration Problem— Periodic System

Refer to Pepper Company transactions described under the Demonstration Problem—Perpetual System to fulfill the following requirements.

Required

1. Open the following general ledger accounts: Cash (101), Accounts Receivable (106), Office Supplies (124), Store Equipment (165), Accounts Payable (201), Long-Term Notes Payable (251), Sales (413), Sales Returns and Allowances (414), Sales Discounts (415), Purchases (505), Purchases Returns and Allowances (506), Purchases Discounts (507), and Sales Salaries Expense (621). Open the following accounts receivable ledger accounts: Marjorie Allen, Dennie Hoskins,

and Jennifer Nelson. Open the following accounts payable ledger accounts: Defore Industries, Mack Company, Schmidt Supply, and Welch Company.

2. Enter the transactions using a sales journal, a purchases journal, a cash receipts journal, a cash disbursements journal, and a general journal similar to the ones illustrated in Appendix 8A. Regularly post to the individual customer and creditor accounts. Also, post any amounts that should be posted as individual amounts to general ledger accounts. Foot and crossfoot the journals and make the month-end postings. *Pepper Co. uses the periodic inventory system in this problem.*

3. Prepare a trial balance and prove the accuracy of subsidiary ledgers by preparing schedules of accounts receivable and accounts payable.

Solution to Demonstration Problem—Periodic System

Sales Journal — Page 2

Date	Account Debited	Invoice Number	PR	Accts. Rec. Dr. Sales Cr.
Mar. 4	Jennifer Nelson	954	✓	16,800
6	Dennie Hoskins	955	✓	10,200
20	Marjorie Allen	956	✓	5,600
31	Totals			32,600
				(106/413)

Cash Receipts Journal — Page 3

Date	Account Credited	Explanation	PR	Cash Debit	Sales Discount Debit	Accts. Rec. Credit	Sales Credit	Other Accts. Credit
Mar. 12	L.T. Notes Payable	Note to bank	251	26,000				26,000
14	Jennifer Nelson	Invoice, 3/4	✓	16,464	336	16,800		
16	Dennie Hoskins	Invoice, 3/6	✓	9,996	204	10,200		
31	Sales	Cash sales	x	134,680			134,680	
31	Totals			187,140	540	27,000	134,680	26,000
				(101)	(415)	(106)	(413)	(x)

Purchases Journal — Page 3

Date	Account	Date of Invoice	Terms	PR	Accts. Payable Credit	Purchases Debit	Office Supplies Debit	Other Accts. Debit
Mar. 6	Office Supplies/Mack Co	3/3	n/30	✓	1,220		1,220	
11	Defore Industries	3/6	2/10, n/30	✓	52,600	52,600		
18	Store Equipment/Schmidt Supp	3/15	n/30	165/✓	22,850			22,850
22	Welch Company	3/18	2/10, n/30	✓	41,625	41,625		
31	Totals				118,295	94,225	1,220	22,850
					(201)	(505)	(124)	(x)

Cash Disbursements Journal — Page 3

Date	Ck. No.	Payee	Account Debited	PR	Cash Credit	Purch. Disc. Credit	Other. Accts. Debit	Accts. Payable Debit
Mar 21	516	Defore Industries	Defore Industries	✓	51,352	1,048		52,400
31	517	Payroll	Sales Salaries Expense	621	15,900		15,900	
31		Totals			67,252	1,048	15,900	52,400
					(101)	(507)	(x)	(201)

General Journal — Page 2

Mar. 16	Accounts Payable—Defore Industries	201/✓	200	
	Purchases Returns and Allowances	506		200
	To record credit memorandum received.			
	Sales Returns and Allowances	414	600	
	Accounts Receivable—Marjorie Allen	106/✓		600
	To record credit memorandum issued.			

Accounts Receivable Ledger

Marjorie Allen

Date	PR	Debit	Credit	Balance
Mar. 20	S2	5,600		5,600
26	G2		600	5,000

Dennie Hoskins

Date	PR	Debit	Credit	Balance
Mar. 6	S2	10,200		10,200
16	R3		10,200	0

Jennifer Nelson

Date	PR	Debit	Credit	Balance
Mar. 4	S2	16,800		16,800
14	R3		16,800	0

Accounts Payable Ledger

Defore Industries

Date	PR	Debit	Credit	Balance
Mar. 11	P3		52,600	52,600
16	G2	200		52,400
21	D3	52,400		0

Mack Company

Date	PR	Debit	Credit	Balance
Mar. 6	P3		1,220	1,220

Schmidt Supply

Date	PR	Debit	Credit	Balance
Mar. 18	P3		22,850	22,850

Welch Company

Date	PR	Debit	Credit	Balance
Mar. 22	P3		41,625	41,625

General Ledger

Cash   Acct. No. 101

Date	PR	Debit	Credit	Balance
Mar. 31	R3	187,140		187,140
31	D4		67,252	119,888

Accounts Receivable   Acct. No. 106

Date	PR	Debit	Credit	Balance
Mar. 26	G2		600	(600)
31	S2	32,600		32,000
31	R3		27,000	5,000

Office Supplies   Acct. No. 124

Date	PR	Debit	Credit	Balance
Mar. 31	P3	1,220		1,220

Store Equipment   Acct. No. 165

Date	PR	Debit	Credit	Balance
Mar. 18	P3	22,850		22,850

Accounts Payable   Acct. No. 201

Date	PR	Debit	Credit	Balance
Mar. 6	G2	200		(200)
31	P3		118,295	118,095
31	D3	52,400		65,695

Long-Term Notes Payable   Acct. No. 251

Date	PR	Debit	Credit	Balance
Mar. 12			26,000	26,000

Sales   Acct. No. 413

Date	PR	Debit	Credit	Balance
Mar. 31	S2		32,600	32,600
31	R3		134,680	167,280

Sales Returns and Allowances   Acct. No. 414

Date	PR	Debit	Credit	Balance
Mar. 26	G2	600		600

Sales Discounts   Acct. No. 415

Date	PR	Debit	Credit	Balance
Mar. 31	R3	540		540

Purchases   Acct. No. 505

Date	PR	Debit	Credit	Balance
Mar. 31	P3	94,225		94,225

Purchases Returns and Allowances   Acct. No. 506

Date	PR	Debit	Credit	Balance
Mar. 6	G2		200	200

Purchases Discounts   Acct. No. 507

Date	PR	Debit	Credit	Balance
Mar. 31	D3		1,048	1,048

Sales Salaries Expense   Acct. No. 621

Date	PR	Debit	Credit	Balance
Mar. 31	D3	15,900		15,900

PEPPER COMPANY
Trial Balance
March 31

	Debit	Credit
Cash	$119,888	
Accounts receivable	5,000	
Office supplies	1,220	
Store equipment	22,850	
Accounts payable		$ 65,695
Long-term notes payable		26,000
Sales		167,280
Sales returns and allowances	600	
Sales discounts	540	
Purchases	94,225	
Purchases returns and allowances		200
Purchases discounts		1,048
Sales salaries expense	15,900	
Totals	$260,223	$260,223

PEPPER COMPANY
Schedule of Accounts Receivable
March 31

Marjorie Allen	$5,000
Total accounts receivable	$5,000

PEPPER COMPANY
Schedule of Accounts Payable
March 31

Mack Company	$ 1,220
Schmidt Supply	22,850
Welch Company	41,625
Total accounts payable	$65,695

Summary

C1 **Identify fundamental principles of accounting information systems.** Accounting information systems are governed by five fundamental principles: control, relevance, compatibility, flexibility, and cost-benefit.

C2 **Identify components of accounting information systems.** The five basic components of an accounting information system are source documents, input devices, information processors, information storage, and output devices.

C3 **Explain the goals and uses of special journals.** Special journals are used for recording transactions of similar type, each meant to cover one kind of transaction. Four of the most common special journals are the sales journal, cash receipts journal, purchases journal, and cash disbursements journal. Special journals are efficient and cost-effective tools in the journalizing and posting processes, and they allow division of labor.

C4 **Describe the use of controlling accounts and subsidiary ledgers.** A general ledger keeps controlling accounts such as Accounts Receivable and Accounts Payable, but details on individual accounts making up the controlling account are kept in subsidiary ledgers (such as an accounts receivable ledger). The balance in a controlling account must equal the sum of its subsidiary account balances after posting is complete.

C5 **Explain how technology-based information systems impact accounting.** Technology-based information systems aim to increase the accuracy, speed, efficiency, and convenience of accounting procedures.

A1 **Analyze a company's performance and financial condition by business segments.** A business segment is a part of a company that is separately identified by its products or services or by the geographic market it serves. Analysis of a company's segments is aided by a segment contribution matrix listing one or more measures such as sales by segments.

P1 **Journalize and post transactions using special journals.** Each special journal is devoted to similar kinds of transactions. Transactions are journalized on one line of a special journal, with columns devoted to specific accounts, dates, names, posting references, explanations, and other necessary information. Posting is threefold: (1) individual amounts in the Other Accounts column are posted to their general ledger accounts on a regular (daily) basis, (2) individual amounts in a column whose total is *not* posted to a controlling account at the end of a period (month) are posted regularly (daily) to their general ledger accounts, and (3) total amounts for all columns except the Other Accounts column are posted at the end of a period (month) to their column's account title in the general ledger.

P2 **Prepare and prove the accuracy of subsidiary ledgers.** Account balances in the general ledger and its subsidiary ledgers are tested for accuracy after posting is complete. This procedure is twofold: (1) prepare a trial balance of the general ledger to confirm that debits equal credits and (2) prepare a schedule to confirm that the controlling account's balance equals the subsidiary ledger's balance.

P3 **Journalize and post transactions using special journals in a periodic inventory system.** Transactions are journalized and posted using special journals in a periodic system. The methods are similar to those in a perpetual system; the primary difference is that both cost of goods sold and inventory are not adjusted at the time of each sale. This usually results in the deletion (or renaming) of one or more columns devoted to these accounts in each special journal.

Guidance Answers to **You Make the Call**

Accountant The main issue is whether commissions have an actual or perceived impact on the integrity and objectivity of your advice. You probably should not accept a commission arrangement (the AICPA Code of Ethics prohibits it when you perform the audit or a review). In any event, you should tell the client of your commission arrangement. Also, you need to seriously examine the merits of agreeing to a commission arrangement when you are in a position to exploit it.

Entrepreneur The accounts receivable ledger has much of the information you need. It lists detailed information for each customer's account, including the amounts, dates for transactions, and dates of payments. It can be reorganized into an "aging schedule" to show how long customers wait before paying their bills. We describe an aging schedule in Chapter 10.

Controller Much of the information you need is in the accounts payable ledger. It contains information for each supplier, the amounts due, and when payments are made. This subsidiary ledger along with information on credit terms should enable you to conduct your analyses.

Banker This merchandiser's segment information is likely to greatly impact your loan decision. The risks associated with the company's two sources of net income are quite different. While net income is up by 10%, U.S. operations are performing poorly and Cuban operations are subject to many uncertainties. These uncertainties depend on political events, legal issues, business relationships, Cuban economic conditions, and a host of other risks. Overall, net income results suggested a low-risk loan opportunity, but the segment information reveals a high-risk situation.

Guidance Answers to **Quick Checks**

1. The five components are source documents, input devices, information processors, information storage, and output devices.

2. An information processor interprets, transforms, and summarizes the recorded accounting information so that it can be used in analysis, interpretation, and decision making.

3. Data saved in information storage are used to prepare periodic financial reports and special-purpose internal reports as well as source documentation for auditors.

4. All cash payments by check are recorded in the cash disbursements journal.

5. Columnar journals allow us to accumulate repetitive debits and credits and post them as column totals rather than as individual amounts from each entry.

6. The equality of debits and credits is kept within the general ledger. The subsidiary ledger keeps the customer's individual account and is used only for supplementary information.

7. An initial and the page number of the journal from which the amount was posted are entered in the PR column of the ledger account next to the amount.

8. A separate column for Sales Taxes Payable can be included in both the cash receipts journal and the sales journal.

9. This refers to a procedure of using copies of sales invoices as a sales journal. Each invoice total is posted directly to the customer's account. All invoices are totaled at month-end for posting to the general ledger accounts.

10. The normal recording and posting procedures are threefold. First, transactions are entered in a special journal column if applicable. Second, individual amounts are posted to the subsidiary ledger accounts. Third, column totals are posted to general ledger accounts.

11. Controlling accounts must be debited periodically for an amount or amounts equal to the sum of their respective debits in the subsidiary ledgers, and they must be credited periodically for an amount or amounts equal to the sum of their respective credits in the subsidiary ledgers.

12. Tests for accuracy of account balances in the general ledger and subsidiary ledgers are twofold. First, we prepare a trial balance of the general ledger to confirm that debits equal credits. Second, we prove the subsidiary ledgers by preparing schedules of accounts receivable and accounts payable.

13. The general journal is still needed for adjusting, closing, and correcting entries and for special transactions such as sales returns, purchases returns, and certain asset purchases.

14. Integrated systems can save time and minimize errors. This is so because actions taken in one part of the system automatically affect and update related parts.

15. Computer systems offer increased accuracy, speed, efficiency, and convenience.

16. Computer networks can create advantages by linking computers, giving different users and different computers access to common databases and programs.

Glossary

Accounting information system people, records, and methods that collect and process data from transactions and events, organize them in useful forms, and communicate results to decision makers. (p. 302).

Accounts payable ledger subsidiary ledger listing individual creditor (supplier) accounts. (p. 306).

Accounts receivable ledger subsidiary ledger listing individual customer accounts. (p. 306).

Batch processing approach that accumulates source documents for a period of time and then processes them all at once such as once a day, week, or month. (p. 317).

Business segment part of a company that can be separately identified by the products or services that it provides or by the geographic markets that it serves. (p. 319).

Cash disbursements journal special journal used to record all payments of cash; also called *cash payments journal*. (p. 315).

Cash receipts journal special journal used to record all receipts of cash. (p. 311).

Check register another name for a cash disbursements journal when the journal has a column for check numbers. (p. 316).

Columnar journal journal with more than one column. (p. 307).

Compatibility principle information system principle that requires an accounting system to conform with a company's activities, personnel, and structure. (p. 302).

Computer hardware physical equipment in a computerized accounting information system. (p. 317).

Computer network linkage giving different users and different computers access to common databases and programs. (p. 318).

Computer software programs that direct operations of computer hardware. (p. 317).

Controlling account general ledger account, the balance of which (after posting) equals the sum of the balances in its related subsidiary ledger. (p. 306).

Control principle information system principle that requires an accounting system to aid managers in controlling and monitoring business activities. (p. 302).

Cost-benefit principle information system principle that requires the benefits from an activity in an accounting system to outweigh the costs of that activity. (p. 303).

Enterprise resource planning (ERP) software programs that manage a company's vital operations, which range from order taking to manufacturing to accounting. (p. 318).

Flexibility principle information system principle that requires an accounting system be able to adapt to changes in the company, business, and needs of decision makers. (p. 302).

Information processor component of an accounting system that interprets, transforms, and summarizes information for use in analysis and reporting. (p. 304).

Information storage component of an accounting system that keeps data in a form accessible to information processors. (p. 304).

Input device means of capturing information from source documents that enables its transfer to information processors. (p. 303).

Online processing approach to inputting data from source documents as soon as a document is available. (p. 317).

Output devices means by which information is taken out of the accounting system and made available for use. (p. 304).

Purchases journal journal used to record all purchases on credit. (p. 313).

Relevance principle information system principle requiring that its reports be useful, understandable, timely, and pertinent for decision making. (p. 302).

Sales journal journal used to record sales of merchandise on credit. (p. 307).

Schedule of accounts payable list of the balances of all accounts in the accounts payable ledger and their total. (p. 314).

Schedule of accounts receivable list of balances for all accounts in the accounts receivable ledger and their total. (p. 309).

Segment contribution matrix list of one or more measures (such as sales) by seg-

ment; usually in dollars and percents along with a growth rate. (p. 319).

Special journal any journal used for recording and posting transactions of a similar type. (p. 305).

Subsidiary ledger list of individual accounts with a common characteristic; linked to a controlling account in the general ledger. (p. 306).

[A superscript ^{A} denotes assignments based on Appendix 8A.]

Questions

1. What are the five fundamental principles of accounting information systems?

2. What are five basic components of an accounting system?

3. What are source documents? Give two examples.

4. What is the purpose of an input device? Give examples of input devices for computer systems.

5. What is the difference between data that are stored off-line and data that are stored online?

6. What purpose is served by the output devices of an accounting system?

7. When special journals are used, they are usually used to record each of four different types of transactions. What are these four common types of transactions?

8. What notations are entered into the Posting Reference column of a ledger account?

9. When a general journal entry is used to record a returned credit sale, the credit of the entry must be posted twice. Does this cause the trial balance to be out of balance? Explain.

10. Describe the procedures involving the use of copies of a company's sales invoices as a sales journal.

11. Credits to customer accounts and credits to other Accounts are individually posted from a cash receipts journal such as the one in Exhibit 8.7. Why not put both types of credits in the same column and save journal space?

12. Why should sales to and receipts of cash from credit customers be recorded and posted daily?

13. Locate the note that discusses **Nike**'s operations by major product lines in Appendix A. In what product line does Nike predominantly operate?

14. Does the income statement of **Reebok** in Appendix A indicate the net income earned by Reebok's business segments? If so, list them.

15. Does the balance sheet of **Gap** in Appendix A indicate the identifiable assets owned by Gap's business segments? If so, list them.

QUICK STUDY

QS 8-1

Accounting information system principles

Place the letter of each systems principle in the blank next to its best description.

A. Control principle   **D.** Flexibility principle

B. Relevance principle   **E.** Cost-benefit principle

C. Compatibility principle

1. _____ The principle requiring the accounting information system to change in response to technological advances and competitive pressures.

2. _____ The principle requiring the accounting information system to help monitor activities.

3. _____ The principle requiring the accounting information system to provide timely information for effective decision making.

4. _____ The principle requiring the accounting information system to adapt to the unique characteristics of the company.

5. _____ The principle that affects all other accounting information system principles.

Fill in the blanks to complete the following descriptions:

1. With _____ processing, source documents are accumulated for a period of time and then processed all at the same time, such as once a day, week, or month.

2. A computer _____ allows different computer users to share access to data and programs.

3. A _____ is an input device that captures writing and other input directly from source documents.

4. _____ _____ _____ software comprises programs that help manage a company's vital operations, from manufacturing to accounting.

QS 8-2
Accounting information system

C2

Identify the most likely role in an accounting system played by each of the lettered items A through L by assigning a number from the list on the left:

1. Source documents

2. Input devices

3. Information processor

4. Information storage

5. Output devices

_____ **A.** Bar code reader

_____ **B.** Filing cabinet

_____ **C.** Bank statement

_____ **D.** Computer scanner

_____ **E.** Computer keyboard

_____ **F.** Zip disc

_____ **G.** Computer monitor

_____ **H.** Invoice from a supplier

_____ **I.** Computer software

_____ **J.** Computer printer

_____ **K.** Digital camera

_____ **L.** MP3 player

QS 8-3
Accounting information system components

C2

Randa Electronics uses a sales journal, a purchases journal, a cash receipts journal, a cash disbursements journal, and a general journal. Randa recently completed the following transactions _a_ through _h_. Identify the journal in which each transaction should be recorded.

a. Paid a creditor.

b. Sold merchandise on credit.

c. Purchased shop supplies on credit.

d. Paid an employee's salary.

e. Borrowed money from the bank.

f. Sold merchandise for cash.

g. Purchased merchandise on credit.

h. Purchased inventory for cash.

QS 8-4
Special journal identification

Buy-The-Book Shop uses a sales journal, a purchases journal, a cash receipts journal, a cash disbursements journal, and a general journal. The following transactions occurred during November. Journalize the November transactions that should be recorded in the general journal.

Nov. 2   Purchased $2,600 of merchandise on credit from the Everly Co., terms 2/10, n/30.

     12   The owner, N. Falco, contributed an automobile worth $17,000 to the business.

     16   Sold $1,200 of merchandise on credit to G. Paltrow, terms n/30.

     19   G. Paltrow returned $175 of (worthless) merchandise originally purchased on November 16.

QS 8-5
Entries in the general journal

C3

Flex is a company with publicly traded securities that operates in more than one industry. Which of the following items of information about each industry segment must the company report?

1. Operating income.

2. Revenues

3. Operating expenses

4. Net sales

5. Cash flows

6. Capital expenditures

7. Identifiable assets

8. Amortization and depreciation

QS 8-6
Required segment reporting

EXERCISES

Exercise 8-1

Sales journal—perpetual

P1

Weaver Company uses a sales journal, a purchases journal, a cash receipts journal, a cash disbursement journal, and a general journal. The following transactions occur in the month of March:

Mar. 2 Sold merchandise costing $300 to K. Kietzman for $450 cash, invoice no. 5703.
5 Purchased $2,400 of merchandise on credit from Tent Corp.
7 Sold merchandise costing $800 to C. Benton for $1,250, terms 2/10, n/30, invoice no. 5704.
8 Borrowed $9,000 cash by giving a note to the bank.
12 Sold merchandise costing $200 to R. Laman for $340, terms n/30, invoice no. 5705.
16 Received $1,225 cash from C. Benton to pay for the purchase of February 7.
19 Sold $900 of used store equipment to Swender, Inc.
25 Sold merchandise costing $500 to T. Docking for $750, terms n/30, invoice no. 5706.

Prepare headings for a sales journal like the one in Exhibit 8.5. Journalize the March transactions that should be recorded in this sales journal.

Exercise 8-2ᴬ

Sales journal—periodic

P3

Prepare headings for a sales journal like the one in Exhibit 8A.1. Journalize the March transactions shown in Exercise 8-1 that should be recorded in the sales journal assuming the periodic inventory system is used.

Exercise 8-3

Cash receipts journal—perpetual

P1

True Co. uses a sales journal, a purchases journal, a cash receipts journal, a cash disbursements journal, and a general journal. The following transactions occur in the month of November.

Nov. 3 Purchased $3,200 of merchandise on credit from Passat Co.
7 Sold merchandise costing $840 on credit to J. Trost for $1,000, subject to a $20 sales discount if paid by the end of the month.
9 Borrowed $3,750 cash by giving a note to the bank.
13 J. Atherton, the owner, contributed $5,000 cash to the company.
18 Sold merchandise costing $250 to B. Baird for $330 cash.
22 Paid Passat Co. $3,200 cash for the merchandise purchased on November 3.
27 Received $980 cash from J. Trost in payment of the November 7 purchase.
30 Paid salaries of $1,650.

Prepare headings for a cash receipts journal like the one in Exhibit 8.7. Journalize the November transactions that should be recorded in the cash receipts journal.

Exercise 8-4ᴬ

Cash receipts journal—periodic P3

Prepare headings for a cash receipts journal like the one in Exhibit 8A.2. Journalize the November transactions shown in Exercise 8-3 that should be recorded in the cash receipts journal assuming the periodic inventory system is used.

Exercise 8-5

Purchases journal—perpetual

P1

Sweeney Company uses a sales journal, a purchases journal, a cash receipts journal, a cash disbursements journal, and a general journal. The following transactions occur in the month of June.

June 1 Purchased $9,100 of merchandise on credit from Lockett, Inc., terms n/30.
8 Sold merchandise on credit to R. Jones for $1,400 subject to a $28 sales discount if paid by the end of the month.
14 Purchased $340 of store supplies from Pak Company on credit, terms n/30.
17 Purchased $380 of office supplies on credit from Stein Company, terms n/30.
24 Sold merchandise to L. Leetch for $630 cash.
28 Purchased store supplies from Quinn's for $90 cash.
29 Paid Lockett, Inc., $9,100 for the merchandise purchased on July 1.

Prepare headings for a purchases journal like the one in Exhibit 8.9. Journalize the June transactions that should be recorded in the purchases journal.

Exercise 8-6ᴬ

Purchases journal—periodic P3

Prepare headings for a purchases journal like the one in Exhibit 8A.3. Journalize the June transactions from Exercise 8-5 that should be recorded in the purchases journal assuming the periodic inventory system is used.

Tucker Supply uses a sales journal, a purchases journal, a cash receipts journal, a cash disbursements journal, and a general journal. The following transactions occur in the month of April.

Apr. 3   Purchased merchandise for $2,950 on credit from Strider, Inc., terms 2/10, n/30.
    9   Issued check no. 210 to Najima Corp. to buy store supplies for $550.
   12   Sold merchandise on credit to C. Kamp for $770, terms n/30.
   17   Issued check no. 211 for $1,400 to repay a note payable to City Bank.
   20   Purchased merchandise for $4,500 on credit from LeDuc, terms 2/10, n/30.
   29   Issued check no. 212 to LeDuc to pay the amount due for the purchase of March 20, less the discount.
   31   Paid salary of $1,800 to B. Deal by issuing check no. 213.
   31   Issued check no. 214 to Strider, Inc., to pay the amount due for the purchase of March 3.

Prepare headings for a cash disbursements journal like the one in Exhibit 8.11. Journalize the April transactions that should be recorded in the cash disbursements journal.

Exercise 8-7

Cash disbursements journal—perpetual

Prepare headings for a cash disbursements journal like the one in Exhibit 8A.4. Journalize the April transactions from Exercise 8-7 that should be recorded in the cash disbursements journal assuming the periodic inventory system is used.

Exercise 8-8ᴬ

Cash disbursements journal—periodic

P3

Roscoe Pharmacy uses the following journals: sales journal, purchases journal, cash receipts journal, cash disbursements journal, and general journal. On June 5, Roscoe purchased merchandise priced at $14,000, subject to credit terms of 2/10, n/30. On June 14, the pharmacy paid the net amount due. In journalizing the payment, the pharmacy debited Accounts Payable for $14,000 but failed to record the cash discount on the purchases. Cash was properly credited for the actual amount paid. In what journals would the June 5 and the June 14 transactions be recorded? What procedure is likely to discover the error in journalizing the June 14 transaction?

Exercise 8-9

Special journal transactions and error discovery

P1

At the end of May, the sales journal of Outdoor Horizon appears as follows:

Exercise 8-10

Posting to subsidiary ledger accounts

P1

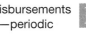

			Sales Journal		
Date	Account Debited	Invoice Number	PR	Accounts Receivable Dr. Sales Cr.	Cost of Good Sold Dr. Inventory Cr.
May 6	Cameron Smith	190		3,880	3,120
10	Deke Harris	191		2,940	2,325
17	Liz Buck	192		1,850	1,480
25	Deke Harris	193		1,340	1,075
31	Totals			10,010	8,000

Outdoor Horizon also recorded the return of certain merchandise with the following entry:

May 20	Sales Returns and Allowances	350	
	Accounts Receivable—Liz Buck		350
	Customer returned (worthless) merchandise.		

Required

1. Open an accounts receivable subsidiary ledger that has a T-account for each customer listed in the sales journal. Post to the customer accounts the entries in the sales journal and any portion of the general journal entry that affects a customer's account.

2. Open a general ledger that has T-accounts for Accounts Receivable, Inventory, Sales, Sales Returns and Allowances, and Cost of Goods Sold. Post the sales journal and any portion of the general journal entry that affects these accounts.

3. Prepare a schedule of accounts in the accounts receivable ledger and add their balances to show that the total equals the balance in the Accounts Receivable controlling account.

Exercise 8-11ᴬ

Posting from special journals to general and subsidiary ledgers—periodic

P1 **P2**

The condensed journals of Tops Trophies follow. The journal column headings are incomplete and do not indicate whether the columns are debit or credit columns.

Sales Journal	
Account	
Jack Elfrink	4,700
Dave Joy	9,400
Ken Stone	2,000
Total	16,100

Purchases Journal	
Account	
Green Corp.	6,400
Sutter, Inc.	5,500
Alli Company	2,700
Total	14,600

Cash Receipts Journal					
Account	**Cash**	**Sales Discounts**	**Accounts Receivable**	**Sales**	**Other Accounts**
Jack Elfrink	4,312	88	4,400		
Sales	3,250			3,250	
Notes Payable	6,000				6,000
Sales	825			825	
Dave Joy	9,212	188	9,400		
Store Equipment	500				500
Totals	24,099	276	13,800	4,075	6,500

Cash Disbursements Journal				
Account	**Cash**	**Purchases Discounts**	**Other Accounts**	**Accounts Payable**
Prepaid Insurance	850		850	
Sutter, Inc.	5,335	165		5,500
Green Corp.	5,537	113		5,650
Store Equipment	1,750		1,750	
Totals	13,472	278	2,600	11,150

General Journal			
Sales Returns and Allowances		300	
Accounts Receivable—Jack Elfrink			300
Accounts Payable—Green Corp.		750	
Purchases Returns and Allowances			750

Prepare T-accounts for the following general ledger and subsidiary ledger accounts. Separate the accounts of each ledger group as follows:

General Ledger Accounts	*Accounts Receivable Ledger Accounts*
Cash	
Accounts Receivable	Jack Elfrink
Prepaid Insurance	Dave Joy
Store Equipment	Ken Stone
Accounts Payable	
Notes Payable	*Accounts Payable Ledger Accounts*
Sales	
Sales Discounts	Green Corp.
Sales Returns and Allowances	Alli Company
Purchases	Sutter, Inc.
Purchase Discounts	
Purchase Returns and Allowances	

Revise and show complete column headings for the special journals, and then post the entries reflected in the journals to their proper T-accounts.

Henderson Company posts its sales invoices directly and then binds them into a Sales Journal. Henderson had the following credit sales to these customers during June:

Exercise 8-12
Accounts receivable ledger

June	2	Jay Hall	. . . .	$ 4,600
	8	Trey Wiltse	. . . .	7,100
	10	Tere Bax	. . . .	14,400
	14	Cindy Smith	. . . .	21,500
	20	Tere Bax	. . . .	12,200
	29	Jay Hall	. . . .	8,300
		Total sales	. . . .	$68,100

Required

1. Open a subsidiary accounts receivable ledger having a T-account for each customer. Post the invoices to the subsidiary ledger.
2. Open an Accounts Receivable controlling T-account and a Sales T-account. Post the end-of-month total from the sales journal to these accounts.
3. Prepare a schedule of accounts in the accounts receivable subsidiary ledger and add their balances to prove that the total equals the Accounts Receivable controlling balance account.

A company that records credit purchases in a purchases journal and records purchases returns in a general journal made the following errors. Indicate when each error should be discovered:

Exercise 8-13
Purchases journal and error identification

1. Posted a purchases return to the Accounts Payable account and to the creditor's subsidiary account but did not post to the purchases return to the Inventory account.
2. Posted a purchases return to the Inventory account and to the Accounts Payable account but did not post to the creditor's subsidiary account.
3. Correctly recorded a $5,000 purchase in the purchases journal but posted it to the creditor's subsidiary account as a $500 purchase.
4. Made an addition error in determining the balance of a creditor's subsidiary account.
5. Made an addition error in totaling the Office Supplies column of the purchases journal.

Exercise 8-14
Analyzing segment information

A1

Refer to Exhibit 8.13 and complete the segment contribution matrix for DogFog Company. Analyze and interpret the matrix, including identification of segments with the highest and lowest growth rates.

Segment	Sales Contribution (in $mil.)		Sales Contribution (in%)		One-Year Growth Rate Percent
	2002	2001	2002	2001	
Segment					
Skiing Group	$6,235	$3,685			
Skating Group	900	500			
Specialty Footwear	2,200	960			
Other specialty	1,075	425			
Subtotal					
General Merchandise					
South America	3,252	1,739			
United States	887	888			
Europe	549	150			
Subtotal					
Total					

PROBLEM SET A

Problem 8-1A
Special journals, subsidiary ledgers, and schedule of accounts receivable—perpetual

P1   P2   C4

Wellington Company completes these transactions during April of the current year (the terms of all credit sales are 2/10, n/30):

Apr. 2 Purchased $14,300 of merchandise on credit from Duncan Company, invoice dated April 2, terms 2/10, n/60.

3 Sold merchandise on credit to Joan Schmidt, Invoice No. 760, for $4,000 (cost is $3,000).

3 Purchased $1,480 of office supplies on credit from Stevens Point, Inc. Invoice dated April 2, terms n/10 EOM.

4 Issued Check No. 587 to *U.S. Times* for advertising expense, $899.

5 Sold merchandise on credit to Paul Kane, Invoice No. 761, for $8,000 (cost is $6,500).

6 Received an $80 credit memorandum from Stevens Point, Inc., for some of the office supplies received on April 3 and returned for credit.

9 Purchased $12,125 of store equipment on credit from Sarah's Supply, invoice dated April 9, terms n/10 EOM.

11 Sold merchandise on credit to Janice Griffin, Invoice No. 762, for $10,500 (cost is $7,000).

12 Issued Check No. 588 to Duncan Company in payment of its April 2 invoice, less the discount.

13 Received payment from Joan Schmidt for the April 3 sale, less the discount.

13 Sold $5,100 of merchandise on credit to Joan Schmidt (cost is $3,600), Invoice No. 763.

14 Received payment from Paul Kane for the April 5 sale, less the discount.

16 Issued Check No. 589, payable to Payroll, in payment of sales salaries for the first half of the month, $10,750. Cashed the check and paid employees.

16 Cash sales for the first half of the month are $52,840 (cost is $35,880). (Cash sales are recorded daily from cash register readings but are recorded only twice in this problem to reduce repetitive entries.)

17 Purchased $13,750 of merchandise on credit from Maben Company, invoice dated April 16, terms 2/10, n/30.

18 Borrowed $60,000 cash from First State Bank by giving a long-term note payable.

20 Received payment from Janice Griffin for the April 11 sale, less the discount.

20 Purchased $830 of store supplies on credit from Sarah's Supply, invoice dated April 19, terms n/10 EOM.

23 Received a $750 credit memorandum from Maben Company for defective merchandise received on April 17 and returned for credit.

23 Received payment from Joan Schmidt for the April 13 sale, less the discount.

25 Purchased $11,375 of merchandise on credit from Duncan Company, invoice dated April 24, terms 2/10, n/60.

26 Issued Check No. 590 to Maben Company in payment of its April 17 invoice, less the return and the discount.

27   Sold $3,170 of merchandise on credit to Paul Kane, Invoice No. 764 (cost is $2,520).
27   Sold $6,700 of merchandise on credit to Janice Griffin, Invoice No. 765 (cost is $4,305).
30   Issued Check No. 591, payable to Payroll, in payment of the sales salaries for the last half of the month, $10,750.
30   Cash sales for the last half of the month are $73,975 (cost is $58,900).

Required

Preparation Component

1. Prepare a sales journal like Exhibit 8.5 and a cash receipts journal like Exhibit 8.7. Number both journal pages as page 3. Then review the transactions of Wellington Company and enter those that should be journalized in the sales journal and those that should be journalized in the cash receipts journal. Ignore any transactions that should be journalized in a purchases journal, a cash disbursements journal, or a general journal.

2. Open the following general ledger accounts: Cash, Accounts Receivable, Inventory, Long-Term Notes Payable, Cost of Goods Sold, Sales, and Sales Discounts. Enter the March 31 balances for Cash ($85,000), Inventory ($125,000), and Long-Term Notes Payable ($210,000). Also open subsidiary accounts receivable ledger accounts for Paul Kane, Joan Schmidt, and Janice Griffin.

3. Post items that should be posted as individual amounts from the journals. (Such items are posted daily but are posted only once here, because they are few in number.) Foot and crossfoot the journals and make the month-end postings.

4. Prepare a trial balance of the general ledger and prove the accuracy of the subsidiary ledger by preparing a schedule of accounts receivable.

Check Trial balance totals, $434,285

Analysis Component

5. Assume that the sum of account balances for the schedule of Accounts Receivable does not equal the balance of the controlling account in the general ledger. Describe steps you would take to discover the error(s).

Assume that Wellington Co. in Problem 8-1A uses the periodic inventory system.

Problem 8-2A^A
Special journals, subsidiary ledgers, and schedule of accounts receivable—periodic

Required

1. Prepare headings for a sales journal like the one in Exhibit 8A.1. Prepare headings for a cash receipts journal like the one in Exhibit 8A.2. Journalize the April transactions shown in Problem 8-1A that should be recorded in the sales journal and the cash receipts journal assuming the *periodic* inventory system is used.

2. Open the general ledger accounts with balances as shown in Problem 8-1A (do not open a Cost of Goods Sold ledger account). Under the periodic system, an Inventory account exists but is inactive until its balance is updated to the correct inventory balance at year-end. In this problem, the Inventory account remains inactive but must be included to correctly complete the trial balance.

3. Complete parts 3, 4, and 5 of Problem 8-1A using the results of parts 1 and 2 of this problem.

Check Trial balance totals, $434,285

The April transactions of Wellington Company are described in Problem 8-1A.

Problem 8-3A
Special journals, subsidiary ledgers, and schedule of accounts payable—perpetual

Required

1. Prepare a general journal, a purchases journal like Exhibit 8.9, and a cash disbursements journal like Exhibit 8.11. Number all journal pages as page 3. Review the April transactions of Wellington Company and enter those transactions that should be journalized in the general journal, the purchases journal, or the cash disbursements journal. Ignore any transactions that should be journalized in a sales journal or cash receipts journal.

2. Open the following general ledger accounts: Cash, Inventory, Office Supplies, Store Supplies, Store Equipment, Accounts Payable, Long-Term Notes Payable, Sales Salaries Expense, and Advertising Expense. Enter the March 31 balances of Cash ($85,000), Inventory ($125,000), and Long-Term Notes Payable ($210,000). Also open accounts payable subsidiary ledger accounts for Sarah's Supply, Duncan Company, Maben Company, and Stevens Point, Inc.

3. Post items that should be posted as individual amounts from the journals. (Such items are posted daily but are posted only once because they are few in number.) Foot and crossfoot the journals and make the month-end postings.

4. Prepare a trial balance of the general ledger and a schedule of accounts payable.

Problem 8-4A^A

Special journals, subsidiary ledgers, and schedule of accounts payable—periodic

The April transactions of Wellington Co. are described in Problem 8-1A.

Required

1. Prepare a general journal, a purchases journal like Exhibit 8A.3, and a cash disbursements journal like Exhibit 8A.4. Number all journal pages as page 3. Review the April transactions of Wellington Company (Problem 8-1A) and enter those transactions that should be journalized in the general journal, the purchases journal, or the cash disbursements journal. Ignore any transaction that should be journalized in a sales journal or cash receipts journal.

2. Open the following general ledger accounts: Cash, Inventory, Office Supplies, Store Supplies, Store Equipment, Accounts Payable, Long-Term Notes Payable, Purchases, Purchases Returns and Allowances, Purchases Discounts, Sales Salaries Expense, and Advertising Expense. Enter the March 31 balances of Cash ($85,000), Inventory ($125,000), and Long-Term Notes Payable ($210,000). Also open accounts payable subsidiary ledger accounts for Sarah's Supply, Duncan Company, Maben Company, and Stevens Point, Inc.

3. Complete parts 3 and 4 of Problem 8-3A using the results of parts 1 and 2 of this problem.

Problem 8-5A

Special journals, subsidiary ledgers, trial balance— perpetual

(If the Working Papers that accompany this textbook are not being used, omit this problem.)

You have just taken over the accounting for Chanute Enterprises, whose annual accounting period ends December 31. The company's previous accountant journalized its transactions through December 15 and posted all items that required posting as individual amounts (see the journals and ledgers in the Working Papers). The company's transactions beginning on December 16 follow (terms of all credit sales are 2/10, n/30):

Dec. 16   Sold merchandise on credit to Marcia Sayles, Invoice No. 916, for $8,700 (cost is $5,600).

17   Received a $1,040 credit memorandum from Ashley Company for merchandise received on December 15 and returned for credit.

17   Purchased $715 of office supplies on credit from BJ's Supply Company, invoice dated December 16, terms n/10 EOM.

18   Received a $40 credit memorandum from BJ's Supply Company for office supplies received on December 17 and returned for credit.

20   Issued a $500 credit memorandum to Margaret Clark for defective (worthless) merchandise sold on December 15 and returned for credit.

21   Purchased $7,700 of store equipment on credit from BJ's Supply Company, invoice dated December 21, terms n/10 EOM.

22   Received payment from Marcia Sayles for the December 12 sale less the discount.

23   Issued Check No. 623 to Sonnenschein Company in payment of its December 15 invoice less the discount.

24   Sold merchandise on credit to Trent Smith, Invoice No. 917, for $1,400 (cost is $800).

24   Issued Check No. 624 to Ashley Company in payment of its December 15 invoice less the return and the discount.

25   Received payment from Margaret Clark for the December 15 sale less the return and the discount.

26   Received $8,400 of merchandise and an invoice dated December 25, terms 2/10, n/60, from Sonnenschein Company.

29   Sold a neighboring merchant five boxes of file folders (office supplies) at their cost of $45 cash.

30   Sandra Meade, the owner of Chanute Enterprises, used Check No. 625 to withdraw $3,500 cash from the business for personal use.

31   Issued Check No. 626 to Jamie Sharp, the company's only sales employee, in payment of her $2,222 salary for the last half of December.

31   Issued Check No. 627 to Rural Electric Company in payment of its $810 December electric bill.

31   Cash sales for the last half of the month are $35,800 (cost is $17,400). (Cash sales are recorded daily but are recorded only twice in this problem to reduce repetitive entries.)

Required

1. Record these transactions in the journals provided in the working papers.

2. Post any amounts that should be posted as individual amounts to the general ledger accounts, including posting to the customer and creditor accounts. (Such items are posted daily but are posted only once here because they are few in number.) Foot and crossfoot the journals and make the month-end postings.

3. Prepare a December 31 trial balance and prove the accuracy of the subsidiary ledgers by preparing schedules of both accounts receivable and accounts payable.

Check Trial balance totals, $228,208

Bishop Company completes these transactions and events during March of the current year (terms of all credit sales are 2/10, n/30):

Mar. 1   Received $43,600 of merchandise and an invoice dated March 1, terms 2/15, n/30, from Fox Industries.

  2   Sold merchandise on credit to Armand Leon, Invoice No. 854, for $16,800 (cost is $8,400).

  3   Purchased $1,230 of office supplies on credit from Hilary Company, invoice dated March 3, terms n/10 EOM.

  3   Sold merchandise on credit to Kit Dean, Invoice No. 855, for $10,200 (cost is $5,800).

  6   Borrowed $82,000 cash by giving Commerce Bank a long-term note payable.

  9   Purchased $21,850 of office equipment on credit from Rose Supply, invoice dated March 9, terms n/10 EOM.

  10   Sold merchandise on credit to Taylor Wood, Invoice No. 856, for $5,600 (cost is $2,900).

  12   Received payment from Armand Leon for the March 2 sale less the discount.

  13   Sent Fox Industries Check No. 416 in payment of the March 1 invoice less the discount.

  13   Received payment from Kit Dean for the March 3 sale less the discount.

  14   Received $32,625 of merchandise and an invoice dated March 13, terms 2/10, n/30, from the LR Company.

  15   Issued Check No. 417, payable to Payroll, in payment of sales salaries for the first half of the month, $18,300. Cashed the check and paid the employees.

  15   Cash sales for the first half of the month are $34,680 (cost is $20,210). (Cash sales are recorded daily, but are recorded only twice here to reduce repetitive entries.)

  15   Post to the customer and creditor accounts, and post any amounts that should be posted as individual amounts to the general ledger accounts. (Such items are posted daily but are posted only twice here because they are few in number.)

  16   Purchased $1,770 of store supplies on credit from Hilary Company, invoice dated March 16, terms n/10 EOM.

  17   Received a $2,425 credit memorandum from LR Company for unsatisfactory merchandise received on March 14 and returned for credit.

  19   Received a $630 credit memorandum from Rose Supply for office equipment received on March 9 and returned for credit.

  20   Received payment from Taylor Wood for the sale of March 10 less the discount.

  23   Issued Check No. 418 to LR Company in payment of the invoice of March 13 less the return and the discount.

  27   Sold merchandise on credit to Taylor Wood, Invoice No. 857, for $14,910 (cost is $7,220).

  28   Sold merchandise on credit to Kit Dean, Invoice No. 858, for $6,315 (cost is $3,280).

  31   Issued Check No. 419, payable to Payroll, in payment of sales salaries for the last half of the month, $18,300. Cashed the check and paid the employees.

  31   Cash sales for the last half of the month are $30,180 (cost is $16,820).

  31   Post to the customer and creditor accounts, and post any amounts that should be posted as individual amounts to the general ledger accounts. Foot and crossfoot the journals and make the month-end postings.

Problem 8-6A

Special journals, subsidiary ledgers, trial balance—perpetual

Required

1. Open the following general ledger accounts: Cash; Accounts Receivable; Inventory (March 1 beg. bal. is $10,000); Office Supplies; Store Supplies; Office Equipment; Accounts Payable; Long-Term Notes Payable; M. Bishop, Capital (March 1 beg. bal. is $10,000); Sales; Sales Discounts; Cost of Goods Sold; and Sales Salaries Expense. Open the following accounts receivable ledger accounts: Taylor Wood, Armand Leon, and Kit Dean. Open the following accounts payable ledger accounts: Hilary Company, Fox Industries, Rose Supply, and LR Company.

2. Enter these transactions in a sales journal like Exhibit 8.5, a purchases journal like Exhibit 8.9, a cash receipts journal like Exhibit 8.7, a cash disbursements journal like Exhibit 8.11, or a general journal. Post when instructed to do so.

Check   Trial balance totals, $234,905

3. Prepare a trial balance of the general ledger and prove the accuracy of the subsidiary ledgers by preparing schedules of both accounts receivable and accounts payable.

Problem 8-7A^A

Special journals, subsidiary ledgers, trial balance—periodic

Assume that Bishop Co. in Problem 8-6A uses the periodic inventory system.

Required

1. Open the following general ledger accounts: Cash; Accounts Receivable; Inventory (March 1 beg. bal. is $10,000); Office Supplies; Store Supplies; Office Equipment; Accounts Payable; Long-Term Notes Payable; M. Bishop, Capital (March 1 beg. bal. is $10,000); Sales; Sales Discounts; Purchases; Purchases Returns and Allowances; Purchases Discounts; and Sales Salaries Expense. Open the following accounts receivable ledger accounts: Taylor Wood, Armand Leon, and Kit Dean. Open the following Accounts Payable ledger accounts: Hilary Company, Fox Industries, Rose Supply, and LR Company.

2. Enter the transactions from Problem 8-6A in a sales journal like Exhibit 8A.1, a purchases journal like Exhibit 8A.3, a cash receipts journal like Exhibit 8A.2, a cash disbursements journal like Exhibit 8A.4, or a general journal. Post when instructed to do so.

Check   Trial balance totals, $238,806

3. Prepare a trial balance of the general ledger and prove the accuracy of the subsidiary ledgers by preparing schedules of both accounts receivable and accounts payable.

PROBLEM SET B

Problem 8-1B

Special journals, subsidiary ledgers, schedule of accounts receivable—perpetual

Best Industries completes these transactions during July of the current year (the terms of all credit sales are 2/10, n/30):

July 1   Purchased $6,500 of merchandise on credit from Torch Company, invoice dated June 30, terms 2/10, n/30.
      3   Issued Check No. 300 to *The Weekly Reader* for advertising expense, $625.
      5   Sold merchandise on credit to Kim Jeffries, Invoice No. 918, for $19,200 (cost is $10,500).
      6   Sold merchandise on credit to Ruth Nyhus, Invoice No. 919, for $7,500 (cost is $4,300).
      7   Purchased $1,250 of store supplies on credit from Prairie, Inc., invoice dated July 7, terms n/10 EOM.
      8   Received a $250 credit memorandum from Prairie, Inc., for store supplies received on July 7 and returned for credit.
      9   Purchased $38,220 of store equipment on credit from Gardner's Supply, invoice dated July 8, terms n/10 EOM.
      10 Issued Check No. 301 to Torch Company in payment of its June 30 invoice, less the discount.
      13 Sold merchandise on credit to Stephanie Davis, Invoice No. 920, $8,550 (cost $5,230).
      14 Sold merchandise on credit to Kim Jeffries, Invoice No. 921, for $5,100 (cost is $3,800).
      15 Received payment from Kim Jeffries for the July 5 sale, less the discount.
      15 Issued Check No. 302, payable to Payroll, in payment of sales salaries for the first half of the month, $31,850. Cashed the check and paid employees.
      15 Cash sales for the first half of the month are $118,350 (cost is $76,330). (Cash sales are recorded daily from the cash registers but are recorded only twice in this problem to reduce repetitive entries.)
      16 Received payment from Ruth Nyhus for the July 6 sale, less the discount.
      17 Purchased $7,200 of merchandise on credit from Adams Company, invoice dated July 17, terms 2/10, n/30.
      20 Purchased $650 of office supplies on credit from Gardner's Supply, invoice dated July 19, terms n/10 EOM.
      21 Borrowed $15,000 cash from College Bank by giving a long-term note payable.
      23 Received payment from Stephanie Davis for the July 13 sale, less the discount.
      24 Received payment from Kim Jeffries for the July 14 sale, less the discount.
      24 Received a $2,400 credit memorandum from Adams Company for defective merchandise received on July 17 and returned for credit.

26   Purchased $9,770 of merchandise on credit from Torch Company, invoice dated July 26, terms 2/10, n/30.

27   Issued Check No. 303 to Adams Company in payment of its July 17 invoice, less the return and the discount.

29   Sold merchandise on credit to Ruth Nyhus, Invoice No. 922, for $17,502 (cost is $10,850).

30   Sold merchandise on credit to Stephanie Davis, Invoice No. 923, for $16,820 (cost is $9,840).

31   Issued Check No. 304, payable to Payroll, in payment of the sales salaries for the last half of the month, $31,850.

31   Cash sales for the last half of the month are $80,244 (cost is $53,855).

Required

Preparation Component

1. Prepare a sales journal like Exhibit 8.5 and a cash receipts journal like Exhibit 8.7. Number both journals as page 3. Then review the transactions of Best Industries and enter those transactions that should be journalized in the sales journal and those that should be journalized in the cash receipts journal. Ignore any transactions that should be journalized in a purchases journal, a cash disbursements journal, or a general journal.

2. Open the following general ledger accounts: Cash, Accounts Receivable, Inventory, Long-Term Notes Payable, Cost of Goods Sold, Sales, and Sales Discounts. Enter the June 30 balances for Cash ($100,000), Inventory ($200,000), and Long-Term Notes Payable ($300,000). Also open subsidiary accounts receivable ledger accounts for Kim Jeffries, Stephanie Davis, and Ruth Nyhus. Post the items that should be posted as individual amounts from the journals. (Such items are posted daily but are posted here only once since they are few in number.) Foot and crossfoot the journals and make the month-end postings.

3. Prepare a trial balance of the general ledger and prove the accuracy of the subsidiary ledger by preparing a schedule of accounts receivable.

Check   Trial balance totals, $588,266

Analysis Component

4. Assume that the sum of account balances on the schedule of Accounts Receivable does not equal the balance of the controlling account in the general ledger. Describe steps you would take to discover the error(s).

Assume that Best Industries in Problem 8-1B uses the periodic inventory system.

Required

1. Prepare headings for a sales journal like the one in Exhibit 8A.1. Prepare headings for a cash receipts journal like the one in Exhibit 8A.2. Journalize the July transactions shown in Problem 8-1B that should be recorded in the sales journal and the cash receipts journal assuming the periodic inventory system is used.

2. Open the general ledger accounts with balances as shown in Problem 8-1B (do not open a Cost of Goods Sold ledger account). Under the periodic system, an Inventory account exists but is inactive until its balance is updated to the correct inventory balance at year-end. In this problem, the Inventory account remains inactive but must be included to correctly complete the trial balance.

3. Complete parts (3, 4, and 5) of Problem 8-1B using the results of parts 1 and 2 of this problem.

Problem 8-2B[A]

Special journals, subsidiary ledgers, and schedule of accounts receivable—periodic

Check   Trial balance totals, $588,266

The July transactions of Best Industries are described in Problem 8-1B

Required

1. Prepare a general journal, a purchases journal like Exhibit 8.9, and a cash disbursements journal like Exhibit 8.11. Number all journal pages as page 3. Review the July transactions of Best Industries and enter those transactions that should be journalized in the general journal, the purchases journal, or the cash disbursements journal. Ignore any transactions that should be journalized in a sales journal or cash receipts journal.

2. Open the following general ledger accounts: Cash, Inventory, Office Supplies, Store Supplies, Store Equipment, Accounts Payable, Long-Term Notes Payable, Sales Salaries Expense, and

Problem 8-3B

Special journals, subsidiary ledgers, and schedule of accounts payable—perpetual

Advertising Expense. Enter the June 30 balances of Cash ($100,000), Inventory ($200,000), and Long-Term Notes Payable ($300,000). Also open accounts payable subsidiary ledger accounts for Gardner's Supply, Torch Company, Adams Company, and Prairie, Inc.

3. Post items that should be posted as individual amounts from the journals. (Such items are posted daily but are posted here only once since they are few in number.) Foot and crossfoot the journals and make the month-end postings.

Check Trial balance totals, $349,640

4. Prepare a trial balance of the general ledger and a schedule of accounts payable.

Problem 8-4B^A

Special journals, subsidiary ledgers, and schedule of accounts payable—periodic

The July transactions of Best Industries are described in Problem 8-1B.

Required

1. Prepare a general journal, a purchases journal like Exhibit 8A.3, and a cash disbursements journal like Exhibit 8A.4. Number all journal pages as page 3. Review the July transactions of Best Company (Problem 8-1B) and enter those transactions that should be journalized in the general journal, the purchases journal, or the cash disbursements journal. Ignore any transaction that should be journalized in a sales journal or cash receipts journal.

2. Open the following general ledger accounts: Cash, Inventory, Office Supplies, Store Supplies, Store Equipment, Accounts Payable, Long-Term Notes Payable, Purchases, Purchases Returns and Allowances, Purchases Discounts, Sales Salaries Expense, and Advertising Expense. Enter the June 30 balances of Cash ($100,000), Inventory ($200,000), and Long-Term Notes Payable ($300,000). Also open accounts payable subsidiary ledger accounts for Torch Company, Prairie, Inc., Gardner's Supply, and Adams Company.

Check Trial balance totals, $352,266

3. Complete parts 3 and 4 of Problem 8-3B using the results of parts 1 and 2 of this problem.

Problem 8-5B

Special journals, subsidiary ledgers, trial balance—perpetual

(If the Working Papers that accompany this textbook are not being used, omit this problem.)

You have just taken over the accounting for EZ Products, whose annual accounting period ends December 31. The company's previous accountant journalized its transactions through December 15 and posted all items that required posting as individual amounts (see the journals and ledgers in the working papers). The company's transactions beginning on December 16 follow (terms of all credit sales are 2/10, n/30):

Dec. 16   Purchased $865 of office supplies on credit from White Supply Company, invoice dated December 16, terms n/10 EOM.

16   Sold merchandise on credit to Brad Farris, Invoice No. 916, for $5,290 (cost is $3,821).

18   Issued a $200 credit memorandum to Leslie Snipes for defective (worthless) merchandise sold on December 15 and returned for credit.

19   Received a $640 credit memorandum from Muser Company for merchandise received on December 15 and returned for credit.

20   Received a $143 credit memorandum from White Supply Company for office supplies received on December 16 and returned for credit.

20   Purchased $7,850 of store equipment on credit from White Supply Company, invoice dated December 19, terms n/10 EOM.

21   Sold merchandise on credit to Joey Cape, Invoice No. 917, for $6,540 (cost is $4,210).

22   Received payment from Brad Farris for the December 12 sale less the discount.

25   Received payment from Leslie Snipes for the December 15 sale less the return and the discount.

25   Issued Check No. 623 to Muser Company in payment of its December 15 invoice less the return and the discount.

25   Issued Check No. 624 to Cloud Company in payment of its December 15 invoice less a 2% discount.

28   Received $7,030 of merchandise with an invoice dated December 28, terms 2/10, n/60, from Cloud Company.

28   Sold a neighboring merchant a carton of calculator tape (store supplies) at its cost of $68 cash.

29   Berneta Swope, the owner of EZ Products, used Check No. 625 to withdraw $5,000 cash from the business for personal use.

30   Issued Check No. 626 to Truman Electric Company in payment of its $970 December electric bill.

30 Issued Check No. 627 to Jamie Ford, the company's only sales employee, in payment of her $2,620 salary for the last half of December.

31 Cash sales for the last half of the month are $65,130 (cost is $32,850). (Cash sales are recorded daily but are recorded only twice here to reduce repetitive entries.)

Required

1. Record these transactions in the journals provided in the working papers.

2. Post any amounts that should be posted as individual amounts to the general ledger accounts, including posting to the customer and creditor accounts. (Normally, these amounts are posted daily but are posted only once here because they are few in number.) Foot and crossfoot the journals and make the month-end postings.

3. Prepare a December 31 trial balance and prove the accuracy of the subsidiary ledgers by preparing schedules of both accounts receivable and accounts payable.

Check Trial balance totals, $258,095

Randa Company completes these transactions during November of the current year (terms of all credit sales are 2/10, n/30):

Nov. 1 Purchased $5,058 of office equipment on credit from Ford Supply, invoice dated November 1, terms n/10 EOM.

2 Borrowed $88,500 cash by giving Missouri Bank a long-term note payable.

4 Received $33,500 of merchandise and an invoice dated November 3, terms 2/10, n/30, from ATX Industries.

5 Purchased $1,040 of store supplies on credit from World Company, invoice dated November 5, terms n/10 EOM.

8 Sold merchandise on credit to Seth Farmer, Invoice No. 439, for $6,550 (cost is $3,910).

10 Sold merchandise on credit to Carlos Beltran, Invoice No. 440, for $13,500 (cost is $8,500).

11 Received $2,557 of merchandise and an invoice dated November 10, terms 2/10, n/30, from Chin Company.

12 Sent ATX Industries Check No. 633 in payment of its November 3 invoice less the discount.

15 Issued Check No. 634, payable to Payroll, in payment of sales salaries for the first half of the month, $6,585. Cashed the check and paid the employees.

15 Cash sales for the first half of the month are $18,170 (cost is $9,000). (Cash sales are recorded daily but are recorded only twice in this problem to reduce repetitive entries.)

15 Post to the customer and creditor accounts, and post any amounts that should be posted as individual amounts to the general ledger accounts. (Normally, these items are posted daily but are posted only twice here because they are few in number.)

15 Sold merchandise on credit to Tony Wood, Invoice No. 441, for $5,250 (cost is $2,450).

16 Purchased $459 of office supplies on credit from World Company, invoice dated November 16, terms n/10 EOM.

17 Received a $557 credit memorandum from Chin Company for unsatisfactory merchandise received on November 11 and returned for credit.

18 Received payment from Seth Farmer for the November 8 sale less the discount.

19 Received payment from Carlos Beltran for the November 10 sale less the discount.

19 Issued Check No. 635 to Chin Company in payment of its invoice of November 10 less the return and the discount.

22 Sold merchandise on credit to Carlos Beltran, Invoice No. 442, for $3,695 (cost is $2,060).

24 Sold merchandise on credit to Tony Wood, Invoice No. 443, for $4,280 (cost is $2,130).

25 Received payment from Tony Wood for the sale of November 15 less the discount.

26 Received a $922 credit memorandum from Ford Supply for office equipment received on November 1 and returned for credit.

30 Issued Check No. 636, payable to Payroll, in payment of sales salaries for the last half of the month, $6,585. Cashed the check and paid the employees.

30 Cash sales for the last half of the month are $16,703 (cost is $10,200).

30 Post to the customer and creditor accounts, and post any amounts that should be posted as individual amounts to the general ledger accounts. Foot and crossfoot the journals and make the month-end postings.

Problem 8-6B
Special journals, subsidiary ledgers, trial balance—perpetual

Required

1. Open the following general ledger accounts: Cash; Accounts Receivable; Inventory (November 1 beg. bal. is $40,000); Office Supplies; Store Supplies; Office Equipment; Accounts Payable; Long-Term Notes Payable; J. Randa, Capital (November 1 beg. bal. is $40,000); Sales; Sales Discounts; Cost of Goods Sold; and Sales Salaries Expense. Open the following accounts receivable ledger accounts: Carlos Beltran, Tony Wood, and Seth Farmer. Open the following accounts payable ledger accounts: World Company, ATX Industries, Ford Supply, and Chin Company.

2. Enter these transactions in a sales journal like Exhibit 8.5, a purchases journal like Exhibit 8.9, a cash receipts journal like Exhibit 8.7, a cash disbursements journal like Exhibit 8.11, or a general journal. Post when instructed to do so.

Check Trial balance totals, $202,283

3. Prepare a trial balance of the general ledger and prove the accuracy of the subsidiary ledgers by preparing schedules of both accounts receivable and accounts payable.

Problem 8-7B^A
Special journals, subsidiary ledgers, trial balance—periodic

Assume that Randa Company in Problem 8-6B uses the periodic inventory system.

Required

1. Open the following general ledger accounts: Cash; Accounts Receivable; Inventory (November 1 beg. bal. is $40,000); Office Supplies; Store Supplies; Office Equipment; Accounts Payable; Long-Term Notes Payable; J. Randa, Capital (November 1 beg. bal. is $40,000); Sales; Sales Discounts; Purchases; Purchases Returns and Allowances; Purchases Discounts; and Sales Salaries Expense. Open the following accounts receivable ledger accounts: Carlos Beltran, Tony Wood, and Seth Farmer. Open the following accounts payable ledger accounts: World Company, ATX Industries, Ford Supply, and Chin Company.

2. Enter the transactions from Problem 8-6B in a sales journal like Exhibit 8A.1, a purchases journal like Exhibit 8A.3, a cash receipts journal like Exhibit 8A.2, a cash disbursements journal like Exhibit 8A.4, or a general journal. Post when instructed to do so.

Check Trial balance totals, $203,550

3. Prepare a trial balance of the general ledger and prove the accuracy of the subsidiary ledgers by preparing schedules of both accounts receivable and accounts payable.

COMPREHENSIVE PROBLEM— PERPETUAL

Spitz Company

Ⓢ Ⓖ *PeachTree*

(*If the Working Papers that accompany this text are not available, omit this comprehensive problem.*) Assume it is Monday, May 1, the first business day of the month, and you have just been hired as the accountant for Spitz Company, which operates with monthly accounting periods. All of the company's accounting work is completed through the end of April and its ledgers show April 30 balances. During your first month on the job, the company experiences the following transactions and events (terms of all credit sales are 2/10, n/30):

May 1　Issued Check No. 3410 to J&K Management Co. in payment of the May rent, $3,710. (Use two lines to record the transaction. Charge 80% of the rent to Rent Expense—Selling Space and the balance to Rent Expense—Office Space.)

　　2　Sold merchandise on credit to Bowman Company, Invoice No. 8785, for $6,100 (cost is $4,100).

　　2　Issued a $175 credit memorandum to Net, Inc., for defective (worthless) merchandise sold on April 28 and returned for credit. The total selling price (gross) was $4,725.

　　3　Received a $798 credit memorandum from Parker Products for merchandise received on April 29 and returned for credit.

　　4　Purchased the following on credit from Gates Supply Co.: merchandise, $37,072; store supplies, $574; and office supplies, $83. Invoice dated May 4, terms n/10 EOM.

　　5　Received payment from Net, Inc., for the balance from the April 28 sale less the May 2 return and the discount.

　　8　Issued Check No. 3411 to Parker Products to pay for the $7,098 of merchandise received on April 29 less the May 3 return and a 2% discount.

　　9　Sold store supplies to the merchant next door at their cost of $350 cash.

　　10　Purchased $4,074 of office equipment on credit from Gates Supply Co., invoice dated May 10, terms n/10 EOM.

　　11　Received payment from Bowman Company for the May 2 sale less the discount.

　　11　Received $8,800 of merchandise and an invoice dated May 10, terms 2/10, n/30, from Gatsby, Inc.

　　12　Received an $854 credit memorandum from Gates Supply Co. for defective office equipment received on May 10 and returned for credit.

15   Issued Check No. 3412, payable to Payroll, in payment of sales salaries, $5,320, and office salaries, $3,150. Cashed the check and paid the employees.

15   Cash sales for the first half of the month are $59,220 (cost is $38,200). (Cash sales are recorded daily but are recorded only twice here to reduce repetitive entries.)

15   Post to the customer and creditor accounts. Also post individual items that are not included in column totals at the end of the month to the general ledger accounts. (Such items are posted daily but are posted only twice each month because they are few in number.)

16   Sold merchandise on credit to Bowman Company, Invoice No. 8786, for $3,990 (cost is $1,890).

17   Received $13,650 of merchandise and an invoice dated May 14, terms 2/10, n/60, from Joey Corp.

19   Issued Check No. 3413 to Gatsby, Inc., in payment of its May 10 invoice less the discount.

22   Sold merchandise to Karim Services, Invoice No. 8787, for $6,850 (cost is $4,990), terms 2/10, n/60.

23   Issued Check No. 3414 to Joey Corp. in payment of its May 14 invoice less the discount.

24   Purchased the following on credit from Gates Supply Co.: merchandise, $8,120; store supplies, $630; and office supplies, $280. Invoice dated May 24, terms n/10 EOM.

25   Received $3,080 of merchandise and an invoice dated May 23, terms 2/10, n/30, from Parker Products.

26   Sold merchandise on credit to Dexter Corp., Invoice No. 8788, for $14,210 (cost is $8,230).

26   Issued Check No. 3415 to Trinity Power in payment of the April electric bill, $1,283.

29   The owner of Spitz Company, Doug Clinton, used Check No. 3416 to withdraw $7,000 cash from the business for personal use.

30   Received payment from Karim Services for the May 22 sale less the discount.

30   Issued Check No. 3417, payable to Payroll, in payment of sales salaries, $5,320, and office salaries, $3,150. Cashed the check and paid the employees.

31   Cash sales for the last half of the month are $66,052 (cost is $42,500).

31   Post to the customer and creditor accounts. Also post individual items that are not included in column totals at the end of the month to the general ledger accounts. Foot and cross-foot the journals and make the month-end postings.

Required

1. Enter these transactions in a sales journal, a purchases journal, a cash receipts journal, a cash disbursements journal, or a general journal. Post when instructed to do so. Assume a perpetual inventory system.

2. Prepare a trial balance in the Trial Balance columns of the work sheet form provided with the working papers. Complete the work sheet using the following information for accounting adjustments:

   a. Expired insurance, $553.

   b. Ending store supplies inventory, $2,632.

   c. Ending office supplies inventory, $504.

   d. Depreciation of store equipment, $567.

   e. Depreciation of office equipment, $329.

   Prepare and post adjusting and closing entries.

3. Prepare a May 2002 multiple-step income statement, a May 2002 statement of changes in owner's equity, and a May 31, 2002, classified balance sheet.

4. Prepare a post-closing trial balance. Also prove the accuracy of subsidiary ledgers by preparing schedules of both accounts receivable and accounts payable.

Beyond the Numbers

BTN 8-1   Refer to the financial statements for **Nike** in Appendix A to answer the following:

1. Identify the note disclosing Nike's revenues by major product lines.

2. For fiscal year ended May 31, 2000, compute the percent of both total revenue and revenue by product line that Nike earns from each segment. Comment on your findings.

Reporting in Action

A1

NIKE

Swoosh Ahead

3. Access Nike's annual report for fiscal years ending after May 31, 2000, from its Web site [www.nike.com] or the SEC's EDGAR database [www.sec.gov]. Complete parts *1* and *2* using the latest data available.

Comparative Analysis

BTN 8-2   Key comparative figures for both **Nike** and **Reebok** follow ($ millions):

Nike			Reebok		
Revenue by Segment	**Current Year**	**Prior Year**	**Revenue by Segment**	**Current Year**	**Prior Year**
United States	$4,732.1	$4,750.7	United States	$1,609.7	$1,858.3
Europe	2,350.9	2,255.8	United Kingdom	545.6	522.4
Asia	955.1	844.5	Europe	476.7	585.7
Americas	550.2	507.1	Other countries	267.9	258.2
Other countries	406.8	418.8			
Total	$8,995.1	$8,776.9	Total	$2,899.9	$3,224.6

Required

1. Compute the percent change in total revenue for each company for the years shown. Comment on your findings.

2. Compute the percent change in revenue by each geographic segment for each company. Comment on your findings.

3. Identify the geographic segment experiencing the largest growth in revenue for each company.

Ethics Challenge

C5

BTN 8-3   Denise Hinson, CPA, is a sole practitioner. She has been practicing as an auditor for 10 years. Recently a long-standing audit client asked Denise to design and implement an integrated computer accounting information system. The fees associated with this additional engagement with the client are very attractive. However, Denise wonders if she can remain objective on subsequent audits in her evaluation of the client's accounting system and its records if she was responsible for its design and implementation. Denise knows that the professional auditing standards require her to remain independent in fact and appearance from her auditing clients.

Required

1. What do you believe auditing standards are concerned with when they require independence in fact? In appearance?

2. Why is it important that auditors remain independent of their clients?

3. Do you think Denise can accept this engagement and remain independent? Justify your response.

Communicating in Practice

C3   C4

BTN 8-4   Your friend, Ivanna B. Sweeter, owns a small retail store that sells candies and nuts. Ivanna acquires her goods from a few select vendors. She generally makes purchase orders by phone and on credit. Sales are primarily for cash. Ivanna keeps her own manual accounting system using a general journal and a general ledger. At the end of each business day, she records one summary entry for cash sales. Ivanna recently began offering goodies in creative gift packages. This has increased sales substantially, and she is now receiving orders from corporate and other clients who order large quantities and prefer to buy on credit. As a result of increased credit transactions in both purchases and sales, keeping the accounting records has become extremely time consuming. Ivanna wants to continue to maintain her own manual system and calls you for advice. Write a memo to her advising how she might modify her current manual accounting system to accommodate the expanded business activities described. Ivanna is accustomed to checking her ledger by using a trial balance. Your memo should explain the advantages of what you propose and of any other verification techniques you recommend.

BTN 8-5   Access the April 14, 2000, filing of the 10-K report for Dell (ticker DELL) at **www.edgar-online.com.** Read the footnote that details Dell's segment information and answer the following:

Taking It to the Net

1. Dell's operations are divided among which three geographic segments?

2. In fiscal year 2000, which geographic area had the largest dollar amount of operating income and identifiable assets?

3. Analyze the net revenue growth for the United States and for foreign countries from 1998 to 1999 and 1999 to 2000. Is Dell growing its revenue faster in domestic markets or foreign markets?

4. For what product groups does Dell provide segment data? What percent of Dell's net revenue is earned by each product group?

BTN 8-6   Each member of the team is to assume responsibility for one of the following tasks:

a. Journalizing in the purchases journal

b. Journalizing in the cash disbursements journal

c. Maintaining and verifying the Accounts Payable ledger

d. Journalizing in the sales and general journal

e. Journalizing in the cash receipts journal

f. Maintaining and verifying the Accounts Receivable ledger

The team should abide by the following procedures in carrying out responsibilities.

Required

1. After tasks (a–f) are assigned, each team member is to quickly read the list of transactions in Problem 8-6A, identifying with initials the journal in which each transaction is to be recorded. Upon completion, the team leader is to read transaction dates, and the appropriate team member is to vocalize responsibility. Any disagreement between teammates must be resolved within the team.

2. Journalize and continually update subsidiary ledgers. Journal recorders should alert teammates assigned to subsidiary ledgers when an entry must be posted to their subsidiary.

3. Team members responsible for tasks (a, b, d, and e) are to summarize and prove journals; members responsible for tasks (c and f) are to prepare both payables and receivables schedules.

4. The team leader is to take charge of the general ledger, rotating team members to obtain amounts to be posted. The person responsible for a journal must complete posting references in the journal. Other team members should verify the accuracy of account balance computations. To avoid any abnormal account balances, post in the following order: P, S, G, R, D. (*Note:* Posting any necessary individual general ledger amounts are also done at this time.)

5. The team leader is to read out general ledger account balances while another team member fills in the trial balance form. Concurrently, one member should keep a running balance of debit account balance totals and another credit account balance totals. Verify the final total of the trial balance and the schedules. If necessary, the team must resolve any errors. Turn in the trial balance and schedules to the instructor.

BTN 8-7   Read the article, "Enterprise Software: A Belated Rush to the Net" in the October 25, 1999, edition of *Business Week*.

***Business Week* Activity**

Required

1. What factor is causing all major enterprise application software makers to substantially revise their software packages?

2. What companies are the major market shareholders in the enterprise application software market?

3. What distinct challenges does each enterprise application software giant face?

Entrepreneurial Decision

P1

e

BTN 8-8 Dakota Rice has operated a local gift shop for two years. Initially, she handled all aspects of the store's accounting manually. Over the past year, she has focused on upgrading the store to a computerized system and has successfully installed software to handle billing, purchasing, and payroll. Dakota hopes this year to move from a periodic inventory system to a perpetual one. She is thinking of investing in a bar code labeler and scanner system to help manage inventory.

Required

1. What are the cost-benefit considerations of a bar code system?
2. How would a bar code system work with the accounting information system to accomplish perpetual inventory accounting?

Cash and Internal Control

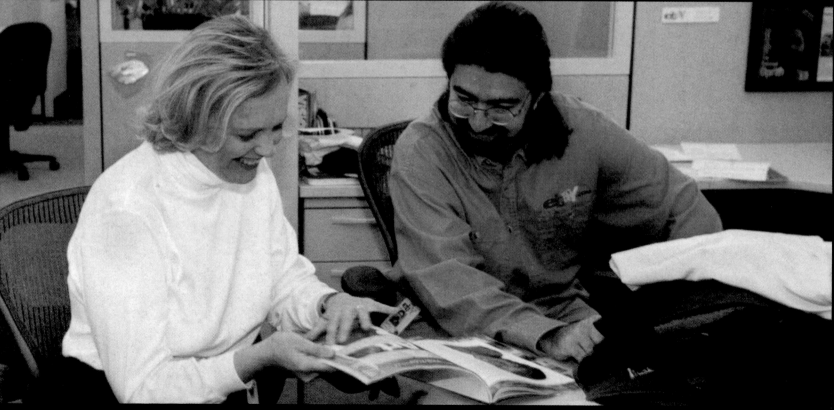

"I hope to make it easier to conduct business with strangers over the Net."—Pierre Omidyar

A Look Back

Chapter 8 focused on accounting information systems. We explained the fundamental principles and components of information systems, the use of special journals and subsidiary ledgers, and technology-

A Look at This Chapter

This chapter extends our study of accounting to the area of internal control and accounting for cash. We describe procedures that are good for internal control. We also explain the control of and accounting for cash.

A Look Ahead

Chapter 10 focuses on receivables and short-term investments. These items are the most liquid assets other than cash. We explain how to account and report for these assets.

Flea Market in Cyberspace

e SAN JOSE, CA—Who ever thought a flea market could be worth $12 billion? Paris-born entrepreneur Pierre Omidyar started his Net auction service, **eBay** (a combination of the words *electronic* and *Bay Area*), five years ago to help his girlfriend collect Pez candy dispensers (**eBay.com**). Omidyar, then 27, saw a need for a Web site where people could buy and sell all kinds of items such as computers, antiques, toys, and music. eBay is now the largest person-to-person auction site on the Web. It creates the marketplace, but buyers and sellers do their own work. eBay never touches the goods or the money. Its earnings derive from commissions, between 1 and 5%, depending on the item's value.

Omidyar calls eBay an experiment in e-commerce. But how does he persuade strangers to trust one another enough to hand over merchandise or cash? "Most people are honest, trustworthy people," says Omidyar. Still, he set up basic controls to establish responsibilities of each party to a trade and to monitor and record transactions. When complications still arose between buyers and sellers, Omidyar had to install a better control system.

Omidyar's response was fourfold. First, he devised a control system whereby buyers and sellers rate their experiences with the other party. This *Feedback Forum* is a public record of past eBay dealings of buyers and sellers. Omidyar says, "It's become a kind of virtuous cycle that's encouraged good behavior." Second, he brought in escrow services to assist traders in making deals. Buyers can have their goods delivered to an escrow service before their money is sent to the seller. Likewise, sellers can require that a buyer send money to the escrow service before sending the goods. Third, he gave traders free insurance against fraud or the mislabeling of goods. Finally, he set up SafeHarbor™, a customer-support team dedicated to providing regular, independent reviews of transactions and users.

Omidyar is confident his new controls will deter fraudulent activities. "By creating an open market that encourages honest dealings," says Omidyar, "I hope to make it easier to conduct business with strangers over the Net." If Omidyar's current record of success is any indication (its said he's made over $3 billion from eBay), he's made Internet *strangers* feel like *bosom buddies*!

[Sources: *Business Week*, January 11, 1999; *eBay Web Site*, May 2001; *USA Today Web Site*, December 30, 1998.]

Chapter Preview

We all are aware of reports and experiences involving theft and fraud. These occurrences affect us in several ways: we lock doors, chain bikes, review sales receipts, and acquire alarm systems. A company also takes actions to safeguard, control, and manage what it owns. Experience tells us small companies are most vulnerable, usually due to weak internal controls. It is management's responsibility to set up policies and procedures to safeguard a company's assets, especially cash. To do so, management and employees must understand and apply principles of internal control. This chapter describes these principles and how to apply them. We focus special attention on cash because it is easily transferable and often at high risk of loss. Several controls for cash are explained, including a voucher system, petty cash funds, and reconciling bank accounts. This chapter also describes a method to account for purchases that helps us decide whether cash discounts on purchases are being lost and, if so, how much is lost. Our understanding of these controls and procedures makes us more secure in carrying out business activities and in assessing those activities of other companies.

Internal Control

This section describes internal control and its fundamental principles. We also discuss the impact of technology on internal control and the limitations of control procedures.

Purpose of Internal Control

C1 Define internal control and its purpose.

Concept 9-1

Managers (or owners) of small businesses often control the entire operation. They supervise workers, participate in all activities, and make major decisions. These managers usually purchase all of the business's assets. They also hire and manage employees, negotiate all contracts, and sign all checks. These managers know from personal contact and observation whether the business is actually receiving the assets and services paid for. Larger companies cannot maintain this close personal supervision. They must delegate responsibilities and rely on formal procedures rather than personal contact in controlling business activities.

Managers use an internal control system to monitor and control business activities. An **internal control system** refers to the policies and procedures managers use to

Did You Know?

Restricted Access Good internal control prevents unauthorized access to assets and accounting records by requiring passwords. It takes a password, for instance, to boot up most office PCs, and logging onto a network calls for another. Then comes voice mail, e-mail, online services, and restricted Web pages—not to mention personal ID numbers on credit and cash cards. Preventing unauthorized access is a crucial goal of internal control experts.

- Protect assets.
- Ensure reliable accounting.
- Promote efficient operations.
- Urge adherence to company policies.

A properly designed internal control system is a key part of systems design, analysis, and performance. Managers place a high priority on internal control systems because they can prevent avoidable losses, help managers plan operations, and monitor company and employee performance. While internal controls do not provide guarantees, they lower the company's risk of loss from not having internal controls.

Principles of Internal Control

C2 Identify principles of internal control.

Internal control policies and procedures vary from company to company. They depend on factors such as the nature of the business and its size. Certain fundamental internal control principles apply to all companies, however. The **principles of internal control** are to

1. Establish responsibilities.
2. Maintain adequate records.
3. Insure assets and bond key employees.
4. Separate recordkeeping from custody of assets.
5. Divide responsibility for related transactions.
6. Apply technological controls.
7. Perform regular and independent reviews.

Point: When the electronic equipment maker Casio [**Casio.com**] started an e-commerce site last year, 13% of the purchases were fraudulent.

In this section, we explain these seven principles and describe how internal control procedures minimize the risk of fraud and theft. These procedures also increase the reliability and accuracy of accounting records.

Establish Responsibilities

Proper internal control means that responsibility for a task is clearly established and assigned to one person. When responsibility is not identified, determining who is at fault is difficult when a problem occurs. For instance, if two salesclerks share the same cash register, identifying which clerk is at fault if there is a cash shortage is difficult. Neither clerk can prove or disprove the alleged shortage. To prevent this problem, one clerk might be given responsibility for handling all cash sales. Alternately, a company can use a register with separate cash drawers for each clerk. Most of us have waited in line at a retail counter during a change of shift while employees swap cash drawers.

Maintain Adequate Records

Good recordkeeping is part of an internal control system. It helps protect assets and ensures that employees use prescribed procedures. Reliable records are also a source of information that managers use to monitor company activities. When detailed records of equipment are kept, for instance, items are unlikely to be lost or stolen without detection. Similarly, transactions are less likely to be entered in wrong accounts if a chart of accounts is set up and used carefully. Many preprinted forms and internal documents are also designed for use in a good internal control system. When sales slips are properly designed, for instance, sales personnel can record needed information efficiently with less chance of errors or delays to customers. When sales slips are prenumbered and controlled, each one issued is the responsibility of one salesperson, preventing the salesperson from pocketing cash by making a sale and destroying the sales slip. Computerized point-of-sales systems achieve the same control results.

Insure Assets and Bond Key Employees

Good internal control means that assets are adequately insured against casualty and that employees handling cash and negotiable assets are bonded. An employee is *bonded* when a company purchases an insurance policy, or a bond, against losses from theft by that employee. Bonding reduces the risk of loss suffered from theft. It also discourages theft because bonded employees know an independent bonding company will be involved when theft is uncovered and is unlikely to be sympathetic with an employee involved in theft.

Separate Recordkeeping from Custody of Assets

An important principle of internal control is that a person who controls or has access to an asset must not keep that asset's accounting records. This principle reduces the risk of theft or waste of an asset because the person with control over it knows that another person keeps its records. Also, a recordkeeper who does not have access to the asset has no reason to falsify records. This means that two people must both agree to commit a fraud, called *collusion*, to steal an asset and hide the theft from the records. Because collusion is necessary to commit this type of fraud, it is less likely to occur.

> ### Did You Know?
>
> **Employee Control**   Do you know what lurks behind that spiffy resume you recently reviewed? The Fraud Defense Network's Fraud Tools page [**www.frauddefense.com**] provides links to free search engines to verify Social Security numbers, addresses, and phone numbers. **KnowX.com** lets you check lawsuits and bankruptcies for under $10. **Employeescreen.com** offers full background searches, including employment verification, for under $100. The Association of Certified Fraud Examiners [**www.cfenet.com**] can also help you find a professional examiner.

> ### Did You Know?
>
> **High-Tech Threads**   Theft and counterfeiting are concerns of most companies. **Tracer Detection Technology** has developed a technique for permanently marking all physical assets. Its technique involves embedding a one-inch-square tag of nylon fibers with different light-absorbing properties. Each pattern of fibers creates a unique optical signature recordable by scanners. It hopes to embed tags in everything from compact disks and credit cards to designer clothes.

Divide Responsibility for Related Transactions

Good internal control divides responsibility for a transaction or a series of related transactions between two or more individuals or departments. This is to ensure that the work of one acts as a check on the other. This principle, often called *separation of duties*, is not a call for duplication of work. Each employee or department should perform unduplicated effort. Examples of transactions with divided responsibility are placing purchase orders, receiving merchandise, and paying vendors. These tasks should not be given to one individual or department. Assigning responsibility for two or more of these tasks to one party increases mistakes and perhaps fraud. Having an independent person, for example, check incoming goods for quality and quantity encourages more care and attention to detail than having the person who placed the order do the checking. Added protection can result from identifying a third person to approve payment of the invoice. We can even designate a fourth person with authority to write checks as another measure of protection.

Apply Technological Controls

Cash registers, check protectors, time clocks, and personal identification scanners are examples of devices that can improve internal control. Technology often improves the effectiveness of controls. A cash register with a locked-in tape or electronic file makes a record of each cash sale. A check protector perforates the amount of a check into its face and makes it difficult to alter the amount. A time clock registers the exact time an employee both arrives at and departs from the job. Mechanical change and currency counters quickly and accurately count amounts, and personal scanners limit access to only authorized individuals. Each of these and other technological controls are an effective part of many internal control systems.

Perform Regular and Independent Reviews

No internal control system is perfect. Changes in personnel and technological advances present opportunities for shortcuts and lapses. So does the stress of time pressures. To counter these factors, regular reviews of internal control systems are needed to ensure that procedures are followed. These reviews are preferably done by internal auditors not directly involved in the activities. Their impartial perspective encourages an evaluation of the efficiency as well as the effectiveness of the internal control system. Many companies also pay for audits by independent, external auditors. These external auditors test the company's financial records to give an opinion as to whether its financial statements are presented fairly. Before external auditors decide on how much testing is needed, they evaluate the effectiveness of the internal control system. In the process of their evaluation, they identify and assess internal controls. This information is often helpful to a client.

You Make the Call *e*

Entrepreneur As owner of a start-up information services company, you hire a systems analyst. One of her first recommendations is to require all employees to take at least one week of vacation per year. Why would she recommend a "forced vacation" policy?

Answer—p. 379

Technology and Internal Control

The fundamental principles of internal control are relevant no matter what the technological state of the accounting system, from purely manual to fully automated systems. Technology impacts an internal control system in several important ways. Perhaps the most obvious is that technology allows us quicker access to databases and information. Used ef-

Point: Information on Internet fraud can be found at these sites: www.ftc.gov/ftc/consumer.htm www.sec.gov/consumer/offertip.htm www.fraud.org

fectively, technology greatly improves managers' abilities to monitor and control business activities. This section describes some technological impacts we must be alert to.

Reduced Processing Errors

Technologically advanced systems reduce the number of errors in processing information. Provided the software and data entry are correct, the risk of mechanical and mathematical errors is nearly eliminated, but erroneous software or data entry does occur and we must be alert to that possibility. Also, less human involvement in data processing also can cause data entry errors to go undiscovered. Similarly, errors in software can produce consistent but erroneous processing of transactions. Continually checking and monitoring all types of systems is important.

> **Did You Know?**
>
> **Shredder or Spy?** That paper shredder in the office could be a high-tech spy tool. A Web site that specializes in gadgets for snooping sold several $5,000 shredders fitted with scanners and wireless transmitters, according to law-enforcement sources. As confidential documents are fed in, they're scanned, and the info is sent to an e-mail address.

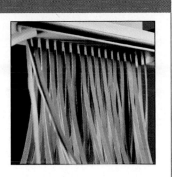

More Extensive Testing of Records

A company's review and audit of electronic records can include more extensive testing when information is easily and rapidly accessed. When accounting records are kept manually, auditors and others likely select only small samples of data to test. When data are accessible with computer technology, however, large samples or even complete data files can be quickly reviewed and analyzed.

Limited Evidence of Processing

Many data processing steps are increasingly done by computer. Accordingly, fewer hard-copy items of documentary evidence are available for review. On the other hand, technologically advanced systems can provide other evidence. They can, for instance, record information such as who made the entries, the date and time, and the source of their entry. Technology can also be designed to require the use of passwords or other identification before access to the system is granted. This means that internal control depends more on the design and operation of the information system and less on the analysis of its resulting documents.

Crucial Separation of Duties

Technological advances in accounting information systems often yield some job eliminations or consolidations. A reduction in workforce carries a risk of losing separation of crucial responsibilities. Companies that use advanced technology also need employees with special skills to operate programs and equipment. The duties of these employees must be controlled and monitored to minimize risk of error and fraud. Better control is maintained if, for instance, the person designing and programming the system does not operate it. The control over programs and files related to cash receipts and disbursements also must be separated. To avoid risk of fraud, the check-writing

> **Did You Know?**
>
> **Accounting Techies** Most internal control systems rely on information technology. A recent study estimates that 200,000 jobs in information technology are vacant. Demand far outstrips supply, producing a bidding war for digital talent in accounting. The most prized recruits are adept at enterprise software, the Web, intranets, and accounting. A recent survey cited the shortage of accounting techies as one of the greatest barriers to company growth.

activities should not be controlled by a computer operator. Achieving acceptable separation of duties can be especially difficult and costly in small companies with few employees.

Limitations of Internal Control

All internal control policies and procedures have limitations. Probably the most serious limitation is the human element. Internal control policies and procedures are applied by people and often impact other people. This human element creates several potential limitations that we can categorize as either (1) human error or (2) human fraud. *Human error* can occur from negligence, fatigue, misjudgment, or confusion. It is a factor when people carry out internal control policies and procedures. *Human fraud* involves intent by people to defeat internal controls for personal gain. Fraud includes collusion to thwart the separation of duties. The human element highlights the importance of establishing an *internal control environment* to convey management's commitment to internal control policies and procedures.

Another important limitation on internal control is the *cost-benefit principle*. This means the costs of internal controls must not exceed their benefits. Analysis of costs and benefits must consider all factors, including the impact on morale. Most companies, for instance, have a legal right to read employees' e-mail, yet companies seldom exercise that right unless they are confronted with evidence of potential harm to the company. The same holds for drug testing, phone tapping, and hidden camera monitoring. The bottom line is that no internal control system is perfect and that managers must establish internal control policies and procedures with a net benefit to the company.

Quick Check

1. Fundamental principles of internal control suggest which of the following:
(a) Responsibility for a series of related transactions (such as placing orders, receiving and paying for merchandise) should be assigned to one employee;
(b) Responsibility for individual tasks should be shared by more than one employee so that one serves as a check on the other; or (c) Employees who handle cash and easily transferable assets should be bonded.

2. What are some impacts of computing technology on internal control?

Answers—p. 380

Control of Cash

Cash is a necessary asset of every company. Most companies include *cash equivalents*, which are similar to cash, as part of cash. Applying principles of internal control to both cash and cash equivalents is important. Cash and cash equivalents are the most liquid of all assets and are easily hidden and moved. An effective system of internal controls protects both cash receipts and cash disbursements and should meet three basic guidelines:

1. Handling cash is separate from recordkeeping of cash.
2. Cash receipts are promptly deposited in a bank.
3. Cash disbursements are made by check.

The first guideline minimizes errors and fraud by separation of duties. As noted earlier, when duties are separated, two or more people must collude to steal cash and conceal this action in the accounting records. The second guideline uses immediate (say, daily) deposits of all cash receipts to produce a timely independent record of the accuracy of the amount of cash received. It also reduces the likelihood of cash theft and loss and the risk that an employee could personally use the money before depositing it. The third guideline uses payments by check to develop an independent bank record of cash disbursements. This guideline also reduces the risk of cash theft and loss.

The exact procedures used to achieve control over cash vary across companies. They depend on factors such as company size, number of employees, volume of cash transactions, and sources of cash. We must therefore view the procedures described in this section as illustrative. This section begins with definitions of cash and cash equivalents. Discussion then focuses on controls and accounting for both cash receipts and disbursements.

Cash, Cash Equivalents, and Liquidity

Define cash and cash equivalents and explain how to report them.

Cash is an important asset for every company and must be managed. Companies also need to carefully control access to cash by employees and others. Good accounting systems both help manage the amount of cash and control who has access to it. The importance of accounting for cash is highlighted by the inclusion of a statement of cash flows in a complete set of financial statements. That statement identifies activities affecting cash.

Point: The most liquid assets are usually reported first on a balance sheet; the least liquid assets are reported last.

Cash and Cash Equivalents Defined

Cash includes currency and coins along with the amounts on deposit in bank accounts, checking accounts (called *demand deposits*), and many savings accounts (called *time deposits*). Cash also includes items that are acceptable for deposit in these accounts such as customers' checks, cashier checks, certified checks, and money orders.

> **Did You Know?**
>
> **Cash Glut   I2 Technologies** reports cash and cash equivalents of $455 million in its recent balance sheet. This amount makes up more than one-half of its total assets.

Cash equivalents are short-term, highly liquid investment assets meeting two criteria: (1) readily convertible to a known cash amount and (2) sufficiently close to their maturity date so that their market value is not sensitive to interest rate changes. Only investments purchased within three months of their maturity dates usually satisfy these criteria. Examples of cash equivalents are short-term investments in assets such as U.S. treasury bills, money market funds, and commercial paper (such as short-term corporate notes payable). To increase their return on investment in cash, many companies invest idle cash in cash equivalents. Most companies combine cash equivalents with cash as a single item on the balance sheet. For example, **Mattel** reports a single cash balance and states that "Cash includes cash equivalents, which are highly liquid investments with maturities of three months or less when purchased. Because of the short maturities of these instruments, the carrying amount is a reasonable estimate of fair value."

Cash is the usual means of payment when paying for other assets, services, or liabilities. **Liquidity** refers to a company's ability to pay for its near term obligations. Cash and similar assets are called **liquid assets** because they can be readily used to settle such obligations. A company needs liquid assets to effectively operate.

> **Did You Know?**
>
> **Cyber-Sleuths**   A team of lawyers at the Federal Trade Commission is on the cutting edge of cybersleuthing. Opportunists in search of easy money on the Internet have been lured to **www.ari.net/NetOpportunities**, where a lurid banner proclaims: "The Internet is a GOLD MINE!!!" It says you can get rich quick—as an "Internet Con$ultant." Take the bait and you get warned—and probably targeted.
>
>
>
> Cyber Fraud on the Rise
> Internet complaints as a percentage of all consumer complaints filed with the FTC
> ▲ Percent
> DATA: FEDERAL TRADE COMMISSION

Control of Cash Receipts

Internal control of cash receipts ensures that cash received is properly recorded and deposited. Cash receipts arise from transactions such as cash sales, collections of customers' accounts, receipts of interest earned, bank loans, sale of assets, and owner investments. The principles of internal control apply to all cash receipts. This section explains internal control over two important types of cash receipts: over-the-counter and by mail.

P1   Apply internal control to cash receipts.

Over-the-Counter Cash Receipts

For purposes of internal control, over-the-counter cash receipts from sales should be recorded on a cash register at the time of each sale. To help ensure that correct amounts are entered, each register should be located so customers can read the amounts entered. Clerks also should be required to enter each sale before wrapping merchandise and to give the customer a receipt for each sale. The design of each cash register should provide a permanent, locked-in record of each transaction. In many systems, the register is directly linked with computing and accounting services. Less advanced registers simply print a record of each transaction on a paper tape or electronic file locked inside the register.

One principle of internal control states that custody over cash should be separate from its recordkeeping. For over-the-counter cash receipts, this separation begins with the cash sale. The clerk who has access to cash in the register should not have access to its locked-in record. At the end of the clerk's work period, the clerk should count the cash in the register, record the amount, and turn over the cash and a record of its amount to the company's cashier. The cashier, like the clerk, has access to the cash but should not have access to accounting records (or the register tape or file). A third employee compares the record of total register transactions (or the register tape or file) with the cash receipts reported by the cashier. This record (or register tape or file) is the basis for a journal entry recording over-the-counter cash receipts. The third employee has access to the records for cash but not to the actual cash. The clerk and the cashier have access to cash but not to the accounting records. None of them can make a mistake or divert cash without the difference being revealed.

Point: Retailers often require cashiers to restrictively endorse checks immediately on receipt by stamping them "For deposit only."

Cash over and short

Sometimes errors in making change are discovered from differences between the cash in a cash register and the record of the amount of cash receipts. Although a clerk is careful, one or more customers can be given too much or too little change. This means that at the end of a work period, the cash in a cash register might not equal the cash receipts entered. This difference is reported in the **Cash Over and Short** account, which is an income statement account recording the income effects of cash overages and cash shortages. To illustrate, if a cash register shows cash receipts of $550 but the count of cash in the register is $555, the entry to record cash sales and its overage is

Assets = Liabilities + Equity
+555   + 5
                      +550

Cash	555	
Cash Over and Short		**5**
Sales		550
To record cash sales and an overage.		

If a cash register shows cash receipts of $625 but the count of cash in the register is $621, the entry to record cash sales and its shortage is:

Assets = Liabilities + Equity
+621   − 4
                      +625

Cash	621	
Cash Over and Short	**4**	
Sales		625
To record cash sales and a shortage.		

Because customers are more likely to dispute being shortchanged, the Cash Over and Short account usually has a debit balance at the end of an accounting period. This debit balance reflects an expense. It can be shown on the income statement as an item in general and administrative expenses. But since the amount is usually small, it is often combined with other small expenses and reported as part of *miscellaneous expenses*. If Cash Over and Short has a credit balance at the end of the period, it usually is shown on the income statement as part of *miscellaneous revenues*.

Cash Receipts by Mail

Control of cash receipts that arrive through the mail starts with the person who opens the mail. Preferably, two people are assigned the task of, and are present for, opening the mail. In this case, theft of cash receipts by mail requires collusion between these two employees. The person opening the mail enters a list (in triplicate) of money received. This list should contain a record of each sender's name, the amount, and an explanation of why the money is sent. The first copy is sent with the money to the cashier. A second copy is sent to the recordkeeper in the accounting area. A third copy is kept by the clerks who opened the mail. The cashier deposits the money in a bank, and the recordkeeper records the amounts received in the accounting records.

Point: A complete set of financial statements includes a statement of cash flows, which provides useful information about a company's sources and uses of cash and cash equivalents during a period of time.

This process reflects good internal control. First, when the bank balance is reconciled by another person (explained later in the chapter), errors or fraud by the mail clerks, the cashier, or the recordkeeper are revealed. They are revealed because the bank's record of cash deposited must agree with the records from each of the three. Moreover, if the mail clerks do not report all receipts correctly, customers will question their account balances. If the cashier does not deposit all receipts, the bank balance does not agree with the recordkeeper's cash balance. The recordkeeper and the person who reconciles the bank balance do not have access to cash and, therefore, have no opportunity to divert cash to themselves. This system makes errors and fraud highly unlikely. The exception is when employees collude.

> **Did You Know?** *e*
>
> **Entrepreneurs, Head West!** In a recent survey by the Small Business Survival Foundation [**www.SBSC.org**], 5 of the top 6 states ranked as most entrepreneur friendly are west of the Mississippi. They are (1) South Dakota, (2) Wyoming, (3) Nevada, (4) New Hampshire, (5) Texas, and (6) Washington. The index is based on several factors including taxes, regulations, compensation costs, and crime.

Control of Cash Disbursements

Control of cash disbursements is especially important for companies. Most large thefts occur from payment of fictitious invoices. One key to controlling cash disbursements is to require all expenditures to be made by check. The only exception is small payments made from petty cash. Another key is to deny access to the accounting records to anyone other than the owner who has the authority to sign checks. The owner of a small business often signs checks and knows from personal contact that the items being paid for are actually received. This arrangement is impossible in large businesses. Instead, internal control procedures must be substituted for personal contact. Such procedures are designed to assure the check signer that the obligations recorded are properly incurred and should be paid. This section describes these and other internal control procedures. They include the voucher system, petty cash system, and the management of cash disbursements for purchases.

> **Did You Know?**
>
> **Paper Chase** Companies are increasingly converting from paper to electronic documents. The basic purposes and features of most paper and electronic documents are the same. But the internal control system must change to reflect different risks and concerns. This includes confidential and competitive-sensitive information that is at greater risk in electronic systems.

Voucher System of Control

A **voucher system** is a set of procedures and approvals designed to control cash disbursements and the acceptance of obligations. The voucher system of control establishes procedures for

P2 Apply the voucher system to control cash disbursements.

- Verifying, approving, and recording obligations for eventual cash disbursement.
- Issuing checks for payment of verified, approved, and recorded obligations.

A reliable voucher system follows standard procedures for every transaction. This applies even when multiple purchases are made from the same supplier.

A voucher system's control over cash disbursements begins when a company incurs an obligation that will result in payment of cash. A key factor in this system is that only approved departments and individuals are authorized to incur such obligations. The system often limits the type of obligations that a department or individual can incur. In a large retail store, for instance, only a purchasing department should be authorized to incur obligations for merchandise inventory. Another key factor is that procedures for purchasing, receiving, and paying for merchandise are divided among several departments (or individuals). These departments include the one requesting the purchase, the purchasing department, the receiving department, and the accounting department. To coordinate and control responsibilities of these departments, several different business documents are used. Exhibit 9.1 shows how documents are accumulated in a **voucher,** which is an internal document (or file) used to accumulate information to control cash disbursements and to ensure that a transaction is properly recorded. Appendix 9A describes each document entering and leaving a voucher system. It also describes the internal control objective served by each document.

Exhibit 9.1

Document Flow in a Voucher System

Sender		Receiver(s)
Cashier	Check	Supplier (vendor)
Accounting	Invoice Approval	Cashier
Receiving	Receiving Report	Accounting, Requesting, and Purchasing
Supplier (vendor)	Invoice	Accounting
Purchasing	Purchase Order	Supplier (vendor), Requesting, and Accounting
Requesting	Purchase Requisition	Purchasing and Accounting

Voucher

A voucher system should be applied not only to purchases but also to all expenses. To illustrate, when a company receives a monthly telephone bill, the charges should be reviewed and verified. A voucher (file) is prepared and the telephone bill is inserted. This transaction is then recorded with a journal entry. If the amount is due at once, a check is issued. If not, the voucher is filed for payment on its due date.

Vouchers should be prepared for all incurred expenses, whether cash payment occurs now or later. This is so because many invoices or bills are often not received until weeks after work is done. If no expense records exist, verifying the invoice and its amount can be difficult. Also, without records, a dishonest employee could collude with a dishonest supplier to get more than one payment for an obligation, payment for excessive amounts, or payment for goods and services not received. An effective voucher system helps prevent such frauds.

Did You Know?

High-Tech Fraud   Weak internal control contributed to a debacle at **Centennial Technologies**, once a high-tech dynamo. Fictitious sales receipts and altered inventory tags deceived auditors, investors, and creditors. Its CEO was eventually indicted on five counts of fraud. Many of these shenanigans could have been avoided with better internal controls.

Point: A voucher is an internal document (file).

Quick Check

3. Why must a company own liquid assets?

4. Why does a company own cash equivalent assets in addition to cash?

5. Identify at least two assets that are classified as cash equivalents.

6. Good internal control procedures for cash include which of the following? (a) All cash disbursements, other than those for very small amounts, are made by check; (b) One employee should count cash received from sales and promptly deposit cash receipts; or (c) Cash receipts by mail should be opened by one employee who is then responsible for recording and depositing receipts.

7. Do all companies require a voucher system? At what point in a company's growth would you recommend a voucher system?

Answers—p. 380

Explain and record petty cash fund transactions.

Petty Cash System of Control

A basic principle for controlling cash disbursements is that all payments must be made by check. An exception to this rule is made for *petty cash disbursements,* which are the small payments required for items such as postage, courier fees, repairs, and low-cost supplies.

Making all small payments by check would require numerous checks for small amounts, and would be both time consuming and expensive. To avoid writing checks for small amounts, a company sets up a petty cash fund and uses the money in this fund to make small payments.

Operating a petty cash fund

Establishing a petty cash fund requires estimating the total amount of small payments likely to be made during a short period such as a week or month. A check is then drawn by the company cashier for an amount slightly in excess of this estimate. This check is recorded with a debit to the Petty Cash account (an asset) and a credit to Cash. The check is cashed, and the currency is given to an employee designated as a *petty cashier,* also called *petty cash custodian.* The petty cashier is responsible for the safekeeping of this cash, making payments from the fund, and its recordkeeping. The petty cashier keeps petty cash and its records in a secure place referred to as the *petty cashbox.*

To illustrate, when each cash disbursement is made, the person receiving payment should sign a *petty cash receipt,* also called *petty cash ticket*—see Exhibit 9.2. The petty cash receipt is then placed in the petty cashbox with the remaining money. Under this system, the sum of all receipts plus the remaining cash equals the total fund amount. A $100 petty cash fund, for instance, contains any combination of cash and petty cash receipts that total $100 (examples are $80 cash plus $20 in receipts, or $10 cash plus $90 in receipts). Each disbursement reduces cash and increases the amount of receipts in the petty cashbox.

Point: A petty cash fund is used only for business expenses.

Petty Cash Receipt		No. 9
Z-Mart		
For ___Freight charges___	Date ___11/5/02___	
Charge to ___Merchandise Inventory___	Amount ___$6.75___	
Approved by ___Jim Gills___	Received by ___Dick Pitch___	

Exhibit 9.2

Petty Cash Receipt

When the petty cash is nearing zero, it should be reimbursed. The petty cashier first sorts the paid receipts by the type of expense or account and then totals the receipts. The petty cashier presents all paid receipts to the company cashier, who stamps all receipts *paid* so they cannot be reused, files them for recordkeeping, and gives the petty cashier a check for their sum. When this check is cashed and the money placed in the cashbox, the total money in the cashbox is restored to its original amount. The fund is now ready for a new cycle of petty cash payments.

Point: Auditors often find misuse of petty cash when petty cash receipts have either no signature or a forged signature. Companies respond with surprise petty cash counts for verification.

Illustration of a petty cash fund

Z-Mart uses a petty cash fund to avoid writing an excessive number of checks for small amounts. To illustrate, assume that Z-Mart establishes a petty cash fund on November 1. It designates one of its office employees as the petty cashier. A $75 check is drawn, cashed, and the proceeds given to the petty cashier. The entry to record the setup of this petty cash fund is

Nov. 1	Petty Cash	75	
	Cash		75
	To establish a petty cash fund.		

Assets = Liabilities + Equity
+75
−75

This entry transfers $75 from the regular Cash account to the Petty Cash account. After the petty cash fund is established, the Petty Cash account is not debited or credited again unless the size of the total fund is changed. A fund probably should be increased if it is being used and reimbursed too frequently. If the fund is too large, some of its money should be redeposited in the Cash account.

Exhibit 9.3

Petty Cash Payments Report

	Z-MART		
	Petty Cash Payments Report		
Miscellaneous Expenses			
Nov. 2	Washing windows	$20.00	
Nov. 27	Printer cartridge	26.50	$46.50
Merchandise Inventory (transportation-in)			
Nov. 5	Transport of merchandise purchased	6.75	
Nov. 20	Transport of merchandise purchased	8.30	15.05
Delivery Expense			
Nov. 18	Customer's package delivered		5.00
Office Expense			
Nov. 15	Purchase of office supplies		4.75
Total			**$71.30**

Point: Although individual petty cash disbursements are not evidenced by a check, the initial petty cash fund is evidenced by a check, and later petty cash expenditures are evidenced by a check to replenish them in total.

During November, the petty cashier makes several payments from petty cash. Each person who received payment is required to sign a receipt. On November 27, after making a $26.50 cash payment for a printer cartridge, only $3.70 cash remains in the fund. The petty cashier then summarizes and totals the petty cash receipts as shown in Exhibit 9.3. This summary and all petty cash receipts are given to the company cashier in exchange for a $71.30 check to reimburse the fund. The petty cashier cashes the check and puts the $71.30 cash in the petty cashbox. The company records the check for reimbursement as follows:

Assets = Liabilities + Equity			
−71.30		−46.50	
		−15.05	
		− 5.00	
		− 4.75	

Nov. 27	Miscellaneous Expenses	46.50	
	Merchandise Inventory	15.05	
	Delivery Expense	5.00	
	Office Expense	4.75	
	Cash		71.30
	To reimburse petty cash.		

Information for this entry is taken from the petty cashier's summary of payments in Exhibit 9.3. The debits in this entry reflect the petty cash payments.

A petty cash fund is often reimbursed at the end of an accounting period even if it is not low on money. This is done to record expenses in the proper period. If the fund is not reimbursed at the end of a period, the financial statements show both an overstated petty cash asset and understated expenses (or assets) that were paid out of petty cash. Some companies do not reimburse the petty cash fund at the end of each period under the assumption that this amount is immaterial to users of financial statements.

Point: To avoid errors in recording petty cash reimbursement, follow these steps: (1) prepare payments report, (2) compute cash needed by subtracting cash remaining from total fund amount, (3) record entry, and (4) check "Dr. = Cr." in entry—any difference is Cash Over and Short.

Increasing or decreasing a petty cash fund

A decision to increase or decrease a petty cash fund is often made when reimbursing it. To illustrate, let's assume Z-Mart decides to *increase* its petty cash fund to $100 on November 27 when it reimburses the fund. The entry to do this is identical to the preceding one except that it includes a (1) debit to Petty Cash for $25 (increasing the fund from $75 to $100) and (2) credit to Cash for $96.30 ($71.30 reimbursement of expenses plus $25 increase in the fund). Alternatively, if Z-Mart *decreases* the petty cash fund from $75 to $55 on November 27, the changes required for the entry on this date

You Make the Call—Ethics

Internal Auditor You are making surprise counts of several $300 petty cash funds. You arrive at one of the petty cashiers when she is on the telephone. She politely asks that you return after lunch so that she can finish her business on the telephone. You agree and return after lunch. In the petty cashbox, you find 14 new $20 bills with consecutive serial numbers plus receipts totaling $20. What is your evaluation?

Answer—p. 380

include a (1) credit to Petty Cash for $20 (decreasing the fund from $75 to $55) and (2) credit to Cash for $51.30 ($71.30 reimbursement of expense minus $20 decrease in the fund).

Cash over and short

Sometimes a petty cashier fails to get a receipt for payment. When this occurs and the fund is later reimbursed, the petty cash payments report plus the cash remaining will not total to the fund balance. This mistake causes the fund to be *short*. If the petty cash fund is short, this shortage is recorded as an expense in the reimbursing entry with a debit to the Cash Over and Short account. (An overage in the petty cash fund is recorded with a credit to Cash Over and Short in the reimbursing entry.)

Example: Prepare the entry to reimburse a $200 petty cash fund when its payments report shows $178 in miscellaneous expenses and $15 cash remains.

Miscel. Expenses	178	
Cash Over & Short	7	
Cash		185

Quick Check

8. Why are some cash payments made from a petty cash fund, and not by check?

9. Why should a petty cash fund be reimbursed at the end of an accounting period?

10. Identify at least two results of reimbursing a petty cash fund.

Answers—p. 380

Control of Purchase Discounts

P4 Apply the net method to control purchase discounts.

This section explains how a company can gain more control over cash *disbursements* to take advantage of favorable purchase discounts. Chapter 6 describes the entries to record the receipt and payment of an invoice for a purchase of merchandise. When Z-Mart purchases merchandise at a $1,200 invoice price with terms of 2/10, n/30, it makes this entry:

Nov. 2	Merchandise Inventory	1,200	
	Accounts Payable		1,200
	Purchased merchandise on credit, invoice dated Nov. 2, terms 2/10, n/30.		

Assets = Liabilities + Equity
+1,200   +1,200

If Z-Mart takes advantage of the discount and pays the amount due on November 12, the entry is

Nov. 12	Accounts Payable	1,200	
	Merchandise Inventory		24
	Cash		1,176
	Paid for the purchase of Nov. 2 less the discount (2% × $1,200).		

Assets = Liabilities + Equity
−24   −1,200
−1,176

These entries reflect the **gross method** of recording purchases, which records the invoice at its *gross* amount of $1,200 *before* recognizing the cash discount. Many companies record invoices in this way.

Another method of recording purchases is the **net method,** which records the invoice at its *net* amount *after* recognizing the cash discount. This method is viewed as providing more useful information to manage cash disbursements. If Z-Mart uses the net method of recording purchases, it deducts the potential $24 cash discount from the gross amount and records the initial purchase at the $1,176 net amount:

Nov. 2	Merchandise Inventory	1,176	
	Accounts Payable		1,176
	Purchased merchandise on credit, invoice dated Nov. 2, terms 2/10, n/30.		

Assets = Liabilities + Equity
+1,176   +1,176

If the invoice for this purchase is paid within the discount period, the entry to record the payment debits Accounts Payable and credits Cash for $1,176. However, if payment is not made within the discount period and the discount is *lost,* the following additional entry must be made either on the date the discount is lost or later when the invoice is paid:

Nov. 13	Discounts Lost	24	
	Accounts Payable		24
	To record the discount lost.		

A check for the full $1,200 invoice amount must be written, recorded, and sent to the creditor.[1] The net method gives management an advantage in controlling and monitoring cash payments involving purchase discounts. When invoices are recorded at *gross* amounts, the amount of any discounts taken is deducted from the balance of the Merchandise Inventory account when cash payment is made. This means that the amount of any discounts lost is not reported in any account or on the income statement. Lost discounts recorded in this way are unlikely to come to the attention of management. However, when purchases are recorded at *net* amounts, a **Discount Lost** expense account is recorded and brought to management's attention as an operating expense. Management can then seek to identify the reason for discounts lost such as oversight, carelessness, or unfavorable terms. This practice gives management better control over persons responsible for paying bills to ensure that they take advantage of favorable discounts.[2]

Banking Activities as Controls

Banks (and other financial institutions) provide many different services. One of their most important services is helping companies control cash and cash transactions. Banks safeguard cash, provide detailed and independent records of cash transactions, and are a source of cash financing. This section describes services and documents provided by banking activities that increase managers' control over cash.

Basic Bank Services

C4 Identify control features of banking activities.

This section explains basic bank services. We include the bank account, the bank deposit, and checking. Each of these services contributes to either or both the control and safeguarding of cash.

Bank Account

A bank account is a record set up by a bank for a customer. It permits a customer to deposit money for safeguarding and helps control withdrawals. To limit access to a bank account, all persons authorized to write checks on the account must sign a **signature card,** which bank employees use to verify signatures on checks. This lowers the risk of loss from forgery. Many companies have more than one bank account to serve different needs and to handle special transactions such as payroll.

Global: If cash is in more than one currency, a company usually translates these amounts into U.S. dollars using the exchange rate as of the balance sheet date.

Bank Deposit

Each bank deposit is supported by a **deposit ticket,** which lists items such as currency, coins, and checks deposited along with their corresponding dollar amounts. The bank gives the customer a copy of the deposit ticket or a deposit receipt as proof of the deposit. Exhibit 9.4 shows one type of deposit ticket.

---

[1] The discount lost can be recorded with the cash payment in a single entry. However, when financial statements are prepared after a discount is lost and before the cash payment is made, an adjusting entry is required to recognize any unrecorded discount lost in the period when incurred.

[2] To help managers assess whether a discount is favorable or not, we compute the *implied interest rate* of not taking the discount: (365 days/[Credit period − Discount period]) × Cash discount percent. For example, if terms are 2/10, n/30, then missing the 2% discount for an additional 20 days implies an annual interest rate of 36.5%, computed as (365 days/[30 days − 10 days]) × 2%. This suggests that if money can be borrowed for less than 36.5%, an entity should take advantage of the discount offered.

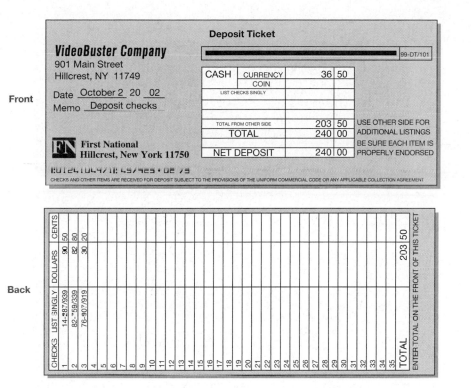

Exhibit 9.4
Deposit Ticket

Bank Check

To withdraw money from an account, the depositor uses a **check,** which is a document signed by the depositor instructing the bank to pay a specified amount of money to a designated recipient. A check involves three parties: a *maker* who signs the check, a *payee* who is the recipient, and a *bank* (or *payer*) on which the check is drawn. The bank provides a depositor the checks that are serially numbered and imprinted with the name and address of both the depositor and bank. Both checks and deposit tickets are imprinted with identification codes in magnetic ink for computer processing. Exhibit 9.5 shows one type of check. It is accompanied with an optional *remittance advice* explaining the payment. When a remittance advice is unavailable, the *memo* line is often used for a brief explanation.

> ### Did You Know?
>
> **Booting Up Your Banker** Many companies are now balancing checkbooks and paying bills via the Web. The convenience and low cost of banking services anytime, anywhere, are attracting customers. Services include the ability to stop payment on a check, move money between accounts, get up-to-date account balances, and identify checks and deposits that have cleared. Even taxes, suppliers, creditors, and employees can be paid electronically.

Electronic Funds Transfer

Electronic funds transfer (EFT) is electronic communication transfer of cash from one party to another. No paper documents are necessary. Banks simply transfer cash from one account to another with a journal entry. Companies are increasingly using EFT because of its covenience and low cost. For instance, it can cost up to one-half dollar to process a check through the banking system, whereas EFT cost is near zero. We now commonly see items such as payroll, rent, utilities, insurance, and interest payments being handled by EFT. The bank statement lists cash withdrawals by EFT with checks and other deductions. Cash receipts by EFT are listed with deposits and other additions. A bank statement is sometimes a depositor's only notice of an EFT.

Bank Statement

Usually once a month, the bank sends each depositor a bank statement showing the activity in the account during the past month. Different banks use different formats for their bank statements, but all of them include the following items of information:

Exhibit 9.5

Check with Remittance Advice

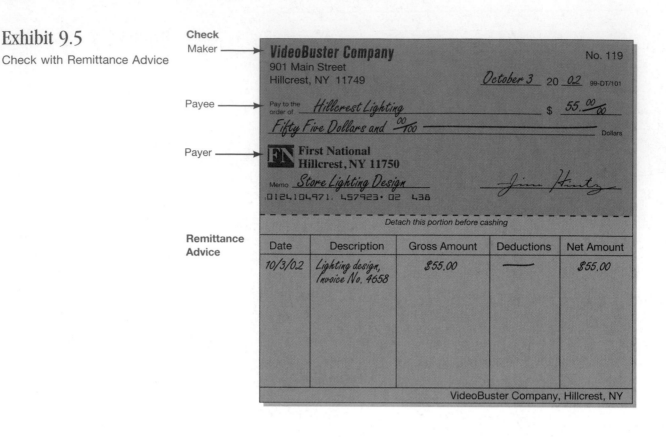

1. Beginning-of-period balance of the depositor's account.
2. Checks and other debits decreasing the account during the period.
3. Deposits and other credits increasing the account during the period.
4. End-of-period balance of the depositor's account.

Point: Good internal control is to deposit all cash receipts daily and make all payments for goods and services by check. This controls access to cash and creates an independent record of all cash activities.

This information reflects the bank's records. Exhibit 9.6 shows one type of bank statement. Identify each of these four items in that statement. Part A of Exhibit 9.6 summarizes changes in the account. Part B lists paid checks along with other debits. Part C lists deposits and credits to the account, and part D shows the daily account balances.

Enclosed with a bank statement is a list of the depositor's canceled checks or the actual canceled checks along with any debit or credit memoranda affecting the account. **Canceled checks** are checks the bank has paid and deducted from the customer's account during the period. Other deductions that can appear on a bank statement include (1) service charges and fees assessed by the bank, (2) checks deposited that are uncollectible, (3) corrections of previous errors, (4) withdrawals through automatic teller machines (ATMs), and (5) periodic payments arranged in advance by a depositor.[3] Except for service charges, the bank notifies the depositor of each deduction with a debit memorandum when the bank reduces the balance. A copy of each debit memorandum is usually sent with the statement.[4]

Global: A company must disclose any restrictions on cash accounts located outside the United States.

Transactions also can increase the depositor's account; such as amounts the bank collects on behalf of the depositor and the corrections of previous errors. Credit memoranda notify the depositor of all increases when they are recorded. A copy of each credit memorandum is often sent with the bank statement. Another item sometimes added to the bank balance is interest earned by the depositor. Banks that pay interest on checking accounts often com-

---

[3] Most business checking accounts do not allow ATM withdrawals because of a desire to make all disbursements by check.

[4] A depositor's account is a liability on the bank's records. This is so because the money belongs to the depositor, not the bank. When a depositor increases the account balance, the bank records it with a *credit* to the account. This means that debit memos from the bank produce *credits* on the depositor's books, and credit memos produce *debits* on the depositor's books.

Exhibit 9.6
Bank Statement

Member FDIC	**First National** Hillcrest, NY 11750		Bank Statement

VideoBuster Company
901 Main Street
Hillcrest, NY 11749

October 31, 2002
Statement Date

494 504 2
Account Number

Previous Balance	Total Checks and Debits	Total Deposits and Credits	Current Balance
1,609.58	723.00	1,163.42	2,050.00

Checks and Debits			Deposits and Credits		Daily Balance	
Date	No.	Amount	Date	Amount	Date	Amount
10/03	119	55.00	10/02	240.00	10/01	1,609.58
10/09	120	200.00	10/09	180.00	10/02	1,849.58
10/10	121	120.00	10/15	100.00	10/03	1,794.58
10/12		23.00 DM	10/16	150.00	10/09	1,774.58
10/14	122	70.00	10/23	485.00 CM	10/10	1,654.58
10/16	123	25.00	10/31	8.42 IN	10/12	1,631.58
10/23	125	15.00			10/14	1,561.58
10/25		20.00 NSF			10/15	1,661.58
		10.00 DM			10/16	1,786.58
10/26	127	50.00			10/23	2,256.58
10/29	128	135.00			10/25	2,226.58
					10/26	2,176.58
					10/29	2,041.58
					10/31	2,050.00

Symbols: **CM**–Credit Memo   **EC**–Error Correction   **NSF**–Non-Sufficient Funds   **SC**–Service Charge
DM–Debit Memo   **IN**–Interest Earned   **OD**–Overdraft

< Reconcile the account immediately. >

pute the amount of interest earned on the average cash balance and credit it to the depositor's account each period. In Exhibit 9.6, the bank credits $8.42 of interest to the account of VideoBuster.

Bank Reconciliation

When a company both deposits all cash receipts and makes all cash payments (except petty cash) by check, it can use the bank statement for proving the accuracy of the depositor's cash records. This is done using a **bank reconciliation,** which is a report explaining any differences between the checking account balance according to the depositor's records and the balance reported on the bank statement.

P5 Prepare a bank reconciliation.

Concept 9-2

Purpose of Bank Reconciliation

The balance of a checking account reported on the bank statement rarely equals the balance in the depositor's accounting records. This is usually due to information that one party has that the other does not. We must therefore prove the accuracy of both the depositor's records and those of the bank. This means we must *reconcile* the two balances and explain or account for any differences in these two balances.

Among the factors causing the bank statement balance to differ from the depositor's book balance are these:

1. **Outstanding checks. Outstanding checks** are checks written (or drawn) by the depositor, deducted on the depositor's records, and sent to the payees but not yet received by the bank for payment at the bank statement date.
2. **Deposits in transit** (also called **outstanding deposits**). **Deposits in transit** are deposits made and recorded by the depositor but not yet recorded on the bank statement. For

example, companies often make deposits at the end of a business day after the bank is closed. The bank does not record a deposit in the bank's night depository on the last day of the period until the next business day, and it does not appear on the bank statement for that period. Deposits mailed to the bank near the end of a period also can be in transit and unrecorded when the statement is prepared.

3. **Deductions for uncollectible items and for services.** A company sometimes deposits another's check that is uncollectible (usually meaning the balance in such an account is not large enough to cover the check). This check is called a *non-sufficient funds (NSF)* check. The bank initially credits the depositor's account for the amount of the deposited check. When the bank learns the check is uncollectible, it debits (reduces) the depositor's account for the amount of that check. The bank may also charge the depositor a fee for processing an uncollectible check and notify the depositor of the deduction by sending a debit memorandum. Each deduction should be recorded by the depositor when a debit memorandum is received, but an entry is sometimes not made until the bank reconciliation is prepared. Other possible bank charges to a depositor's account that are reported on a bank statement include printing new checks and service for maintaining the account. Notification of these charges is typically first made in the bank statement.

4. **Additions for collections and for interest.** Banks sometimes act as collection agents for their depositors by collecting notes and other items. Banks can also receive electronic fund transfers to the depositor's account. When a bank collects an item, it is added to the depositor's account, less any service fee. The bank also sends a credit memorandum to notify the depositor of the transaction. When the memorandum is received, the depositor should record it; yet it sometimes remains unrecorded until the bank reconciliation is prepared. If an account earns interest, the bank statement includes a credit for the amount earned.

5. **Errors.** Both banks and depositors can make errors. Bank errors might not be discovered until the depositor prepares the bank reconciliation. Also, depositor errors are sometimes discovered when the bank balance is reconciled.

Reconciling a Bank Balance

The employee who prepares the bank reconciliation should not be responsible for cash receipts, processing checks, or maintaining cash records. A reconciliation requires this person to

■ Compare deposits on the bank statement with deposits in the accounting records. Identify any discrepancies and determine which is correct. List any errors and unrecorded deposits.

■ Inspect all credits on the bank statement and determine whether each is recorded. Examples are collections by the bank, correction of previous bank statement errors, and interest earned by the depositor. List any unrecorded credits.

■ Compare canceled checks on the bank statement with actual checks returned (if provided) with the statement. For each check, make sure the bank deducts the correct amount and properly charges it to the account. List any discrepancies.

■ Compare canceled checks on the bank statement with checks recorded. List any outstanding checks. Inspect and list any canceled checks unrecorded.

■ Identify any outstanding checks listed on the previous period's bank reconciliation that are not included in the canceled checks on this period's bank statement. List those checks that still remain outstanding. Send the list to the cashier for follow-up with payees to see if the checks were received.

■ Inspect all debits on the bank statement and determine whether each is recorded. Examples are bank charges for newly printed checks, NSF checks, and monthly service charges. List any unrecorded debits.

Point: Small businesses with few employees often allow recordkeepers to both write checks and keep the general ledger. If this is done, it is essential that the owner do the bank reconciliation.

When these tasks are complete, the employee can then prepare the reconciliation.

Illustrating a Bank Reconciliation

We follow nine steps in preparing the bank reconciliation. It is helpful to refer to the bank reconciliation for VideoBuster shown in Exhibit 9.7 when studying steps ① through ⑨.

① Identify the bank balance of the cash account (*balance per bank*).

② Identify and list any unrecorded deposits and any bank errors understating the bank balance. Add them to the bank balance.

③ Identify and list any outstanding checks and any bank errors overstating the bank balance. Deduct them from the bank balance.

④ Compute the *adjusted bank balance,* also called *corrected* or *reconciled balance.*

⑤ Identify the company's book balance of the cash account (*balance per book*).

⑥ Identify and list any unrecorded credit memoranda from the bank, interest earned, and errors understating the book balance. Add them to the book balance.

⑦ Identify and list any unrecorded debit memoranda from the bank, service charges, and errors overstating the book balance. Deduct them from the book balance.

⑧ Compute the *adjusted book balance,* also called *corrected* or *reconciled balance.*

⑨ Verify that the two adjusted balances from steps 4 and 8 are equal. If so, they are reconciled. If not, check for accuracy and missing data to achieve reconciliation.

In reconciling the bank account, VideoBuster gathered the following data:

■ Bank balance shown on the bank statement is $2,050.

■ Book balance shown in the accounting records is $1,404.58.

■ A $145 deposit placed in the bank's night depository on October 31 is not recorded on the bank statement.

■ A comparison of canceled checks with the company's books showed two checks outstanding—No. 124 for $150 and No. 126 for $200.

■ Enclosed with the bank statement is a credit memorandum showing the bank collected a note receivable for the company on October 23. The note's proceeds of $500 (minus a $15 collection fee) are credited to the company's account. The company has not yet recorded this credit memorandum.

■ The bank statement shows a credit of $8.42 for interest earned on the average cash balance. There was no prior notification of this item, and it is not yet recorded.

■ Other debits on the bank statement that are not recorded include (1) a $23 charge for checks printed by the bank and (2) a NSF check for $20 plus a related $10 processing fee. The NSF check is dated October 16 and included in that day's deposit.

The bank reconciliation in Exhibit 9.7 reflects these items. The circled numbers in this reconciliation correspond to the nine steps listed.

Recording Adjusting Entries from a Bank Reconciliation

A bank reconciliation helps identify any errors by both the bank and the depositor. It also identifies unrecorded items that need recording by the company. In VideoBuster's reconciliation, the adjusted balance of $1,845 is the correct balance as of October 31. But the company's accounting records show a $1,404.58 balance. We must prepare journal entries to adjust the book balance to the correct balance. *It is important to remember that only the items reconciling the book balance require adjustment.* A review of Exhibit 9.7 indicates that four entries are required for VideoBuster.

VIDEOBUSTER
Bank Reconciliation
October 31, 2002

①	Bank statement balance		$2,050.00	⑤ Book balance		$1,404.58
②	Add			⑥ Add		
	Deposit of 10/31 in transit		145.00	Collect $500 note less $15 fee . .	$485.00	
			2,195.00	Interest earned	8.42	493.42
③	Deduct					1,898.00
	Outstanding checks			⑦ Deduct		
	No. 124	$150.00		Check printing charge	23.00	
	No. 126	200.00	350.00	NSF check plus service fee	30.00	53.00
④	**Adjusted bank balance**		**$1,845.00**	⑧ **Adjusted book balance . . . .**		**$1,845.00**

⑨ Balances are equal (reconciled)

Exhibit 9.7

Bank Reconciliation

Collection of note

The first entry is to record the proceeds of VideoBuster's note receivable collected by the bank less the expense of having the bank perform that service:

Assets = Liabilities + Equity
+485 −15
−500

Oct. 31	Cash	485	
	Collection Expense	15	
	Notes Receivable		500
	To record the collection fee and proceeds of a note collected by the bank.		

Interest earned

The second entry records the interest credited to VideoBuster's account by the bank:

Assets = Liabilities + Equity
+8.42 +8.42

Oct. 31	Cash	8.42	
	Interest Earned		8.42
	To record interest earned on the cash balance in the checking account.		

Check printing

The third entry debits Miscellaneous Expenses for the check printing charge:

Assets = Liabilities + Equity
−23 −23

Oct. 31	Miscellaneous Expenses	23	
	Cash		23
	Check printing charge.		

NSF check

The fourth entry records the NSF check that is returned as uncollectible. The $20 check was originally received from F. Heflin in payment of his account and then deposited. The bank charged $10 for handling the NSF check and deducted $30 total from VideoBuster's account. This means the entry must reverse the effects of the original entry made when the check was received and also must record the $10 fee:

Assets = Liabilities + Equity
+30
−30

Oct. 31	Accounts Receivable—F. Heflin	30	
	Cash		30
	To charge Heflin's account for $20 NSF check and $10 bank fee.		

This entry reflects normal business practice by adding the NSF $10 fee to Heflin's account. The company will try to collect the entire $30 from Heflin. After these four entries are recorded, the book balance of cash is adjusted to the correct amount of $1,845 ($1,404.58 + $485 + $8.42 − $23 − $30).

Quick Check

11. What is a bank statement?

12. What is the meaning of the phrase *to reconcile a bank balance?*

13. Why do we reconcile the bank statement balance of cash and the depositor's book balance of cash?

14. List at least two items affecting the bank side of a bank reconciliation and indicate whether the items are added or subtracted.

15. List at least three items affecting the book side of a bank reconciliation and indicate whether the items are added or subtracted.

Answers—p. 380

Days' Sales Uncollected

Using the Information

Many companies attract customers by selling to them on credit. This means that cash receipts from customers are delayed until accounts receivable are collected. Users of accounting information often want to know how quickly a company can convert its accounts receivable into cash. This is important for evaluating a company's liquidity. One measure of the liquidity of receivables is the **days' sales uncollected,** also called *days' sales in receivables*. This measure is computed by dividing the current balance of receivables by net credit sales over the year just completed and then multiplying by 365 (number of days in a year). Since net credit sales usually are not reported to external users, the net sales (or revenues) figure is commonly used in the computation. This formula for days' sales uncollected is shown in Exhibit 9.8.

A1 Compute the days' sales uncollected ratio and use it to analyze liquidity.

$$\text{Days' sales uncollected} = \frac{\text{Accounts receivable}}{\text{Net sales}} \times 365$$

Exhibit 9.8

Days' Sales Uncollected

We use days' sales uncollected to estimate how much time is likely to pass before the current amount of accounts receivable is received in cash. For evaluation purposes, we need to compare this estimate to that for other companies in the same industry. We also make comparisons between current and prior periods.

To illustrate, we select data from the annual reports of two toy manufacturers, **Hasbro** and **Mattel**. Their days' sales uncollected figures are shown in Exhibit 9.9.

Exhibit 9.9

Analysis Using Days' Sales Uncollected ($ millions)

Company	Figure	1999	1998	1997
Hasbro	Accounts receivable	$1,084	$ 959	$ 783
	Net sales	$4,232	$3,304	$3,189
	Days' sales uncollected	93 days	106 days	90 days
Mattel	Accounts receivable	$1,270	$1,150	$1,253
	Net sales	$5,515	$5,621	$5,456
	Days' sales uncollected	84 days	75 days	84 days

Days' sales uncollected for Hasbro in 1999 is computed as ($1,084/$4,232) × 365 days = 93 days. This means it will take about 93 days to collect cash from ending accounts receivable. This number reflects one or more of the following factors: a company's ability to collect receivables, customer financial health, customer payment strategies, and discount terms. To further assess days' sales uncollected for Hasbro, we compare it to the numbers for two prior years and to those of Mattel. We see that Hasbro's days' sales uncollected varies from 90 to 106 days. In comparison to Mattel, Hasbro takes longer to collect cash from its receivables. Days' sales uncollected for Mattel varies from 75 days to 84 days. This higher liquidity in receivables for Mattel often translates into increased profitability. Running a successful company requires monitoring the liquidity of assets.

You Make the Call

Sales Representative The sales staff is told to take action to reduce days' sales uncollected. What can you, a salesperson, do to reduce days' sales uncollected?

Answer—p. 380

Demonstration Problem

Prepare a bank reconciliation for Jamboree Enterprises for the month ended November 30, 2002. The following information is available to reconcile Jamboree Enterprises' book balance of cash with its bank statement balance as of November 30, 2002:

a. After all posting is complete on November 30, the company's book balance of Cash has a $16,380 debit balance, but its bank statement shows a $38,520 balance.

b. Checks No. 2024 for $4,810 and No. 2036 for $5,000 are outstanding.

c. In comparing the canceled checks returned by the bank with the entries in the accounting records, it is found that Check No. 2025 in payment of rent is correctly drawn for $1,000 but is erroneously entered in the accounting records as $880.

d. The November 30 deposit of $17,150 was placed in the night depository after banking hours on that date, and this amount does not appear on the bank statement.

e. In reviewing the bank statement, a check belonging to Jumbo Enterprises in the amount of $160 was erroneously drawn against Jamboree's account.

f. A credit memorandum enclosed with the bank statement indicates that the bank collected a $30,000 note and $900 of related interest on Jamboree's behalf. This transaction was not recorded by Jamboree before receiving the statement.

g. A debit memorandum for $1,100 lists a $1,100 NSF check received from a customer, Marilyn Welch. Jamboree had not recorded the return of this check before receiving the statement.

h. Bank service charges for November total $40. These charges were not recorded by Jamboree before receiving the statement.

Planning the Solution

• Set up a bank reconciliation as follows with a bank side and a book side (see Exhibit 9.7). Leave room to both add and deduct items. Each column will result in a reconciled, equal balance.

Bank statement balance	Book balance. . . . .
Add:.	Add:
Deduct:	Deduct:
Adjusted bank balance	Adjusted book balance . . . .

• Examine each item (a) through (h) to determine whether it affects the book or the bank balance and whether it should be added or deducted from the bank or book balance.

• After all items are analyzed, complete the reconciliation and arrive at a reconciled balance between the bank side and the book side.

• For each reconciling item on the book side, prepare an adjusting entry. Additions to the book side require an adjusting entry that debits Cash. Deductions on the book side require an adjusting entry that credits Cash.

Solution to Demonstration Problem

JAMBOREE ENTERPRISES
Bank Reconciliation
November 30, 2002

Bank statement balance		$38,520	Book balance		$16,380	
Add			Add			
Deposit of Nov. 30. . . .	$17,150		Collection of note . .	$30,000		
Bank error.	160	17,310	Interest earned	900	30,900	
		55,000			47,280	
Deduct			Deduct			
Outstanding checks		9,810	NSF check	1,100		
			Recording error	120		
			Service charge	40	1,260	
Adjusted bank balance		**$46,020**	**Adjusted book balance**		**$46,020**	

Required Adjusting Entries for Jamboree

Nov. 30	Cash	30,900	
	Notes Receivable		30,000
	Interest Earned		900
	To record collection of note with interest.		
Nov. 30	Accounts Receivable—M. Welch	1,100	
	Cash		1,100
	To reinstate account due from an NSF check.		
Nov. 30	Rent Expense	120	
	Cash		120
	To correct recording error on check no. 2025.		
Nov. 30	Bank Service Charges	40	
	Cash		40
	To record bank service charges.		

APPENDIX

Document Flow in a Voucher System

9A

This appendix describes the important documents in and their flow through a voucher system of control. We explain how this system is useful in controlling cash disbursements.

Purchase Requisition

Department managers are usually not allowed to place orders directly with suppliers. If each manager were allowed to deal directly with suppliers, the merchandise purchased and the resulting lia-

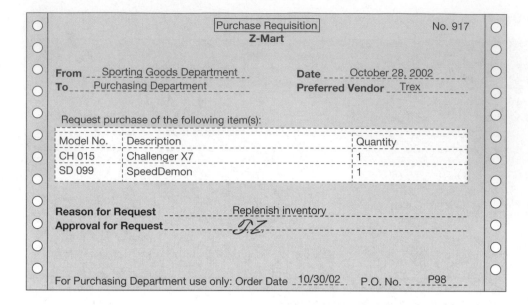

Model No.	Description	Quantity
CH 015	Challenger X7	1
SD 099	SpeedDemon	1

(Purchase Requisition, Z-Mart, No. 917)

From ___ Sporting Goods Department ___   Date ___ October 28, 2002 ___
To ___ Purchasing Department ___   Preferred Vendor ___ Trex ___

Request purchase of the following item(s):

Reason for Request ___ Replenish inventory ___
Approval for Request ___ J.Z. ___

For Purchasing Department use only: Order Date _10/30/02_.   P.O. No. ___P98___

bilities would not be well-controlled. To gain control over purchases, department managers are usually required to place all orders through a purchasing department. When merchandise is needed, a department manager must inform the purchasing department of its needs by preparing and signing a **purchase requisition,** which lists the merchandise needed and requests that it be purchased—see Exhibit 9A.1. Two copies of the purchase requisition are sent to the purchasing department. The purchasing department then sends one copy to the accounting department. When the accounting department receives a purchase requisition, it creates and maintains a voucher for this transaction. A third copy of the requisition is kept by the requesting department as backup.

Purchase Order

A **purchase order** is a document the purchasing department uses to place an order with a seller (**vendor**). A vendor usually is a manufacturer or wholesaler. A purchase order authorizes a vendor to ship ordered merchandise at the stated price and terms—see Exhibit 9A.2. When the purchasing department receives a purchase requisition, it prepares at least four copies of a purchase order. The copies are distributed as follows: *copy 1* is sent to the vendor as a purchase request and as authority to ship

Purchase Order   No. P98
Z-Mart
10 Michigan Street
Chicago, Illinois 60521

To: Trex
     W9797 Cherry Road
     Antigo, Wisconsin 54409

Date ___ 10/30/02 ___
FOB ___ Destination ___
Ship by _ As soon as possible _
Terms ___ 2/15, n/30 ___

Request shipment of the following item(s):

Model No.	Description	Quantity	Price	Amount
CH 015	Challenger X7	1	490	490
SD 099	SpeedDemon	1	710	710

All shipments and invoices must
include purchase order number

Ordered by

___ J.W. ___

merchandise; *copy 2* is sent, along with a copy of the purchase requisition, to the accounting department where it is entered in the voucher and used in approving payment of the invoice; *copy 3* is sent
to the requesting department to inform its manager that action is being taken; and *copy 4* is retained
on file by the purchasing department.

Invoice

An **invoice** is an itemized statement of goods prepared by the vendor (supplier) listing the customer's
name, items sold, sales prices, and terms of sale. An invoice is also a bill sent to the buyer from the
supplier. From the vendor's point of view, it is a *sales invoice*. The vendor sends the invoice to a
buyer, or **vendee,** who treats it as a *purchase invoice*. When receiving a purchase order, the vendor
ships the ordered merchandise to the buyer and includes or mails a copy of the invoice covering the
shipment to the buyer. The invoice is sent to the buyer's accounting department where it is placed in
the voucher. Exhibit 6.6 shows Z-Mart's purchase invoice.

Receiving Report

Many companies maintain a separate department to receive all merchandise and purchased assets.
When each shipment arrives, this receiving department counts the goods and checks them for damage and agreement with the purchase order. It then prepares four or more copies of a **receiving report,** which is used within the company to notify the appropriate persons that ordered goods have
been received and to describe the quantities and condition of the goods. One copy is placed in the
voucher. Copies are also sent to the requesting department and the purchasing department to notify
them that the goods have arrived. The receiving department retains a copy in its files.

Invoice Approval

When a receiving report arrives, the accounting department should have copies of the following documents in the voucher: purchase requisition, purchase order, and invoice. With the information in
these documents, the accounting department can record the purchase and approve its payment. In approving an invoice for payment, the department checks and compares information across all documents. To facilitate this checking and to ensure that no step is omitted, the department often uses an
invoice approval, also called *check authorization*—see Exhibit 9A.3. An invoice approval is a checklist of steps necessary for approving an invoice for recording and payment. It is a separate document
either filed in the voucher or preprinted (or stamped) on the voucher.

Point: Recording a purchase is
initiated by an invoice approval, not
an invoice. An invoice approval
verifies that the amount is consistent
with that requested, ordered, and
received. This controls and verifies
purchases and related liabilities.

Invoice Approval			
Document		By	Date
Purchase requisition	917	7.'-	10/28/02
Purchase order	P98	9w	10/30/02
Receiving report	R85	2K	11/3/02
Invoice:	4657		11/12/02
Price		Cl-	11/12/02
Calculations		Cl-	11/12/02
Terms		Cl-	11/12/02
Approved for payment		a--	

Exhibit 9A.3

Invoice Approval

As each step in the checklist is approved, the person initials the invoice approval and records the
current date. Final approval implies the following steps have occurred:

1. **Requisition check:** Items on invoice are requested per purchase requisition.
2. **Purchase order check:** Items on invoice are ordered per purchase order.
3. **Receiving report check:** Items on invoice are received, per receiving report.
4. **Invoice check: Price:** Invoice prices are as agreed with the vendor.
   Calculations: Invoice has no mathematical errors.
   Terms: Terms are as agreed with the vendor.

Voucher

Once an invoice has been checked and approved, the voucher is complete. A complete voucher is a
record summarizing a transaction. Once the voucher certifies a transaction as correct, it authorizes

Exhibit 9A.4

Inside of a Voucher

Z-Mart			Voucher No. 4657
Chicago, Illinois			

Date   Oct. 28, 2002

Pay to   Trex

City   Antigo   State   Wisconsin

For the following: (attach all invoices and supporting documents)

Date of Invoice	Terms	Invoice Number and Other Details	Terms
Nov. 2, 2002	2/15, n/30	Invoice No. 4657	1,200
		Less discount	24
		Net amount payable	1,176

Payment approved

N. O. Neal

Auditor

recording an obligation. A voucher also contains approval for paying the obligation on an appropriate date. The physical form of a voucher varies across companies. Many are designed so that the invoice and other related source documents are placed inside the voucher, which is often a folder.

Completion of a voucher usually requires a person to enter certain information on both the inside and outside of the voucher. Typical information required on the inside of a voucher is shown in Exhibit 9A.4, and that for the outside is shown in Exhibit 9A.5. This information is taken from the invoice and the supporting documents filed in the voucher. A complete voucher is sent to an authorized individual (often called an *auditor*). This person performs a final review, approves the accounts and amounts for debiting (called the *accounting distribution*), and authorizes recording of the voucher.

After a voucher is approved and recorded, it is filed until its due date, when it is sent to the cashier for payment. The person issuing checks relies on the approved voucher and its signed supporting documents as proof that an obligation has been incurred and must be paid. The purchase requisition and purchase order confirm the purchase was authorized. The receiving report shows items have been received, and the invoice approval form verifies that the invoice has been checked for errors. There is little chance for error and even less chance for fraud without collusion unless all the documents and signatures are forged.

Exhibit 9A.5

Outside of a Voucher

Voucher No. 4657

Accounting Distribution

Account Debited	Amount
Merch. Inventory	1,200
Store Supplies	
Office Supplies	
Sales Salaries	
Other	
Total Vouch. Pay. Cr.	1,200

Due Date   November 12, 2002

Pay to   Trex

City   Antigo

State   Wisconsin

Summary of charges:

Total charges   1,200

Discount   24

Net payment   1,176

Record of payment:

Paid

Check No.

Summary

C1 **Define internal control and its purpose.** An internal control system consists of the policies and procedures managers use to protect assets, ensure reliable accounting, promote efficient operations, and urge adherence to company policies. It can prevent avoidable losses and help managers both plan operations and monitor company and human performance.

C2 **Identify principles of internal control.** Principles of good internal control include establishing responsibilities, maintaining adequate records, insuring assets and bonding employees, separating recordkeeping from custody of assets, dividing responsibilities for related transactions, applying technological controls, and performing regular independent reviews.

C3 **Define cash and cash equivalents and explain how to report them.** Cash includes currency, coins, and amounts on (or acceptable for) deposit in checking and savings accounts. Cash equivalents are short-term, highly liquid investment assets readily convertible to a known cash amount and sufficiently close to their maturity date so that market value is not sensitive to interest rate changes. Cash and cash equivalents are liquid assets because they are readily converted into other assets or can be used to pay for goods, services, or liabilities.

C4 **Identify control features of banking activities.** Banks offer several services that promote the control and safeguarding of cash. A bank account is a record set up by a bank permitting a customer to deposit money for safeguarding and to draw checks on it. A bank deposit is money contributed to the account with a deposit ticket as proof. A check is a document signed by the depositor instructing the bank to pay a specified amount of money to a designated recipient.

A1 **Compute the days' sales uncollected ratio and use it to analyze liquidity.** Many companies attract customers by selling to them on credit. This means that cash flows from customers are delayed until accounts receivable are collected. Users of accounting information often want to know how quickly a company can convert its accounts receivable into cash. This is important for evaluating a company's liquidity. The days' sales uncollected ratio, one measure reflecting liquidity, is computed by dividing the ending balance of receivables by annual net sales, and then multiplying by 365.

P1 **Apply internal control to cash receipts.** Internal control of cash receipts ensures all cash received is properly recorded and deposited. Attention is focused on two important types of cash receipts: over-the-counter and by mail. Good internal control for over-the-counter cash receipts includes use of a cash register, customer review, use of receipts, a permanent transaction record, and separation of the custody of cash from its recordkeeping. Good internal control for cash receipts by mail includes at least two people assigned to open mail and prepare a list with each sender's name, amount, and explanation.

P2 **Apply the voucher system to control cash disbursements.** A voucher system is a set of procedures and approvals designed to control cash disbursements and acceptance of obligations. The voucher system of control relies on several important documents, including the voucher and its supporting files. A key factor in this system is that only approved departments and individuals are authorized to incur certain obligations. To coordinate and control responsibilities, several documents are used.

P3 **Explain and record petty cash fund transactions.** Petty cash disbursements are payments of small amounts for items such as postage, courier fees, repairs, and supplies. A company usually sets up one or more petty cash funds. A petty fund cashier is responsible for safekeeping the cash, making payments from this fund, and keeping receipts and records. A Petty Cash account is debited only when the fund is established or increased in size. The cashier presents all paid receipts to the company cashier for reimbursement. When the fund is replenished, petty cash disbursements are recorded with debits to expense (or asset) accounts and a credit to cash.

P4 **Apply the net method to control purchase discounts.** The net method aids management in monitoring and controlling purchase discounts. When invoices are recorded at gross amounts, the amount of discounts taken is deducted from the balance of the Merchandise Inventory account. This means the amount of any discounts lost is not reported in any account and is unlikely to come to the attention of management. But when purchases are recorded at net amounts, a Discounts Lost account is brought to management's attention as an operating expense. Management can then seek to identify the reason for discounts lost, such as oversight, carelessness, or unfavorable terms.

P5 **Prepare a bank reconciliation.** A bank reconciliation proves the accuracy of the depositor's and the bank's records. The bank statement balance is adjusted for items such as outstanding checks and unrecorded deposits made on or before the bank statement date but not reflected on the statement. The book balance also often requires adjustment for items such as service charges, bank collections for the depositor, and interest earned on the account.

Guidance Answers to **You Make the Call**

Entrepreneur A forced vacation policy is part of a good system of internal controls. When employees are forced to take vacations, their ability to hide any fraudulent behavior decreases because others must perform the duties of the people on vacation. A replacement employee potentially can uncover fraudulent behavior or falsified records. A forced vacation policy is especially important for employees in more sensitive positions of handling money or in control of easily transferable assets.

Internal Auditor Your decision is whether to accept the situation or to dig further to see whether the petty cashier is abusing petty cash. Since you were asked to postpone your count, along with the fact the fund consists of 14 new $20 bills, you have legitimate concerns about whether money is being used for personal use. It is possible the most recent reimbursement of the fund was for $280 (14 × $20) or more. In that case, this reimbursement can leave the fund with sequentially numbered $20 bills. But if the most recent reimbursement was for less than $280, the presence of 14 sequentially numbered $20 bills suggests that the new bills were obtained from a bank as replacement for bills that had been removed. Neither situation shows the cashier is stealing money, but the second case indicates the cashier "borrowed" the cash and later replaced it af-

ter the auditor showed up. In writing your report, you must not conclude the cashier is unethical unless other evidence supports it. You also might consider additional surprise counts of this petty cashier over the next few weeks.

Sales Representative A salesperson can take several steps to reduce days' sales uncollected. These include (1) decreasing the proportion of sales on account to total sales by encouraging more cash sales, (2) identifying customers most delayed in their payments and encouraging earlier payments or cash sales, and (3) implementing stricter credit policies to eliminate credit sales to customers that never pay.

Guidance Answers to **Quick Checks**

1. c

2. Technology reduces processing errors. It also allows more extensive testing of records, limits the amount of hard evidence, and highlights the importance of separation of duties.

3. A company owns liquid assets so that it can purchase other assets, buy services, and pay obligations.

4. A company owns cash equivalents because they yield a return greater than what cash earns (and are readily exchanged for cash).

5. Examples of cash equivalents are 90-day U.S. treasury bills, money market funds, and commercial paper (notes).

6. a

7. A voucher system is used when an owner/manager can no longer control purchasing procedures through personal supervision and direct participation.

8. If all cash payments are made by check, numerous checks for small amounts must be written. Because this practice is expensive and time consuming, a petty cash fund is often established for making small cash payments.

9. If the petty cash fund is not reimbursed at the end of an accounting period, the transactions involving petty cash are not yet recorded, and the petty cash asset is overstated.

10. First, when the petty cash fund is reimbursed, the petty cash transactions are recorded. Second, reimbursement provides cash to allow the fund to continue being used. Third, reimbursement identifies any cash shortage or overage in the fund.

11. A bank statement is a report prepared by the bank describing the activities in a depositor's account.

12. To reconcile a bank balance means to explain the difference between the cash balance in the depositor's accounting records and the balance on the bank statement.

13. The purpose of the bank reconciliation is to determine whether the bank or the depositor has made any errors and whether the bank has entered any transactions affecting the account that the depositor has not recorded.

14. Outstanding checks—subtracted
Unrecorded deposits—added

15. Debit memos—subtracted   Interest earned—added
NSF checks—subtracted   Credit memos—added
Bank service charges—subtracted

Glossary

Bank reconciliation report that explains the difference between the book balance of cash and the balance reported on the bank statement. (p. 369).

Canceled checks checks that the bank has paid and deducted from the depositor's account. (p. 368).

Cash includes currency, coins, and amounts on deposit in bank checking or savings accounts. (p. 359).

Cash equivalents short-term, investment assets that are readily convertible to a known cash amount and sufficiently close to their maturity date so that market value

is not sensitive to interest rate changes. (p. 359).

Cash Over and Short income statement account used to record cash overages and cash shortages arising from missing petty cash receipts or simple errors. (p. 360).

Check document signed by the depositor instructing the bank to pay a specified amount to a designated recipient. (p. 367).

Days' sales uncollected measure of the liquidity of receivables computed by dividing the current balance of receivables by the annual credit (or net) sales, and then mul-

tiplying by 365; also called *days' sales in receivables*. (p. 373).

Deposit in Transit A deposit recorded by the company but not yet by its bank. (p. 369).

Deposit ticket lists items such as currency, coins, and checks deposited and their corresponding dollar amounts. (p. 366).

Discounts Lost expense resulting from a failure to take advantage of cash discounts on purchases. (p. 366).

Electronic funds transfer (EFT) use of electronic communication to transfer cash from one party to another. (p. 367).

Gross method method of recording purchases at the full invoice price without deducting any cash discounts. (p. 365).

Internal control system all policies and procedures used to protect assets, ensure reliable accounting, promote efficient operations, and urge adherence to company policies. (p. 354).

Invoice itemized record of goods prepared by the vendor that lists the customer's name, the items sold, the sales prices, and the terms of sale. (p. 377).

Invoice approval document containing a checklist of steps necessary for approving an invoice for recording and payment; also called *check authorization* (p. 377).

Liquid asset resources such as cash that are easily converted into other assets or used to pay for goods, services, or liabilities. (p. 359).

Liquidity company's ability to pay for its short-term obligations. (p. 359).

Net method method of recording purchases at the full invoice price less any cash discounts. (p. 365).

Outstanding checks checks written and recorded by the depositor but not yet paid by the bank at the bank statement date (p. 369).

Principles of internal control principles requiring management to establish responsibility, maintain records, insure assets, separate recordkeeping from custody of assets, divide responsibility for related transactions, apply technological controls, and perform reviews. (p. 354).

Purchase order document used by the purchasing department to place an order with a seller (vendor). (p. 376).

Purchase requisition document listing merchandise needed by a department and requesting it be purchased. (p. 376).

Receiving report form used to report that ordered goods are received and to describe their quantity and condition. (p. 377).

Signature card includes the signatures of each person authorized to sign checks on the account. (p. 366).

Vendee buyer or purchaser of goods or services. (p. 377).

Vendor seller of goods or services. (p. 376).

Voucher internal file used to store documents and information to control cash disbursements and to ensure that a transaction is properly recorded. (p. 361).

Voucher system procedures and approvals designed to control cash disbursements and acceptance of obligations. (p. 361).

[The Superscript letter ^{A} denotes assignments based on Appendix 9A.]

Questions

1. List the seven broad principles of internal control.

2. Why should responsibility for related transactions be divided among different departments or individuals?

3. Internal control procedures are important in every business, but at what stage in the development of a business do they become especially critical?

4. Which of the following assets is most liquid? Which is least liquid? Inventory, building, accounts receivable, cash?

5. Why should the person who keeps the records of an asset not be the person responsible for its custody?

6. When a store purchases merchandise, why are individual departments not allowed to directly deal with suppliers?

7. What is a petty cash receipt? Who should sign it?

8. Why should all cash receipts be deposited on the day of receipt?

9. **Nike**'s statement of cash flows in Appendix A describes changes in cash and cash equivalents for the year ended May 31, 2000. What amount is provided (used) by investing activities? What amount is provided (used) by financing activities?

10. **Reebok**'s balance sheet in Appendix A reports cash and cash equivalents as of December 31, 1999 and 1998. Compare and discuss the amount of cash and cash equivalents with the other current assets as of December 31, 1999. Compare and assess the amount of cash and cash equivalents as of December 31, 1999 with its amount at December 31, 1998.

11. Why does **Gap**'s balance sheet in Appendix A not report Accounts Receivable?

---

1. What is the main objective of internal control procedures, and how is it achieved?

2. Why should recordkeeping for assets be separated from custody over the assets?

QUICK STUDY

QS 9-1
Internal control objective C1 C2

A good system of internal control for cash provides adequate procedures for protecting both cash receipts and cash disbursements. What are three basic guidelines that help achieve this protection?

QS 9-2
Internal control for cash P1

What is the difference between the terms *liquidity* and *cash equivalent*?

QS 9-3
Terminology C1

QS 9-4
Purchase discounts **P4**

Which accounting method uses a Discounts Lost account? What is the advantage of this method?

QS 9-5
Petty cash accounting

P3

1. The petty cash fund of the Roberts Agency is established at $85. At the end of the period, the fund contained $14.80 and had the following receipts: film rentals, $21.30; refreshments for meetings, $30.85 (both expenditures to be classified as Entertainment Expense); postage, $8.95; and printing, $9.10. Prepare journal entries to record (a) establishment of the fund and (b) reimbursement of the fund at the end of the period.

2. Identify the two event(s) that cause a Petty Cash account to be credited in a journal entry.

QS 9-6
Bank reconciliation

P5

1. For each of the following items indicate whether its amount (i) affects the bank or book side of a bank reconciliation and (ii) represents an addition or a subtraction in a bank reconciliation:

   (a) Outstanding checks   **(e)** Interest on cash balance
   (b) Debit memos   **(f)** Credit memos
   (c) NSF checks   **(g)** Bank service charges
   (d) Unrecorded deposits

2. Which of the items in part (1) require an adjusting journal entry?

QS 9-7
Days' sales uncollected

A1

The following annual account balances are taken from Daredevil Sports at December 31:

	2002	2001
Accounts receivable	$ 85,692	$ 80,485
Net sales	2,691,855	2,396,858

What is the change in the number of days' sales uncollected between years 2002 and 2001? According to this analysis, is the company's collection of receivables improving? Explain your answer.

EXERCISES

Exercise 9-1
Recommend internal control procedures **C2**

What internal control procedures would you recommend in each of the following situations?

1. A concession company has one employee who sells T-shirts and sunglasses at the beach. Each day, the employee is given enough shirts and sunglasses to last through the day and enough cash to make change. The money is kept in a box at the stand.

2. An antique store has one employee who is given cash and sent to garage sales each weekend. The employee pays cash for this merchandise that the antique store resells.

Exercise 9-2
Internal control of cash **P1**
receipts by mail

Some of O'Hara Co.'s cash receipts from customers are sent to the company with the regular mail. O'Hara's recordkeeper opens these letters and deposits the cash received each day. Identify any internal control problem(s) in this arrangement. What changes do you recommend?

Exercise 9-3
Analyzing internal control

C2

Folkerts Company is a rapidly growing start-up business. Its recordkeeper, who was hired one year ago, left town after the company's manager discovered that a large sum of money had disappeared over the past six months. An audit disclosed that the recordkeeper had written and signed several checks made payable to the recordkeeper's fiancé and then recorded the checks as salaries expense. The fiancé, who cashed the checks but never worked for the company, left town with the recordkeeper. As a result, the company incurred an uninsured loss of $184,000. Evaluate Folkerts's internal control system and indicate which principles of internal control appear to have been ignored.

Exercise 9-4
Petty cash fund with a shortage

P3

Brady Company establishes a $350 petty cash fund on September 9. On September 30, the fund shows $103.25 in cash along with receipts for the following expenditures: transportation-in, $39.85; office supplies, $123.55; and miscellaneous expenses, $80.00. The petty cashier could not account for a $3.35 shortage in the fund. Brady uses the perpetual system in accounting for merchandise inventory. Prepare (1) the September 9 entry to establish the fund and (2) the September 30 entry to reimburse the fund and reduce it to $250.

Eanes Co. establishes a $200 petty cash fund on January 1. One week later, the fund shows $38 in cash along with receipts for the following expenditures: postage, $74; transportation-in, $29; store supplies, $16; and miscellaneous expenses, $43. Eanes uses the perpetual system in accounting for merchandise inventory. Prepare journal entries to (1) establish the fund on January 1, (2) reimburse it on January 8, and (3) reimburse the fund and increase it to $400 on January 8 assuming no entry in part (2).

Exercise 9-5
Petty cash fund

Prepare a table with the following headings for a bank reconciliation dated September 30:

Exercise 9-6
Bank reconciliation and
adjusting entries
P5

| Bank Balance | | Book Balance | | | Not Shown on the Reconciliation |
Add	Deduct	Add	Deduct	Adjust	

For each item following, place an *x* in the appropriate column to indicate whether the item should be added to or deducted from the book or bank balance, or whether it should not appear on the reconciliation. If the book balance is to be adjusted, place a *Dr.* or *Cr.* in the Adjust column to indicate whether the Cash balance should be debited or credited. At the left side of your table, number the items to correspond to the following list.

1. Bank service charge.
2. Checks written and mailed to payees on October 5.
3. Checks written by another depositor but charged against this company's account.
4. Principal and interest collected by the bank but not yet recorded by the company.
5. Special charge for collection of note in part (4) on this company's behalf.
6. Check written against the account and cleared by the bank; erroneously not recorded by the company recordkeeper.
7. Interest earned on the cash balance in the bank.
8. Night deposit made on September 30 after the bank closed.
9. Checks outstanding on August 31 that cleared the bank in September.
10. NSF check from customer returned on September 15 but not yet recorded by this company.
11. Checks written and mailed to payees on September 30.
12. Deposit made on September 5 and processed on September 8.

Ashley Clinic deposits all cash receipts on the day when they are received and makes all cash payments by check. On June 30, 2002, after all posting is complete, its Cash account shows an $11,589 debit balance. Ashley Clinic's June 30 bank statement shows $10,555 on deposit in the bank on that day. Prepare a bank reconciliation for Ashley Clinic using the following information:

Exercise 9-7
Bank reconciliation

a. Outstanding checks total $1,829.
b. The bank statement for June included a $16 debit memorandum for bank services.
c. Check No. 919, returned with the canceled checks, was correctly drawn for $467 in payment of a utility bill on June 15. Ashley Clinic mistakenly recorded it with a debit to Utilities Expense and a credit to Cash in the amount of $476.
d. The June 30 cash receipts of $2,856 were placed in the bank's night depository after banking hours and were not recorded on the June 30 bank statement.

Give the adjusting journal entries that Ashley Clinic must record as a result of preparing the bank reconciliation in Exercise 9-7.

Exercise 9-8
Adjusting entries from
bank reconciliation   P5

Union Merchandise Co. reported annual net sales for 2001 and 2002 of $665,000 and $747,000, respectively. Also, its year-end balances of accounts receivable were as follows: December 31, 2001, $61,000; and December 31, 2002, $93,000. Calculate the days' sales uncollected at the end of each year and comment on any changes in the liquidity of this company's receivables.

Exercise 9-9
Liquidity of accounts
receivable   A1

Exercise 9-10
Record invoices at gross
or net amounts

P4

Pelkner's Imports uses the perpetual system in accounting for merchandise inventory and had the following transactions during the month of October. Prepare entries to record these transactions assuming Pelkner's records invoices (a) at gross amounts and (b) at net amounts.

Oct.   2   Received merchandise purchased at a $3,000 invoice price, invoice dated October 2, terms 2/10, n/30.

     10   Received a $500 credit memorandum (at full invoice price) for merchandise received on October 2 and returned for credit.

     17   Received merchandise purchased at a $5,400 invoice price, invoice dated October 16, terms 2/10, n/30.

     26   Paid for the merchandise received on October 17, less the discount.

     28   Paid for the merchandise received on October 2. Payment was delayed because the invoice was mistakenly filed for payment today. This error caused the discount to be lost.

Exercise 9-11^A
Documents in a
voucher system   **P2**

Management uses a voucher system to help control and monitor cash disbursements. Identify at least four key documents that are part of a voucher system of control. Explain each document's purpose, where it originates, and how it flows through the voucher system (including the flow of copies).

PROBLEM SET A

Problem 9-1A
Establish, reimburse, and
adjust petty cash; accounting
adjustments

P3

G

Roosevelt Co. set up a petty cash fund for payments of small amounts. The following petty cash transactions are reported by the petty cashier as occurring in May (the last month of the company's fiscal year):

May   1   Received a company check for $250 to establish the petty cash fund.

     15   Received a company check to replenish the fund for the following expenditures made since April 1 and to increase the fund to $500.

        a.   Paid $88 for janitorial service.

        b.   Purchased office supplies for $53.68.

        c.   Purchased postage stamps for $53.50.

        d.   Paid $47.15 to *The County Crier* for an advertisement in the newspaper.

        e.   Counted $11.15 remaining in the petty cash box.

     31   The petty cashier reports that $293.39 remains in the fund and decides that the May 15 increase in the fund was too large. A company check is drawn to replenish the fund for the following expenditures made since May 15 and to reduce the fund to $400.

        f.   Purchased office supplies for $147.36.

        g.   Reimbursed office manager for business mileage, $23.50.

        h.   Paid $34.75 courier charges to deliver merchandise to a customer, terms FOB destination.

Required

Preparation Component

Check   Cash Cr.: May 15, $488.85;
May 31, $106.61

1. Prepare journal entries to establish the fund on May 1 and to replenish it on May 15 and on May 31 along with any increase or decrease in the fund balance.

Analysis Component

2. Explain how the company's financial statements are affected if the petty cash fund is not replenished and no entry is made on May 31. (*Hint:* The amount of office supplies that appears on a balance sheet is determined by a physical count of office supplies.)

Problem 9-2A
Establish, reimburse, and
increase petty cash

P3

Metro Art Gallery had the following petty cash transactions in February of the current year:

Feb.   2   Wrote a $400 check, cashed it, and gave the proceeds and the petty cashbox to Kareena White, the petty cashier.

     5   Purchased paper for the copier, $14.15.

     9   Paid $32.50 COD shipping charges on merchandise purchased for resale, terms FOB shipping point. Metro uses the perpetual system to account for merchandise inventory.

     12   Paid $7.95 postage to express mail a contract to a client.

     14   Reimbursed Liz Walcotte, the manager, $68 for business mileage on her car.

     20   Purchased stationery, $67.77.

     23   Paid a courier $20 to deliver merchandise sold to a customer, terms FOB destination.

25   Paid $13.10 COD shipping charges on merchandise purchased for resale, terms FOB shipping point.

27   Paid $54 for postage stamps.

28   Sorted the petty cash receipts by accounts affected and exchanged them for a check to both reimburse the fund for expenditures and increase the amount of the fund to $500. There was $121.53 cash in the fund.

Required

1. Prepare the journal entry to establish the petty cash fund.

2. Prepare a petty cash payments report for February with these categories: delivery expense, mileage expense, postage expense, merchandise inventory (transportation-in), and office supplies. Sort the payments into the appropriate categories and total the expenditures in each category.

3. Prepare the journal entry to both reimburse and increase the amount in the fund.

Check Feb. 28 entry, Cash, $378.47 Cr.

For each of these five separate cases, identify the principle of internal control that is violated. Recommend what the business should do to ensure adherence to principles of internal control.

1. Heather Hawthorne records all incoming customer cash receipts for her employer and posts the customer payments to their accounts.

2. At Cunningham Company, Jack and Jo alternate lunch hours. Jack is the petty cash custodian, but if someone needs petty cash when he is at lunch, Jo fills in as custodian.

3. Marcia Diamond does all the posting of patient charges and payments at the Provincetown Medical Clinic. Each night Marcia backs up the computerized accounting system to a tape and stores the tape in a locked file at her desk.

4. Bob Magee prides himself on hiring quality workers who require little supervision. As office manager, Bob gives his employees full discretion over their tasks and has seen no reason to perform independent reviews of their work for years.

5. Susan Smith's manager has told her to reduce costs. Susan decides to raise the deductible on the plant's property insurance from $5,000 to $10,000. This cuts the property insurance premium in half. In a related move, she decides that bonding the plant's employees is a waste of money since the company has not experienced any losses due to employee theft. Susan saves the entire amount of the bonding insurance premium by dropping the bonding insurance.

Problem 9-3A
Analyzing internal control

The following information is available to reconcile Colin Company's book balance of cash with its bank statement cash balance as of July 31, 2002:

a. After all posting is complete on July 31, the company's Cash account has a $27,497 debit balance, but its bank statement shows a $27,233 balance.

b. Check No. 3031 for $1,482 and Check No. 3040 for $558 were outstanding on the June 30 bank reconciliation. Check No. 3040 is returned with the July canceled checks, but Check No. 3031 is not. Also, Check No. 3065 for $382 and Check No. 3069 for $2,281, both written in July, are not among the canceled checks returned with the July 31 statement.

c. In comparing the canceled checks returned by the bank with the entries in the accounting records, it is found that Check No. 3056 for July rent was correctly written and drawn for $1,270 but was erroneously entered in the accounting records as $1,250.

d. A credit memorandum enclosed with the bank statement indicates the bank collected an $8,000 noninterest-bearing note for Colin, deducted a $45 collection fee, and credited the remainder to its account. Colin had not recorded this event before receiving the statement.

e. A debit memorandum for $805 lists a $795 NSF check plus a $10 NSF charge. The check had been received from a customer, Jason White. Colin has not yet recorded this check as NSF.

f. Enclosed with the statement is a $25 debit memorandum for bank services. It has not yet been recorded because no previous notification had been received.

g. The July 31 daily cash receipts of $11,514 were placed in the bank's night depository on that date but do not appear on the July 31 bank statement.

Problem 9-4A
Prepare a bank reconciliation and record adjustments

Required

Preparation Component

1. Prepare a bank reconciliation for this company as of July 31, 2002.

Check Reconciled balance, $34,602

2. Prepare the journal entries necessary to bring the company's book balance of cash into conformity with the reconciled cash balance as of July 31, 2002.

Analysis Component

3. Assume that the July 31, 2002, bank reconciliation for this company is prepared and some items are treated incorrectly. For each of the following errors, explain the effect of the error on (i) the adjusted bank statement cash balance and (ii) the adjusted cash account book balance.

    a. The company's unadjusted cash account balance of $27,497 is listed on the reconciliation as $27,947.

    b. The bank's collection of the $8,000 note less the $45 collection fee is added to the bank statement cash balance.

Problem 9-5A

Prepare a bank reconciliation and record adjustments

Clarke Company most recently reconciled its bank statement and book balances of cash on August 31 and it showed two checks outstanding, No. 5888 for $1,028.05 and No. 5893 for $493.95. The following information is available for its September 30, 2002, reconciliation:

From the September 30 Bank Statement

Previous Balance	Total Checks and Debits	Total Deposits and Credits	Current Balance
16,800.45	9,620.05	11,272.85	18,453.25

Checks and Debits			Deposits and Credits		Daily Balance	
Date	No.	Amount	Date	Amount	Date	Amount
09/03	5888	1,028.05	09/05	1,103.75	08/31	16,800.45
09/04	5902	719.90	09/12	2,226.90	09/03	15,772.40
09/07	5901	1,824.25	09/21	4,093.00	09/04	15,052.50
09/17		600.25 NSF	09/25	2,351.70	09/05	16,156.25
09/20	5905	937.00	09/30	12.50 IN	09/07	14,332.00
09/22	5903	399.10	09/30	1,485.00 CM	09/12	16,558.90
09/22	5904	2,090.00			09/17	15,958.65
09/28	5907	213.85			09/20	15,021.65
09/29	5909	1,807.65			09/21	19,114.65
					09/22	16,625.55
					09/25	18,977.25
					09/28	18,763.40
					09/29	16,955.75
					09/30	18,453.25

From Clarke Company's Accounting Records

Cash Receipts Deposited				Cash Disbursements		
Date			Cash Debit	Check No.		Cash Credit
Sept.	5		1,103.75	5901		1,824.25
	12		2,226.90	5902		719.90
	21		4,093.00	5903		399.10
	25		2,351.70	5904		2,060.00
	30		1,682.75	5905		937.00
			11,458.10	5906		982.30
				5907		213.85
				5908		388.00
				5909		1,807.65
						9,332.05

Cash					Acct. No. 101
Date		**Explanation**	**PR**	**Debit**	**Credit**	**Balance**
Aug.	31	Balance				15,278.45
Sept.	30	Total receipts	R12	11,458.10		26,736.55
	30	Total disbursements	D23		9,332.05	17,404.50

Other Information

Check No. 5904 is correctly drawn for $2,090 to pay for computer equipment; however, the record-keeper misread the amount and entered it in the accounting records with a debit to Computer Equipment and a credit to Cash of $2,060. The NSF check shown in the statement was originally received from a customer, S. Nilson, in payment of her account. Its return had not been recorded when the bank first notified the company. The credit memorandum is from the collection of a $1,500 note for Clarke Company by the bank. The bank deducted a $15 collection fee. The collection and fee are not yet recorded.

Required

Preparation Component

1. Prepare the September 30, 2002, bank reconciliation for this company.

2. Prepare the journal entries to adjust the book balance of cash to the reconciled balance.

Check   Reconciled balance, $18,271.75

Analysis Component

3. The bank statement reveals that some of the prenumbered checks in the sequence are missing. Describe three possible situations that could explain this.

Cashco Co. establishes a petty cash fund for payments of small amounts. The following transactions involving the petty cash fund occurred in January (the last month of the company's fiscal year).

Jan. 3   A company check for $150 is written and made payable to the petty cashier to establish the petty cash fund.

14   A company check is written to replenish the fund for the following expenditures made since January 3 and to increase the fund to $200.
  a.   Purchased office supplies, $14.29.
  b.   Paid $19.60 COD shipping charges on merchandise purchased for resale, terms FOB shipping point. Cashco uses the perpetual system to account for inventory.
  c.   Paid $38.57 to All-Tech for minor repairs to a computer.
  d.   Paid $12.82 for items classified as miscellaneous expenses.
  e.   Counted $62.28 remaining in the petty cash box.

31   The petty cashier reports that $17.35 remains in the fund and decides that the February 14 increase in the fund was not large enough. A company check is written to replenish the fund for the following expenditures made since January 14 and to increase it to $250.
  f.   Paid $50 to *The Smart Saver* for an advertisement in this monthly newsletter.
  g.   Paid $48.19 for office supplies.
  h.   Paid $78 to *3 Men and a Truck* for delivery of merchandise to a customer, terms FOB destination.

PROBLEM SET B

Problem 9-1B

Establishing, reimbursing, and adjusting petty cash; accounting adjustments

Required

Preparation Component

1. Prepare journal entries to establish the fund on January 3 and to replenish it on January 14 and January 31 along with any increase or decrease in the fund balance.

Check   Cr. Cash: Jan. 14, $137.72; Jan. 31, $232.65

Analysis Component

2. Explain how the company's financial statements are affected if the petty cash fund is not replenished and no entry is made on January 31. (*Hint:* The amount of Office Supplies that appears on a balance sheet is determined by a physical count of office supplies.)

Problem 9-2B
Establish, reimburse, and increase petty cash

P3

Carousel Music Center had the following petty cash transactions in March of the current year:

March 5   Wrote a $250 check, cashed it, and gave the proceeds and the petty cashbox to Claire Mane, the petty cashier.

       6   Paid $12.50 COD shipping charges on merchandise purchased for resale, terms FOB shipping point. Carousel uses the perpetual system to account for merchandise inventory.

     11   Paid $10.75 delivery charges on merchandise sold to a customer, terms FOB destination.

     12   Purchased file folders, $14.13.

     14   Reimbursed Trisha Cox, the manager, $11.65 for office supplies purchased.

     18   Purchased paper for printer, $20.54.

     27   Paid $45.10 COD shipping charges on merchandise purchased for resale, terms FOB shipping point.

     28   Purchased postage stamps, $18.

     30   Reimbursed Trisha Cox $56.80 for business car mileage.

     31   Sorted the petty cash receipts by accounts affected and exchanged them for a check to both reimburse the fund for expenditures and increase the amount of the fund to $300. There was $61.53 cash in the fund.

Required

1. Prepare the general journal entry to establish the petty cash fund.

Check (2) Total expenses $189.47   **2.** Prepare a petty cash payments report for March with these categories: delivery expense, mileage expense, postage expense, merchandise inventory (transportation-in), and office supplies. Sort the payments into the appropriate categories and total the expenses in each category.

3. Prepare the general journal entry to both reimburse and increase the amount in the fund.

Problem 9-3B
Analyzing internal control

C2

For each of these five separate cases, identify the principle of internal control that is violated. Recommend what the business should do to ensure adherence to principles of internal control.

1. Sue Stanley is the company's computer specialist and oversees the company's computerized payroll system. Her boss recently asked her to put password protection on all office computers. Sue has put a password in place that allows only the boss access to the file where pay rates are changed and personnel are added or deleted from the payroll.

2. Park Theater has a computerized order-taking system for its tickets. The system is active all week and backed up every Friday night.

3. B2B Company has two employees handling acquisitions of inventory. One employee places purchase orders and pays vendors. The second employee receives the merchandise.

4. The owner of Rite-Aid uses a check protector to perforate checks, making it difficult for anyone to alter the amount of the check. The check protector sits on the owner's desk in an office that contains company checks and is often unlocked.

5. Rison Company is a small organization but has separated the duties of cash receipts and cash disbursements. Also, the employee responsible for cash disbursements reconciles the bank account monthly.

Problem 9-4B
Prepare a bank reconciliation and record adjustments

P5

The following information is available to reconcile Steele Co.'s book balance of cash with its bank statement cash balance as of December 31, 2002:

a. After posting is complete, the December 31 cash balance according to the accounting records is $32,878.30, and the bank statement cash balance for that date is $46,822.40.

b. Check No. 1273 for $4,589.30 and Check No. 1282 for $400.00, both written and entered in the accounting records in December, are not among the canceled checks returned. Two checks, No. 1231 for $2,289.00 and No. 1242 for $410.40, were outstanding on the most recent November 30 reconciliation. Check No. 1231 is returned with the December canceled checks, but Check No. 1242 is not.

c. When the December checks are compared with entries in the accounting records, it is found that Check No. 1267 had been correctly drawn for $3,456 to pay for office supplies but was erroneously entered in the accounting records as $3,465.

d. Two debit memoranda are included with the returned checks and are unrecorded at the time of the reconciliation. One of the debit memoranda is for $762.50 and dealt with an NSF check for $745.00 that had been received from a customer, Tidwell Industries, in payment of its account. The bank assessed a $17.50 fee for processing it. The second debit memorandum is a $99.00 charge for check printing. Steele did not record these transactions before receiving the statement.

e. A credit memorandum indicates that the bank collected a $19,000 note receivable for the company, deducted a $20 collection fee, and credited the balance to the company's cash account. Steele did not record this transaction before receiving the statement.

f. The December 31 daily cash receipts of $9,583.10 were placed in the bank's night depository on that date but do not appear on the December 31 bank statement.

Required

Preparation Component

1. Prepare a bank reconciliation for this company as of December 31, 2002.

2. Prepare the journal entries necessary to bring the company's book balance of cash into conformity with the reconciled cash balance as of December 31, 2002.

Check   Reconciled bal., $51,005.80

Analysis Component

3. Explain the nature of the communications conveyed by a bank when the bank sends the depositor (a) a debit memorandum and (b) a credit memorandum.

Sure Systems most recently reconciled its bank balance on April 30 and showed two checks outstanding at that time, No. 1771 for $781.00 and No. 1780 for $1,425.90. The following information is available for its May 31, 2002, reconciliation:

Problem 9-5B
Prepare a bank reconciliation and record adjustments

From the May 31 Bank Statement

Previous Balance	Total Checks and Debits	Total Deposits and Credits	Current Balance
18,290.70	13,094.80	16,566.80	21,762.70

Checks and Debits			Deposits and Credits		Daily Balance	
Date	No.	Amount	Date	Amount	Date	Amount
05/01	1771	781.00	05/04	2,438.00	04/30	18,290.70
05/02	1783	382.50	05/14	2,898.00	05/01	17,509.70
05/04	1782	1,285.50	05/22	1,801.80	05/02	17,127.20
05/11	1784	1,449.60	05/25	7,350.00 CM	05/04	18,279.70
05/18		431.80 NSF	05/26	2,079.00	05/11	16,830.10
05/25	1787	8,032.50			05/14	19,728.10
05/26	1785	63.90			05/18	19,296.30
05/29	1788	654.00			05/22	21,098.10
05/31		14.00 SC			05/25	20,415.60
					05/26	22,430.70
					05/29	21,776.70
					05/31	21,762.70

From Sure Systems' Accounting Records

Cash Receipts Deposited			Cash Disbursements		
Date		Cash Debit	Check No.		Cash Credit
May	4	2,438.00	1782		1,285.50
	14	2,898.00	1783		382.50
	22	1,801.80	1784		1,449.60
	26	2,079.00	1785		63.90
	31	2,727.30	1786		353.10
			1787		8,032.50
		11,944.10	1788		644.00
			1789		639.50
					12,850.60

Cash						Acct. No. 101
Date		**Explanation**	**PR**	**Debit**	**Credit**	**Balance**
Apr.	30	Balance				16,083.80
May	31	Total receipts	R7	11,944.10		28,027.90
	31	Total disbursements	D8		12,850.60	15,177.30

Other Information

Check No. 1788 is correctly drawn for $654 to pay for May utilities; however, the recordkeeper mis-read the amount and entered it in the accounting records with a debit to Utilities Expense and a credit to Cash for $644. The bank paid and deducted the correct amount. The NSF check shown in the state-ment was originally received from a customer, D. Hunt, in payment of her account. Its return has not yet been recorded. The credit memorandum is from a $7,400 note that the bank collected for the com-pany. The bank deducted a $50 collection fee and deposited the remainder in the company's account. The collection and fee are not yet recorded.

Required

Preparation Component

Check Reconciled balance, $22,071.50

1. Prepare the May 31, 2002, bank reconciliation for Sure Systems.
2. Prepare the journal entries to adjust the book balance of cash to the reconciled balance.

Analysis Component

3. The bank statement reveals that some of the prenumbered checks in the sequence are missing. Describe three possible situations that might explain this.

Beyond the Numbers

Reporting in Action

C3 A1

NIKE

BTN 9-1   Refer to the financial statements for **Nike** in Appendix A to answer the following:

1. For both fiscal year-end 2000 and 1999, determine the total amount of cash and cash equivalents. Determine the percent this amount represents of total current assets, total current liabilities, total shareholders' equity, and total assets for both years. Comment on any trends.
2. For both fiscal 2000 and 1999, use the information in the statement of cash flows to determine the percent change between the beginning and ending year amounts of cash and cash equivalents.
3. Compute the days' sales uncollected as of May 31, 2000, and May 31, 1999. Has the collection of receivables improved?

Swoosh Ahead

4. Access Nike's annual report for fiscal years ending after May 31, 2000, from its Web site [www.nike.com] or the SEC EDGAR database [www.sec.gov]. Recompute the days' sales un-collected for fiscal years ending after May 31, 2000. Compare this to the days' sales uncollected for 2000 and 1999.

Comparative Analysis

A1

NIKE

BTN 9-2   Key comparative figures ($ in millions) for both **Nike** and **Reebok** follow:

Key Figures	Nike		Reebok	
	Current Year	**Prior Year**	**Current Year**	**Prior Year**
Accounts receivable	$1,567.2	$1,540.1	$ 417.4	$ 517.8
Net sales	$8,995.1	$8,776.9	$2,899.9	$3,224.6

Required

Compute days' sales uncollected for both companies for the two years shown. Comment on any trends for both companies. Which company has the larger percent change in days' sales uncollected?

BTN 9-3 Susie Martin, Dot Night, and Colleen Walker work for a family physician, Dr. Gillbanks, who is in private practice. Dr. Gillbanks is knowledgeable about office management practices and has segregated the cash receipt duties as follows. Susie opens the mail and prepares a triplicate list of money received. She sends one copy of the list to Dot, the cashier, who deposits the receipts daily in the bank. Colleen, the recordkeeper, receives a copy of the list and posts payments to patients' accounts. About once a month the office clerks have an expensive lunch they pay for as follows. First, Dot endorses a patient's check in Dr. Gillbank's name and cashes it at the bank. Susie then destroys the remittance advice accompanying the check. Finally, Colleen posts payment to the customer's account as a miscellaneous credit. The three justify their actions by their relatively low pay and knowledge that Dr. Gillbanks will likely never miss the money.

Required

1. Who is the best person in Dr. Gillbank's office to reconcile the bank statement?
2. Would a bank reconciliation uncover this office fraud?
3. What are some ways to detect this type of fraud?
4. Suggest additional internal controls that Dr. Gillbanks may want to implement.

BTN 9-4 Assume you are a business consultant. The owner of a company sends you an e-mail expressing concern that the company is not taking advantage of discounts offered by vendors. The company currently uses the gross method of recording purchases. The owner is considering a review of all invoices and payments from the previous period. Due to the volume of purchases, however, the owner recognizes this is time consuming and costly. The owner seeks your advice about monitoring purchase discounts in the future. Provide a response in memorandum form.

BTN 9-5 Visit the Association of Certified Fraud Examiners Web site at **www.cfenet.com.** Research the fraud facts presented at this site and fill in the blanks in the following factual statements.

1. Fraud and abuse cost U.S. organizations more than $_____ billion annually.
2. The average organization loses more than $_____ per day per employee to fraud and abuse.
3. The average organization loses about _____% of its total annual revenue to fraud and abuse committed by its own employees.
4. The median fraud loss by males is about $_____; by females, about $_____.
5. Men commit nearly _____% of the offenses.
6. Losses caused by managers are _____ times those caused by employees.
7. Median fraud losses caused by executives are _____ times those of their employees.
8. The most costly abuses occur in organizations with less than _____ employees.
9. The _____ industry experiences the lowest median losses.
10. Occupational fraud and abuse fall into three main categories:_____.

BTN 9-6 Each team must prepare a list of 10 internal controls a consumer could observe in a typical retail department store. When called upon, the team's spokesperson must be prepared to share controls identified by the team that have not been shared by another team's spokesperson.

BTN 9-7 Read the article "Fraud on the Net" in the April 3, 2000, issue of *Business Week*.

Required

1. In 1997, 3% of all consumer complaints were about the Internet. How large is the percent now?
2. What percentage of Nike.com's purchase requests are estimated to be fraudulent?
3. Is the government making progress in detecting Internet fraud? Explain.
4. What are 5 of the top 10 scams on the net?

Entrepreneurial Decision

C2   P1

e

BTN 9-8   Steffi Kraff is setting up operations for her new carry-out business to sells subs and salads to mainly college students. Customers will order and receive their food at the counter, where a cashier will exchange food for cash. From the counter, customers will be able to see other employees making subs and salads.

Required

Identify the seven principles of internal control along with examples of each that the owner should implement.

Receivables and Short-Term Investments

"Everything we make is whimsical and unusual"—Tarina Tarantino.

A Look Back

Chapter 9 focused on internal control and accounting for cash. We described

A Look at This Chapter

This chapter emphasizes receivables and short-term investments. We explain

A Look Ahead

Chapter 11 focuses on plant assets, natural resources, and intangible

Learning Objectives

Conceptual

C1 Describe accounts receivable and how they occur and are recorded.

C2 Describe a note receivable and the computation of its maturity date and interest.

C3 Explain how receivables can be converted to cash before maturity.

C4 Describe short-term investments in debt and equity securities.

Analytical

A1 Compute accounts receivable turnover and use it to analyze liquidity.

Procedural

P1 Apply the direct write-off and allowance methods to account for accounts receivable.

P2 Estimate uncollectibles using methods based on sales and accounts receivable.

P3 Record the receipt of a note receivable.

P4 Record the honoring and dishonoring of a note and adjustments for interest on a note.

P5 Record short-term investment transactions.

Tarina Tarantino

e HOLLYWOOD, CA—Tarina Tarantino had always made jewelry for herself. Having grown up with "artistic hippie parents," Tarantino says she's always been attracted to the bold and offbeat. She and her husband, Alfonso Campos, knew they were unto something when Tarantino would wear her creations to work and return home jewelry-less as customers would buy the jeweled treasures off her hands and head. Campos decided to call some of the best stores and designers in L.A. "I'd tell them all I needed was one minute of their time, and it would be the best minute of their lives," says Campos.

Orders soon flooded in—more than they could handle. **Tarina Tarantino Designs [TarinaTarantino.com]** was launched with $400 in cash and a car that they sold. Not surprisingly, banks scoffed at a loan request. "We had $50,000 worth of orders, and we thought 'Wow! This is going to be it'," says Campos. "They looked at us like '$50,000 is nothing kids. Do you have any collateral?'" Still, they pushed forward, setting up shop in the dining room of their apartment. Both quit jobs to devote all their attention to the business. "Letting go of the security of a paycheck was really the best thing we ever did," says Tarantino.

Tarantino now sells her creations over the Web and in retail stores. "My typical customer is an urban princess," says Tarantino. "She wants something glamorous and funky, something that makes her feel unique." Tarantino also accepts credit cards along with money orders and cashier's checks to encourage sales. Although noncash sales have costs, Tarantino and Campos believe the benefits outweigh them. However, personal checks are not accepted to avoid uncollectible accounts receivable. Tarantino admits entrepreneurship is tough, "It looks easy, but really it's a lot of blood, sweat, and tears." But it has paid off—Tarantino expects sales to exceed $5 million this year. That's a lot of funky jewelry. [Sources: *Tarina Tarantino Web site*, May 2001; *Entrepreneur*, November, 1999; *First Jewelry Web site*, March 2001]

Chapter Preview

This chapter focuses on accounts receivable, short-term notes receivable, and short-term investments. We describe each of these assets, their uses, and how they are accounted for and reported in financial statements. This knowledge helps us use accounting information to make better decisions. It can also help in predicting future company performance and financial condition.

Accounts Receivable

 C1 Describe accounts receivable and how they occur and are recorded.

A *receivable* refers to an amount due from another party. Receivables, cash, cash equivalents, and short-term investments make up the most liquid assets of a company. The two most common receivables are accounts receivable and notes receivable. Other receivables include interest receivable, rent receivable, tax refund receivable, and receivables from officers and employees.

Accounts receivable refer to amounts due from customers for credit sales. This section begins by describing how accounts receivable occur. It includes receivables that occur when customers use credit cards issued by third parties and when a company gives credit directly to customers. When a company does extend credit directly to customers, it must (1) maintain a separate account receivable for each customer and (2) account for bad debts from credit sales.

Recognizing Accounts Receivable

Accounts receivable occur from credit sales to customers. The amount of credit sales has increased in recent years, reflecting several factors including an efficient financial system and a sound economy. Retailers such as **The Limited**, **Chic by H.I.S**, **Best Buy**, and **CompUSA** hold millions of dollars in accounts receivable. Similar amounts are held by wholesalers such as **Nike**, **Reebok**, **SUPERVALU**, **SYSCO**, and **Ace Hardware**. Exhibit 10.1 shows recent dollar amounts of accounts receivable and their percent of total assets for four well-known companies.

Exhibit 10.1

Accounts Receivable for Selected Companies

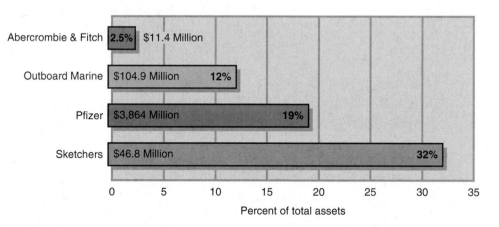

Sales on Credit

Credit sales are recorded by increasing (debiting) Accounts Receivable. A company must also maintain a separate account for each customer that tracks how much that customer purchases, has already paid, and still owes. This information provides the basis for sending bills to customers and for other business analyses. To maintain this information, companies that extend credit directly to their customers keep a separate account receivable for each one of them. The general ledger continues to have a single Accounts Receivable account along with the other financial statement accounts, but a supplementary record is created to maintain a separate account for each customer. This supplementary record is called the *accounts receivable ledger*.

Exhibit 10.2 shows the relation between the Accounts Receivable account in the general ledger and its individual customer accounts in the accounts receivable ledger for **TechCom**, a small electronics wholesaler. This exhibit reports a $3,000 ending balance of TechCom's

Exhibit 10.2

General Ledger and the
Accounts Receivable Ledger
(before July 1 transactions)

accounts receivable for June 30. TechCom's transactions are mainly in cash, but it has two major credit customers: CompStore and RDA Electronics. Its schedule of accounts receivable shows that the $3,000 balance of the Accounts Receivable account in the general ledger equals the total of its two customers' balances in the accounts receivable ledger.

To see how accounts receivable from credit sales are recognized in the accounting records, we look at two transactions on July 1 between TechCom and its credit customers. The first is a credit sale of $950 to CompStore. A credit sale is posted with both a debit to the Accounts Receivable account in the general ledger and a debit to the customer account in the accounts receivable ledger. The second transaction is a collection of $720 from RDA Electronics from a prior credit sale. Cash receipts from a credit customer are posted with credits to both the Accounts Receivable account in the general ledger and to the customer account in the accounts receivable ledger.[1] Both transactions are journalized in Exhibit 10.3.

July 1	Accounts Receivable—CompStore	950	
	Sales		950
	*To record credit sales**		
July 1	Cash	720	
	Accounts Receivable—RDA Electronics . . .		720
	To record collection of credit sales.		

Exhibit 10.3

Accounts Receivable
Transactions

* We omit the entry to Dr. Cost of Sales and Cr. Merchandise Inventory to focus on sales and receivables.

Exhibit 10.4 shows the general ledger and the accounts receivable ledger after recording the two July 1 transactions. The general ledger shows the effects of the sale, the collection, and the resulting balance of $3,230. These events are also reflected in the individual customer accounts: RDA Electronics has an ending balance of $280, and CompStore's ending balance is $2,950. The $3,230 sum of the individual accounts equals the debit balance of the Accounts Receivable account in the general ledger.

Point: New software helps merchants build Web storefronts quickly and easily. Merchants simply enter product details such as names and prices, and out comes a respectable-looking Web site complete with order forms. They also offer security with credit card orders and can track sales and site visits.

---

[1] Posting debits or credits to Accounts Receivable in two separate ledgers does not violate the requirement that debits equal credits. The equality of debits and credits is maintained in the general ledger. The accounts receivable ledger is a supplementary record providing detailed information on each customer.

Exhibit 10.4

General Ledger and the
Accounts Receivable Ledger
(after July 1 transactions)

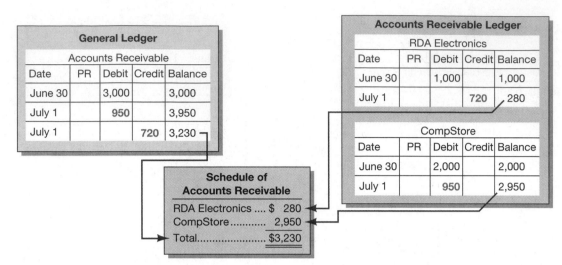

General Ledger

Accounts Receivable

Date	PR	Debit	Credit	Balance
June 30		3,000		3,000
July 1		950		3,950
July 1			720	3,230

Schedule of Accounts Receivable

RDA Electronics .... $ 280
CompStore............   2,950
Total..................... $3,230

Accounts Receivable Ledger

RDA Electronics

Date	PR	Debit	Credit	Balance
June 30		1,000		1,000
July 1			720	280

CompStore

Date	PR	Debit	Credit	Balance
June 30		2,000		2,000
July 1		950		2,950

Many large retailers such as **Sears** and **JCPenney** maintain their own credit cards. This allows them to grant credit to approved customers and to earn interest on any balance not paid within a specified period of time. It also allows them to avoid the fee charged by credit card companies. The entries in this case are the same as those for TechCom except for the possibility of added interest revenue. If a customer owes interest on a bill, we debit Interest Receivable and credit Interest Revenue for that amount.

Credit Card Sales

Many companies allow their customers to pay for products and services using credit cards and bankcards such as **Visa**, **MasterCard**, or **American Express**. This practice gives customers the ability to make purchases without cash or checks. Once credit is established with a credit card company or bank, the customer does not have to open an account with each store. Customers using these cards can make single monthly payments instead of several payments to different creditors. They also can defer their payments.

There are several reasons why sellers allow customers to use credit cards and bankcards instead of granting credit directly. First, the seller does not have to evaluate each customer's credit standing or make decisions about who gets credit and how much. Second, the seller avoids the risk of extending credit to customers who cannot or do not pay. This risk is transferred to the card company. Third, the seller typically receives cash from the credit card company and bank sooner than had it granted credit directly to customers. Fourth, a variety of credit options for customers offers a potential increase in sales volume. **Sears** historically offered credit only to customers using a Sears card, but later changed its policy to permit customers to charge purchases to third-party credit card companies in a desire to increase sales. It reported that: "SearsCharge increased its share of Sears retail sales even as the company expanded the payment options available to its customers with the acceptance . . . of VISA, MasterCard, and American Express in addition to the Discover Card."

There are guidelines in how companies account for credit card and bankcard sales. Some credit cards, but mostly bankcards, credit a seller's Cash account immediately upon deposit. In this case the seller deposits a copy of each credit card sales receipt in its bank account just as it deposits a customer's check. Some other credit cards require the seller to remit a copy (often electronically) of each receipt to the credit card company. Until payment is received, the seller has an account receivable from the credit card company. In both cases, the seller pays a fee for services provided by the card company, often ranging from 2% to 5% of card sales. This charge is deducted from the credit to the seller's account or the cash payment to the seller.

The procedures used in accounting for credit card sales depend on whether cash is received immediately on deposit or cash receipt is delayed until the credit card company makes the payment. To illustrate, if TechCom has $100 of credit card sales with a 4% fee, and its cash is received immediately on deposit, the entry is

July 15	Cash	96	
	Credit Card Expense	4	
	Sales		100
	To record credit card sales less a 4% credit card expense.		

Assets = Liabilities + Equity
+96 −4
+100

However, if TechCom must remit copies of the credit card sales receipts to the credit card company and wait for payment, the entry on the date of sale is

July 15	Accounts Receivable—Credit Card Co.	96	
	Credit Card Expense	4	
	Sales		100
	To record credit card sales less 4% credit card expense.		

Assets = Liabilities + Equity
+96 +100
−4

When cash is received from the credit card company, the entry to record the receipt is

July 25	Cash	96	
	Accounts Receivable—Credit Card Co.		96
	To record cash receipt.		

Assets = Liabilities + Equity
+96
96

Some firms report credit card expense in the income statement as a type of discount deducted from sales to get net sales. Other companies classify it as a selling expense or even as an administrative expense. Arguments can be made for each alternative.

Answer—p. 421

You Make the Call

Entrepreneur   As a small retailer, you are considering allowing customers to purchase merchandise using credit cards. Until now, your store accepted only cash and checks. What form of analysis do you use to make this decision?

Point: Third-party credit card costs can be large. JCPenney recently reported sales of $32,510 million. Beyond its bad debt expenses, it reported third-party credit costs of nearly $100 million.

Quick Check

1. In recording credit card sales, when do you debit Accounts Receivable and when do you debit Cash?
2. When are credit card expenses recorded when sales receipts are accumulated and remitted to the credit card company for payment? When are these expenses incurred?

Answers—p. 421

Valuing Accounts Receivable

When a company directly grants credit to its customers, some customers do not always pay what they promised. The accounts of these customers are *uncollectible accounts,* commonly called **bad debts.** The total amount of uncollectible accounts is an expense of selling on credit. Why do companies sell on credit if they expect some accounts to be uncollectible? The answer is that companies believe that granting credit will increase sales and net income enough to offset bad debts. They are willing to incur bad debts losses if the net effect is to increase sales and net income. Companies use two methods to account for uncollectible accounts: (1) direct write-off method and (2) allowance method. We describe both.

Direct Write-Off Method

P1 Apply the direct write-off and allowance methods to account for accounts receivable.

The **direct write-off method** of accounting for bad debts records the loss from an uncollectible account receivable when it is determined to be uncollectible. No attempt is made to predict bad debts expense. Bad debts expense is recorded when specific accounts are written off as uncollectible. To illustrate, if TechCom determines on January 23 that it cannot collect $520 owed to it by its customer Jack Kent, it recognizes the loss using the direct write-off method as follows:

Assets = Liabilities + Equity
−520   −520

Jan. 23	Bad Debts Expense	520	
	Accounts Receivable—J. Kent		520
	To write off an uncollectible account.		

The debit in this entry charges the uncollectible amount directly to the current period's Bad Debts Expense account. The credit removes its balance from the Accounts Receivable account in the general ledger (and its subsidiary ledger).

Sometimes an account written off is later collected. This can be due to factors such as continual collection efforts or customer's good fortune. If the account of Jack Kent that was written off directly to Bad Debts Expense is later collected in full, the following two entries record this recovery:

Assets = Liabilities + Equity
+520   +520

Assets = Liabilities + Equity
+520
−520

Mar. 11	Accounts Receivable—J. Kent	520	
	Bad Debts Expense		520
	To reinstate account previously written off.		
Mar. 11	Cash	520	
	Accounts Receivable—J. Kent		520
	To record full payment of account.		

Companies must weigh at least two accounting principles when considering the use of the direct write-off method: the (1) matching principle and (2) materiality principle.

Matching Principle Applied to Bad Debts

The **matching principle** requires expenses to be reported in the same accounting period as the sales they helped produce. This means that if extending credit to customers helped produce sales, the bad debts expense linked to those sales is matched and reported in the same period. The direct write-off method usually does not best match sales and expenses because bad debts expense is not recorded until an account becomes uncollectible, which often does not occur in the same period as the credit sale. However, applying the matching principle to bad debts presents challenges. Managers realize that some portion of credit sales will be uncollectible, but which credit sales are uncollectible is unknown. If a customer fails to pay within the credit period, most companies send out repeated billings and make other efforts to collect. They do not accept that a customer is not going to pay until they take every reasonable means of collection. This decision point may not be reached until one or more accounting periods after the sale is made. Matching bad debts expense with the sales it produces therefore requires a company to estimate uncollectibles.

Point: Pier 1 Imports reports $4.7 million of bad debts expense is matched against $300.5 million of credit sales in a recent fiscal year.

Materiality Principle Applied to Bad Debts

The **materiality principle** states that an amount can be ignored if its effect on the financial statements is unimportant to users' business decisions. The materiality principle permits the use of the direct write-off method when bad debts expenses are very small in relation to a company's other financial statement items such as sales and net income.

Allowance Method

The **allowance method** of accounting for bad debts matches the *expected* loss from uncollectible accounts receivable against the sales they helped produce. We must use expected losses since management cannot exactly identify the customers who will not pay their bills at the time of sale. This means that at the end of each period, the allowance method requires an estimate of the total bad debts expected to result from that period's sales. An allowance is then recorded for this expected loss. This method has two advantages over the direct write-off method: (1) it charges bad debts expense to the period when it recognizes the related sales and (2) it reports accounts receivable on the balance sheet at the estimated amount of cash to be collected.

Point: Under the direct write-off method, expense is recorded each time an account is written off. Under the allowance method, expense is recorded with an adjusting entry equal to the total estimated uncollectibles for that period's sales.

Concept 10-1

Recording Estimated Bad Debts Expense

The allowance method estimates bad debts expense at the end of each accounting period and records it with an adjusting entry. TechCom, for instance, had credit sales of approximately $300,000 during its first year of operations. At the end of the first year, $20,000 of credit sales remained uncollected. Based on the experience of similar businesses, TechCom estimated that $1,500 of its accounts receivable would be uncollectible. This estimated expense is recorded with the following adjusting entry:

Point: The Office of the Comptroller of the Currency reports that losses from bad debts led to the collapse of 98% of failed banks.

Dec. 31	Bad Debts Expense	1,500	
	Allowance for Doubtful Accounts		1,500
	To record estimated bad debts.		

Assets	= Liabilities +	Equity
1,500		1,500

The estimated Bad Debts Expense of $1,500 from selling on credit is reported on the income statement and matched with the $300,000 credit sales it helped produce. The credit in this entry is to a contra asset account called **Allowance for Doubtful Accounts.** A contra account is used because at the time of the adjusting entry, the company does not know which customers will not pay. Bad Debts Expense often appears on the income statement as an administrative expense rather than a selling expense. The process of evaluating and approving customers for credit is usually not assigned to the selling department because its main goal is to increase sales, and it may approve customers for credit at the expense of increased bad debts. Therefore, responsibility for granting credit is assigned to a separate credit-granting or other administrative department.

Point: Bad Debts Expense is also called *Uncollectible Accounts Expense.* The Allowance for Doubtful Accounts is also called *Allowance for Uncollectible Accounts.*

Bad Debts Related Accounts in Financial Statements

Recall that TechCom has $20,000 of outstanding accounts receivable at the end of its first year of operations. After the bad debts adjusting entry is posted, TechCom's Accounts Receivable and its Allowance for Doubtful Accounts appear as shown in Exhibit 10.5.

Accounts Receivable			Allowance for Doubtful Accounts		
Dec. 31	20,000			Dec. 31	1,500

Exhibit 10.5

General Ledger Balances after Bad Debts Adjusting Entry

The Allowance for Doubtful Accounts credit balance of $1,500 has the effect of reducing accounts receivable (net of the allowance) to its estimated realizable value. **Realizable value** is the expected proceeds from converting an asset into cash. Although credit customers owe $20,000 to TechCom, only $18,500 is expected to be realized in cash collections from these customers. In the balance sheet, the Allowance for Doubtful Accounts is subtracted from Accounts Receivable to show the amount expected to be realized. This information is often reported as shown in Exhibit 10.6.

Exhibit 10.6

Balance Sheet Presentation of the Allowance for Doubtful Accounts

Current assets		
Accounts receivable	**$20,000**	
Less allowance for doubtful accounts	**(1,500)**	**$18,500**

Sometimes the Allowance for Doubtful Accounts is not reported separately. This alternative presentation is shown in Exhibit 10.7.

Exhibit 10.7

Alternative Presentation of the Allowance for Doubtful Accounts

Current assets	
Accounts receivable (net of $1,500 estimated uncollectible accounts)	**$18,500**

Writing Off a Bad Debt

When specific accounts are identified as uncollectible, they are written off against the Allowance for Doubtful Accounts. To illustrate, after spending some time trying to collect from Jack Kent, TechCom decides that Kent's $520 account is uncollectible and makes the following entry to write it off:

Assets = Liabilities + Equity
+520
−520

Jan. 23	Allowance for Doubtful Accounts	520	
	Accounts Receivable—J. Kent		520
	To write off an uncollectible account.		

Posting this write-off entry to the Accounts Receivable account removes the amount of the bad debt from the general ledger. Posting it to Kent's individual account removes the amount of the bad debt from the subsidiary ledger. The general ledger accounts now appear as in Exhibit 10.8 (assuming no other transactions affecting these accounts).

Exhibit 10.8

General Ledger Balances after Write-Off

Accounts Receivable					Allowance for Doubtful Accounts			
Dec. 31	20,000						Dec. 31	1,500
		Jan. 23	520		Jan. 23	520		

Point: In posting a write-off of an uncollectible, we use the Explanation column in the ledger to indicate the reason for this credit. Otherwise, this credit might be misinterpreted as payment in full.

Note two points with the write-off entry. First, although bad debts are an expense of selling on credit, the allowance account is debited in the write-off. The expense account is not debited because bad debts expense is previously estimated and recorded with an adjusting entry in the period when the sales occurred. Second, while the write-off removes the uncollectible account receivable from the ledgers, it does not affect the realizable value of TechCom's accounts receivable as shown in Exhibit 10.9. Neither total assets nor net income is affected by the write-off of a specific account. Instead, both assets and net income are affected in the period when bad debts expense is recorded with an adjusting entry.

Exhibit 10.9

Realizable Value before and after Write-Off

	Before Write-Off	After Write-Off
Accounts receivable	$20,000	$19,480
Less allowance for doubtful accounts	1,500	980
Estimated realizable accounts receivable	**$18,500**	**$18,500**

Recovery of a Bad Debt

When a customer fails to pay and the account is written off as uncollectible, his or her credit standing is jeopardized. To help restore credit standing, a customer sometimes chooses to voluntarily pay all or part of the amount owed. A company makes two entries when collecting an account previously written off by the allowance method. The first is to reverse the write-off and reinstate the customer's account. The second entry records the collection of the reinstated account. To illustrate, if on March 11 Kent pays in full his account previously written off, the entries to record this recovery are

Mar. 11	Accounts Receivable—J. Kent	520	
	Allowance for Doubtful Accounts		520
	To reinstate account previously written off.		
Mar. 11	Cash	520	
	Accounts Receivable—J. Kent		520
	To record full payment of account.		

Assets = Liabilities + Equity
+520
−520

Assets = Liabilities + Equity
+520
−520

In this illustration, Kent paid the entire amount previously written off, but sometimes a customer pays only a portion of the amount owed. A question then arises as to whether the entire balance of the account is returned to accounts receivable or just the amount paid. This is a matter of judgment. If we believe this customer will later pay in full, we return the entire amount owed to accounts receivable, but if we expect no further collection, we return only the amount paid.

Example: If TechCom used a collection agency and paid a 35% commission on $520 collected from J. Kent, how is this recorded?
Answer:
Cash 338
Collection Expense 182
   Accts. Recble.—J. Kent . . 520

Quick Check

3. Why must bad debts expense be estimated if possible?

4. What term describes the balance sheet valuation of Accounts Receivable less the Allowance for Doubtful Accounts?

5. Why is estimated bad debts expense credited to a contra account (Allowance for Doubtful Accounts) rather than to the Accounts Receivable account?

Answers—p. 421

Estimating Bad Debts Expense

Companies with direct credit sales must attempt to estimate bad debts expense. They do this to help them manage their receivables and to set credit policies. The allowance method also requires an estimate of bad debts expense to prepare an adjusting entry at the end of each accounting period. There are two common methods to estimate bad debts expense. One is based on the income statement relation between bad debts expense and sales. The second is based on the balance sheet relation between accounts receivable and the allowance for doubtful accounts. Both methods require an analysis of past experience.

P2 Estimate uncollectibles using methods based on sales and accounts receivable.

Percent of Sales Method

The *percent of sales method* uses income statement relations to estimate bad debts. It is based on the idea that a given percent of a company's credit sales for the period are uncollectible.[2] The income statement then reports that percent of sales as the amount of bad debts expense. To illustrate, assume that **MusicLand** has credit sales of $400,000 in year 2002. Based on past experience, MusicLand estimates 0.6% of credit sales to be uncollectible.

Point: When using the percent of sales method for estimating uncollectibles, the amount of the bad debts estimate is the number used in the adjusting entry.

---

[2] The focus is on *credit* sales. Cash sales do not produce bad debts, and they are generally not used in this estimation. If cash sales are small compared to credit sales, there usually is no major impact from including them.

This implies that MusicLand expects $2,400 of bad debts expense from its sales (computed as $400,000 × 0.006 = $2,400). The adjusting entry to record this estimated expense is

Assets = Liabilities + Equity
−2,400   −2,400

Dec. 31	Bad Debts Expense	2,400	
	Allowance for Doubtful Accounts.		2,400
	To record estimated bad debts.		

This entry does not mean the December 31, 2002, balance in Allowance for Doubtful Accounts will be $2,400. A $2,400 balance occurs only if the account had a zero balance prior to posting the adjusting entry. Unless a company is in its first period of operations, its allowance account has a zero balance only if the prior amounts written off as uncollectible *exactly* equal the prior estimated bad debts expenses. This means the allowance account balance reported on the balance sheet would rarely equal the amount of expense reported on the income statement. Note that expressing bad debts expense as a percent of sales is based on past experience. As new experience is obtained, we often find the percent to be too high or too low. When this happens, we adjust the percent for future periods.

Did You Know?

eBay of Deadbeats   Want to pick up some cheap debt? The Web is the place to do it. **Sprint** recently put $145 million of its unpaid telephone bills up for sale on **DebtAuction.com,** and **Bank One** listed $211 million of unpaid credit card receivables on rival **DebtForSale.com.** Insiders say Sprint's $145 million portfolio fetched $2 million—better low margins than none at all.

Bum Loans on the Net
E-Debt.com
DistressDebt.com
DebtForSale.com
DebtAuction.com
CollectionsX.com

Accounts Receivable Methods

The *accounts receivable methods* use balance sheet relations to estimate bad debts—mainly the relation between accounts receivable and the allowance amount. These methods focus on some portion of the end-of-period accounts receivable balance that is not collectible. The objective of the bad debts adjusting entry in this case is to make the Allowance for Doubtful Accounts balance equal to the portion of outstanding accounts receivable estimated as uncollectible. To obtain this balance for the Allowance for Doubtful Accounts, we compare its balance before the adjustment with the estimated balance. The estimated balance for the allowance account is obtained in one of two ways: (1) computing the percent uncollectible from the total outstanding accounts receivable or (2) aging accounts receivable.

Point: When using an accounts receivable method for estimating uncollectibles, the allowance account balance is adjusted so as to equal the estimate of uncollectibles when recording the adjusting entry.

Percent of accounts receivable method

The *percent of accounts receivable method* assumes a given percent of a company's outstanding receivables to be uncollectible. This percent is based on past experience and is impacted by current conditions such as economic trends and difficulties faced by customers. The total dollar amount of all outstanding receivables is multiplied by this percent to get the estimated dollar amount of uncollectible accounts. This amount is reported in the balance sheet as the Allowance for Doubtful Accounts. To achieve this result, we prepare an adjusting entry debiting Bad Debts Expense and crediting Allowance for Doubtful Accounts. The amount of the adjustment is the amount necessary to yield a balance in the Allowance for Doubtful Accounts that equals the estimated amount of uncollectibles.

Global: In China, government regulation constrains the *percents* used to estimate bad debts.

To illustrate, assume that **MusicLand** has $50,000 of outstanding accounts receivable on December 31, 2002. Past experience suggests 5% of outstanding receivables are uncollectible. This means that after the adjusting entry is posted, we want the Allowance for Doubtful Accounts to show a $2,500 credit balance (computed as 5% of $50,000). Before the adjustment the account appears as follows

Allowance for Doubtful Accounts			
		Dec. 31, 2001, bal.	2,000
Feb. 6	800		
July 10	600		
Nov. 20	400		
		Unadjusted bal.	200

The $2,000 beginning balance is from the December 31, 2001, balance sheet. During 2002, accounts of customers are written off on February 6, July 10, and November 20. The account has a $200 credit balance prior to the December 31, 2002, adjustment. The adjusting entry to give the allowance account the estimated $2,500 balance is

Dec. 31	Bad Debts Expense	2,300	
	Allowance for Doubtful Accounts.		2,300
	To record estimated bad debts.		

Assets − Liabilities + Equity
−2,300   −2,300

After this entry the allowance has a $2,500 credit balance as shown in Exhibit 10.10.

Aging of accounts receivable method

Both the percent of sales (income statement) method and the percent of accounts receivable (balance sheet) method use information from *past* experience to estimate the amount of bad debts expense. Another balance sheet method, called the **aging of accounts receivable** method, uses both past and current receivables information to produce a more precise estimate. It reviews *each* account receivable to estimate the amount uncollectible. Each receivable is classified by how long it is past its due date. Then estimates of uncollectible amounts are made assuming that the longer an amount is past due, the more likely it is to be uncollectible. Classifications are often based on 30-day (or one-month) periods. After the amounts are classified (or aged), past experience is used to estimate the percent of each class that is uncollectible. These percents are applied to the amounts in each class to get the estimated balance of the Allowance for Doubtful Accounts. This computation is performed by setting up a schedule such as Exhibit 10.11 for MusicLand.

Allowance for Doubtful Accounts			
		Dec. 31, 2001, bal.	2,000
Feb. 6	800		
July 10	600		
Nov. 20	400		
		Unadjusted bal.	200
		Dec. 31 adjustment	**2,300**
		Dec. 31, 2002, bal.	2,500

Exhibit 10.10

Allowance for Doubtful Accounts after Bad Debts Adjusting Entry

Did You Know?

Smart e-Commerce When you buy online with a credit card, you put your account number at risk. If, however, you slide a smart card into a reader on your PC and enter your password, the merchant never gets your account number but only a code authorizing the sale. Since **American Express** launched the first major U.S. smart card last year, an estimated 2 million consumers have signed up.

Exhibit 10.11

Aging of Accounts Receivable

			MUSICLAND				
			Schedule of Accounts Receivable by Age				
	Customer	Totals	Not Yet Due	1 to 30 Days Past Due	31 to 60 Days Past Due	61 to 90 Days Past Due	Over 90 Days Past Due
7	Charles Abbot	$ 450	$ 450				
8	Frank Allen	710			$ 710		
9	George Arden	500	300	$ 200			
10	Paul Baum	740				$ 100	$ 640
23	ZZ Services	1,000	810	190			
24	Totals	$ 49,900	$ 37,000	$ 6,500	$ 3,500	$ 1,900	$ 1,000
25	Percent uncollectible		x 2%	x 5%	x 10%	x 25%	x 40%
26	Estimated uncollectible	$ 2,290	$ 740	$ 325	$ 350	$ 475	$ 400

Point: Experience shows the longer a receivable is past due, the lower is the likelihood of collection. An aging schedule exploits this relation and yields useful information to evaluate credit policies.

Exhibit 10.11 lists each customer's total account balance. Then each individual balance is assigned to one of five classes based on its days past due. In computerized systems, this task can be programmed. When all accounts are aged, the amounts in each class are

Point: Spreadsheet software is especially useful for estimating bad debts. Using both current and past data, estimates of bad debts are obtained under different assumptions and economic trends.

totaled and multiplied by the estimated percent of uncollectible accounts for each class. The reasonableness of the percents used is regularly reviewed to reflect changes in the company and economy.

To illustrate the aging method, notice that MusicLand has $3,500 in accounts receivable that are 31 to 60 days past due. Its management estimates 10% of the amounts in this age class are not collectible, or a total of $350 (computed as $3,500 × 10%). Similar analysis is done for each of the other four classes. The final total of $2,290 ($740 + $325 + $350 +

Exhibit 10.12

Computation of the Required Adjustment for an Accounts Receivable Method

Unadjusted balance	$ 200 credit
Estimated balance	2,290 credit
Required adjustment	**$2,090 credit**

$475 + $400) shown in the first column is the estimated balance for the Allowance for Doubtful Accounts. Since the allowance account has an unadjusted credit balance of $200, the required adjustment to the Allowance for Doubtful Accounts is $2,090.

This computation is shown in Exhibit 10.12.

To obtain the estimated balance of $2,290, MusicLand prepares the following end-of-period adjusting entry:

Assets = Liabilities + Equity
−2,090   −2,090

Dec. 31	Bad Debts Expense	2,090	
	Allowance for Doubtful Accounts		2,090
	To record estimated bad debts.		

Alternatively, if the allowance account had an unadjusted *debit* balance of $500 (instead of the $200 credit balance), its required adjustment is computed as follows:

Unadjusted balance	$ 500 debit
Estimated balance	2,290 credit
Required adjustment	**$ 2,790 credit**

The entry to record the end-of-period adjustment for this alternative case is

Assets = Liabilities + Equity
−2,790   −2,790

Dec. 31	Bad Debts Expense	2,790	
	Allowance for Doubtful Accounts		2,790
	To record estimated bad debts.		

Global: International practices vary as to when receivables should be written off. Some do not write off an account until it is one to two years past due.

To sum up the MusicLand case, when the percent of sales (income statement) method is used, MusicLand's bad debts expense is estimated at $2,400. When the percent of accounts receivable method is used, the expense is $2,300. When the aging of accounts receivable method is used, the expense is $2,090. We expect these amounts to differ since each method gives only an estimate of future payments. The aging of accounts receivable method is a more detailed examination of specific accounts and is usually the most reliable.[3] Exhibit 10.13 summarizes the principles guiding all three estimation methods and their focus of analysis.

Exhibit 10.13

Methods to Estimate Bad Debts

---

[3] Aging analysis often is supplemented with information about specific customers, allowing management to decide whether those accounts should be classified as uncollectible. This information usually is supplied by the sales and credit departments.

Quick Check

6. SnoBoard Company's year-end balance in its Allowance for Doubtful Accounts is a credit of $440. By aging accounts receivable, it estimates that $6,142 is uncollectible. Prepare SnoBoard's year-end adjusting entry for bad debts.

7. Record entries for these transactions assuming the allowance method is used:

Jan. 10   The $300 account of customer Cool Jam is determined uncollectible.

April 12   Cool Jam unexpectedly pays in full the account that was deemed uncollectible on January 10.

Answers—p. 421

Installment Accounts Receivable

Many companies allow their credit customers to make periodic payments over several months. For example, **Harley-Davidson** reports more than $400 million in installment receivables. The seller refers to such assets as *installment accounts receivable,* which are amounts owed by customers from credit sales for which payment is required in periodic amounts over an extended time period. Source documents for installment accounts receivable include sales slips or invoices describing the sales transactions. The customer is usually charged interest. Although installment accounts receivable may have credit periods of more than one year, they are classified as current assets if the seller regularly offers customers such terms.

You Make the Call

Labor Union Chief   A week prior to contract negotiations, financial statements are released showing no growth in income. A 10% growth was predicted. In your analysis, you find that the company increased its allowance for uncollectibles from 1.5% to 4.5% of accounts receivable. Without this change, income would show a 9% growth. Does this analysis impact your negotiations?

Answer—p. 421

Notes Receivable

A **promissory note** is a written promise to pay a specified amount of money either on demand or at a definite future date. Promissory notes are used in many transactions, including paying for products and services, lending and borrowing money, and paying for accounts receivable. Sellers sometimes allow customers to sign a note for sales. Sellers also sometimes ask for a note to replace an account receivable when a customer requests additional time to pay a past-due account. Most notes include interest charges. If a seller regularly offers customers this option, such notes are classified as current assets even when their credit period is longer than one year. For legal reasons, sellers generally prefer to receive notes when the credit period is long and when the receivable is for a large amount. If a lawsuit is needed to collect from a customer, a note is the buyer's written acknowledgment of the debt, its amount, and its terms.

Exhibit 10.14 shows a promissory note dated July 10, 2002. For this note, Julia Browne promises to pay TechCom or to its order (according to TechCom's instructions) a specified

C2   Describe a note receivable and the computation of its maturity date and interest.

Concept 10-2

Exhibit 10.14

Promissory Note

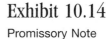

Principal

Promissory Note

$1,000   July 10, 2002
Amount   **Date**

Ninety days   after date _____ I _____ promise to pay to the order of
          TechCom Company
          Los Angeles, CA

One thousand and no/100 --------------------------------- Dollars

for value received with interest at the annual rate of _12%_
payable at First National Bank of Los Angeles, CA

_____ *Julia Browne*

Date of note
Due date
Payee
Interest rate
Maker

amount of money ($1,000), called the **principal of a note,** at a definite future date (October 8, 2002). As the one who signed the note and promised to pay it at maturity, Browne is the **maker of the note.** As the person to whom the note is payable, TechCom is the **payee of the note.** To Browne, the note is a liability called a *note payable*. To TechCom, the same note is an asset called a *note receivable*. This note bears interest at 12%, as written on the note. **Interest** is the charge for using (not paying) the money until a later date. To a borrower, interest is an expense. To a lender, it is revenue.

Computations for Notes

This section describes key computations for notes including the determination of maturity date, period covered, and interest computation.

Maturity Date and Period

The **maturity date of a note** is the day the note (principal and interest) must be repaid. The *period* of a note is the time from the note's (contract) date to its maturity date. Many notes mature in less than a full year, and the period they cover is often expressed in days. When the time of a note is expressed in days, its maturity date is the specified number of days after the note's date. As an example, a five-day note dated June 15 matures and is due on June 20. A 90-day note dated July 10 matures on October 8. This October 8 due date is computed as shown in Exhibit 10.15.

Exhibit 10.15

Maturity Date Computation

Days in July	31
Minus the date of the note	10
Days remaining in July	21
Add days in August	31
Add days in September	30
Days to equal 90 days, or **maturity date of October 8**	8
Period of the note in days	90

The period of a note is sometimes expressed in months or years. When months are used, the note matures and is payable in the month of its maturity on the *same day of the month* as its original date. A nine-month note dated July 10, for instance, is payable on April 10. The same analysis applies when years are used.

Interest Computation

Interest is the cost of borrowing money for the borrower or, alternatively, the profit from lending money for the lender. Unless otherwise stated, the rate of interest on a note is the rate charged for the use of the principal for one year. The formula for computing interest on a note is shown in Exhibit 10.16.

Exhibit 10.16

Computation of Interest Formula

$$\begin{array}{ccc} \textbf{Principal} & \textbf{Annual} & \textbf{Time} \\ \textbf{of the} & \times \textbf{ interest } \times & \textbf{expressed } = \textbf{Interest} \\ \textbf{note} & \textbf{rate} & \textbf{in years} \end{array}$$

To simplify interest computations for notes with periods expressed in days, a year is commonly treated as having 360 days (called the *banker's rule*). **We treat a year as having 360 days in the examples and in the assignments.** Using the promissory note in Exhibit 10.14 where we have a 90-day, 12%, $1,000 note, the total interest is computed as follows:

$$\$1,000 \times 12\% \times \frac{90}{360} = \$1,000 \times .12 \times .25 = \$30$$

Receipt of a Note

Notes receivable are usually recorded in a single Notes Receivable account to simplify recordkeeping. We need only one account because the original notes are kept on file. This means the maker, rate of interest, due date, and other information are available by examining the actual note.[4] To illustrate the recording for the receipt of a note, we use the $1,000, 90-day, 12% promissory note in Exhibit 10.14. TechCom received this note at the time of a product sale to Julia Browne. This transaction is recorded as follows:

P3   Record the receipt of a note receivable.

July 10	Notes Receivable	1,000	
	Sales		1,000
	Sold goods in exchange for a 90-day, 12% note.		

Assets = Liabilities + Equity
+1,000   +1,000

Companies sometimes accept a note from an overdue customer as a way to grant a time extension on a past-due account receivable. When this occurs, a company might collect part of the past-due balance in cash. This partial payment forces a concession from the customer, reduces the customer's debt (and the seller's risk), and produces a note for a smaller amount. To illustrate, TechCom agreed to accept $232 in cash along with a $600, 60-day, 15% note from Jo Cook to settle her $832 past-due account. TechCom made the following entry to record receipt of this cash and note:

Oct. 5	Cash	232	
	Notes Receivable	600	
	Accounts Receivable—J. Cook		832
	Received cash and note to settle account.		

Assets = Liabilities + Equity
+232
+600
−832

Honoring and Dishonoring a Note

The principal and interest of a note are due on its maturity date. The maker of the note usually *honors* the note and pays it in full. But sometimes a maker *dishonors* the note and does not pay it at maturity.

P4   Record the honoring and dishonoring of a note and adjustments for interest on a note.

Recording an Honored Note

We use the preceding TechCom note transaction to illustrate the honoring of a note. When Cook pays the note on its due date, TechCom records it as follows:

Dec. 4	Cash	615	
	Notes Receivable		600
	Interest Revenue		15
	Collect note with interest of $600 × 15% × 60/360.		

Assets = Liabilities + Equity
+615   +15
−600

Interest Revenue, also called Interest Earned, is reported on the current period's income statement.

Recording a Dishonored Note

When a note's maker is unable or refuses to pay at maturity, the note is dishonored. The act of dishonoring a note does not relieve the maker of the obligation to pay. The payee should use every legitimate means to collect. But how do companies report this event? The balance of the Notes Receivable account should include only those notes that have not matured. When a note is dishonored, we therefore remove the amount of this note from the Notes Receivable account and charge it back to an account receivable from its maker. To illustrate,

Point: When posting a dishonored note to a customer's account, an explanation is included. Otherwise, a later review of the account might misinterpret the debit as a sale on account.

---

[4] When a company holds a large number of notes, it sometimes sets up a controlling account and a subsidiary ledger for notes. This is similar to the handling of accounts receivable.

TechCom holds an $800, 12%, 60-day note of Greg Hart. At maturity, Hart dishonors the note. TechCom records this dishonoring of the note as follows:

Oct. 14	Accounts Receivable—G. Hart	816	
	Interest Revenue		16
	Notes Receivable		800
	To charge account of G. Hart for a dishonored note and interest of $800 × 12% × 60/360.		

Charging a dishonored note back to the account of its maker serves two purposes. First, it removes the amount of the note from the Notes Receivable account and records the dishonored note in the maker's account. Second, and more important, if the maker of the dishonored note applies for credit in the future, his or her account will show all past dealings, including the dishonored note. Restoring the account also reminds the company to continue collection efforts from Hart for both principal and interest. The entry records the full amount, including interest to ensure that it is included in collection efforts.

End-of-Period Interest Adjustment

When notes receivable are outstanding at the end of a period, accrued interest is computed and recorded. This recognizes the interest earned by the note's holder. To illustrate, on December 16, TechCom accepts a $3,000, 60-day, 12% note from a customer in granting an extension on a past-due account. When TechCom's accounting period ends on December 31, $15 of interest has accrued on this note ($3,000 × 12% × 15/360). The following adjusting entry records this revenue:

Dec. 31	Interest Receivable	15	
	Interest Revenue		15
	To record accrued interest earned.		

Interest Revenue then appears on the income statement for the period when it is earned, and Interest Receivable appears on the balance sheet as a current asset. When the December 16 note is collected on February 14, TechCom's entry to record the cash receipt is

Feb. 14	Cash	3,060	
	Interest Revenue		45
	Interest Receivable		15
	Notes Receivable		3,000
	Received payment of note and its interest.		

Total interest earned on the note is $60. The $15 credit to Interest Receivable on February 14 reflects the collection of the interest accrued from the December 31 adjusting entry. The $45 interest earned reflects TechCom's revenue from holding the note from January 1 to February 14 of the current period.

Quick Check

8. Irwin purchases $7,000 of merchandise from Stamford on December 16, 2002. Stamford accepts Irwin's $7,000, 90-day, 12% note as payment. Stamford's accounting period ends on December 31, and it does not make reversing entries. Prepare entries for Stamford on December 16, 2002, and December 31, 2002.

9. Using the information in Quick Check 8, prepare Stamford's March 16, 2003, entry if Irwin dishonors the note.

Answers—p. 422

Sometimes companies convert receivables to cash before they are due. Reasons for this include the need for cash or the desire not to be involved in collection activities. Converting receivables is usually done either by (1) selling them or (2) using them as security for a loan. A recent survey shows that about 20% of large companies obtain cash from either selling of receivables or pledging them as security. In some industries such as textiles and furniture, this is common practice. Recently, this practice has become common for other industries, especially the apparel industry.

Converting Receivables to Cash before Maturity

C3 Explain how receivables can be converted to cash before maturity.

Selling Accounts Receivable

A company can sell all or a portion of its accounts receivable to a finance company or bank. The buyer, called a *factor,* charges the seller a *factoring fee* and then receives cash from the receivables as they come due. By incurring a factoring fee, the seller receives cash earlier and can pass the risk of bad debts to the factor. The seller can also choose to avoid costs of billing and accounting for the receivables. To illustrate, if TechCom sells $20,000 of its accounts receivable and is charged a 4% factoring fee, it records this sale as follows:

Aug. 15	Cash.	19,200	
	Factoring Fee Expense.	800	
	Accounts Receivable		20,000
	Sold accounts receivable for cash, less a 4% factoring fee.		

Assets = Liabilities + Equity
+19,200   −800
−20,000

Factoring is a major business today. **CIT Group** is a large factoring firm with annual volume of about $8 billion. Interestingly, about 90% of the factoring industry's business comes from textile, furniture, and apparel businesses.

Global: Companies in export sales increasingly sell their receivables to factors.

Pledging Accounts Receivable

A company can also raise cash by borrowing money and *pledging* its accounts receivable as security for the loan. Pledging receivables does not transfer the risk of bad debts to the lender because the borrower retains ownership of the receivables. If the borrower defaults on the loan, the lender has a right to be paid from the cash receipts of the accounts receivable when collected. To illustrate, when TechCom borrows $35,000 and pledges its receivables as security, it records this transaction as follows:

Point: When accounts receivable are sold, each subsidiary ledger account is credited along with the controlling account for the total.

Aug. 20	Cash.	35,000	
	Notes Payable.		35,000
	Borrowed money with a note secured by pledging accounts receivable.		

Assets = Liabilities + Equity
+35,000   +35,000

Since pledged receivables are committed as security for a specific loan, the borrower's financial statements should disclose the pledging of accounts receivable. TechCom, for instance, includes the following note with its financial statements: *Accounts receivable in the amount of $40,000 are pledged as security for a $35,000 note payable.* Another example is from the notes of **Chock Full O'Nuts**: "Outstanding borrowings . . . are collateralized by, among other things, the trade accounts receivable."

Did You Know?

Cash Poor? Both **Zenith** and **Packard Bell** used receivables to get much needed cash. **Zenith** obtained a three-year, $60 million credit agreement by pledging accounts receivable as collateral. **Intel** converted accounts receivable to a note receivable for a customer—widely assumed to be **Packard Bell**.

Discounting Notes Receivable

Notes receivable can be converted to cash before they mature. This can be done by discounting them at a financial institution. To illustrate, TechCom discounts a $3,000, 90-day, 10% note receivable at National Bank. TechCom had held the note for 50 of its 90 days before discounting it. The bank applies a 12% rate in discounting the note, and TechCom receives proceeds of $3,034 from the bank. It recorded the discounting of this note as follows:[5]

Assets = Liabilities + Equity
+3,034   +34
−3,000

Aug. 25	Cash.......................................	3,034	
	Interest Revenue*........................		34
	Notes Receivable.........................		3,000
	Discounted a note receivable.		

* If the cash proceeds are less than the Note Receivable balance, the difference (a debit) is recorded as Interest Expense.

Notes receivable are discounted without recourse or with recourse. When a note is discounted *without recourse,* the bank assumes the risk of a bad debt loss, and the original payee does not have a contingent liability. A **contingent liability** is an obligation to make a future payment if, and only if, an uncertain future event occurs. Examples are potential tax assessments, debts of others guaranteed by the company, and outstanding lawsuits against the company. A note discounted without recourse is like an outright sale of an asset. If a note is discounted *with recourse* and the original maker of the note fails to pay the bank when it matures, the original payee of the note must pay for it. This means a company discounting a note with recourse has a contingent liability until the bank is paid. A company should disclose contingent liabilities in notes to its financial statements. TechCom included the following note: "The Company is contingently liable for a $3,000 note receivable discounted with recourse." A similar example of a receivables sale with recourse is from the notes of **Tyco:** "The Company entered into an agreement pursuant to which it sold . . . receivables. The Company has retained substantially the same risk of credit loss as if the receivables had not been sold."

The disclosure of contingencies in notes is consistent with the **full disclosure principle,** which requires financial statements (including notes) to report all relevant information about a company's operations and financial position. Relevance is judged by whether a company's disclosure impacts users' business decisions. Besides contingent liabilities, other items often reported to satisfy the full disclosure principle are long-term commitments under contracts (such as long-term leases and the pledging of assets) and the accounting methods used.

Point: Notes receivable often are a major part of a company's assets. Likewise, notes payable often are a large part of a company's liabilities.

Point: Much of the information required by the full disclosure principle is in notes to financial statements. This information is critical to financial analysis.

Did You Know?   *e*

No Place Like Home   Home is where the business is—that according to nearly one-half (49%) of entrepreneurs in a recent survey with annual sales between $50,000 to $500,000. More similarities exist between home-based and not home-based entrepreneurships than commonly assumed. Interestingly, the majority of these companies are set up as proprietorships.

	Home-Based	Not Home-Based
Similarities:		
Years in business . . .	13.9 yrs.	14.5 yrs.
Checking acct. bal. . . .	$ 14,700	$ 15,200
Household income	$108,400	$113,200
Differences		
Importance of growth . .	11%	21%
Proprietorship .	72%	52%

---

[5] Cash proceeds from the bank are computed as follows:

Principal of note	$3,000
+ Interest from note ($3,000 × 10% × 90/360) ...	+ 75
= Maturity value of note	$3,075
− Bank discount ($3,075 × 12% × 40/360)	− (41)
= Cash proceeds	$3,034

The net Interest Revenue ($34) equals the total interest from the note ($75) less the bank's discount ($41). If the bank's discount exceeds the note's total interest, Interest Expense is debited for the difference.

Recall from Chapter 9 that cash equivalents are investments readily converted to known amounts of cash and that mature within three months. Many investments, however, mature between 3 and 12 months. These investments are **short-term investments,** also called *temporary investments,* or *marketable securities.* Specifically, short-term investments are securities that (1) management intends to convert to cash within one year or the operating cycle, whichever is longer, and (2) are readily convertible to cash. Short-term investments are current assets and serve a purpose similar to cash equivalents. Short-term investments can include both debt and equity securities. *Debt securities* reflect a creditor relationship such as investments in notes, bonds, and certificates of deposit. Debt securities are issued by governments, companies, and individuals. *Equity securities* reflect an ownership relationship such as shares of stock issued by companies.

Short-Term Investments

C4 Describe short-term Investments in debt and equity securities.

Accounting for Short-Term Investments

This section explains the basics of accounting for short-term investments in both debt and equity securities. Chapter 16 will further explain the accounting for investments.

Debt Securities

Short-term investments in debt (and equity) securities are recorded at cost when purchased. To illustrate, TechCom purchases **Intel** short-term notes payable for $4,000 on January 10. TechCom's entry to record this purchase is

Jan. 10	Short-Term Investments	4,000	
	Cash		4,000
	Bought $4,000 of Intel notes maturing May 10.		

Assets = Liabilities + Equity
+4,000
−4,000

These notes mature on May 10. When the cash proceeds of $4,000 plus the $120 interest ($4,000 $\times$ 9% $\times \frac{120}{360}$) are received at maturity, TechCom records this as:

May 10	Cash.	4,120	
	Short-Term Investments		4,000
	Interest Revenue		120
	Received cash proceeds from matured notes.		

Assets = Liabilities + Equity
+4,120   +120
−4,000

Equity Securities

The cost of a short-term investment in equity securities includes all necessary costs to acquire it, including commissions paid. To illustrate, TechCom purchases 100 shares of Nike common stock as a short-term investment for $50 per share plus $100 in commissions. The entry to record this purchase is

Example: What is cost per share? *Answer:* Cost per share is the total cost of acquisition, inclusive of fees, divided by number of shares acquired.

June 2	Short-Term Investments	5,100	
	Cash		5,100
	Bought 100 shares of Nike stock at $50 per share plus $100 commission.		

Assets = Liabilities + Equity
+5,100
−5,100

The commission is recorded as part of the investment cost. TechCom also receives a $0.40 per share cash dividend on its Nike stock during the current period. This dividend is recorded in a revenue account as follows:

Dec. 12	Cash.	40	
	Dividend Revenue		40
	Received dividend of $0.40 per share on 100 shares of Nike stock.		

Assets = Liabilities + Equity
+40   +40

Valuing and Reporting Short-Term Investments

Companies must value and report most short-term investments at their fair values. *Fair value* of a security is its market value. Accounting requirements vary depending on whether short-term investments are classified as (1) held-to-maturity, (2) trading, or (3) available-for-sale securities. This section describes the financial statement presentation for each of these classifications.

Held-to-Maturity Securities

Held-to-maturity securities are *debt securities* that the company has the intent and ability to hold until they mature. **Dairy Queen**, for instance, in notes to its financial statements, states: "Management determines the appropriate classification of debt securities at the time of purchase and reevaluates such designation as of each balance sheet date. Debt securities are classified as held-to-maturity because the Company has the positive intent and ability to hold such securities to maturity." Held-to-maturity securities are reported in current assets if their maturity dates are within the longer of one year or the operating cycle. Held-to-maturity securities are reported at cost (plus accrued interest).

Point: Only debt securities are classified as *held-to-maturity*. Equity securities have no maturity date.

Trading Securities

Trading securities are *debt and equity securities* that the company intends to actively manage and trade for profit. This means that frequent purchases and sales are made to earn profits on short-term price changes. Trading securities are especially common with financial institutions such as banks and insurance companies.

Valuing and reporting trading securities

Point: The phrase *unrealized* gain or loss refers to a change in an item's market value when the change in value is not yet realized through an actual sale.

The entire portfolio of trading securities is reported at its market (fair) value with a "market adjustment" to the cost of the portfolio. The term *portfolio* refers to a group of securities. Any unrealized gain or loss from a change in the market value of the portfolio of trading securities during a period is reported on the income statement. Most users believe accounting reports are more useful when changes in market value for a portfolio of trading securities are reported in income. To illustrate, TechCom's portfolio of trading securities has a total cost of $11,500 and a market value of $13,000 on December 31, 2002 (this is the first year it held trading securities). The difference between the $11,500 cost and the $13,000 market value reflects a $1,500 gain. This gain is an **unrealized gain** because it is not yet confirmed by actual sales of these securities. TechCom records this gain as:

Point: Market Adjustment—Trading is a *permanent account*, shown as a deduction or addition to Short-Term Investments—Trading.

Assets = Liabilities + Equity
+1,500　　　　　　　+1,500

Dec. 31	Market Adjustment—Trading	1,500	
	Unrealized Gain—Income		1,500
	To reflect an unrealized gain in market values of trading securities.		

Point: Unrealized Gain (or Loss)—Income is a *temporary account* that is closed to Income Summary at the end of each period.

The Unrealized Gain (or Loss) is reported in the Other Revenues and Gains (or Expenses and Losses) section on the income statement. After posting this entry, TechCom's investment in trading securities is reported in the current assets section of its balance sheet as shown:

Example: If TechCom's portfolio of trading securities has a cost of $14,800 and a market value of $16,100 at December 31, 2003, its adjusting entry is
Unrealized Loss—Income . 200
　Mkt. Adj.—Trading 200
This entry revises the current balance in the market adjustment account to reflect the market difference from cost ($1,500 Dr. + $200 Cr. = $1,300 Dr.).

Current Assets		
Short-Term Investments—Trading (at cost)	$11,500	
Market Adjustment—Trading	1,500	
Short-Term Investments—Trading (at market)		$13,000

The total cost of the portfolio of trading securities is maintained in one account and the market adjustment is recorded in a separate account. The market adjustment is revised at the end of each period to equal the difference between the cost and market values.

Selling trading securities

When individual trading securities are sold, the difference between the net proceeds from the sale (sale price less fees) and the cost of the individual trading securities that are sold is recognized as a gain or a loss. To illustrate, when TechCom sells its $5,100 short-term investment in Nike stock on December 15 for net proceeds of $5,400, it recognizes a gain of $300. The entry to record this sale is

Point: The price of a security is sometimes listed in fraction form. For example, an equity security with a price of $22\frac{1}{4}$, is the same as saying its price is $22.25.

Dec. 15	Cash	5,400	
	Gain on Sale of Short-Term Investments		300
	Short-Term Investments		5,100
	To record sale of 100 shares of Nike stock.		

Assets = Liabilities + Equity
+5,400   +300
−5,100

This gain is reported in the Other Revenues and Gains section on the income statement. If a loss is recorded, it is shown in Other Expenses and Losses. When TechCom computes its market adjustment for trading securities at the end of the period, it excludes the cost and market values of the Nike stock since it has been sold.

Available-for-Sale Securities

Available-for-sale securities are *debt and equity securities* not classified as trading or held-to-maturity securities. Available-for-sale securities are purchased to yield interest, dividends, or increases in market value. They are not actively managed like trading securities.

> **Did You Know?**
>
> **Back to the Future** About 70 years ago banks switched from reporting market values for their short-term investments to reporting them at cost. We now see a return to market value reporting for many short-term investments. This is driven by S&L and other banking failures in disclosing market value changes. Ironically, the Great Depression fueled the conversion from market values to costs out of concern for the lack of reliability of market values.

Valuing and reporting available-for-sale securities

Similar to trading securities, companies adjust the cost of the portfolio of available-for-sale securities to reflect changes in market value. This is done with a market adjustment to its total portfolio cost. However, any unrealized gain or loss for the portfolio of available-for-sale securities is *not* reported on the income statement. Instead, it is reported in the equity section of the balance sheet (and is part of comprehensive income—explained in Chapter 16). Many users believe that since available-for-sale securities are not actively traded, including changes in market value would unnecessarily increase the variability of income and decrease its usefulness. To illustrate, TechCom's portfolio of available-for-sale securities had a total cost of $15,400 and a market value of $14,500 on December 31, 2002 (this is the first year it held such securities). The difference between the $15,400 cost and the $14,500 market value reflects a $900 unrealized loss. TechCom records this loss as:

Point: Unrealized Gain (or Loss)— Equity is a permanent account reported in the equity section.

Dec. 31	Unrealized Loss—Equity	900	
	Market Adjustment—Available-for-Sale		900
	To reflect an unrealized loss in market values of available-for-sale securities.		

Assets = Liabilities + Equity
−900   −900

This is reported in TechCom's current asset and equity sections of its balance sheet as follows:

Current Assets		
Short-Term Investments—Available-for-sale (at cost)	$15,400	
Market Adjustment—Available-for-sale	(900)	
Short-Term Investments—Available-for-sale (at market)		$14,500
Equity		
... usual equity and capital accounts ...		
Less: Unrealized loss on available-for-sale securities		$ 900

Example: If TechCom's portfolio of available-for-sale securities has a cost of $7,500 and a market value of $8,500 at December 31, 2003, its adjusting entry is
Mkt. Adj.—AFS 1,900
    Unreal. Loss—Equity 900
    Unreal. Gain—Equity 1,000
This entry revises the balance in the market adjustment account. It also removes the unrealized loss and records the unrealized gain.

Selling available-for-sale securities

Accounting for the sale of individual available-for-sale securities is identical to that described for the sale of trading securities. When individual available-for-sale securities are sold, the difference between the cost of the individual securities sold and the net proceeds from the sale (sale price less fees) is recognized as a gain or loss.

Summary of Accounting for Short-Term Investments

Exhibit 10.17 summarizes the accounting for short-term investments in securities.

Exhibit 10.17

Accounting for Short-Term Investments in Securities

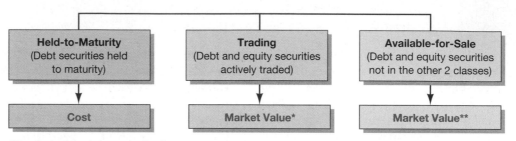

*Unrealized gains or losses reported on income statement.
**Unrealized gains or losses reported in equity section on balance sheet and in comprehensive income.

The balance sheet presentation of short-term investments usually reports the market value for the sum *total* of all three classes of securities instead of each individual class. The cost is also usually reported and the details are sometimes disclosed in the notes. A typical presentation of short-term investments is shown in Exhibit 10.18.

Exhibit 10.18

Statement Presentation of Short-Term Investments

Current assets	
Short-term investments, at market value (cost is $16,200)	**$14,500**

Although the contra account to Short-Term Investments is not shown, we can determine its balance as $1,700 by comparing the $16,200 cost with the $14,500 market value.

Quick Check

10. How are held-to-maturity securities reported (valued) on the balance sheet?

11. How are trading securities reported (valued) on the balance sheet?

12. Where are unrealized gains and losses on available-for-sale securities reported?

13. Where are unrealized gains and losses on trading securities reported?

14. A company has substantial accounts receivable but needs cash. What alternatives are available for getting cash from its accounts receivable prior to receiving payments from credit customers? Show the entry made for each alternative.

Answers—p. 422

Using the Information   Accounts Receivable Turnover

A1 Compute accounts receivable turnover and use it to analyze liquidity.

For a company selling on credit, we want to assess both the quality and liquidity of its accounts receivable. *Quality* of receivables refers to the likelihood of collection without loss. Experience shows the longer receivables are outstanding beyond their due date, the lower the likelihood of collection. *Liquidity* of receivables refers to the speed of collection. **Accounts receivable turnover** is a measure of both the quality and liquidity of accounts receivable. It indicates how often, on average, receivables are received and collected during the period. The formula for this ratio is shown in Exhibit 10.19.

$$\text{Accounts receivable turnover} = \frac{\text{Net sales}}{\text{Average accounts receivable}}$$

Exhibit 10.19
Accounts Receivable Turnover

We prefer to use net *credit* sales in the numerator because cash sales do not create receivables. Since financial statements rarely report net credit sales, our analysis uses net sales. The denominator is the *average* accounts receivable balance, computed as (Beginning balance I Ending balance) ÷ 2. TechCom has an accounts receivable turnover of 5.1. This indicates its average accounts receivable balance is converted into cash 5.1 times during the period. Exhibit 10.20 shows graphically this turnover activity for TechCom.

Exhibit 10.20
Rate of Accounts Receivable Turnover for TechCom

Accounts receivable turnover also reflects how well management is doing in granting credit to customers in a desire to increase sales. A high turnover in comparison with competitors suggests management should consider using more liberal credit terms to increase sales. A low turnover suggests management should consider stricter credit terms and more aggressive collection efforts to avoid having its resources tied up in accounts receivable.

To illustrate its application, we take data from two competitors: **Dell Computer** and **Apple Computer**. Exhibit 10.21 shows accounts receivable turnover for both companies.

Exhibit 10.21
Analysis Using Accounts Receivable Turnover

Company	Figure ($ in millions)	1999	1998	1997
Dell	Net sales	$25,265	$18,243	$12,327
	Average accounts receivable	$ 2,351	$ 1,790	$ 1,195
	Accounts receivable turnover	**10.7**	**10.2**	**10.3**
Apple	Net sales	$ 6,134	$ 5,941	$ 7,081
	Average accounts receivable	$ 818	$ 995	$ 1,266
	Accounts receivable turnover	**7.5**	**6.0**	**5.6**

Dell's 1999 turnover is computed ($ in millions) as $25,265/$2,351 = 10.7. This means Dell's average accounts receivable balance was converted into cash 10.7 times in 1999. Also, its turnover slightly improved in 1999 (versus its prior two years), and it is superior to Apple. Is Dell's turnover too high? Since sales are markedly growing over this time period, Dell's turnover does not appear to be too high. Instead, its management seems to be doing a good job managing receivables. Similarly, Apple has improved its management of receivables during this period. Turnover for competitors is generally in the range of 6 to 8 for this same period.[6]

> ### You Make the Call
>
> **Family Physician** Your practice has turned less profitable so you hire a health care analyst to make recommendations. The analyst highlights several points including the following ". . . *accounts receivable turnover is too low. Tighter credit policies are recommended along with discontinuing service to those most delayed in payments.*" How do you interpret these recommendations? What actions do you take?

Answer—p. 421

---

[6] As an approximation of *average days' sales uncollected* (see Chapter 9), we can estimate how many days (*on average*) it takes to collect receivables as follows: 365 days ÷ accounts receivable turnover.

Demonstration Problem

Garden Company completes the following selected transactions during year 2002.

May   8   Purchases 300 shares of Federal Express stock as a short-term investment in available-for-sale securities at a cost of $40 per share plus $975 in broker fees.

July   14   Writes off a $750 account receivable arising from a sale to Briggs Company that dates to 13 months ago. (Garden Company uses the allowance method.)

        30   Garden Company receives a $1,000, 90-day, 10% note from a product sale to Sumrell Company.

Aug.   15   Receives $2,000 cash plus a $10,000 note from JT Co. in exchange for merchandise that sells for $12,000. The note is dated August 15, bears 12% interest, and matures in 180 days.

Sept.   2   Sells 100 shares of its investment in Federal Express stock at $47 per share and holds the remaining 200 shares. The broker's commission on this sale is $225.

        15   Receives $9,850 cash in exchange for discounting without recourse the $10,000 note (dated August 15) at the local bank.

Oct.   2   Purchases 400 shares of McDonald's stock for $60 per share plus $1,600 in commissions. The stock is held as a short-term investment in available-for-sale securities.

Nov.   1   Completed a $200 credit card sale with a 4% fee. The cash is received immediately from the credit card company.

         5   Completed a $500 credit card sale with a 5% fee. The payment from the credit card company is received on Nov. 7.

        15   Received the full amount of $750 from Briggs Company that was previously written off on July 14. Record the bad debts recovery.

        20   Sumrell Company refuses to pay the note that was due to Garden Company on October 28. Prepare the journal entry to charge the dishonored note plus accrued interest to Sumrell Company's accounts receivable.

Required

1. Prepare journal entries to record these transactions on Garden Company's books.

2. Prepare an adjusting journal entry as of December 31, 2002, assuming the following:

   a. Bad debts expense is estimated by an aging of accounts receivable. The unadjusted balance of the Allowance for Doubtful Accounts is a $1,000 debit, and it is estimated to be a $20,400 credit.

   b. Alternatively, assume that bad debts expense is estimated using the percent of sales method. The Allowance for Doubtful Accounts had a $1,000 debit balance before adjustment, and the company estimates bad debts to be 1% of its credit sales of $2,000,000.

3. Prepare an adjusting journal entry as of December 31, 2002, if the market prices of the equity securities held by Garden Company are $48 per share for Federal Express and $55 per share for McDonald's. (Year 2002 is Garden Co.'s first year of operations.)

Planning the Solution

- Examine each transaction to determine the accounts affected and then record the entries.
- For the year-end adjustment, record the bad debts expense for the two approaches.

Solution to Demonstration Problem

1.

May 8	Short-Term Investments	12,975	
	Cash		12,975
	Purchased 300 shares of Federal Express stock (300 × $40) + $975.		
July 14	Allowance for Doubtful Accounts	750	
	Accounts Receivable—Briggs Co.		750
	Wrote off an uncollectible account.		
July 30	Notes Receivable—Sumrell Co.	1,000	
	Sales		1,000
	Sold merchandise for a 90-day, 10% note.		

Aug. 15	Cash	2,000	
	Notes Receivable—JT Co....................	10,000	
	Sales		12,000
	Sold merchandise to customer for $2,000 *cash and $10,000 note.*		
Sept. 2	Cash	4,475	
	Gain on Sale of Short-term Investment		150
	Short-Term Investments....................		4,325
	Sold 100 shares of Federal Express for *$47 per share less a $225 commission. The* *original cost is ($12,975 × 100/300).*		
Sept. 15	Cash	9,850	
	Interest Expense	150	
	Notes Receivable—JT Co.		10,000
	Discounted note receivable dated August 15.		
Oct. 2	Short-Term Investments	25,600	
	Cash		25,600
	Purchased 400 shares of McDonald's for *$60 per share plus $1,600 in commissions.*		
Nov. 1	Cash	192	
	Credit Card Expense	8	
	Sales		200
	To record credit card sale less a 4% credit *card expense.*		
Nov. 5	Accounts Receivable—Credit Card Co...........	475	
	Credit Card Expense	25	
	Sales		500
	To record credit card sale less a 5% credit *card expense.*		
Nov. 7	Cash..	475	
	Accounts Receivable—Credit Card Co........		475
	To record cash receipt.		
Nov. 15	Accounts Receivable—Briggs Co..............	750	
	Allowance for Doubtful Accounts		750
	To reinstate the account of Briggs Company *previously written off.*		
Nov. 15	Cash	750	
	Accounts Receivable—Briggs Co.		750
	Cash received in full payment of account.		
Nov. 20	Accounts Receivable—Sumrell Co..............	1,025	
	Interest Revenue.........................		25
	Notes Receivable—Sumrell Co.		1,000
	To charge account of Sumrell Company for *a $1,000 dishonored note and interest of* *$1,000 × 10% × 90/360.*		

> Interest Expense of $150 is the *net* of interest revenue from the note *less* the bank discounting charge.

2a. Aging of accounts receivable method:

Dec. 31	Bad Debts Expense	21,400	
	Allowance for Doubtful Accounts		21,400
	To adjust allowance account from a $1,000 *debit balance to a $20,400 credit balance.*		

2b. Percent of sales method:

Dec. 31	Bad Debts Expense.....................	20,000	
	Allowance for Doubtful Accounts		20,000
	To provide for bad debts as 1% × $2,000,000 ..... in credit sales.		

(*Note:* For the income statement approach, which requires estimating bad debts as a percent of sales or credit sales, the Allowance account balance is **not** considered when making the adjusting entry.)

3. Computation of unrealized gain or loss:

Short-Term Investments in Available-for-Sale Securities	Shares	Cost per Share	Total Cost	Market Value per Share	Total Market Value	Unrealized Gain (Loss)
Federal Express	200	$43.25	$ 8,650	$ 48.00	$ 9,600	
McDonald's	400	64.00	25,600	55.00	22,000	
Total			$ 34,250		$31,600	$(2,650)

Adjusting entry:

Dec. 31	Unrealized Loss—Equity	2,650	
	Market Adjustment—Available-for-Sale		2,650
	To reflect an unrealized loss in market values of available-for-sale securities.		

Summary

C1 **Describe accounts receivable and how they occur and are recorded.** Accounts receivable are amounts due from customers for credit sales. A subsidiary ledger lists amounts owed by individual customers. Credit sales arise from at least two sources: (1) sales on credit and (2) credit card sales. Sales on credit refer to a company's granting credit directly to customers. Credit card sales involve customers' use of third party credit cards.

C2 **Describe a note receivable and the computation of its maturity date and interest.** A note receivable is a written promise to pay a specified amount of money at a definite future date. The maturity date is the day the note (principal and interest) must be repaid. Interest rates are normally stated in annual terms. The amount of interest on the note is computed by expressing time as a fraction of one year and multiplying the note's principal by this fraction and the annual interest rate.

C3 **Explain how receivables can be converted to cash before maturity.** Receivables can be converted to cash before maturity in three ways. First, a company can sell accounts receivable to a factor, who charges a factoring fee. Second, a company can borrow money by signing a note payable that is se-

cured by pledging the accounts receivable. Third, notes receivable can be discounted at a bank, with or without recourse.

C4 **Describe short-term investments in debt and equity securities.** Short-term investments can include both debt and equity securities. *Debt securities* reflect a creditor relationship and include investments in notes, bonds, and certificates of deposit. *Equity securities* reflect an ownership relationship and include shares of stock issued by other companies.

A1 **Compute accounts receivable turnover and use it to analyze liquidity.** Accounts receivable turnover is a measure of both the quality and liquidity of accounts receivable. The accounts receivable turnover measure indicates how often, on average, receivables are received and collected during the period. Accounts receivable turnover is computed as net sales divided by average accounts receivable.

P1 **Apply the direct write-off and allowance methods to account for accounts receivable.** The direct write-off method charges Bad Debts Expense when accounts are written off as uncollectible. This method is acceptable only when the amount of bad debts expense is immaterial. Under the allowance method, bad debts expense is recorded with an adjustment at the end of each accounting period that debits the Expense account and credits the Allowance for Doubtful Accounts. The uncollectible accounts are later written off with a debit to the Allowance for Doubtful Accounts.

P2 **Estimate uncollectibles using methods based on sales and accounts receivable.** Uncollectibles are estimated by focusing on either (1) the income statement relation between bad debts expense and credit sales or (2) the balance sheet relation between accounts receivable and the allowance for doubtful accounts. The first approach emphasizes the matching principle using the income statement. The second approach emphasizes realizable value of accounts receivable using the balance sheet.

P3 **Record the receipt of a note receivable.** A note received is recorded at its principal amount by debiting the Notes Receivable account. The credit amount is to the asset, product, or service provided in return for the note.

P4 **Record the honoring and dishonoring of a note and adjustments for interest on a note.** When a note is honored, the payee debits the money received and credits both Notes Receivable and Interest Revenue. Dishonored notes are credited to Notes Receivable and debited to Accounts Receivable (to the account of the maker in an attempt to collect). Interest earned from holding a note is recorded for the amount of time the note is held.

P5 **Record short-term investment transactions.** Short-term investments are initially recorded at cost, and any dividends or interest from these investments is recorded in the income statement. Short-term investments are classified as held-to-maturity securities, trading securities, or available-for-sale securities. Held-to-maturity securities are reported at cost on the balance sheet. Trading securities and available-for-sale securities are reported at their fair (market) values. Unrealized gains and losses on trading securities are reported in income. Unrealized gains and losses on available-for-sale securities are reported in the equity section of the balance sheet. When short-term investments are sold, the difference between the net proceeds from the sale and the cost of the securities is recognized as a gain or loss.

Guidance Answers to **You Make the Call**

Entrepreneur Your analysis of allowing credit card sales should weigh the benefits against the costs. The primary benefit is the potential to increase sales by attracting customers who prefer the convenience of credit cards. The primary cost is the fee charged by the credit card company for providing this service to your store. Your analysis should therefore estimate the expected increase in sales dollars from allowing credit card sales and then subtract (1) the normal costs and expenses and (2) the credit card fees associated with this expected increase in sales dollars. If your analysis shows an increase in profit from allowing credit card sales, your store should probably accept them.

Labor Union Chief Yes, this information is likely to impact your negotiations. The obvious question is why the company increased this allowance to such a large extent. The major increase in this allowance means a substantial increase in bad debts expense *and* a decrease in earnings. Coming immediately prior to labor contract discussions, this change also raises concerns since it reduces the union's bargaining power for increased compensation. You want to ask management for supporting documentation justifying this increase. You also want data for two or three prior years and similar data from competitors. These data should give you some sense of whether the change in the allowance for uncollectibles is justified.

Family Physician The recommendations are twofold. First, the analyst suggests more stringent screening of patients' credit standing. Second, the analyst suggests dropping patients who are most overdue in payments. You are likely bothered by both suggestions. While they are probably financially wise recommendations, you are troubled by eliminating services to those less able to pay. One alternative is to follow the recommendations while implementing a care program directed at patients less able to pay for services. This allows you to continue services to patients less able to pay and lets you discontinue services to patients able but unwilling to pay.

Guidance Answers to **Quick Checks**

1. If cash is received when credit card sales receipts are deposited in the bank, the company debits Cash at the time of sale. If the company does not receive payment until after it submits receipts to the credit card company, it debits Accounts Receivable at the time of sale (cash is later debited when payment is received from the credit card company).

2. Credit card expenses are usually *recorded* and *incurred* at the time of their related sales; not when cash is received from the credit card company.

3. If possible, bad debts expense must be matched with the sales that gave rise to the accounts receivable. This requires that companies estimate future bad debts at the end of each period before they learn which accounts are uncollectible.

4. Realizable value (also called *net realizable value*).

5. The estimated amount of bad debts expense cannot be credited to the Accounts Receivable account because the specific customer accounts that will prove uncollectible cannot be identified and removed from the subsidiary Accounts Receivable Ledger. Moreover, if only the Accounts Receivable account is credited its balance would not equal the sum of its subsidiary account balances.

6.

Dec. 31	Bad Debts Expense	5,702	
	Allowance for Doubtful Accounts		5,702

7.

Jan. 10	Allowance for Doubtful Accounts. . . .	300	
	Accounts Receivable—Cool Jam		300
Apr. 12	Accounts Receivable—Cool Jam. . . .	300	
	Allowance for Doubtful Accounts.		300
Apr. 12	Cash	300	
	Accounts Receivable—Cool Jam		300

8.

Dec. 16	Note Receivable	7,000	
	Sales		7,000
Dec. 31	Interest Receivable	35	
	Interest Revenue		35
	($7,000 × 12% × 15/360)		

9.

Mar. 16	Accounts Receivable—Irwin	7,210	
	Interest Revenue		175
	Interest Receivable		35
	Notes Receivable		7,000

10. Held-to-maturity securities are reported at cost.

11. Trading securities are reported at fair (market) value.

12. The equity section of the balance sheet (and in comprehensive income).

13. The income statement.

14. Alternatives are (1) selling their accounts receivable to a factor and (2) pledging accounts receivable as loan security. The entries to record these transactions take the following form:

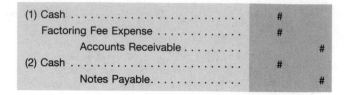

(1) Cash	#	
Factoring Fee Expense	#	
Accounts Receivable		#
(2) Cash	#	
Notes Payable		#

Glossary

Accounts receivable amounts due from customers for credit sales. (p. 396).

Accounts receivable turnover measure of both the quality and liquidity of accounts receivable; indicates how often receivables are received and collected during the period; computed by dividing net sales by average accounts receivable. (p. 416).

Aging of accounts receivable process of classifying accounts receivable by how long they are past due for purposes of estimating uncollectible accounts. (p. 405).

Allowance for Doubtful Accounts contra asset account with a balance approximating uncollectible accounts receivable; also called *Allowance for Uncollectible Accounts*. (p. 401).

Allowance method procedure that (1) estimates and matches bad debts expense with its sales for the period and (2) reports accounts receivable at estimated realizable value. (p. 401).

Available-for-sale securities investments in debt and equity securities that are not classified as trading securities or held-to-maturity securities. (p. 415).

Bad debts accounts of customers who do not pay what they have promised to pay; an expense of selling on credit; also called *uncollectible accounts*. (p. 399).

Contingent liability obligation to make a future payment if, and only if, an uncertain future event occurs. (p. 412).

Direct write-off method method that records the loss from an uncollectible account receivable at the time it is determined to be uncollectible; no attempt is made to estimate bad debts. (p. 400).

Full disclosure principle principle that requires financial statements (including notes) to report all relevant information about an entity's operations and financial condition. (p. 412).

Held-to-maturity securities debt securities that a company has the intent and ability to hold until they mature. (p. 414).

Interest charge for using money (or other assets) until repaid at a future date. (p. 408).

Maker of a note entity who signs a note and promises to pay it at maturity. (p. 408).

Matching principle requires expenses to be reported in the same period as the sales they helped produce. (p. 400).

Materiality principle implies an amount can be ignored if its effect on financial statements is unimportant to users. (p. 401).

Maturity date of a note date when principal and interest of a note are due. (p. 408).

Payee of a note entity to whom a note is made payable. (p. 408).

Principal of a note amount that the signer of a note agrees to pay back when it matures, not including interest. (p. 408).

Promissory note (or **note**) written promise to pay a specified amount either on demand or at a definite future date. (p. 407).

Realizable value expected proceeds from converting an asset into cash. (p. 401).

Short-term investments debt and equity securities that management expects to convert to cash within the next 3 to 12 months (or the operating cycle if longer); also called *temporary investments*. (p. 413).

Trading securities investments in debt and equity securities that the company intends to actively trade for profit. (p. 414).

Unrealized gain (loss) gain (loss) not yet realized by an actual transaction or event such as a sale. (p. 414).

Questions

1. How do sellers benefit from allowing their customers to use credit cards?

2. Why does the direct write-off method of accounting for bad debts usually fail to match revenues and expenses?

3. Explain the accounting principle of materiality.

4. Explain why writing off a bad debt against the Allowance account does not reduce the estimated realizable value of a company's accounts receivable.

5. Why does the Bad Debts Expense account usually not have the same adjusted balance as the Allowance for Doubtful Accounts?

6. Why might a business prefer a note receivable to an account receivable?

7. What does it mean to sell a receivable without recourse?

8. Under what two conditions should investments be classified as current assets?

9. On a balance sheet, what valuation must be reported for short-term investments in trading securities?

10. If a short-term investment in available-for-sale securities costs $6,780 and is sold for $7,500, how should the difference between these two amounts be recorded?

11. Refer to **Nike**'s balance sheet in Appendix A. What percent of accounts receivable at May 31, NIKE

2000, has been set aside as an allowance for doubtful accounts? How does this percent compare to the prior year?

12. Refer to the balance sheet of **Reebok** in Appendix A. Does it use the direct write-off method or allowance method to account for doubtful accounts? What is the realizable value of its accounts receivable as of December 31, 1999? What is another name for the Allowance for Doubtful Accounts?

13. Refer to the balance sheet of **Gap** in Appendix A. Why does it not show any accounts receivable in its current asset section? GAP

Fortune Corp. uses the allowance method to account for uncollectibles. On October 31, it wrote off an $800 account of a customer, Christina Rowland. On December 9, it receives a $300 payment from Rowland.

1. Make the appropriate entry or entries for October 31.

2. Make the appropriate entry or entries for December 9.

QUICK STUDY

QS 10-1

Allowance method for bad debts P1

Blazek Company's year-end unadjusted trial balance shows accounts receivable of $99,000, allowance for doubtful accounts of $600 (credit), and sales of $280,000. Uncollectibles are estimated to be 1.5% of accounts receivable.

1. Prepare the December 31 year-end adjusting entry for uncollectibles.

2. What amount would have been used in the year-end adjustment if the allowance account had a year-end unadjusted debit balance of $300?

3. Assume the same facts as in part (1), except that Blazek estimates uncollectibles as 1% of sales. What amount is used in the year-end adjustment?

QS 10-2

Percent of accounts receivable method

P1

Journalize the following transactions:

1. Sold $20,000 in merchandise on MasterCard credit cards. The net cash receipts from sales are immediately deposited in the seller's bank account. MasterCard charges a 5% fee.

2. Sold $5,000 on an assortment of credit cards. Net cash receipts are received 10 days later, and a 4% fee is charged.

QS 10-3

Credit card sales

C1

On August 2, 2002, PSI Co. receives a $6,000, 90-day, 12% note from customer Tom Cather as payment on his account. Prepare journal entries for August 2 and for the note's maturity date assuming the note is honored by Cather.

QS 10-4

Note receivable P3 P4

Snyder Company's December 31 year-end unadjusted trial balance shows a $10,000 balance in Notes Receivable. This balance is from one 6% note dated December 1, with a period of 45 days. Prepare necessary journal entries for December 31 and for the note's maturity date assuming it is honored.

QS 10-5

Note receivable P3 P4

On April 18, Derek Co. made a short-term investment in 300 shares of Computer Advantage common stock. Their purchase price is $42.5 per share and the broker's fee is $250. The intent is to actively manage these shares. On June 30, Derek Co. receives $1 per share from Computer Advantage in dividends. Prepare the April 18 and June 30 journal entries.

QS 10-6

Short-term equity investments C4

Cooper Co. purchases short-term investments in available-for-sale securities at a cost of $50,000 on November 25, 2002. At December 31, 2002, these securities had a market value of $47,000.

1. Prepare the December 31, 2002 year-end adjusting entry for these securities.

2. For each account in the entry for part (1), explain how it is reported in financial statements.

3. Prepare the April 6, 2003, entry when Cooper sells these securities for $52,000.

QS 10-7

Available-for-Sale Securities C4 P5

QS 10-8
Accounts receivable turnover

The following data are taken from the comparative balance sheets of Fuqua Co.:

	2002	2001
Accounts receivable......	$153,400	$138,500
Net sales.............	854,200	910,600

Compute the accounts receivable turnover for year 2002.

EXERCISES

Exercise 10-1
Accounts receivable
subsidiary ledger

Taku Company recorded the following transactions during November 2002:

Nov. 5	Accounts Receivable—Paint Shop	4,615	
	Sales		4,615
10	Accounts Receivable—Cool Enterprises	1,350	
	Sales		1,350
13	Accounts Receivable—Matt Mahoney	832	
	Sales		832
21	Sales Returns and Allowances	209	
	Accounts Receivable—Matt Mahoney		209
30	Accounts Receivable—Paint Shop	2,713	
	Sales		2,713

1. Open a general ledger having T-accounts for Accounts Receivable, Sales, and Sales Returns and Allowances. Also open a subsidiary accounts receivable ledger having a T-account for each customer. Post these entries to both the general ledger and the accounts receivable ledger.

2. Prepare a schedule of accounts receivable (see Exhibit 10.4) and compare its total with the balance of the Accounts Receivable controlling account as of November 30.

Exercise 10-2
Allowance for doubtful
accounts entries

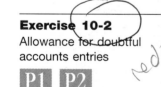

At year-end, Cayman Company estimates its bad debts as 0.5% of its $975,000 of annual credit sales. On December 31, Cayman adjusts its Allowance for Doubtful Accounts for that amount. On the following February 1, Cayman decides the $580 account of P. Snoop is uncollectible and writes it off as a bad debt. On June 5, Snoop unexpectedly pays the amount previously written off. Prepare the journal entries of Cayman to record these events.

Exercise 10-3
Percent of accounts
receivable method

At year-end, Bayoo Supply Co. uses the percent of accounts receivable method to estimate bad debts. On December 31, 2002, it has outstanding accounts receivable of $55,000, and it estimates that 2% will be uncollectible. Give the entry to record bad debts expense for year 2002 under the assumption that the Allowance for Doubtful Accounts has (1) a $415 credit balance before the adjustment and (2) a $291 debit balance before the adjustment.

Exercise 10-4
Selling and pledging accounts
receivable

On June 30, Koby Co. has $128,700 of accounts receivable. Prepare journal entries to record the following July transactions. Also prepare any footnotes to the July 31 financial statements that result from these transactions.

July 4   Sold $7,245 of merchandise to customers on credit.
     9   Sold $20,000 of accounts receivable to Nations Bank. Nations charges a 4% fee.
   17   Received $5,859 cash from customers in payment on their accounts.
   27   Borrowed $10,000 cash from Nations Bank, pledging $12,500 of accounts receivable as security for the loan.

Busch Company allows customers to use two credit cards in charging purchases. With the NuWay Card, Busch receives an immediate credit when it deposits sales receipts in its checking account. NuWay Card assesses a 4% service charge for credit card sales. The second credit card that Busch accepts is the Continental Bank Card. Busch sends its accumulated receipts to Continental Bank on a weekly basis and is paid by Continental about 10 days later. Continental Bank charges 2.5% of sales for using its card. Prepare journal entries to record the following selected credit card transactions of Busch Company:

Apr. 8   Sold merchandise for $8,400 accepting the customer's NuWay Card. At the end of the day, the NuWay receipts are deposited in Busch's account at the bank.

12   Sold merchandise for $5,602, accepting the customer's Continental Bank Card. Transferred $5,602 of credit card receipts to Continental Bank, requesting payment.

20   Received Continental Bank's check for the April 12 billing, less the service charge.

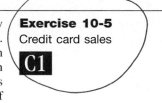

Exercise 10-5
Credit card sales

Prepare journal entries for the following selected transactions of Chandra Company:

2002

Dec. 13   Accepted a $9,600, 60-day, 8% note dated this day in granting Tom Alcox a time extension on his past-due account receivable.

31   Made an adjusting entry to record the accrued interest on the Alcox note.

31   Closed the Interest Revenue account to Income Summary.

2003

Feb. 11   Received Alcox's payment for principal and interest on the note dated December 13.

Mar. 12   Accepted a $5,000, 10%, 90-day note dated this day in granting a time extension on the past-due account receivable of BAX Company.

17   Accepted a $1,800, 30-day, 9% note dated this day in granting Bill Connors a time extension on his past-due account receivable.

Apr. 16   Connors dishonors his note when presented for payment.

May 1   Wrote off the Connors account against the Allowance for Doubtful Accounts.

June 10   Received the BAX payment for principal and interest on the note dated March 12.

Exercise 10-6
Notes receivable transactions and entries

Prepare journal entries to record these selected transactions for Venus Company:

Nov. 1   Accepts a $6,000, 180-day, 8% note dated today from Shelia Denton in granting a time extension on her past-due account receivable.

Dec. 31   Adjusts the accounts for the accrued interest earned on the Denton note.

Apr. 30   Denton honors her note when presented for payment.

Exercise 10-7
Honoring a note

Prepare journal entries to record the following selected transactions of Warren Company:

Mar. 21   Accepts a $2,500, 180-day, 8% note dated today from Tina Adams in granting a time extension on her past-due account receivable.

Sept. 17   Adams dishonors her note when it is presented for payment.

Dec. 31   After exhausting all legal means of collection, Warren Company writes off Adams's account against the Allowance for Doubtful Accounts.

Exercise 10-8
Dishonoring a note

Prepare journal entries to record the following transactions involving the short-term investments of Morford Co., all of which occurred during year 2002:

a. On February 15, paid $120,000 cash to purchase $120,000 of MRI's 90-day short-term debt securities, which are dated February 15 and pay 8% interest.

b. On March 22, bought 700 shares of GRE Company stock at $27.50 plus a $150 brokerage fee.

c. On May 16, received a check from MRI in payment of the principal and 90 days' interest on the debt securities purchased in transaction *a*.

d. On August 1, paid $80,000 cash to purchase $80,000 of Flash Electronics' 10% debt securities, dated July 30, 2002, and maturing January 30, 2003.

e. On September 1, received a $1.00 per share cash dividend on the GRE Company stock purchased in transaction *b*.

Exercise 10-9
Short-term investment transactions

f. On October 8, sold 350 shares of GRE Co. stock for $34 per share, less a $140 brokerage fee.

g. On October 30, received a check from Flash Electronics for 90 days' interest on the debt securities purchased in transaction *d*.

Exercise 10-10
Trading securities

C4 **P5**

Focus Co. purchases short-term investments in trading securities at a cost of $66,000 on December 27, 2002. At December 31, 2002, these securities had a market value of $72,000.

1. Prepare the December 31, 2002, year-end adjusting entry for these securities.
2. For each account in the entry for part (1), explain how it is reported in financial statements.
3. Prepare the January 3, 2003, entry when Focus sells one-half of these securities for $35,000.

Exercise 10-11
Market values of short-term investments

C4 **P5**

On December 31, 2002, Quaker Company held the following short-term investments in its securities available-for-sale:

	Cost	Market Value
T.R. Rowe Company common stock	$38,200	$42,100
Valdez Corporation bonds payable	51,400	49,500
Transunion Corporation notes payable	70,600	62,900
Lake Placid Company common stock	86,500	83,100

Quaker had no short-term investments in its prior accounting periods. Prepare the December 31, 2002, adjusting entry to record the market value of these investments.

Exercise 10-12
Accounts receivable turnover

A1

The following information is from the annual financial statements of Whipple Company:

	2003	2002	2001
Net sales	$405,000	$336,000	$388,000
Accounts receivable (December 31)	44,800	41,400	34,800

Compute Whipple's accounts receivable turnover for 2002 and 2003. Compare the two results and give a possible explanation for any major change.

PROBLEM SET A

Problem 10-1A
Estimating bad debts

P1 **P2**

On December 31, 2002, MidComm's records show the following results for the year:

Cash sales	$1,905,000
Credit sales	5,682,000

In addition, its unadjusted trial balance includes the following items:

Accounts receivable	$1,270,100 debit
Allowance for doubtful accounts	16,580 debit

Required

1. Prepare the adjusting entry for MidComm to recognize bad debts under each of the following independent assumptions:

   a. Bad debts are estimated to be 2% of credit sales.

   b. Bad debts are estimated to be 1% of total sales.

   c. Analysis suggests 5% of accounts receivable at year-end are uncollectible.

2. Show how Accounts Receivable and the Allowance for Doubtful Accounts appear on the December 31, 2002, balance sheet given the facts in part (1a).

3. Show how Accounts Receivable and the Allowance for Doubtful Accounts appear on the December 31, 2002, balance sheet given the facts in part (1c).

Check (1a) Bad Debts Expense, $113,640 Dr.

Hawkins Company has credit sales of $3.6 million for year 2002. On December 31, 2002, the company's Allowance for Doubtful Accounts has a credit balance of $14,500. Hawkins prepares a schedule of its December 31, 2002, accounts receivable by age. On the basis of past experience, it also estimates the percent of receivables in each age category that will become uncollectible. This information is summarized here:

December 31, 2002 Accounts Receivable	Age of Accounts Receivable	Expected Percent Uncollectible
$830,000	Not due (under 30 days)	1.25%
254,000	1 to 30 days past due	2.00
86,000	31 to 60 days past due	6.50
38,000	61 to 90 days past due	32.75
12,000	Over 90 days past due	68.00

Required

Preparation Component

1. Estimate the amount needed in the Allowance for Doubtful Accounts at December 31, 2002, using the aging of accounts receivable method.

2. Prepare the journal entry to record bad debts expense at December 31, 2002.

Check   (2) Bad Debts Expense, $27,150 Dr.

Analysis Component

3. On June 30, 2003, Hawkins Company concludes that a customer's $4,750 receivable (created in 2002) is uncollectible and that the account should be written off. What effect will this action have on Hawkins' 2003 net income? Explain.

Heche Company began operations on January 1, 2002. During its first two years, the company completed a number of transactions involving sales on credit, accounts receivable collections, and bad debts. These transactions are summarized as follows:

Problem 10-3A
Accounts receivable transactions and bad debts adjustments

2002

a. Sold $1,345,400 of merchandise on credit, terms n/30.

b. Wrote off $18,300 of uncollectible accounts receivable.

c. Received $669,200 cash in payment of accounts receivable.

d. In adjusting the accounts on December 31, the company concluded that 1.5% of accounts receivable will be uncollectible.

2003

e. Sold $1,525,600 of merchandise on credit, terms n/30.

f. Wrote off $27,800 of uncollectible accounts receivable.

g. Received $1,204,666 cash in payment of accounts receivable.

h. In adjusting the accounts on December 31, the company concluded that 1.5% of accounts receivable will be uncollectible.

Check   (h) 2003 Bad Debts Expense, $32,197 Dr.

Required

Prepare journal entries to record Heche's 2002 and 2003 summarized transactions and its year-end adjustments to record bad debts expense.

American Co. allows select customers to make purchases on credit. The other customers can use either of two credit cards: Zip Bank or OneCharge. Zip Bank deducts a 3% service charge for sales on its credit card but credits the checking account of American immediately when credit card receipts are deposited. American deposits the Zip Bank credit card receipts at the close of each business day. When customers use OneCharge credit cards, American accumulates the receipts for several days before submitting them to OneCharge for payment. OneCharge deducts a 2% service charge and usually pays within one week of being billed. American completes the following transactions in the month of June. (The terms of all credit sales are 2/15, n/30, and all sales are recorded at the gross price.)

Problem 10-4A
Sales on credit and credit card sales

C1

	June 4	Sold $650 of merchandise on credit to Anne Klein.
	5	Sold merchandise for $6,900 to customers who used their Zip Bank credit cards.
	6	Sold merchandise for $5,872 to customers who used their OneCharge credit cards.
	8	Sold merchandise for $4,335 to customers who used their OneCharge credit cards.
	10	Submitted OneCharge card receipts accumulated since June 6 to the credit card company for payment.
	13	Wrote off the account of Mandy Smith against the Allowance for Doubtful Accounts. The $429 balance in Smith's account stemmed from a credit sale in October of last year.

Check June 17, Dr. Cash $10,003

| | 17 | Received the amount due from OneCharge. |
| | 18 | Received Klein's check paying for the purchase of June 4. |

Required

Prepare journal entries to record the preceding transactions and events.

Problem 10-5A

Analyzing and journalizing notes receivable transactions

The following selected transactions are from Van Dyken Company:

2002

Dec. 16 Accepted a $10,800, 60-day, 8% note dated this day in granting Roy Williams a time extension on his past-due account receivable.

31 Made an adjusting entry to record the accrued interest on the Williams note.

31 Closed the Interest Revenue account to Income Summary.

2003

Feb. 14 Received Williams' payment for principal and interest on the note dated December 16.

Mar. 2 Accepted a $6,120, 8%, 90-day note dated this day in granting a time extension on the past-due account receivable from DST Company.

17 Accepted a $2,400, 30-day, 7% note dated this day in granting Penny Kleen a time extension on her past-due account receivable.

Apr. 16 Kleen dishonored her note when presented for payment.

Check April 21, Dr. Interest Expense $60

21 Discounted, with recourse, the DST Company note at BancFirst at a net interest cost of $60 (the $60 is the net of interest from note and the bank discount) receiving cash proceeds of $6,060.

June 2 Received notice from BancFirst that DST Company had dishonored the note due May 31. Paid the bank the principal plus interest due on the note. (*Hint:* Create an account receivable for the maturity value of the note.)

July 17 Received payment from DST Company for the maturity value of its dishonored note plus interest for 46 days beyond maturity at 8%.

Aug. 7 Accepted a $7,450, 90-day, 10% note dated this day in granting a time extension on the past-due account receivable of Mentzer and Oak.

Sept. 3 Accepted a $2,120, 60-day, 10% note dated this day in granting Keva Whitehouse a time extension on her past-due account receivable.

18 Discounted, without recourse, the Whitehouse note at BancFirst at a net interest cost of $30 (the net of interest from note and the bank discount) receiving cash proceeds of $2,090.

Nov. 5 Received payment of principal plus interest from Mentzer and Oak for the note of August 7.

Dec. 1 Wrote off the Penny Kleen account against Allowance for Doubtful Accounts.

Required

Preparation Component

Prepare journal entries to record these transactions and events.

Analysis Component

What reporting is necessary when a business discounts notes receivable with recourse and these notes have not reached maturity by the end of the period? Explain the reason for this requirement and the accounting principle being satisfied.

Problem 10-6A

Short-term investment transactions and entries

Elliott Company, which began operations in 2002, invests its idle cash in trading securities. The following transactions are from the company's short-term investments in its trading securities:

2002

Jan. 20 Purchased 800 shares of Ford Motor Co. at $26 per share plus a $125 commission.

Feb. 9   Purchased 2,200 shares of Lucent Technology at $44.25 per share plus a $578 commission.
Oct. 12   Purchased 750 shares of Z-Seven at $7.55 per share plus a $200 commission.

2003

Apr. 15   Sold 800 shares of Ford Motor Co. at $29 per share less a $285 commission.
July 5   Sold 750 shares of Z-Seven at $10.25 per share less a $102.50 commission.
      22   Purchased 1,600 shares of Hunt Corp. at $30 per share plus a $444 commission.
Aug. 19   Purchased 1,800 shares of Donna Karan at $8.15 per share plus a $290 commission.

2004

Feb. 27   Purchased 3,400 shares of HCA at $34 per share plus a $420 commission.
Mar. 3   Sold 1,600 shares of Hunt at $25 per share less a $250 commission.
June 21   Sold 2,200 shares of Lucent Technology at $42 per share less a $420 commission.
      30   Purchased 1,200 shares of Black & Decker at $47.50 per share plus a $595 commission.
Nov. 1   Sold 1,800 shares of Donna Karan at $18.25 per share less a $309 commission.

Required

1. Prepare journal entries to record these short-term investment activities for the years shown. (Ignore the year end adjusting entries.)

2. On December 31, 2004, prepare the adjusting entry to record the market value of these investments: HCA's share price was $36 and Black & Decker's share price was $43.50. (The Market Adjustment—Trading account had an unadjusted balance of zero.)

Check Dr. Market Adjustment—Trading $985

Boca Company had no short-term investments prior to year 2002, but it had the following transactions involving short-term investments in available-for-sale securities during 2002:

Apr. 16   Purchased 4,000 shares of Gem Co. stock at $24.25 per share plus a $180 brokerage fee.
May   1   Paid $100,000 to buy 90-day U.S. Treasury bills (debt securities): $100,000 principal amount, 6% interest, dated May 1.
July 7   Purchased 2,000 shares of PepsiCo stock at $49.25 per share plus a $175 brokerage fee.
      20   Purchased 1,000 shares of Xerox stock at $16.75 per share plus a $205 brokerage fee.
Aug. 3   Received a check for principal and accrued interest on the U.S. Treasury bills that matured on July 29.
      15   Received an $0.85 per share cash dividend on the Gem Co. stock.
      28   Sold 2,000 shares of Gem Co. stock at $30 per share less a $225 brokerage fee.
Oct. 1   Received a $1.90 per share cash dividend on the PepsiCo shares.
Dec. 15   Received a $1.05 per share cash dividend on the remaining Gem Co. stock owned.
      31   Received a $1.30 per share cash dividend on the PepsiCo shares.
      31   Market values per share are Gem Co., $26.50; PepsiCo, $46.50; and Xerox, $13.75.

Problem 10-7A
Short-term investment transactions and entries

Required

Preparation Component

1. Prepare journal entries to record these preceding transactions and events.

2. Prepare a schedule to compare the cost and market values of Boca's short-term investments in available-for-sale securities.

3. Prepare an adjusting entry, if necessary, to record the market adjustment to the short-term investments in available-for-sale securities.

Check (3) Dr. Unrealized Loss—Equity $4,470

Analysis Component

4. Explain the balance sheet presentation of a market adjustment to short-term investments.

5. How do these short-term investments affect Boca's income statement for year 2002 and the equity section of its balance sheet at the end of year 2002?

On December 31, 2002, Sherman Service Co.'s records show the following results for the year:

PROBLEM SET B

Problem 10-1B
Estimating bad debts

Cash sales	$1,025,000
Credit sales	1,342,000

In addition, its unadjusted trial balance includes the following items:

Accounts receivable	$575,000 debit
Allowance for doubtful accounts	7,500 credit

Required

1. Prepare the adjusting entry for Sherman Service Co. to recognize bad debts under each of the following independent assumptions:

a. Bad debts are estimated to be 2.5% of credit sales.

Check   (1b) Bad debts expense, $35,505

b. Bad debts are estimated to be 1.5% of total sales.

c. Analysis suggests 6% of accounts receivable at year-end are uncollectible.

2. Show how Accounts Receivable and the Allowance for Doubtful Accounts appear on the December 31, 2002, balance sheet given the facts in part (1a).

3. Show how Accounts Receivable and the Allowance for Doubtful Accounts appear on the December 31, 2002, balance sheet given the facts in part (1c).

Problem 10-2B

Aging accounts receivable

Quest Company has credit sales of $4.5 million for year 2002. On December 31, 2002, the company's Allowance for Doubtful Accounts has a debit balance of $3,400. Quest prepares a schedule of its December 31, 2002, accounts receivable by age. On the basis of past experience, it also estimates the percent of receivables in each age category that will become uncollectible. This information is summarized here:

December 31, 2002 Accounts Receivable	Age of Accounts Receivable	Expected Percent Uncollectible
$396,400	Not due (under 30 days)	2.0%
277,800	1 to 30 days past due	4.0
48,000	31 to 60 days past due	8.5
6,600	61 to 90 days past due	39.0
2,800	Over 90 days past due	82.0

Required

Preparation Component

1. Compute the amount needed in the Allowance for Doubtful Accounts at December 31, 2002, using the aging of accounts receivable method.

Check   (2) Bad Debts Expense, $31,390 Dr.

2. Prepare the journal entry to record bad debts expense at December 31, 2002.

Analysis Component

3. On July 31, 2003, Quest concludes that a customer's $3,455 receivable (created in 2002) is uncollectible and that the account should be written off. What effect will this action have on Quest's 2003 net income? Explain.

Problem 10-3B

Accounts receivable transactions and bad debts adjustments

Wergeles Co. began operations on January 1, 2002, and completed several transactions during 2002 and 2003 that involve sales on credit, accounts receivable collections, and bad debts. These transactions are summarized as follows:

2002

a. Sold $685,320 of merchandise on credit, terms n/30.

b. Received $482,300 cash in payment of accounts receivable.

c. Wrote off $9,350 of uncollectible accounts receivable.

d. In adjusting the accounts on December 31, the company concluded that 1% of accounts receivable will be uncollectible.

2003

e. Sold $870,200 of merchandise on credit, terms n/30.

f. Received $990,800 cash in payment of accounts receivable.

g. Wrote off $11,090 of uncollectible accounts receivable.

h. In adjusting the accounts on December 31, the company concludes that 1% of accounts receivable will be uncollectible.

Check (h) 2003 Bad Debts
Expense, $9,773.10 Dr.

Required

Prepare journal entries to record the 2002 and 2003 summarized transactions of Wergeles Co. along with its year-end adjusting entry to record bad debts expense.

King Supply Co. allows select customers to make purchases on credit. The other customers can use either of two credit cards: Commerce Bank or Via. Commerce Bank deducts a 3% service charge for sales on its credit card but immediately credits the checking account of King when credit card receipts are deposited. King deposits the Commerce Bank credit card receipts at the close of each business day. When customers use the Via card, King accumulates the receipts for several days and then submits them to Via for payment. Via deducts a 2% service charge and usually pays within one week of being billed. King completed the following transactions in August (terms of all credit sales are 2/10, n/30; and all sales are recorded at the gross price).

Problem 10-4B
Sales on credit and credit
card sales

Aug. 4   Sold $3,700 of merchandise on credit to Tess Wright.
    10   Sold merchandise for $5,200 to customers who used their Commerce Bank credit cards.
    11   Sold merchandise for $1,250 to customers who used their Via cards.
    14   Received Wright's check paying for the purchase of August 4.
    15   Sold merchandise for $3,240 to customers who used their Via cards.
    18   Submitted Via card receipts accumulated since August 11 to the credit card company for payment.
    22   Wrote off the account of Silver City against the Allowance for Doubtful Accounts. The $498 balance in Silver City's account stemmed from a credit sale in November of last year.
    25   Received the amount due from Via.

Check Aug. 25, Dr. Cash $4,400

Required

Prepare journal entries to record the preceding transactions and events.

The following selected transactions are from Cruiser Company:

Problem 10-5B
Analyzing and journalizing
notes receivable transactions

2002

Nov. 1   Accepted a $4,800, 90-day, 10% note dated this day in granting Terry Mullen a time extension on her past-due account receivable.
Dec. 31   Made an adjusting entry to record the accrued interest on the Mullen note.
    31   Closed the Interest Revenue account to Income Summary.

2003

Jan. 30   Received Mullen's payment for principal and interest on the note dated November 1.
Feb. 28   Accepted a $12,600, 8%, 30-day note dated this day in granting a time extension on the past-due account receivable from Coffey Co.
Mar. 1   Accepted a $6,200, 60-day, 12% note dated this day in granting Staci Case a time extension on her past-due account receivable.
    23   Discounted, without recourse, the Case note at Firstar Bank at a net interest cost of $60 (the net of interest from note and the bank discount) receiving cash proceeds of $6,140.
    30   The Coffey Co. dishonored its note when presented for payment.
June 15   Accepted a $2,000, 60-day, 8% note dated this day in granting a time extension on the past-due account receivable of Sarah Morris.
    21   Accepted a $9,500, 90-day, 14% note dated this day in granting Vinnie May a time extension on his past-due account receivable.
July 5   Discounted, with recourse, the V. May note at Firstar Bank at a net interest cost of $200 (the net of interest from note and the bank discount) receiving cash proceeds of $9,300.
Aug. 14   Received payment of principal plus interest from Morris for the note of June 15.
Sept. 25   Received notice from Firstar Bank that the V. May note had been paid.
Nov. 30   Wrote off Coffey Co.'s account against Allowance for Doubtful Accounts.

Check March 23, Dr. Interest
Expense $60

Required

Preparation Component

Prepare journal entries to record these transactions and events.

Analysis Component

What reporting is necessary when a business discounts notes receivable with recourse and these notes have not reached maturity by the end of the period? Explain the reason for this requirement and the accounting principle being satisfied.

Problem 10-6B

Short-term investment transactions and entries

Dryfus Enterprises, which began operations in 2002, invests its idle cash in trading securities. The following transactions relate to the company's short-term investments in its trading securities.

2002

Mar. 10   Purchased 2,400 shares of AOL at $59.15 per share plus a $1,545 commission.
May   7   Purchased 5,000 shares of Motorola at $36.25 per share plus a $2,855 commission.
Sept. 1   Purchased 1,200 shares of UPS at $57.25 per share plus a $1,250 commission.

2003

Apr. 26   Sold 5,000 shares of Motorola at $34.50 per share less a $2,050 commission.
      27   Sold 1,200 shares of UPS at $60.50 per share less a $1,788 commission.
June 2   Purchased 3,600 shares of SPW Int'l. at $172 per share plus a $3,250 commission.
      14   Purchased 900 shares of Wal-Mart at $50.25 per share plus a $1,082 commission.

2004

Jan. 28   Purchased 2,000 shares of PepsiCo at $43 per share plus a $2,890 commission.
      31   Sold 3,600 shares of SPW at $168 per share less a $2,040 commission.
Aug. 22   Sold 2,400 shares of AOL at $56.75 per share less a $2,480 commission.
Sept. 3   Purchased 1,500 shares of Vodaphone at $40.50 per share plus a $1,680 commission.
Oct.   9   Sold 900 shares of Wal-Mart at $53.75 per share less a $1,220 commission.

Required

1. Prepare journal entries to record these short-term investment activities for the years shown. (Ignore any year-end adjusting entries.)

Check Cr. Market Adjustment—Trading $13,820

2. On December 31, 2004, prepare the adjusting entry to record the market value of these investments: PepsiCo's share price was $41 and Vodaphone's share price was $37. (The Market Adjustment—Trading account had an unadjusted balance of zero.)

Problem 10-7B

Short-term investment transactions and entries

Corbin Systems had no short-term investments on December 31, 2001, but it had the following transactions involving short-term investments in available-for-sale securities during 2002.

Feb. 6   Purchased 3,400 shares of Nokia stock at $41.25 per share plus a $3,000 brokerage fee.
      15   Paid $20,000 to buy six-month U.S. Treasury bills (debt securities): $20,000 principal amount, 6% interest, dated February 15.
Apr. 7   Purchased 1,200 shares of Dell Co. stock at $39.50 per share plus a $1,255 brokerage fee.
June 2   Purchased 2,500 shares of Merck stock at $72.50 per share plus a $3,890 brokerage fee.
      30   Received a $0.19 per share cash dividend on the Nokia shares.
Aug. 11   Sold 850 shares of Nokia stock at $46 per share less a $1,050 brokerage fee.
      16   Received a check for principal and accrued interest on the U.S. Treasury bills purchased February 15.
      24   Received a $0.10 per share cash dividend on the Dell shares.
Nov. 9   Received a $0.20 per share cash dividend on the remaining Nokia shares.
Dec. 18   Received a $0.15 per share cash dividend on the Dell shares.
      31   Market values per share are Nokia, $40.25; Dell, $40.50; and Merck, $59.

Required

Preparation Component

1. Prepare journal entries to record these preceding transactions and events.

2. Prepare a schedule to compare the cost and market values of the short-term investments in available-for-sale securities.

3. Prepare an adjusting entry, if necessary, to record the market adjustment to the short-term investments account in available-for-sale securities.

Check (3) Dr. Unrealized Loss— Equity, $42,495

Analysis Component

4. Explain the balance sheet presentation of a market adjustment to short-term investments.

5. How do these short-term investments affect its income statement for year 2002 and the equity section of its balance sheet at the end of year 2002?

Beyond the Numbers

BTN 10-1 Refer to **Nike**'s financial statements in Appendix A to answer the following:

1. What is the amount of accounts receivable (net) on May 31, 2000?

2. Nike's most liquid assets include "cash and equivalents" and "accounts receivable." Compute its most liquid assets as of May 31, 2000, as a percent of current liabilities. Do the same for May 31, 1999. Comment on the company's ability to satisfy current liabilities at the end of the fiscal year 2000 as compared to the end of fiscal year 1999.

3. What criteria did Nike use to classify items as cash equivalents?

4. Compute Nike's accounts receivable turnover as of May 31, 2000.

Swoosh Ahead

5. Access Nike's annual report for fiscal years ending after May 31, 2000, at its Web site [**www.nike.com**] or the SEC's EDGAR database [**www.sec.gov**]. Recompute parts (2) and (4) and comment on any changes since May 31, 2000.

Reporting in Action

NIKE

BTN 10-2 Key comparative figures ($ in millions) for both **Nike** and **Reebok** follow:

| Key Figures | Nike | | | Reebok | | |
	Current Year	One-Year Prior	Two-Years Prior	Current Year	One-Year Prior	Two-Years Prior
Allowance for doubtful accounts	$ 65.4	$ 73.2	$ 71.4	$ 46.2	$ 47.4	$ 44.0
Accounts receivable, net ..	1,567.2	1,540.1	1,674.4	417.4	517.8	561.7
Net sales	9,995.1	8,776.9	9,663.1	2,891.2	3,205.4	3,643.6

Comparative Analysis

NIKE

Required

1. Compute the accounts receivable turnover for both Nike and Reebok for each of the two most recent years using the data shown.

2. Using results from part (1), compute how many days it takes each company, *on average,* to collect receivables.

3. Which company is more efficient in collecting its accounts receivable?

4. Which company estimates a higher percent of uncollectible accounts receivable?

BTN 10-3 Susie Norton is the manager of a medium-size company. A few years ago, Susie persuaded the owner to base a part of her compensation on the net income the company earns each year. Each December Susie estimates year-end financial figures in anticipation of the bonus she will receive. If the bonus is not as high as she would like, she offers several recommendations to the accountant for year-end adjustments. One of her favorite recommendations is for the controller to reduce the estimate of doubtful accounts.

Ethics Challenge
P1 P2

Required

1. What effect does lowering the estimate for doubtful accounts have on the income statement and balance sheet?

2. Do you think Susie's recommendation to adjust the allowance for doubtful accounts is within her right as manager, or do you think this action is an ethics violation? Justify your response.

3. What type of internal control(s) might be useful for this company in overseeing the manager's recommendations for accounting changes?

Communicating in Practice

P1   P2

BTN 10-4   As the accountant for Bel-Air Distributing, you attend a sales managers' meeting devoted to a discussion of credit policies. At the meeting, you report that bad debts expense is estimated to be $59,000 and accounts receivable at year-end amount to $1,750,000 less a $43,000 allowance for doubtful accounts. Stan Waters, a sales manager, expresses confusion over why bad debts expense and the allowance for doubtful accounts are different amounts. Write a one-page memorandum to him explaining why a difference in bad debts expense and the allowance for doubtful accounts is not unusual. The company estimates bad debts expense as 2% of sales.

Taking It to the Net

C4   P5

BTN 10-5   Access the September 28, 1999, 10-K Filing of **Microsoft** (MSFT) at **www.edgar-online.com**. Identify Microsoft's equity and other investments footnote.

Required

1. As of June 30, 1999, did Microsoft's debt securities that were recorded at market show a net unrealized gain or net unrealized loss? What was the amount of this gain or loss?

2. As of June 30, 1999, did Microsoft's equity securities that were recorded at market show a net unrealized gain or net unrealized loss? What was the amount of this gain or loss?

3. Identify two common stocks that Microsoft had in its investment portfolio as of June 30, 1999.

Teamwork in Action

P2

BTN 10-6   Each member of a team is to participate in estimating uncollectibles using the aging schedule and percents shown in Problem 10-2A. The division of labor is up to the team. Your goal is to accurately complete this task as soon as possible. After estimating uncollectibles, check your estimate with the instructor. If the team's estimate is correct, the team then should prepare the adjusting entry and the presentation of net realizable accounts receivable for the December 31, 2002, balance sheet.

Business Week Activity

P1   C1

BTN 10-7   Read the article "For CFS, Bad Debts Are Sweet Profits" in the August 11, 1997, issue of **Business Week**.

Required

1. How does CFS make money by collecting bad debts for others?

2. What was CFS's net margin in 1996? Why is the margin so large?

3. Who are CFS's main competitors?

4. To what does CFS's CEO attribute the company's success?

Entrepreneurial Decision

C1

e

BTN 10-8   Kimberly Mills operates Musician Memorabilia, a merchandising business that buys and sells souvenirs and mementos linked with contemporary musicians. Mills accepts only cash from buyers. Her monthly cash sales are $25,000, with a net profit margin of 30%. However, buyers are increasingly requesting either to use credit cards with their purchases or to buy on credit. Therefore, Mills has decided to pursue one of two plans (neither plan will impact cash sales nor alter current costs as a percent of sales):

Plan A. *Mills accepts credit cards.* This plan is expected to yield new credit sales equal to 20% of current cash sales. Cost estimates of this plan as a percent of net credit sales are: credit card fee, 4.8%; recordkeeping, 1.2%.

Plan B. *Mills grants credit directly to qualified buyers.* This plan is expected to yield new credit sales equal to 24% of current cash sales. Cost estimates of this plan as a percent of net credit sales are: uncollectibles, 6.7%; collection expenses, 1.3%; recordkeeping, 2.0%.

Required

1. Compute the added monthly net income (loss) expected under (a) Plan A and (b) Plan B.
2. Should Mills pursue either plan? Discuss the financial and nonfinancial factors relevant to this decision.

Plant Assets, Natural Resources, and Intangibles

A Look Back

Chapters 9 and 10 focused on short-term assets: cash, cash equivalents, receivables, and short-term investments. We explained why they are known as liquid assets and described how companies account and report for them.

A Look at This Chapter

This chapter introduces us to long-term assets, including plant assets, natural resource assets, and intangible assets. We explain how to record a long-term asset's cost, the allocation of an asset's cost to periods benefiting from it, the recording of additional asset costs after an asset is purchased, and the disposal of an asset.

A Look Ahead

Chapter 12 introduces us to both current and long-term liabilities. We explain how they are computed, recorded, and reported in financial statements. We also explain accounting for payroll.

"What everybody else did was overlook the obvious."—John Schnatter

Learning Objectives

Conceptual

C1 Describe plant assets and issues in accounting for them.

C2 Explain depreciation and the factors affecting its computation.

C3 Explain depreciation for partial years and changes in estimates.

C4 Identify cash flow impacts of long-term asset transactions.

Analytical

A1 Compare and analyze depreciation for different methods.

A2 Compute total asset turnover and apply it to analyze a company's use of assets.

Procedural

P1 Apply the cost principle to compute the cost of plant assets.

P2 Compute and record depreciation using the straight-line, units-of-production, and declining-balance methods.

P3 Distinguish between revenue and capital expenditures, and account for these expenditures.

P4 Account for asset disposal through discarding, selling, and exchanging an asset.

P5 Account for natural resource assets and their depletion.

P6 Account for intangible assets and their amortization.

No Stoppa' da Papa

e LOUISVILLE, KY—It began with vision, determination, and a sledge-hammer. While running Mick's Tavern, a bar owned by his father in their hometown of Jeffersonville, Ind., 22-year-old John Schnatter knocked down a broom closet with a sledgehammer and installed a pizza oven. As a teenager, he had worked at several pizzerias, learning the art of pizza making. Now it was Schnatter's chance to show everyone he could make a better pizza. His pizza business soon outgrew the tavern. Today, his pizza company, **Papa John's** (**www.PapaJohns.com**), commands 5% of the market, trailing only Pizza Hut and Domino's.

Being a little company among giants, Schnatter had to do more with less. He began with just $1,600 cash and sold 300 to 400 pizzas a week. To save on rent, he slept in the back room of the pizzeria. "You have to keep things simple and focused," says Schnatter. This translates into selling only core products—pizza, breadsticks, cheesesticks, and soft drinks. Schnatter's skill at managing plant assets and intangibles has led to a regular 20 to 40 percent growth in both sales and income. Whereas competitors often earn under $2 in sales per dollar of assets, Papa John's earns about $2.20 in sales per dollar of assets. Schnatter also works at managing two other assets—employees and brand loyalty. His company's mission statements declare that "people are our most important [unrecorded] asset" and that the company "will create superior brand loyalty [intangible asset]." This focus on asset management is a winning recipe for Papa John's.

What's next? Schnatter proclaims, "The stage is set for us to become the No. 1 pizza brand in the world!" To do that, Schnatter must manage plant as-set growth, being sure to cover depreciation while not cutting into profits. He must also manage repairs and additions to restaurant equipment and build-ings. With success, annual revenues are likely to approach $1 billion. There aren't many pizzerias with dough that rises like that! [Sources: *Papa John's Web Site,* May 2001; *Time,* October 26, 1998; *Entrepreneur,* November 1997]

Chapter Preview

This chapter focuses on long-term assets used in the operation of a company. These assets can be grouped into plant assets, natural resource assets, and intangible assets. Plant assets are a major investment for most companies. They make up a large part of assets on most balance sheets, and they yield depreciation, often one of the largest expenses on income statements. They also affect the statement of cash flows when cash is paid to acquire plant assets or is received from their sale. When companies acquire or build a plant asset, it is often referred to as a *capital expenditure*. Capital expenditures are important events because they impact both the short- and long-term success of a company. Natural resource assets and intangible assets have similar impacts. Because of these and other reasons, it is important that we understand the accounting for and analysis of these assets. This chapter describes the purchase and use of these assets. We also explain what distinguishes these assets from other types of assets, how to determine their cost, how to allocate their costs to periods benefiting from their use, and how to dispose of them.

Section 1— Plant Assets

C1 Describe plant assets and issues in accounting for them.

Plant assets are tangible assets used in a company's operations that have a useful life of more than one accounting period. Plant assets are also called *plant and equipment; property, plant, and equipment;* and *fixed assets.* For many companies, plant assets make up the single largest asset they own. Exhibit 11.1 shows plant assets as a percent of total assets for several companies. They make up a large percent of these companies' assets, and their dollar values are large. **McDonald's** plant assets, for instance, are reported at more than $16 billion, and **Wal-Mart** reports plant assets of more than $32 billion.

Exhibit 11.1

Plant Assets of Selected Companies

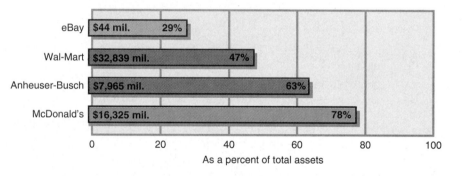

As a percent of total assets

Concept 11-1

Point: Amazon.Com's plant assets of $318 million make up 13% of its total assets, and Priceline.Com's plant assets of $28 million make up 6% of its total assets.

Point: It often helps to view plant assets as prepaid expenses that benefit several future accounting periods.

Plant assets are set apart from other assets by two important features. First, *plant assets are used in operations.* This makes them different from, for instance, inventory that is held for sale and not used in operations. The distinctive feature here is use, not type of asset. A company that purchases a computer for purposes of reselling it reports it on the balance sheet as inventory. If the same company purchases this computer to use in operations, however, it is a plant asset. Another example is a long-term investment such as land held for future expansion. However, if this land holds a factory used in operations, the land is part of plant assets. Another example is equipment held for use in the event of a breakdown or for peak periods of production. This equipment is reported in plant assets. If this same equipment is removed from use and held for sale, however, it is not reported in plant assets.

The second important feature is that *plant assets have useful lives extending over more than one accounting period.* This makes plant assets different from current assets such as supplies that are usually consumed in a short time after they are placed in use. The cost of current assets is assigned to that one period when they are used. Many prepaid expenses are distinguished from plant assets by the length of their useful lives.

The accounting for plant assets reflects these two important features. Since plant assets are used in operations, we try to match their costs against the revenues they generate. Also, since plant assets' useful lives extend over more than one period, our matching of costs and revenues must extend over several periods. We measure plant assets (balance sheet effect) and allocate assets' cost to periods benefiting from their use (income statement effect).

Exhibit 11.2 shows four main accounting issues with plant assets:

1. Compute the costs of plant assets.
2. Allocate the costs of plant assets (less any salvage amounts) against revenues for the periods they benefit.
3. Account for expenditures such as repairs and improvements to plant assets.
4. Record the disposal of plant assets.

Exhibit 11.2

Issues in Accounting for Plant Assets

This chapter focuses on the decisions and factors surrounding each of these four important accounting issues.

Cost of Plant Assets

Plant assets are recorded at cost when purchased. This is consistent with the *cost principle.* **Cost** includes all normal and reasonable expenditures necessary to get the asset in place and ready for its intended use. The cost of a factory machine, for instance, includes its invoice price less any cash discount for early payment, plus any necessary freight, unpacking, and assembling costs. A plant asset's cost also includes any necessary costs to install and test it before placing it in use. Examples are the costs of building a base or foundation for a machine, providing electrical hook-ups, and adjusting the asset before using it in operations.

> **P1** Apply the cost principle to compute the cost of plant assets.

To be charged to and reported as part of the cost of a plant asset, an expenditure must be normal, reasonable, and necessary in preparing it for its intended use. If an asset is damaged during unpacking, the repairs are not added to its cost. Instead, they are charged to an expense account. Nor is a traffic fine paid for moving heavy machinery on city streets without a proper permit part of the machinery's cost, but payment for a proper permit is included in the cost of machinery. Charges in addition to the purchase price are sometimes incurred to modify or customize a new plant asset. These charges are added to the asset's cost. We explain in this section how to determine the cost of plant assets for each of the four major classes of plant assets.

Global: Many countries including Switzerland, Brazil, the Netherlands, and the United Kingdom permit asset revaluations under certain conditions. This is a deviation from the cost principle.

Land

When land is purchased for a building site, its cost includes the total amount paid for the land, including any real estate commissions. Its cost also includes fees for insuring the title, legal fees, and any accrued property taxes paid by the purchaser. Payments for surveying, clearing, grading, draining, and landscaping also are included in the cost of land. Other costs include local government assessments, whether incurred at the time of purchase or later, for items such as public roadways, sewers, and sidewalks. These assessments are included because they permanently add to the land's value.

Land purchased as a building site sometimes includes structures that must be removed. In such cases, the total purchase price is charged to the Land account along with the cost of removing the structures, less any amounts recovered through sale of salvaged materials. To illustrate, assume **Gap** paid $167,000 cash to acquire land for a retail store. This land contains an old service garage that is removed at a net cost of $13,000 ($15,000 in costs

Exhibit 11.3

Computing Cost of Land

Cash price of land	$167,000
Net cost of garage removal	13,000
Closing costs	10,000
Cost of land	**$190,000**

less $2,000 proceeds from salvaged materials). Additional closing costs total $10,000, consisting of brokerage fees ($8,000), legal fees ($1,500), and title costs ($500). The cost of this land to Gap is $190,000 and is computed as shown in Exhibit 11.3.

Land Improvements

Because land has an unlimited life and is not usually used up over time, it is not subject to depreciation. **Land improvements** such as parking lot surfaces, driveways, fences, and lighting systems, however, have limited useful lives and are used up. While the costs of these improvements increase the usefulness of the land, they are charged to a separate Land Improvement account so their costs can be allocated to the periods they benefit.

Buildings

A Building account is charged for the costs of purchasing or constructing a building that is used in operations. When purchased, a building's costs usually include its purchase price, brokerage fees, taxes, title fees, and attorney costs. Its costs also include all expenditures to make it ready for its intended use, including any necessary repairs or renovations such as wiring, lighting, flooring, and wall coverings.

When a company constructs a building or any plant asset for its own use, its costs include materials and labor plus a reasonable amount of indirect overhead cost. Overhead includes the costs of items such as heat, lighting, power, and depreciation on machinery used to construct the asset. Costs of construction also include design fees, building permits, and insurance during construction. **Amazon.com** reports more than $83 million of construction in progress for its plant assets. However, costs such as insurance to cover the asset *after* it is placed in use are operating expenses.

Machinery and Equipment

The costs of machinery and equipment consist of all costs normal and necessary to purchase them and prepare them for their intended use. These include the purchase price, taxes, transportation charges, insurance while in transit, and installing, assembling, and testing machinery and equipment. **Sony**, for instance, disclosed in a recent annual report that: "capital expenditures [most of this for machinery and equipment] during the year under review increased . . . Sony intends to further increase its capital expenditures."

Example: If appraised values in Exhibit 11.4 are land, $24,000; land improvements, $12,000; and building, $84,000, what cost is assigned to the building? *Answer* (3 steps):.
(1) $24,000 + $12,000 + $84,000 = $120,000 (total appraisal)
(2) $84,000/$120,000 = 70% (building's percent of total)
(3) 70% × $90,000 = $63,000 (building's apportioned cost)

Lump-Sum Purchase

Plant assets sometimes are purchased as a group in a single transaction for a lump-sum price. This transaction is called a *lump-sum purchase,* or *group, bulk,* or *basket purchase.* When this occurs, we allocate the cost of the purchase among the different types of assets acquired based on their *relative market values.* Their market values can be estimated by appraisal or by using the tax-assessed valuations of the assets. To illustrate, Cola Company paid $90,000 cash to acquire a group of items consisting of land appraised at $30,000, land improvements appraised at $10,000, and a building appraised at $60,000. The $90,000 cost is allocated on the basis of appraised values as shown in Exhibit 11.4.

Exhibit 11.4

Computing Costs in a Lump-Sum Purchase

	Appraised Value	Percent of Total	Apportioned Cost
Land	$ 30,000	30% ($30,000/$100,000)	**$27,000** ($90,000 × 30%)
Land improvements. . . .	10,000	10 ($10,000/$100,000)	**9,000** ($90,000 × 10%)
Building	60,000	60 ($60,000/$100,000)	**54,000** ($90,000 × 60%)
Totals.	$100,000	100%	$90,000

Quick Check

1. Identify the asset category for each of the following: (a) office supplies, (b) office equipment, (c) merchandise, (d) land for future expansion, and (e) trucks used in operations.

2. Identify the account charged for each of the following: (a) purchase price of a vacant lot to be used in operations and (b) cost of paving that same vacant lot.

3. What amount is recorded as the cost of a new machine given the following payments related to its purchase: gross purchase price, $700,000; sales tax, $40,000; purchase discount taken, $21,000; freight to move machine to plant— terms FOB shipping point, $3,500; normal assembly costs, $3,000; cost of necessary foundation for machine, $2,500; cost of parts used in maintaining the machine, $4,200?

Answers—p. 464

Depreciation

C2 Explain depreciation and the factors affecting its computation.

We explained in the prior section that plant assets are tangible assets purchased to use in operations for more than one period. It is helpful to think of a plant asset as an amount of "usefulness" contributing to a company's operations throughout the asset's useful life. Because the lives of all plant assets other than land are limited, the amount of usefulness expires as an asset is used. This expiration of a plant asset's usefulness is called **depreciation,** which is the process of allocating the cost of a plant asset to expense in the accounting periods benefiting from its use. For instance, when a company buys a delivery truck to use as a plant asset, it acquires an amount of usefulness in the sense that it obtains a quantity of transportation. The total cost of this transportation is the cost of the truck less the proceeds expected to be received when the truck is sold or traded in at the end of its useful life. This net cost is allocated to the periods that benefit from the truck's use. This allocation of the truck's cost is depreciation.

Note that depreciation does not measure the decline in the truck's market value each period, nor does it measure the truck's physical deterioration. Depreciation is a process of allocating a plant asset's cost to expense over its useful life, nothing more. Because depreciation reflects the cost of using a plant asset, we do not begin recording depreciation charges until the asset is actually put into service. This section describes the factors we must consider in computing depreciation, the depreciation methods used, revisions in depreciation, and depreciation for partial periods.

Global: International accounting standards encourage use of the cost principle for plant assets. Plant asset revaluation is permitted provided it is consistently applied across periods.

Factors in Computing Depreciation

Three factors are relevant in determining depreciation: (1) cost, (2) salvage value, and (3) useful life.

Concept 11-2

Cost

The cost of a plant asset consists of all necessary and reasonable expenditures to acquire it and to prepare it for its intended use. We described the computation of cost earlier in this chapter.

Salvage Value

The total amount of depreciation to be charged off over an asset's benefit period equals the asset's cost minus its salvage value. **Salvage value,** also called *residual value* or *scrap value,* is an estimate of the asset's value at the end of its benefit period. This is the amount we expect to receive from disposing of the asset at the end of its benefit period. If we expect an asset to be traded in on a new asset, its salvage value is the expected trade-in value.

Point: If we expect additional costs in preparing a plant asset for disposal, the salvage value equals the expected amount from disposing of the asset less the disposal preparation costs.

Useful (Service) Life

The **useful life** of a plant asset is the length of time it is productively used in a company's operations. Useful life, also called **service life,** might not be as long as the asset's total productive life. For example, the productive life of a computer is often four to eight years

Point: Useful life and salvage value are estimates. Estimates require judgment based on consideration of all available information.

Global: While accounting in the U.S. must consider inadequacy and obsolescence in estimating useful life, the accounting in many other countries does not.

or more. Some companies, however, trade in old computers for new ones every two years. In this case, these computers have a two-year useful life, meaning the cost of these computers (less their expected trade-in values) is charged to depreciation expense over a two-year period.

Several variables often make the useful life of a plant asset difficult to predict. A major variable is the wear and tear from use in operations. Two other variables, inadequacy and obsolescence, also demand consideration. **Inadequacy** refers to the capacity of a company's plant assets that is unable to meet the company's growing productive demands. **Obsolescence** refers to a plant asset that is no longer useful in producing goods or services with a competitive advantage because of new inventions and improvements. Both inadequacy and obsolescence are difficult to predict because the timing of demand changes, new inventions, and improvements normally cannot be predicted. A company usually disposes of an inadequate or obsolete asset before it wears out.

A company is often able to better predict a new asset's useful life when it has past experience with a similar asset. When it has no such experience, a company relies on the experience of others or on engineering studies and judgment. In note 4 of its annual report, **Coca-Cola Bottling** reports the following useful lives:

> The principal categories and estimated useful
> lives of property, plant and equipment were:
>
> Buildings . . . .   10–50 years
> Machinery and equipment . . . . .   5–20 years
> Transportation equipment . . . . . .   4–10 years
> Furniture and fixtures . . . .   7–10 years
> Vending equipment . . . .   6–13 years

Did You Know?

Life Expectancy The life expectancy of plant assets is often in the eye of the beholder. For instance, both **Converse** and **Stride Rite** compete in the athletic shoe market, yet their buildings' life expectancies are quite different. Converse depreciates buildings over 5 to 10 years, but Stride Rite depreciates its buildings over 10 to 40 years. Such differences can dramatically impact financial statements.

P2 Compute and record depreciation using the straight-line, units-of-production, and declining-balance methods.

Depreciation Methods

Many *depreciation methods* are used to allocate a plant asset's cost over the accounting periods in its useful life. The most frequently used method of depreciation is the straight-line method. Another common depreciation method is the units-of-production method. We explain both of these methods in this section. This section also describes accelerated depreciation methods, with a focus on the declining-balance method.

The computations in this section use information from an athletic shoe manufacturer. In particular, we look at a machine used for inspecting athletic shoes before packaging. Manufacturers such as **Converse**, **Reebok**, **Adidas**, and **Fila** use this machine. Data for its depreciation are in Exhibit 11.5.

Exhibit 11.5

Data for Athletic Shoe-Inspecting Machine

Cost	$10,000
Salvage value	1,000
Depreciable cost	$ 9,000
Useful life	
Accounting periods	5 years
Units inspected	36,000 shoes

Straight-Line Method

Straight-line depreciation charges the same amount of expense to each period of the asset's useful life. A two-step process is used. We first compute the *depreciable cost* of the asset; this amount is also called the *cost to be depreciated*. It is computed by subtracting the asset's salvage value from its total cost. Second, depreciable cost is divided by the number of accounting periods in the asset's useful life. The formula for straight-line depreciation, along with its computation for the inspection machine described above, are shown in Exhibit 11.6.

Exhibit 11.6

Straight-Line Depreciation Formula

$$\frac{\text{Cost} - \text{Salvage value}}{\text{Useful life in periods}} = \frac{\$10,000 - \$1,000}{5 \text{ years}} = \$1,800 \text{ per year}$$

If this machine is purchased on December 31, 2000, and used throughout its predicted useful life of five years, the straight-line method allocates an equal amount of depreciation to each of the years 2001 through 2005. We make the following adjusting entry at the end of each of the five years to record straight-line depreciation of this machine:

Dec. 31	Depreciation Expense	1,800	
	Accumulated Depreciation—Machinery ...		1,800
	To record annual depreciation.		

Assets = Liabilities + Equity
−1,800   −1,800

The $1,800 Depreciation Expense is reported on the income statement among operating expenses. The $1,800 Accumulated Depreciation is a contra asset account to the Machinery account in the balance sheet.

The graph on the left in Exhibit 11.7 shows the $1,800 per year expense amount reported in each of the five years. The graph on the right shows the amounts reported on each of the six December 31 balance sheets while the company owns the asset.

Example. If salvage value of the machine is estimated to be $2,500, what is the annual depreciation expense? *Answer:*
($10,000 − $2,500)/5 years
= $1,500.

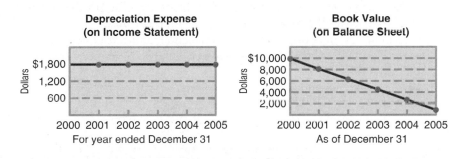

Exhibit 11.7

Financial Statement Effects of Straight-Line Depreciation

The net balance sheet amount is the asset's **book value** and is computed as the asset's total cost less its accumulated depreciation. For example, at the end of year 2 (December 31, 2002), its book value is $6,400 and is reported in the balance sheet as follows:

| Machinery .... | $10,000 | |
| Less accumulated depreciation ...... | 3,600 | $6,400 |

The book value of this machine declines by $1,800 each year due to depreciation. From the graphs in Exhibit 11.7 we can see why this method is called straight line.

We also can compute the *straight-line depreciation rate,* defined as 100% divided by the number of periods in the asset's useful life. For the inspection machine, this rate is 20% (100% ÷ 5 years). We use this rate along with other information to compute the machine's *straight-line depreciation schedule* shown in Exhibit 11.8. Note three points in Exhibit 11.8. First, depreciation expense is the same each period. Second, accumulated depreciation is the

| | Depreciation for the Period | | | End of Period | |
Annual Period	Depreciable Cost*	Depreciation Rate	Depreciation Expense	Accumulated Depreciation	Book Value†
2000	—	—	—	—	$10,000
2001	$9,000	20%	$1,800	$1,800	8,200
2002	9,000	20	1,800	3,600	6,400
2003	9,000	20	1,800	5,400	4,600
2004	9,000	20	1,800	7,200	2,800
2005	9,000	20	1,800	9,000	1,000

Exhibit 11.8

Straight-Line Depreciation Schedule

* $10,000 − $1,000.   † Book value is cost minus accumulated depreciation.

sum of current and prior periods' depreciation expense. Third, book value declines each period until it equals salvage value at the end of its useful life.

Units-of-Production Method

The straight-line method charges an equal share of an asset's cost to each period. If plant assets are used up in about equal amounts each accounting period, this method produces a reasonable matching of expenses with revenues. The use of some plant assets varies greatly, however, from one period to the next. A builder, for instance, might use a piece of construction equipment for a month and then not use it again for several months. When equipment use varies from period to period, the units-of-production depreciation method can better match expenses with revenues than can straight-line depreciation. **Units-of-production depreciation** charges a varying amount to expense for each period of an asset's useful life depending on its usage.

A two-step process is used to compute units-of-production depreciation. We first compute *depreciation per unit* by subtracting the asset's salvage value from its total cost and then dividing by the total number of units expected to be produced during its useful life. Units of production can be expressed in product or other units such as hours used or miles driven. The second step is to compute depreciation expense for the period by multiplying the units produced in the period by the depreciation per unit.

The formula for units-of-production depreciation, along with its computation for the machine described in Exhibit 11.5, are shown in Exhibit 11.9. (*Note:* 7,000 shoes are inspected and sold in its first year.)

Exhibit 11.9

Units-of-Production Depreciation Formula

Step 1

$$\text{Depreciation per unit} = \frac{\text{Cost} - \text{Salvage value}}{\text{Total units of production}} = \frac{\$10,000 - \$1,000}{36,000 \text{ shoes}} = \$0.25 \text{ per shoe}$$

Step 2

$$\text{Depreciation expense} = \text{Depreciation per unit} \times \text{Units produced in period}$$

$$\$0.25 \text{ per shoe} \times 7,000 \text{ shoes} = \$1,750$$

Using actual data on the number of shoes inspected by the machine, we can compute the *units-of-production depreciation schedule* shown in Exhibit 11.10. For example, depreciation for the first year is $1,750 (7,000 shoes at $0.25 per shoe). Depreciation for the second year is $2,000 (8,000 shoes at $0.25 per shoe). The other years are similarly computed. Notice in Exhibit 11.10 that (1) depreciation expense depends on unit output, (2) accumulated depreciation is the sum of current and prior periods' depreciation expense, and (3) book value declines each period until it equals salvage value at the end of the asset's useful life.

Exhibit 11.10

Units-of-Production Depreciation Schedule

| | Depreciation for the Period | | | End of Period | |
Annual Period	Number of Units	Depreciation per Unit	Depreciation Expense	Accumulated Depreciation	Book Value
2000	—	—	—	—	$10,000
2001	7,000	$0.25	**$1,750**	$1,750	8,250
2002	8,000	0.25	**2,000**	3,750	6,250
2003	9,000	0.25	**2,250**	6,000	4,000
2004	7,000	0.25	**1,750**	7,750	2,250
2005	5,000	0.25	**1,250**	9,000	**1,000**

Boise Cascade is one of many companies using the units-of-production depreciation method. It reports that "substantially all of the Company's paper and wood products manufacturing facilities determine depreciation by the units-of-production method."

Declining-Balance Method

An **accelerated depreciation method** yields larger depreciation expenses in the early years of an asset's life and smaller charges in later years. Of several accelerated methods, the most common is the **declining-balance method** of depreciation, which uses a depreciation rate of up to twice the straight-line rate and applies it to the asset's beginning-of-period book value. The amount of depreciation declines each period because book value *declines* each period.

A common depreciation rate for the declining balance method is double the straight-line rate. This is called the *double-declining-balance* or *DDB* method. This method is applied in three steps: (1) compute the asset's straight-line depreciation rate, (2) double the straight-line rate, and (3) compute depreciation expense by multiplying this rate by the asset's beginning-of-period book value.

To illustrate, let's return to the machine in Exhibit 11.5 and apply the double-declining-balance method to compute depreciation expense. Exhibit 11.11 shows the first year depreciation computation for the machine. The three-step process is to (1) divide 100% by five years to determine the straight-line rate of 20% per year, (2) double this 20% rate to get the declining-balance rate of 40% per year, and (3) compute depreciation expense as 40% multiplied by the beginning-of-period book value.

Global: German accounting permits accelerated depreciation of up to three times the straight-line rate.

Point: In the DDB method, *double* refers to the rate and *declining balance* refers to book value. The rate is applied to beginning book value each period.

Exhibit 11.11
Double-Declining-Balance Depreciation Formula

Step 1

Straight-line rate = 100% ÷ Useful life = 100% ÷ 5 years = 20%

Step 2

Double-declining-balance rate = 2 × Straight-line rate = 2 × 20% = 40%

Step 3

Depreciation expense = Double-declining-balance rate × Beginning-period book value

40% × \$10,000 = \$4,000 (for 2001)

The *double-declining-balance depreciation schedule* is shown in Exhibit 11.12. The schedule follows the formula except for year 2005, when depreciation expense is \$296. This \$296 is not equal to 40% × \$1,296, or \$518.40. If we had used the \$518.40 for depreciation

Point: Graph and describe the asset's book value over its useful life using the DDB method.

Exhibit 11.12
Double-Declining-Balance Depreciation Schedule

| | Depreciation for the Period | | | End of Period | |
Annual Period	Beginning of Period Book Value	Depreciation Rate	Depreciation Expense	Accumulated Depreciation	Book Value
2000	—	—	—	—	\$10,000
2001	\$10,000	40%	**\$4,000**	\$4,000	6,000
2002	6,000	40	**2,400**	6,400	3,600
2003	3,600	40	**1,440**	7,840	2,160
2004	2,160	40	864	8,704	1,296
2005	1,296	40	296*	9,000	**1,000**

* Year 2005 depreciation is \$1,296 − \$1,000 = \$296 (never depreciate book value below salvage value).

Example: What is DDB depreciation expense in year 2004 if the salvage value is $2,000?
Answer: $2,160 − $2,000 = $160

expense in 2005, ending book value would equal $777.60, which is less than the $1,000 salvage value. Instead, the $296 is computed by subtracting the $1,000 salvage value from the $1,296 book value at the beginning of the fifth year (the year when DDB depreciation cuts into salvage value). This is done so that an asset is never depreciated below its salvage value.

A1 Compare and analyze depreciation for different methods.

Comparing Depreciation Methods

Exhibit 11.13 shows depreciation expense for the machine under each of the three depreciation methods.

Exhibit 11.13

Depreciation Expense for the Different Methods

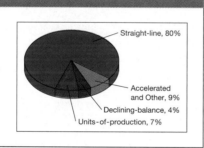

Period	Straight-Line	Units-of-Production	Double-Declining-Balance
2001	$1,800	$1,750	$4,000
2002	1,800	2,000	2,400
2003	1,800	2,250	1,440
2004	1,800	1,750	864
2005	1,800	1,250	296
Totals	$9,000	$9,000	$9,000

While the amount of depreciation expense per period differs for different methods, total depreciation expense is the same over the machine's useful life. Each method starts with a total cost of $10,000 and ends with a salvage value of $1,000. The difference is the pattern in depreciation expense over the useful life. The book value of the asset when using straight-line is always greater than the book value from using double-declining-balance, except at the beginning and end of the asset's useful life, when it is the same. Also, the straight-line method yields a steady pattern of depreciation expense while the units-of-production depreciation depends on the number of units produced. Each of these methods is acceptable because it allocates cost in a systematic and rational manner.

Did You Know?

Trends Approximately 80% of companies use straight-line depreciation for their plant assets, 7% use units-of-production, and 4% use declining balance. Another 9% use an unspecified accelerated method—most of these probably are declining balance.

Straight-line, 80%
Accelerated and Other, 9%
Declining-balance, 4%
Units-of-production, 7%

Depreciation for Tax Reporting

Global: Some Canadian companies are permitted to use an "increasing charge" depreciation (the opposite of accelerated depreciation).

Point: Differences between financial accounting and tax accounting records are normal and expected.

Point: Understanding depreciation for financial accounting will help in learning MACRS for tax accounting. Rules for MACRS are available from www.IRS.com.

The records a company keeps for financial accounting purposes are usually separate from the records it keeps for tax accounting purposes. This is so because financial accounting aims to report useful information on financial performance and position, whereas tax accounting reflects government objectives in raising revenues. Differences between these two accounting systems are normal and expected. Depreciation is a common example of how the records usually differ. For example, many companies use accelerated depreciation in computing taxable income. This reduces taxable income in the early years of an asset's life because higher depreciation expense is reported in these early years. On the other hand, the lower depreciation expense in later years means that taxable income is higher in later years. A company's goal here is to *postpone* its tax payments. This means a company can use these resources now to earn additional income before payment is due.

The U.S. federal income tax law has rules for depreciating assets. These rules include the **Modified Accelerated Cost Recovery System (MACRS).** MACRS allows straight-line depreciation for some assets, but it requires accelerated depreciation for most kinds of assets. MACRS separates depreciable assets into different classes and defines the depreciable life and rate for each class. MACRS is not acceptable for financial reporting because it often al-

Did You Know?

Depreciation Technology Computer technology greatly simplifies depreciation computations and revisions. Many inexpensive, off-the-shelf software packages and business calculators allow a user to choose from a variety of depreciation methods for each asset entered. Depreciation schedules for both financial reporting and income tax reporting are quickly and accurately generated.

locates costs over an arbitrary period that is less than the asset's useful life. Details of MACRS are covered in tax accounting.

Partial Year Depreciation

Plant assets are purchased and disposed of at various times. When an asset is purchased (or disposed of) at a time other than the beginning or end of an accounting period, depreciation is recorded for part of a year. This is done so that the year of purchase or the year of disposal is charged with its share of the asset's depreciation.

To illustrate, let's return to the machine described in Exhibit 11.5. Assume that this machine is purchased and placed in service on October 8, 2000, and the annual accounting period ends on December 31. This machine costs $10,000, has a useful life of five years, and a salvage value of $1,000. Because this machine is purchased and used for nearly three months in 2000, the calendar-year income statement should report depreciation expense on the machine for that part of the year. Normally, the amount of depreciation is based on the assumption that the asset is purchased on the first day of the month nearest the actual date of purchase. In this case, since the purchase occurred on October 8, we assume an October 1 purchase date. This means that three months' depreciation is recorded in 2000. Using straight-line depreciation, we compute three months' depreciation of $450 as follows:

$$\frac{\$10,000 - \$1,000}{5 \text{ years}} \times \frac{3}{12} = \$450$$

A similar computation is necessary when an asset disposal occurs during a period. For example, let's suppose the machine is sold on June 24, 2005. Depreciation is recorded for the period January 1 through June 24 when it is disposed of. This partial year's depreciation, computed to the nearest whole month, is

$$\frac{\$10,000 - \$1,000}{5 \text{ years}} \times \frac{6}{12} = \$900$$

Revising Depreciation

Because depreciation is based on predictions of salvage value and useful life, depreciation expense is an estimate. During the useful life of an asset, new information may indicate that the original estimates are inaccurate. If our estimate of an asset's useful life and/or salvage value changes, what should we do? The answer is to use the new estimate to compute depreciation for current and future periods. This means we revise depreciation expense computation by spreading the cost yet to be depreciated over the useful life remaining. This approach is used for all depreciation methods.

Let's return to our machine described in Exhibit 11.8 using straight-line depreciation. At the beginning of this asset's third year, its book value is $6,400, computed as:

Cost	$10,000
Less two years' accumulated depreciation	3,600
Book value	$6,400

Assume that at the beginning of its third year, the estimated number of years remaining in its useful life changes from three to four years *and* its estimate of salvage value changes from $1,000 to $400. Straight-line depreciation for each of the four remaining years is computed as shown in Exhibit 11.14.

$$\frac{\textbf{Book value} - \textbf{Revised salvage value}}{\textbf{Revised remaining useful life}} = \frac{\$6,400 - \$400}{4 \text{ years}} = \$1,500 \text{ per year}$$

Exhibit 11.14

Computing Revised
Straight-Line Depreciation

Global: Some countries require the depreciation method chosen for financial reporting to match the method chosen for tax reporting.

C3 Explain depreciation for partial years and changes in estimates.

Example: If the machine's salvage value is zero and purchase occurs on Oct. 8, 2000, how much depreciation is recorded at Dec. 31, 2000?
Answer: $10,000/5 × 3/12 = $500

Point: Remaining depreciable cost equals book value less revised salvage value at the point of revision.

This means $1,500 of depreciation expense is recorded for the machine at the end of the third through sixth years of its remaining useful life. Since this asset was depreciated at $1,800 per year for the first two years, it is tempting to conclude that depreciation expense was overstated in the first two years. However, these expenses reflected the best information available at that time. We do not go back and restate prior years' financial statements for this type of new information. Instead, we adjust the current and future periods' statements to reflect this new information. Revising an estimate of the useful life or salvage value of a plant asset is referred to as a **change in an accounting estimate** and is reflected in current and future financial statements, not in prior statements.

Reporting Depreciation

Both the cost and accumulated depreciation of plant assets are reported on the balance sheet or in its notes. **Arctic Cat**, for instance, reports the following in its balance sheet:

Property and equipment ($ thousands):	
Machinery, equipment, and tooling	$71,936
Land, buildings, and improvements	16,861
	$88,797
Less accumulated depreciation	(52,411)
Total	$36,386

Many companies also show plant assets on one line with the net amount of cost less accumulated depreciation. When this is done, the amount of accumulated depreciation is disclosed in a note. **Nike** reports only the net amount of its property, plant, and equipment in its balance sheet in Appendix A. To satisfy the *full-disclosure principle,* Nike describes its depreciation methods in its Note 1 and the individual amounts comprising plant assets in its Note 3.

Reporting both the cost and accumulated depreciation of plant assets helps users compare the assets of different companies. For example, a company holding assets costing $50,000 and accumulated depreciation of $40,000 is likely in a situation different from a company with new assets costing $10,000. While the net undepreciated cost of $10,000 is the same in both cases, the first company may have more productive capacity available but likely is facing the need to replace older assets. These insights are not provided if the two balance sheets report only the $10,000 book values.

Depreciation is a process of cost allocation. Plant assets are reported on a balance sheet at their undepreciated costs (book value), not at market values. This emphasis on costs rather than market values is based on the *going-concern principle* described in Chapter 2. This principle states that, unless there is evidence to the contrary, we assume that a company continues in business. This implies that plant assets are held and used long enough to recover their cost through the sale of products and services. Since plant assets are not for sale, their market values are not reported in financial statements. Instead, assets are reported on a balance sheet at cost less accumulated depreciation.

Accumulated depreciation is a contra asset account with a normal credit balance. It does not reflect funds accumulated to buy new assets when the assets currently owned are replaced. If a company has funds available to buy assets, the funds are shown on the balance sheet among liquid assets such as Cash or Investments.

You Make the Call—Ethics

Controller You are the controller for Fascar, a struggling company. Fascar's operations require regular investments in equipment, and depreciation is its largest expense. Competitors also frequently replace equipment, which is typically depreciated over three years. Fascar's president instructs you to revise useful lives of equipment from three to six years and to use a six-year life on all new equipment. You suspect these instructions are motivated by a desire to improve reported income. What actions do you take?

Answer—p. 464

Quick Check

4. On January 1, 2002, a company pays $77,000 to purchase office furniture with a zero salvage value. The furniture's useful life is somewhere between 7 and 10 years. What is the year 2002 straight-line depreciation on the furniture using a (a) 7-year useful life and (b) 10-year useful life?

5. What does the term *depreciation* mean in accounting?

6. A company purchases a machine for $96,000 on January 1, 2003. Its useful life is five years or 100,000 units of product, and its salvage value is $8,000. During 2003, 10,000 units of product are produced. Compute the book value of this machine on December 31, 2003, assuming (a) straight-line depreciation and (b) units-of-production depreciation.

7. In early January 2002, a company acquires equipment for $3,800. The company estimates this equipment to have a useful life of three years and a salvage value of $200. Early in 2004, the company changes its estimates to a total four-year useful life and zero salvage value. Using straight-line, what is depreciation for the year ended 2004?

Answers—p. 464

Acquiring a plant asset and putting it into service often cause additional expenditures to operate, maintain, repair, and improve it. In recording these expenditures, we must decide whether to capitalize or expense them. To capitalize an expenditure is to debit the asset account. The issue is whether more useful information is provided by reporting these expenditures as current period expenses or by adding them to the plant asset's cost and depreciating them over its remaining useful life.

Revenue expenditures, also called *income statement expenditures,* are additional costs of plant assets that do not materially increase the asset's life or productive capabilities. They are recorded as expenses and deducted from revenues in the current period's income statement. Examples of revenue expenditures are cleaning, repainting, adjustments, and lubricants. **Capital expenditures,** also called *balance sheet expenditures,* are additional costs of plant assets that provide benefits extending beyond the current period. They are debited to asset accounts and reported on the balance sheet. Capital expenditures increase or improve the type or amount of service an asset provides. Examples are roofing replacement, plant expansion, and major overhauls of machinery and equipment.

Financial statements are affected for several years by the accounting choice of recording costs as either revenue expenditures or capital expenditures. Managers must be careful in classifying them. This classification decision is helped by identifying these expenditures as either ordinary repairs or as betterments and extraordinary repairs.

Ordinary Repairs

Ordinary repairs are expenditures to keep the asset in normal, good operating condition. They are necessary if an asset is to perform to expectations over its useful life. Ordinary repairs do not extend an asset's useful life beyond its original estimate or increase its productivity beyond original expectations. Examples are normal costs of cleaning, lubricating, adjusting, and replacing (small) parts of a machine. Ordinary repairs are treated as *revenue expenditures.* This means their costs are reported as expenses on the current period income statement. Following this rule, **America West Airlines** reports "routine maintenance and repairs are charged to expense as incurred."

Few companies keep records for assets costing less than some minimum amount such as $500. Instead, these *low-cost plant assets* are treated as a revenue expenditure. This means their costs are charged to an expense account at the time of purchase. This practice is acceptable under the

Revenue and Capital Expenditures

P3 Distinguish between revenue and capital expenditures, and account for these expenditures.

Point: If a manager's compensation is tied to net income, evidence suggests this can influence a manager's classification of expenditures.

Point: When an amount is said to be *capitalized* to an account, the amount is added to the account's normal balance.

Financial Statement Effect			
Treatment	**Accounting**	**Expense**	**Current Income**
Revenue expenditure	Income stmt. account debited	Currently recognized	Lower
Capital expenditure	Balance sheet account debited	Deferred to future	Higher

Point: Expenditures for both extraordinary repairs and betterments require revision of depreciation schedules.

Example: A company purchases a Web server. Identify each item as a revenue or capital expenditure: (1) purchase price, (2) necessary wiring, (3) platform for operation, (4) circuits to increase capacity, (5) cleaning after each three months use, (6) repair of a faulty connection, and (7) replaced a cooling fan. *Answer:* Capital expenditures: 1, 2, 3, 4; Revenue expenditures: 5, 6, 7.

Assets = Liabilities + Equity
+1,800
−1,800

materiality principle. Treating immaterial capital expenditures as revenue expenditures is unlikely to mislead users of financial statements. As an example, **Coca-Cola Bottling** capitalizes only major, or material, asset replacement: "minor replacements are charged to expense when incurred."

Betterments and Extraordinary Repairs

Betterments, also called *improvements,* are expenditures that make a plant asset more efficient or productive. A betterment often involves adding a component to an asset or replacing one of its old components with a better one. A betterment does not always increase an asset's useful life. An example is replacing manual controls on a machine with automatic controls to reduce labor costs. This machine will still wear out as fast as it would with manual controls. One special type of betterment is an *addition.* Examples are a new wing to a factory or a new dock to a warehouse.

Because a betterment benefits future periods, it is debited to the asset account as a capital expenditure. The new book value (less salvage value) is then depreciated over the asset's remaining useful life. To illustrate, suppose a company pays $8,000 for a machine with an eight-year useful life and no salvage value. After three years and $3,000 of depreciation, it adds an automated system to the machine at a cost of $1,800. This results in reduced labor costs when operating the machine in future periods. The cost of this betterment is added to the Machinery account with this entry:

Jan. 2	Machinery	1,800	
	Cash		1,800
	To record installation of automated system.		

After the betterment, the remaining cost to be depreciated is $6,800, computed as $8,000 − $3,000 + $1,800. Depreciation expense for the remaining five years is $1,360 per year, computed as $6,800/5 years.

Extraordinary repairs are expenditures extending the asset's useful life beyond its original estimate. Costs of extraordinary repairs are *capital expenditures* because they benefit future periods. As with betterments, they can be debited to the asset account. For example, **American West Airlines** reports: "the cost of major scheduled airframe, engine and certain component overhauls are capitalized (and expensed) . . . over the periods benefited." Extraordinary repairs also can be debited to the asset's accumulated depreciation account to reverse some effects of past depreciation—this approach is described in advanced courses.

You Make the Call

Entrepreneur Your start up Internet services company needs cash, and you are preparing financial statements to apply for a short-term loan. A friend suggests you treat as many expenses as possible as capital expenditures. What are the impacts on financial statements of this suggestion? What do you think is the aim of your friend's proposal?

Answer—p. 464

Disposals of Plant Assets

Plant assets are disposed of for several reasons. For example, many assets are eventually discarded because they wear out or become obsolete. Other assets are sold because of changing business plans, and sometimes an asset is exchanged for another asset. Regardless of the reason, disposals of plant assets occur in one of three basic ways: discarding, sale, or exchange. The general approach to accounting for each of these three types of disposals of plant assets is described in Exhibit 11.15.

Exhibit 11.15

Accounting for Disposals of Plant Assets

1. Record depreciation up to the date of disposal—this also updates Accumulated Depreciation.
2. Remove account balances of the disposed asset—including its Accumulated Depreciation.
3. Record any cash (and/or other assets) received or paid in the disposal.
4. Record any gain or loss—computed by comparing the disposed asset's book value with the market value of any assets received.*

* One exception to step 4 is the case of a gain on an asset exchange—it is described later in this section.

Discarding Plant Assets

A plant asset is *discarded* when it is no longer useful to the company and it has no market value. To illustrate, assume that a machine costing $9,000 with accumulated depreciation of $9,000 is discarded. When accumulated depreciation equals the asset's cost, it is said to be *fully depreciated* (zero book value). The entry to record the discarding of this asset is

June 5	Accumulated Depreciation—Machinery	9,000	
	Machinery		9,000
	To discard fully depreciated machinery.		

P4 Account for asset disposal through discarding, selling, and exchanging an asset.

Assets = Liabilities + Equity
+9,000
−9,000

This entry reflects all four steps of Exhibit 11.15. Step 1 is unnecessary since the machine is fully depreciated. Step 2 is reflected in the debit to Accumulated Depreciation and credit to Machinery. Since no other asset is involved, step 3 is irrelevant. Also, since book value is zero and no other asset is involved, no gain or loss is recorded in step 4.

How do we account for discarding an asset that is not fully depreciated? Or one whose depreciation is not up to date? To answer this, consider equipment costing $8,000 with accumulated depreciation of $6,000 on December 31 of the prior fiscal year-end. This equipment is being depreciated using straight line over eight years with zero salvage value. On July 1 it is discarded. Step 1 is to bring depreciation expense up to date:

Point: Recording depreciation expense up to date gives an up-to-date book value for determining gain or loss.

July 1	Depreciation Expense	500	
	Accumulated Depreciation—Equipment		500
	To record 6 months' depreciation ($1,000 × 6/12).		

Assets = Liabilities + Equity
−500   −500

Steps 2 through 4 of Exhibit 11.15 are reflected in the second (and final) entry:

July 1	Accumulated Depreciation—Equipment	6,500	
	Loss on Disposal of Equipment	1,500	
	Equipment		8,000
	To discard equipment with a $1,500 book value.		

Assets = Liabilities + Equity
+6,500   −1,500
−8,000

The loss is computed by comparing the equipment's $1,500 ($8,000 − $6,000 − $500) book value with the zero net cash proceeds. This loss is reported in the Other Expenses and Losses section of the income statement. Discarding an asset can sometimes require a cash payment that would increase the loss. More generally, the income statement reports any gain or loss from discarding the asset, and the balance sheet reports the changes in the asset and accumulated depreciation accounts.

Point: Gain or loss is determined by comparing "value given" (book value) to "value received."

Selling Plant Assets

Companies often sell plant assets when they restructure or downsize operations. To illustrate the accounting for selling plant assets, we consider BTO's March 31 sale of equipment that cost $16,000 and has accumulated depreciation of $12,000 at December 31 of the prior calendar year-end. Annual depreciation on this equipment is $4,000 computed using straight-line depreciation. Step 1 of this sale is to record depreciation expense and update accumulated depreciation to March 31 of the current year:

March 31	Depreciation Expense	1,000	
	Accumulated Depreciation—Equipment		1,000
	To record 3 months' depreciation ($4,000 × 3/12).		

Assets = Liabilities + Equity
−1,000   −1,000

Steps 2 through 4 of Exhibit 11.15 can be reflected in one entry that depends on the amount received from the asset's sale. We consider three different possibilities.

Sale at Book Value

If BTO receives $3,000, an amount equal to the equipment's book value as of March 31, no gain or loss occurs on disposal. The accounting in this case is

Assets   = Liabilities + Equity
+3,000
+13,000
−16,000

March 31	Cash	3,000	
	Accumulated Depreciation—Equipment	13,000	
	Equipment		16,000
	To record sale of equipment for no gain or loss.		

Sale above Book Value

If BTO receives $7,000, an amount that is $4,000 above the equipment's book value as of March 31, a gain on disposal occurs. The entry is

Assets   = Liabilities + Equity
+7,000   +4,000
+13,000
−16,000

March 31	Cash	7,000	
	Accumulated Depreciation—Equipment	13,000	
	Gain on Disposal of Equipment		4,000
	Equipment		16,000
	To record sale of equipment for a $4,000 gain.		

Sale below Book Value

If BTO receives $2,500, an amount that is $500 below the equipment's book value as of March 31, a loss on disposal occurs. The entry is

Assets   = Liabilities + Equity
+2,500   −500
+13,000
−16,000

March 31	Cash	2,500	
	Loss on Disposal of Equipment	500	
	Accumulated Depreciation—Equipment	13,000	
	Equipment		16,000
	To record sale of equipment for a $500 loss.		

Exchanging Plant Assets

Many plant assets such as machinery, automobiles, and office equipment often are disposed of by exchanging them for newer assets. In a typical exchange of plant assets, a trade-in allowance is received on the old asset and the balance is paid in cash. Accounting for the exchange of assets is similar to any other disposal unless the old and the new assets are similar in the functions they perform. Trading an old truck for a new truck is an exchange of similar assets, whereas trading a truck for a machine is an exchange of dissimilar assets. This section describes the accounting for the exchange of similar assets. Similar asset exchanges are common, whereas dissimilar asset exchanges are not (the latter are discussed in advanced courses).

Accounting for exchanges of similar assets depends on whether the book value of the asset(s) given up is less or more than the market value of the asset(s) received. When the market value of the asset(s) received is less than the book value of the asset(s) given up, the difference is recognized as a loss. But when the value of the asset(s) received is more than the asset's book value given up, the gain is *not* recognized.

Receiving Less in Exchange: A Loss

Let's assume a company exchanges both old equipment and $33,000 in cash for new equipment. The old equipment originally cost $36,000 and has accumulated depreciation of $20,000 at the time of exchange. The new equipment has a market value of $42,000. These details are reflected in the middle ("Loss") columns of Exhibit 11.16.

Exhibit 11.16

Computing Gain or Loss on *Similar* Asset Exchange

Similar Plant Asset Exchange		Loss		Gain	
Market value of asset(s) received			$42,000		$52,000
Book value of asset(s) given up:					
Equipment ($36,000 − $20,000)	$16,000			$16,000	
Cash	33,000		49,000	33,000	49,000
Gain (loss) on exchange			$ (7,000)		$ 3,000

The entry to record this similar asset exchange is

Jan. 3	Equipment (**new**)	42,000	
	Loss on Exchange of Assets	7,000	
	Accumulated Depreciation—Equipment	20,000	
	Equipment (**old**)		36,000
	Cash		33,000
	To record exchange of old equipment and cash for new equipment.		

Assets = Liabilities + Equity
+42,000   −7,000
+20,000
−36,000
−33,000

The book value of the assets given up is $49,000. This includes the $33,000 cash and the $16,000 ($36,000 − $20,000) book value of the old equipment. The $49,000 book value of assets given up is compared to the market value of the new equipment received ($42,000). This yields a loss of $7,000 ($42,000 − $49,000).

Point: Parenthetical journal entry notes to "new" and "old" equipment are for illustration only. Both the debit and credit are to the same Equipment account in the general ledger.

Receiving More in Exchange: A Gain

Let's assume the same facts as in the preceding similar asset exchange *except* that the new equipment received has a market value of $52,000 instead of $42,000. The entry to record this similar asset exchange is

Jan. 3	Equipment (**new**)	49,000	
	Accumulated Depreciation—Equipment	20,000	
	Equipment (**old**)		36,000
	Cash		33,000
	To record exchange of old equipment and cash for new equipment.		

Assets = Liabilities + Equity
+49,000
+20,000
−36,000
−33,000

We show how to compute the gain from this exchange in the far right ("Gain") columns of Exhibit 11.16. This gain is *not* recognized in the entry because of a rule prohibiting recognizing a gain on similar asset exchanges.[1] The $49,000 recorded for the new equipment equals its cash price ($52,000) less the unrecognized gain ($3,000) on the exchange. The $49,000 cost recorded is called the *cost basis* of the new machine. This cost basis is the amount we use to compute depreciation and its book value. The cost basis of the new asset also can be computed by summing the book values of the assets given up as shown in Exhibit 11.17.

Point: No gain is recognized for similar asset exchanges.

Cost of old equipment	$36,000
Less accumulated depreciation ...	20,000
Book value of old equipment	$16,000
Cash paid in the exchange	33,000
Cost recorded for new equipment	**$49,000**

Exhibit 11.17

Cost Basis of New Asset when Gain Not Recognized

Example: Assume this old equipment is sold for $19,000 and, in a separate transaction, new equipment is purchased for $52,000. Record both transactions. *Answer:*
Cash 19,000
Accum. Depr—Eq. . 20,000
   Equipment (old) 36,000
   Gain on Sale of Eq. 3,000
Equipment (new) ... 52,000
   Cash 52,000

[continued on next page]

Quick Check

8. Early in the fifth year of a machine's 6-year useful life, it is overhauled, and its useful life is extended to nine years. This machine originally cost $108,000 and the overhaul cost is $12,000. Prepare the entry to record the overhaul cost.

9. Explain the difference between revenue expenditures and capital expenditures and how both are recorded.

10. What is a betterment? How is a betterment recorded?

---

[1] The reason a gain from a similar asset exchange is not recognized is that the earnings process is not considered complete for the exchanged asset. The decision to recognize a loss from a similar asset exchange is an application of *accounting conservatism* in measuring and recording asset values.

[continued from previous page]

> **11.** A company acquires equipment on January 10, 2002, at a cost of $42,000. Straight-line depreciation is used with a five-year life and $7,000 salvage value. On June 27, 2003, the company sells this equipment for $32,000. Prepare the entry(ies) for June 27, 2003.
>
> **12.** A company trades an old Web server for a new one. The cost of the old server is $30,000, and its accumulated depreciation at the time of the trade is $23,400. The new server has a cash price of $45,000. Prepare entries to record the trade under two different assumptions: the company receives a trade-in allowance of (a) $3,000 and (b) $7,000.

Answers—p. 465

Section 2— Natural Resources

 Account for natural resource assets and their depletion.

Natural resources are assets that are physically consumed when used. Examples are standing timber, mineral deposits, and oil and gas fields. Because they are consumed when used, they are often called *wasting assets*. These assets represent soon-to-be inventories of raw materials that will be converted into one or more products by cutting, mining, or pumping. Until that conversion takes place, they are noncurrent assets and are shown in a balance sheet using titles such as timberlands, mineral deposits, or oil reserves. Natural resources are reported under either plant assets or its own separate category. **Alcoa**, for instance, reports its natural resources under the balance sheet title *Properties, plants and equipment*. In a note to its financial statements, Alcoa reports a separate amount for *Land and land rights, including mines*. **Weyerhaeuser**, on the other hand, reports its huge timber holdings in a separate balance sheet category titled *Timber and timberlands*.

Acquisition Cost and Depletion

Natural resources are recorded at cost, which includes all expenditures necessary to acquire the resource and prepare it for its intended use. **Depletion** is the process of allocating the cost of a natural resource to the period when it is consumed, known as the resource's *useful life*. Natural resources are reported on the balance sheet at cost less *accumulated depletion*. The depletion expense per period is usually based on units extracted from cutting, mining, or pumping. This is similar to units-of-production depreciation. **Exxon Mobil** uses this approach to amortize the costs of discovering and operating its oil wells.

To illustrate depletion of natural resources, let's consider a mineral deposit with an estimated 500,000 tons of available ore. It is purchased for $500,000, and we expect zero salvage value. The depletion charge per ton of ore mined is $1, computed as $500,000 ÷ 500,000 tons. If 85,000 tons are mined and sold in the first year, the depletion charge for that year is $85,000. These computations are detailed in Exhibit 11.18.

Exhibit 11.18

Depletion Formula and Computations

Step 1

$$\text{Depletion per unit} = \frac{\text{Cost} - \text{Salvage value}}{\text{Total units of capacity}} = \frac{\$500,000 - \$0}{500,000 \text{ tons}} = \$1 \text{ per ton}$$

Step 2

$$\text{Depletion expense} = \text{Depletion per unit} \times \text{Units extracted in period}$$

$$= \$1 \times 85,000 = \$85,000$$

Depletion expense for the period is recorded as follows:

Assets = Liabilities + Equity
−85,000   −85,000

Dec. 31	Depletion Expense—Mineral Deposit	85,000	
	Accumulated Depletion—Mineral Deposit . .		85,000
	To record depletion of the mineral deposit.		

The period-end balance sheet reports the mineral deposit as shown in Exhibit 11.19.

Mineral deposit	$500,000	
Less accumulated depletion	**85,000**	$415,000

Exhibit 11.19

Balance Sheet Presentation of Natural Resources

Since all 85,000 tons of the mined ore are sold during the year, the entire $85,000 of depletion is reported on the income statement. If some of the ore remains unsold at year-end, however, the depletion related to the unsold ore is carried forward on the balance sheet and reported as Ore Inventory, a current asset.

Plant Assets Used in Extracting Resources

The conversion of natural resources by mining, cutting, or pumping usually requires machinery, equipment, and buildings. When the usefulness of these plant assets is directly related to the depletion of a natural resource, their costs are depreciated over the useful life of the natural resource in proportion to its depletion. This means depreciation is computed using the units-of-production method. For example, if a machine is permanently installed in a mine and 10% of the its ore is mined and sold in the period, then 10% of the machine's cost (less any salvage value) is allocated to depreciation expense. The same procedure is used when a machine is abandoned once resources are extracted. On the other hand, if a machine will be moved to and used at another site when extraction is complete, the machine is depreciated over its useful life.

Section 3— Intangible Assets

Intangible assets are long-term rights, privileges, or competitive advantages that belong to the owner of such nonphysical assets used in operations. Examples are patents, copyrights, licenses, leaseholds, franchises, goodwill, and trademarks. Lack of physical substance is not sufficient for an asset to be an intangible. Notes and accounts receivable, for instance, lack physical substance, but they are not intangibles. This section identifies the more common types of intangible assets and explains the accounting for them.

P6 Account for intangible assets and their amortization.

Accounting for Intangible Assets

Accounting for intangible assets is similar to that for plant assets. An intangible asset is recorded at cost when purchased. Its cost must be systematically allocated to expense over its estimated useful life through the process of **amortization.** The amortization period for an intangible asset must be 40 years or less. The eventual disposal of an intangible asset involves removing its book value, recording any other asset(s) received or given up, and recognizing any gain or loss for the difference.

Amortization of intangible assets is similar to depreciation of plant assets and the depletion of natural resources in that it is a process of cost allocation. However, only the straight-line method is used for amortizing intangibles *unless* the company can show that another method is preferred. Another difference is that although the effects of depreciation and depletion are recorded in a contra account (Accumulated Depreciation or Accumulated Depletion), amortization is usually credited directly to the intangible asset account. This means the original cost of intangible assets is rarely reported on the balance sheet. Instead, only the net amount of unamortized cost (its book value) is reported.

Some intangibles have limited useful lives due to laws, contracts, or other asset characteristics. Examples are patents, copyrights, and leaseholds. Other intangibles such as goodwill, trademarks, and trade names have useful lives that cannot be easily determined. The cost of intangible assets is amortized over the periods expected to benefit by their use, but in no case can this period be longer than the asset's legal existence or longer than 40 years even when the life of an asset (for example, goodwill) can continue indefinitely into the future.

Intangible assets are often shown in a separate section of the balance sheet immediately after plant assets. **Callaway Golf**, for instance, follows this approach in reporting more than

Point: The cost to acquire a Web site address is an intangible asset.

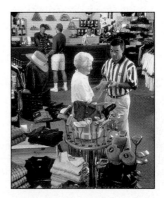

Global: Japan permits recording the costs of both externally purchased and internally developed intangible assets.

$100 million of *intangible assets* in its recent balance sheet. Companies usually disclose the amortization periods they apply to intangibles. **Corning**'s annual report, for instance, says it amortizes intangible assets over a maximum of 15 years except for goodwill, which it amortizes over 40 years. The remainder of our discussion focuses on accounting for specific types of intangible assets.

Patents

The federal government grants patents to encourage the invention of new technology, mechanical devices, and production processes. A **patent** is an exclusive right granted to its owner to manufacture and sell a patented item, or to use a process for 17 years. When patent rights are purchased, the cost to acquire the rights is debited to an account called *Patents.* If the owner engages in lawsuits to successfully defend a patent, the cost of lawsuits is debited to the Patents account. However, the costs of research and development leading to a new patent are expensed when incurred.

A patent gives its owner exclusive rights to it for 17 years, but its cost is amortized over its estimated useful life (not to exceed 17 years). If we purchase a patent costing $25,000 with a useful life of 10 years, we make the following adjusting entry at the end of each of the 10 years to amortize one-tenth of its cost:

Did You Know?

Drug War   Mention "drug war" and most people think of fighting cocaine or heroin use. But another drug war is under way: Brand-name drugmakers are fighting to stop generic copies of their products from hitting the market once their patents expire. Successfully delaying a generic rival can mean hundreds of millions of dollars in extra sales.

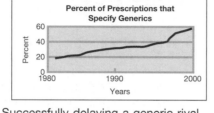

Percent of Prescriptions that Specify Generics

Assets = Liabilities + Equity
−2,500   −2,500

Dec. 31	Amortization Expense—Patents	2,500	
	Patents		2,500
	To amortize patent costs over its useful life.		

The $2,500 debit to Amortization Expense appears on the income statement as a cost of the product or service provided under protection of the patent. This entry uses the common practice of crediting the Patents account rather than using a contra account.

Copyrights

A **copyright** gives its owner the exclusive right to publish and sell a musical, literary, or artistic work during the life of the creator plus 50 years, although the useful life of most copyrights is much shorter. The costs of a copyright are amortized over its useful life. The only identifiable cost of many copyrights is the fee paid to the Copyright Office of the federal government or international agency granting the copyright. If this fee is immaterial, it is charged directly to an expense account, but if the identifiable costs of a copyright are material, they are capitalized (recorded in an asset account) and periodically amortized by debiting an account called *Amortization Expense—Copyrights.*

Did You Know?

Go PHISH!   MP3 allows users to download and upload full-length, CD-quality sound recordings. Popular groups and individual artists, such as PHISH, Pearl Jam, Van Halen, and Madonna have found their songs freely circulating on the Web months before their official release. The industry now uses an automated Web crawler to electronically scan for online pirates.

Leaseholds

Property is rented under a contract called a **lease.** The property's owner, called the **lessor,** grants the lease. The one who secures the right to possess and use the property is called the **lessee. A leasehold** refers to the rights the lessor grant to the lessee under the terms of the lease. A leasehold is an intangible asset for the lessee.

Point: A leasehold implies existence of future benefits that the lessee controls because of a prepayment. It also meets the definition of an asset.

Certain leases require no advance payment from the lessee but require monthly rent payments. In this case, we do not set up a Leasehold account. Instead, the monthly payments are debited to a Rent Expense account. If a long-term lease requires the lessee to pay the final period's rent in advance when the lease is signed, the lessee records this advance payment with a debit to a leasehold account. Because the advance payment is not used until the final period, the Leasehold account balance remains intact until that time. Then its balance is transferred to Rent Expense.[2]

A long-term lease can increase in value when current rental rates for similar property rise while the required payments under the lease remain constant. This increase in value of a lease is not reported on the lessee's balance sheet since no extra cost is incurred to acquire it. However, if the property is subleased and the new tenant makes a cash payment to the original lessee for the rights under the old lease, the new tenant debits this payment to a Leasehold account. The balance of this Leasehold account is amortized to Rent Expense of the new tenant over the remaining life of the lease.

Point: Capital leases are recorded by the lessee similar to a purchase; see Chapter 12.

To illustrate how the changing value of a lease can affect business decisions, consider **La Côte Basque**, a historic restaurant in New York. A few years ago, it sold the two years remaining on its lease to **Walt Disney Company**. La Côte Basque already knew it could not renew the lease when it expired because Disney had negotiated a long-term lease of the property with the building owner, **Coca-Cola Company**. La Côte Basque had been operating in this location for 36 years but could not compete with Disney's offer. The restaurant sold the remainder of its lease for a sizable amount and relocated earlier than required.

Leasehold Improvements

Long-term leases sometimes require the lessee to pay for alterations or improvements to the leased property such as partitions, painting, and storefronts. These alterations and improvements are called **leasehold improvements,** and their costs are debited to a *Leasehold Improvements* account. Since leasehold improvements become part of the property and revert to the lessor at the end of the lease, the lessee amortizes these costs over the life of the lease or the life of the improvements, whichever is shorter. The amortization entry debits Rent Expense and credits Leasehold Improvements.

Did You Know?

Employee Assets Be nice to your employees says a recent study. Focusing on entrepreneurs who make accommodations to employees, the study confirms such employees are more productive and loyal and work to solve problems. One entrepreneur even lists employees' personal appointments on the company calendar so everyone can plan around those dates.

Franchises and Licenses

Franchises and **licenses** are rights that a company or government grants an entity to deliver a product or service under specified conditions. Many organizations, including **McDonald's, Pizza Hut**, **Major League Baseball**, and professional football and basketball, grant franchise and license rights. The costs of franchises and licenses are debited to a *Franchises and Licenses* asset account and are amortized over the lives of the agreements, not to exceed 40 years.

Did You Know?

Logo Hold The **World Wrestling Federation** (WWF) licenses its mark and logo on thousands of retail products, including toys, video games, and apparel. Its licensing agreements yield it a percent of revenues; license revenues totaled more than $600 million this past year.

Goodwill

Goodwill has a specific meaning in accounting. **Goodwill** is the amount by which a company's value exceeds the value of its individual assets and liabilities. This usually implies that the company as a whole has certain valuable attributes not measured among its individual assets and liabilities. These can include superior management, skilled work force, good supplier or customer relations, quality products or services, good location, or other competitive advantages.

Point: IBM's balance sheet includes an item called *Investments and Sundry Assets*. A note to this item reports that it includes more than $1 billion of goodwill.

Point: Accounting for goodwill is different for financial accounting and tax accounting. The IRS requires the amortization of goodwill over a period not to exceed 15 years.

---

[2] Some long-term leases give the lessee essentially the same rights as a purchaser. This results in tangible assets and liabilities reported by the lessee. Chapter 12 describes these so-called *capital leases.*

Goodwill Illustration

Conceptually, a company has goodwill when its expected future income is greater than the normal income for its industry (competitors). To illustrate, consider the information in Exhibit 11.20 for two competing companies (Z2 and Burton) of roughly equal size in the snowboard industry.

Exhibit 11.20

Data for Goodwill Illustration

	Z2	Burton
Net assets* (excluding goodwill)	$190,000	$190,000
Normal return on net assets in the industry	10%	10%
Normal net income	$ 19,000	$ 19,000
Expected net income	24,000	19,000
Expected net income above normal	**$ 5,000**	**$ 0**

* Net assets (also called *equity*) equal total assets minus total liabilities.

The expected net income for Z2 is $24,000. This is $5,000 higher than the $19,000 industry norm based on the 10% return on net assets (equity) for its competitors. This implies that Z2 has goodwill that yields above normal net income. In contrast, Burton's expected income of $19,000 equals the norm for this industry. This implies zero goodwill for Burton. For Z2, it implies we are willing to pay more than just the value of its net assets—specifically, to acquire its goodwill asset.

In accounting, goodwill is usually recorded only when an entire company or business segment is purchased. The buyer and seller can estimate goodwill in more than one way. For instance, how do we value Z2's $5,000 per year above normal net income? One method is to value goodwill at some *multiple* of above normal net income. If we choose a multiple of 6, our goodwill estimate for Z2 is 6 times $5,000 (or $30,000). Another method is to assume the $5,000 above normal net income continues indefinitely (often called *capitalizing*). This is like an *annuity*. For example, if we assume a 16% discount (interest) rate, the goodwill estimate is $5,000/16%, or $31,250. Whatever method we choose, the value of goodwill is confirmed only by the price the seller is willing to accept and the buyer is willing to pay.

Global: In some countries, including the United Kingdom, the entire cost of goodwill can be charged against equity and, therefore, does not affect current or future earnings.

Accounting for Goodwill

Global: International accounting standards call for charging goodwill against income. The amortization period suggested is 5 or fewer years unless a longer period (up to 20 years) is justified.

To keep accounting information from being too subjective, goodwill is not recorded unless it is purchased. Purchased goodwill is measured by taking the purchase price of the company and subtracting the market value of its individual net assets (excluding goodwill). Goodwill is a major part of many company purchases. For instance, **Yahoo!** paid nearly $3.0 billion in stock and options to acquire **GeoCities**; where about $2.8 of the $3.0 billion was for goodwill and other intangibles.

Goodwill is amortized on a straight-line basis over its estimated useful life just as other intangible assets are. Since estimating the useful life of goodwill is difficult, estimates range widely. Exhibit 11.21 shows results from a recent survey on the goodwill amortization period. The most common amortization period is 40 years. If we assume that most companies that report "not exceeding 40" actually use 40 years, then nearly 60% of companies appear to choose the longest amortization period permitted. This is not surprising because it allows companies to spread goodwill costs over more years.

Exhibit 11.21

Goodwill Amortization Period

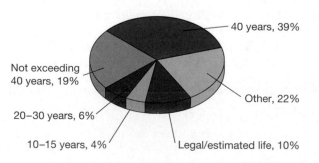

40 years, 39%
Not exceeding 40 years, 19%
20–30 years, 6%
10–15 years, 4%
Legal/estimated life, 10%
Other, 22%

Trademarks and Trade Names

Companies often adopt unique symbols or select unique names and brands in marketing their products. A **trademark** or **trade (brand) name** is a symbol, name, phrase, or jingle identified with a company, product, or service. Examples are Nike swoosh, Marlboro Man, Big Mac, Coca-Cola, and Corvette. Ownership and exclusive right to use a trademark or trade name is often established by showing that one company used it before another. Ownership is best established by registering a trademark or trade name with the government's Patent Office. The cost of developing, maintaining, or enhancing the value of a trademark or trade name (such as advertising) is charged to expense when incurred. If a trademark or trade name is purchased, however, its cost is debited to an asset account and then amortized.

Did You Know?

What's in a Name?   When it comes to branding, nobody does it better than **Nike**. Its swoosh is one of the world's best-known trademarks. It has helped Nike pump out sales and earnings growth exceeding its competitors. Equally impressive is the brand identity that the "**Intel Inside**" campaign created for a product that consumers never see and few understand.

Quick Check

13. Give an example of both a natural resource and an intangible asset.

14. A company pays $650,000 for an ore deposit. The deposit is estimated to have 325,000 tons of ore that will be mined over the next 10 years. During the first year, it mined, processed, and sold 91,000 tons. What is that year's depletion expense?

15. On January 6, 2002, a company pays $120,000 for a patent with a 17-year legal life to produce a toy expected to be marketable for three years. Prepare entries to record its acquisition and the December 31, 2002, adjustment.

Answers—p. 465

Most long-term asset acquisitions and disposals impact the statement of cash flows. Cash acquisitions of long-term assets are reported in the investing section of the statement of cash flows. Most acquisitions are an immediate *use* of cash, and the amount paid at acquisition is deducted in the statement. **Nike**, for instance, reports the following under investing activities in its statement of cash flows in Appendix A: "Additions to property, plant and equipment ($ millions) . . . $(419.9)."

Disposals of long-term assets usually create an immediate receipt of cash. When they do, they are reported as a *source* of cash (an addition) in the investing section of the statement of cash flows. Nike reports its disposals in Appendix A as follows: "Disposals of property, plant and equipment ($ millions) . . . $ 25.3." Note that a gain or loss from an asset disposal is the difference between an asset's book value and the value received. Neither reflects any cash flows. Depreciation and amortization also do *not* yield cash flows.

Cash Flow Impacts of Long-Term Assets

C4 Identify cash flow impacts of long-term asset transactions.

Total Asset Turnover

A company's assets are important in determining its ability to generate sales and earn income. Managers devote much attention to deciding what assets a company acquires, how much it invests in assets, and how to use assets most efficiently and effectively. One important measure of a company's ability to use its assets is **total asset turnover.** The formula for total asset turnover is in Exhibit 11.22.

A2 Compute total asset turnover and apply it to analyze a company's use of assets.

$$\text{Total asset turnover} = \frac{\text{Net sales}}{\text{Average total assets}}$$

Exhibit 11.22

Total Asset Turnover

Total asset turnover can be computed for any type of company, including manufacturing, merchandising, and service companies. The numerator, net sales, reflects amounts earned from the sale of products and services. The denominator, average total assets, reflects the total resources devoted to operating the company.

To illustrate, let's look at total asset turnover for two competing companies: **Coors** and **Anheuser-Busch**. Exhibit 11.23 reports total asset turnover for these two companies.

Exhibit 11.23

Analysis Using Total Asset Turnover

Company	($ in millions)	1999	1998	1997
Coors	Net sales	$ 2,057	$ 1,900	$ 1,821
	Total assets	$ 1,546	$ 1,461	$ 1,412
	Total asset turnover	1.37	1.32	1.31
Anheuser-Busch	Net sales	$11,704	$11,246	$11,066
	Total assets	$12,640	$12,484	$11,727
	Total asset turnover	0.93	0.93	1.00

To show how we compute and use total asset turnover, let's look at the numbers for Coors. We compute Coors's 1999 total asset turnover as follows: $2,057/[($1,546 + $1,461)/2] = 1.37. We express Coors's use of assets in generating net sales by saying "it turned its assets over 1.37 times during the year." This means that each $1.00 of assets produced $1.37 of net sales for the year. Is a total asset turnover of 1.37 good or bad? It is safe to say that all companies desire a high total asset turnover. Like many ratio analyses, however, a company's total asset turnover must be interpreted in comparison with that of prior years and of its competitors. Interpreting the total asset turnover also requires an understanding of the company's operations. Some operations are capital intensive, meaning a relatively large amount is invested in assets to generate sales. This suggests a relatively lower total asset turnover. Other companies' operations are labor intensive, meaning they generate sales more by the efforts of people than the use of assets. In that case, we expect a higher total asset turnover.[3] Coors's turnover has been steady over the past three years and is superior to that for Anheuser-Busch. Total asset turnover for Coors's competitors, available in industry publications such as Dun & Bradstreet, is generally in the range of 1.0 to 1.1 over this same period. Overall, Coors appears to be competitive and doing slightly better than its competitors on total asset turnover.

You Make the Call

Environmentalist   A paper manufacturer claims it cannot afford more environmental controls. It points to its low total asset turnover of 1.9 and argues that it cannot compete with companies whose total asset turnover is much higher. Examples cited are food stores (5.5) and auto dealers (3.8). How do you respond?

Answer—p. 464

Demonstration Problem

On July 14, 2002, Tulsa Company pays $600,000 to acquire a fully equipped factory. The purchase involves the following assets:

Asset	Appraised Value	Salvage Value	Useful Life	Depreciation Method
Land	$160,000			Not depreciated
Land improvements	80,000	$ 0	10 years	Straight-line
Building	320,000	100,000	10 years	Double-declining-balance
Machinery	240,000	20,000	10,000 units	Units-of-production*
Total	$800,000			

* The machinery is used to produce 700 units in 2002 and 1,800 units in 2003.

---

[3] There is a relation between total asset turnover and profit margin. Companies with low total asset turnover require higher profit margins (examples are hotels and real estate); companies with high total asset turnover can succeed with lower profit margins (examples are food stores and toy merchandisers).

Required

1. Allocate the total $600,000 purchase cost among the separate assets.

2. Compute the 2002 (six months) and 2003 depreciation expense for each asset and compute total depreciation expense for both years.

3. On the first day of 2004, Tulsa exchanged the machinery that was acquired on July 14, 2002, and $5,000 cash for similar machinery with a $210,000 market value. Journalize the exchange of these similar assets.

4. On the last day of calendar year 2004, Tulsa discarded machinery that had been on its books for five years. The machinery's original cost is $12,000 (estimated life of five years) and its salvage value is $2,000. No depreciation had been recorded for the fifth year when the disposal occurred. Journalize the fifth year of depreciation (straight-line method) and the asset's disposal.

5. At the beginning of year 2004, Tulsa purchased with cash a patent for $100,000. The company estimated the patent's useful life to be 10 years. Journalize the patent acquisition and its amortization for the year 2004.

6. Late in the year 2004, Tulsa acquired an ore deposit for $600,000 cash. It added roads and shafts for an additional cost of $80,000. Salvage value of the mine is estimated to be $20,000. The company estimated 330,000 tons of available ore. In year 2004, Tulsa mined and sold 10,000 tons of ore. Journalize the mine's acquisition and its first year's depletion.

Planning the Solution

• Complete a three-column schedule showing these amounts for each asset: appraised value, percent of total value, and apportioned cost.

• Using allocated costs, compute depreciation for 2002 (only one-half year) and 2003 (full year) for each asset. Summarize those computations in a table showing total depreciation for each year.

• Remember that gains on exchanges of similar assets are not recognized. Make a journal entry to add the acquired machinery to the books and to remove the old machinery, along with its accumulated depreciation, and the cash given in the exchange.

• Remember that depreciation must be recorded up to date before discarding an asset. Calculate and record depreciation expense for the fifth year using the straight-line method. Since salvage value is not received at the end of a discarded asset's life, the amount of any salvage value becomes a loss on disposal. Record the loss on the disposal as well as the removal of the discarded asset and its related accumulated depreciation.

• Record the patent (an intangible asset) at its purchase price. Use straight-line amortization over its useful life to calculate amortization expense. Remember that no accumulated amortization account is used. Instead, the intangible asset account is credited directly.

• Record the ore deposit (a natural resource asset) at its cost, including any added costs to ready the mine for use. Calculate depletion per ton using the depletion formula. Multiply the depletion per ton by the amount of tons mined and sold this year to calculate depletion expense for the year.

Solution to Demonstration Problem

1. Allocation of the total cost of $600,000 among the separate assets:

Asset	Appraised Value	Percent of Total Value	Apportioned Cost
Land	$160,000	20%	**$120,000** ($600,000 × 20%)
Land improvements	80,000	10	**60,000** ($600,000 × 10%)
Building	320,000	40	**240,000** ($600,000 × 40%)
Machinery	240,000	30	**180,000** ($600,000 × 30%)
Total	$800,000	100%	$600,000

2. Depreciation for each asset. (*Note:* Land is not depreciated.)

Land Improvements

Cost	$ 60,000
Salvage value	0
Depreciable cost	$ 60,000
Useful life	10 years
Annual depreciation expense ($60,000/10 years)	$ 6,000
2002 depreciation ($6,000 × 6/12)	**$ 3,000**
2003 depreciation	**$ 6,000**

Building

Straight-line rate = 100%/10 years = 10%
Double-declining-balance rate = 10% × 2 = 20%

2002 depreciation ($240,000 × 20% × 6/12)	**$ 24,000**
2003 depreciation [($240,000 − $24,000) × 20%]	**$ 43,200**

Machinery

Cost	$180,000
Salvage value	20,000
Depreciable cost	$160,000
Total expected units of production	10,000 units
Depreciation per unit ($160,000/10,000 units)	$ 16
2002 depreciation ($16 × 700 units)	**$ 11,200**
2003 depreciation ($16 × 1,800 units)	**$ 28,800**

Total depreciation expense:

	2002	2003
Land improvements	$ 3,000	$ 6,000
Building	24,000	43,200
Machinery	11,200	28,800
Total	$38,200	$78,000

3. Record the exchange of similar assets (machinery) with a gain on the exchange: The book value on the exchange date is $180,000 (cost) − $40,000 (accumulated depreciation). The book value of the machinery given up in the exchange ($140,000) plus the $5,000 cash paid is less than the $210,000 value of the machine acquired. The entry to record this exchange of similar assets does not recognize the $65,000 gain on exchange:

Machinery (new)	145,000*	
Accumulated Depreciation—Machinery (old)	40,000	
Machinery (old)		180,000
Cash		5,000
To record exchange of similar assets.		

* Fair market value of acquired asset of $210,000 minus $65,000 gain.

4. Record the depreciation up to date on the discarded asset:

Depreciation Expense—Equipment	2,000	
Accumulated Depreciation—Equipment		2,000
To record depreciation of date of disposal: ($12,000 − $2,000)/5		

Record the removal of the discarded asset and its loss on disposal:

Accumulated Depreciation—Machinery	10,000	
Loss on Disposal of Machinery	2,000	
Machinery		12,000
To record the discarding of machinery with a $2,000 book value.		

5.

Patent	100,000	
Cash		100,000
To record patent acquisition.		

Amortization Expense—Patent	10,000	
Patent		10,000
To record amortization expense: $100,000/10 years = $10,000.		

6.

Ore Deposit	680,000	
Cash		680,000
To record ore deposit acquisition and its related costs.		

Depletion Expense—Ore Deposit	20,000	
Accumulated Depletion—Ore Deposit		20,000
To record depletion expense: ($680,000 – $20,000)/330,000 tons = *$2 per ton. 10,000 tons mined and sold × $2 = $20,000 depletion.*		

Summary

C1 Describe plant assets and issues in accounting for them. Plant assets are tangible assets used in the operations of a company that have a useful life of more than one accounting period. Plant assets are set apart from other tangible assets by two important features: use in operations and useful lives longer than one period. The four main accounting issues with plant assets are (1) computing their costs, (2) allocating their costs to the periods they benefit, (3) accounting for subsequent expenditures, and (4) recording their disposal.

C2 Explain depreciation and the factors affecting its computation. Depreciation is the process of allocating to expense the cost of a plant asset over the accounting periods that benefit from its use. Depreciation does not measure the decline in a plant asset's market value or its physical deterioration. Three factors determine depreciation: cost, salvage value, and useful life. Salvage value is an estimate of the asset's value at the end of its benefit period. Useful (service) life is the length of time an asset is productively used.

C3 Explain depreciation for partial years and changes in estimates. Partial year depreciation is often required because assets are bought and sold throughout the year. Depreciation is revised when changes in estimates such as salvage value and useful life occur. If the useful life of a plant asset changes, for instance, the remaining cost to be depreciated is spread over the remaining (revised) useful life of the asset.

C4 Identify cash flow impacts of long-term asset transactions. Acquisition and disposal of long-term assets for cash impact the investing section of the statement of cash flows. Acquisitions are a use of cash; disposals are a source of cash.

A1 Compare and analyze depreciation for different methods. The amount of depreciation expense per period is usually different for different methods, yet total depreciation expense over an asset's life is the same for all methods. Each method starts with the same total cost and ends with the same salvage value. The difference is in the pattern of depreciation expense over the asset's life. Common methods are straight-line, double-declining-balance, and units-of-production.

A2 Compute total asset turnover and apply it to analyze a company's use of assets. Total asset turnover measures a company's ability to use its assets to generate sales. Total asset turnover is defined as net sales divided by average total assets. While all companies desire a high total asset turnover, it must be interpreted in comparison with that for prior years and its competitors.

P1 Apply the cost principle to compute the cost of plant assets. Plant assets are recorded at cost when purchased. Cost includes all normal and reasonable expenditures necessary to get the asset in place and ready for its intended use. The cost of a lump-sum purchase is allocated among its individual assets.

P2 **Compute and record depreciation using the straight-line, units-of-production, and declining-balance methods.** The straight-line method divides cost less salvage value by the asset's useful life to determine depreciation expense per period. The units-of-production method divides cost less salvage value by the estimated number of units the asset will produce over its life to determine depreciation per unit. The declining-balance method multiplies the asset's book value by a factor that is usually double the straight-line rate.

P3 **Distinguish between revenue and capital expenditures, and account for these expenditures.** Revenue expenditures expire in the current period and are debited to expense accounts and matched with current revenues. Ordinary repairs are an example of revenue expenditures. Capital expenditures benefit future periods and are debited to asset accounts. Examples of capital expenditures are extraordinary repairs and betterments.

P4 **Account for asset disposal through discarding, selling, or exchanging an asset.** When a plant asset is discarded, sold, or exchanged, its cost and accumulated depreciation are removed from the accounts. Any cash proceeds from discarding or selling an asset are recorded and compared to the asset's book value to determine gain or loss. When similar assets are exchanged, losses are recognized but gains are not. When gains are not recognized, the new asset account is debited for the book value of the old asset plus any cash paid.

P5 **Account for natural resource assets and their depletion.** The cost of a natural resource is recorded in a noncurrent asset account. Depletion of a natural resource is recorded by allocating its cost to depletion expense using the units-of-production method. Depletion is credited to an Accumulated Depletion account.

P6 **Account for intangible assets and their amortization.** An intangible asset is recorded at the cost incurred to purchase it. The cost of an intangible asset is allocated to expense using the straight-line method and is called *amortization*. Amortization is recorded with a credit directly to the asset account. Intangible assets include patents, copyrights, leaseholds, goodwill, and trademarks.

Guidance Answers to **You Make the Call**

Controller You might tell the president of your concern that the longer estimate does not seem realistic in light of past experience. You might ask if the change implies a new replacement plan. Depending on the president's response, such a conversation might eliminate your concern. It is possible the president's instruction reflects an honest and reasonable prediction of the future. Since the company is struggling financially, the president may have concluded the normal pattern of replacing assets every three years cannot continue. Perhaps the strategy is to avoid costs of frequent replacements and stretch use of the equipment a few years longer until financial conditions improve. You should consider the possibility the president has a more complete understanding of the situation and honestly believes a six-year life is a good estimate. On the downside, you may be correct in suspecting the president is acting unethically. If you conclude the president's decision is unethical, you might confront the president with your opinion that it is unethical to change the estimate to increase income. Another possibility is to wait and see whether the auditor will insist on not changing the estimate. In either case, you should insist that the statements be based on reasonable estimates.

Entrepreneur Treating an expense as a capital expenditure means reported expenses will be lower and income higher in the short run. This is so because a capital expenditure is not expensed immediately but is spread over the asset's useful life. Treating an expense as a capital expenditure also means asset and equity totals are reported at larger amounts in the short run. This continues until the asset is fully depreciated. Your friend is probably trying to help, but the suggestion hints at unethical behavior. Only an expenditure benefiting future periods is a capital expenditure.

Environmentalist You must point out that the paper manufacturer's comparison of its total asset turnover with food stores and auto dealers is misdirected. Explain that these other industries' turnovers are higher because their profit margins are lower (about 2%). Profit margins for the paper industry are usually 3% to 3.5%. You need to collect data from competitors in the paper industry to show that a 1.9 total asset turnover is about right for this industry. You might also want to collect data on this company's revenues and expenses, along with compensation data for its high-ranking officers and employees.

Guidance Answers to **Quick Checks**

1. **a.** Office supplies—current assets
   b. Office equipment—plant assets
   c. Merchandise—current assets (inventory)
   d. Land for future expansion—long-term investments
   e. Trucks used in operations—plant assets
2. **a.** Land   **b.** Land Improvements
3. $700,000 + $49,000 − $21,000 + $3,500 + $3,000 + $2,500 = $737,000
4. **a.** Straight-line with 7-year life: ($77,000/7) = $11,000
   b. Straight-line with 10-year life: ($77,000/10) = $7,700

5. Depreciation is a process of allocating the cost of plant assets to the accounting periods that benefit from the assets' use.
6. **a.** Book value using straight-line depreciation:
   $96,000 − [($96,000 − $8,000)/5] = $78,400
   b. Book value using units of production:
   $96,000 − [($96,000 − $8,000) × (10,000/100,000)] = $87,200
7. ($3,800 − $200)/3 = $1,200 (original depreciation per year)
   $1,200 × 2 = $2,400 (accumulated depreciation)
   ($3,800 − $2,400)/2 = $700 (revised depreciation)

8.

Machinery	12,000	
Cash		12,000

9. A revenue expenditure benefits only the current period and should be charged to expense in the current period. A capital expenditure yields benefits that extend beyond the end of the current period and should be charged to an asset.

10. A betterment involves modifying an existing plant asset to make it more efficient, usually by replacing part of the asset with an improved or superior part. The cost of a betterment should be debited to the asset's account.

11.

Depreciation Expense	3,500	
Accumulated Depreciation		3,500
Cash	32,000	
Accumulated Depreciation	10,500	
Gain on Sale of Equipment		500
Equipment		42,000

12.

(a) Equipment	45,000	
Loss on Exchange of Assets	3,600	
Accumulated Depreciation, Equip.	23,400	
Equipment		30,000
Cash ($45,000 − $3,000)		42,000

(b) Equipment (reflects $400 unrecog. gain)	44,600	
Accumulated Depreciation, Equip.	23,400	
Equipment		30,000
Cash ($45,000 − $7,000)		38,000

13. Examples of intangibles are patents, copyrights, leaseholds, leasehold improvements, goodwill, trademarks, and licenses. Examples of natural resources are timberlands, mineral deposits, and oil reserves.

14. ($650,000/325,000 tons) × 91,000 tons = $182,000

15.

Jan. 6	Patents	120,000	
	Cash		120,000
Dec. 31	Amortization Expense	40,000*	
	Patents		40,000

* $120,000/3 years = $40,000.

Glossary

Accelerated depreciation method method that produces larger depreciation charges during the early years of an asset's life and smaller charges in its later years. (p. 445).

Amortization process of allocating the cost of an intangible asset to expense over its estimated useful life. (p. 455).

Betterment expenditure to make a plant asset more efficient or productive; also called *improvement*. (p. 450).

Book value total cost of an asset less its accumulated depreciation (or depletion, or amortization). (p. 443).

Capital expenditure additional costs of plant assets that provide material benefits extending beyond the current period; also called *balance sheet expenditure*. (p. 449).

Change in an accounting estimate change in an accounting estimate that results from new information, subsequent developments, better insight, or improved judgment. (p. 448).

Copyright right giving the owner the exclusive privilege to publish and sell musi-cal, literary, or artistic work during the creator's life plus 50 years. (p. 456).

Cost all normal and reasonable expenditures necessary to get a plant asset in place and ready for its intended use. (p. 439).

Declining-balance method method that determines depreciation charge for the period by multiplying a depreciation rate (up to twice the straight-line rate) by the asset's beginning-period book value. (p. 445).

Depletion process of allocating the cost of natural resources to periods when they are consumed. (p. 454).

Depreciation process of allocating the cost of a plant asset to expense in the periods benefiting from its use. (p. 441).

Extraordinary repairs major repairs that extend the useful life of a plant asset beyond prior expectations; treated as a capital expenditure. (p. 450).

Franchises, Licenses privileges granted by a company or government to sell a product or service under specified conditions. (p. 457).

Goodwill amount by which a company's value exceeds the value of its individual assets and liabilities. (p. 457).

Inadequacy condition in which the capacity of plant assets is too small to meet the company's productive demands. (p. 442).

Intangible assets long-term rights, privileges, or competitive advantages that belong to the owner of these nonphysical assets used in operations. (p. 455).

Land improvements assets that increase the benefits of land, have a limited useful life, and are depreciated. (p. 440).

Lease contract specifying the rental of property. (p. 456).

Leasehold rights the lessor grants to the lessee under the terms of a lease. (p. 456).

Leasehold improvements alterations or improvements to leased property such as partitions and storefronts. (p. 457).

Lessee party to a lease who secures the right to possess and use the property from another party (the lessor). (p. 456).

Lessor party to a lease who grants another party (the lessee) the right to possess and use property. (p. 456).

Modified Accelerated Cost Recovery System (MACRS) depreciation system required by federal income tax law. (p. 446).

Natural resources assets physically consumed when used; examples are timber, mineral deposits, and oil and gas fields; also called *wasting assets*. (p. 454).

Obsolescence condition in which, because of new inventions and improvements, a plant asset can no longer be used to produce goods or services with a competitive advantage. (p. 442).

Ordinary repairs repairs to keep a plant asset in normal, good operating condition; treated as a revenue expenditure. (p. 449).

Patent exclusive right granted to its owner to manufacture and sell an item or to use a process for 17 years. (p. 456).

Plant assets tangible assets used in a company's operations that have a useful life of more than one period. (p. 438).

Revenue expenditure expenditure reported on the current income statement as an expense because it does not provide benefits in future periods. (p. 449).

Salvage value estimate of amount to be recovered at the end of an asset's useful life; also called *residual*, or *scrap, value*. (p. 441).

Straight-line depreciation method that allocates an equal portion of the total depreciation for a plant asset (cost minus salvage) to each accounting period in its useful life. (p. 442).

Total asset turnover measure of a company's ability to use its assets to generate sales; computed by dividing net sales by average total assets. (p. 459).

Trademark or **trade (brand) name** symbol, name, phrase, or jingle identified with a company, product, or service. (p. 459).

Units-of-production depreciation method that charges a varying amount to depreciation expense for each period of an asset's useful life depending on its usage. (p. 444).

Useful (or service) life length of time an asset will be productively used in the operations of a business. (p. 441).

Questions

1. What is the general rule for costs included in a plant asset?
2. What characteristics of a plant asset make it different from other assets?
3. What is the balance sheet classification for land that is held for future expansion? Why is such land not classified as a plant asset?
4. What is different between land and land improvements?
5. Why is the Modified Accelerated Cost Recovery System not generally accepted for financial accounting purposes?
6. Does the balance in the Accumulated Depreciation— Machinery account represent funds to replace the machinery when it wears out? If not, what does it represent?
7. What accounting principle justifies charging low-cost plant asset purchases immediately to an expense account?
8. What is the difference between ordinary repairs and extraordinary repairs? How should each be recorded?
9. Identify events that might lead to disposal of a plant asset.
10. What is the process of allocating the cost of natural resources to expense as they are used?
11. What are the characteristics of an intangible asset?
12. Is the declining-balance method an acceptable way to compute depletion of natural resources?

13. What general procedures are followed in accounting for the acquisition and cost allocation of intangible assets?
14. When do we know a company has goodwill? When can goodwill appear in a company's balance sheet?
15. A company buys another business and pays for its goodwill. If the company plans to incur costs each year to maintain the value of the goodwill, must it also amortize goodwill?
16. How does accounting for long-term assets impact the statement of cash flows?
17. How is total asset turnover computed? Why would a financial statement user be interested in total asset turnover?
18. Refer to **Nike**'s balance sheet in Appendix A. **NIKE** What title does Nike use for its plant assets? What is its book value of plant assets as of May 31, 2000, and May 31, 1999?
19. Refer to **Reebok**'s balance sheet in Appendix **Reebok** A. How are Reebok's plant assets and intangibles reported (with amounts) on its 1999 balance sheet?
20. Refer to the January 29, 2000, balance sheet of **Gap** in Appendix A. What long-term assets discussed in this chapter are reported?

QUICK STUDY

QS 11-1
Cost of plant assets **C1**

U-Bowl installs automatic score-keeping equipment with an invoice price of $190,000. The electrical work required for the installation costs $20,000. Additional costs are $4,000 for delivery and $13,700 for sales tax. During the installation, a component of the equipment is carelessly left on a lane and hit by the automatic lane-cleaning machine. The cost of repairing the component is $1,850. What is the recorded cost of the automatic score-keeping equipment?

QS 11-2
Depreciation methods **P2**

On January 2, 2002, Young Country acquires sound equipment for concert performances at a cost of $65,800. The band estimates it will use this equipment for four years, during which time it anticipates performing about 200 concerts. It estimates at that point it can sell the equipment for $2,000. During year 2002, the band performs 45 concerts. Compute the year 2002 depreciation using the (1) straight-line method and (2) units-of-production method.

Identify the main difference between (1) plant assets and current assets, (2) plant assets and inventory, and (3) plant assets and long-term investments.

QS 11-3
Defining assets **C1**

A fleet of refrigerated delivery trucks is acquired on January 5, 2002, at a cost of $830,000 with an estimated useful life of eight years and an estimated salvage value of $75,000. Compute the depreciation expense for the first three years using the double-declining-balance method.

QS 11-4
Double-declining- **P2** balance method

Refer to the facts in QS 11–2. Assume that Young Country chose straight-line depreciation but realizes early in the second year that due to concert bookings beyond expectations, this equipment will last only a total of three years. The salvage value remains unchanged. Compute the revised depreciation for both the second and third years.

QS 11-5
Computing revised depreciation **C3**

For each of the following investing activities, identify whether it is a source (A) or use (B) of cash.
A. Cash provided by investing activities.
B. Cash used by investing activities.
1. _AB_ Purchase of timberland for cash   **3.** _B_ Cash purchase of machinery
2. _BA_ Cash sale of factory warehouse   **4.** _B_ Sale of patents for cash

QS 11-6
Cash impacts from acquisitions and disposals

C4

Fife Co. owns a machine that costs $42,400 with accumulated depreciation of $18,400. Fife exchanges the machine for a similar but newer model that has a market value of $52,000. Record the exchange assuming Fife also paid cash of (1) $30,000 and (2) $22,000.

QS 11-7
Similar asset **P4** exchange

---

1. Classify the following as either a revenue or a capital expenditure:
   a. Completed an addition to an office building for $225,000 cash. _Cap_
   b. Monthly cost of replacement filters on an air conditioning system, $175. _Rev_
   c. Cost of annual tune-ups for delivery trucks, $200 cash per truck. _Rev_
   d. Replaced a compressor for a refrigeration system that extends its useful life by four years, $40,000 cash cost. _Cap_
2. Prepare the journal entries to record items (a) and (d) of part (1).

QS 11-8
Revenue and capital expenditures

P3

Outback Company acquires an ore mine at a cost of $1,400,000. It incurs additional costs of $400,000 to access the mine, which is estimated to hold 1,000,000 tons of ore. The estimated value of the land after the ore is removed is $200,000.
1. Prepare the entry to record the cost of the ore mine.
2. Prepare the year-end adjusting entry if 180,000 tons of ore are mined and sold the first year.

QS 11-9
Natural resources and depletion

P5

Which of the following assets are reported on the balance sheet as intangible assets? Which are reported as natural resources? (a) Oil well, (b) Trademark, (c) Leasehold, (d) Gold mine, (e) Building.

QS 11-10
Classify assets **P6**

On January 4 of this year, Belair Boutique incurs a $105,000 cost to modernize its store. Improvements include new floors, ceilings, wiring, and wall coverings. These improvements are estimated to yield benefits for 10 years. Belair leases its store and has eight years remaining on the lease. Prepare the entry to record both the cost of modernization and the amortization at the end of this year.

QS 11-11
Intangible assets **P6** and amortization

Eastman Company reports the following: net sales of $14,880 million for 2003 and $13,990 million for 2002; end-of-year total assets of $15,869 million for 2003 and $17,819 million for 2002. Compute its total asset turnover for 2003.

QS 11-12
Computing total **A2** asset turnover

EXERCISES

Exercise 11-1
Recording costs of real estate **C1**

Ashgrove Manufacturing purchases a large lot on which an old building is located as part of its plans to build a new plant. The negotiated purchase price for this real estate is $280,000 for the lot plus $110,000 for the old building. The company pays $33,500 to tear down the old building and $47,000 to landscape the lot. It also pays a total of $1,540,000 in construction costs—this amount consists of the cost of the new building and $87,800 for lighting and paving a parking area next to the building. Prepare a single journal entry to record these costs incurred by Ashgrove, all of which are paid in cash.

Exercise 11-2
Cost of plant asset
C1

Bottalico Co. purchases a machine for $12,500, terms 2/10, n/60, FOB shipping point. The seller prepaid the freight charges, $360, adding the amount to the invoice and bringing its total to $12,860. The machine requires special steel mounting and power connections costing $895. Another $475 is paid to assemble the machine and get it into operation. In moving the machine to its steel mounting, $180 in damages occurred. Later, $40 of materials is used in adjusting the machine to produce a satisfactory product. The adjustments are normal for this machine and are not the result of the damages. Compute the cost recorded for this machine. (Assume Bottalico pays for this machine within the cash discount period.)

Exercise 11-3
Lump-sum purchase of plant assets **C1**

Reese Company pays $375,280 for real estate plus $20,100 in closing costs. The real estate consists of land appraised at $156,820; land improvements appraised at $57,540; and a building appraised at $178,300. Allocate the total cost among the three purchased assets and prepare the journal entry to record the purchase.

Exercise 11-4
Depreciation methods
P2

In early January 2002, LabOne purchases computer equipment for $154,000 to use in research and development activities for four years. It will then sell it at a $25,000 estimated salvage value. Prepare schedules showing the depreciation and book values for the four years assuming (1) straight-line and (2) double-declining-balance depreciation.

Exercise 11-5
Depreciation methods
C2

Duce Company installs a computerized manufacturing machine in its factory at a cost of $43,500. The machine's useful life is estimated at 10 years, or 385,000 units of product, with a $5,000 salvage value. During its second year, the machine produces 32,500 units of product. Determine the machine's second-year depreciation under the (1) straight-line, (2) units-of-production, and (3) double-declining-balance methods.

Exercise 11-6
Depreciation methods; partial year depreciation **C3**

On April 1, 2002, Admiral's Backhoe Co. purchases a trencher for $280,000. The machine is expected to last five years and have a salvage value of $40,000. Compute depreciation expense for year 2003 using the (1) straight-line and (2) double-declining-balance methods.

Exercise 11-7
Revising depreciation
C3

Top Notch Fitness Club uses straight-line depreciation for a machine costing $23,860, with an estimated four-year life and a $2,400 salvage value. After two years, Top Notch determines that the machine still has three more years of remaining useful life, after which it will have an estimated $2,000 salvage value. Compute (1) the machine's book value at the end of its second year and (2) the amount of depreciation for each of the final three years given the revised estimates.

Exercise 11-8
Income effects of depreciation methods **A1**

MES Enterprises pays $238,400 for equipment that will last five years and have a $43,600 salvage value. By using the machine in its operations for five years, the company expects to earn $88,500 annually, after deducting all expenses except depreciation. Prepare a schedule showing income before depreciation, depreciation expense, and net income for each year and the total five-year period, assuming (1) straight-line depreciation and (2) double-declining-balance depreciation.

Exercise 11-9
Extraordinary repairs; computations and entries **P3**

Mustang Company owns a building that appears on its prior year's balance sheet at its original $572,000 cost less $429,000 accumulated depreciation. The building is depreciated on a straight-line basis assuming a 20-year life and no salvage value. During the first week in January of the current year, major structural repairs are completed on the building at a $68,350 cost. The repairs extend its useful life for 7 years beyond the 20 years originally estimated.

1. Determine the building's age as of the end of the prior year.
2. Prepare the entry to record the cost of the structural repairs that are paid in cash.
3. Determine the book value of the building immediately after the repairs are recorded.
4. Prepare the entry to record the current year's depreciation.

Archer Company pays $264,000 for equipment expected to last four years and have a $25,000 salvage value. Prepare journal entries to record the following costs related to the equipment:

1. During the second year of the equipment's life, $22,000 cash is paid for a new component expected to increase the equipment's productivity by 10% a year.
2. During the third year, $6,250 cash is paid for normal repairs necessary to keep the equipment in good working order.
3. During the fourth year, $14,870 is paid for repairs expected to increase the useful life of the equipment from four to five years.

Exercise 11-10
Ordinary repairs, extraordinary repairs, and betterments

Blackbelt Construction trades in an old tractor for a new tractor, receiving a $29,000 trade-in allowance and paying the remaining $83,000 in cash. The old tractor cost $96,000, and straight-line accumulated depreciation of $52,500 had been recorded under the assumption that it would last eight years and have a $12,000 salvage value. Answer the following questions:

1. What is the book value of the old tractor at the time of exchange?
2. What is the loss on this similar asset exchange?
3. What amount should be recorded (debited) in the asset account for the new tractor?

Exercise 11-11
Exchanging similar assets

P4

On January 2, 2002, Ritchfield Co. disposes of a machine costing $44,000 with accumulated depreciation of $24,625. Prepare the entries to record the disposal under each of the following separate assumptions:

a. Machine is sold for $18,250 cash.
b. Machine is traded in on a similar but newer machine having a $60,200 cash price. A $25,000 trade-in allowance is received, and the balance is paid in cash.
c. Machine is traded in on a similar but newer machine having a $60,200 cash price. A $15,000 trade-in allowance is received, and the balance is paid in cash.

Exercise 11-12
Recording plant asset disposals

P4

Finesse Co. purchases and installs a machine on January 1, 2002, at a total cost of $105,000. Straight-line depreciation is taken each year for four years assuming a seven-year life and no salvage value. The machine is disposed of on July 1, 2006, during its fifth year of service. Prepare entries to record the partial year's depreciation on July 1, 2006, and to record the disposal under the following separate assumptions: (a) the machine is sold for $45,000 cash, and (b) Finesse receives an insurance settlement of $25,000 resulting from the total destruction of the machine in a fire.

Exercise 11-13
Partial year depreciation; disposal of plant asset

P4

On April 2, 2002, Cascade Mining Co. pays $3,736,250 for an ore deposit containing 1,525,000 tons. The company installs machinery in the mine costing $213,500, with an estimated seven-year life and no salvage value. The machinery will be abandoned when the ore is completely mined. Cascade began mining on May 1, 2002, and mined and sold 166,200 tons of ore during the remaining eight months of 2002. Prepare the December 31, 2002, entries to record both the ore deposit depletion and the mining machinery depreciation. Mining machinery depreciation should be in proportion to the mine's depletion.

Exercise 11-14
Depletion of natural resources

P5

Uptown Gallery purchases the copyright on an oil painting for $418,000 on January 1, 2002. The copyright legally protects its owner for 19 more years. However, the company plans to market and sell prints of the original for only 12 years. Prepare entries to record the purchase of the copyright on January 1, 2002, and its annual amortization on December 31, 2002.

Exercise 11-15
Amortization of intangible assets   P6

Exercise 11-16
Goodwill estimation

P6

Tracey Losh has devoted years to developing a profitable business that earns an attractive return. Losh is now considering selling the business and is attempting to estimate its goodwill. The value of the business's net assets (excluding goodwill) is $537,000, and in a typical year net income is about $90,000. Most businesses of this type are expected to earn a return of about 10% on their net assets. Estimate the value of this business's goodwill for the following separate cases assuming it is (a) equal to 10 times the amount that net income is above normal and (b) computed by capitalizing the amount that net income is above normal at a rate of 8%.

Exercise 11-17
Cash flows related to plant assets

C4

GAP

Refer to the statement of cash flows for **Gap** in Appendix A for the 52 week period ended January 29, 2000, to answer the following:

1. What amount of cash is used to purchase property and equipment?

2. How much depreciation and amortization are recorded?

3. What total amount of net cash is used in investing activities?

4. What amount of cash is used to acquire lease rights?

Exercise 11-18
Evaluating efficient use of assets   A2

Klink Co. reports net sales of $5,865,000 for 2002 and $8,689,000 for 2003. End-of-year balances for total assets are: 2001, $1,686,000; 2002, $1,800,000; and 2003, $1,982,000. Compute Klink's total asset turnover for 2002 and 2003 and comment on its efficiency in using assets.

PROBLEM SET A

Problem 11-1A ✓
Plant asset costs; depreciation methods

C1   C2   C3

A1   P1   P2

G   S

Check   (3) Depreciation, $9,624

Gunner Construction negotiates a lump-sum purchase of several assets from a company that is going out of business. The purchase is completed on January 1, 2002, at a total cash price of $802,000 for a building, land, land improvements, and six vehicles. The estimated market values of the assets are building, $506,000; land, $302,000; land improvements, $28,500; and six vehicles, $124,500. The company's fiscal year ends on December 31.

Required

Preparation Component

1. Prepare a table to allocate the lump-sum purchase price to the separate assets purchased (round percents to whole numbers). Prepare the journal entry to record the purchase.

2. Compute the depreciation expense for year 2002 on the building using the straight-line method, assuming a 15-year life and a $26,000 salvage value.

3. Compute the depreciation expense for year 2002 on the land improvements assuming a five-year life and double-declining-balance depreciation.

Analysis Component

4. Defend or refute this statement: Accelerated depreciation results in payment of less taxes over the asset's life.

Problem 11-2A
Real estate costs; depreciation

C1   C2   C3

P1   P2

S

In January 2002, Moonscapes pays $3,200,000 for a tract of land with two buildings on it. It plans to demolish Building 1 and build a new store in its place. Building 2 will be a company office; it is appraised at $645,000, with a useful life of 20 years and a $60,000 salvage value. A lighted parking lot near Building 1 has improvements (Land Improvements 1) valued at $420,000 and expected to last another 14 years with no salvage value. Without the buildings and improvements, the tract of land is valued at $1,785,000. Moonscapes also incurs the following additional costs:

Cost to demolish Building 1	$ 328,400
Cost of additional landscaping	175,400
Cost to construct new building (Building 3), having a useful life of 25 years and a $392,000 salvage value	2,202,000
Cost of new land improvements (Land Improvements 2) near Building 2 having a 20-year useful life and no salvage value	164,000

Required

1. Prepare a table with the following column headings: Land, Building 2, Building 3, Land Improvements 1, and Land Improvements 2. Allocate the costs incurred by Moonscapes to the appropriate columns and total each column.

2. Prepare a single journal entry to record all the incurred costs assuming they are paid in cash on January 1, 2002.

3. Using the straight-line method, prepare the December 31 adjusting entries to record depreciation for the 12 months of 2002 when these assets were in use.

Check (3) Cr. Accum. depr.—Land Improvements 2, $8,200

Clampett Contractors completed the following transactions and events involving the purchase and operation of equipment in its business:

2002

Jan. 1   Paid $287,600 cash plus $11,504 in sales tax and $1,500 in transportation (FOB shipping point) for a new loader. The loader is estimated to have a four-year life and a $20,604 salvage value. Loader costs are recorded in the Equipment account.

Jan. 3   Paid $4,800 to enclose the cab and install air conditioning in the loader to enable operations under harsher conditions. This increased the estimated salvage value of the loader by another $1,396.

Dec. 31   Recorded annual straight-line depreciation on the loader.

2003

Jan. 1   Paid $5,400 to overhaul the loader's engine, which increased the loader's estimated useful life by two years.

Feb. 17   Paid $820 to repair the loader after the operator backs it into a tree.

Dec. 31   Recorded annual straight-line depreciation on the loader.

Required

Prepare journal entries to record these transactions and events.

Problem 11-3A
Computing and revising depreciation; revenue and capital expenditures

Check Dec. 31, 2003, Dr. Depr. Expense—Equip., $43,591

ACT Company completed the following transactions and events involving its delivery trucks:

2002

Jan. 1   Paid $20,515 cash plus $1,485 in sales tax for a new delivery truck estimated to have a five-year life and a $2,000 salvage value. Delivery truck costs are recorded in the Trucks account.

Dec. 31   Recorded annual straight-line depreciation on the truck.

2003

Dec. 31   Recorded annual straight-line depreciation on the truck. Due to new information obtained earlier in the year, the truck's estimated useful life was changed from five to four years, and the estimated salvage value was increased to $2,500.

2004

Dec. 31   Recorded annual straight-line depreciation on the truck.

Dec. 31   Sold the truck for $5,200 cash.

Required

Prepare journal entries to record these transactions and events.

Problem 11-4A
Computing and revising depreciation; selling plant assets

Check Dec. 31, 2004, Dr. Loss on Sale of Trucks, $2,466

Part 1. A machine costing $257,500 with a four-year life and an estimated $20,000 salvage value is installed in Carlton Company's factory on January 1. The factory manager estimates the machine will produce 475,000 units of product during its life. It actually produces the following units: year 1, 220,000; year 2, 124,600; year 3, 121,800; and year 4, 15,200. The total number of units produced by the end of year 4 exceeds the original estimate—this difference was not predicted. (The machine must not be depreciated below its estimated salvage value.)

Required

Prepare a table with the following column headings:

Year	Straight-Line	Units-of-Production	Double-Declining-Balance

Problem 11-5A
Depreciation methods; disposal of plant asset

Check   Year 4, Units-of-Production
Depreciation, $4,300

Compute depreciation for each year and the total depreciation of all years combined for the machine under each depreciation method.

Part 2. Casablanca purchases a used machine for $178,000 cash on January 2 and readies it for use the next day at a $2,840 cost. It is installed on a new platform costing $1,160. The company predicts the machine will be used for six years and have a $15,000 salvage value. Depreciation is to be charged on a straight-line basis. A full year's depreciation is charged on December 31, the end of the first year of the machine's use. On December 31 of its fifth year in use, it is disposed of.

Required

a. Prepare journal entries to record the machine purchase and cost to ready and install it. Cash is paid for all costs incurred.

b. Prepare journal entries to record depreciation of the machine at December 31 of its first year and at December 31 in the year of its disposal.

Check   (iii) Dr. Loss from Fire,
$12,835

c. Prepare journal entries to record the machine's disposal under each of the following unrelated assumptions: (i) it is sold for $15,000 cash; (ii) it is sold for $50,000 cash; and (iii) it is destroyed in a fire and the insurance company pays $30,000 to settle the loss claim.

Problem 11-6A
Intangible assets and
natural resources

Part 1. On July 1, 2002, Sweetman Company signs a contract to lease space in a building for 15 years. The lease contract calls for annual rental payments of $80,000 on each July 1 throughout the life of the lease, and that the lessee will pay for all additions and improvements to the leased property. On June 20, 2007, Sweetman decides to sublease the space to Kirk & Associates for the remaining 10 years of the lease—Kirk pays $200,000 to Sweetman for the right to sublease and it agrees to assume the obligation to pay the $80,000 annual rent to the building owner beginning July 1, 2007. After taking possession of the leased space, Kirk pays for improving the office portion of the leased space at a $130,000 cost. The improvements are paid for on July 5, 2007 and are estimated to have a useful life equal to the 16 years remaining in the life of the building.

Required

Check   (f) Dr. Rent Expense,
$40,000

Prepare entries for Kirk to record (a) its payment to Sweetman for the right to sublease the building space, (b) its payment of the 2007 annual rent to the building owner, and (c) its payment for the office improvements. Prepare Kirk's year-end adjusting entries required at December 31, 2007, to (d) amortize the $200,000 cost of the sublease, (e) amortize the office improvements, and (f) record rent expense.

Part 2. On July 3 of the current year, Denver Mining Co. pays $4,725,000 for land estimated to contain 5.125 million tons of recoverable ore. It installs machinery costing $400,000 that has a 10-year life and no salvage value and is capable of mining the ore deposit in eight years. The machinery is paid for on July 25, seven days before mining operations begin. The company removes and sells 480,000 tons of ore during its first five months of operations. Depreciation of the machinery is in proportion to the mine's depletion as the machinery will be abandoned after the ore is mined.

Required

Preparation Component

Check   (c) Depletion, $442,560

Prepare entries to record (a) the purchase of the land, (b) the cost and installation of machinery, (c) the first five months' depletion assuming the land has a net salvage value of zero after the ore is mined, and (d) the first five months' depreciation on machinery.

Analysis Component

Describe both the similarities and differences in amortization, depletion, and depreciation.

Rent-A-Way, an equipment rental business, has the following balance sheet on December 31, 2002:

Problem 11-7A
Goodwill estimation
and amortization

Assets		
Cash		$ 87,800
Equipment	$725,300	
Accumulated depreciation—Equipment	303,500	421,800
Buildings	360,000	
Accumulated depreciation—Buildings	160,000	200,000
Land		102,000
Total assets		$811,600
Liabilities and Equity		
Accounts payable		$100,400
Long-term note payable		285,400
J. Reynolds, Capital		425,800
Total liabilities and equity		$811,600

In this industry, normal annual net income averages 20% of equity. Rent-A-Way regularly expects to earn $100,000 annually. The balance sheet amounts are reasonable estimates of market values for both assets (except goodwill) and liabilities. In negotiations to sell the business, Rent-A-Way proposes to measure goodwill by capitalizing the amount of above-normal net income at a rate of 15%. The potential buyer thinks that goodwill should be valued at five times the amount of above-normal net income.

Required

1. Compute the amount of goodwill as proposed by Rent-A-Way.
2. Compute the amount of goodwill as proposed by the potential buyer.
3. The buyer purchases the business for the net asset amount (assets less liabilities) reported on the December 31, 2002, balance sheet plus the amount proposed by Rent-A-Way for goodwill. What is the buyer's purchase price?
4. If the buyer earns $100,000 of net income *before* amortization of goodwill in its first year after acquiring the business under the terms in part (3), and goodwill is amortized over the longest permissible time period, what amount of net income is reported for the first year?
5. What rate of return does the buyer's investment earn for the first year given the facts in parts (3) and (4)?

Check (1) $98,933 and (2) $74,200

Asheville Company negotiates a lump-sum purchase of several assets from a contractor who is relocating. The purchase is completed on January 1, 2002, at a total cash price of $1,720,000 for a building, land, land improvements, and six trucks. The estimated market values of the assets are building, $895,400; land, $430,200; land improvements, $248,200; and six trucks, $203,900. The company's fiscal year ends on December 31.

PROBLEM SET B

Problem 11-1B
Plant asset costs;
depreciation methods

Required

Preparation Component

1. Prepare a table to allocate the lump-sum purchase price to the separate assets purchased (round percents to whole numbers). Prepare the journal entry to record the purchase.
2. Compute the depreciation expense for year 2002 on the building using the straight-line method, assuming a 12-year life and a $120,000 salvage value.
3. Compute the depreciation expense for year 2002 on the land improvements assuming a 10-year life and double-declining-balance depreciation.

Check (3) Depreciation, $48,160

Analysis Component

4. Defend or refute this statement: Accelerated depreciation results in payment of more taxes over the assets life.

In January 2002, BuyTech pays $1,550,000 for a tract of land with two buildings. It plans to demolish Building A and build a new shop in its place. Building B will be a company office; it is appraised at a $489,900 value, with a useful life of 15 years and a $100,000 salvage value. A lighted parking lot near Building B has improvements (Land Improvements B) valued at $127,200 and expected to

Problem 11-2B
Real estate
costs; depreciation

last another six years with no salvage value. Without the buildings and improvements, the tract of land is valued at $802,549. BuyTech also incurs the following additional costs:

Cost to demolish Building A	$ 122,000
Cost of additional landscaping	174,500
Cost to construct new building (Building C), having a useful life of 20 years and a $258,000 salvage value	1,458,000
Cost of new land improvements (Land Improvements C) near building C, having a 10-year useful life and no salvage value	103,500

Required

1. Prepare a table with the following column headings: Land, Building B, Building C, Land Improvements B, and Land Improvements C. Allocate the costs incurred by BuyTech to the appropriate columns and total each column.

2. Prepare a single journal entry to record all incurred costs assuming they are paid in cash on January 1, 2002.

Check (3) Cr. Accum. depr.—Land Improvements C, $10,350

3. Using the straight-line method, prepare the December 31 adjusting entries to record depreciation for the 12 months of 2002 when these assets were in use.

Problem 11-3B

Computing and revising depreciation; revenue and capital expenditures

Pronto Delivery Service completed the following transactions and events involving the purchase and operation of its equipment for its business:

2002

Jan.   1   Paid $25,860 cash plus $1,810 in sales tax for a new delivery van that was estimated to have a five-year life and a $3,670 salvage value. Van costs are recorded in the Equipment account.

Jan.   3   Paid $1,850 to install sorting racks in the van for more accurate and quicker delivery of packages. This increases the estimated salvage value of the van by another $230.

Dec. 31   Recorded annual straight-line depreciation on the van.

2003

Jan.   1   Paid $2,080 to overhaul the van's engine, which increased the van's estimated useful life by two years.

May 10   Paid $800 to repair the van after the driver backed it into a loading dock.

Check Dec. 31, 2003, Dr. Depr. Expense—Equip., $3,763

Dec. 31   Record annual straight-line depreciation on the van.

Required

Prepare journal entries to record these transactions and events.

Problem 11-4B

Computing and revising depreciation; selling plant assets

Precision Instruments completed the following transactions and events involving its machinery:

2002

Jan.   1   Paid $107,800 cash plus $6,470 in sales tax for a new machine. The machine is estimated to have a six-year life and a $10,270 salvage value.

Dec. 31   Recorded annual straight-line depreciation on the machinery.

2003

Dec. 31   Recorded annual straight-line depreciation on the machine. Due to new information obtained earlier in the year, the machine's estimated useful life was changed from six to four years, and the estimated salvage value was increased to $14,100.

2004

Dec. 31   Recorded annual straight-line depreciation on the machine.

Check Dec. 31, 2004, Dr. Loss on Sale of Machine, $16,473

Dec. 31   Sold the machine for $25,240 cash.

Required

Prepare journal entries to record these transactions and events.

Part 1. On January 2, Brodie Co. purchases and installs a new machine costing $324,000 with a five-year life and an estimated $30,000 salvage value. Management estimates the machine will produce 1,470,000 units of product during its life. Actual production of units is as follows: year 1, 355,600; year 2, 320,400; year 3, 317,000; year 4, 342,600; and year 5, 138,500. The total number of units produced by the end of year 5 exceeds the original estimate—this difference was not predicted. (The machine must not be depreciated below its estimated salvage value.)

Problem 11-5B

Depreciation methods; disposal of plant assets

Required

Prepare a table with the following column headings:

Year	Straight-Line	Units-of-Production	Double-Declining-Balance

Compute depreciation for each year and total depreciation of all years combined for the machine under each depreciation method.

Check DDB depreciation, Year 3, $46,656

Part 2. On January 1, Trek purchases a used machine for $150,000 and readies it for use the next day at a cost of $3,510. It is mounted on a new platform costing $4,600. Management estimates the machine will be used for seven years and have an $18,110 salvage value. Depreciation is to be charged on a straight-line basis. A full year's depreciation is charged on December 31 of the first through fifth years of the machine's use. On December 31 of its sixth year of use, the machine is disposed of.

Required

a. Prepare journal entries to record the machine purchase and the cost to ready and install it. Cash is paid for all costs incurred.

b. Prepare journal entries to record depreciation of the machine at December 31 of its first year and at December 31 in the year of its disposal.

c. Prepare journal entries to record the machine's disposal under each of the following unrelated assumptions: (i) it is sold for $28,000 cash; (ii) it is sold for $52,000 cash; and (iii) it is destroyed in a fire and the insurance company pays $25,000 to settle the loss claim.

Check (iii) Dr. Loss from Fire, $13,110

Part 1. On January 1, 2002, Grandview Co. enters into a 12-year lease on a building. The lease contract requires: (1) annual rental payments of $36,000 each Jan. 1 throughout the life of the lease and (2) that the lessee will pay for all additions and improvements to the leased property. On January 1, 2009, Grandview decides to sublease the space to Moberly Co. for the remaining five years of the lease—Moberly pays $40,000 to Grandview for the right to sublease and agrees to assume the obligation to pay the $36,000 annual rent to the building owner beginning Jan. 1, 2009. After taking possession of the leased space, Moberly pays for improving the office portion of the leased space at a $20,000 cost. The improvements are paid for on Jan. 3, 2009, and are estimated to have a useful life equal to the 13 years remaining in the life of the building.

Problem 11-6B

Intangible assets and natural resources

P5 P6 A1

Required

Prepare entries for Moberly to record (a) its payment to Grandview for the right to sublease the building space, (b) its payment of the 2009 annual rent to the building owner, and (c) its payment for the office improvements. Prepare Moberly's year-end adjusting entries required on December 31, 2009, to (d) amortize the $40,000 cost of the sublease, (e) amortize the office improvements, and (f) record rent expense.

Check (e) Dr. Rent Expense, $4,000

Part 2. On February 19 of the current year, Rock Solid Co. pays $5,400,000 for land estimated to contain 4 million tons of recoverable ore. It installs machinery costing $400,000 that has a 16-year life and no salvage value and is capable of mining the ore deposit in 12 years. The machinery is paid for on March 21, 11 days before mining operations begin. The company removes and sells 254,000 tons of ore during its first nine months of operations. Depreciation of the machinery is in proportion to the mine's depletion as the machinery will be abandoned after the ore is mined.

Required

Preparation Component

Prepare entries to record (a) the purchase of the land, (b) the cost and installation of machinery, (c) the first nine months' depletion assuming the land has a net salvage value of zero after the ore is mined, and (d) the first nine months' depreciation on machinery.

Analysis Component

Describe both the similarities and differences in amortization, depletion, and depreciation.

Problem 11-7B
Goodwill estimation
and amortization

P6

Tiki Casual Wear has the following balance sheet on December 31, 2003:

Assets		
Cash		$ 148,700
Merchandise inventory		608,950
Buildings	$ 452,800	
Accumulated depreciation—Buildings	212,800	240,000
Land		185,900
Total assets		$1,183,550
Liabilities and Equity		
Accounts payable		$ 108,520
Long-term note payable		415,975
M. Hepperly, Capital		659,055
Total liabilities and equity		$1,183,550

In this industry, normal annual net income averages 28% of equity. Tiki regularly expects to earn $200,000 annually. The balance sheet amounts are reasonable estimates of market values for both assets (except goodwill) and liabilities. In negotiations to sell the business, Tiki proposes to measure goodwill by capitalizing the amount of above-normal net income at a rate of 10%. The potential buyer believes that goodwill should be valued at eight times the amount of above-normal net income.

Required

1. Compute the amount of goodwill as proposed by Tiki.
2. Compute the amount of goodwill as proposed by the potential buyer.
3. The buyer purchases the business for the net asset amount (assets less liabilities) reported on the December 31, 2003, balance sheet plus the amount proposed by Tiki for goodwill. What is the buyer's purchase price?
4. If the buyer earns $200,000 of net income *before* amortization of goodwill in its first year after acquiring the business under the terms in part (3), and goodwill is amortized over the longest permissible time period, what amount of net income is reported for the first year?
5. What rate of return does the buyer's investment earn for the first year given the facts in parts (3) and (4)?

Beyond the Numbers

**Reporting in
Action**

A1   A2

NIKE

BTN 11-1   Refer to the financial statements for **Nike** in Appendix A to answer the following:

1. What percent of the original cost of Nike's property, plant, and equipment remains to be depreciated as of May 31, 2000, and May 31, 1999? Assume these assets have no salvage value.
2. Over what length(s) of time is Nike amortizing its intangible assets and goodwill?
3. What is the change in total property, plant, and equipment (before accumulated depreciation) for the year ended May 31, 2000? What is the amount of cash provided (used) by investing activities for property, plant, and equipment for the year ended May 31, 2000? What is one possible explanation for the difference between these two amounts?
4. Compute Nike's total asset turnover for the year ended May 31, 2000.

Swoosh Ahead

5. Access **Nike**'s annual report for fiscal years ending after May 31, 2000, at its Web site [**www.nike.com**] or the SEC's EDGAR database [**www.sec.gov**]. Recompute Nike's total asset turnover for the additional years' data you collect. Comment on any differences relative to the turnover computed in part (4).

BTN 11-2   Key comparative figures ($ in millions) for **Nike** and **Reebok** follow:

| Key Figures | Nike | | | Reebok | | |
	Current Year	One Year Prior	Two Years Prior	Current Year	One Year Prior	Two Years Prior
Total assets	$5,856.9	$5,247.7	$5,397.4	$1,564.1	$1,684.6	$1,756.1
Net sales	8,995.1	8,776.9	9,553.1	2,899.9	3,224.6	3,643.6

Comparative Analysis

A2

NIKE

Reebok

Required

1. Compute total asset turnover for the most recent two years for both Nike and Reebok using the data shown.

2. Which company is more efficient in generating net sales given the total assets it employs?

BTN 11-3   Janice Griffin owns a small business and manages its accounting. Her company just finished a year in which a large amount of borrowed funds were invested in a new building addition as well as in equipment and fixture additions. Janice's banker requires her to submit semiannual financial statements so he can monitor the financial health of her business. He has warned her that if profit margins erode, he might raise the interest rate on the borrowed funds to reflect the increased loan risk from the bank's point of view. Janice knows profit margin is likely to decline this year. As she prepares year-end adjusting entries, she decides to apply the following depreciation rule: all asset additions are considered to be in use on the first day of the following month.

Ethics Challenge

C1 C2

Required

1. Identify decisions that managers like Janice must make in applying depreciation methods.

2. Is Janice's rule an ethical violation, or is it a legitimate decision in computing depreciation?

3. How will Janice's depreciation rule affect the profit margin of her business?

BTN 11-4   Teams are to select an industry, and each team member is to select a different company in that industry. Each team member is to acquire the annual report (form 10-K) of the company selected. Annual reports can be obtained at the company's Web site or the SEC's EDGAR database [**www.sec.gov**]. Use the annual report to compute total asset turnover. Communicate with teammates via a meeting, e-mail, or telephone to discuss the meaning of this ratio, how different companies compare to each other, and the industry norm. The team must prepare a one-page report that describes the ratios for each company and identifies the conclusions reached during the team's discussion.

Communicating in Practice

A2

BTN 11-5   Access **Adaptec**'s (ticker: ADPT) 10-K report filed on June 27, 2000, at www.edgar-online.com to answer the following.

Taking It to the Net

C1 P6

Required

1. Read the overview of Adaptec's business and briefly describe the types of products it produces.

2. On page 7 of the 10-K, what information is provided regarding the company's patents?

3. Does Adaptec show any patent-related revenue or expense on its consolidated statement of operations (income statement)?

4. How much goodwill did Adaptec amortize in year 2000 and year 1999?

Teamwork in Action

C2 **A1** **P2**

Point: This activity can follow an overview of each method. Step 1 allows for three areas of expertise. Larger teams will have some duplication of areas, but the straight-line choice should not be duplicated. The instructor should specify time allowed for each step. Expert teams can use the book and consult with the instructor.

BTN 11-6   Each team member is to become an expert on one depreciation method to facilitate teammates' understanding of that method. Follow these procedures:

a. Each team member is to select an area for expertise from one of the following depreciation methods: straight-line, units-of-production, and declining-balance.

b. Expert teams are to be formed from those who have selected the same area of expertise. The instructor will identify the location where each expert team meets.

c. Using the following data, expert teams are to collaborate and develop a presentation answering the requirements. Expert team members must write the presentation in a format they can show to their learning teams.

Presentation Data and Requirements

Data: On January 8, 2002, Whitewater Riders purchase a van to transport rafters back to the point of departure at the conclusion of the rafting adventures they operate. The cost of the van is $44,000. It has an estimated salvage value of $2,000 and is expected to be used for four years and driven 60,000 miles. The van is expected to be driven 12,000 miles in 2002, 18,000 miles in 2003, 21,000 in 2004, and 10,000 in 2005.

1. Compute annual depreciation expense for each year of the van's estimated useful life.

2. Explain when and how annual depreciation is recorded.

3. Explain the impact of this depreciation method versus others on income over the van's life.

4. Identify the van's book value for each year of its life and illustrate the reporting of this amount for any one year.

d. Reform original learning teams. In rotation, experts are to present to their teams the results from part (c). Experts are to encourage and respond to questions.

Business Week Activity

C1 **P6**

BTN 11-7   Read the commentary "Goodwill Accounting" in the August 30, 1999, issue of *Business Week*.

Required

1. Explain how goodwill is calculated in accounting terms?

2. Describe how goodwill was accounted for prior to 1970.

3. How is goodwill accounted for under existing accounting standards?

4. What proposal is the FASB seriously considering regarding the write-off period for goodwill?

5. What plan do the two accounting professors at Southern Methodist University propose in accounting for goodwill?

Entrepreneurial Decision

A2

e

BTN 11-8   Jason Gannon is an entrepreneur and owner of **Game Haven**, which is a gameroom gallery providing high-tech action games aimed at teenagers and young adults. Game Haven consistently earns annual net sales of $350,000 on an average total asset investment of $100,000. To increase sales, Gannon proposes to expand the gameroom, which would increase average total assets by $50,000. This expansion is expected to increase net sales by $250,000.

Required

1. Compute this company's total asset turnover under (a) current conditions and (b) proposed conditions.

2. Evaluate and comment on the merits of Gannon's proposal given your analysis in part (1). Identify any concerns you would express about the proposal.

12

Current Liabilities

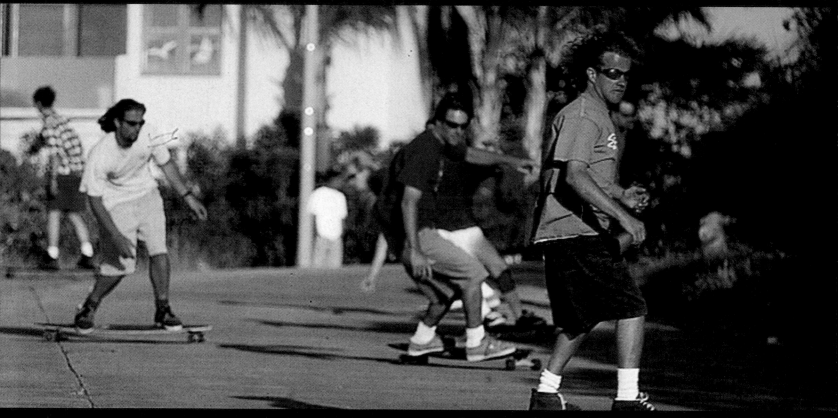

"Look for something missing in a given market."—Dennis Telfer

A Look Back

Chapter 11 focused on long-term assets including plant assets, natural resources, and intangibles. We showed how to record their costs, allocate their costs to periods benefiting from their use, and record their disposal.

A Look at This Chapter

This chapter emphasizes current liabilities and introduces long-term liabilities. We explain how to identify, compute, record, and report current liabilities in financial statements.

A Look Ahead

Chapter 13 explains the partnership form of organization. Important characteristics of this form of organization are described as are the accounting concepts and procedures for its basic transactions.

Conceptual

C1 Describe current and long-term liabilities and their characteristics.

C2 Identify and describe known current liabilities.

C3 Explain how to account for contingent liabilities.

C4 Describe accounting for long-term liabilities.

Analytical

A1 Compute the times interest earned ratio and use it to analyze liabilities.

Procedural

P1 Prepare entries to account for short-term notes payable.

P2 Compute and record *employee* payroll deductions and liabilities.

P3 Compute and record *employer* payroll expenses and liabilities.

P4 Account for estimated liabilities, including warranties and income taxes.

Carve and Slide

e LA JOLLA, CA—What do you get when you mix untamed ambition with a wild urge to carve, slide, and cross-step? The answer is **Sector 9 (Sector9.com)**, a skateboard manufacturer that traces its roots to three 20-something mavericks messing around in a backyard in La Jolla. Back then there wasn't anyone making long board skateboards. But Sector 9 changed all that when three skateboarding pals—Dennis Telfer, Dave Klimkiewicz, and Steve Lake—launched their skateboard manufacturing company. "It was something that was really different," says Telfer, describing how they did not focus on today's downscaled models but instead revived the long boards reminiscent of the 1970s. Skateboard manufacturers "pretty much laughed at us," recalls Telfer. But laugh no more. What started as a desire to skate more like one would surf or snowboard has developed into a craze for a growing number of skateboarders—and Sector 9 leads the way. Telfer says, "Our style of riding has opened up a totally new niche in the industry."

Still, it takes more than ideas and ambition to launch a company. The three worked hard testing different designs in Telfer's backyard before moving their fledgling skateboard craftsmanship to an indoor facility. Today, Sector 9, a company of 25 people, has a common goal of introducing the world to its style of skateboarding. Along the way, the friends learned to handle many aspects of business, including the crucial task of managing their liabilities, as well as obligations for payroll, skateboard materials, warranties, worker benefits, and taxes. Without effective management of liabilities, Sector 9 would not be where it is today. "It's pretty crazy," says Telfer, who recognizes that liability management continues to be crucial to the success of Sector 9. "As stressed as I am, though, I always love it." The three visionaries of Sector 9 continue to roll.

The market has embraced Sector 9 skateboards. Sector 9's annual sales projections are close to $5 million and its management of liabilities is first rate. Taking the skateboard path less traveled is proving rewarding for these three ardent skateboarders with humble beginnings. [Sources: *Sector 9 Web Site*, May 2001; *Entrepreneur*, November 12, 1998.]

Chapter Preview

Previous chapters introduced us to liabilities such as accounts payable, notes payable, wages payable, and unearned revenues. In this chapter, we learn more about these liabilities and additional ones such as warranties, taxes, payroll, vacation pay, and leases. We also describe contingent liabilities and look at some long-term liabilities. Our focus is on how to define, classify, measure, and analyze liabilities in order to report useful information about them to business decision makers.

Characteristics of Liabilities

This section discusses important characteristics of liabilities and how they are classified and reported.

Defining Liabilities

C1 Describe current and long-term liabilities and their characteristics.

A liability is a probable future payment of assets or services that a company is presently obligated to make as a result of past transactions or events. This definition includes three crucial factors:

- ■ Due to a past transaction or event.
- ■ Present obligation.
- ■ Future payment of assets or services.

Exhibit 12.1

Characteristics of a Liability

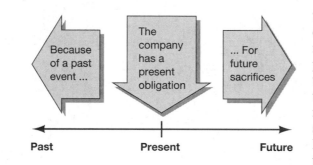

These three important elements are portrayed visually in Exhibit 12.1. Liabilities do not include all expected future payments. For example, most companies expect to pay wages to their employees in upcoming months and years, but these future payments are not liabilities because no past event such as employee work resulted in a present obligation. Instead, the liabilities arise when employees perform their work and earn the wages.

Classifying Liabilities

Information about liabilities is more useful when the balance sheet identifies them as either current or long term. Decision makers need to know when obligations are due so they can plan for them and take appropriate action.

Current Liabilities

Point: Improper classification of liabilities can distort key ratios used in financial statement analysis and decision making.

Current liabilities, also called *short-term liabilities,* are obligations due within one year or the company's operating cycle, whichever is longer. They are expected to be paid using current assets or by creating other current liabilities. Common examples of current liabilities are accounts payable, short-term notes payable, wages payable, warranty liabilities, lease liabilities, taxes payable, and unearned revenues.

Current liabilities are different across companies. A company's current liabilities depend on its type of operations. **Harley-Davidson,** for instance, recently included the following current accrued liabilities related to its motorcycle operations ($000s):

Warranty/recalls	$14,655
Dealer incentive programs	40,322

Global: In some countries such as France, the balance sheet does not separate current liabilities into their own category.

Univision, the leading Spanish-language television broadcaster, reports a much different set of current liabilities. For instance, it reports more than $140 million in current liabilities made up of items such as television programming and license fee liabilities.

482

Long-Term Liabilities

A company's obligations not expected to be paid within the longer of one year or the company's operating cycle are reported as **long-term liabilities.** They can include long-term notes payable, warranty liabilities, lease liabilities, and bonds payable. They are sometimes reported on the balance sheet in a single long-term liabilities total or in multiple categories. **Domino's**, for instance, reports long-term liabilities in its recent balance sheet of ($ millions): long-term debt, $696; insurance reserves, $15; other, $22. They are reported after current liabilities. A single liability also can be divided between the current and noncurrent sections if a company expects to make payments toward it in both the short- and long-term. In the case of Domino's, it reports ($ millions) long-term debt, $696; and current portion of long-term debt, $21. The second item is reported in current liabilities. We sometimes see liabilities that do not have a fixed due date but are payable on the creditor's demand. These are reported as current liabilities because of the possibility of payment in the near-term. Exhibit 12.2 shows amounts of current and long-term liabilities for selected companies.

Point: The current ratio will be overstated by a failure to classify the portion of long-term debt due next period as a current liability.

Exhibit 12.2

Current and Long-Term Liabilities ($ millions)

Uncertainty in Liabilities

Accounting for liabilities involves addressing three important questions: Whom to pay? When to pay? How much to pay? Answers to these questions are often decided when a liability is incurred. For example, if a company has a $100 account payable to a specific individual, payable on March 15, the answers are clear. The company knows whom to pay, when to pay, and how much to pay. However, the answers to one or more of these three questions are uncertain for some liabilities.

Uncertainty in Whom to Pay

Liabilities can involve uncertainty in whom to pay. For instance, a company can create a liability with a known amount when issuing a note that is payable to its holder. In this case, a specific amount is payable to the note's holder at a specified date, but the company does not know who the holder is until that date. Despite this uncertainty, the company reports this liability on its balance sheet.

Uncertainty in When to Pay

A company can have an obligation of a known amount to a known creditor but not know when it must be paid. For example, a legal services firm can accept fees in advance from a client who plans to use the firm's services in the future. This means that the firm has a liability that it settles by providing services at an unknown future date. Although this uncertainty exists, the firm's balance sheet must report this liability. These types of obligations are reported as current liabilities because they are likely to be settled in the short term.

Uncertainty in How Much to Pay

A company can be aware of an obligation but not know how much will be required to settle it. For example, a company using electrical power is billed only after the meter has been read. This cost is incurred and the liability created before a bill is received. A liability to the power company is reported as an estimated amount if the balance sheet is prepared before a bill arrives.

Quick Check

1. What is a liability?

2. Is every expected future payment a liability?

3. If a liability is payable in 15 months, is it classified as current or long-term?

Answers—p. 509

Known (Determinable) Liabilities

C2 Identify and describe known current liabilities.

Most liabilities arise from situations with little uncertainty. They are set by agreements, contracts, or laws and are measurable. These liabilities are **known liabilities,** also called *definitely determinable liabilities.* Known liabilities include accounts payable, notes payable, payroll, sales taxes, unearned revenues, and leases. We describe how to account for these known liabilities in this section.

Accounts Payable

Accounts payable, or trade accounts payable, are amounts owed to suppliers for products or services purchased with credit. Accounting for accounts payable is explained and illustrated in several prior chapters. Much of our discussion of merchandising activities in Chapters 6 and 7, for instance, dealt with accounts payable.

Sales Taxes Payable

Nearly every state and many cities levy taxes on retail sales. Sales taxes are stated as a percent of selling prices. The retailer (seller) collects sales taxes from customers when sales occur and remits these collections (often monthly) to the proper government agency. Since retailers currently owe these collections to the government, this amount is a current liability for retailers. **Home Depot**, for instance, reports sales taxes payable of $269 million in its recent annual report. To illustrate, if Home Depot sells materials on August 31 worth $6,000 that are subject to a 5% sales tax, its entry is

Assets = Liabilities + Equity
+6,300   +300   +6,000

Aug. 31	Cash	6,300	
	Sales		6,000
	Sales Taxes Payable ($6,000 × 0.05)		300
	To record cash sales and 5% sales tax.		

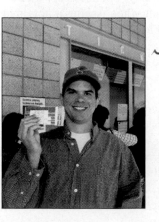

Sales Taxes Payable is debited and Cash credited when it remits these collections to the government. Sales Taxes Payable is not an expense. It arises because laws require retailers to collect this cash from customers for the government.

Unearned Revenues

Point: To *defer* a revenue means to postpone recognition of a revenue collected in advance until it is earned. Sport teams must defer recognition of ticket sales until games are played.

Unearned revenues (also called *deferred revenues, collections in advance,* and *prepayments*) are amounts received in advance from customers for future products or services. Advance ticket sales for sporting events or music concerts are examples. The **Boston Celtics**, for instance, reported "deferred game revenues" including advance ticket sales of $10.4 million in its recent balance sheet. When the Celtics sell $5 million of season tickets, its entry is

June 30	Cash	5,000,000	
	Unearned Season Ticket Revenue		5,000,000
	To record sale of Celtic season tickets.		

Assets = Liabilities + Equity
+5,000,000 +5,000,000

When each game is played, the Celtics record revenue for the portion earned:

Oct. 31	Unearned Season Ticket Revenue	60,000	
	Season Ticket Revenue		60,000
	To record Celtic season ticket revenues earned.		

Assets = Liabilities + Equity
−60,000 +60,000

Unearned Season Ticket Revenue is an unearned revenue account and is reported as a current liability. Unearned revenues also arise with airline ticket sales, magazine subscriptions, construction projects, hotel reservations, and custom orders.

Short-Term Notes Payable

A **short-term note payable** is a written promise to pay a specified amount on a definite future date within one year or the company's operating cycle, whichever is longer. These promissory notes are negotiable (as are checks), meaning they can be transferred from party to party by endorsement. The written documentation provided by notes is helpful in resolving disputes and for pursuing legal actions involving these liabilities. Most notes payable bear interest to compensate for use of the amount until payment is made. Short-term notes payable can arise from many transactions. A company that purchases merchandise on credit can sometimes extend the credit period by signing a note to replace an account payable. They also can arise when money is borrowed from a bank. We describe both of these cases in this section.

P1 Prepare entries to account for short-term notes payable.

Point: Required characteristics for negotiability of a note: (1) unconditional promise, (2) in writing, (3) specific amount, and (4) definite due date.

Note Given to Extend Credit Period

A company can replace an account payable with a note payable. A common example is a creditor that requires the substitution of an interest-bearing note for an overdue account payable that does not bear interest. A less common situation occurs when a debtor's weak financial condition motivates the creditor to obtain a note, sometimes for a lesser amount, and to close the account to ensure that this customer makes no additional credit purchases.

Illustration of note to extend credit period

To illustrate, let's assume that on August 23, Irwin asks to extend its past-due $600 account payable to McGraw. After some negotiations, McGraw agrees to accept $100 cash and a 60-day, 12%, $500 note payable to replace the account payable. Irwin records the transaction with this entry:

Aug. 23	Accounts Payable—McGraw	600	
	Cash		100
	Notes Payable		500
	Gave $100 cash and a 60-day, 12% note for payment on account.		

Assets = Liabilities + Equity
−100   −600
        +500

Signing the note does not pay Irwin's debt. Instead, the form of debt is changed from an account payable to a note payable. McGraw prefers the note payable over the account payable because it earns interest and it is written documentation of the debt's existence, term, and amount. When the note comes due, Irwin pays the note and interest by giving McGraw a check for $510. This payment is recorded with this entry:

Point: Accounts payable are detailed in a subsidiary ledger, but notes payable are usually not. This means a creditor's name is not often necessary in an entry. A file with copies of notes often serves as a subsidiary ledger.

Oct. 22	Notes Payable	500	
	Interest Expense	10	
	Cash		510
	Paid note with interest ($500 × 12% × 60/360).		

Assets = Liabilities + Equity
−510   −500   −10

Interest expense is computed by multiplying the principal of the note ($500) by the annual interest rate (12%) for the fraction of the year the note is outstanding (60 days/360 days).

Note Given to Borrow from Bank

A bank nearly always requires a borrower to sign a promissory note when making a loan. When the note matures, the borrower repays the note with an amount larger than the amount borrowed. The difference between the amount borrowed and the amount repaid is *interest*. This section considers two types of notes. The first note type often states that the note's signer promises to pay *principal* (the amount borrowed) plus interest. In this case, the *face value* of the note equals principal. Face value is the value shown on the face (front) of the note. The second note type occurs when a bank has a borrower sign a note with a face value that includes both principal and interest. In this case, the note's signer receives *less* than the note's face value. The difference between the borrowed amount and the note's face value is interest. Since the borrowed amount is less than the note's face value, the difference is called **discount on note payable.** To illustrate these two types of notes, assume that a company needs $2,000 for a project and borrows this money from a bank at 12% annual interest. The loan is made on September 30, 2002, and is due in 60 days.

Face value equals amount borrowed

In many cases the borrowing company signs a note with its face value equal to the amount borrowed. The note includes a statement similar to this: *"I promise to pay $2,000 plus interest at 12% within 60 days after September 30."* This note is shown in Exhibit 12.3.

Exhibit 12.3

Note with Face Value Equal to Amount Borrowed

Promissory Note

$2,000   Sept. 30, 2002
Face Value   **Date**

Sixty days   after date, _____ *I* _____ **promise to pay to the order of**

National Bank
Boston, MA

Two thousand and no/100 ------------------------------- **Dollars**

plus interest at the annual rate of _12%_ .

Janet Lee

The borrower records its receipt of cash and the new liability with this entry:

Sept. 30	Cash	2,000	
	Notes Payable		2,000
	Borrowed $2,000 cash with a 60-day, 12%, $2,000 note.		

When principal and interest are paid, the borrower records payment with this entry:

Nov. 29	Notes Payable	2,000	
	Interest Expense	40	
	Cash		2,040
	Paid note with interest ($2,000 × 12% × 60/360).		

Face value equals amount borrowed plus interest

In some cases the borrower signs a note with the interest included in its face value. This type of note includes a promise similar to this: *"I promise to pay $2,040 within 60 days after September 30."* This note is shown in Exhibit 12.4. The borrower receives $2,000 cash, and the note does not refer to the rate used to compute the $40 of interest included in the $2,040 face value. In other respects, this note is similar to the one in Exhibit 12.3. Since this note lacks a stated interest rate, it is sometimes called a **noninterest-bearing note,** which can be misleading since the note does bear interest that is included in the face value.

Exhibit 12.4

Note with Face Value Equal to Amount Borrowed plus Interest

Promissory Note

$2,040   Sept. 30, 2002

Face Value   **Date**

Sixty days   after date, _____ I _____ promise to pay to the order of

National Bank
Boston, MA

Two thousand forty and no/100 ------------------- **Dollars.**

Janet Lee

When the face value of a note includes principal and interest, the borrower usually records this note with an entry to credit Notes Payable for its face value and to record the interest in a Discount on Notes Payable account as follows:

Point: Use of a contra liability account allows us to always enter face value when recording notes payable.

Sept. 30	Cash	2,000	
	Discount on Notes Payable	40	
	Notes Payable		2,040
	Borrowed $2,000 cash with a 60-day, $2,040 note.		

Assets = Liabilities + Equity
+2,000   +2,040
              −40

Discount on Notes Payable is a contra liability account to the Notes Payable account. If a balance sheet is prepared after this transaction on September 30, the $40 discount is subtracted from the $2,040 note to reflect the $2,000 net amount borrowed:[1]

Point: A discount reflects deferred interest expense. The matching principle supports regular recognition of this expense over time.

| Notes payable .... | $2,040 | |
| Less discount on notes payable ...... | 40 | $2,000 |

When this note matures 60 days later on November 29, the entry to record the company's $2,040 payment to the bank is

Nov. 29	Notes Payable	2,040	
	Interest Expense	40	
	Cash		2,040
	Discount on Notes Payable		40
	Paid note with interest.		

Assets = Liabilities + Equity
−2,040   −2,040   −40
              +40

End-of-Period Adjustment to Notes

When the end of an accounting period falls between the signing of a note payable and its maturity date, the *matching principle* requires us to record the accrued but unpaid interest on the note. To illustrate, let's return to the earlier short-term note and assume the company borrows $2,000 cash on December 16, 2002, instead of September 30. This 60-day note

You Make the Call

Rock Band   Your band needs $30,000 to upgrade equipment. You receive loan approvals for $30,000 cash at two banks. One bank's proposed loan contract reads: "Band promises to pay $30,000 plus interest at 14% within 6 months." The competing bank's loan contract reads: "Band promises to pay $32,000 within 6 months." Which loan do you prefer?

Answer—p. 509

---

[1] We can approximate the annual interest rate on a short-term loan as **(Interest paid ÷ Amount received) ×**
(360 days ÷ Loan period in days).

Assets = Liabilities + Equity
           +10   −10

Assets = Liabilities + Equity
−2,040   −10   −30
           −2000

matures on February 14, 2003, and the company's fiscal year ends on December 31. Thus, we need to record interest expense for the final 15 days in December. The adjusting entry depends on the type of note.

Face value equals amount borrowed

When the note's face value equals the amount borrowed, any accrued interest is charged to expense and credited to an Interest Payable account. Specifically, we know that 15 days of the 60-day loan period for the $2,000, 12% note have elapsed by December 31. This means one-fourth (15 days/60 days) of the $40 total interest is an expense of year 2002. The borrower records this expense with the following adjusting entry:

2002			
Dec. 31	Interest Expense	10	
	Interest Payable		10
	To record accrued interest on note ($2,000 × 12% × 15/360).		

When this note matures on February 14, the borrower must recognize 45 days of interest expense for year 2003 and remove the balances of the two liability accounts:

2003			
Feb. 14	Interest Expense*	30	
	Interest Payable	10	
	Notes Payable	2,000	
	Cash		2,040
	*Paid note with interest. *($2,000 × 12% × 45/360)*		

Face value equals amount borrowed plus interest

When the face value of the note *includes* interest, any accrued interest is charged to Interest expense with an adjustment to the Discount on Notes Payable account. Specifically, for the $2,040 noninterest-bearing note entered into on December 16, the adjusting entry on December 31 needs to record the accrual for 15 days of interest. Accrued interest is recorded by reducing the balance of the contra liability account from $40 to $30. This adjustment increases the net liability to $2,010 ($2,040 note less $30 discount):

Assets = Liabilities + Equity
           +10   −10

2002			
Dec. 31	Interest Expense	10	
	Discount on Notes Payable		10
	To record accrued interest on note ($40 × 15/60).		

When this note matures, we need an entry both to accrue interest expense for its last 45 days and to record payment of both principal and interest:

Assets = Liabilities + Equity
−2,040   −2,040   −30
           +30

2003			
Feb. 14	Interest Expense*	30	
	Notes Payable	2,040	
	Discount on Notes Payable		30
	Cash		2,040
	*Paid note with interest. *($40 × 45/60)*		

Answers—p. 509

Quick Check

4. Why does a creditor prefer a note payable to a past-due account payable?

5. A company borrows money by signing a $1,050, 6-month note payable. In recording the transaction, the company correctly debits $50 to Discount on Notes Payable. How much cash is borrowed? What annual rate of interest is charged?

Payroll Liabilities

An employer incurs several expenses and liabilities from having employees. These expenses and liabilities are often large and arise from salaries and wages earned, from employee benefits, and from payroll taxes levied on the employer. **Anheuser-Busch**, for instance, reports payroll-related current liabilities of more than $250 million from "accrued salaries, wages and benefits." We discuss payroll liabilities and related accounts in this section. The appendix to this chapter describes important details about payroll reports, records, and procedures.

P2 Compute and record *employee* payroll deductions and liabilities.

Employee Payroll Deductions

Gross pay is the total compensation an employee earns including wages, salaries, commissions, bonuses, and any compensation earned before deductions such as taxes.[2] **Net pay,** also called *take-home pay,* is gross pay less all deductions. **Payroll deductions,** commonly called *withholdings,* are amounts withheld from an employee's gross pay, either required or voluntary. Required deductions result from laws and include income taxes and Social Security taxes. Voluntary deductions, at an employee's option

Did You Know?

Pay or Else Delay or failure to pay withholding taxes to government agencies has severe consequences. For example, a 100% penalty can be levied, with interest, on the unpaid balance. The government can even close the company, take its assets, and pursue legal actions against those involved.

include pension and health contributions, union dues, and charitable giving. Exhibit 12.5 shows the typical payroll deductions of an employee. The employer withholds payroll

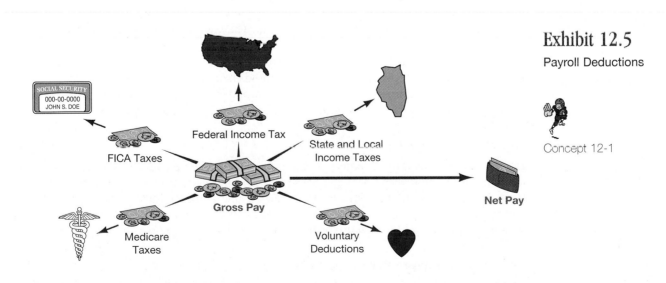

Exhibit 12.5

Payroll Deductions

Concept 12-1

---

[2] *Wages* usually refer to payments to employees at an hourly rate. *Salaries* usually refer to payments to employees at a monthly or yearly rate.

deductions from employees' pay and is obligated to transmit this money to the designated organization. The employer records payroll deductions as current liabilities until these amounts are transmitted. This section discusses the major payroll deductions.

Employee FICA taxes

The federal Social Security system provides retirement, disability, survivorship, and medical benefits to qualified workers. Laws *require* employers to withhold **Federal Insurance Contributions Act (FICA) taxes** from employees' pay to cover costs of the system. Employers usually separate FICA taxes into two groups: (1) retirement, disability, and survivorship and (2) medical. For the first group, the Social Security system provides monthly cash payments to qualified retired workers for the rest of their lives. These payments are often called *Social Security benefits.* Taxes related to this group are often called *Social Security taxes.* For the second group, the system provides monthly payments to deceased workers' surviving families and to disabled workers who qualify for assistance. These payments are commonly called *Medicare benefits,* which like those in the first group, are paid with *Medicare taxes* (part of FICA taxes).

Law requires employers to withhold FICA taxes from each employee's salary or wages on each payday. The taxes for Social Security and Medicare are computed separately. For example, for 2000, the amount withheld from each employee's pay for Social Security tax is 6.2% of the first $76,200 the employee earns in the calendar year, or a maximum of $4,724.40. The Medicare tax is 1.45% of *all* wages the employee earns. Medicare tax has no maximum amount because the government wants to maintain solvency of this program. For any changes in rates or with the maximum earnings level, check the IRS Web site at **www.IRS.USTreas.gov**.

Employers must pay withheld taxes to the Internal Revenue Service (IRS) on specific filing dates during the year. Employers who fail to send the withheld taxes to the IRS on time can be assessed substantial penalties. Until all the taxes are sent to the IRS, they are included in employers' current liabilities.

Employee income tax

Most employers are required to withhold federal income tax from each employee's paycheck. The amount withheld is computed using tables published by the IRS. The amount depends on the employee's annual earnings rate and the number of *withholding allowances* the employee claims. Allowances reduce the amount of taxes you owe the government. The more allowances you claim, the less tax your employer will withhold. Employees can claim allowances for themselves and their dependents. They also can claim additional allowances if they expect major declines in their taxable income for medical expenses. (An employee who claims more allowances than appropriate is subject to a fine.) Most states and many local governments require employers to withhold their income taxes from employees' pay and to remit them promptly to the proper government agency. Until they are paid, withholdings are reported as a current liability on the employer's balance sheet.

Point: Part-time employees may claim "exempt from withholding" if they did not have any income tax liability in the prior year and do not expect any in the current year.

Point: IRS withholding tables are based on projecting weekly (or other period) pay into an annual figure.

Employee voluntary deductions

Beyond Social Security, Medicare, and income taxes, employers often withhold other amounts from employees' earnings. These withholdings arise from employee requests, contracts, unions, or other agreements. They can include amounts for charitable giving, medical insurance premiums, pension contributions, and union dues. Until they are paid, these withholdings are employers' current liabilities.

Recording <u>Employee</u> Payroll Deductions

Employers must accrue payroll expenses and liabilities at the end of each pay period. To illustrate, assume that an employee earns a salary of $2,000 per month. At the end of January, the employer's entry to accrue payroll expenses and liabilities for this employee is

Jan. 31	Salaries Expense	2,000	
	FICA—Social Security Taxes Payable (6.2%)		124
	FICA—Medicare Taxes Payable (1.45%) . . .		29
	Employee Federal Income Taxes Payable* . .		213
	Employee Medical Insurance Payable*		85
	Employee Union Dues Payable*		25
	Accrued Payroll Payable		1,524
	To record payroll for January.		

Assets = Liabilities + Equity
+124   −2,000
+29
+213
+85
+25
+1,524

* Amounts taken from employer's accounting records.

Salaries Expense (debit) shows the employee earns a gross salary of $2,000. The first five payables (credits) show liabilities the employer owes on behalf of this employee to cover FICA taxes, income taxes, medical insurance, and union dues. The Accrued Payroll Payable account (credit) records the $1,524 net pay the employee receives from the $2,000 gross pay earned. When the employee is paid, another entry (or a series of entries) is required to record the check written and distributed (or funds transferred). The entry to record cash payment to this employee is to debit Accrued Payroll Payable and credit Cash for $1,524.

Employer Payroll Taxes

Employers must pay payroll taxes in addition to those required of employees. These employer taxes include FICA and unemployment taxes.

Employer FICA tax

Employers must pay FICA taxes *equal in amount to* the FICA taxes withheld from their employees. An employer's tax is credited to the same FICA Taxes Payable accounts used to record the Social Security and Medicare taxes withheld from employees. (A self-employed person must pay both the employee and employer FICA taxes.)

Federal and state unemployment taxes

The federal government participates with states in a joint federal–state unemployment insurance program. Each state administers its own program. These programs provide unemployment benefits to qualified workers. The federal government approves state programs and pays a portion of their administrative expenses.

Federal Unemployment Taxes (FUTA). Employers are subject to a federal unemployment tax on wages and salaries paid to their employees. For 2000, an employer is required to pay FUTA taxes of as much as 6.2% of the first $7,000 earned by each employee. This federal tax can be reduced by a credit of up to 5.4% for taxes paid to a state program. As a result, the net federal unemployment tax is often only 0.8%.

State Unemployment Taxes (SUTA). All states support their unemployment insurance programs by placing a payroll tax on employers. (A few states require employees to make a contribution. In our assignments, we assume this tax is only on the employer.) In most states, the base rate for SUTA taxes is 5.4% of the first $7,000 paid each employee. This base rate is adjusted according to an employer's merit rating. The state assigns a **merit rating** that reflects a company's stability or instability in employing workers. A good rating reflects stability in employment and means an employer can pay less than the 5.4% base rate. A low

Did You Know?

Payroll Control   More than $600 million is lost annually to check schemes. Companies are fighting back with an internal control method called *positive pay*. Here's how it works: A company regularly (daily) sends the bank a "positive file" listing all checks written. When a check reaches the bank for payment, the bank compares the check against the positive file. This flags any forged checks, as well as authentic checks that have been altered. Discrepancies are reported to the company, which can stop payment.

P3   Compute and record *employer* payroll expenses and liabilities.

Did You Know?

Tax Aid   Technology helps reduce errors and increase speed in computing taxes as compared with manual use of tax tables. Tax tables can also be stored on computer or downloaded off the Web [**www.IRS.USTreas.gov**] and then used to accurately and quickly compute payroll taxes.

You Make the Call—Ethics

Web Designer You take a summer job working for a family friend who runs a small IT service. When the time arrives for your first paycheck, the owner slaps you on the back, gives you full payment in cash, winks, and adds: "No need to pay those high taxes, eh." What action do you take?

Answer—p. 509

rating reflects high turnover or seasonal hirings and layoffs. A favorable merit rating translates into cash savings from lower taxes. To illustrate, an employer with 100 employees who each earn $7,000 or more per year saves $30,800 annually if it has a merit rating of 1.0% versus 5.4%. This is computed by comparing taxes of $37,800 at the 5.4% rate to only $7,000 at the 1.0% rate.

Recording Employer Payroll Taxes

Employer payroll taxes are an added expense beyond the wages and salaries earned by employees. These taxes are often recorded in an entry separate from the one recording payroll expenses and deductions. To illustrate, assume that the $2,000 recorded salaries expense on the previous page is earned by an employee whose earnings have not yet reached $5,000 for the year. Also assume that the federal unemployment tax rate is 0.8% and the state unemployment tax rate is 5.4%. The FICA portion of the employer's tax is $153, computed by multiplying both the 6.2% and 1.45% by the $2,000 gross pay. State unemployment (SUTA) taxes are $108 (5.4% of the $2,000 gross pay). Federal unemployment (FUTA) taxes are $16 (0.8% of $2,000). The entry to record the employer's payroll tax expense and related liabilities is

Example: If the employer's merit rating in this example reduces its SUTA rate to 2.9%, what is its SUTA liability? *Answer:* SUTA payable = $2,000 × 2.9% = $58

Assets = Liabilities + Equity
+124   −277
+29
+108
+16

Jan. 31	Payroll Taxes Expense	277	
	FICA—Social Security Taxes Payable (6.2%)		124
	FICA—Medicare Taxes Payable (1.45%) . .		29
	State Unemployment Taxes Payable		108
	Federal Unemployment Taxes Payable		16
	To record employer payroll taxes.		

Quick Check

6. A company pays its one employee $3,000 per month. This company's FUTA rate is 0.8% on the first $7,000 earned, its SUTA rate is 4.0% on the first $7,000, its Social Security tax rate is 6.2% of the first $76,200, and its Medicare tax rate is 1.45% of all amounts earned. The entry to record this company's March payroll includes what amount for total payroll taxes expense?

7. Identify whether the employer or employee or both pays each of the following: (a) FICA taxes; (b) FUTA taxes; (c) SUTA taxes; and (d) withheld income taxes.

Answers—p. 509

Estimated Liabilities

P4 Account for estimated liabilities, including warranties and income taxes.

An **estimated liability** is a known obligation of an uncertain amount, but one that can be reasonably estimated. Common examples are employee benefits such as pensions, health care and vacation pay, warranties offered by a seller, and income taxes. We discuss each of these in this section. Other examples of estimated liabilities include property taxes and certain contracts to provide future services.

Health and Pension Benefits

Many companies provide **employee benefits** beyond salaries and wages. An employer often pays all or part of medical, dental, life, and disability insurance. Many employers also contribute to *pension plans,* which are agreements by employers to provide benefits (payments) to employees after retirement. Many companies also provide medical care and insurance benefits to their retirees. When payroll taxes and charges for employee benefits are totaled, payroll cost often exceeds employees' gross earnings by 25% or more.

To illustrate, assume an employer agrees to (1) pay an amount for medical insurance equal to $8,000 and (2) contribute an additional 10% of employees' $120,000 gross salary to a retirement program. The entry to record these benefits is

Did You Know?

Post Game Benefits Several ex-players are suing Major League Baseball over a pension system they say unfairly excludes them and fails to reward their contributions to the game. Gripes include failure to extend pensions to players whose careers ended before 1947, were interrupted by World War II, or were spent in the Negro League. A full pension is about $120,000 a year.

Jan. 31	Employee Benefits Expense.	20,000	
	Employee Medical Insurance Payable		8,000
	Employee Retirement Program Payable . . .		12,000
	To record costs of employee benefits.		

Assets = Liabilities + Equity
+8,000   −20,000
+12,000

Vacation Pay

Many employers offer paid vacation benefits. For example, many employees earn 2 weeks' vacation by working 50 weeks. This benefit increases employers' payroll expenses because employees are paid for 52 weeks but work for only 50 weeks. Total annual salary is the same, but the cost per week worked is greater than the amount paid per week. To illustrate, if an employee is paid $20,800 for 52 weeks but works only 50 weeks, the weekly salary expense to the employer is $416 ($20,800/50 weeks) instead of the $400 paid weekly to the employee ($20,800/52 weeks). The $16 difference between these two amounts is recorded weekly to Salary Expense and Vacation Pay Liability. When the employee takes a vacation, the employer reduces the vacation pay liability but does not record any additional expense.

Global: Bonuses are considered part of salary expense in most countries. In Japan, bonuses to members of the board of directors and to external auditors are directly charged against equity rather than treated as an expense.

Bonus Plans

Many companies offer bonuses to employees, and many of the bonuses depend on net income. To illustrate, assume an employer offers a bonus to its employees equal to 5% of the company's annual net income (to be equally shared). The company's expected annual net income is $210,000. The year-end adjusting entry to record this benefit is

Dec. 31	Employee Bonus Expense*	10,000	
	Bonus Payable		10,000
	To record expected bonus costs.		

Assets = Liabilities + Equity
+10,000   −10,000

* Bonus Expense is deducted in computing net income. This means it equals 5% of $210,000 *less the bonus*—computed as:

$$B = 0.05 (\$210,000 - B)$$
$$B = \$10,500 - 0.05B$$
$$1.05B = \$10,500$$
$$\mathbf{B = \$10,000}$$

When the bonus is paid, Bonus Payable is debited and Cash is credited for $10,000.

Warranty Liabilities

A **warranty** is a seller's obligation to replace or correct a product (or service) that fails to perform as expected within a specified period. Most new cars, for instance, are sold with a warranty covering parts for a specified period of time. **Ford Motor Co**. reported more than $10 billion in "dealer and customer allowances and claims" in its recent annual report. To comply with the *full disclosure* and *matching principles,* the seller reports the expected warranty expense in the period when revenue from the sale of the product or service is reported.

Point: Zenith recently reported $32.1 million on its balance sheet for warranties.

The seller reports this warranty obligation as a liability, although the existence, amount, payee, and date of future sacrifices are uncertain. Still, such future sacrifices are probable, and the amount of this liability can be estimated using, for instance, past experience with warranties.

Illustration of Warranty Liabilities

To illustrate, consider a dealer who sells a used car for $16,000 on December 1, 2002, with a maximum of one-year or 12,000-mile warranty covering parts. This dealer's experience shows warranty expense averages about 4% of a car's selling price, or $640 in this case ($16,000 × 4%). The dealer records the estimated expense and liability related to this sale with this entry:

Assets = Liabilities + Equity
+640   −640

2002 Dec. 1	Warranty Expense	640	
	Estimated Warranty Liability		640
	To record estimated warranty expense.		

This entry alternatively could be made as part of end-of-period adjustments. Either way, the estimated warranty expense is reported on the 2002 income statement. It also results in a warranty liability on the balance sheet. To further extend this example, suppose the customer returns the car for warranty repairs on January 9, 2003. The dealer performs this work by replacing parts costing $200. The entry to record partial settlement of the estimated warranty liability is

Point: Recognition of expected warranty liabilities is necessary to comply with the matching and full disclosure principles.

Assets = Liabilities + Equity
−200   −200

2003 Jan. 9	Estimated Warranty Liability.	200	
	Auto Parts Inventory.		200
	To record costs of warranty repairs.		

This entry reduces the balance of the estimated warranty liability. Warranty expense was previously recorded in 2002, the year the car was sold with the warranty. What happens if total warranty expenses are more or less than the estimated 4%, or $640? The answer is that management should monitor actual warranty expenses to see whether the 4% rate is accurate. If experience reveals a large difference from the estimate, the rate for current and future sales should be changed. Differences are expected, but they should be small.

Income Tax Liabilities

Financial statements of both proprietorships and partnerships do not include income taxes because these organizations do not directly pay income taxes. Instead, taxable income for these organizations is carried to the owners' personal tax return and taxed at that level. However, corporations are subject to income taxes and must estimate their income tax liability when preparing financial statements.

Illustration of Income Tax Liabilities

Income tax expense for a corporation creates a liability until payment is made to the government. Because this tax is created by earning income, a liability is incurred when income is earned. This tax must be paid quarterly under federal regulations. To illustrate, consider a corporation that prepares monthly financial statements. Based on its income in January 2002, this corporation estimates that it owes income taxes of $12,100. The following adjusting entry records this estimate:

Assets = Liabilities + Equity
+12,100   −12,100

Jan. 31	Income Taxes Expense	12,100	
	Income Taxes Payable		12,100
	To accrue January income taxes.		

The tax liability is recorded each month until the first quarterly payment is made. If estimated taxes for this first quarter total $30,000, the entry to record its payment is

Apr. 10	Income Taxes Payable.	30,000	
	Cash		30,000
	Paid estimated quarterly income taxes based on first quarter income.		

Assets − Liabilities + Equity
−30,000   −30,000

This process of accruing and then paying estimated income taxes continues through the year. When annual financial statements are prepared at year-end, the corporation knows its actual total income and the actual amount of income taxes it must pay. This information allows it to properly record Income Taxes Expense for the quarter so that the total of the four quarters' expense amounts equals the taxes paid to the government.

Deferred Income Tax Liabilities

An income tax liability for corporations can arise when the amount of income before taxes that the corporation reports on its income statement is not the same as the amount of income reported on its income tax return. This difference occurs because income tax laws and GAAP measure income differently.[3]

Some differences between tax laws and GAAP are temporary. *Temporary differences* arise when the tax return and the income statement report a revenue or expense in different years. As an example, companies are often able to deduct higher amounts of depreciation in the early years of an asset's life and smaller amounts in later years for tax reporting in comparison to GAAP. This means in the early years, depreciation for tax reporting is often more than depreciation on the income statement. In later years, depreciation for tax reporting is often less than depreciation on the income statement. When temporary differences exist between taxable income on the tax return and the income before taxes on the income statement, corporations compute Income Taxes Expense based on the income reported on the income statement. The result is that Income Taxes Expense reported in the income statement is often different than the amount of Income Taxes Payable to the government. This difference is called *Deferred Income Tax*.

Illustration of Deferred Income Tax

To illustrate, assume that in recording its usual quarterly income tax payments, a corporation computes $25,000 of income taxes expense. It also determines that only $21,000 is currently due and $4,000 is deferred to future years (a timing difference). The entry to record this end-of-period adjustment is

Dec. 31	Income Taxes Expense	25,000	
	Income Taxes Payable		21,000
	Deferred Income Tax Liability.		4,000
	To record tax expense and deferred tax liability.		

Assets = Liabilities + Equity
+21,000   −25,000
+4,000

The credit to Income Taxes Payable reflects the amount currently due to be paid. The credit to **Deferred Income Tax Liability** reflects tax payments deferred until future years when the temporary difference reverses. **Coca-Cola Bottling**, for instance, reports deferred income taxes of $125 million among its liabilities on its recent balance sheet.

Temporary differences also can cause a company to pay income taxes *before* they are reported on the income statement as expense. If so, the company reports a *Deferred Income Tax Asset* on its balance sheet. **Dell**, for instance, reports deferred income taxes of $535 million as an asset in its recent balance sheet.

---

[3] Differences between tax laws and GAAP arise because Congress uses tax laws to generate receipts, stimulate the economy, and influence behavior, whereas GAAP are intended to provide financial information useful for decision making. Also, tax accounting often follows the cash basis, whereas GAAP follows the accrual basis.

Answers—p. 509

Contingent Liabilities

 Explain how to account for contingent liabilities.

	Probable	Reasonably Possible	Remote
Amount estimable	Record contingent liability	Disclose liability in notes	No action
Amount not estimable	Disclose liability in notes	Disclose liability in notes	No action

Point: Point out that a contingency is an *IF*. Namely, if a future event occurs, then financial consequences are likely for the entity.

A contingent liability is a potential obligation that depends on a future event arising from a past transaction or event. An example is a lawsuit pending in court. Here, a past transaction or event leads to a lawsuit whose result depends on the court's decision. Generally, future payment of a contingent liability depends on whether an uncertain future event occurs.

Accounting for Contingent Liabilities

Accounting for contingent liabilities depends on the likelihood that a future event will occur and the ability to estimate the future amount owed if this event occurs. Three categories are identified. (1) The future event is *probable* (likely) and the amount owed can be *reasonably estimated*. We record this amount as a liability. Examples are the estimated liabilities described earlier such as warranties, vacation pay, and income taxes. (2) The future event is *remote* (unlikely). We do not record or disclose information regarding these contingent liabilities. (3) Likelihood of the future event is between these two extremes. That is, if the future event is *reasonably possible* (could occur), we disclose information about the contingent liability in notes to the financial statements. The next section identifies contingent liabilities that often fall in the third category—when the future event is reasonably possible. Disclosing information about contingencies in the third category is motivated by the *full-disclosure principle*, which requires information relevant to decision makers be reported.

Reasonably Possible Contingent Liabilities

This section discusses common examples of reasonably possible contingent liabilities.

Point: A discounted note receivable is a contingent liability. It becomes a liability only if the original signer of the note fails to pay it at maturity.

Potential Legal Claims. Many companies are sued or at risk of being sued. The accounting question is: whether the defendant should recognize a liability on its balance sheet or disclose a contingent liability in its notes while a lawsuit is outstanding and not yet settled. The answer is that a potential claim is recorded in the accounts *only* if payment for damages is probable and the amount can be reasonably estimated. If the potential claim cannot be reasonably estimated or is less than probable but reasonably possible, it is disclosed. **Ford Motor Company**, for example, includes the following note in its recent annual report: "Various legal actions, governmental investigations and proceedings and claims are pending . . . against the company . . . arising out of alleged defects in the company's products."

Did You Know?

Boiling Mad   Remember the infamous lawsuit against **McDonald's** that awarded an 81-year-old New Mexico woman $2.9 million—later reduced to $640,000—after spilling hot coffee in her lap? Well, copycat litigation is booming. Fast-food chains are beset by suits over hot-drink and food spills. Companies from **Burger King** to **Starbucks** now print cautions on coffee cups, chili bowls, and so forth.

Debt Guarantees. Sometimes a company guarantees the payment of debt owed by a supplier, customer, or another company. The guarantor usually discloses the guarantee in its financial statement notes as a contingent liability. If it is probable that the debtor will default, the guarantor needs to record and report the guarantee in its financial statements as a liability. The **Boston Celtics** report a unique guarantee when it comes to coaches and players: "Certain of the contracts provide for guaranteed payments which must be paid even if the employee is injured or terminated."

Other Contingencies. Other examples of contingencies include environmental damages, possible tax assessments, insurance losses, and government investigations. **Sun**, for instance, reports "federal, state, local and foreign laws . . . result in loss contingencies . . . at Sun's refineries, service stations, terminals, pipelines and truck transportation facilities." Many of these contingencies require disclosure in notes to financial statements since they are reasonably possible. These contingencies can sometimes carry characteristics that cause them to be recorded as liabilities or, alternatively, omitted altogether.

Uncertainties. All organizations face uncertainties from future events such as natural disasters and the development of new competing products or services. If these events occur, they can damage a company's assets or drive it out of business. These uncertainties are not contingent liabilities because they are future events *not* arising from past transactions. Financial statements are not useful if they unduly speculate about the effects of possible future uncertainties such as these.

> ### Did You Know?
>
> **Eco Cops** What's it worth to see from one side of the Grand Canyon to the other? What's the cost when beaches are closed due to pollution? One method to measure these environmental liabilities is called **contingent valuation** by which people are surveyed and asked to answer such questions. Regulators use their answers to levy fines, assess punitive damages, measure costs of clean-up, and assign penalties.

Point: Auditors and managers often have different views about whether a contingency is recorded, disclosed, or omitted.

Global: Accounting for contingencies varies across countries. Germany, for example, permits the recording of contingent liabilities that are reasonably possible.

Quick Check

11. A future payment is reported as a liability on the balance sheet if payment is contingent on a future event that (a) Is reasonably possible but the payment cannot be reasonably estimated; (b) Is probable and the payment can be reasonably estimated; or (c) Is not probable but the payment is known.

12. Under what circumstances is a future payment reported in the notes to the financial statements as a contingent liability?

Concept 12-2

Answers—p. 509

Long-term liabilities are a company's obligations not requiring a payment within one year or its operating cycle, whichever is longer. Long-term liabilities often are identical to current liabilities except for the longer time interval until the obligation comes due. Long-term liabilities can arise from many different transactions and events. Probably their most common source is money borrowed from a bank in return for a note. They also occur when a company enters into a multiyear lease agreement similar to buying an asset. We explain long-term liabilities in the context of discussing known, estimated, and contingent long-term liabilities. The main discussion of accounting for long-term liabilities is in Chapter 15.

Long-Term Liabilities

C4 Describe accounting for long-term liabilities.

Known Long-Term Liabilities

Many known or determinable liabilities are long term. These include most unearned revenues and notes payable. For example, if **Sports Illustrated** sells a five-year magazine subscription, it records amounts received for this subscription in an Unearned Subscription Revenues account. Amounts in this account are liabilities, but are they current or long term? They are *both*. The portion of the Unearned

> ### Did You Know?   *e*
>
> **Entrepreneurial Financing** The Small Business Administration [www.sba.gov] publishes a yearly report of likely sources of small business loans by state. The report shows that small businesses number more than 25 million, employ 53% of the private work force, make 47% of all sales, create most new jobs, and produce 55% of innovations. It also shows that about 70% of small businesses with loans obtain this money from commercial banks.

Subscription Revenues account that will be fulfilled in the next year is reported as a current liability. The remaining portion is reported as a long-term liability.

The same analysis applies to notes payable. For example, a borrower reports a three-year note payable as a long-term liability in the first two years it is outstanding. In the third year, the borrower reclassifies this note as a current liability since it is due within one year or the operating cycle, whichever is longer. The **current portion of long-term debt** refers to that part of long-term debt due within one year or the operating cycle, whichever is longer. Long-term debt is reported under long-term liabilities, but the *current portion due* is reported under current liabilities. To illustrate, assume that a $7,500 debt is paid in installments of $1,500 per year for five years. The $1,500 due within the year is reported as a current liability. No journal entry is necessary. Instead, we simply classify the amounts for debt as either current or long term when the balance sheet is prepared.

Some known liabilities are rarely reported in long-term liabilities. These include accounts payable, sales taxes, and wages and salaries.

Estimated Long-Term Liabilities

Estimated liabilities are both current and long term. Examples include employee benefits and deferred income taxes. Pension liabilities to employees are long term to workers who will not retire within the next period. For employees who are retired or will retire within the next period, a portion of pension liabilities is current. The same analysis applies to employee health benefits, deferred income taxes payable for corporations, and warranties. For example, many warranties are for 30 or 60 days in length. Estimated costs under these warranties are properly reported in current liabilities, yet many automobile warranties are for three years or 36,000 miles. A portion of these warranties is reported as long-term.

Contingent Long-Term Liabilities

Contingent liabilities can be either, or both, current and long-term in nature. This extends to nearly every contingent liability, including litigation, debt guarantees, environmental clean-up, government investigations, and tax assessments.

Using the Information　　　　　　　　　　　　　　　　**Times Interest Earned**

| A1 | Compute the times interest earned ratio and use it to analyze liabilities. |

A company incurs interest expense on many of its current and long-term liabilities. Examples extend from its short-term notes and the current portion of long-term liabilities to its long-term notes and bonds. The amount of these liabilities is likely to remain in one form or another for a substantial period of time. Because of this, interest expense is often viewed as a *fixed expense*. This means the amount of interest is unlikely to fluctuate much from changes in sales or other operating activities. While fixed costs can be advantageous when a company is growing, they create risk. This risk stems from the possibility a company might be unable to pay fixed expenses if sales decline. To illustrate, consider **X-Caliber**'s results for year 2002 and two possible outcomes for year 2003 shown in Exhibit 12.6. X-Caliber manufactures water sports equipment and remains a family-owned operation.

Exhibit 12.6

X-Caliber's Actual and Projected Results

		Year 2003	
($ thousands)	**Year 2002**	**Sales Increase**	**Sales Decrease**
Sales	$600	$900	$300
Expenses (75% of sales)	450	675	225
Income before interest	150	225	75
Interest expense (fixed)	60	60	60
Net income	$ 90	$165	$ 15

Expenses excluding interest are at, and expected to remain at, 75% of sales. Expenses such as these that change with sales volume are called *variable expenses*. Interest expense is at, and expected to remain at, $60,000 per year due to its fixed nature.

The middle numerical column of Exhibit 12.6 shows that X-Caliber's income nearly doubles if sales increase by 50% to $900,000. The far right column shows that its profits fall sharply if sales decline by 50% to $300,000.

These results show that the amount of fixed interest expense it incurs each period affects a company's risk. The risk from fixed expenses is numerically reflected in the **times interest earned** ratio defined in Exhibit 12.7.

$$\text{Times interest earned} = \frac{\text{Income before interest expense}}{\text{Interest expense}}$$

Exhibit 12.7
Times Interest Earned

For 2002, X-Caliber's income before interest is $150,000. Its times interest earned is computed as $150,000/$60,000, or 2.5 times. This ratio suggests that X-Caliber faces low to moderate risk because its sales must decline sharply before it would be unable to cover its interest expenses.

We must use special care when computing the times interest earned ratio for a corporation. Since interest is deducted in determining taxable income for a corporation, the numerator for this ratio is *adjusted for a corporation* and expressed as

$$\begin{array}{c}\text{Times interest earned} \\ \text{(corporation)}\end{array} = \frac{\text{Income before interest expense and income taxes}}{\text{Interest expense}}$$

Exhibit 12.8 shows **Circuit City**'s times interest earned ratio for 1998–2000. Its ratio ranged from 3.2 to 14.0. Most competitors' ratios ranged from 3.0 to 9.0 during this period. Experience shows when this ratio falls below 1.5 to 2.0 and remains at that level or lower for several periods, the default rate on liabilities increases sharply. This reflects increased risk for such companies and their creditors. We also must interpret the times interest earned ratio in light of information about the variability of a company's income before interest. If this amount is stable from year to year or if income is growing, the company can afford to take on added risk by borrowing. If its income before interest greatly varies from year to year, fixed interest expense can increase the risk that it will not earn a positive return and be unable to pay interest expense.

Exhibit 12.8
Circuit City's Times Interest Earned

Demonstration Problem

The following transactions and events took place at Kern Company during its recent calendar year reporting period (Kern does not use reversing entries):

a. In September 2002, Kern sold $140,000 of merchandise covered by a 180-day warranty. Prior experience shows that costs of the warranty equal 5% of sales. Compute September's warranty expense and prepare the adjusting journal entry for the warranty liability as recorded at September 30. Also prepare the journal entry on October 8 to record a $300 cash expenditure to provide warranty service on an item sold in September.

b. On October 12, 2002, Kern arranged with a supplier to replace Kern's overdue $10,000 account payable by paying $2,500 cash and signing a note for the remainder. The note matures in 90 days and has a 12% interest rate. Prepare the entries recorded on October 12, December 31, and January 10, 2003, related to this transaction.

c. In late December, Kern learns it is facing a product liability suit filed by an unhappy customer. Kern's lawyer advises that although it will probably suffer a loss from the lawsuit, it is not possible to estimate the amount of damages at this time.

d. Kern's net income for the year is $1,000,000. Its interest expense for the year is $275,000. Calculate Kern's times interest earned ratio.

e. Sally Kline works for Kern. For the pay period ended November 30, her gross earnings are $3,000. Sally has $800 deducted for federal income taxes and $200 for state income taxes from each paycheck. Additionally, a $35 premium for her health care insurance and a $10 donation for the United Way are deducted. Sally pays FICA Social Security taxes at a rate of 6.2% and FICA Medicare taxes at a rate of 1.45%. She has not earned enough this year to be exempt from FICA taxes. Journalize the payment of Sally's wages by Kern.

f. On November 1, Kern borrows $5,000 from a bank in return for a 60-day, 14%, $5,000 note. Record the note's issuance on November 1 and its repayment with interest on December 31.

g. On December 16, Kern issues a noninterest-bearing note promising to pay $2,050 within 60 days. Record the issuance of the note, the interest accrual on December 31, and the repayment of the note on February 14 ($50 of interest is included in the note's face value of $2,050).

h. (*Assume that Kern is a corporation for parts* h *and* i.) Kern has made and recorded its quarterly income tax payments. In reviewing its year-end tax adjustments, it identifies an additional $50,000 of income tax expense that should be recorded. A portion of this additional expense, $10,000, is deferrable to future years. Record this year-end income taxes expense adjusting entry.

i. Income taxes expense for the year is $225,000. Calculate Kern's time interest earned ratio.

Planning the Solution

- For *a*, compute the warranty expense for September and record it with an estimated liability. Record the October expenditure as a decrease in the liability.
- For *b*, eliminate the liability for the account payable and create the liability for the note payable. Compute interest expense for the 80 days that the note is outstanding in 2002 and record it as an additional liability. Record the payment of the note, being sure to include the interest for the 10 days in 2003.
- For *c*, decide whether the company's contingent liability needs to be disclosed or accrued (recorded) according to the two necessary criteria: probable loss and reasonably estimable.
- For *d*, calculate times interest earned according to the formula in the chapter.
- For *e*, set up payable accounts for all items in Sally's paycheck that require deductions. After deducting all necessary items, credit the remaining amount to Accrued Payroll Payable.
- For *f*, record the issuance of the note. Calculate 60 days' interest due using the 360-day convention in the interest formula.
- For *g*, record the note as a noninteresting-bearing note. Use the contra account Discount on Notes Payable for the interest portion of the proceeds upon issuance. Make the year-end adjustment for 15 days' interest to Interest Expense and Discount on Notes Payable. Record the repayment of the note, being sure to include the interest for the 45 days in 2003.
- For *h*, determine how much of the income taxes expense is payable in the current year and how much needs to be deferred.
- For *i*, apply and compute times interest earned.

Solution to Demonstration Problem

a. Warranty expense = 5% × $140,000 = $7,000

Sept. 30	Warranty Expense.	7,000	
	Estimated Warranty Liability.		7,000
	To record warranty expense for the month.		
Oct. 8	Estimated Warranty Liability	300	
	Cash		300
	To record the cost of the warranty service.		

b. Interest expense for 2002 = 12% × $7,500 × 80/360 = $200
Interest expense for 2003 = 12% × $7,500 × 10/360 = $25

Oct. 12	Accounts Payable	10,000	
	Notes Payable		7,500
	Cash		2,500
	Paid $2,500 cash and gave a 90-day, 12% note		
	to extend the due date on the account.		
Dec. 31	Interest Expense	200	
	Interest Payable		200
	To accrue interest on note payable.		
Jan. 10	Interest Expense	25	
	Interest Payable	200	
	Notes Payable	7,500	
	Cash		7,725
	Paid note with interest, including the accrued		
	interest payable.		

c. Disclose the pending lawsuit in the financial statement notes. Although the loss is probable, no liability can be accrued since the loss cannot be reasonably estimated.

d. Times interest earned $= \dfrac{\text{Income before interest expense}}{\text{Interest expense}}$

$$= \dfrac{\$1,000,000 + \$275,000}{\$275,000} = 4.64 \text{ times}$$

e.

Nov. 30	Salaries Expense	3,000.00	
	FICA—Social Security Taxes Payable (6.2%)		186.00
	FICA—Medicare Taxes Payable (1.45%) . .		43.50
	Employee Federal Income Taxes Payable . .		800.00
	Employee State Income Taxes Payable . . .		200.00
	Employee Medical Insurance Payable		35.00
	Employee United Way Payable		10.00
	Accrued Payroll Payable		1,725.50
	To record Kline's pay.		

f.

Nov. 1	Cash	5,000	
	Notes Payable		5,000
	Borrowed cash with a 60-day, 14% note.		

When the note and interest are paid 60 days later, Kern Company records this entry:

Dec. 31	Notes Payable	5,000.00	
	Interest Expense	116.67	
	Cash		5,116.67
	Paid note with interest ($5,000 × 14% × 60/360).		

g.

Dec. 16	Cash	2,000.00	
	Discount on Notes Payable	50.00	
	Notes Payable		2,050.00
	Borrowed cash with a 60-day note.		
Dec. 31	Interest Expense	12.50	
	Discount on Notes Payable		12.50
	To record accrued interest (15/60 days × $50).		

When the note matures on February 14, 2003, Kern records this entry:

Feb. 14	Interest Expense (45/60 days × $50)	37.50	
	Notes Payable	2,050.00	
	Cash		2,050.00
	Discount on Notes Payable		37.50
	Paid note with interest.		

h.

Dec. 31	Income Taxes Expense	50,000	
	Income Taxes Payable		40,000
	Deferred Income Tax Liability		10,000
	To record added income taxes expense and the deferred tax liability.		

i. Times interest earned $= \dfrac{\$1,000,000 + \$275,000 + \$225,000}{\$275,000} = \underline{\underline{5.45 \text{ times}}}$

APPENDIX

12A Payroll Reports, Records and Procedures

Understanding payroll procedures and keeping adequate payroll reports and records is essential to a company's success. Many companies now use accounting software to maintain their payroll records. This appendix focuses on payroll accounting and its reports, records, and procedures.

Payroll Reports

Most employees and employers are required to pay local, state, and federal payroll taxes. Payroll expenses involve liabilities to individual employees, to federal and state governments, and to other organizations such as insurance companies. Beyond paying these liabilities, employers are required to prepare and submit reports explaining how they computed these payments.

Reporting FICA Taxes and Income Taxes

Identify and describe payroll records.

The Federal Insurance Contributions Act (FICA) requires each employer to file an Internal Revenue Service (IRS) **Form 941,** the *Employer's Quarterly Federal Tax Return,* within one month after the end of each calendar quarter. A form 941 is shown in Exhibit 12A.1 for Phoenix Sales & Service, a landscape design company. Accounting information and software are helpful in tracking payroll transactions and reporting the accumulated information on Form 941. Specifically, the employer reports total wages subject to income tax withholding on line 2 of Form 941. (For simplicity, this appendix uses *wages* to refer to both wages and salaries.) The income tax withheld is reported on lines 3 and 5. The combined amount of employees' and employer's FICA (Social Security) taxes for Phoenix Sales & Service is reported on line 6a (taxable Social Security wages, $36,599 × 12.4% = $4,538.28).

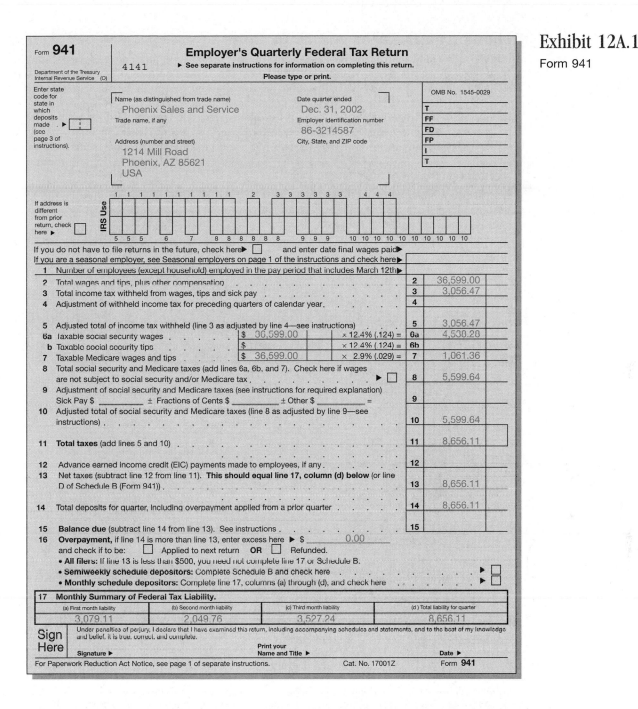

Exhibit 12A.1

Form 941

The 12.4% is the sum of the Social Security tax withheld, computed as 6.2% tax withheld from the employees' wages for the quarter plus the 6.2% tax levied on the employer. The combined amount of employees' Medicare wages is reported on line 7. The 2.9% is the sum of 1.45% withheld from employees' wages for the quarter plus 1.45% tax levied on the employer. Total FICA taxes are reported on lines 8 and 10 and are added to the total income taxes withheld of $3,056.47 to yield a total of $8,656.11. For this year, assume that income up to $76,200 is subject to Social Security tax. There is no income limit on amounts subject to Medicare tax. Congress sets annual limits on the amount owed for Social Security tax.

The total of amounts deposited in a **federal depository bank** is subtracted to determine whether a balance remains to be paid. Federal depository banks are authorized to accept deposits of amounts payable to the federal government. Deposit requirements depend on the amount of tax owed. For example, when the sum of FICA taxes plus the employees' income taxes is less than $500 for a quarter, the taxes can be paid when Form 941 is filed. Companies with large payrolls are often required to pay monthly or semiweekly. If taxes owed are $100,000 or more at the end of any day, they must be paid by the end of the next banking day.

Reporting FUTA Taxes and SUTA Taxes

An employer's federal unemployment taxes (FUTA) are reported on an annual basis by filing an *Annual Federal Unemployment Tax Return,* IRS **Form 940.** It must be mailed on or before January 31 following the end of each tax year. Ten more days are allowed if all required tax deposits are filed on a timely basis and the full amount of tax is paid on or before January 31. FUTA payments are made quarterly to a federal depository bank if the total amount due exceeds $100. If $100 or less is due, the taxes are remitted annually. Requirements for paying and reporting state unemployment taxes (SUTA) vary depending on the laws of each state. Most states require quarterly payments and reports.

Reporting Wages and Salaries

Employers are required to give each employee an annual report of his/her wages subject to FICA and federal income taxes along with the amounts of these taxes withheld. This report is called a *Wage and Tax Statement,* or **Form W-2.** It must be given to employees before January 31 following the year covered by the report. Exhibit 12A.2 shows Form W-2 for one of the employees at Phoenix Sales & Service.

Exhibit 12A.2

Form W-2

a Control number			
AR101		OMB No. 1545-0008	
b Employer's identification number		1 Wages, tips, other compensation	2 Federal income tax withheld
86-3214587		4910.00	333.37
c Employer's name, address, and ZIP code		3 Social security wages	4 Social security tax withheld
Phoenix Sales and Service		4910.00	304.42
1214 Mill Road		5 Medicare wages and tips	6 Medicare tax withheld
Phoenix, AZ 85621		4910.00	71.20
USA		7 Social security tips	8 Allocated tips
d Employee's social security number		9 Advance EIC payment	10 Dependent care benefits
333-22-9999			
e Employee's name, address, and ZIP code		11 Nonqualified plans	12 Benefits included in box 1
Robert Austin		13	14 Other
18 Roosevelt Blvd., Apt C			
Tempe, AZ 86322			

15 Statutory employee	Deceased	Pension plan	Legal rep.	Hshld. emp.	Subtotal	Deferred compensation

16 State	Employer's state I.D. No.	17 State wages, tips, etc.	18 State income tax	19 Locality name	20 Local wages, tips, etc.	21 Local income tax
AZ	13-902319	4910.00	26.68			

Department of the Treasury—Internal Revenue Service

Form **W-2** Wage and Tax Statement

Copy 1 For State, City, or Local Tax Department

Copies of the W-2 Form must be sent to the Social Security Administration. There they post to each employee's Social Security account the amount of the employee's wages subject to FICA taxes and FICA taxes withheld. These posted amounts become the basis for determining an employee's retirement and survivors' benefits. The Social Security Administration also transmits to the IRS the amount of each employee's wages subject to federal income taxes and the amount of taxes withheld.

Payroll Records

C6 Identify and describe payroll records.

Employers must keep certain payroll records in addition to reporting and paying taxes. These records usually include a payroll register. Good records also require an individual earnings report for each employee.

Payroll Register

A **payroll register** shows the pay period dates, hours worked, gross pay, deductions, and net pay of each employee for each pay period. Exhibit 12A.3 shows a payroll register for Phoenix Sales &

Exhibit 12A.3

Payroll Register

```
Peachtree Accounting: Exhibit 12a-3                                    _ □ ×
File  Edit  Maintain  Tasks  Analysis  Options  Reports  Window  Help
                    Phoenix Sales and Service                          _ □ ×
                         Payroll Register
                    For the Week Ending Oct. 8, 2002
```

Employee ID Employee SS No. Refer., Date	Pay Type	Pay Hours	Gross Pay	FIT	SIT	FICA-SS_EE	FICA-Med_EE	Net Pay
				FUTA	SUTA	FICA-SS_ER	FICA-Med_ER	
AR101 Robert Austin 333-22-9999 9001, 10/8/02	Regular Overtime	40.00	400.00 —	-28.99	-2.32	-24.80	-5.80	336.09
			400.00	-3.20	-10.80	-24.80	-5.80	
CJ102 Judy Cross 299-11-9201 9002, 10/8/02	Regular Overtime	40.00 1.00	560.00 21.00	-52.97	-4.24	-36.02	-8.42	479.35
			581.00	-4.65	-15.69	-36.02	-8.42	
DJ103 John Diaz 444-11-9090 9003, 10/8/02	Regular Overtime	40.00 2.00	560.00 42.00	-48.33	-3.87	-37.32	-8.73	503.75
			602.00	-4.82	-16.25	-37.32	-8.73	
KK104 Kay Koifo 909-11-3344 9004, 10/8/02	Regular Overtime	40.00	560.00 —	-68.57	-5.49	-34.72	-8.12	443.10
			560.00	-4.48	-15.12	-34.72	-8.12	
ML105 Lee Miller 444-56-3211 9005, 10/8/02	Regular Overtime	40.00	560.00 —	-34.24	-2.74	-34.72	-8.12	480.18
			560.00	-4.48	-15.12	-34.72	-8.12	
SD106 Dale Sears 909-33-1234 9006, 10/8/02	Regular Overtime	40.00	560.00 —	-68.57	-5.49	-34.72	-8.12	443.10
			560.00	-4.48	-15.12	-34.72	-8.12	
Totals	Regular Overtime	240.00 3.00	3,200.00 63.00	-301.67	-24.15	-202.30	-47.31	2,687.57
			3,263.00	-26.11	-86.10	-202.30	-47.31	

```
Sales    Purchases    General Ledger    Payroll    Inventory    Company    Analysis
```

Service. It has a three-line heading and a four-line explanation of the information and data that make up this report. It is organized into nine columns:

Col. 1 Employee identification (ID); Employee name; Social Security number (SS No.); Reference (check number) and Date (date check issued)

Col. 2 Pay Type (regular and overtime)

Col. 3 Pay Hours (number of hours worked as regular and overtime)

Col. 4 Gross Pay (amount of gross pay)[4]

Col. 5 FIT (federal income taxes withheld); FUTA (federal unemployment taxes)

Col. 6 SIT (state income taxes withheld); SUTA (state unemployment taxes)

Col. 7 FICA-SS_EE (social security taxes withheld, employee); FICA-SS_ER (social security taxes, employer)

Col. 8 FICA-Med_EE (medicare tax withheld, employee); FICA-Med_ER (medicare tax, employer)

Col. 9 Net pay (Gross pay less amounts withheld from employees)

Net pay for each employee is computed as gross pay minus the items on the first line of columns 5–8. The employer's payroll tax for each employee is computed as the sum of items on the third line of columns 5–8. A payroll register includes all data necessary to record payroll in the general journal. In some software programs the entries to record payroll are made in a *payroll journal.*

Payroll Check

Payment of payroll is usually done by check or funds transfer. Exhibit 12A.4 shows a *payroll check* for a Phoenix employee. This check is accompanied with a detachable *statement of earnings* (at top) showing gross pay, deductions, and net pay.

---

[4] The Gross Pay column shows regular hours worked on the first line multiplied by the regular pay rate. This equals regular pay. Overtime hours multiplied by the overtime premium rate equals overtime premium pay reported on the second line. If employers are engaged in interstate commerce, federal law sets a minimum overtime rate of pay to employees. For this company, it is 50% of the regular rate for hours worked in excess of 40 per week. This means workers earn at least 150% of their regular rate for hours in excess of 40 per week.

Exhibit 12A.4

Check and Statement of
Earnings

EMPLOYEE NO.	EMPLOYEE NAME		SOCIAL SECURITY NO.	PAY PERIOD END	CHECK DATE
AR101	Robert Austin		333-22-9999	10/8/02	10/8/02

ITEM	RATE	HOURS	TOTAL	ITEM	THIS CHECK	YEAR TO DATE
Regular	10.00	40.00	400.00	Gross	400.00	400.00
Overtime	15.00			Fed. Income tax	-28.99	-28.99
				FICA-Soc. Sec.	-24.80	-24.80
				FICA-Medicare	-5.80	-5.80
				State Income tax	-2.32	-2.32

HOURS WORKED	GROSS THIS PERIOD	GROSS YEAR TO DATE	NET CHECK	CHECK No.
40.00	400.00	400.00	$338.09	9001

(Detach and retain for your records)

PHOENIX SALES AND SERVICE
1214 Mill Road
Phoenix, AZ 85621
602-555-8900

Phoenix Bank and Trust
Phoenix, AZ 85621
3312-87044

9001

CHECK NO.	DATE	AMOUNT
9001	Oct 8, 2002	*************$338.09*

Three Hundred Thirty–Eight and 9/100 Dollars

PAY TO THE ORDER OF

Robert Austin
18 Roosevelt Blvd., Apt C
Tempe, AZ 86322

Mary Wills
AUTHORIZED SIGNATURE

Employee Earnings Report

An **employee earnings report** is a cumulative record of an employee's hours worked, gross earnings, deductions, and net pay. Payroll information on this report is taken from the payroll register. The employee earnings report for R. Austin at Phoenix Sales & Service is shown in Exhibit 12A.5.

Exhibit 12A.5

Employee Earnings Report

Peachtree Accounting: Exhibit 12a-5
File Edit Maintain Tasks Analysis Options Reports Window Help

Phoenix Sales and Service
Employee Earnings Report
For the Month Ending Dec. 31, 2002

Employee ID Employee SS No.	Date Reference	Gross Pay	FIT	SIT	FICA-SS_EE	FICA-Med_EE	Net Pay
			FUTA	SUTA	FICA-SS_ER	FICA-Med_ER	
Beginning Balance for Robert Austin		2,910.00	-188.42	-15.08	-160.42	-42.20	2,483.88
			-23.28	-78.57	-180.42	-42.20	
AR101 Robert Austin 333-22-9999	12/3/02 9049	400.00	-28.99	-2.32	-24.80	-5.80	338.09
			-3.20	-10.80	-24.80	-5.80	
AR101 Robert Austin 333-22-9999	12/10/02 9055	400.00	-28.99	-2.32	-24.80	-5.80	338.09
			-3.20	-10.80	-24.80	-5.80	
AR101 Robert Austin 333-22-9999	12/17/02 9061	400.00	-28.99	-2.32	-24.80	-5.80	338.09
			-3.20	-10.80	-24.80	-5.80	
AR101 Robert Austin 333-22-9999	12/24/02 9067	400.00	-28.99	-2.32	-24.80	-5.80	338.09
			-3.20	-10.80	-24.80	-5.80	
AR101 Robert Austin 333-22-9999	12/31/02 9073	400.00	-28.99	-2.32	-24.80	-5.80	338.09
			-3.20	-10.80	-24.80	-5.80	
Total 12/1/02 thru 12/31/02		2,000.00	-144.95	-11.60	-124.00	-29.00	1,690.45
			-16.00	-54.00	-124.00	-29.00	
Year-to-date Total for Robert Austin		4,910.00	-333.37	-26.68	-304.42	-71.20	4,174.33
			-39.28	-132.57	-304.42	-71.20	

Sales   Purchases   General Ledger   Payroll   Inventory   Company   Analysis

This employee earnings report accumulates information that can show when an employee's earnings reach the tax-exempt points for FICA, FUTA, and SUTA taxes. It also gives data employers need to prepare Form W-2.

Employers must be able to compute federal income tax for payroll purposes. This section explains how we compute this tax and how to use a payroll bank account.

Payroll Procedures

Computing Federal Income Taxes

To compute the amount of taxes withheld from each employee's wages, we need to determine both the employee's wages earned and the employee's number of *withholding allowances*. Each employee records the number of withholding allowances claimed on a withholding allowance certificate, **Form W-4,** filed with the employer. When the number of withholding allowances increases, the amount of income taxes withheld decreases.

 P5   Compute payroll taxes.

Employers often use a **wage bracket withholding table** similar to the one shown in Exhibit 12A.6 to compute the federal income taxes withheld from each employee's gross pay. The table in Exhibit 12A.6 is for a single employee paid weekly. Tables are also provided for married employees and for biweekly, semimonthly, and monthly pay periods (most payroll software includes these tables). When using a wage bracket withholding table to compute federal income tax withheld from an employee's gross wages, we need to locate an employee's wage bracket within the first two columns of the table. We then find the amount withheld by looking in the withholding allowance column for that employee.

Exhibit 12A.6

Wage Bracket Withholding Table

SINGLE Persons—WEEKLY Payroll Period
(For Wages Paid)

If the wages are –		And the number of withholding allowances claimed is —										
At least	But less than	0	1	2	3	4	5	6	7	8	9	10
		The amount of income tax to be withheld is —										
$600	$610	95	80	68	60	52	44	36	29	21	13	5
610	620	97	83	69	61	53	46	38	30	22	15	7
620	630	100	86	71	63	55	47	39	32	24	16	8
630	640	103	88	74	64	56	49	41	33	25	18	10
640	650	106	91	77	66	58	50	42	35	27	19	11
650	660	109	94	79	67	59	52	44	36	28	21	13
660	670	111	97	82	69	61	53	45	38	30	22	14
670	680	114	100	85	70	62	55	47	39	31	24	16
680	690	117	102	88	73	64	56	48	41	33	25	17
690	700	120	105	91	76	65	58	50	42	34	27	19
700	710	123	108	93	79	67	59	51	44	36	28	20
710	720	125	111	96	82	68	61	53	45	37	30	22
720	730	128	114	99	84	70	62	54	47	39	31	23
730	740	130	116	102	87	73	64	56	48	40	33	25
740	750	134	119	105	90	76	65	57	50	42	34	26

Payroll Bank Account

Companies with few employees often pay them with checks drawn on the company's regular bank account. Companies with many employees often use a special **payroll bank account** to pay employees. When this account is used, a company either (1) draws one check for total payroll on the regular bank account and deposits it in the payroll bank account or (2) executes an *electronic funds transfer* to the payroll bank account. The entry to record this transaction is

P6   Record payment of payroll.

Oct. 8	Accrued Payroll Payable	2,687.57	
	Cash		2,687.57
	To transfer cash to the payroll bank account.		

Assets   = Liabilities + Equity
−2,687.57   −2,687.57

Individual payroll checks are then drawn on this payroll bank account. Because only one check for the total payroll is drawn on the regular bank account each payday, use of a special payroll bank account helps with internal control. It also helps in reconciling the regular bank account. When companies use a payroll bank account, they usually include check numbers in the payroll register. The payroll register in Exhibit 12A.3 shows check numbers in column 1. For instance, Check No. 9001 is issued to Robert Austin. With this information, the payroll register serves as a supplementary record of wages earned by and paid to employees.

Quick Check

13. What two items determine the amount deducted from an employee's wages for federal income taxes?

[continued on next page]

[continued from previous page]

14. What amount of income tax is withheld from the salary of an employee who is single with three withholding allowances and earnings of $675 in a week? (*Hint:* Use the wage bracket withholding table in Exhibit 12A.6.)

15. Which of the following steps are executed when a company draws one check for total payroll and deposits it in a special payroll bank account? (a) Write a check to the payroll bank account for the total payroll and record it with a debit to Accrued Payroll Payable and a credit to Cash. (b) Deposit a check (or transfer funds) for the total payroll in the payroll bank account. (c) Issue individual payroll checks drawn on the payroll bank account. (d) All of the above.

Answer—p. 509

Summary

 Describe current and long-term liabilities and their characteristics. Liabilities are probable future payments of assets or services that past transactions or events presently obligate an entity to make. Current liabilities are due within one year or the operating cycle, whichever is longer. All other liabilities are long term.

C2 **Identify and describe known current liabilities.** Known (determinable) current liabilities are set by agreements or laws and are measurable with little uncertainty. They include accounts payable, sales taxes payable, unearned revenues, notes payable, payroll liabilities, and the current portion of long-term debt.

C3 **Explain how to account for contingent liabilities.** If an uncertain future payment depends on a probable future event and the amount can be reasonably estimated, the payment is recorded as a liability. The uncertain future payment is reported as a contingent liability (in the notes) if (a) the future event is reasonably possible but not probable or (b) the event is probable but the payment amount cannot be reasonably estimated.

C4 **Describe accounting for long-term liabilities.** Long-term liabilities are obligations *not* requiring payment within one year or the operating cycle, whichever is longer. Long-term liabilities are similar to current liabilities except for the length of time until payment and the likely use of present value concepts.

C5 **Identify and describe payroll reporting.** Employers report FICA taxes and federal income tax withholdings using Form 941. FUTA taxes are reported on Form 940. Earnings and deductions are reported to each employee and the federal government on Form W-2.

C6 **Identify and describe payroll records.** An employer's payroll records include a payroll register for each pay period, payroll checks and statements of earnings, and individual employee earnings reports.

 Compute the time interest earned ratio and use it to analyze liabilities. Times interest earned is computed by dividing a company's net income before interest by the amount of fixed interest expenses. For a corporation, the numerator is net income before interest *and* taxes. Times interest earned ratio reflects a company's ability to pay fixed interest obligations.

P1 **Prepare entries to account for short-term notes payable.** Short-term notes payable are current liabilities; most bear interest. When a short-term note's face value equals the amount borrowed, it identifies a rate of interest to be paid at maturity. When a short-term note's face value equals the amount to be paid at maturity, its face value includes interest.

P2 **Compute and record *employee* payroll deductions and liabilities.** Employee payroll deductions include FICA taxes, income taxes, and voluntary deductions such as for pensions and charitable giving. They make up the difference between gross and net pay.

P3 **Compute and record *employer* payroll expenses and liabilities.** An employer's payroll expenses include employees' gross earnings, and benefits, and payroll taxes levied on the employer. Payroll liabilities include employees' net pay amounts withheld from their wages and benefits, and the employer's payroll taxes.

P4 **Account for estimated liabilities, including warranties and income taxes.** Liabilities for health and pension benefits, warranties, bonuses, and income taxes are recorded with estimated amounts. These items are recognized as expenses when incurred.

P5 **Compute payroll taxes.** Federal income tax deductions depend on the employee's earnings and the number of withholding allowances claimed. Wage bracket withholding tables are available for different pay periods and employee classes.

P6 **Record payment of payroll.** Employers with a large number of employees often use a separate payroll bank account. When this is done, the payment of employees is recorded with a transfer of cash from the regular bank account to the payroll bank account.

Guidance Answers to **You Make the Call**

Rock Band Both banks agree to give the band $30,000 cash and require repayment in six months. Provided terms in these contracts are similar, the only potential difference is in the amount of interest the band must pay. The second bank's contract makes this clear—since $30,000 is borrowed and the band must pay $32,000, the interest charged is $2,000. For the first bank, we must compute interest on the contract. It is $2,100, computed as $30,000 × 14% × 6/12. The band prefers the contract requiring less interest, which is the one reading: "Band promises to pay $32,000 within 6 months."

Web Designer You need to be concerned about being an accomplice to unlawful payroll activities. Not paying federal and state taxes on wages earned is illegal and unethical. Such payments also will not provide the employee with Social Security and some Medicare credits. The best course of action is to request payment by check. If this fails to change the owner's payment practices, you must consider quitting this job.

Entrepreneur Risk is partly reflected by the times interest earned ratio. This ratio for the first franchise is 1.5 [($100,000 + $200,000)/$200,000], whereas the ratio for the second franchise is 3.5 [($100,000 + $40,000)/$40,000]. This analysis shows that the first franchise is more at risk of incurring a loss if its sales decline. The second question asks about variability of income before interest. If income before interest greatly varies, this increases the risk an owner will not earn sufficient income to cover interest. Since the first franchise has the greater variability, it is a riskier investment.

Guidance Answers to **Quick Checks**

1. A liability involves a probable future payment of assets or services that an entity is presently obligated to make as a result of past transactions or events.

2. No, an expected future payment is not a liability unless an existing obligation was created by a past event or transaction.

3. In most cases, a liability due in 15 months is classified as long term. It is classified as a current liability if the company's operating cycle is 15 months or longer.

4. A creditor prefers a note payable instead of an account payable so as to (a) charge interest and/or (b) have evidence of the debt and its terms for potential litigation or disputes.

5. The amount borrowed is $1,000 cash ($1,050 − $50). The rate of interest is 5% ($50/$1,000) for six months, which approximates an annual rate of 10%.

6. $1,000(.008) + $1,000(.04) + $3,000(.062) + $3,000(.0145) = $277.50

7. (a) FICA taxes are paid by both the employee and employer. (b) FUTA taxes are paid by the employer.

(c) SUTA taxes are paid by the employer.
(d) Withheld income taxes are paid by the employee.

8. (a)

9. (a) (Warranty expense was previously estimated.)

10. A corporation accrues an income tax liability for its quarterly financial statements because income tax expense is incurred when income is earned, not just at year-end.

11. (b)

12. A future payment is reported in the notes as a contingent liability if (a) the uncertain future event is probable but the amount of payment cannot be reasonably estimated or (b) the uncertain future event is not probable but has a reasonable possibility of occurring.

13. An employee's gross earnings and number of withholding allowances determine the deduction for federal income taxes.

14. $70

15. (d)

Glossary

Contingent liability potential liability that depends on a future event arising from a past transaction. (p. 496).

Current liability an obligation due within a year or the company's operating cycle, whichever is longer; paid using current assets or by creating other current liabilities, (p. 482).

Current portion of long-term debt portion of long-term debt due within one year or the operating cycle, whichever is longer; reported under current liabilities. (p. 498).

Deferred income tax liability corporation income taxes that are deferred until future years because of temporary differences between GAAP and tax rules. (p. 495).

Discount on note payable difference between the face value of a note payable and the amount borrowed; is interest to be paid on the note over its life. (p. 486).

Employee benefits additional compensation paid to or on behalf of employees, such as premiums for medical, dental, life, dis-

ability insurance, and contributions to pension plans. (p. 492).

Employee earnings report record of an employee's net pay, gross pay, deductions, and year-to-date information. (p. 506).

Estimated liability obligation of an uncertain amount that can be reasonably estimated. (p. 492).

Federal depository bank bank authorized to accept deposits of amounts payable to the federal government. (p. 503).

Federal Insurance Contributions Act (FICA) Taxes taxes assessed on both employers and employees; for Social Security and Medicare programs. (p. 490).

Federal Unemployment Taxes (FUTA) payroll taxes on employers assessed by the federal government to support the federal unemployment insurance program. (p. 491).

Form 940 IRS form used to report an employer's federal unemployment taxes (FUTA) on an annual filing basis. (p. 504).

Form 941 IRS form filed to report FICA taxes owed and remitted. (p. 502).

Form W-2 annual report by an employer to each employee showing the employee's wages subject to FICA and federal income taxes along with amounts withheld. (p. 504).

Form W-4 a withholding allowance certificate, filed with the employer, identifying the number of withholding allowances claimed. (p. 507).

Gross pay total compensation earned by an employee. (p. 489).

Known liabilities obligations of a company with little uncertainty; set by agreements, contracts, or laws; also called *definitely determinable liabilities*. (p. 484).

Long-term liability obligations *not* requiring payment within one year or the operating cycle, whichever is longer. (p. 483).

Merit rating rating assigned to an employer by a state based on the employer's record of employment. (p. 491).

Net pay gross pay less all deductions; also called *take-home pay*. (p. 489).

Noninterest-bearing note note with no stated rate of interest; interest is included in the face value of the note. (p. 487).

Payroll bank account bank account used solely for paying employees; each pay period an amount equal to the total employees' net pay is deposited in it and the employees' payroll checks are drawn on it. (p. 507).

Payroll deductions amounts withheld from an employee's gross pay; also called *withholdings*. (p. 489).

Payroll register record for a pay period that shows the pay period dates, regular and overtime hours worked, gross pay, net pay, and deductions. (p. 504).

Short-term note payable current obligation in the form of a written promissory note. (p. 485).

State Unemployment Taxes (SUTA) state payroll taxes on employers to support unemployment programs. (p. 491).

Times interest earned ratio of income before interest expense (and any income taxes) divided by interest expense; reflects risk of interest commitments when income varies. (p. 499).

Wage bracket withholding table table of the amounts of income tax withheld from employees' wages. (p. 507).

Warranty agreement that obligates the seller to correct or replace a product or service when it fails to perform properly within a specified period. (p. 493).

[Superscript letter ^A denotes assignments based on Appendix 12A.]

Questions

1. What are the three important questions concerning the uncertainty of liabilities?
2. What is the difference between a current and a long-term liability?
3. What is an estimated liability?
4. What is the combined amount (in percent) of the employees' and employer's Social Security tax rate?
5. What is the current Medicare tax rate?
6. What determines the amount deducted from an employee's wages for federal income taxes?
7. Which payroll taxes are the employee's responsibility and which are the employer's responsibility?
8. What is an employer's unemployment merit rating? How are these ratings assigned to employers?
9. Why are warranty liabilities usually recognized on the balance sheet as liabilities even when they are uncertain?
10. Suppose that a company has a facility located where disastrous weather conditions often occur. Should it report a probable loss from a future disaster as a liability on its balance sheet? Explain.

11.^A What is a wage bracket withholding table?
12.^A What amount of income tax is withheld from the salary of an employee who is single with two withholding allowances and earning $725 per week? What if the employee earned $625 and has no withholding allowances? (Use Exhibit 12A.6.)
13. Refer to **Nike**'s financial statements in **NIKE** Appendix A. Explain the change in current notes payable for 2000 with reference to a statement other than the balance sheet.
14. Refer to **Reebok**'s balance sheet in Appendix A. **Reebok** What accounts related to income taxes are on the balance sheet? Identify the meaning of each income tax account you identify.
15. Refer to **Gap**'s balance sheet in Appendix A. Which current liability account reports the payroll-related liabilities (if any) of Gap as of January 29, 2000?

Which of the following items are normally classified as a current liability for a company that has a 15-month operating cycle?

1. Bonds payable maturing in 2 years.

2. Note payable due in 11 months.

3. Portion of long-term note due in 15 months.

4. Salaries payable.

5. Note payable due in 18 months.

6. FICA taxes Payable.

Cube Computing sells $6,000 of merchandise for cash on September 30. The sales tax law requires Cube to collect 4% sales tax on every dollar of merchandise sold. Record the entry for the $6,000 sale and its applicable sales tax. Also record the entry that shows the remittance of the 4% tax on this sale to the state government on October 15.

Ticketmaster receives $5,000,000 in advance ticket sales for a four-date tour of the Rolling Stones. Record the advance ticket sales on October 31. Record the revenue earned for the first concert date of November 5 assuming it represents one-fourth of the advance ticket sales.

Regis Co. has five employees, each of whom earns $2,500 per month and has been employed since January 1. FICA Social Security taxes are 6.2% of gross pay and FICA Medicare taxes are 1.45% of gross pay. FUTA taxes are 0.8% and SUTA taxes are 2.8% of the first $7,000 paid to each employee. Prepare the March 31 journal entry to record March payroll taxes expense.

On November 7, 2002, Eager Company borrows $160,000 cash by signing a 90-day, 8% note payable with a face value of $160,000. (1) Compute the accrued interest payable on December 31, 2002, and (2) present the journal entry to record the payment of the note at maturity.

Hamm Company signs a noninterest-bearing note promising to pay $5,125 within 60 days after December 16. Record the signing of the note, the interest accrual on December 31, and the repayment of the note on February 14. (The note's face value of $5,125 includes $125 of interest.)

On September 11, 2002, Maxims sells a mower for $500 with a one-year warranty that covers parts. Warranty expense is estimated at 5% of sales. On July 24, 2003, the mower is brought in for repairs covered under the warranty requiring $55 in materials taken from the repair parts inventory. Prepare the July 24, 2003, entry to record the warranty repairs.

Ivanhoe Corporation has made and recorded its quarterly income tax payments. After a final review of taxes for the year, the company identifies an additional $40,000 of income tax expense that should be recorded. A portion of this additional expense, $6,000, is deferrable to future years. Record the year-end income tax expense adjusting entry for Ivanhoe.

The following legal claims exist for Kalamazoo Co. Identify the accounting treatment for each claim as either (a) a liability that is recorded or (b) an item described in notes to its financial statements.

1. Kalamazoo Company (defendant) estimates that a pending lawsuit could result in damages of $1,250,000; it is reasonably possible that the plaintiff will win the case.

2. Kalamazoo Company faces a probable loss on a pending lawsuit; the amount is not reasonably estimable.

3. Kalamazoo Company estimates damages in a case at $3,500,000 with a high probability of losing the case.

Fabrique Company offers an annual bonus to employees if it meets certain net income goals. Prepare the journal entry to record a $15,000 bonus owed to workers (to be shared equally) at year-end.

Compute the times interest earned for Sarafin Company, which reports income after interest expense of $1,675,500 and interest expense of $145,000. Sarafin Company is a proprietorship.

EXERCISES

Exercise 12-1
Financial statement presentation—current liabilities

Rahid Company has the following selected accounts and balances after its adjusting entries:

Accounts payable	$ 60,000
Note payable, 6-month	5,000
Accumulated depreciation—Equipment	22,000
Accrued payroll payable	4,750
Estimated warranty liability	11,000
Discount on 6-month note payable	500
Payroll taxes expense	3,000
Long-term debt	105,000

Prepare the current liability section of Rahid Company's balance sheet, assuming $15,000 of the long-term debt is due within the next year.

Exercise 12-2
Classifying liabilities

C1

The following items appear on the balance sheet of a company with a two-month operating cycle. Identify the proper classification of each item as follows: *C* if it is a current liability, *L* if it is a long-term liability, or *N* if it is not a liability.

_____ **1.** Notes payable (due in 6 to 12 months).
_____ **2.** Bonds payable (mature in five years).
_____ **3.** Mortgage payable (due in 12 months).
_____ **4.** Notes receivable (due in 30 days).
_____ **5.** Income taxes payable.
_____ **6.** Notes payable (due in 120 days).
_____ **7.** Mortgage payable (due after 13 months).
_____ **8.** Accounts receivable.
_____ **9.** Wages payable.
_____ **10.** Notes payable (due in 13 to 24 months).

Exercise 12-3
Warranty expense and liability

P4

Yoko Co. sold a copier costing $4,800 with a two-year parts warranty to a customer on August 16, 2002, for $6,000 cash. Yoko uses the perpetual inventory system. Based on experience, Yoko expects to incur warranty costs equal to 4% of selling price. Warranty expense is recorded with an adjusting entry at the end of each year. On November 22, 2003, the copier requires on-site repairs that are completed the same day. The repairs cost $209 for materials taken from the parts inventory. These are the only repairs required in 2003 for this copier.

1. How much warranty expense does the company report in 2002 for this copier?
2. How much is the estimated warranty liability for this copier as of December 31, 2002?
3. How much warranty expense does the company report in 2003 for this copier?
4. How much is the estimated warranty liability for this copier as of December 31, 2003?
5. Prepare journal entries to record (a) the sale; (b) the adjustment on December 31, 2002, to recognize the warranty expense; and (c) the repairs that occur in November 2003.

Exercise 12-4
Accounting for income taxes

P4

Caper Corporation prepares financial statements each month. As part of its accounting process, estimated income taxes are accrued each month for 30% of the current month's net income. The estimated income taxes are paid in the first month of each quarter for the amount accrued in the prior quarter. The following information is available for the last quarter of year 2002:

October net income	28,600
November net income	19,100
December net income	34,600

After all tax computations are completed in mid-January, Caper determines that the quarter's Income Taxes Payable account balance should be $28,300 on December 31.

Required

1. Determine the amount of the adjustment needed on December 31 to produce the proper ending balance in the Income Taxes Payable account.

2. Prepare journal entries to record (a) the December 31, 2002, adjustment to the Income Taxes Payable account and (b) the January 15, 2003, payment of the fourth-quarter taxes.

Peerless Systems borrows $104,000 cash on May 15, 2002, by signing a 60-day, 12% note.

1. On what date will this note mature?

2. How much interest expense results from this note? (Assume a 360 day year.)

3. Suppose the face value of the note equals $104,000, the principal of the loan. Prepare the journal entries to record issuance of the note and its payment at maturity.

4. Suppose the face value of the note is $106,080, which includes both the principal of the loan ($104,000) and the interest to be paid at maturity. Prepare the journal entries to record issuance of the note and its payment at maturity.

Exercise 12-5
Interest-bearing and noninterest-bearing notes payable

Excel Co. borrows $200,000 cash on November 1, 2002, by signing a 90-day, 9% note.

1. On what date will this note mature?

2. How much interest expense results from this note in 2002? (Assume a 360-day year.)

3. How much interest expense results from this note in 2003? (Assume a 360-day year.)

4. Suppose the face value of the note equals $200,000, the principal of the loan. Prepare journal entries to record issuance of the note, accrual of interest at the end of 2002, and payment of the note at maturity.

5. Suppose the face value of the note is $204,500, which includes both the principal of the loan ($200,000) and its interest ($4,500). Prepare journal entries to record issuance of the note, accrual of interest at the end of 2002, and payment of the note at maturity.

Exercise 12-6
Interest-bearing and noninterest-bearing short-term notes payable with year-end adjustments

---

TSI Co. has one employee. The employee and the company are subject to the following taxes:

Exercise 12-7
Computing payroll taxes

Tax	Rate	Applied To
FICA—Social Security	6.20%	First $76,200
FICA—Medicare	1.45	Gross pay
FUTA	0.80	First $7,000
SUTA	2.90	First $7,000

Compute TSI's amounts for these four taxes applied to the employee's gross earnings for September under each of three separate situations (a), (b), and (c):

	Gross Pay through August	Gross Pay for September
a.	$ 6,800	$ 900
b.	19,200	2,200
c.	71,200	8,000

Using the data in situation (a) of Exercise 12-7, prepare the employer's September 30 journal entries to record (1) salary expense and its related payroll liabilities for this employee and (2) the employer's payroll taxes expense and its related liabilities. The employee's federal income taxes withheld by the employer are $100.

Exercise 12-8
Payroll-related journal entries

Exercise 12-9
Adjusting entries for liabilities

P4

Prepare any necessary adjusting entries at December 31, 2002, for Delta Company's year-end financial statements given the following information:

1. During December, Delta Company sold 4,000 units of a product that carries a 60-day warranty. December sales for this product total $150,000. The company expects 8% of the units to need repair under warranty, and it estimates the average repair cost per unit will be $17.

2. A disgruntled employee is suing Delta Company. Legal advisers believe that the company will probably have to pay damages, but the amount cannot be reasonably estimated.

3. Employees earn vacation pay at a rate of one day per month. During December, 20 employees qualify for vacation pay. Their average daily wage is $105 per employee.

4. Delta Company guarantees the $7,500 debt of a supplier. The supplier will probably not default on the debt.

5. Delta Company records an adjusting entry for $1,750,000 of previously unrecorded cash sales along with the sales taxes of 5%.

6. $75,000 of $100,000 previously received in advance for products is now earned.

Exercise 12-10
Computing and recording bonuses

C2

For the year ended December 31, 2002, Warner Company has implemented an employee bonus program equal to 3% of Warner's net income that employees will share equally. Warner's net income is expected to be $500,000, and bonus expense is deducted in computing net income.

1. Compute the amount of the bonus payable to the employees at year-end (use the method described in the chapter and round to the nearest dollar).

2. Prepare the journal entry at December 31, 2002, to record the bonus due the employees.

3. Prepare the journal entry at January 19, 2003, to record payment of the bonus to employees.

Exercise 12-11
Computing and interpreting times interest earned

A1

Use the following information from proprietorships (a) through (f) to compute times interest earned:

	Net Income (Loss)	Interest Expense
a.	$150,000	$44,000
b.	160,000	10,000
c.	170,000	12,000
d.	365,000	14,000
e.	89,000	14,000
f.	⟨5,000⟩	10,000

Which of the cases demonstrates the strongest ability to pay interest expenses as they come due?

Exercise 12-12[A]
Net pay computation

P5

The payroll records of Classic Software show the following information about Trish Nyhart, an employee, for the weekly pay period ending September 30, 2002:

Total (gross) earnings for current pay period . . .	$ 725
Cumulative earnings previous pay periods	9,600

Trish is single and claims one allowance. Compute her Social Security tax (6.2%), Medicare tax (1.45%), federal income tax withholding, state income tax (0.5%), and net pay for the current pay period. The state income tax is 0.5 percent on $9,000 maximum. (Use the withholding table in Exhibit 12A.6.)

Exercise 12-13[A]
Gross and net pay computation

P5 P6

Wendy Geiger, an unmarried employee, works 48 hours in the week ended January 12. Her pay rate is $14 per hour, and her wages are subject to no deductions other than FICA—Social Security, FICA—Medicare, and federal income taxes. She claims two withholding allowances. Compute her regular pay, overtime pay (overtime premium is 50% of regular rate for hours in excess of 40 per week), and gross pay. Then compute her FICA tax deduction (use 6.2% for the Social Security portion and 1.45% for the Medicare portion), income tax deduction (use the wage bracket withholding table of Exhibit 12A.6), total deductions, and net pay.

Exercise 12-14[A]   P6
Payroll entry

Using Exercise 12-13, prepare the journal entry to record the transfer of $573.30 cash to a payroll bank account.

Langholz Co. entered into the following transactions involving short-term liabilities in 2002 and 2003.

PROBLEM SET A

Problem 12-1A
Short-term notes payable transactions and entries

2002

Apr. 20	Purchased $40,250 of merchandise on credit from Fitz, terms are 1/10, n/30. Langholz uses the perpetual inventory system.
May 19	Replaced the account payable to Fitz with a 90-day, $35,000 note bearing 10% annual interest along with paying $5,250 in cash.
July 8	Borrowed $80,000 cash from Firstar Bank by signing a 120-day interest-bearing note for $80,000. The note's annual interest rate is 9%.
?	Paid the amount due on the note to Fitz at maturity.
?	Paid the amount due on the note to Firstar Bank at maturity.
Nov. 28	Borrowed $42,000 cash by signing a noninterest-bearing note with a face value of $42,560 to UMB Bank that matures in 60 days. The face value includes a principal amount of $42,000 and interest of $560.
Dec. 31	Recorded an adjusting entry for the accrual of interest on the note to UMB Bank.

2003

?	Paid the amount due on the note to UMB Bank at maturity.

Required

1. Determine the maturity dates for each of the three notes described.

2. Determine the interest due at maturity for the three notes. (Assume a 360-day year.)

3. Determine the interest to be recorded in the adjusting entry at the end of 2002.

4. Determine the interest to be recorded in 2003.

Check   (4) Year 2003 interest, $252

5. Prepare journal entries for all the preceding transactions and events for years 2002–2003.

On October 29, 2002, Close Shave Products began operations by purchasing electric razors for resale at $75 each. Close Shave uses the perpetual inventory method. The razors are covered under a warranty that requires the company to replace any nonworking razor within 90 days. When a razor is returned, the company discards it and mails a new one from inventory to the customer. The company's cost for a new razor is $20 in both 2002 and 2003. The manufacturer has advised the company to expect warranty costs to equal 8% of dollar sales. The following transactions and events occurred in 2002 and 2003:

Problem 12-2A
Warranty expenses and liabilities estimation

2002

Nov.	11	Sold 105 razors for $7,875 cash.
	30	Recognized warranty expense for November with an adjusting entry.
Dec.	9	Replaced 15 razors that were returned under the warranty.
	16	Sold 220 razors for $16,500 cash.
	29	Replaced 30 razors that were returned under the warranty.
	31	Recognized warranty expense for December with an adjusting entry.

2003

Jan.	5	Sold 150 razors for $11,250 cash.
	17	Replaced 50 razors that were returned under the warranty.
	31	Recognized warranty expense for January with an adjusting entry.

Required

1. Prepare journal entries to record these transactions and adjustments for 2002 and 2003.

2. How much warranty expense is reported for November 2002 and December 2002?

3. How much warranty expense is reported for January 2003?

4. What is the balance of the Estimated Warranty Liability account as of December 31, 2002?

5. What is the balance of the Estimated Warranty Liability account as of January 31, 2003?

Check   (4) 12/31/02 Estim. Warranty Liab. bal., $1,050 Cr.

Problem 12-3A
Computing and analyzing
times interest earned

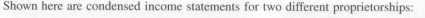
A1

Shown here are condensed income statements for two different proprietorships:

Acme Co.	
Sales	$1,000,000
Variable expenses (80%)	800,000
Income before interest	$ 200,000
Interest expense (fixed)	60,000
Net income	$ 140,000

Nadir Co.	
Sales	$1,000,000
Variable expenses (60%)	600,000
Income before interest	$ 400,000
Interest expense (fixed)	260,000
Net income	$ 140,000

Required

Preparation Component

1. Compute times interest earned for Acme Co.

2. Compute times interest earned for Nadir Co.

Check (3) Net income for Acme, $200,000 (43% increase)

3. What happens to each company's net income if sales increase by 30%?

4. What happens to each company's net income if sales increase by 50%?

5. What happens to each company's net income if sales increase by 80%?

6. What happens to each company's net income if sales decrease by 10%?

7. What happens to each company's net income if sales decrease by 20%?

8. What happens to each company's net income if sales decrease by 40%?

Analysis Component

9. Comment on what you observe in relation to the fixed cost strategies of the two companies and the ratio values you computed in parts (1) and (2).

Problem 12-4A
Payroll expenses,
withholdings, and taxes

P2 P3

$

Legal Eagles pays its employees every week. Employees' gross pay is subject to these taxes:

Tax	Rate	Applied To
FICA—Social Security	6.20%	First $76,200
FICA—Medicare	1.45	Gross pay
FUTA	0.80	First $7,000
SUTA	2.15	First $7,000

The company is preparing its payroll calculations for the week ended August 25. Payroll records show the following information for the company's four employees:

	A	B	C	D
1				**Current Week**
2		**Gross Pay**		
3	**Name**	**through 8/18**	**Gross Pay**	**Income Tax Withholding**
4	Chip	$78,200	$2,000	$278
5	Todd	31,700	1,000	109
6	Mary	6,850	550	60
7	Skip	1,250	500	45
8				

In addition to gross pay, the company must pay one-half of the $34 per employee weekly health insurance; each employee pays the remaining one-half. The company also contributes an extra 8% of each employee's gross pay (at no cost to employees) to a pension fund.

Required

Compute the following for the week ended August 25 (round amounts to the nearest cent):

1. Each employee's FICA withholdings for Social Security.

2. Each employee's FICA withholdings for Medicare.

3. Employer's FICA taxes for Social Security.

4. Employer's FICA taxes for Medicare.

5. Employer's FUTA taxes.

6. Employer's SUTA taxes.

7. Each employee's net (take-home) pay.

8. Employer's total payroll-related expense for each employee.

Check   (7) Total net pay, $3,304.17

On January 8, the end of the first weekly pay period of the year, Kidwear Company's payroll register showed that its employees earned $22,760 of office salaries and $65,840 of sales salaries. Withholdings from the employees' salaries include FICA Social Security taxes at the rate of 6.2%, FICA Medicare taxes at the rate of 1.45%, $12,860 of federal income taxes, $1,340 of medical insurance deductions, and $840 of union dues. No employee earned more than $7,000 in this first period.

Problem 12-5A^A

Entries for payroll transactions

Required

1. Calculate FICA Social Security taxes payable and FICA Medicare taxes payable. Prepare the journal entry to record Kidwear Company's January 8 payroll expenses and liabilities.

2. Prepare the journal entry to record Kidwear's payroll taxes resulting from the January 8 payroll. Kidwear's merit rating reduces its state unemployment tax rate to 4.0% of the first $7,000 paid each employee. The federal unemployment tax rate is 0.8%.

3. Kidwear Company uses a payroll bank account and special payroll checks in paying its employees. Prepare the journal entry to transfer funds equal to the payroll from the regular bank account to the payroll bank account.

4. After the entry in part (3) is journalized and posted, are additional journal entries required to record the payroll checks and pay the employees?

Check   (3) Dr. Accrued Payroll Payable, $66,782.10

Friesen Company has 10 employees, each of whom earns $2,700 per month and is paid on the last day of each month. All 10 have been employed continuously at this amount since January 1. Friesen uses a payroll bank account and special payroll checks to pay its employees. On March 1, the following accounts and balances exist in its general ledger:

a. FICA—Social Security Taxes Payable, $3,348; FICA—Medicare Taxes Payable, $783 (The balances of these accounts represent total liabilities for *both* the employer's and employees' FICA taxes for the February payroll only.)

b. Employees' Federal Income Taxes Payable, $4,000 (liability for February only).

c. Federal Unemployment Taxes Payable, $432 (liability for January and February together).

d. State Unemployment Taxes Payable, $2,160 (liability for January and February together).

During March and April, the company had the following payroll transactions:

Problem 12-6A^A

Entries for payroll transactions

Mar. 15   Issued check payable to Fleet Bank, a federal depository bank authorized to accept employers' payments of FICA taxes and employee income tax withholdings. The $8,131 check is in payment of the February FICA and employee income taxes.

   31   Recorded the March payroll and transferred funds from the regular bank account to the payroll bank account. The payroll register shows the following summary totals for the March pay period:

Salaries and Wages				Federal	
Office Salaries	Shop Wages	Gross Pay	FICA Taxes*	Income Taxes	Net Pay
$10,800	$16,200	$27,000	$1,674.00	$4,000	$20,934.50
			$ 391.50		

* FICA taxes are Social Security and Medicare, respectively.

   31   Issued checks payable to each employee in payment of the March payroll.

   31   Recorded the employer's payroll taxes resulting from the March payroll. The company has a merit rating that reduces its state unemployment tax rate to 4.0% of the first $7,000 paid each employee. The federal rate is 0.8%.

Check   Dr. Payroll Taxes Expenses, $2,833.50

Apr. 15   Issued check to Fleet Bank in payment of the March FICA and employee income taxes.
     15   Issued check to the State Tax Commission for the January, February, and March state un-
           employment taxes. Mailed the check and the first quarter tax return to the Commission.
     30   Issued check payable to Fleet Bank in payment of the employer's FUTA taxes for the first
           quarter of the year.
     30   Mailed Form 941 to the IRS, reporting the FICA taxes and the employees' federal income
           tax withholdings for the first quarter.

Required

Prepare journal entries to record the transactions and events for both March and April.

PROBLEM SET B

Quinn Co. entered into the following transactions involving short-term liabilities in 2002 and 2003.

Problem 12-1B

Short-term notes payable
transactions and entries

P1

2002

Apr. 22   Purchased $5,000 of merchandise on credit from Cascade Products, terms are 1/10, n/30.
           Quinn uses the perpetual inventory system.
May 23   Replaced the account payable to Cascade Products with a 60-day, $4,600 note bearing 15%
           annual interest along with paying $400 in cash.
July 15   Borrowed $12,000 cash from Fall River Bank by signing a 120-day interest-bearing note
           for $12,000. The note's annual interest rate is 10%.
     ?   Paid the amount due on the note to Cascade Products at maturity.
     ?   Paid the amount due on the note to Fall River Bank at maturity.
Dec. 6   Borrowed $8,000 cash by signing a noninterest-bearing note with a face value of $8,090
           to City Bank that matures in 45 days. The principal amount on the note is $8,000 and in-
           terest is $90.
     31   Recorded an adjusting entry for the accrual of interest on the note to City Bank.

2003

     ?   Paid the amount due on the note to City Bank at maturity.

Required

1. Determine the maturity dates for each of the three notes described.
2. Determine the interest due at maturity for the three notes. (Assume a 360-day year.)
3. Determine the interest to be recorded in the adjusting entry at the end of 2002.
Check   (4) Year 2003 interest, $40
4. Determine the interest to be recorded in 2003.
5. Prepare journal entries for all the preceding transactions and events for years 2002–2003.

Problem 12-2B

Warranty expenses and
liabilities estimation

P4

On November 10, 2002, Maleta Co. began operations by purchasing electric coffee grinders for resale at $50 each. Maleta uses the perpetual inventory method. The grinders are covered under a war-
ranty that requires the company to replace any nonworking grinder within 60 days. When a grinder
is returned, the company discards it and mails a new one from inventory to the customer. The company's cost for a new grinder is $24 in both 2002 and 2003. The manufacturer has advised the com-
pany to expect warranty costs to equal 10% of dollar sales. The following transactions and events
occurred in 2002 and 2003.

2002

Nov. 16   Sold 50 grinders for $2,500 cash.
     30   Recognized warranty expense for November with an adjusting entry.
Dec. 12   Replaced six grinders that were returned under the warranty.
     18   Sold 200 grinders for $10,000 cash.
     28   Replaced 17 grinders that were returned under the warranty.
     31   Recognized warranty expense for December with an adjusting entry.

2003

Jan. 7   Sold 40 grinders for $2,000 cash.
     21   Replaced 38 grinders that were returned under the warranty.
     31   Recognized warranty expense for January with an adjusting entry.

Required

1. Prepare journal entries to record these transactions and adjustments for 2002 and 2003.
2. How much warranty expense is reported for November 2002 and December 2002?
3. How much warranty expense is reported for January 2003?
4. What is the balance of the Estimated Warranty Liability account as of December 31, 2002?
5. What is the balance of the Estimated Warranty Liability account as of January 31, 2003?

Check   (4) 12/31/02 Estim.
Warranty Liab. bal., $698 Cr.

Shown here are condensed income statements for two different proprietorships:

Problem 12-3B
Computing and analyzing
times interest earned

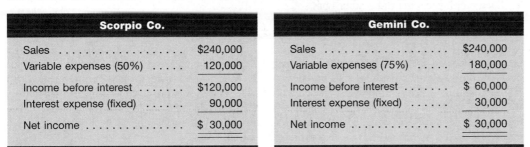

Scorpio Co.	
Sales	$240,000
Variable expenses (50%)	120,000
Income before interest	$120,000
Interest expense (fixed)	90,000
Net income	$ 30,000

Gemini Co.	
Sales	$240,000
Variable expenses (75%)	180,000
Income before interest	$ 60,000
Interest expense (fixed)	30,000
Net income	$ 30,000

Required

Preparation Component

1. Compute times interest earned for Scorpio.
2. Compute times interest earned for Gemini.
3. What happens to each company's net income if sales increase by 10%?
4. What happens to each company's net income if sales increase by 40%?
5. What happens to each company's net income if sales increase by 90%?
6. What happens to each company's net income if sales decrease by 20%?
7. What happens to each company's net income if sales decrease by 50%?
8. What happens to each company's net income if sales decrease by 80%?

Check   (4) Net income of Scorpio,
$78,000 (160% increase)

Analysis Component

9. Comment on what you observe in relation to the fixed cost strategies of the two companies and
the ratio values you computed in parts (1) and (2).

Seahawk Company pays its employees every week. Employees' gross pay is subject to these taxes:

Problem 12-4B
Payroll expenses,
withholdings, and taxes

P2 P3

Tax	Rate	Applied To
FICA—Social Security	6.20%	First $76,200
FICA—Medicare	1.45	Gross pay
FUTA	0.80	First $7,000
SUTA	1.75	First $7,000

The company is preparing its payroll calculations for the week ended September 30. Payroll records
show the following information for the company's four employees:

	A	B	C	D
1				Current Week
2		Gross Pay		
3	Name	through 9/23	Gross Pay	Income Tax Withholding
4	Axle	$78,400	$2,500	$198
5	Fred	58,700	1,245	163
6	Celine	5,350	525	55
7	Anne	24,300	700	52

In addition to gross pay, the company must pay one-half of the $40 per employee weekly health in-
surance; each employee pays the remaining one-half. The company also contributes an extra 5% of
each employee's gross pay (at no cost to employees) to a pension fund.

Required

Compute the following for the week ended September 30 (round amounts to the nearest cent):

1. Each employee's FICA withholdings for Social Security.

2. Each employee's FICA withholdings for Medicare.

3. Employer's FICA taxes for Social Security.

4. Employer's FICA taxes for Medicare.

5. Employer's FUTA taxes.

6. Employer's SUTA taxes.

Check   (7) Total net pay, $4,196.80   **7.** Each employee's net (take-home) pay.

8. Employer's total payroll-related expense for each employee.

Problem 12-5B[A]

Entries for payroll transactions

Genie Company's first weekly pay period of the year ends on January 8. On that date, the column totals in Genie's payroll register indicate its sales employees earned $34,745, its office employees earned $21,225, and its delivery employees earned $1,030. The employees are to have withheld from their wages FICA Social Security taxes at the rate of 6.2%, FICA Medicare taxes at the rate of 1.45%, $8,625 of federal income taxes, $1,160 of medical insurance deductions, and $138 of union dues. No employee earned more than $7,000 in the first pay period.

Required

1. Calculate FICA Social Security taxes payable and FICA Medicare taxes payable. Prepare the journal entry to record Genie Company's January 8 payroll expenses and liabilities.

2. Prepare the journal entry to record Genie's payroll taxes resulting from the January 8 payroll. Genie's merit rating reduces its state unemployment tax rate to 3.4% of the first $7,000 paid each employee. The federal unemployment tax rate is 0.8%.

Check   (3) Dr. Accrued Payroll
Payable, $42,716.50

3. Genie Company uses special payroll checks and a payroll bank account in paying its employees. Prepare the journal entry to transfer funds equal to the payroll from the regular bank account to the payroll bank account.

4. After the entry in part (3) is journalized and posted, are additional journal entries required to record the payroll checks and pay the employees?

Problem 12-6B[A]

Entries for payroll transactions

CMI Company has five employees, each of whom earns $1,400 per month and is paid on the last day of each month. All five have been employed continuously at this amount since January 1. CMI uses a payroll bank account and special payroll checks to pay its employees. On June 1, the following accounts and balances exist in its general ledger:

a. FICA—Social Security Taxes Payable, $868; FICA—Medicare Taxes Payable, $203. (The balances of these accounts represent total liabilities for *both* the employer's and employees' FICA taxes for the May payroll only.)

b. Employees' Federal Income Taxes Payable, $1,050 (liability for May only).

c. Federal Unemployment Taxes Payable, $112 (liability for April and May together).

d. State Unemployment Taxes Payable, $560 (liability for April and May together).

During June and July, the company had the following payroll transactions:

June 15   Issued check payable to Security Bank, a federal depository bank authorized to accept employers' payments of FICA taxes and employee income tax withholdings. The $2,121 check is in payment of the May FICA and employee income taxes.

    30   Recorded the June payroll and transferred funds from the regular bank account to the payroll bank account. The payroll register shows the following summary totals for the June pay period:

Salaries and Wages					
Office Salaries	Shop Wages	Gross Pay	FICA Taxes*	Federal Income Taxes	Net Pay
$2,800	$4,200	$7,000	$434.00 $101.50	$1,050	$5,414.50

* FICA taxes are Social Security and Medicare, respectively.

30   Issued checks payable to each employee in payment of the June payroll.

30   Recorded the employer's payroll taxes resulting from the June payroll. The company has a merit rating that reduces its state unemployment tax rate to 4.0% of the first $7,000 paid each employee. The federal rate is 0.8%.

July 15   Issued check payable to Security Bank in payment of the June FICA and employee income taxes.

15   Issued check to the State Tax Commission for the April, May, and June state unemployment taxes. Mailed the check and the second quarter tax return to the State Tax Commission.

31   Issued check payable to Security Bank in payment of the employer's FUTA taxes for the second quarter of the year.

31   Mailed Form 941 to the IRS, reporting the FICA taxes and the employees' federal income tax withholdings for the second quarter.

Check   Dr. Payroll Taxes Expenses, $535.50

Required

Prepare journal entries to record the transactions and events for both June and July.

BeGone Exterminators provides pest control services and also sells extermination products manufactured by other companies. The following six-column table contains the company's unadjusted trial balance as of December 31, 2002.

COMPREHENSIVE PROBLEM

BeGone Exterminators
(Review of Chapters 1–12)

BEGONE EXTERMINATORS December 31, 2002					
	Unadjusted Trial Balance		Adjustments	Adjusted Trial Balance	
Cash	$ 18,000				
Accounts receivable	5,000				
Allowance for doubtful accounts .		$ 928			
Merchandise inventory	12,700				
Trucks	40,000				
Accum. depreciation—Trucks		0			
Equipment	55,000				
Accum. depreciation—Equip.		14,400			
Accounts payable		4,800			
Estimated warranty liability		1,400			
Unearned services revenue		0			
Long-term notes payable		15,000			
Discount on notes payable	3,974				
T. Bugg, Capital		62,600			
T. Bugg, Withdrawals	10,000				
Extermination services revenue . .		70,000			
Interest earned		872			
Sales		80,000			
Cost of goods sold	54,017				
Depreciation expense—Trucks . . .	0				
Depreciation expense—Equip. . . .	0				
Wages expense	32,500				
Interest expense	0				
Rent expense	10,000				
Bad debts expense	0				
Miscellaneous expense	1,338				
Repairs expense	671				
Utilities expense	6,800				
Warranty expense	0				
Totals	$250,000	$250,000			

The following information applies to the company at the end of the current year:

a. The bank reconciliation as of December 31, 2002, includes these facts:

Balance per bank	$16,100
Balance per books	18,000
Outstanding checks	1,800
Deposit in transit	1,450
Interest earned	52
Service charges (miscellaneous expense)	15

Included with the bank statement is a canceled check that the company failed to record. (Information from the bank reconciliation allows you to determine the amount of this check, which is a payment on account.)

b. An examination of customers' accounts shows that accounts totaling $779 should be written off as uncollectible. Using an aging of receivables, the company determines that the ending balance of the Allowance for Doubtful Accounts should be $800.

c. A truck is purchased and placed in service on January 1, 2002. Its cost is being depreciated with the straight-line method using these facts and estimates:

Original cost	$40,000
Expected salvage value	5,000
Useful life (years)	5

d. Two items of equipment (a sprayer and an injector) were purchased and put into service early in January 2000. They are being depreciated with the straight-line method using these facts and estimates:

	Sprayer	Injector
Original Cost	$35,000	$20,000
Expected salvage value	3,000	4,000
Useful life (years)	8	5

e. On August 1, 2002, the company is paid $7,680 in advance to provide monthly service for an apartment complex for one year. The company began providing the services in August. When the cash was received, the full amount was credited to the Extermination Services Revenue account.

f. The company offers a warranty for the services it sells. The expected cost of providing warranty service is 2.5% of sales. No warranty expense has been recorded for 2002. All costs of servicing warranties in 2002 were properly debited to the Estimated Warranty Liability account.

g. The $15,000 long-term note is a five-year, noninterest-bearing note that was issued to First National Bank on December 31, 2000. The market interest rate on the issuance of the loan was 8% and interest expense (not yet recorded) is $882 for year 2002.

h. The ending inventory of merchandise is counted and determined to have a cost of $12,700. BeGone uses a perpetual inventory system.

Required

1. Use the preceding information to determine amounts for the following items:

   a. Correct ending balance of Cash and the amount of the omitted check.

   b. Adjustment needed to obtain the correct ending balance of the Allowance for Doubtful Accounts.

   c. Depreciation expense for the truck acquired in January.

   d. Depreciation expense for the two items of equipment used during year 2002.

   e. Adjusted ending balances of the Extermination Services Revenue and Unearned Services Revenue accounts.

   f. Adjusted ending balances of the accounts for Warranty Expense and Estimated Warranty Liability.

   g. Adjusted ending balances of the accounts for Interest Expense and Discount on Notes Payable. (Round amounts to nearest whole dollar.)

Check Adjustments Column
Totals, $25,294

2. Use the results of part (1) to complete the six-column table by first entering the appropriate adjustments for items (a) through (g) and then completing the adjusted trial balance columns. (*Hint*: Item (b) requires two adjustments.)

3. Present journal entries to record the adjustments entered on the six-column table. Assume BeGone's adjusted balance for Merchandise Inventory matches the year-end physical count.

4. Prepare a single-step income statement, a statement of changes in owner's equity, and a classified balance sheet.

Check   Net income, $23,370; Total assets, $98,271

Beyond the Numbers

BTN 12-1   Refer to the financial statements for **Nike** in Appendix A to respond to the following:

1. Compute times interest earned for the years ended May 31, 2000, 1999, and 1998. Comment on Nike's ability to cover its interest expense for this period.

2. What evidence can you identify for an indication that Nike has temporary differences between income reported on its income statement and income reported on its tax return?

Reporting in Action

C3   A1

NIKE

Swoosh Ahead

3. Access Nike's annual report for fiscal years ending after May 31, 2000, at its Web site [**www.nike.com**] or the SEC's EDGAR database [**www.sec.gov**]. Compute Nike's times interest earned for years ending after May 31, 2000, that you have access to.

BTN 12-2   Key comparative figures ($ millions) for both **Nike** and **Reebok** follow:

Comparative Analysis

A1

NIKE

Reebok

Key Figures	NIKE			REEBOK		
	Current Year	One Year Prior	Two Years Prior	Current Year	One Year Prior	Two Years Prior
Net income	$579.1	$451.4	$399.6	$11.0	$23.9	$135.1
Income taxes ...	340.1	294.7	253.4	10.1	11.9	12.5
Interest expense .	45.0	44.1	60.0	49.7	60.7	64.4

Required

1. Compute times interest earned for the three years' data shown for each company.

2. Comment on which company appears stronger in its ability to pay interest obligations if income should decline.

BTN 12-3   Mike Gates is a sales manager for an automobile dealership. He earns a bonus each year based on revenue from the number of autos sold in the year less related warranty expenses. Actual warranty expenses have varied over the prior 10 years from a low of 3% of an automobile's selling price to a high of 10%. In the past, Mike has tended to estimate warranty expenses on the high end to be conservative. He must work with the dealership's accountant at year-end to arrive at the warranty expense accrual for cars sold this year.

Ethics Challenge

P4

1. Does the warranty accrual decision create any ethical dilemma for Gates?

2. Since warranty expenses vary, what percent do you think Gates should choose for this year? Justify your response.

BTN 12-4   Matthew Stafford is the accounting and finance manager for a manufacturer. At year-end, he must determine how to account for the company's contingencies. His manager, John Harris, objects to Matthew's proposal to recognize an expense and a liability for warranty service on units of a new product introduced in the fourth quarter. John comments, "There's no way we can estimate this warranty cost. We don't owe anyone anything until a product breaks and is returned. Let's report an expense if and when we do repairs."

Communicating in Practice

C3

Required

Prepare a one-page memorandum for Matthew to send to John defending his proposal.

Taking It to the Net

C1 **C4** **A1**

BTN 12-5   Access the March 28, 2000, filing of the 10-K of **McDonald's Corporation** (Ticker: MCD), which is available from **www.edgar-online.com.**

Required

1. Identify the current liabilities on McDonald's balance sheet as of December 31, 1999.
2. What portion (in percent) of McDonald's long-term debt matures within the next 12 months?
3. Use the consolidated statement of income for the year ended December 31, 1999, to compute McDonald's times interest earned ratio.

Teamwork in Action

P1 **C2**

BTN 12-6   Your team is in business and you need to borrow $6,000 cash for short-term needs. You have been shopping banks for a loan, and you have the following two options:

A. Sign a $6,000, 90-day, 11% interest-bearing note dated June 1.
B. Sign a $6,172.50, 90-day, noninterest-bearing note dated June 1.

Required

1. Discuss these two options and determine the best choice. Ensure that all teammates concur with the decision and understand the rationale.
2. Each member of the team is to prepare *one* of the following journal entries:
   a. Option A—at date of issuance.
   b. Option B—at date of issuance.
   c. Option A—at maturity date.
   d. Option B—at maturity date.
3. In rotation, each member is to explain the entry he/she prepared in part (2) to the team. Ensure that all team members concur with and understand the entries.
4. Assume that the funds are borrowed on December 1 (instead of June 1) and your business operates on a calendar-year reporting period. Each member of the team is to prepare *one* of the following entries:
   a. Option A—the year-end adjustment.
   b. Option B—the year-end adjustment.
   c. Option A—at maturity date.
   d. Option B—at maturity date.
5. In rotation, each member is to explain the entry he/she prepared in part (4) to the team. Ensure that all team members concur with and understand the entries.

Business Week Activity

P4

BTN 12-7   Read the article "The Second Income: Is It Worth It?" in the August 25, 1997, issue of *Business Week*.

Required

1. What assumptions does the article's analysis make regarding the couple's location, income, family members, mortgage, and 401(k) plans?
2. Based on the analysis in the table, what is the couple's take-home pay when the husband works and the wife stays home? What is the pretax value of the 401(k) savings in this first scenario?
3. Based on the analysis reported in the table, what is the couple's take-home pay when both the husband and the wife work? What is the pretax value of the 401(k) savings in this second scenario?
4. What conclusions can you draw from this one example of whether it pays for both members of this couple to work full-time?

BTN 12-8   Shania Swain is an entrepreneur and owner of **The Edge**, a manufacturer of skateboards and accesssories. The Edge is considering a major technological investment in its manufacturing process. This investment would cut variable costs from 60% of sales to 45% of sales. However, fixed interest expense would increase from $90,000 per year to $190,000 per year to fund the $800,000 plant asset investment (with zero salvage, 50-year life, and depreciated using straight-line). Its recent income statement follows:

Entrepreneurial Decision

THE EDGE Income Statement For Year Ended January 31, 2002	
Sales	$500,000
Depreciation	10,000
Variable expenses (60%)	300,000
Income before interest	$190,000
Interest expense (fixed)	90,000
Net income	$100,000

Required

1. Compute The Edge's times interest earned ratio at January 31, 2002.

2. If the Edge expects sales to remain at $500,000, what would net income equal if it makes the investment?

3. What would net income equal if sales increase to $600,000 and the investment is (a) not made and (b) made?

4. What would net income equal if sales increase to $773,333 and the investment is (a) not made and (b) made? (Round amounts to the nearest thousand dollar.)

5. What would net income equal if sales increase to $900,000 and the investment is (a) not made and (b) made?

6. Comment on the results from parts (1) through (5) and their relation to the times interest earned ratio.

13

Partnerships

"Work with something that you love."—Amy Nye Wolf

A Look Back

Chapter 12 primarily focused on current liabilities and secondarily on long-term liabilities. We explained how liabilities are identified, computed, recorded, and reported in financial statements.

A Look at This Chapter

This chapter explains the partnership form of organization. Important characteristics of this form of organization are described along with the accounting concepts and procedures for its most fundamental transactions.

A Look Ahead

Chapter 14 extends our discussion to the corporate form of organization. We describe the accounting for stock issuances, dividends, and other equity transactions. We also explain how income, earnings per share, and retained earnings are reported.

Carry-On Music

e NEW YORK—Amy Nye Wolf knows the value of a good idea and a partnership. Wolf was only 17 years old and hiking across Europe when she bought a cassette at a London airport musicstand. "Even though they were overpriced and it was a lousy selection, I bought one anyway," says Wolf. This experience planted the seeds of selling CDs to U.S. air travelers. A few years later, using her savings and a loan from her parents, Wolf set up a partnership called **AltiTUNES Partners LP** [**www.AltiTUNES.com**] to pursue her idea—selling CDs and portable electronic products from stands in airport terminals.

Wolf believes knowledge of financial analysis and partnerships is crucial to her business activities. "I don't think I could do what I'm doing today without having worked as an analyst. I mean, they [accounting professionals] teach you everything from cash flow analysis and literally how to put together an Excel spreadsheet, which is a key tool." Wolf also emphasizes the importance of partnership formation, agreements, and financial statements to stay afloat. "There's a lot of other things you can do in life rather than risk everything and start your own business. We were fortunate in that the business started to throw off cash pretty much in its first week."

After a few lean years, AltiTUNES is a hit with travelers. It currently operates music outlets in more than 25 airport locations as well as its first train station outlet in New York's Grand Central Terminal. This year's revenues are expected to exceed $10 million. With little competition, low overhead, captive buyers, and a nearly 40% gross margin, the ride ahead looks smooth for AltiTUNES. [Sources: *AltiTUNES Web site*, May 2001; *CNN Business Unusual*, November 1997; *Forbes.Com*, May 1999]

The three common types of business organizations are proprietorships, partnerships, and corporations. Partnerships are similar to proprietorships, except they have more than one owner. This chapter explains partnerships and looks at several variations of them. These variations include limited partnerships, limited liability partnerships, S corporations, and limited liability companies. Understanding the advantages and disadvantages of the partnership form of business organization is important for making informed business decisions. This chapter gives us information to make such decisions.

Partnership Form of Organization

A **partnership** is an unincorporated association of two or more people to pursue a business for profit as co-owners. Many businesses are organized as partnerships. They are especially common in small retail and service businesses. Many professional practitioners also organize their practices as partnerships, including physicians, lawyers, investors, and accountants.

Characteristics of Partnerships

C1 Identify characteristics of partnerships and similar organizations.

Partnerships are an important type of organization because they offer certain advantages with their unique characteristics. We describe these characteristics in this section.

Voluntary Association

A partnership is a voluntary association between partners. Joining a partnership increases the risk to one's personal financial position in a desire for financial or other rewards. Note that some courts have ruled that partnerships are created by the actions of individuals even when there is no expressed agreement to form one.

Partnership Agreement

Point: When a new partner is admitted, all parties usually must agree to the admission.

Forming a partnership requires that two or more legally competent people (who are of age and of sound mental capacity) agree to be partners. Their agreement becomes a **partnership contract,** also called *articles of copartnership.* While it should be in writing, the contract is binding even if it is only expressed verbally. Partnership agreements normally include details of the partners' (1) names and contributions, (2) rights and duties, (3) sharing of income and losses, (4) withdrawal arrangement, (5) dispute procedures, (6) admission and withdrawal of partners, and (7) rights and duties in the event a partner dies.

Limited Life

Point: The end of a partnership is referred to as its *dissolution.*

The life of a partnership is limited. Death, bankruptcy, or any event taking away the ability of a partner to enter into or fulfill a contract ends a partnership. Any one of the partners can also terminate a partnership at will.

Taxation

Point: Partners are taxed on their share of partnership income, not on their withdrawals.

A partnership has the same tax status as a proprietorship and is not subject to taxes on its income. The income or loss of a partnership is allocated to the partners according to the partnership agreement, and it is included in determining the taxable income for each partner's tax return. Partnership income or loss is allocated each year whether or not cash is distributed to partners.

Mutual Agency

Mutual agency implies that each partner is a fully authorized agent of the partnership. As its agent, a partner can commit or bind the partnership to any contract within the scope of the partnership business. For instance, a partner in a merchandising business can sign contracts binding the partnership to buy merchandise, lease a store building, borrow money, or hire employees. These activities are all within the scope of a merchandising firm. A partner in a law firm, acting alone, however, cannot bind the other partners to a contract to buy snowboards for resale or rent an apartment for parties. These actions are outside the normal scope of a law firm's business. Partners also can agree to limit the power of any one or more of the partners to negotiate contracts for the partnership. This agreement is binding on the partners and on outsiders who know it exists. It is not binding on outsiders who do not know it exists. Outsiders unaware of the agreement have the right to assume each partner has normal agency powers for the partnership. Mutual agency exposes partners to the risk of unwise actions by any one partner.

Point: The majority of states adhere to the Uniform Partnership Act for the basic rules of partnership formation, operation, and dissolution.

Unlimited Liability

Unlimited liability implies that each partner can be called on to pay a partnership's debts. When a partnership cannot pay its debts, creditors usually can apply their claims to partners' *personal* assets. If a partner does not have enough assets to meet his/her share of the partnership debt, the creditors can apply their claims to the assets of the other partners. Partnerships in which all partners have *mutual agency* and *unlimited liability* are called **general partnerships.** Mutual agency and unlimited liability are two main reasons that most general partnerships have only a few members.

Co-Ownership of Property

Partnership assets are owned jointly by all partners. Any investment by a partner becomes the joint property of all partners. Partners have a claim on partnership assets based on their capital account and the partnership contract.

Organizations with Partnership Characteristics

Organizations exist that combine certain characteristics of partnerships with other forms of organizations. We discuss several of these forms in this section.

Limited Partnerships

Some individuals who want to invest in a partnership are unwilling to accept the risk of unlimited liability. Their needs may be met with a **limited partnership.** This type of organization is identified in its name with the words "Limited Partnership," or "Ltd.," or "L.P." A limited partnership has two classes of partners, general and limited. At least one partner must be a **general partner** who assumes management duties and unlimited liability for the debts of the partnership. The **limited partners** have no personal liability beyond the amounts they invest in the partnership. The general partner(s) manages a limited partnership. Limited partners have no active role except as specified

> **Did You Know?**
>
> **Celtic Partners**   The **Boston Celtics** is organized as a limited partnership. It owns and operates the Boston Celtics NBA team. The general partner of the Boston Celtics is Celtics, Inc., and Paul E. Gaston is chairman of the board of Celtics, Inc.
>
>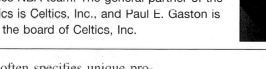

in the partnership agreement. A limited partnership agreement often specifies unique procedures for allocating income and losses between general and limited partners. The accounting procedures are similar for both limited and general partnerships.

Limited Liability Partnerships

Most states allow individuals to form a **limited liability partnership.** This is identified in its name with the words "Limited Liability Partnership" or by "L.L.P." This type of partnership is designed to protect innocent partners from malpractice or negligence claims resulting from the acts of another partner. When a partner provides service resulting in a malpractice claim, that partner has personal liability for the claim. The remaining partners who were not responsible for the actions resulting in the claim are not personally liable for it. However, most states hold all partners personally liable for other partnership debts. Accounting for a limited liability partnership is the same as for a general partnership.

S Corporations

Certain corporations with 75 or fewer stockholders can elect to be treated as a partnership for income tax purposes. These corporations are called Sub-Chapter S or simply **S corporations.** This distinguishes them from other corporations, called Sub-Chapter C or simply **C corporations.** S corporations provide stockholders the same limited liability feature that C corporations do. The advantage of an S corporation is that it does not pay income taxes.

If stockholders work for an S corporation, their salaries are treated as expenses of the corporation. The remaining income or loss of the corporation is allocated to stockholders for inclusion on their personal tax returns. Except for C corporations having to account for income tax expenses and liabilities, the accounting procedures are the same for both S and C corporations.

Limited Liability Companies

Point: The majority of proprietorships and partnerships that are being organized today are being set up as an LLC.

A relatively new form of business organization is the **limited liability company.** The names of these businesses usually include the words "Limited Liability Company" or an abbreviation such as "L.L.C." or "L.C." This form of business has certain features similar to a corporation and others similar to a limited partnership. The owners, who are called *members,* are protected with the same limited liability feature as owners of corporations. While limited partners cannot actively participate in the management of a limited partnership, the members of a limited liability company can assume an active management role. A limited liability company usually has a limited life. For income tax purposes, a limited liability company is typically treated as a partnership. This treatment depends on factors such as whether the members' equity interests are freely transferable and whether the company has continuity of life. A limited liability company's accounting system is designed to help management comply with the dictates of the articles of organization and company regulations adopted by its members. The accounting system also must provide information to support the company's compliance with state and federal laws, including taxation.

> ### Did You Know?
>
> **Tax Relief** A recent IRS rule lets individuals set themselves up as LLCs. Previously, an LLC needed to have at least two people. There is also a PLLC for professionals.

Point: Accounting for LLCs is similar to that for proprietorships and partnerships. One difference is that Owner (Partner), Capital is usually called Members, Capital for LLCs.

Choosing a Business Form

Choosing the proper business form is crucial. Many factors should be considered, including taxes, liability risk, tax and fiscal year-end, ownership structure, estate planning, business risks, and earnings and property distributions. The following table summarizes several important characteristics of business organizations:

	Proprietorship	Partnership	LLP	LLC	S Corp.	Corporation
Business entity	yes	yes	yes	yes	yes	yes
Legal entity	no	no	no	yes	yes	yes
Limited liability	no	no	limited*	yes	yes	yes
Business taxed	no	no	no	no	no	yes
One owner allowed	yes	no	no	yes	yes	yes

* A partner's personal liability for LLP debts is limited. Most LLPs carry insurance to protect against malpractice.

We must remember that this table is a summary, not a detailed list. Many details underlie each of these business forms, and several details differ across states. Also, state and federal laws change, and a body of law is still developing around LLCs. Business owners should look at these details and consider unique business arrangements such as organizing various parts of their businesses in different forms.

> ### Quick Check
>
> 1. A partnership is terminated in the event (a) a partnership agreement is not in writing, (b) a partner dies, (c) a partner exercises mutual agency.
> 2. What does the term *unlimited liability* mean when applied to a general partnership?
> 3. Which of the following forms of organization do not provide limited liability to all of its owners: (a) S corporation, (b) limited liability company, (c) limited partnership?

Answers—p. 544

Accounting for a partnership is the same as accounting for a proprietorship with the exception for transactions directly affecting partners' equity. Because ownership rights in a partnership are divided among partners, partnership accounting

Basic Partnership Accounting

- Uses a capital account for each partner.
- Uses a withdrawals account for each partner.
- Allocates net income or loss to partners according to the partnership agreement.

This section describes partnership accounting for organizing a partnership, distributing income and loss, and preparing financial statements.

Organizing a Partnership

When partners invest in a partnership, their capital accounts are credited for the invested amounts. Partners can invest both assets and liabilities. Each partner's investment is recorded at an agreed-upon value, normally the market values of the contributed assets and liabilities at the date of contribution.

P1 Prepare entries for partnership formation.

To illustrate, Kate Steeley and David Breck organize a partnership called **BOARDS** that offers year-round facilities for skateboarding and snowboarding. Steeley's initial net investment in BOARDS is $30,000, made up of cash ($7,000), boarding facilities ($33,000), and a note payable reflecting a bank loan for the new business ($10,000). Breck's initial investment is cash of $10,000. These amounts are the values agreed upon by both partners. The entries to record these investments follow:

Steeley's Investment

Jan. 11	Cash	7,000	
	Boarding facilities	33,000	
	Note payable		10,000
	K. Steeley, Capital		30,000
	To record the investment of Steeley.		

Assets − Liabilities + Equity
+7,000   +10,000   +30,000
+33,000

Breck's Investment

Jan. 11	Cash	10,000	
	D. Breck, Capital		10,000
	To record the investment of Breck.		

Assets = Liabilities + Equity
+10,000   +10,000

Once a partnership is formed, accounting for its transactions is similar to accounting for those of a proprietorship. Chapters 2, 3, and 4 describe the basic accounting procedures for a proprietorship, and they apply here as well. Minor differences include the following:

Point: Both equity and cash are reduced when a partner withdraws cash from a partnership.

1. Partners' withdrawals are debited to their own separate withdrawals accounts.
2. Partners' capital accounts are credited (or debited) for their shares of net income (or net loss) when closing the accounts at the end of a period.
3. Each partner's withdrawals account is closed to that partner's capital account.

These procedures are similar to those used for a proprietorship, except that separate capital and withdrawals accounts are kept for each partner.

Did You Know?

Nutty Partners The Hawaii-based **ML Macadamia Orchards LP** is one of the world's largest growers of macadamia nuts. It reported the following partners' capital balances ($ thousands) in its recent balance sheet:

| General Partners . . . . | $ 613 |
| Limited Partners . . . . | $60,657 |

P2 Allocate and record income and loss among partners.

Concept 13-1

Dividing Income or Loss

Partners are not employees of the partnership but are its owners. If partners devote their time and services to their partnership, they are understood to do so for profit, not for salary. This means there are no salaries to partners that are reported as expenses on the partnership income statement. However, when net income or loss of a partnership is allocated among partners, the partners can agree to allocate "salary allowances" reflecting the relative value of services provided. Partners also can agree to allocate "interest allowances" based on the amount invested. For instance, since Steeley contributes three times the investment of Breck, it is only fair that this be considered when allocating income between them. Like salary allowances, these interest allowances are not expenses on the income statement.

Point: Partners can agree on one ratio to divide income and another ratio to divide a loss.

Partners can agree to any method of dividing income or loss. In the absence of an agreement, the law says that the partners share income or loss of a partnership equally. If partners agree on how to share income but say nothing about losses, they share losses the same way that income is shared. Several methods of sharing partnership income or loss are used. Three common methods to divide income or loss use (1) a stated fractional basis, (2) the ratio of capital investments, or (3) salary and interest allowances and any remainder according to a fixed ratio. We explain each of these methods in this section.

Allocation on Stated Ratios

Point: The fractional basis can be stated as a proportion, ratio, or percent. For example, a 3:2 basis is the same as ⅗ and ⅖, or 60% and 40%.

The *stated ratio* (also called the *income and loss ratio*, the *profit and loss ratio*, or the *P&L ratio*) method of allocating partnership income or loss gives each partner a fraction of the total. Partners must agree on the fractional share each receives. To illustrate, assume the partnership agreement of K. Steeley and D. Breck says Steeley receives two-thirds and Breck one-third of partnership income and loss. If their partnership's net income is $60,000, it is allocated to the partners when the Income Summary account is closed as follows:

Assets = Liabilities + Equity
−60,000
+40,000
+20,000

Dec. 31	Income Summary	60,000	
	K. Steeley, Capital		40,000
	D. Breck, Capital		20,000
	To allocate income and close Income Summary.		

Allocation on Capital Balances

Point: To determine the percent of income received by each partner, divide an individual partner's share by total net income.

The *capital balances* method of allocating partnership income or loss assigns an amount based on the ratio of each partner's relative capital balance. If Steeley and Breck agree to share income and loss on the ratio of their beginning capital balances—Steeley's $30,000 and Breck's $10,000—Steeley receives three-fourths of any income or loss ($30,000/$40,000) and Breck receives one-fourth ($10,000/$40,000). The journal entry follows the same format as that using stated ratios.

Allocation on Services, Capital, and Stated Ratios

The *services, capital, and stated ratio* method of allocating partnership income or loss recognizes that service and capital contributions of partners often are not equal. Salary allowances can make up for differences in service contributions. Interest allowances can make up for unequal capital contributions. Also, the allocation of income and loss can include *both* salary and interest allowances. To illustrate, assume that the partnership agreement of K. Steeley and D. Breck reflects differences in service and capital contributions as follows:

1. Annual salary allowances of $36,000 to Steeley and $24,000 to Breck.
2. Annual interest allowances of 10% of a partner's beginning-year capital balance.
3. Any remaining balance of income or loss is shared equally.

These salaries and interest allowances are *not* reported as expenses on the income statement. They are simply a means of dividing partnership income or loss. The remainder of this section provides two illustrations using this 3-point allocation agreement.

	Steeley	Breck	Total
Net income			$70,000
Salary allowances			
Steeley	$36,000		
Breck		$24,000	
Interest allowances			
Steeley (10% × $30,000)	3,000		
Breck (10% × $10,000)		1,000	
Total salaries and interest	39,000	25,000	64,000
Balance of income			6,000
Balance allocated equally			
Steeley	3,000 ←		
Breck		3,000 ←	
Total allocated			6,000
Balance of income			$ 0
Income of each partner	$42,000	$28,000	

Exhibit 13.1

Dividing Income When Income Exceeds Allowances

Illustration when income exceeds allowance

If BOARDS has first-year net income of $70,000, and Steeley and Breck apply the 3-point partnership agreement at the bottom of the prior page, then income is allocated as shown in Exhibit 13.1. Steeley gets $42,000 and Breck gets $28,000 of the $70,000 total.

Illustration when allowances exceed income

The sharing agreement between Steeley and Breck must be followed even if net income is less than the total of the allowances. For example, if BOARDS' first year net income is $50,000 instead of $70,000, it is allocated to the partners as shown in Exhibit 13.2. Computations for salaries and interest are identical to those in Exhibit 13.1. However, when we apply the total allowances against income, the balance of income is negative. This $(14,000) negative balance is allocated in the same manner as a positive balance.

Point: When allowances exceed income, the amount of this negative balance often is referred to as a *sharing agreement loss* or *deficit*.

	Steeley	Breck	Total
Net income			$50,000
Salary allowances			
Steeley	$36,000		
Breck		$24,000	
Interest allowances			
Steeley (10% × $30,000)	3,000		
Breck (10% × $10,000)		1,000	
Total salaries and interest	39,000	25,000	64,000
Balance of income			(14,000)
Balance allocated equally			
Steeley	(7,000) ←		
Breck		(7,000) ←	
Total allocated			14,000
Balance of income			$ 0
Income of each partner	$32,000	$18,000	

Exhibit 13.2

Dividing Income When Allowances Exceed Income

Point: Check to make sure the sum of the dollar amounts allocated to each partner equals net income or loss.

Point: When a loss occurs, it is possible for a specific partner's capital to increase (when closing income summary) if that partner's allowance is in excess of his or her share of the negative balance. This implies that decreases to the capital balances of other partners exceed the partnership's loss amount.

Accordingly, the equal sharing agreement for the remaining balance means a negative $(7,000) is allocated to each partner. In this case, Steeley ends up with $32,000 and Breck gets $18,000. If BOARDS had experienced a loss, Steeley and Breck would share it in the same manner as the $50,000 income. The only difference is that they would have begun with a negative amount because of the loss. Specifically, the partners would still have been allocated their salary and interest allowances, further adding to the negative balance of the loss. This *total* negative balance *after* salary and interest allowances would have been allocated equally between the partners. These allocations would have been applied against the positive numbers from any allowances to determine each partner's share of the loss.

Quick Check

4. Ben and Jerry form a partnership by contributing $70,000 and $35,000, respectively. They agree to an interest allowance equal to 10% of each partner's capital balance at the beginning of the year, with the remaining income shared equally. Allocate first-year income of $40,000 to each partner.

Answer—p. 544

Partnership Financial Statements

Partnership financial statements are very similar to those of a proprietorship. The **statement of changes in partners' equity,** also called *statement of partners' capital,* is one exception. It shows *each* partner's beginning capital balance, additional investments, allocated income or loss, withdrawals, and ending capital balance. To illustrate, Exhibit 13.3 shows the statement of changes in partners' equity for BOARDS prepared using the sharing agreement of Exhibit 13.1. Recall that BOARDS' income was $70,000 and that Steeley withdrew $20,000 and Breck $12,000 at year-end.

The equity section of the balance sheet of a partnership usually shows the separate capital account balance of each partner. In the case of BOARDS, both K. Steeley, Capital, and D. Breck, Capital, are listed in the owner's equity section along with their balances of $52,000 and $26,000, respectively.

Did You Know?

Hotel California The **Casa Munras Hotel Partners LP** operates the Casa Munras Garden Hotel and several leased retail stores in Monterey, California. Its recent statement of changes in partners' equity reports that total partners' withdrawals (distributions) equal $270,000, of which $2,700 is distributed to general partners and the remainder of $267,300 to limited partners.

Exhibit 13.3

Statement of Changes in Partners' Equity

BOARDS Statement of Changes in Partners' Equity For Year Ended December 31, 2002			
	Steeley	**Breck**	**Total**
Beginning capital balances	$ 0	$ 0	$ 0
Plus			
Investments by owners	30,000	10,000	40,000
Net income			
Salary allowances $36,000		$24,000	
Interest allowances 3,000		1,000	
Balance allocated 3,000		3,000	
Total net income	42,000	28,000	70,000
	72,000	38,000	110,000
Less partners' withdrawals	(20,000)	(12,000)	(32,000)
Ending capital balances	**$52,000**	**$26,000**	**$78,000**

A partnership is based on a contract between individuals. When a partner is admitted or withdraws, the present partnership ends. Still, the business can continue to operate as a new partnership consisting of the remaining partners. This section considers how to account for the admission and withdrawal of partners.

Admission of a Partner

A new partner is admitted in one of two ways: by purchasing an interest from one or more current partners, or by investing cash or other assets.

Purchase of Partnership Interest

The purchase of partnership interest is a *personal transaction between one or more current partners and the new partner.* To become a partner, the current partners must accept the purchaser. Accounting for the purchase of partnership interest involves reallocating current partners' capital to reflect the transaction. To illustrate, at the end of BOARDS' first year, D. Breck sells one-half of his partnership interest to Cris Davis for $18,000. This means Breck gives up a $13,000 recorded interest ($26,000 × 1/2) in the partnership (see the ending capital balance in Exhibit 13.3). The partnership records this as follows:

Jan. 4	D. Breck, Capital	13,000	
	C. Davis, Capital		13,000
	To record admission of Davis by purchase.		

After this entry is posted, BOARDS' equity shows K. Steeley, Capital; D. Breck, Capital; and C. Davis, Capital, and their respective balances of $52,000, $13,000, and $13,000.

Two aspects of this transaction are important. First, the partnership, does *not* record the $18,000 Davis paid Breck regardless of the amount Davis paid Breck. The partnership's assets, liabilities, and *total* equity are unaffected by this transaction among partners. Second, Steeley and Breck must agree if Davis is to become a partner. If they agree to accept Davis, a new partnership is formed and a new contract with a new income-and-loss-sharing agreement is prepared. If Steeley or Breck refuses to accept Davis as a partner, then (under the Uniform Partnership Act), Davis gets Breck's sold share of partnership income and loss. If the partnership is liquidated, Davis gets Breck's sold share of partnership assets. Davis gets no voice in managing the company unless he is admitted as a partner.

Investing Assets in a Partnership

Admitting a partner by accepting assets is a *transaction between the new partner and the partnership.* The invested assets become partnership property. To illustrate, if Steeley (with a $52,000 interest) and Breck (with a $26,000 interest) agree to accept Davis as a partner in BOARDS with her investment of $22,000 cash, this is recorded as

Jan. 4	Cash	22,000	
	C. Davis, Capital		22,000
	To record admission of Davis by investment.		

After this entry is posted, both assets (cash) and equity (C. Davis, Capital) increase by $22,000. Davis now has a 22% equity in the assets of the business, computed as $22,000 divided by the entire partnership equity ($52,000 + $26,000 + $22,000). She does not necessarily have a right to 22% of income. Dividing income and loss is a separate matter on which partners must agree.

Bonus to old partners

When the current value of a partnership is greater than the recorded amounts of equity, the partners usually require a new partner to pay a bonus for the privilege of joining. To illustrate, assume that Steeley and Breck agree to accept Davis as a partner with a 25% interest in BOARDS if she invests $42,000. Recall the partnership's accounting records show

P3 Account for the admission and withdrawal of partners.

Concept 13-2

Assets = Liabilities + Equity
  −13,000
  +13,000

Point: Partners' withdrawals are not constrained by the partnership's annual income or loss.

Assets = Liabilities + Equity
+22,000   +22,000

Steeley's recorded equity in the business is $52,000 and Breck's recorded equity is $26,000 (see Exhibit 13.3). Davis's equity is determined as follows:

Equities of existing partners ($52,000 + $26,000)	$ 78,000
Investment of new partner	42,000
Total partnership equity	$120,000
Equity of Davis (25% × $120,000)	$ 30,000

Although Davis invests $42,000, her equity in the new partnership is only $30,000. The $12,000 difference is called a *bonus* and is allocated to existing partners (Steeley and Breck) according to their income-and-loss-sharing agreement. A bonus is shared in this way because it is viewed as an increase in the value of the partnership that is not yet reflected in income. The entry to record this transaction follows:

Assets = Liabilities + Equity
+42,000   +30,000
                          +6,000
                          +6,000

Jan. 4	Cash	42,000	
	C. Davis, Capital		30,000
	K. Steeley, Capital ($12,000 × ½)		6,000
	D. Breck, Capital ($12,000 × ½)		6,000
	To record admission of Davis and bonus.		

Bonus to new partner

Alternatively, existing partners can grant a bonus to a new partner. This usually occurs when they need additional cash or the new partner has exceptional talents. The bonus to the new partner is in the form of a larger share of equity than the amount invested. To illustrate, assume Steeley and Breck agree to accept Davis as a partner with a 25% interest in the partnership, but they require Davis to invest only $18,000. Davis's equity is determined as follows:

Equities of existing partners ($52,000 + $26,000)	$78,000
Investment of new partner	18,000
Total partnership equity	$96,000
Equity of Davis (25% × $96,000)	$24,000

The old partners contribute the $6,000 bonus (computed as $24,000 minus $18,000) to Davis according to their income-and-loss-sharing ratio. Moreover, Davis's 25% equity does not necessarily entitle her to 25% of future income or loss. This is a separate matter for agreement by the partners. The entry to record the admission and investment of Davis is

Assets = Liabilities + Equity
+18,000   −3,000
                          −3,000
                          +24,000

Jan. 4	Cash	18,000	
	K. Steeley, Capital ($6,000 × ½)	3,000	
	D. Breck, Capital ($6,000 × ½)	3,000	
	C. Davis, Capital		24,000
	To record Davis's admission and bonus.		

Withdrawal of a Partner

A partner generally withdraws from a partnership in one of two ways. (1) First, the withdrawing partner can sell his/her interest to another person who pays for it in cash or other assets. For this, we need only debit the withdrawing partner's capital account and credit the new partner's capital account. (2) The second case is when cash or other assets of the partnership are distributed to the withdrawing partner in settlement of his/her interest. To illustrate these cases, assume that Breck withdraws from the partnership of BOARDS in some future period. Their partnership shows the following capital balances at the date of Breck's withdrawal: K. Steeley, $84,000; D. Breck, $38,000; and C. Davis, $38,000. The partners (Steeley, Breck, and Davis) share income and loss equally. Accounting for Breck's withdrawal depends on whether a bonus is paid. We describe three possibilities.

No Bonus

If Breck withdraws and takes cash equal to his capital balance, the entry is

Oct. 31	D. Breck, Capital	38,000	
	Cash		38,000
	To record withdrawal of Breck from partnership with no bonus.		

Assets = Liabilities + Equity
−38,000   −38,000

Breck can take any combination of assets to which the partners agree to settle his equity. Breck's withdrawal creates a new partnership between the remaining partners. A new partnership contract and a new income-and-loss-sharing agreement are required.

Bonus to Remaining Partners

A withdrawing partner is sometimes willing to take less than the recorded value of his/her equity to get out of the partnership or because the recorded value is overstated. Whatever the reason, when this occurs, the withdrawing partner in effect gives the remaining partners a bonus equal to the equity left behind. The remaining partners share this unwithdrawn equity in their income-and-loss-sharing ratio. To illustrate, if Breck withdraws and agrees to take $34,000 cash in settlement of his capital balance, the entry is

Oct. 31	D. Breck, Capital	38,000	
	Cash		34,000
	K. Steeley, Capital		2,000
	C. Davis, Capital		2,000
	To record withdrawal of Breck and bonus to remaining partners.		

Assets = Liabilities + Equity
−34,000   −38,000
                         +2,000
                         +2,000

Breck withdrew $4,000 less than his recorded equity of $38,000. This $4,000 is divided between Steeley and Davis according to their income-and-loss-sharing ratio.

Bonus to Withdrawing Partner

A withdrawing partner may be able to receive more than his/her recorded equity for at least two reasons. First, the recorded equity may be understated. Second, the remaining partners may agree to remove this partner by giving assets of greater value than this partner's recorded equity. In either case, the withdrawing partner receives a bonus. The remaining partners reduce their equity by the amount of this bonus according to their income-and-loss-sharing ratio. To illustrate, if Breck withdraws and receives $40,000 cash in settlement of his capital balance, the entry is

Assets = Liabilities + Equity
−40,000   −38,000
                         −1,000
                         −1,000

Oct. 31	D. Breck, Capital	38,000	
	K. Steeley, Capital	1,000	
	C. Davis, Capital	1,000	
	Cash		40,000
	To record Breck's withdrawal from partnership with a bonus to Breck.		

Falcon Communications LP has a partnership withdrawal agreement. Falcon owns and operates cable television systems in 25 states, and it has two managing general partners. The partnership agreement states that "at any time after September 30, 2005, either [partner] . . . can offer to sell to the other partner the offering partner's entire partnership interest . . . for a negotiated price. If the partner receiving such an offer rejects it, the offering partner may elect to cause [the partnership] . . . to be liquidated and dissolved."

Answer—p. 543

Death of a Partner

A partner's death dissolves a partnership. A deceased partner's estate is entitled to receive his/her equity. The partnership contract should contain provisions for settlement in this case. These provisions usually require (1) closing the books to determine income or loss since the end of the previous period and (2) determining and recording current market values for both assets and liabilities. The remaining partners and the deceased partner's estate then must agree to a settlement of the deceased partner's equity. This can involve selling the equity to remaining partners or to an outsider, or it can involve withdrawing assets.

Liquidation of a Partnership

P4	Prepare entries for partnership liquidation.

When a partnership is liquidated, its business ends and four concluding steps are required:

1. Record the sale of noncash assets for cash and any gain or loss from their liquidation.
2. Allocate any gain or loss from liquidation of the assets in step (1) to the partners using their income-and-loss sharing ratio.
3. Pay or settle all partner liabilities.
4. Distribute any remaining cash to partners based on their capital balances.

Partnership liquidation usually falls into one of two cases as described in the following sections.

No Capital Deficiency

No capital deficiency means that all partners have a zero or credit balance in their capital accounts for final distribution of cash. To illustrate, assume that Steeley, Breck, and Davis operate their partnership in BOARDS for several years, sharing income and loss equally. The partners then decide to liquidate. On the liquidation date, the current period's income or loss is transferred to the partners' capital accounts according to the sharing agreement. After that transfer assume the partners' recorded equity balances (immediately prior to liquidation) are Steeley, $70,000; Breck, $66,000; and Davis, $62,000.

Next, assume that BOARDS sells its noncash assets for a net gain of $6,000. In a liquidation, gains or losses usually result from the sale of noncash assets, which are called *losses and gains from liquidation*. Partners share losses and gains from liquidation according to their income-and-loss-sharing agreement (equal for these partners) yielding the partners' revised equity balances of Steeley, $72,000; Breck, $68,000; and Davis, $64,000.[1] Then,

---

[1] The concepts behind these entries are not new. For example, assume BOARDS has two noncash assets recorded as boarding facilities, $15,000, and land, $25,000. The entry to sell these assets for $46,000 is

Jan. 15	Cash..............................	46,000	
	Boarding facilities		15,000
	Land		25,000
	Gain from Liquidation		6,000
	Sold noncash assets at a gain.		

We then record the allocation of any loss or gain (a gain in this case) from liquidation according to the partners' income-and-loss sharing agreement as follows:

Jan. 15	Gain from Liquidation	6,000	
	K. Steeley, Capital		2,000
	D. Breck, Capital		2,000
	C. Davis, Capital		2,000
	To allocate liquidation gain to partners.		

after partnership assets are sold and any gain or loss is allocated, the liabilities must be paid. After creditors are paid, any remaining cash is divided among the partners according to their capital account balances. BOARDS' only liability at liquidation is $20,000 in accounts payable. The entries to record the payment to creditors and the final distribution to partners are

Jan. 15	Accounts Payable....................	20,000	
	Cash		20,000
	To pay claims of creditors.		
Jan. 15	K. Steeley, Capital.....................	72,000	
	D. Breck, Capital	68,000	
	C. Davis, Capital.....................	64,000	
	Cash		204,000
	To distribute remaining cash to partners.		

Assets   = Liabilities + Equity
−20,000   −20,000

Assets   = Liabilities + Equity
−204,000   −72,000
                         −68,000
                         −64,000

It is important to remember that the final cash payment is distributed to partners according to their capital account balances, whereas gains and losses from liquidation are allocated according to the income-and-loss-sharing ratio.

Capital Deficiency

Capital deficiency means that at least one partner has a debit balance in his/her capital account at the point of final cash distribution. This can arise from liquidation losses, excessive withdrawals before liquidation, or recurring losses in prior periods. A partner with a capital deficiency must, if possible, cover the deficit by paying cash into the partnership.

   To illustrate, assume that Steeley, Breck, and Davis operate their partnership in BOARDS for several years, sharing income and losses equally. The partners then decide to liquidate. Immediately prior to the final distribution of cash, the partners' recorded capital balances are Steeley, $19,000; Breck, $8,000; and Davis, $(3,000). Davis's capital deficiency means she owes the partnership $3,000. Both Steeley and Breck have a legal claim against Davis's personal assets. The final distribution of cash in this case depends on how this capital deficiency is handled. Two possibilities exist.

Partner Pays Deficiency

Davis is obligated to pay $3,000 into the partnership to cover the deficiency. If she is willing and able to pay, the entry to record receipt of her payment is

Jan. 15	Cash	3,000	
	C. Davis, Capital		3,000
	To record payment of deficiency by Davis.		

Assets   = Liabilities + Equity
+3,000   +3,000

After the $3,000 payment, the partners' capital balances are Steeley, $19,000; Breck, $8,000; and Davis, $0. The entry to record the final cash distributions to partners is

Jan. 15	K. Steeley, Capital......................	19,000	
	D. Breck, Capital	8,000	
	Cash		27,000
	To distribute remaining cash to partners.		

Assets   = Liabilities + Equity
−27,000   −19,000
                        −8,000

Partner Cannot Pay Deficiency

The remaining partners with credit balances absorb any partner's unpaid deficiency according to their income-and-loss-sharing ratio. To illustrate, if Davis is unable to pay the $3,000 deficiency, Steeley and Breck absorb it. Since they share equally, Steeley and Breck each absorb $1,500 of the deficiency. This is recorded as follows:

Assets = Liabilities + Equity
−1,500
−1,500
+3,000

Jan. 15	K. Steeley, Capital.	1,500	
	D. Breck, Capital	1,500	
	C. Davis, Capital		3,000
	To transfer Davis deficiency to Steeley and Breck.		

After Steeley and Breck absorb Davis's deficiency, the capital accounts of the partners are Steeley, $17,500; Breck, $6,500; and Davis, $0. The entry to record the final cash distributions to the partners is

Assets = Liabilities + Equity
−24,000   −17,500
                 −6,500

Jan. 15	K. Steeley, Capital.	17,500	
	D. Breck, Capital	6,500	
	Cash		24,000
	To distribute remaining cash to partners.		

Davis's inability to cover her deficiency does not relieve her of the liability. If she becomes able to pay at some future date, Steeley and Breck can each collect $1,500 from her.

Using the Information   Partner Return on Equity

A1   Compute partner return on equity and use it to evaluate partnership performances.

As with proprietorships, an important role of partnership financial statements is to aid current and potential partners in evaluating partnership success compared with other opportunities. One measure of this success is the **partner return on equity** ratio:

$$\text{Partner return on equity} = \frac{\text{Partner net income}}{\text{Average partner equity}}$$

This measure is separately computed for each partner. To illustrate, Exhibit 13.4 reports selected data from the **Boston Celtics LP** for 2000. The return on equity for the *total* partnership is computed as $452/[(\$1,188,074 + \$1,144,780)/2] = 0.04\%$. However, return on equity can be quite different across partners. For example, the **Celtics LP** partner return on equity is computed as $43,491/[(\$223,298 + \$266,789)/2] = 17.75\%$, whereas the **Boston Celtics Communications LP** partner return on equity is computed as $380/[(\$641,574 + \$641,954)/2] = 0.06\%$. Partner return on equity provides each partner an assessment of its return on its equity invested in the partnership. A specific partner often uses this return to decide whether additional investment or withdrawal of resources is best for that partner. Exhibit 13.4 reveals that year 2000 produced poor returns for all partners except Celtics LP.

Exhibit 13.4

Selected Data from Boston Celtics LP

	Total	Boston Celtics LP I	Boston Celtics LP II	Celtics LP	Boston Celtics Communications LP
Balance at June 30, 1999	$1,188,074	$189,968	$133,234	$223,298	$641,574
Net income (loss) for year	452	(33,636)	(9,783)	43,491	380
Cash distribution	(43,746)	—	(43,746)	—	—
Balance at June 30, 2000	$1,144,780	$156,332	$ 79,705	$266,789	$641,954
Partner return on equity	0.04%	(19.43)%	(9.19)%	17.75%	0.06%

The following transactions and events affect the partners' capital accounts in several successive partnerships. Prepare a table with six columns, one for each of the five partners along with a total column to show the effects of the following events on the five partners' capital accounts.

Demonstration Problem

Part 1

4/13/2002	Ries and Bax create R&B Company. Each invests $10,000, and they agree to share profits equally.
12/31/2002	R&B Co. earns $15,000 in its first year. Ries withdraws $4,000 from the partnership, and Bax withdraws $7,000.
1/1/2003	Royce is made a partner in RB&R Company after contributing $12,000 cash. The partners agree that a 10% interest allowance will be given on each partner's beginning capital balance. In addition, Bax and Royce are to receive $5,000 salary allowances. The remainder of the income is to be divided evenly.
12/31/2003	The partnership's income for the year is $40,000, and withdrawals at year-end are Ries, $5,000; Bax, $12,500; and Royce, $11,000.
1/1/2004	Ries sells her interest for $20,000 to Murdock, whom Bax and Royce accept as a partner in the new BR&M Co. Income is to be shared equally after Bax and Royce each receive $25,000 salary allowances.
12/31/2004	The partnership's income for the year is $35,000, and year-end withdrawals are Bax, $2,500, and Royce, $2,000.
1/1/2005	Elway is admitted as a partner after investing $60,000 cash in the new Elway & Associates partnership. He is given a 50% interest in capital after the other partners transfer $3,000 to his account from each of theirs. A 20% interest allowance (on the beginning-of-year capital balances) will be used in sharing profits, there will be no salary allowances, and Elway will receive 40% of the remaining balance—the other three partners will each get 20%.
12/31/2005	Elway & Associates earns $127,600 for the year, and year-end withdrawals are Bax, $25,000; Royce, $27,000; Murdock, $15,000; and Elway, $40,000.
1/1/2006	Elway buys out Bax and Royce for the balances of their capital accounts after a revaluation of the partnership assets. The revaluation gain is $50,000, which is divided in the previous 1:1:1:2 ratio. Elway pays the others from personal funds. Murdock and Elway will share profits on a 1:9 ratio.
2/29/2006	The partnership earns $10,000 of income since the beginning of the year. Murdock retires and receives partnership cash equal to her capital balance. Elway takes possession of the partnership assets in his own name, and the company is dissolved.

Part 2

Journalize the events affecting the partnership for the year ended December 31, 2003.

Planning the Solution

- Evaluate each transaction's effects on the capital accounts of the partners.

- Each time a new partner is admitted or a partner withdraws, allocate any bonus based on the income-or-loss-sharing agreement.

- Each time a new partner is admitted or a partner withdraws, allocate subsequent net incomes or losses in accordance with the new partnership agreement.

- Prepare entries to (1) record Royce's initial investment; (2) record the allocation of interest, salaries, and remainder; (3) show the cash withdrawals from the partnership; and (4) close the withdrawal accounts on December 31, 2003.

Solution to Demonstration Problem

Part 1

Event	Ries	Bax	Royce	Murdock	Elway	Total
4/13/2002						
Initial Investment	$10,000	$10,000				$ 20,000
12/31/2002						
Income (equal)	7,500	7,500				15,000
Withdrawals	(4,000)	(7,000)				(11,000)
Ending balance	$13,500	$10,500				$ 24,000
1/1/2003						
New investment			$12,000			$ 12,000
12/31/2003						
10% interest	1,350	1,050	1,200			3,600
Salaries		5,000	5,000			10,000
Remainder (equal)	8,800	8,800	8,800			26,400
Withdrawals	(5,000)	(12,500)	(11,000)			(28,500)
Ending balance	$18,650	$12,850	$16,000			$ 47,500
1/1/2004						
Transfer interest	(18,650)			$18,650		$ 0
12/31/2004						
Salaries		25,000	25,000			50,000
Remainder (equal)		(5,000)	(5,000)	(5,000)		(15,000)
Withdrawals		(2,500)	(2,000)			(4,500)
Ending balance	$ 0	$30,350	$34,000	$13,650		$ 78,000
1/1/2005						
New investment					$ 60,000	60,000
Bonuses to Elway		(3,000)	(3,000)	(3,000)	9,000	0
Adjusted balance		$27,350	$31,000	$10,650	$ 69,000	$138,000
12/31/2005						
20% interest		5,470	6,200	2,130	13,800	27,600
Remainder (1:1:1:2) . . .		20,000	20,000	20,000	40,000	100,000
Withdrawals		(25,000)	(27,000)	(15,000)	(40,000)	(107,000)
Ending Balance		$27,820	$30,200	$17,780	$ 82,800	$158,600
1/1/2006						
Gain (1:1:1:2)		10,000	10,000	10,000	20,000	50,000
Adjusted balance		$37,820	$40,200	$27,780	$102,800	$208,600
Transfer interests		(37,820)	(40,200)		78,020	0
Adjusted balance		$ 0	$ 0	$27,780	$180,820	$208,600
2/29/2006						
Income (1:9)				1,000	9,000	10,000
Adjusted balance				$28,780	$189,820	$218,600
Settlements				(28,780)	(189,820)	(218,600)
Final balance				$ 0	$ 0	$ 0

Part 2

2003			
Jan. 1	Cash	12,000	
	Royce, Capital		12,000
	To record investment of Royce.		
Dec. 31	Income Summary	40,000	
	Ries, Capital		10,150
	Bax, Capital		14,850
	Royce, Capital		15,000
	To allocate interest, salaries, and remainders.		
Dec. 31	Ries, Withdrawals	5,000	
	Bax, Withdrawals	12,500	
	Royce, Withdrawals	11,000	
	Cash		28,500
	To record cash withdrawals by partners.		
Dec. 31	Ries, Capital	5,000	
	Bax, Capital	12,500	
	Royce, Capital	11,000	
	Ries, Withdrawals		5,000
	Bax, Withdrawals		12,500
	Royce, Withdrawals		11,000
	To close withdrawal accounts.		

Summary

C1 Identify characteristics of partnerships and similar organizations. Partnerships are voluntary associations, involve partnership agreements, have limited life, are not subject to income tax, include mutual agency, and have unlimited liability. Organizations that combine selected characteristics of partnerships and corporations include limited partnerships, limited liability partnerships, S corporations, and limited liability companies.

A1 Compute partner return on equity and use it to evaluate partnership performance. Partner return on equity provides each partner an assessment of his/her return on equity invested in the partnership.

P1 Prepare entries for partnership formation. A partner's initial investment is recorded at the fair market value of the assets contributed to the partnership.

P2 Allocate and record income and loss among partners. A partnership agreement should specify how to allocate partnership income or loss among partners. Allocation can be based on a stated ratio, capital balances, or salary and interest allowances to compensate partners for differences in their service and capital contributions.

P3 Account for the admission and withdrawal of partners. When a new partner buys a partnership interest directly from one or more existing partners, the amount of cash paid from one partner to another does not affect the partnership total recorded equity. When a new partner purchases equity by investing additional assets in the partnership, the new partner's investment can yield a bonus either to existing partners or to the new partner. The entry to record a withdrawal can involve payment from either (1) the existing partners' personal assets or (2) partnership assets. The latter can yield a bonus to either the withdrawing or remaining partners.

P4 Prepare entries for partnership liquidation. When a partnership is liquidated, losses and gains from selling partnership assets are allocated to the partners according to their income-and-loss-sharing ratio. If a partner's capital account has a deficiency that the partner cannot pay, the other partners share the deficit according to their relative income-and-loss-sharing ratio.

Guidance Answer to **You Make the Call**

Financial Planner The partnership agreement apparently fails to mention liabilities or use the term *net assets.* To give the estate one-third of total assets is not fair to the remaining partners because if the partner had lived and the partners had decided to liquidate, the liabilities would need to be paid out of assets before any liquidation. Also, a settlement based on the deceased partner's recorded equity would fail to recognize excess of current value over book value. These value increases would be realized if the partnership were liquidated. A fair settlement would seem to be a payment to the estate for the balance of the deceased partner's equity based on the *current value of net assets.*

Guidance Answers to **Quick Checks**

1. (b)

2. Unlimited liability means that the creditors of a partnership require each partner to be personally responsible for all partnership debts.

3. (c)

4.

	Ben	Jerry	Total
Net Income			$40,000
Interest allowance (10%)	$ 7,000	$ 3,500	10,500
Balance of income			**$29,500**
Balance allocated equally . . .	14,750	14,750	29,500
Balance of income			$ 0
Income of partners	**$21,750**	**$18,250**	

Glossary

C corporation corporation that does not qualify for and elect to be treated as a partnership for income tax purposes and therefore is subject to income taxes. (p. 529).

General partner partner who assumes unlimited liability for the debts of the partnership; responsible for partnership management. (p. 529).

General partnership partnership in which all partners have mutual agency and unlimited liability for partnership debts. (p. 529).

Limited liability company form of organization that combines corporation and limited partnership features, provides limited liability to its members (owners), and allows members to actively participate in management. (p. 530).

Limited liability partnership partnership in which a partner is not personally liable for malpractice or negligence unless that partner is responsible for providing the service that resulted in the claim. (p. 529).

Limited partners partners who have no personal liability for partnership debts beyond the amounts they invested in the partnership. (p. 529).

Limited partnership partnership that has two classes of partners, limited partners and general partners. (p. 529).

Mutual agency legal relationship among partners whereby each partner is an agent of the partnership and is able to bind the partnership to contracts within the scope of the partnership's business. (p. 528).

Partner return on equity partner net income divided by average partner equity. (p. 540).

Partnership unincorporated association of two or more persons to pursue a business for profit as co-owners. (p. 528).

Partnership contract agreement among partners that sets terms under which the affairs of the partnership are conducted. (p. 528).

Partnership liquidation dissolution of a partnership by (1) selling noncash assets and allocating any gain or loss according to partners' income-and-loss ratio, (2) paying liabilities, and (3) distributing any remaining cash according to partners' capital balances. (p. 538).

S corporation corporation that meets special tax qualifications so as to be treated like a partnership for income tax purposes. (p. 529).

Statement of changes in partners' equity financial statement that shows total capital balances at the beginning of the period, any additional investment by partners, the income or loss of the period, the partners' withdrawals, and the partners' ending capital balances; also called *statement of partners' capital*. (p. 534).

Unlimited liability legal relationship among general partners that makes each of them responsible for partnership debts if the other partners are unable to pay their shares. (p. 529).

Questions

1. If a partnership contract does not state the period of time the partnership is to exist, when does the partnership end?

2. What does the term *mutual agency* mean when applied to a partnership?

3. Can partners limit the right of a partner to commit their partnership to contracts? Would the agreement be binding (a) on the partners and (b) on outsiders?

4. Assume Amey and Lacey are partners. Lacey dies, and her son claims the right to take his mother's place in the partnership. Does he have this right? Why or why not?

5. Assume the Barnes and Ardmore partnership agreement provides for a two-thirds/one-third sharing of income but says nothing about losses. The first year of partnership operation resulted in a loss, and Barnes argues that the loss should be shared equally because the partnership agreement said nothing about sharing losses. Is Barnes correct? Explain.

6. Allocation of partnership income among the partners appears on what financial statement?

7. What does the term *unlimited liability* mean when it is applied to partnership members?

8. How does a general partnership differ from a limited partnership?

9. George, Burton, and Dillman have been partners for three years. The partnership is being dissolved. George is leaving the firm, but Burton and Dillman plan to carry on the business. In the final settlement, George places a $75,000 salary claim against the partnership. He contends that he has a claim for a salary of $25,000 for each year because he devoted all of his time for three years to the affairs of the partnership. Is his claim valid? Why or why not?

10. Kay, Kat, and Kim are partners. In a liquidation, Kay's share of partnership losses exceeds her capital account balance.

Moreover, she is unable to meet the deficit from her personal assets, and her partners shared the excess losses. Does this relieve Kay of liability?

11. After all partnership assets have been converted to cash and all liabilities paid, the remaining cash should equal the sum of the balances of the partners' capital accounts. Why?

12. Assume a partner withdraws from a partnership and receives assets of greater value than the book value of his equity. Should the remaining partners share the resulting reduction in their equities in the ratio of their relative capital balances or according to their income-and-loss-sharing ratio?

Jim and Jon are partners who agree that Jim will receive a $100,000 salary allowance after which any remaining income or loss will be shared equally. If Jon's capital account is credited $2,000 as his share of the net income in a given period, how much net income did the partnership earn?

QUICK STUDY

QS 13-1
Partnership income allocation
P2

Ann Martin and Susie Meyer are partners in a business they started two years ago. The partnership agreement states that Ann should receive a salary allowance of $15,000 and that Susie should receive a $20,000 salary allowance. Any remaining income or loss is to be shared equally. Determine each partner's share of the current year's net income of $52,000.

QS 13-2
Partnership income allocation
P2

Steve and Jack are partners in operating a store. Without consulting Steve, Jack enters into a contract to purchase merchandise for the store. Steve contends that he did not authorize the order and refuses to take delivery. The vendor sues the partners for the contract price of the merchandise. (*a*) Will the partnership have to pay? Why? (*b*) Does your answer differ if Steve and Jack are partners in a public accounting firm?

QS 13-3
Partnership liability

C1

Lemm organized a limited partnership and is the only general partner. Moxie invested $20,000 in the partnership and was admitted as a limited partner with the understanding that he would receive 10% of the profits. After two unprofitable years, the partnership ceased doing business. At that point, partnership liabilities were $85,000 larger than partnership assets. How much money can the partnership's creditors obtain from Moxie's personal assets to satisfy the unpaid partnership debts?

QS 13-4
Liability in limited partnerships

P1

Tomm agrees to pay Lennox and Bradley $10,000 each for a one-third (33⅓%) interest in the Lennox and Bradley partnership. When Tomm is admitted, each partner has a $30,000 capital balance. Make the journal entry to record Tomm's purchase of the partners' interest.

QS 13-5
Partner admission through purchase of interest
P3

Chung and Choi are partners, each with $40,000 in their partnership capital accounts. Kwon is admitted to the partnership by investing $40,000 cash. Make the entry to show Kwon's admission to the partnership.

QS 13-6
Admission of a partner
P3

Sig and Freed's company is organized as a partnership. At the prior year-end, partnership equity totals $150,000 ($100,000 from Sig and $50,000 from Freed). For the current year, partnership net income is $25,000 ($20,000 allocated to Sig and $5,000 allocated to Freed), and year-end total partnership equity is $200,000 ($140,000 from Sig and $60,000 from Freed). Compute the total partnership *and* individual partner return on equity ratios.

QS 13-7
Partner return on equity

A1

EXERCISES

Exercise 13-1

Characteristics of partnerships

Next to the following list of eight characteristics of business organizations, write a brief description of how each characteristic applies to general partnerships.

Characteristic	Implication to General Partnerships
1. Life	
2. Owners' liability	
3. Legal status	
4. Tax status of income	
5. Owners' authority	
6. Ease of formation	
7. Transferability of ownership	
8. Ability to raise large amounts of capital	

Exercise 13-2

Forms of organization

C1

For each of the following separate cases, recommend a form of business organization. With each recommendation, explain how business profits would be taxed if the owners adopt the form of organization recommended. Also list several advantages that the owners will enjoy from the form of business organization that you recommend.

1. Meg, Liz, and Chris are recent college graduates in computer science. They want to start a Web site development company. They all have college debts and currently do not own any substantial computer equipment needed to get the company started.

2. Dr. Fromm and Dr. Morris are recent graduates from medical residency programs. Both are family practice physicians and would like to open a clinic in an underserved rural area. Although neither has any funds to bring to the new venture, a banker has expressed interest in making a loan to provide start-up funds for their practice.

3. Phil has been out of school for about five years and has become quite knowledgeable about the commercial real estate market. He would like to organize a company that buys and sells real estate. Phil believes he has the expertise to manage the company but needs funds to invest in commercial property.

Exercise 13-3

Journalizing partnership transactions

P2

On March 1, 2002, Favor and Alcox formed a partnership. Favor contributed $80,000 cash and Alcox contributed land valued at $60,000 and a building valued at $100,000. The partnership also assumed responsibility for Alcox's $80,000 long-term note payable associated with the land and building. The partners agreed to share profits as follows: Favor is to receive an annual salary allowance of $25,000, both are to receive an annual interest allowance of 10% of their beginning-year capital investment, and any remaining profit or loss is to be shared equally. On October 20, 2002, Favor withdrew cash of $34,000 and Alcox withdrew $20,000. After the adjusting and closing entries are made to the revenue and expense accounts at December 31, the Income Summary account had a credit balance of $90,000.

Required

1. Prepare journal entries to record the partners' initial capital investments, their cash withdrawals, and the December 31 closing of both the Withdrawals and Income Summary accounts.

2. Determine the balances of the partners' capital accounts as of December 31, 2002.

Exercise 13-4

Income allocation in a partnership

Cosmo and George began a partnership by investing $60,000 and $80,000, respectively. During its first year, the partnership earned $160,000. Prepare calculations showing how the $160,000 income should be allocated to the partners under each of the following three separate plans for sharing income and loss: (1) the partners failed to agree on a method to share income; (2) the partners agreed to share income and loss in proportion to their initial investments (round proportions to the nearest hundredth); and (3) the partners agreed to share income by granting a $50,000 per year salary allowance to Cosmo, a $40,000 per year salary allowance to George, 10% interest on their initial capital investments, and the remaining balance shared equally.

Assume that the partners of Exercise 13-4 agreed to share net income and loss by granting annual salary allowances of $50,000 to Cosmo and $40,000 to George, 10% interest allowances on their investments, and any remaining balance shared equally.

Exercise 13-5

Income allocation in a partnership

P2

Required

1. Determine the partners' shares of Cosmo and George given a first-year net income of $98,800.

2. Determine the partners' shares of Cosmo and George given a first-year net loss of $16,800.

The partners in the Biz Partnership have agreed that partner Madonna may sell her $100,000 equity in the partnership to Streisand, for which Streisand will pay Madonna $85,000. Present the partnership's journal entry to record the sale of Madonna's interest to Streisand on September 30.

Exercise 13-6

Sale of partnership Interest

P3

The E-O Partnership has total partners' equity of $510,000, which is made up of Elm, Capital, $400,000, and Oak, Capital, $110,000. The partners share net income and loss in a ratio of 80% to Elm and 20% to Oak. On November 1, Ash is admitted to the partnership and given a 15% interest in equity and income and loss. Prepare the journal entry to record the admission of Ash under each of the following separate assumptions: Ash invests cash of (1) $90,000; (2) $120,000; and (3) $80,000.

Exercise 13-7

Admission of new partner

P3

Holland, Flowers, and Wood have been partners sharing net income and loss in a 5:3:2 ratio. On January 31, the date Wood retires from the partnership, the equities of the partners are Holland, $150,000; Flowers, $90,000; and Wood, $60,000. Present journal entries to record Wood's retirement under each of the following separate assumptions: Wood is paid for his equity using partnership cash of (1) $60,000, (2) $80,000, (3) $30,000.

Exercise 13-8

Retirement of partner

P3

The Red, White & Blue partnership was begun with investments by the partners as follows: Red, $180,000; White, $240,000; and Blue, $210,000. The operations did not go well, and the partners eventually decided to liquidate the partnership, sharing all losses equally. On August 31, after all assets were converted to cash and all creditors were paid, only $60,000 in partnership cash remained.

Exercise 13-9

Liquidation of partnership

P4

Required

1. Compute the capital account balances of the partners after the liquidation of assets and the payment of creditors.

2. Any partner with a deficit agrees to pay cash to the partnership to cover the deficit. Present the journal entries on August 31 to record (a) the cash receipt from the deficient partner(s) and (b) the final disbursement of cash to the partners.

3. Assume that any partner with a deficit is not able to reimburse the partnership. Present journal entries (a) to transfer the deficit of any deficient partners to the other partners and (b) to record the final disbursement of cash to the partners.

Tuttle, Ritter, and Lee are partners who share income and loss in a 1:4:5 ratio. After lengthy disagreements among the partners and several unprofitable periods, the partners decided to liquidate the partnership. Before liquidation, the partnership balance sheet shows total assets, $126,000; total liabilities, $78,000; Tuttle, Capital, $2,500; Ritter, Capital, $14,000; and Lee, Capital, $31,500. The cash proceeds from selling the assets were sufficient to repay all but $28,000 to the creditors. Calculate the loss from selling the assets, allocate the loss to the partners, and determine how much of the remaining liability should be paid by each partner.

Exercise 13-10

Liquidation of partnership

P4

Assume that the Tuttle, Ritter, and Lee partnership of Exercise 13-10 is a limited partnership. Tuttle and Ritter are general partners and Lee is a limited partner. How much of the remaining $28,000 liability should be paid by each partner?

Exercise 13-11

Liquidation of limited partnership

P4

Hunt Sports Enterprises LP is organized as a limited partnership consisting of two individual partners: Soccer LP and Football LP. Both partners separately operate a minor league soccer team and a semipro football team. Compute partner return on equity for each limited partnership (and the total)

Exercise 13-12

Partner return on equity

A1

for the year ended June 30, 2002, using the following selected data on partner capital balances from Hunt Sports Enterprises LP:

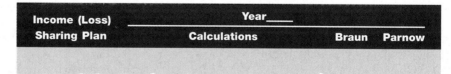

	Soccer LP	Football LP	Total
Balance at 6/30/01	$189,000	$ 758,000	$ 947,000
Annual net income	22,134	445,898	468,032
Cash distribution	—	(50,000)	(50,000)
Balance at 6/30/02	$211,134	$1,153,898	$1,365,032

PROBLEM SET A

Problem 13-1A
Allocating partnership income

P2 G

Check   (3) Simms, Capital, $97,800

Kim Ries, Tere Bax, and Kurt Simms invested $80,000, $112,000, and $128,000, respectively, in a partnership. During its first year, the firm earned $249,000.

Required

Prepare the entry to close the firm's Income Summary account as of its December 31 year-end and to allocate the $249,000 net income to the partners under each of the following separate assumptions: The partners (1) have no agreement on the method of sharing income and loss; (2) agreed to share income and loss in the ratio of their beginning capital investments; and (3) agreed to share income and loss by providing annual salary allowances of $66,000 to Ries, $56,000 to Bax, and $80,000 to Simms; granting 10% interest on the partners' beginning capital investments; and sharing the remainder equally.

Problem 13-2A
Allocating partnership income and loss; sequential years

P2

S

Sid Braun and Ty Parnow are forming a partnership to which Braun will devote one-half time and Parnow will devote full time. They have discussed the following alternative plans for sharing income and loss: (a) in the ratio of their initial capital investments, which they have agreed will be $42,000 for Braun and $63,000 for Parnow; (b) in proportion to the time devoted to the business; (c) a salary allowance of $6,000 per month to Parnow and the balance in accordance with the ratio of their initial capital investments; or (d) a salary allowance of $6,000 per month to Parnow, 10% interest on their initial capital investments, and the balance shared equally. The partners expect the business to perform as follows: Year 1, $36,000 net loss; Year 2, $90,000 net income; and Year 3, $150,000 net income.

Required

Prepare three tables with the following column headings:

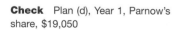

Income (Loss) Sharing Plan	Year_____ Calculations	Braun	Parnow

Check   Plan (d), Year 1, Parnow's share, $19,050

Complete the tables, one for each of the first three years, by showing how to allocate partnership income or loss to the partners under each of the four plans being considered. (Round answers to the nearest whole dollar.)

Problem 13-3A
Partnership income allocation, statement of changes in partners' equity, and closing entries

P2

S

Trey Wiltse, Ron Buck, and Esther Ray formed the WBR Partnership by making capital contributions of $367,500, $262,500, and $420,000, respectively. They predict annual partnership net income of $450,000 and are considering the following alternative plans of sharing income and loss: (a) equally; (b) in the ratio of their initial capital investments; or (c) salary allowances of $80,000 to Wiltse, $60,000 to Buck, and $90,000 to Ray; interest allowances of 10% on their initial capital investments; and the balance shared equally.

Required

1. Prepare a table with the following column headings:

Income (Loss) Sharing Plan	Calculations	Wiltse	Buck	Ray	Total

Use the table to show how to distribute net income of $450,000 for the calendar year under each of the alternative plans being considered. (Round answers to the nearest whole dollar.)

2. Prepare a statement of changes in partners' equity showing the allocation of income to the partners assuming they agree to use plan (c), that income earned is $209,000, and that Wiltse, Buck, and Ray withdraw $34,000, $48,000, and $64,000, respectively, at year-end.

3. Prepare the December 31 journal entry to close Income Summary assuming they agree to use plan (c) and that net income is $209,000. Also close the withdrawals accounts.

Check   (2) Ray, Ending Capital, $446,000

Part 1. Goering, Gore, and Schmit are partners with capital balances as follows: Goering, $168,000; Gore, $138,000; and Schmit, $294,000. The partners share income and loss in a 3:2:5 ratio. Gore decides to withdraw from the partnership, and the partners agree to not have the assets revalued upon his retirement. Prepare journal entries to record Gore's February 1 withdrawal from the partnership under each of the following separate assumptions: Gore (a) sells his interest to Getz for $160,000 after Goering and Schmit approve the entry of Getz as a partner; (b) gives his interest to a son-in-law, Swanson, and thereafter Goering and Schmit accept Swanson as a partner; (c) is paid $138,000 in partnership cash for his equity; (d) is paid $214,000 in partnership cash for his equity; and (e) is paid $30,000 in partnership cash plus equipment recorded on the partnership books at $70,000 less its accumulated depreciation of $23,200.

Problem 13-4A
Withdrawal of a partner

Check   (e) Cr. Schmit, Capital, $38,250

Part 2. Assume that Gore does not retire from the partnership described in Part (1). Instead, Ford is admitted to the partnership on February 1 with a 25% equity. Prepare journal entries to record Ford's entry into the partnership under each of the following separate assumptions: Ford invests (a) $200,000; (b) $145,000; and (c) $262,000.

Quick, Drake, and Sage plan to liquidate their partnership. They share income and loss in a 3:2:1 ratio. On the day of liquidation their balance sheet appears as follows:

Problem 13-5A
Liquidation of a partnership

QUICK, DRAKE, AND SAGE			
Balance Sheet			
May 31			
Assets		**Liabilities and Equity**	
Cash	$180,800	Accounts payable	$245,500
Inventory	537,200	Quick, Capital	93,000
		Drake, Capital	212,500
		Sage, Capital	167,000
Total assets	$718,000	Total liabilities and equity	$718,000

Required

Prepare the journal entries for the sale of inventory, the allocation of its gain or loss, and the distribution of cash in each of the following separate cases: Inventory is sold for (1) $600,000; (2) $500,000; (3) $320,000 and any partners with capital deficits pay in the amount of their deficits; and (4) $250,000 and the partners have no assets other than those invested in the partnership.

Check   (4) Cash distribution, Sage, $102,266.67

Kelli Cook, Ryan Moore, and Seth Davis invested $164,000, $98,400, and $65,600, respectively, in a partnership. During its first year, the firm earned $270,000.

PROBLEM SET B

Problem 13-1B
Allocating partnership income

Required

Prepare the entry to close the firm's Income Summary account as of its December 31 year-end and to allocate the $270,000 net income to the partners under each of the following separate assumptions. (Round answers to whole dollars.) The partners (1) have no agreement on the method of sharing income and loss; (2) agreed to share income and loss in the ratio of their beginning capital investments; and (3) agreed to share income and loss by providing annual salary allowances of $96,000 to Cook, $72,000 to Moore, and $50,000 to Davis; granting 10% interest on the partners' beginning capital investments; and sharing the remainder equally.

Check   (3) Davis, Capital, $62,960

Problem 13-2B

Allocating partnership income and loss; sequential years

P2

Maria Barto and J. R. Black are forming a partnership to which Barto will devote one-third time and Black will devote full time. They have discussed the following alternative plans for sharing income and loss: (a) in the ratio of their capital initial investments, which they have agreed will be $104,000 for Barto and $156,000 for Black; (b) in proportion to the time devoted to the business; (c) a salary allowance of $4,000 per month to Black and the balance in accordance with the ratio of their initial capital investments; or (d) a salary allowance of $4,000 per month to Black, 10% interest on their initial capital investments, and the balance shared equally. The partners expect the business to perform as follows: Year 1, $36,000 net loss; Year 2, $76,000 net income; and Year 3, $188,000 net income.

Required

Prepare three tables with the following column headings:

Income (Loss) Sharing Plan	Year____ Calculations	Barto	Black

Check Plan (d), Year 1, Black's share, $8,600

Complete the tables, one for each of the first three years, by showing how to allocate partnership income or loss to the partners under each of the four plans being considered. (Round answers to the nearest whole dollar.)

Problem 13-3B

Partnership income allocation, statement of changes in partners' equity, and closing entries

P2

Staci Long, Rachel Xi, and Ron Stack formed the LXS Partnership by making capital contributions of $144,000, $216,000, and $120,000, respectively. They predict annual partnership net income of $240,000 and are considering the following alternative plans of sharing income and loss: (a) equally; (b) in the ratio of their initial capital investments; or (c) salary allowances of $40,000 to Long, $30,000 to Xi, and $80,000 to Stack; interest allowances of 12% on their initial capital investments; and the balance shared equally.

Required

1. Prepare a table with the following column headings:

Income (Loss) Sharing Plan	Calculations	Long	Xi	Stack	Total

Use the table to show how to distribute net income of $240,000 for the calendar year under each of the alternative plans being considered. (Round answers to the nearest whole dollar.)

Check (2) Stack, Ending Capital, $150,400

2. Prepare a statement of changes in partners' equity showing the allocation of income to the partners assuming they agree to use plan (c), that income earned is $87,600, and that Long, Xi, and Stack withdraw $18,000, $38,000, and $24,000, respectively, at year-end.

3. Prepare the December 31 journal entry to close Income Summary assuming they agree to use plan (c) and that net income is $87,600. Also close the withdrawals accounts.

Problem 13-4B

Withdrawal of a partner

P3

Part 1. Adams, Allen, and Aates are partners with capital balances as follows: Adams, $606,000; Allen, $148,000; and Aates, $446,000. The partners share income and loss in a 5:1:4 ratio. Adams decides to withdraw from the partnership, and the partners agree to not have the assets revalued upon her retirement. Prepare journal entries to record Adams's April 30 withdrawal from the partnership under each of the following separate assumptions: Adams (a) sells her interest to Adrian for $250,000 after Allen and Aates approve the entry of Adrian as a partner; (b) gives her interest to a daughter-in-law, Asp, and thereafter Allen and Aates accept Asp as a partner; (c) is paid $606,000 in partnership cash for her equity; (d) is paid $350,000 in partnership cash for her equity; and (e) is paid $200,000 in partnership cash plus manufacturing equipment recorded on the partnership books at $538,000 less its accumulated depreciation of $336,000.

Check (e) Cr. Aates, Capital, $163,200

Part 2. Assume that Adams does not retire from the partnership described in Part (1). Instead, Appier is admitted to the partnership on April 30 with a 20% equity. Prepare journal entries to record the entry of Appier under each of the following separate assumptions: Appier invests (a) $300,000; (b) $196,000; (c) $426,000.

Laman, Hinson, and Roney, who share income and loss in a 2:1:2 ratio, plan to liquidate their partnership. At liquidation, their balance sheet appears as follows:

Problem 13-5B
Liquidation of a partnership
P4

LAMAN, HINSON, AND RONEY
Balance Sheet
January 18

Assets		Liabilities and Equity	
Cash	$348,600	Accounts payable	$342,600
Equipment	617,200	Laman, Capital	300,400
		Hinson, Capital	195,800
		Roney, Capital	127,000
Total assets	$965,800	Total liabilities and equity	$965,800

Required

Prepare journal entries for the sale of equipment, the allocation of its gain or loss, and the distribution of cash in each of the following separate cases: Equipment is sold for (1) $650,000; (2) $530,000; (3) $200,000 and any partners with capital deficits pay in the amount of their deficits; and (4) $150,000, and the partners have no assets other than those invested in the partnership.

Check (4) Cash distribution, Laman, $73,600

Beyond the Numbers

BTN 13-1 Take a step back in time and imagine that **Nike** is in its infancy as a company. The year is 1965 and Nike is called BRS (Blue Ribbon Sports). BRS is organized as a partnership between two general partners, Bill Bowerman and Phil Knight.

Reporting in Action
C1
NIKE

Required

1. Refer to Nike's income statement in Appendix A. It varies in several key ways from what it would have shown for the BRS partnership. Explain how a corporate income statement differs from a partnership income statement.

2. Compare the Nike balance sheet in Appendix A to what the BRS partnership balance sheet would have shown in 1965. Identify and explain any differences you would anticipate.

BTN 13-2 Over the last 20 to 30 years, **Nike** and **Reebok** have evolved into large corporations. Today it is hard to imagine them as fledgling startups. Research Nike's history online. Numerous Web pages chronicle its beginnings. Also, research Reebok's history online.

Comparative Analysis
C1

Required

1. Which company is older?
2. Which company was not started in the United States?
3. Which company started as a partnership between two men?
4. Which company was devised, in part, as a result of a classroom assignment?
5. Which company paid $35 to develop its logo?

BTN 13-3 Doctors Fair, Melchor, and Chandra have been in a group practice for several years. Fair and Melchor are family practice physicians, and Chandra is a general surgeon. Chandra receives many referrals for surgery from his family practice partners. Upon the partnership's original formation, the three doctors agreed to a two-part formula to share income. Every month each doctor receives a salary allowance of $4,000. Additional income is divided according to a percent of patient charges the doctors generate for the month. In the current month, Fair generated 10% of the billings, Melchor 30%,

Ethics Challenge
P2

and Chandra 60%. The group's income for this month is $60,000. Chandra has expressed dissatisfaction with the income-sharing formula and asks that income be split entirely on patient charge percents.

Required

1. Compute the income allocation for the current month using the original agreement.
2. Compute the income allocation for the current month using Chandra's proposed agreement.
3. Identify the ethical components of this partnership decision for the doctors.

Communicating in Practice
C1

BTN 13-4   Assume that you are studying for an upcoming accounting exam with a good friend. Your friend says that she has a solid understanding of general partnerships but is less sure that she understands organizations that combine certain characteristics of partnerships with other forms of business organization. You offer to make some study notes for your friend to help her learn about limited partnerships, limited liability partnerships, S Corporations, and limited liability companies. Prepare a 2-page set of well-organized, complete study notes on these four forms of business organization.

Taking It to the Net
P1 **P2**

BTN 13-5   Access the September 15, 2000, 10-K filing of the **Boston Celtics Limited Partnership** at **www.edgar-online.com**.

Required

1. Locate the June 30, 2000, balance sheet for the Boston Celtics Limited Partnership. List the account titles used in the equity section of this balance sheet.
2. How many units of limited partnership interest are authorized, issued, and outstanding as of June 30, 2000?
3. What are the equity balances of the general partners and limited partners as of June 30, 2000?
4. What is the partnership's largest asset as of June 30, 2000?

Teamwork in Action
P2

BTN 13-6   This activity requires teamwork to reinforce understanding of accounting for partnerships.

Required

1. Assume that Baker, Warner, and Rice form the BWR Partnership by making capital contributions of $200,000, $300,000, and $500,000, respectively. BWR predicts annual partnership net income of $600,000. The partners are considering various plans for sharing income and loss. Assign a different team member to compute how the projected $600,000 income would be shared under each of the following separate plans:
   a. Shared equally.
   b. In the ratio of the partners' initial capital investments.
   c. Salary allowances of $50,000 to Baker, $60,000 to Warner, and $70,000 to Rice, with the remaining balance shared equally.
   d. Interest allowances of 10% on the partners' initial capital investments, with the remaining balance shared equally.
2. In sequence, each member is to present his/her income-sharing calculations with the team.
3. As a team, identify and discuss at least one other possible way that income could be shared.

Business Week Activity
C1

BTN 13-7   Read the article "I've Got the Horse Right Here" in the October 9, 2000, issue of *Business Week*.

Required

1. How does the article characterize the recent health of the horse racing industry?
2. What was the average price of a yearling in 2000 and in 1995?
3. The article states that investors may purchase shares of stallions through partnership interests. Explain what form these partnerships would likely take, general or limited.
4. If you were to invest in horses, which horses carry the least risk according to this article?

BTN 13-8   Ricky Dee wants to form a general partnership with his good friend Buddy Stanton to operate a Web programming and consulting service. Neither Ricky nor Buddy has organized a partnership business before.

Required

1. What details should Ricky and Buddy specify in their general partnership agreement?
2. What advantages should Ricky and Buddy be aware of with respect to organizing as a general partnership?
3. What disadvantages should Rick and Buddy be aware of with respect to organizing as a general partnership?

Entrepreneurial Decision

Appendix

A

Financial Statement Information

This appendix includes financial information for (1) **Nike**, (2) **Reebok**, and (3) **Gap**. This information is taken from their annual reports. An **annual report** is a summary of a company's financial results for the year, along with its current financial condition and future plans. This report is directed to external users of financial information, but it also affects the actions and decisions of internal users.

A company uses an annual report to showcase itself and its products. Many annual reports include attractive photos, diagrams, and illustrations related to the company. The primary objective of annual reports, however, is the *financial section,* which communicates much information about a company, with most data drawn from the accounting information system. The layout of an annual report's financial section is fairly established and typically includes the following:

- Letter to Shareholders
- Financial History and Highlights
- Management Discussion and Analysis
- Management's Report
- Report of Independent Accountants (Auditor's Report)
- Financial Statements
- Notes to Financial Statements
- List of Directors and Officers

This appendix provides the financial statements for Nike (plus selected notes), Reebok, and Gap. The appendix is organized as follows:

- Nike   **A-2** through **A-10**
- Reebok   **A-11** through **A-14**
- Gap   **A-15** through **A-18**

Many assignments at the end of each chapter refer to information in this appendix. We encourage readers to spend time with these assignments; they are especially useful in showing the relevance and diversity of financial accounting and reporting.

Special note: The SEC maintains the EDGAR (**E**lectronic **D**ata **G**athering, **A**nalysis, and **R**etrieval) database at **www.sec.gov.** The **Form 10-K** is the annual report form for most companies. It provides electronically accessible information. The **Form 10-KSB** is the annual report form filed by "small businesses." It requires slightly less information than the Form 10-K. Both forms must be filed within 90 days after the company's fiscal year-end. (Forms 10-K405, 10-KT, 10-KT405, and 10-KSB405 are slight variations of the usual form due to certain regulations or rules.)

NIKE

Financial History

(in millions, except per share data, financial ratios and number of shareholders)

YEAR ENDED MAY 31,	2000	1999	1998	1997	1996	1995
Revenues	$8,995.1	$8,776.9	$9,553.1	$9,186.5	$6,470.6	$4,760.8
Gross margin	3,591.3	3,283.4	3,487.6	3,683.5	2,563.9	1,895.6
Gross margin %	39.9%	37.4%	36.5%	40.1%	39.6%	39.8%
Restructuring charge	(2.5)	45.1	129.9	—	—	—
Net income	579.1	451.4	399.6	795.8	553.2	399.7
Basic earnings per common share	2.10	1.59	1.38	2.76	1.93	1.38
Diluted earnings per common share	2.07	1.57	1.35	2.68	1.88	1.36
Average common shares outstanding	275.7	283.3	288.7	288.4	286.6	289.6
Diluted average common shares outstanding	279.4	288.3	295.0	297.0	293.6	294.0
Cash dividends declared						
per common share	0.48	0.48	0.46	0.38	0.29	0.24
Cash flow from operations	759.9	961.0	517.5	323.1	339.7	254.9
Price range of common stock						
High	64.125	65.500	64.125	76.375	52.063	20.156
Low	26.563	31.750	37.750	47.875	19.531	14.063

MAY 31,						
Cash and equivalents	$ 254.3	$ 198.1	$ 108.6	$ 445.4	$ 262.1	$ 216.1
Inventories	1,446.0	1,170.6	1,396.6	1,338.6	931.2	629.7
Working capital	1,456.4	1,818.0	1,828.8	1,964.0	1,259.9	938.4
Total assets	5,856.9	5,247.7	5,397.4	5,361.2	3,951.6	3,142.7
Long-term debt	470.3	386.1	379.4	296.0	9.6	10.6
Redeemable Preferred Stock	0.3	0.3	0.3	0.3	0.3	0.3
Shareholders' equity	3,136.0	3,334.6	3,261.6	3,155.9	2,431.4	1,964.7
Year-end stock price	42.875	60.938	46.000	57.500	50.188	19.719
Market capitalization	11,559.1	17,202.2	13,201.1	16,633.0	14,416.8	5,635.2

FINANCIAL RATIOS						
Return on equity	17.9%	13.7%	12.5%	28.5%	25.2%	21.6%
Return on assets	10.4%	8.5%	7.4%	17.1%	15.6%	14.5%
Inventory turns	4.1	4.3	4.4	4.8	5.0	5.2
Current ratio at May 31	1.7	2.3	2.1	2.1	1.9	1.8
Price/Earnings ratio at May 31 (diluted)	20.7	38.8	34.1	21.5	26.6	14.5

GEOGRAPHIC REVENUES						
United States	$5,017.4	$5,042.6	$5,460.0	$5,538.2	$3,964.7	$2,997.9
Europe	2,350.9	2,255.8	2,096.1	1,789.8	1,334.3	980.4
Asia Pacific	955.1	844.5	1,253.9	1,241.9	735.1	515.6
Americas (exclusive of United States)	671.7	634.0	743.1	616.6	436.5	266.9
Total Revenues	$8,995.1	$8,776.9	$9,553.1	$9,186.5	$6,470.6	$4,760.8

All per common share data has been adjusted to reflect the 2-for-1 stock splits paid October 23, 1996, October 30, 1995 and October 5, 1990. The Company's Class B Common Stock is listed on the New York and Pacific Exchanges and trades under the symbol NKE. At May 31, 2000, there were approximately 153,000 shareholders of Class A and Class B common stock.

Nike, Inc. Consolidated Statement of Income

(in millions, except per share data)

YEAR ENDED MAY 31,	2000	1999	1998
Revenues	$8,995.1	$8,776.9	$9,553.1
Costs and expenses:			
Cost of sales	5,403.8	5,493.5	6,065.5
Selling and administrative	2,606.4	2,426.6	2,623.8
Interest expense (Notes 4 and 5)	45.0	44.1	60.0
Other income/expense, net (Notes 1, 10 and 11)	23.2	21.5	20.9
Restructuring charge, net (Note 13)	(2.5)	45.1	129.9
Total costs and expenses	8,075.9	8,030.8	8,900.1
Income before income taxes	919.2	746.1	653.0
Income taxes (Note 6)	340.1	294.7	253.4
Net income	$ 579.1	$ 451.4	$ 399.6
Basic earnings per common share (Notes 1 and 9)	$ 2.10	$ 1.59	$ 1.38
Diluted earnings per common share (Notes 1 and 9)	$ 2.07	$ 1.57	$ 1.35

NIKE

Nike, Inc. Consolidated Balance Sheet

(in millions)

MAY 31,	2000	1999
ASSETS		
Current Assets:		
Cash and equivalents	$ 254.3	$ 198.1
Accounts receivable, less allowance for doubtful accounts of $65.4 and $73.2	1,567.2	1,540.1
Inventories (Note 2)	1,446.0	1,170.6
Deferred income taxes (Notes 1 and 6)	111.5	120.6
Income taxes receivable	2.2	15.9
Prepaid expenses (Note 1)	215.2	219.6
Total current assets	3,596.4	3,264.9
Property, plant and equipment, net (Note 3)	1,583.4	1,265.8
Identifiable intangible assets and goodwill (Note 1)	410.9	426.6
Deferred income taxes and other assets (Notes 1 and 6)	266.2	290.4
Total assets	$5,856.9	$5,247.7
LIABILITIES AND SHAREHOLDERS' EQUITY		
Current Liabilities:		
Current portion of long-term debt (Note 5)	$ 50.1	$ 1.0
Notes payable (Note 4)	924.2	419.1
Accounts payable (Note 4)	543.8	473.6
Accrued liabilities	621.9	553.2
Total current liabilities	2,140.0	1,446.9
Long-term debt (Notes 5 and 14)	470.3	386.1
Deferred income taxes and other liabilities (Notes 1 and 6)	110.3	79.8
Commitments and contingencies (Notes 12 and 15)	—	—
Redeemable Preferred Stock (Note 7)	0.3	0.3
Shareholders' Equity :		
Common stock at stated value (Note 8):		
Class A convertible – 99.2 and 100.7 shares outstanding	0.2	0.2
Class B – 170.4 and 181.6 shares outstanding	2.6	2.7
Capital in excess of stated value	369.0	334.1
Unearned stock compensation	(11.7)	—
Accumulated other comprehensive income	(111.1)	(68.9)
Retained earnings	2,887.0	3,066.5
Total shareholders' equity	3,136.0	3,334.6
Total liabilities and shareholders' equity	$5,856.9	$5,247.7

Nike, Inc. Consolidated Statement of Cash Flows
(in millions)

YEAR ENDED MAY 31,	2000	1999	1998
Cash provided (used) by operations:			
Net income	$579.1	$451.4	$399.6
Income charges (credits) not affecting cash:			
Depreciation	188.0	198.2	184.5
Non-cash portion of restructuring charge	—	28.0	59.3
Deferred income taxes	36.8	37.9	(113.9)
Amortization and other	35.6	30.6	49.0
Changes in certain working capital components:			
(Increase) decrease in inventories	(275.4)	226.0	(58.0)
(Increase) decrease in accounts receivable	(27.1)	134.3	79.7
Decrease (increase) in other current assets and income taxes receivable	65.6	25.0	(12.6)
Increase (decrease) in accounts payable, accrued liabilities and income taxes payable	157.3	(170.4)	(70.1)
Cash provided by operations	759.9	961.0	517.5
Cash provided (used) by investing activities:			
Additions to property, plant and equipment	(419.9)	(384.1)	(505.9)
Disposals of property, plant and equipment	25.3	27.2	16.8
Increase in other assets	(51.3)	(60.8)	(87.4)
Increase (decrease) in other liabilities	5.9	1.2	(18.5)
Cash used by investing activities	(440.0)	(416.5)	(595.0)
Cash provided (used) by financing activities:			
Additions to long-term debt	0.1	—	101.5
Reductions in long-term debt including current portion	(1.8)	(1.5)	(2.5)
Increase (decrease) in notes payable	505.1	(61.0)	(73.0)
Proceeds from exercise of options	23.9	54.4	32.2
Repurchase of stock	(646.3)	(299.8)	(202.3)
Dividends – common and preferred	(133.1)	(136.2)	(127.3)
Cash used by financing activities	(252.1)	(444.1)	(271.4)
Effect of exchange rate changes on cash	(11.6)	(10.9)	12.1
Net increase (decrease) in cash and equivalents	56.2	89.5	(336.8)
Cash and equivalents, beginning of year	198.1	108.6	445.4
Cash and equivalents, end of year	$254.3	$198.1	$108.6
Supplemental disclosure of cash flow information:			
Cash paid during the year for:			
Interest	$ 45.0	$ 47.1	$ 52.2
Income taxes	221.1	231.9	360.5
Non-cash investing and financing activity:			
Assumption of long-term debt to acquire property, plant, and equipment	$108.9	—	—

NIKE

NIKE

Nike, Inc. Consolidated Statement of Shareholders' Equity
(in millions)

| | COMMON STOCK | | | | CAPITAL IN EXCESS OF STATED VALUE | UNEARNED STOCK COMPENSATION | ACCUMULATED OTHER COMPREHENSIVE INCOME | RETAINED EARNINGS | TOTAL |
| | CLASS A | | CLASS B | | | | | | |
	SHARES	AMOUNT	SHARES	AMOUNT					
BALANCE AT MAY 31, 1997	101.7	$0.2	187.6	$2.7	$210.6	$ —	$ (31.3)	$2,973.7	$3,155.9
Stock options exercised			2.1		57.2				57.2
Conversion to Class B Common Stock	(0.2)		0.2						
Repurchase of Class B Common Stock			(4.4)		(5.3)			(197.0)	(202.3)
Dividends on common stock								(132.9)	(132.9)
Comprehensive income:									
Net income								399.6	399.6
Foreign currency translation (net of tax benefit of $3.7)							(15.9)		(15.9)
Comprehensive income							(15.9)	399.6	383.7
BALANCE AT MAY 31, 1998	101.5	0.2	185.5	2.7	262.5	—	(47.2)	3,043.4	3,261.6
Stock options exercised			2.7		80.5				80.5
Conversion to Class B Common Stock	(0.8)		0.8						
Repurchase of Class B Common Stock			(7.4)		(8.9)			(292.7)	(301.6)
Dividends on common stock								(135.6)	(135.6)
Comprehensive income:									
Net income								451.4	451.4
Foreign currency translation (net of tax benefit of $12.5)							(21.7)		(21.7)
Comprehensive income							(21.7)	451.4	429.7
BALANCE AT MAY 31, 1999	100.7	0.2	181.6	2.7	334.1	—	(68.9)	3,066.5	3,334.6
Stock options exercised			1.3		38.7				38.7
Conversion to Class B Common Stock	(1.5)		1.5						
Repurchase of Class B Common Stock			(14.5)	(0.1)	(17.3)			(627.1)	(644.5)
Dividends on common stock								(131.5)	(131.5)
Issuance of shares to employees			0.5		13.5	(13.5)			—
Amortization of unearned compensation						1.8			1.8
Comprehensive income:									
Net income								579.1	579.1
Foreign currency translation (net of tax benefit of $9.3)							(42.2)		(42.2)
Comprehensive income							(42.2)	579.1	536.9
BALANCE AT MAY 31, 2000	99.2	$0.2	170.4	$2.6	$369.0	$ (11.7)	$(111.1)	$2,887.0	$3,136.0

Nike, Inc. Notes to Consolidated Financial Statements

NOTE 1—SUMMARY OF SIGNIFICANT ACCOUNTING POLICIES:

Basis of consolidation: The consolidated financial statements include the accounts of NIKE, Inc. and its subsidiaries (the Company). All significant intercompany transactions and balances have been eliminated.

Recognition of revenues: Revenues recognized include sales and fees earned on sales by licensees. Revenues are recognized when title passes based on the terms of the sale, which are generally upon shipment.

Advertising and promotion: Advertising production costs are expensed the first time the advertisement is run. Media (TV and print) placement costs are expensed in the month the advertising appears. Accounting for endorsement contracts, the majority of the Company's promotional expenses, is based upon specific contract provisions. Generally, endorsement payments are expensed uniformly over the term of the contract after giving recognition to periodic performance compliance provisions of the contracts. Contracts requiring prepayments are included in prepaid expenses or other assets depending on the length of the contract. Total advertising and promotion expenses were $978.2 million, $978.6 million and $1,129.1 million for the years ended May 31, 2000, 1999 and 1998, respectively. Included in prepaid expenses and other assets was $158.7 million and $180.9 million at May 31, 2000 and 1999, respectively, relating to prepaid advertising and promotion expenses.

Cash and equivalents: Cash and equivalents represent cash and short-term, highly liquid investments with original maturities of three months or less.

Inventory valuation: Inventories are stated at the lower of cost or market. Inventories are valued on a first-in, first-out (FIFO) basis. In the fourth quarter of fiscal year 1999, the Company changed its method of determining cost for substantially all of its U.S. inventories from last-in, first-out (LIFO) to FIFO. See Note 11.

Property, plant and equipment and depreciation: Property, plant and equipment are recorded at cost. Depreciation for financial reporting purposes is determined on a straight-line basis for buildings and leasehold improvements over 2 to 30 years and principally on a declining balance basis for machinery and equipment over 2 to 8 years. Computer software is depreciated on a straight-line basis over 3 to 7 years.

Identifiable intangible assets and goodwill: At May 31, 2000 and 1999, the Company had patents, trademarks and other identifiable intangible assets with a value of $215.2 million and $213.0 million, respectively. The Company's excess of purchase cost over the fair value of net assets of businesses acquired (goodwill) was $323.5 million and $324.8 million at May 31, 2000 and 1999, respectively.

Identifiable intangible assets and goodwill are being amortized over their estimated useful lives on a straight-line basis over five to forty years. Accumulated amortization was $127.8 million and $111.2 million at May 31, 2000 and 1999, respectively. Amortization expense, which is included in other income/expense, was $18.5 million, $19.4 million and $19.8 million for the years ended May 31, 2000, 1999 and 1998, respectively. Intangible assets are periodically reviewed by the Company for impairments to assess if the fair value is less than the carrying value.

Foreign currency translation: Adjustments resulting from translating foreign functional currency financial statements into U.S. dollars are included in the currency translation adjustment, a component of accumulated other comprehensive income in shareholders' equity.

Derivatives: The Company enters into foreign currency contracts in order to reduce the impact of certain foreign currency fluctuations. Firmly committed transactions and the related receivables and payables may be hedged with forward exchange contracts or purchased options. Anticipated, but not yet firmly committed, transactions may be hedged through the use of purchased options. Premiums paid on purchased options and any realized gains are included in prepaid expenses or accrued liabilities and are recognized in earnings when the transaction being hedged is recognized. Gains and losses arising from foreign currency forward and option contracts, and cross-currency swap transactions are recognized in income or expense as offsets of gains and losses resulting from the underlying hedged transactions. Hedge effectiveness is determined by evaluating whether gains and losses on hedges will offset gains and losses on the underlying exposures. This evaluation is performed at inception of the hedge and periodically over the life of the hedge. Occasionally, hedges may cease to be effective and are thus terminated prior to recognition of the underlying transaction. Gains and losses on these hedges are deferred until the point in time ineffectiveness is determined and will be included in the basis of the underlying transaction. Hedges will also be terminated if the underlying transaction is no longer expected to occur. When this occurs all related deferral gains and losses are recognized in earnings immediately. Cash flows from risk management activities are classified in the same category as the cash flows from the related investment, borrowing or foreign exchange activity. See Note 15 for further discussion.

Income taxes: Income taxes are provided currently on financial statement earnings of non-U.S. subsidiaries expected to be repatriated. The Company intends to determine annually the amount of undistributed non-U.S. earnings to invest indefinitely in its non-U.S. operations. The Company accounts for income taxes using the asset and liability method. This approach requires the recognition of deferred tax assets and liabilities for the expected future tax consequences of temporary differences between the carrying amounts and the tax bases of other assets and liabilities. See Note 6 for further discussion.

Earnings per share: Basic earnings per common share is calculated by dividing net income by the average number of common shares outstanding during the year. Diluted earnings per common share is calculated by adjusting outstanding shares, assuming conversion of all potentially dilutive stock options and awards. See Note 9 for further discussion.

Management estimates: The preparation of financial statements in conformity with generally accepted accounting principles requires management to make estimates, including estimates relating to assumptions that affect the reported amounts of assets and liabilities and disclosure of contingent assets and liabilities at the date of financial statements and the reported amounts of revenues and expenses during the reporting period. Actual results could differ from these estimates.

Reclassifications: Certain prior year amounts have been reclassified to conform to fiscal year 2000 presentation. These changes had no impact on previously reported results of operations or shareholders' equity.

NOTE 2 – INVENTORIES:

Inventories by major classification are as follows:

(in millions)

MAY 31,	2000	1999
Finished goods	$1,416.6	$1,127.6
Work-in-progress	17.3	21.2
Raw materials	12.1	21.8
	$1,446.0	$1,170.6

As stated in Note 1, the Company changed its inventory valuation method for substantially all U.S. inventories in fiscal year 1999.

NOTE 3 – PROPERTY, PLANT AND EQUIPMENT:

Property, plant and equipment includes the following:

(in millions)

MAY 31,	2000	1999
Land	$ 180.6	$ 99.6
Buildings	503.4	374.2
Machinery and equipment	981.9	923.3
Leasehold improvements	279.6	273.4
Construction in process	448.3	330.8
	2,393.8	2,001.3
Less accumulated depreciation	810.4	735.5
	$1,583.4	$1,265.8

Capitalized interest expense incurred was $4.8 million, $6.9 million and $6.5 million for the fiscal years ended May 31, 2000, 1999 and 1998, respectively.

NOTE 7 – REDEEMABLE PREFERRED STOCK:

NIAC is the sole owner of the Company's authorized Redeemable Preferred Stock, $1 par value, which is redeemable at the option of NIAC at par value aggregating $0.3 million. A cumulative dividend of $0.10 per share is payable annually on May 31 and no dividends may be declared or paid on the common stock of the Company unless dividends on the Redeemable Preferred Stock have been declared and paid in full. There have been no changes in the Redeemable Preferred Stock in the three years ended May 31, 2000. As the holder of the Redeemable Preferred Stock, NIAC does not have general voting rights but does have the right to vote as a separate class on the sale of all or substantially all of the assets of the Company and its subsidiaries, on merger, consolidation, liquidation or dissolution of the Company or on the sale or assignment of the NIKE trademark for athletic footwear sold in the United States.

NOTE 9 – EARNINGS PER SHARE:

The following represents a reconciliation from basic earnings per share to diluted earnings per share. Options to purchase 9.7 million and 3.3 million shares of common stock were outstanding at May 31, 2000 and May 31, 1998, respectively, but were not included in the computation of diluted earnings per share because the options' exercise prices were greater than the average market price of the common shares and, therefore, the effect would be antidilutive. No such antidilutive options were outstanding at May 31, 1999.

(in millions, except per share data)

YEAR ENDED MAY 31,	2000	1999	1998
Determination of shares:			
Average common shares outstanding	275.7	283.3	288.7
Assumed conversion of dilutive stock options and awards	3.7	5.0	6.3
Diluted average common shares outstanding	279.4	288.3	295.0
Basic earnings per common share	$ 2.10	$ 1.59	$ 1.38
Diluted earnings per common share	$ 2.07	$ 1.57	$ 1.35

NOTE 10 – BENEFIT PLANS:

The Company has a profit sharing plan available to substantially all employees. The terms of the plan call for annual contributions by the Company as determined by the Board of Directors. Contributions of $15.7 million, $12.8 million and $11.2 million to the plan are included in other expense in the consolidated financial statements for the years ended May 31, 2000, 1999 and 1998, respectively. The Company has a voluntary 401(k) employee savings plan. The Company matches a portion of employee contributions with common stock, vesting that portion over 5 years. Company contributions to the savings plan were $6.7 million, $7.4 million and $8.1 million for the years ended May 31, 2000, 1999 and 1998, respectively, and are included in selling and administrative expenses.

NOTE 11 – OTHER INCOME/EXPENSE, NET:

Included in other income/expense for the years ended May 31, 2000, 1999, and 1998, was interest income of $13.6 million, $13.0 million and $16.5 million, respectively. In addition, included in other income/expense in fiscal 1999 was income of $15.0 million related to the change in accounting for inventories in the U.S. from the LIFO to the FIFO method. The change was effected in the fourth quarter of fiscal 1999 and was not considered significant to show the cumulative effect or to restate comparable income statements as dictated by Accounting Principles Board Opinion No. 20.

NOTE 12 – COMMITMENTS AND CONTINGENCIES:

The Company leases space for its offices, warehouses and retail stores under leases expiring from one to seventeen years after May 31, 2000. Rent expense aggregated $145.5 million, $129.5 million and $129.6 million for the years ended May 31, 2000, 1999 and 1998, respectively. Amounts of minimum future annual rental commitments under non-cancelable operating leases in each of the five fiscal years 2001 through 2005 are $121.1 million, $107.3 million, $89.0 million, $69.9 million, $59.3 million, respectively, and $299.5 million in later years.

At May 31, 2000, the Company had letters of credit outstanding totaling $678.2 million. These letters of credit were issued for the purchase of inventory.

Lawsuits arise during the normal course of business. In the opinion of management, none of the pending lawsuits will result in a significant impact on the consolidated results of operations or financial position.

NOTE 16 – OPERATING SEGMENTS AND RELATED INFORMATION:

Revenues by Major Product Lines: Revenues to external customers for NIKE Brand products are attributable to sales of Footwear, Apparel, and Equipment & Other NIKE Brand. Revenues to external customers for Other Brands include external sales by the non-NIKE brand subsidiaries.

(in millions)

YEAR ENDED MAY 31,	2000	1999	1998
Footwear	$5,561.5	$5,218.4	$5,959.0
Apparel	2,698.6	2,822.9	2,885.7
Equipment	328.2	316.8	277.4
Other brands	406.8	418.8	431.0
	$8,995.1	$8,776.9	$9,553.1

Report of Independent Accountants

Portland, Oregon
June 29, 2000
To the Board of Directors and
Shareholders of NIKE, Inc.

In our opinion, the accompanying consolidated balance sheet and the related consolidated statements of income, of cash flows and of shareholders' equity present fairly, in all material respects, the financial position of NIKE, Inc. and its subsidiaries at May 31, 2000 and 1999, and the results of their operations and their cash flows for each of the three years in the period ended May 31, 2000 in conformity with accounting principles generally accepted in the United States. These financial statements are the responsibility of the Company's management; our responsibility is to express an opinion on these financial statements based on our audits. We conducted our audits of these statements in accordance with auditing standards generally accepted in the United States, which require that we plan and perform the audit to obtain reasonable assurance about whether the financial statements are free of material misstatement. An audit includes examining, on a test basis, evidence supporting the amounts and disclosures in the financial statements, assessing the accounting principles used and significant estimates made by management, and evaluating the overall financial statement presentation. We believe that our audits provide a reasonable basis for the opinion expressed above.

PricewaterhouseCoopers LLP

REEBOK INTERNATIONAL LTD.

CONSOLIDATED STATEMENTS OF INCOME

	Year Ended December 31		
	1999	**1998**	**1997**
	(Amounts in thousands, except per share data)		
Net sales	$2,899,872	$3,224,592	$3,643,599
Other income (expense)	(8,635)	(19,167)	(6,158)
	2,891,237	3,205,425	3,637,441
Costs and expenses:			
Cost of sales	1,783,914	2,037,465	2,294,049
Selling, general and administrative expenses	971,945	1,043,199	1,069,433
Special charges	61,625	35,000	58,161
Amortization of intangibles	5,183	3,432	4,157
Interest expense	49,691	60,671	64,366
Interest income	(9,159)	(11,372)	(10,810)
	2,863,199	3,168,395	3,479,356
Income before income taxes and minority interest	28,038	37,030	158,085
Income taxes	10,093	11,925	12,490
Income before minority interest	17,945	25,105	145,595
Minority interest	6,900	1,178	10,476
Net income	$ 11,045	$ 23,927	$ 135,119
Basic earnings per share	$ .20	$ .42	$ 2.41
Diluted earnings per share	$ .20	$ .42	$ 2.32

Reebok

Reebok

REEBOK INTERNATIONAL LTD.
CONSOLIDATED BALANCE SHEETS

	December 31	
	1999	1998
	(Amounts in thousands, except share data)	
Assets		
Current assets:		
Cash and cash equivalents	$ 281,744	$ 180,070
Accounts receivable, net of allowance for doubtful accounts (1999, $46,217; 1998, $47,383)	417,404	517,830
Inventory	414,616	535,168
Deferred income taxes	88,127	79,484
Prepaid expenses and other current assets	41,227	50,309
Total current assets	1,243,118	1,362,861
Property and equipment, net	178,111	172,585
Other non-current assets:		
Intangibles, net of amortization	68,892	68,648
Deferred income taxes	43,868	43,147
Other	30,139	37,383
	142,899	149,178
Total Assets	$1,564,128	$1,684,624
Liabilities and Stockholders' Equity		
Current liabilities:		
Notes payable to banks	$ 27,614	$ 48,070
Current portion of long-term debt	185,167	86,640
Accounts payable	153,998	203,144
Accrued expenses	248,822	177,133
Income taxes payable	8,302	27,597
Total current liabilities	623,903	542,584
Long-term debt, net of current portion	370,302	554,432
Minority interest and other long-term liabilities	41,107	46,672
Commitments and contingencies		
Outstanding redemption value of equity put options		16,559
Stockholders' equity:		
Common stock, par value $.01; authorized 250,000,000 shares; issued shares 92,985,737 in 1999; 93,306,642 shares in 1998	930	933
Retained earnings	1,170,885	1,156,739
Less 36,716,227 shares in treasury at cost	(617,620)	(617,620)
Unearned compensation		(26)
Accumulated other comprehensive income (expense)	(25,379)	(15,649)
	528,816	524,377
Total Liabilities and Stockholders' Equity	$1,564,128	$1,684,624

REEBOK INTERNATIONAL LTD.
CONSOLIDATED STATEMENTS OF STOCKHOLDERS' EQUITY

	Shares	Total	Common Stock (Par Value $.01)	Retained Earnings	Treasury Stock	Unearned Compensation	Accumulated Other Comprehensive Income (Expense)
			(Dollar amounts in thousands)				
Balance, December 31, 1996	92,556,295	$381,234	$926	$ 992,563	$(617,620)	$(283)	$ 5,648
Comprehensive income:							
Net income		135,119		135,119			
Adjustment for foreign currency translation		(26,933)					(26,933)
Comprehensive income		108,186					
Issuance of shares to certain employees	9,532			431		(431)	
Amortization of unearned compensation		566				566	
Shares repurchased and retired	(313)	8				8	
Shares issued under employee stock purchase plans	151,210	4,363	1	4,362			
Shares issued upon exercise of stock options	399,111	10,044	4	10,040			
Income tax reductions relating to exercise of stock options		2,756		2,756			
Balance, December 31, 1997	93,115,835	507,157	931	1,145,271	(617,620)	(140)	(21,285)
Comprehensive income:							
Net income		23,927		23,927			
Adjustment for foreign currency translation		5,636					5,636
Comprehensive income		29,563					
Issuance of shares to certain employees	14,704			458		(458)	
Amortization of unearned compensation		387				387	
Shares repurchased and retired	(114,920)	(3,181)	(1)	(3,365)		185	
Shares issued under employee stock purchase plans	223,583	3,821	2	3,819			
Shares issued upon exercise of stock options	67,440	1,187	1	1,186			
Put option contracts outstanding		(16,559)		(16,559)			
Premium received from unexercised equity put options		2,002		2,002			
Balance, December 31, 1998	93,306,642	524,377	933	1,156,739	(617,620)	(26)	(15,649)
Comprehensive income:							
Net income		11,045		11,045			
Adjustment for foreign currency translation		(9,730)					(9,730)
Comprehensive income		1,315					
Issuance of shares to certain employees	4,449			116		(116)	
Amortization of unearned compensation		142				142	
Shares repurchased pursuant to equity put options	(625,000)	0	(6)	6			
Shares issued under employee stock purchase plans	292,432	2,885	3	2,882			
Shares issued upon exercise of stock options	7,214	97		97			
Balance, December 31, 1999	92,985,737	$528,816	$930	$1,170,885	$(617,620)	$ (0)	$(25,379)

REEBOK INTERNATIONAL LTD.
CONSOLIDATED STATEMENTS OF CASH FLOWS

	Year Ended December 31		
	1999	1998	1997
	(Amounts in thousands)		
Cash flows from operating activities:			
Net income	$ 11,045	$ 23,927	$ 135,119
Adjustments to reconcile net income to net cash provided by operating activities:			
Depreciation and amortization	48,643	48,017	47,423
Minority interest	6,900	1,178	10,476
Deferred income taxes	(9,364)	(28,074)	(17,285)
Special charges	61,625	35,000	58,161
Changes in operating assets and liabilities:			
Accounts receivable	85,698	63,951	(13,915)
Inventory	109,381	39,134	(47,937)
Prepaid expenses and other	5,986	8,626	(4,155)
Accounts payable and accrued expenses	(18,338)	(65,616)	18,295
Income taxes payable	(19,951)	25,634	(59,257)
Total adjustments	270,580	127,850	(8,194)
Net cash provided by operating activities:	281,625	151,777	126,925
Cash flows from investing activity:			
Payments to acquire property and equipment	(51,197)	(53,616)	(23,910)
Net cash used for investing activity	(51,197)	(53,616)	(23,910)
Cash flows from financing activities:			
Net borrowings (repayments) of notes payable to banks	(22,269)	2,048	27,296
Repayments of long-term debt	(85,020)	(121,016)	(156,966)
Proceeds from issuance of common stock to employees	2,982	5,008	17,163
Proceeds from premium on equity put options		2,002	
Dividends to minority shareholders	(17,966)	(6,649)	(3,900)
Repurchases of common stock	(16,559)	(3,366)	
Net cash used for financing activities	(138,832)	(121,973)	(116,407)
Effect of exchange rate changes on cash	10,078	(5,884)	(9,207)
Net increase (decrease) in cash and cash equivalents	101,674	(29,696)	(22,599)
Cash and cash equivalents at beginning of year	180,070	209,766	232,365
Cash and cash equivalents at end of year	$ 281,744	$ 180,070	$ 209,766
Supplemental disclosures of cash flow information:			
Interest paid	$ 43,620	$ 58,224	$ 59,683
Income taxes paid	35,147	26,068	115,985

GAP, Inc.

CONSOLIDATED STATEMENTS OF EARNINGS

($000 except per share amounts)	52 Weeks Ended Jan. 29, 2000	Percentage to Sales	52 Weeks Ended Jan. 30, 1999	Percentage to Sales	52 Weeks Ended Jan. 31, 1998	Percentage to Sales
Net sales	$11,635,398	100.0%	$ 9,054,462	100.0%	$ 6,507,825	100.0%
Costs and expenses						
Cost of goods sold and occupancy expenses	6,775,262	58.2	5,318,218	58.7	4,021,541	61.8
Operating expenses	3,043,432	26.2	2,403,365	26.5	1,635,017	25.1
Net interest expense (income)	31,755	0.3	13,617	0.2	(2,975)	0.0
Earnings before income taxes	1,784,949	15.3	1,319,262	14.6	854,242	13.1
Income taxes	657,884	5.6	494,723	5.5	320,341	4.9
Net earnings	$ 1,127,065	9.7%	$ 824,539	9.1%	$ 533,901	8.2%
Weighted-average number of shares–basic	853,804,924		864,062,060		891,404,945	
Weighted-average number of shares–diluted	895,029,176		904,374,383		922,951,706	
Earnings per share–basic	$ 1.32		$ 0.95		$ 0.60	
Earnings per share–diluted	1.26		0.91		0.58	

See Notes to Consolidated Financial Statements.

GAP, Inc.

CONSOLIDATED BALANCE SHEETS

($000 except par value)	Jan. 29, 2000	Jan. 30, 1999
Assets		
Current Assets		
Cash and equivalents	$ 450,352	$ 565,253
Merchandise inventory	1,462,045	1,056,444
Other current assets	285,393	250,127
Total current assets	2,197,790	1,871,824
Property and Equipment		
Leasehold improvements	1,426,537	1,040,959
Furniture and equipment	2,083,604	1,601,572
Land and buildings	278,422	160,776
Construction-in-progress	414,725	245,020
	4,203,288	3,048,327
Accumulated depreciation and amortization	(1,487,973)	(1,171,957)
Property and equipment, net	2,715,315	1,876,370
Lease rights and other assets	275,651	215,725
Total assets	$5,188,756	$3,963,919
Liabilities and Shareholders' Equity		
Current Liabilities		
Notes payable	$ 168,961	$ 90,690
Accounts payable	805,945	684,130
Accrued expenses and other current liabilities	751,710	655,770
Income taxes payable	26,263	122,513
Total current liabilities	1,752,879	1,553,103
Long-Term Liabilities		
Long-term debt	784,925	496,455
Deferred lease credits and other liabilities	417,907	340,682
Total long-term liabilities	1,202,832	837,137
Shareholders' Equity		
Common stock $.05 par value		
Authorized 2,300,000,000 shares; issued 1,007,356,790 and 997,496,214 shares; outstanding 850,498,941 and 857,960,032 shares	50,368	49,875
Additional paid-in capital	669,490	349,037
Retained earnings	4,172,796	3,121,360
Accumulated other comprehensive loss	(6,759)	(12,518)
Deferred compensation	(23,150)	(31,675)
Treasury stock, at cost	(2,629,700)	(1,902,400)
Total shareholders' equity	2,233,045	1,573,679
Total liabilities and shareholders' equity	$5,188,756	$3,963,919

See Notes to Consolidated Financial Statements.

GAP, Inc.

CONSOLIDATED STATEMENTS OF CASH FLOWS

($000)	52 Weeks Ended Jan. 29, 2000	52 Weeks Ended Jan. 30, 1999	52 Weeks Ended Jan. 31, 1998
Cash Flows from Operating Activities			
Net earnings	$1,127,065	$ 824,539	$ 533,901
Adjustments to reconcile net earnings to net cash provided by operating activities:			
Depreciation and amortization	436,184	326,447	269,706
Tax benefit from exercise of stock options and vesting of restricted stock	211,891	79,808	23,682
Deferred income taxes	2,444	(34,766)	(13,706)
Change in operating assets and liabilities:			
Merchandise inventory	(404,211)	(322,287)	(156,091)
Prepaid expenses and other	(55,519)	(77,292)	(44,736)
Accounts payable	118,121	265,296	63,532
Accrued expenses	89,071	231,178	107,365
Income taxes payable	(94,893)	38,805	(8,214)
Deferred lease credits and other long-term liabilities	47,775	62,433	69,212
Net cash provided by operating activities	1,477,928	1,394,161	844,651
Cash Flows from Investing Activities			
Net purchase of property and equipment	(1,238,722)	(797,592)	(465,843)
Acquisition of lease rights and other assets	(39,839)	(28,815)	(19,779)
Net maturity of short-term investments	—	—	174,709
Net purchase of long-term investments	—	—	(2,939)
Net cash used for investing activities	(1,278,561)	(826,407)	(313,852)
Cash Flows from Financing Activities			
Net increase in notes payable	84,778	1,357	44,462
Net issuance of long-term debt	311,839	—	495,890
Issuance of common stock	76,211	36,655	23,309
Net purchase of treasury stock	(707,125)	(879,383)	(585,798)
Cash dividends paid	(75,795)	(76,888)	(79,503)
Net cash used for financing activities	(310,092)	(918,259)	(101,640)
Effect of exchange rate fluctuations on cash	(4,176)	2,589	(1,634)
Net (decrease) increase in cash and equivalents	(114,901)	(347,916)	427,525
Cash and equivalents at beginning of year	565,253	913,169	485,644
Cash and equivalents at end of year	$ 450,352	$ 565,253	$ 913,169

See Notes to Consolidated Financial Statements.

GAP, Inc.

CONSOLIDATED STATEMENTS OF SHAREHOLDERS' EQUITY

($000 except share and per share amounts)	Common Stock		Additional Paid-in Capital	Retained Earnings	Accumulated Other Comprehensive Loss	Deferred Compensation	Treasury Stock		Total	Comprehensive Earnings
	Shares	Amount					Shares	Amount		
Balance at January 31, 1998	989,826,394	$ 49,491	$ 205,393	$2,392,750	$ (15,230)	$ (38,167)	(105,277,081)	$(1,010,251)	$1,583,986	$ 523,858
Issuance of common stock pursuant to stock option plans	7,575,195	380	46,709			(10,351)			36,738	
Net issuance of common stock pursuant to management incentive restricted stock plans	94,625	4	4,361			(3,873)			492	
Tax benefit from exercise of stock options by employees and from vesting of restricted stock			79,808						79,808	
Adjustments for foreign currency translation ($1,893) and fluctuations in fair market value of financial instruments ($819)					2,712				2,712	2,712
Amortization of restricted stock and discounted stock options						20,716			20,716	
Purchase of treasury stock							(35,714,475)	(910,387)	(910,387)	
Reissuance of treasury stock			12,766				1,455,374	18,238	31,004	
Net earnings				824,539					824,539	824,539
Cash dividends ($.11 per share)				(95,929)					(95,929)	
Balance at January 30, 1999	997,496,214	$ 49,875	$ 349,037	$3,121,360	$ (12,518)	$ (31,675)	(139,536,182)	$(1,902,400)	$1,573,679	$ 827,251
Issuance of common stock pursuant to stock option plans	9,933,713	497	81,456			(9,186)			72,767	
Net cancellations of common stock pursuant to management incentive restricted stock plans	(73,137)	(4)	2,583			(3,411)			(832)	
Tax benefit from exercise of stock options by employees and from vesting of restricted stock			211,891						211,891	
Adjustments for foreign currency translation ($3,305) and fluctuations in fair market value of financial instruments ($2,454)					5,759				5,759	5,759
Amortization of restricted stock and discounted stock options			72			21,122			21,194	
Purchase of treasury stock			4,276				(18,500,000)	(745,056)	(740,780)	
Reissuance of treasury stock			20,175				1,178,333	17,756	37,931	
Net earnings				1,127,065					1,127,065	1,127,065
Cash dividends ($.09 per share)				(75,629)					(75,629)	
Balance at January 29, 2000	1,007,356,790	$ 50,368	$ 669,490	$4,172,796	$ (6,759)	$ (23,150)	(156,857,849)	$(2,629,700)	$2,233,045	$1,132,824

See Notes to Consolidated Financial Statements.

B

Present and Future Values

Learning Objectives

Conceptual

C1 Describe the earning of interest and the concepts of present and future values.

Procedural

P1 Apply present value concepts to a single amount by using interest tables.

P2 Apply future value concepts to a single amount by using interest tables.

P3 Apply present value concepts to an annuity by using interest tables.

P4 Apply future value concepts to an annuity by using interest tables.

Appendix Preview

The concepts of present and future values are important to modern business activity. The purpose of this appendix is to explain, illustrate, and compute present and future values. We apply these concepts to both business and everyday activities.

Present and Future Value Concepts

C1 Describe the earning of interest and the concepts of present and future values.

There's an old saying, *"Time is money."* This saying reflects the notion that as time passes, the value of our assets and liabilities changes. This change is due to *interest,* which is the payment to the owner of an asset for its use by a borrower. The most common example of interest is a savings account asset. As we keep a balance of cash in the account, it earns interest that the financial institution pays us. An example of a liability is a car loan. As we carry the balance of the loan, we accumulate interest costs on it. We must ultimately repay this loan with interest.

Present and future value computations enable us to measure or estimate the interest component of holding assets or liabilities over time. The present value computation is important when we want to know the value of future-day assets *today.* The future value computation is important when we want to know the value of present-day assets *at a future date.* The first section focuses on the present value of a single amount. The second section focuses on the future value of a single amount. Then both the present and future values of a series of amounts (called an *annuity*) are defined and explained.

Present Value of a Single Amount

Exhibit B.1

Present Value of a Single Amount Diagram

We graphically express the present value, called p, of a single future amount, called f, that is received or paid at a future date in Exhibit B.1.

The formula to compute the present value of a single amount is shown in Exhibit B.2 where p = present value; f = future value; i = rate of interest per period; and n = number of periods. (Interest is also called the *discount,* and an interest rate is also called the *discount rate.*)

Exhibit B.2

Present Value of a Single Amount Formula

$$p = \frac{f}{(1 + i)^n}$$

To illustrate present value concepts, assume we need $220 one period from today. We want to know how much we must invest now, for one period, at an interest rate of 10% to provide for this $220. For this illustration, the p, or present value, is the unknown amount—the specifics are shown graphically as follows:

Conceptually, we know p must be less than $220. This is obvious from the answer to this question: Would we rather have $220 today or $220 at some future date? If we had $220 today, we could invest it and see it grow to something more than $220 in the future. Therefore, we would prefer the $220 today. This means if we were promised $220 in the future, we would take less than $220 today. But how much less? To answer that question, we compute an estimate of the present value of the $220 to be received one period from now using the formula in Exhibit B.2 as follows:

$$p = \frac{f}{(1 + i)^n} = \frac{\$220}{(1 + 0.10)^1} = \$200$$

We interpret this result to say that given an interest rate of 10%, we are indifferent between $200 today or $220 at the end of one period.

We can also use this formula to compute the present value for *any number of periods.* To illustrate, consider a payment of $242 at the end of two periods at 10% interest. The present value of this $242 to be received two periods from now is computed as follows:

$$p = \frac{f}{(1 + i)^n} = \frac{\$242}{(1 + 0.10)^2} = \$200$$

Together, these results tell us we are indifferent between $200 today, or $220 one period from today, or $242 two periods from today given a 10% interest rate per period.

The number of periods (n) in the present value formula does not have to be expressed in years. Any period of time such as a day, a month, a quarter, or a year can be used. Whatever period is used, the interest rate (i) must be compounded for the same period. This means if a situation expresses n in months and i equals 12% per year, then i is transformed into interest earned per month (or 1%). In this case, interest is said to be *compounded monthly.*

I will pay your allowance at the end of the month. Do you want to wait or receive its present value today?

A present value table helps us with present value computations. It gives us present values (factors) for a variety of both interest rates (i) and periods (n). Each present value in a present value table assumes the future value (f) equals 1. When the future value (f) is different from 1, we need simply multiply the present value (p) from the table by that future value to give us the estimate. The formula used to construct a table of present values for a single future amount of 1 is shown in Exhibit B.3.

P1 Apply present value concepts to a single amount by using interest tables.

$$p = \frac{1}{(1 + i)^n}$$

Exhibit B.3
Present Value of 1 Formula

This formula is identical to that in Exhibit B.2 except that f equals 1. Table B.1 at the end of this appendix is such a present value table. It is often called a **present value of 1 table**. A present value table involves three factors: p, i, and n. Knowing two of these three factors allows us to compute the third. (A fourth is f, but as already explained, we need only multiply the 1 used in the formula by f.) To illustrate the use of a present value table, consider three cases.

Case 1 (solve for p when knowing i and n). To show how we use a present value table, let's again look at how we estimate the present value of $220 (the f value) at the end of one period ($n = 1$) where the interest rate (i) is 10%. To solve this case, we go to the present value table (Table B.1) and look in the row for 1 period and in the column for 10% interest. Here we find a present value (p) of 0.9091 based on a future value of 1. This means, for instance, that $1 to be received 1 period from today at 10% interest is worth $0.9091 today. Since the future value in this case is not $1 but $220, we multiply the 0.9091 by $220 to get an answer of $200.

Case 2 (solve for n when knowing p and i). To illustrate, assume a $100,000 future value ($f$) that is worth $13,000 today ($p$) using an interest rate of 12% (i) but where n is unknown. In particular, we want to know how many periods (n) there are between the present value

and the future value. To put this in context, it would fit a situation in which we want to retire with $100,000 but currently have only $13,000 that is earning a 12% return. How long
will it be before we can retire? To answer this, we go to Table B.1 and look in the 12% interest column. Here we find a column of present values (p) based on a future value of 1.
To use the present value table for this solution, we must divide $13,000 ($p$) by $100,000
(f), which equals 0.1300. This is necessary because *a present value table defines f equal to
1, and p as a fraction of 1*. We look for a value nearest to 0.1300 (p), which we find in the
row for 18 periods (n). This means the present value of $100,000 at the end of 18 periods
at 12% interest is $13,000 or, alternatively stated, we must work 18 more years.

Case 3 (solve for i when knowing p and n). In this case, we have, say, a $120,000 fu-
ture value (f) that is worth $60,000 today ($p$) when there are nine periods (n) between the
present and future values but the interest rate is unknown. As an example, suppose we want
to retire with $120,000, but we have only $60,000 and hope to retire in nine years. What
interest rate must we earn to retire with $120,000 in nine years? To answer this, we go to
the present value table (Table B.1) and look in the row for nine periods. To use the present
value table, we must divide $60,000 ($p$) by $120,000 ($f$), which equals 0.5000. Recall that
this step is necessary because a present value table defines f equal to 1, and p as a fraction
of 1. We look for a value in the row for nine periods that is nearest to 0.5000 (p), which
we find in the column for 8% interest (i). This means the present value of $120,000 at the
end of nine periods at 8% interest is $60,000 or, in our example, we must earn 8% annual
interest to retire in nine years.

Answer—p. B-8

Quick Check

1. A company is considering an investment expected to yield $70,000 after six years.
If this company demands an 8% return, how much is it willing to pay for this
investment?

Future Value of a Single Amount

Exhibit B.4

Future Value of a Single
Amount Formula

We must modify the formula for the present value of a single amount to obtain the formula
for the future value of a single amount. In particular, we multiply both sides of the equation in Exhibit B.2 by $(1 + i)^n$ to get the result shown in Exhibit B.4.

$$f = p \times (1 + i)^n$$

The future value (f) is defined in terms of p, i, and n. We can use this formula to determine
that $200 ($p$) invested for 1 ($n$) period at an interest rate of 10% (i) yields a future value of
$220 as follows:

$$
\begin{aligned}
f &= p \times (1 + i)^n \\
&= \$200 \times (1 + 0.10)^1 \\
&= \$220
\end{aligned}
$$

This formula can also be used to compute the future value of an amount for *any number of
periods* into the future. To illustrate, assume that $200 is invested for three periods at 10%.
The future value of this $200 is $266.20, computed as follows:

$$
\begin{aligned}
f &= p \times (1 + i)^n \\
&= \$200 \times (1 + 0.10)^3 \\
&= \$266.20
\end{aligned}
$$

A future value table makes it easier for us to compute future values (f) for many different combinations of interest rates (i) and time periods (n). Each future value in a future value table assumes the present value (p) is 1. As with a present value table, if the future amount is something other than 1, we simply multiply our answer by that amount. The formula used to construct a table of future values (factors) for a single amount of 1 is in Exhibit B.5.

P2 Apply future value concepts to a single amount by using interest tables.

$$f = (1 + i)^n$$

Exhibit B.5

Future Value of 1 Formula

Table B.2 at the end of this appendix shows a table of future values for a current amount of 1. This type of table is called a **future value of 1 table**.

There are some important relations between Tables B.1 and B.2. In Table B.2, for the row where $n = 0$, the future value is 1 for each interest rate. This is so because no interest is earned when time does not pass. Also notice that Tables B.1 and B.2 report the same information but in a different manner. In particular, one table is simply the *inverse* of the other. To illustrate this inverse relation, let's say we invest $100 annually for a period of five years at 12% per year. How much do we expect to have after five years? We can answer this question using Table B.2 by finding the future value (f) of 1, for five periods from now, compounded at 12%. From that table we find $f = 1.7623$. If we start with $100, the amount it accumulates to after five years is $176.23 ($100 × 1.7623). We can alternatively use Table B.1. Here we find that the present value (p) of 1, discounted five periods at 12%, is 0.5674. Recall the inverse relation between present value and future value. This means $p = 1/f$ (or equivalently, $f = 1/p$). This means we can compute the future value of $100 invested for five periods at 12% as follows: $f = $100 × (1/0.5674) = 176.24.

A future value table involves three factors: f, i, and n. Knowing two of these three factors allows us to compute the third. To illustrate, consider these three possible cases.

Case 1 (solve for f when knowing i and n). Our preceding example fits this case in which we need to solve for f when knowing i and n. We found that $100 invested for five periods at 12% interest accumulates to $176.24.

Case 2 (solve for n when knowing f and i). In this case, we have, say, $2,000 ($p$) and we want to know how many periods (n) it will take to accumulate to $3,000 ($f$) at 7% ($i$) interest. To answer this, we go to the future value table (Table B.2) and look in the 7% interest column. Here we find a column of future values (f) based on a present value of 1. To use a future value table, we must divide $3,000 ($f$) by $2,000 ($p$), which equals 1.500. This is necessary because *a future value table defines p equal to 1, and f as a multiple of 1*. We look for a value nearest to 1.50 (f), which we find in the row for six periods (n). This means that $2,000 invested for six periods at 7% interest accumulates to $3,000.

Case 3 (solve for i when knowing f and n). In this case, we have, say, $2,001 ($p$) and in nine years ($n$), we want to have $4,000 ($f$). What rate of interest must we earn to accomplish this? To answer that, we go to Table B.2 and search in the row for nine periods. To use a future value table, we must divide $4,000 ($f$) by $2,001 ($p$), which equals 1.9990. Recall that this is necessary because a future value table defines p equal to 1 and f as a multiple of 1. We look for a value nearest to 1.9990 (f), which we find in the column for 8% interest (i). This means that $2,001 invested for nine periods at 8% interest accumulates to $4,000.

Quick Check

2. Assume that you win a $150,000 cash sweepstakes. You decide to deposit this cash in an account earning 8% annual interest, and you plan to quit your job when the account equals $555,000. How many years will it be before you can quit working?

Answer—p. B-8

Present Value of an Annuity

An annuity is a series of equal payments occurring at equal intervals. One example is a series of three annual payments of $100 each. An *ordinary annuity* is defined as equal end-of-period payments at equal intervals. An ordinary annuity of $100 for 3 periods and its present value (*p*) are illustrated in Exhibit B.6.

Exhibit B.6

Present Value of an Ordinary Annuity Diagram

P3 Apply present value concepts to an annuity by using interest tables.

One way for us to compute the present value of an ordinary annuity is to find the present value of each payment using our present value formula from Exhibit B.3. We then add each of the three present values. To illustrate, let's look at three $100 payments at the end of each of the next three periods with an interest rate of 15%. Our present value computations are

$$ p = \frac{\$100}{(1 + 0.15)^1} + \frac{\$100}{(1 + 0.15)^2} + \frac{\$100}{(1 + 0.15)^3} = \$228.32 $$

This computation is identical to computing the present value of each payment (from Table B.1) and taking their sum or, alternatively, adding the values from Table B.1 for each of the three payments and multiplying their sum by the $100 annuity payment.

A more direct way is to use a present value of annuity table. Table B.3 at the end of this appendix is one such table. This table is called a **present value of an annuity of 1 table**. If we look at Table B.3 where $n = 3$ and $i = 15\%$, we see the present value is 2.2832. This means the present value of an annuity of 1 for three periods, with a 15% interest rate, equals 2.2832.

A present value of an annuity formula is used to construct Table B.3. It can also be constructed by adding the amounts in a present value of 1 table. To illustrate, we use Table B.1 and B.3 to confirm this relation for the prior example:

From Table B.1		From Table B.3	
$i = 15\%, n = 1$	0.8696		
$i = 15\%, n = 2$	0.7561		
$i = 15\%, n = 3$	0.6575		
Total	2.2832	$i = 15\%, n = 3$	2.2832

We can also use business calculators or spreadsheet programs to find the present value of an annuity.

The future value of an *ordinary annuity* is the accumulated value of each annuity payment with interest as of the date of the final payment. To illustrate, let's consider the earlier annuity of three annual payments of $100. Exhibit B.7 shows the point in time for the future value (f). The first payment is made two periods prior to the point when future value is determined, and the final payment occurs on the future value date.

Future Value of an Annuity

Exhibit B.7

Future Value of an Ordinary Annuity Diagram

One way to compute the future value of an annuity is to use the formula to find the future value of *each* payment and add them. If we assume an interest rate of 15%, our calculation is

$$f = \$100 \times (1 + 0.15)^2 + \$100 \times (1 + 0.15)^1 + \$100 \times (1 + 0.15)^0 = \$347.25$$

This is identical to using Table B.2 and summing the future values of each payment, or by adding the future values of the three payments of 1 and multiplying the sum by $100.

A more direct way is to use a table showing future values of annuities. Such a table is called a **future value of an annuity of 1 table**. Table B.4 at the end of this appendix is one such table. Note that in Table B.4 when $n = 1$, the future values equal 1 ($f = 1$) for all rates of interest. This is so because such an annuity consists of only one payment and the future value is determined on the date of that payment—no time passes between the payment and its future value. The future value of an annuity formula is used to construct Table B.4. We can also construct it by adding the amounts from a future value of 1 table. To illustrate, we use Tables B.2 and B.4 to confirm this relation for the prior example:

P4 Apply future value concepts to an annuity by using interest tables.

From Table B.2		From Table B.4	
$i = 15\%, n = 0$	1.0000		
$i = 15\%, n = 1$	1.1500		
$i = 15\%, n = 2$	1.3225		
Total............	3.4725	$i = 15\%, n = 3$	3.4725

Note that the future value in Table B.2 is 1.0000 when $n = 0$, but the future value in Table B.4 is 1.0000 when $n = 1$. Is this a contradiction? No. When $n = 0$ in Table B.2, the future value is determined on the date when a single payment occurs. This means that no interest is earned, since no time has passed, and the future value equals the payment. Table B.4 describes annuities with equal payments occurring at the end of each period. When $n = 1$, the annuity has one payment, and its future value equals 1 on the date of its final and only payment. Again, no time passes from the payment and its future value date.

Quick Check

4. A company invests $45,000 per year for five years at 12% annual interest. Compute the value of this annuity investment at the end of five years.

Answer—p. B-8

Summary

C1 **Describe the earning of interest and the concepts of present and future values.** Interest is payment by a borrower to the owner of an asset for its use. Present and future value computations are a way for us to estimate the interest component of holding assets or liabilities over a period of time.

P1 **Apply present value concepts to a single amount by using interest tables.** The present value of a single amount received at a future date is the amount that can be invested now at the specified interest rate to yield that future value.

P2 **Apply future value concepts to a single amount by using interest tables.** The future value of a single amount

invested at a specified rate of interest is the amount that would accumulate by the future date.

P3 **Apply present value concepts to an annuity by using interest tables.** The present value of an annuity is the amount that can be invested now at the specified interest rate to yield that series of equal periodic payments.

P4 **Apply future value concepts to an annuity by using interest tables.** The future value of an annuity invested at a specific rate of interest is the amount that would accumulate by the date of the final payment.

Guidance Answers to **Quick Checks**

1. $70,000 \times 0.6302 = \$44,144$ (use Table B.1, $i = 8\%$, $n = 6$).

2. $555,000/\$150,000 = 3.7000$; Table B.2 shows this value is not achieved until after 17 years at 8% interest.

3. $10,000 \times 5.2421 = \$52,421$ (use Table B.3, $i = 4\%$, $n = 6$).

4. $45,000 \times 6.3528 = \$285,876$ (use Table B.4, $i = 12\%$, $n = 5$).

QUICK STUDY

QS B-1

Identifying interest rates in tables   **C1**

You must make future value estimates using the *future value of 1 table* (Table B.2). Which interest rate column do you use when working with the following rates?

1. 8% compounded quarterly

2. 12% compounded annually

3. 6% compounded semiannually

4. 12% compounded monthly

QS B-2

Interest rate on an investment   **P1**

Ken Francis is offered the possibility of investing $2,745 today and then in return receiving $10,000 after 15 years. What is the annual rate of interest for this investment? (Use Table B.1.)

QS B-3

Number of periods of an investment   **P1**

Megan Brink is offered the possibility of investing $6,651 today at 6% interest per year in a desire to have $10,000. How many years must Brink wait to accumulate $10,000? (Use Table B.1.)

QS B-4

Present value of an amount   **P1**

Flaherty is considering an investment which, if paid for immediately, is expected to return $140,000 five years from now. If Flaherty demands a 9% return, how much is she willing to pay for this investment?

CII, Inc., invests $630,000 in a project expected to earn a 12% annual rate of return. The earnings will be reinvested in the project each year until the entire investment is liquidated 10 years later. What will the cash proceeds be when the project is liquidated?

QS B-5
Future value of an amount
P2

Beene Distributing is considering a project that will return $150,000 annually at the end of each year for six years. If Beene demands an annual return of 7% and pays for the project immediately, how much is it willing to pay?

QS B-6
Present value of an annuity
P3

Claire Fitch is planning to begin an individual retirement program in which she will invest $1,500 annually at the end of each year. Fitch plans to retire after making 30 annual investments in the program earning a return of 10%. What is the value of the program on the date of the last payment?

QS B-7
Future value of an annuity
P4

Bill Thompson expects to invest $10,000 at 12% and, at the end of a certain period, receive $96,463. How many years will it be before Thompson receives the payment? (Use Table B.2.)

EXERCISES

Exercise B-1
Number of periods of an investment
P2

Ed Summers expects to invest $10,000 for 25 years, after which he wants to receive $108,347. What rate of interest must Summers earn? (Use Table B.2.)

Exercise B-2
Interest rate on an investment
P2

Jones expects an immediate investment of $57,466 to return $10,000 annually for eight years, with the first payment to be received one year from now. What rate of interest must Jones earn? (Use Table B.3.)

Exercise B-3
Interest rate on an investment
P3

Keith Riggins expects an investment of $82,014 to return $10,000 annually for several years. If Keith earns a return of 10%, how many annual payments will he receive? (Use Table B.3.)

Exercise B-4
Number of periods of an investment
P3

Algoe expects to invest $1,000 annually for 40 years to yield an accumulated value of $154,762 on the date of the last investment. For this to occur, what rate of interest must Algoe earn? (Use Table B.4.)

Exercise B-5
Interest rate on an investment
P4

Kate Beckwith expects to invest $10,000 annually that will earn 8%. How many annual investments must Kate make to accumulate $303,243 on the date of the last investment? (Use Table B.4.)

Exercise B-6
Number of periods of an investment
P4

Sam Weber finances a new automobile by paying $6,500 cash and agreeing to make 40 monthly payments of $500 each, the first payment to be made one month after the purchase. The loan bears interest at an annual rate of 12%. What is the cost of the automobile?

Exercise B-7
Present value of an annuity
P3

Spiller Corp. plans to issue 10%, 15-year, $500,000 par value bonds payable that pay interest semi-annually on June 30 and December 31. The bonds are dated December 31, 2002, and are issued on that date. If the market rate of interest for the bonds is 8% on the date of issue, what will be the total cash proceeds from the bond issue?

Exercise B-8
Present value of bonds
P1 P3

McAdams Company expects to earn 10% per year on an investment that will pay $606,773 six years from now. Use Table B.1 to compute the present value of this investment.

Exercise B-9
Present value of an amount
P1

Exercise B-10

Present value of an amount and an annuity

P1 P3

Compute the amount that can be borrowed under each of the following circumstances:

1. A promise to pay $90,000 in seven years hence at an interest rate of 6%.

2. An agreement made on February 1, 2002, to make three separate payments of $20,000 on February 1 of 2003, 2004, and 2005. The annual interest rate is 10%.

Exercise B-11

Present value of an amount

P1

On January 1, 2002, a company agrees to pay $20,000 in three years. If the annual interest rate is 10%, determine how much cash the company can borrow with this agreement.

Exercise B-12

Present value of an amount

P1

Find the amount of money that can be borrowed today with each of the following separate debt agreements *a* through *f*:

Case	Single Future Payment	Number of Periods	Interest Rate
a.	$40,000	3	4%
b.	75,000	7	8
c.	52,000	9	10
d.	18,000	2	4
e.	63,000	8	6
f.	89,000	5	2

Exercise B-13

Present values of annuities

P3

C&H Ski Club recently borrowed money and agrees to pay it back with a series of six annual payments of $5,000 each. C&H subsequently borrows more money and agrees to pay it back with a series of four annual payments of $7,500 each. The annual interest rate for both loans is 6%.

1. Use Table B.1 to find the present value of these two separate annuities. (Round amounts to the nearest dollar.)

2. Use Table B.3 to find the present value of these two separate annuities.

Exercise B-14

Present value with semiannual compounding

C1 P3

Otto Co. borrows money on April 30, 2002, by promising to make four payments of $13,000 each on November 1, 2002, May 1, 2003, November 1, 2003, and May 1, 2004.

1. How much money is Otto able to borrow if the interest rate is 8%, compounded semiannually?

2. How much money is Otto able to borrow if the interest rate is 12%, compounded semiannually?

3. How much money is Otto able to borrow if the interest rate is 16%, compounded semiannually?

Exercise B-15

Future value of an amount

P2

Mark Welsch deposits $7,200 in an account that earns interest at an annual rate of 8%, compounded quarterly. The $7,200 plus earned interest must remain in the account 10 years before it can be withdrawn. How much money will be in the account at the end of 10 years?

Exercise B-16

Future value of an annuity

P4

Kelly Malone plans to have $50 withheld from her monthly paycheck and deposited in a savings account that earns 12% annually, compounded monthly. If Kelly continues with her plan for two and one half years, how much will be accumulated in the account on the date of the last deposit?

Exercise B-17

Future value of an amount plus an annuity

P2 P4

Starr Company decides to establish a fund that it will use 10 years from now to replace an aging production facility. The company will make an initial contribution of $100,000 to the fund and plans to make quarterly contributions of $50,000 beginning in three months. The fund earns 12%, compounded quarterly. What will be the value of the fund 10 years from now?

Exercise B-18

Future value of an amount

P2

Catten, Inc., invests $163,170 today earning 7% per year for nine years. Use Table B.2 to compute the future value of the investment nine years from now.

For each of the following situations, identify (1) it as either a (a) present or future value and (b) single amount or annuity case, (2) the table you would use in your computations (but do not solve the problem), and (3) the interest rate and time periods you would use.

a. You need to accumulate $10,000 for a trip you wish to take in four years. You are able to earn 8% compounded semiannually on your savings. You plan to make only one deposit and let the money accumulate for four years. How would you determine the amount of the one-time deposit?

b. Assume the same facts as in part (a) except you will make semiannual deposits to your savings account.

c. You want to retire after working 40 years with savings in excess of $1,000,000. You expect to save $4,000 a year for 40 years and earn an annual rate of interest of 8%. Will you be able to retire with more than $1,000,000 in 40 years?

d. A sweepstakes agency names you a grand prize winner. You can take $225,000 immediately or elect to receive annual installments of $30,000 for 20 years. You can earn 10% annually on any investments you make. Which prize do you choose to receive?

Exercise B-19

Using present and future value tables

Table B.1

Present Value of 1

$$p = 1/(1 + i)^n$$

	Rate											
Periods	**1%**	**2%**	**3%**	**4%**	**5%**	**6%**	**7%**	**8%**	**9%**	**10%**	**12%**	**15%**
1	0.9901	0.9804	0.9709	0.9615	0.9524	0.9434	0.9346	0.9259	0.9174	0.9091	0.8929	0.8696
2	0.9803	0.9612	0.9426	0.9246	0.9070	0.8900	0.8734	0.8573	0.8417	0.8264	0.7972	0.7561
3	0.9706	0.9423	0.9151	0.8890	0.8638	0.8396	0.8163	0.7938	0.7722	0.7513	0.7118	0.6575
4	0.9610	0.9238	0.8885	0.8548	0.8227	0.7921	0.7629	0.7350	0.7084	0.6830	0.6355	0.5718
5	0.9515	0.9057	0.8626	0.8219	0.7835	0.7473	0.7130	0.6806	0.6499	0.6209	0.5674	0.4972
6	0.9420	0.8880	0.8375	0.7903	0.7462	0.7050	0.6663	0.6302	0.5963	0.5645	0.5066	0.4323
7	0.9327	0.8706	0.8131	0.7599	0.7107	0.6651	0.6227	0.5835	0.5470	0.5132	0.4523	0.3759
8	0.9235	0.8535	0.7894	0.7307	0.6768	0.6274	0.5820	0.5403	0.5019	0.4665	0.4039	0.3269
9	0.9143	0.8368	0.7664	0.7026	0.6446	0.5919	0.5439	0.5002	0.4604	0.4241	0.3606	0.2843
10	0.9053	0.8203	0.7441	0.6756	0.6139	0.5584	0.5083	0.4632	0.4224	0.3855	0.3220	0.2472
11	0.8963	0.8043	0.7224	0.6496	0.5847	0.5268	0.4751	0.4289	0.3875	0.3505	0.2875	0.2149
12	0.8874	0.7885	0.7014	0.6246	0.5568	0.4970	0.4440	0.3971	0.3555	0.3186	0.2567	0.1869
13	0.8787	0.7730	0.6810	0.6006	0.5303	0.4688	0.4150	0.3677	0.3262	0.2897	0.2292	0.1625
14	0.8700	0.7579	0.6611	0.5775	0.5051	0.4423	0.3878	0.3405	0.2992	0.2633	0.2046	0.1413
15	0.8613	0.7430	0.6419	0.5553	0.4810	0.4173	0.3624	0.3152	0.2745	0.2394	0.1827	0.1229
16	0.8528	0.7284	0.6232	0.5339	0.4581	0.3936	0.3387	0.2919	0.2519	0.2176	0.1631	0.1069
17	0.8444	0.7142	0.6050	0.5134	0.4363	0.3714	0.3166	0.2703	0.2311	0.1978	0.1456	0.0929
18	0.8360	0.7002	0.5874	0.4936	0.4155	0.3503	0.2959	0.2502	0.2120	0.1799	0.1300	0.0808
19	0.8277	0.6864	0.5703	0.4746	0.3957	0.3305	0.2765	0.2317	0.1945	0.1635	0.1161	0.0703
20	0.8195	0.6730	0.5537	0.4564	0.3769	0.3118	0.2584	0.2145	0.1784	0.1486	0.1037	0.0611
25	0.7798	0.6095	0.4776	0.3751	0.2953	0.2330	0.1842	0.1460	0.1160	0.0923	0.0588	0.0304
30	0.7419	0.5521	0.4120	0.3083	0.2314	0.1741	0.1314	0.0994	0.0754	0.0573	0.0334	0.0151
35	0.7059	0.5000	0.3554	0.2534	0.1813	0.1301	0.0937	0.0676	0.0490	0.0356	0.0189	0.0075
40	0.6717	0.4529	0.3066	0.2083	0.1420	0.0972	0.0668	0.0460	0.0318	0.0221	0.0107	0.0037

Table B.2

Future Value of 1

$$f = (1 + i)^n$$

	Rate											
Periods	**1%**	**2%**	**3%**	**4%**	**5%**	**6%**	**7%**	**8%**	**9%**	**10%**	**12%**	**15%**
0	1.0000	1.0000	1.0000	1.0000	1.0000	1.0000	1.0000	1.0000	1.0000	1.0000	1.0000	1.0000
1	1.0100	1.0200	1.0300	1.0400	1.0500	1.0600	1.0700	1.0800	1.0900	1.1000	1.1200	1.1500
2	1.0201	1.0404	1.0609	1.0816	1.1025	1.1236	1.1449	1.1664	1.1811	1.2100	1.2544	1.3225
3	1.0303	1.0612	1.0927	1.1249	1.1576	1.1910	1.2250	1.2597	1.2950	1.3310	1.4049	1.5209
4	1.0406	1.0824	1.1255	1.1699	1.2155	1.2625	1.3108	1.3605	1.4116	1.4641	1.5735	1.7490
5	1.0510	1.1041	1.1593	1.2167	1.2763	1.3382	1.4026	1.4693	1.5386	1.6105	1.7623	2.0114
6	1.0615	1.1262	1.1941	1.2653	1.3401	1.4185	1.5007	1.5869	1.6771	1.7716	1.9738	2.3131
7	1.0721	1.1487	1.2299	1.3159	1.4071	1.5036	1.6058	1.7138	1.8280	1.9487	2.2107	2.6600
8	1.0829	1.1717	1.2668	1.3686	1.4775	1.5938	1.7182	1.8509	1.9926	2.1436	2.4760	3.0590
9	1.0937	1.1951	1.3048	1.4233	1.5513	1.6895	1.8385	1.9990	2.1719	2.3579	2.7731	3.5179
10	1.1046	1.2190	1.3439	1.4802	1.6289	1.7908	1.9672	2.1589	2.3674	2.5937	3.1058	4.0456
11	1.1157	1.2434	1.3842	1.5395	1.7103	1.8983	2.1049	2.3316	2.5804	2.8531	3.4785	4.6524
12	1.1268	1.2682	1.4258	1.6010	1.7959	2.0122	2.2522	2.5182	2.8127	3.1384	3.8960	5.3503
13	1.1381	1.2936	1.4685	1.6651	1.8856	2.1329	2.4098	2.7196	3.0658	3.4523	4.3635	6.1528
14	1.1495	1.3195	1.5126	1.7317	1.9799	2.2609	2.5785	2.9372	3.3417	3.7975	4.8871	7.0757
15	1.1610	1.3459	1.5580	1.8009	2.0789	2.3966	2.7590	3.1722	3.6425	4.1772	5.4736	8.1371
16	1.1726	1.3728	1.6047	1.8730	2.1829	2.5404	2.9522	3.4259	3.9703	4.5950	6.1304	9.3576
17	1.1843	1.4002	1.6528	1.9479	2.2920	2.6928	3.1588	3.7000	4.3276	5.0545	6.8660	10.7613
18	1.1961	1.4282	1.7024	2.0258	2.4066	2.8543	3.3799	3.9960	4.7171	5.5599	7.6900	12.3755
19	1.2081	1.4568	1.7535	2.1068	2.5270	3.0256	3.6165	4.3157	5.1417	6.1159	8.6128	14.2318
20	1.2202	1.4859	1.8061	2.1911	2.6533	3.2071	3.8697	4.6610	5.6044	6.7275	9.6463	16.3665
25	1.2824	1.6406	2.0938	2.6658	3.3864	4.2919	5.4274	6.8485	8.6231	10.8347	17.0001	32.9190
30	1.3478	1.8114	2.4273	3.2434	4.3219	5.7435	7.6123	10.0627	13.2677	17.4494	29.9599	66.2118
35	1.4166	1.9999	2.8139	3.9461	5.5160	7.6861	10.6766	14.7853	20.4140	28.1024	52.7996	133.176
40	1.4889	2.2080	3.2620	4.8010	7.0400	10.2857	14.9745	21.7245	31.4094	45.2593	93.0510	267.864

$$n = \left[1 - \frac{1}{\quad} \right]$$

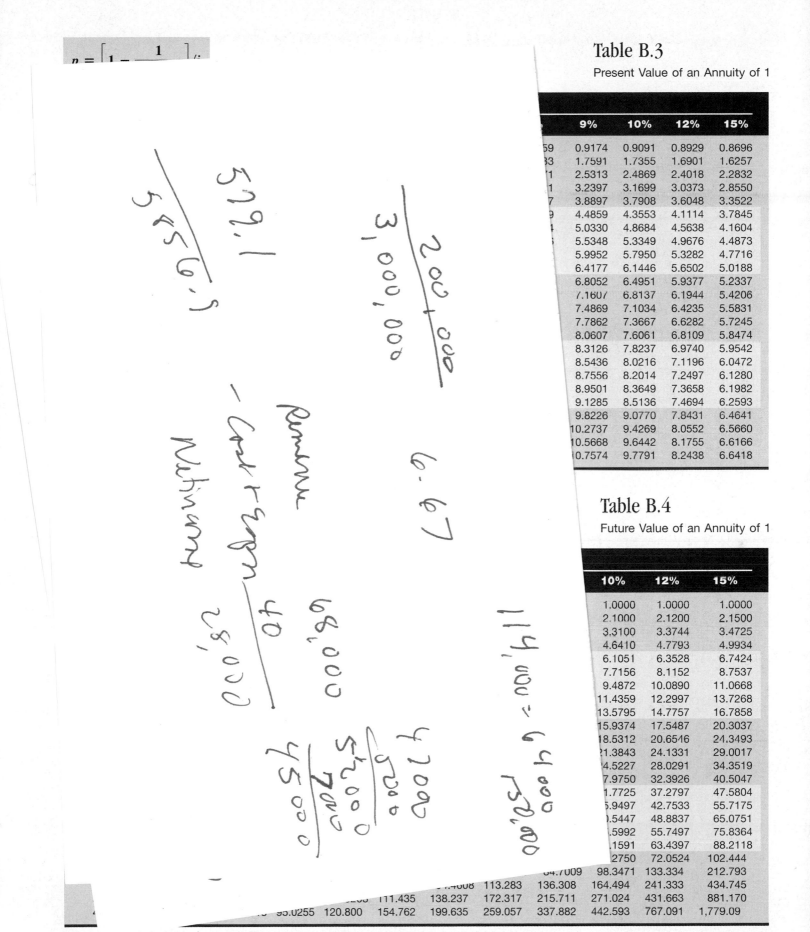

Table B.3

Present Value of an Annuity of 1

	9%	10%	12%	15%
59	0.9174	0.9091	0.8929	0.8696
33	1.7591	1.7355	1.6901	1.6257
1	2.5313	2.4869	2.4018	2.2832
1	3.2397	3.1699	3.0373	2.8550
7	3.8897	3.7908	3.6048	3.3522
9	4.4859	4.3553	4.1114	3.7845
4	5.0330	4.8684	4.5638	4.1604
5	5.5348	5.3349	4.9676	4.4873
	5.9952	5.7950	5.3282	4.7716
	6.4177	6.1446	5.6502	5.0188
	6.8052	6.4951	5.9377	5.2337
	7.1607	6.8137	6.1944	5.4206
	7.4869	7.1034	6.4235	5.5831
	7.7862	7.3667	6.6282	5.7245
	8.0607	7.6061	6.8109	5.8474
	8.3126	7.8237	6.9740	5.9542
	8.5436	8.0216	7.1196	6.0472
	8.7556	8.2014	7.2497	6.1280
	8.9501	8.3649	7.3658	6.1982
	9.1285	8.5136	7.4694	6.2593
	9.8226	9.0770	7.8431	6.4641
	10.2737	9.4269	8.0552	6.5660
	10.5668	9.6442	8.1755	6.6166
	10.7574	9.7791	8.2438	6.6418

Table B.4

Future Value of an Annuity of 1

	10%	12%	15%
	1.0000	1.0000	1.0000
	2.1000	2.1200	2.1500
	3.3100	3.3744	3.4725
	4.6410	4.7793	4.9934
	6.1051	6.3528	6.7424
	7.7156	8.1152	8.7537
	9.4872	10.0890	11.0668
	11.4359	12.2997	13.7268
	13.5795	14.7757	16.7858
	15.9374	17.5487	20.3037
	18.5312	20.6546	24.3493
	21.3843	24.1331	29.0017
	24.5227	28.0291	34.3519
	27.9750	32.3926	40.5047
	31.7725	37.2797	47.5804
	35.9497	42.7533	55.7175
	40.5447	48.8837	65.0751
	45.5992	55.7497	75.8364
	51.1591	63.4397	88.2118
	57.2750	72.0524	102.444
64.7009	98.3471	133.334	212.793
113.283	136.308	164.494	241.333	434.745
111.435	138.237	172.317	215.711	271.024	431.663	881.170
95.0255	120.800	154.762	199.635	259.057	337.882	442.593	767.091	1,779.09

Credits

Index

D

Chart of Accounts

Assets

Current Assets

101 Cash
102 Petty cash
103 Cash equivalents
104 Short-term investments
105 Market adjustment, _____ securities (S-T)
106 Accounts receivable
107 Allowance for doubtful accounts
108 Legal fees receivable
109 Interest receivable
110 Rent receivable
111 Notes receivable
115 Subscriptions receivable, Common stock
116 Subscriptions receivable, Preferred stock
119 Merchandise inventory
120 _____ inventory
121 _____ inventory
124 Office supplies
125 Store supplies
126 _____ supplies
128 Prepaid insurance
129 Prepaid interest
131 Prepaid rent
132 Raw materials inventory
133 Goods in process inventory, _____
134 Goods in process inventory, _____
135 Finished goods inventory

Long-Term Investments

141 Long-term investments
142 Market adjustment, _____ securities (L-T)
144 Investment in _____
145 Bond sinking fund

Plant Assets

151 Automobiles
152 Accumulated depreciation, Automobiles
153 Trucks
154 Accumulated depreciation, Trucks
155 Boats
156 Accumulated depreciation, Boats
157 Professional library
158 Accumulated depreciation, Professional library
159 Law library
160 Accumulated depreciation, Law library
161 Furniture
162 Accumulated depreciation, Furniture
163 Office equipment
164 Accumulated depreciation, Office equipment
165 Store equipment
166 Accumulated depreciation, Store equipment
167 _____ equipment
168 Accumulated depreciation, _____ equipment
169 Machinery
170 Accumulated depreciation, Machinery
173 Building _____
174 Accumulated depreciation, Building _____
175 Building _____
176 Accumulated depreciation, Building _____
179 Land improvements _____
180 Accumulated depreciation, Land improvements _____
181 Land improvements _____
182 Accumulated depreciation, Land improvements _____
183 Land

Natural Resources

185 Mineral deposit
186 Accumulated depletion, Mineral deposit

Intangible Assets

191 Patents
192 Leasehold
193 Franchise
194 Copyrights
195 Leasehold improvements
196 Organization costs

Liabilities

Current Liabilities

201 Accounts payable
202 Insurance payable
203 Interest payable
204 Legal fees payable
207 Office salaries payable
208 Rent payable
209 Salaries payable
210 Wages payable
211 Accrued payroll payable
214 Estimated warranty liability
215 Income taxes payable
216 Common dividend payable
217 Preferred dividend payable
218 State unemployment taxes payable
219 Employee federal income taxes payable
221 Employee medical insurance payable
222 Employee retirement program payable
223 Employee union dues payable
224 Federal unemployment taxes payable
225 FICA taxes payable
226 Estimated vacation pay liability

Unearned Revenues

230 Unearned consulting fees
231 Unearned legal fees
232 Unearned property management fees
233 Unearned _____ fees
234 Unearned _____ fees
235 Unearned janitorial revenue
236 Unearned _____ revenue
238 Unearned rent

Notes Payable

240 Short-term notes payable
241 Discount on short-term notes payable
245 Notes payable
251 Long-term notes payable
252 Discount on long-term notes payable

Long-Term Liabilities

253 Long-term lease liability
255 Bonds payable
256 Discount on bonds payable
257 Premium on bonds payable
258 Deferred income tax liability

Equity

Owner's Equity

301 _____, Capital
302 _____, Withdrawals
303 _____, Capital
304 _____, Withdrawals
305 _____, Capital
306 _____, Withdrawals

Contributed Capital

307 Common stock, $ _____ par value
308 Common stock, no par
309 Common stock subscribed
310 Common stock dividend distributable
311 Contributed capital in excess of par value, Common stock
312 Contributed capital in excess of stated value, No-par common stock
313 Contributed capital from retirement of common stock
314 Contributed capital, Treasury stock
315 Preferred stock
316 Contributed capital in excess of par value, Preferred stock
317 Preferred stock subscribed

Retained Earnings

318 Retained earnings
319 Cash dividends declared
320 Stock dividends declared

Other Equity Accounts

321 Treasury stock, Common
322 Unrealized gain—Equity
323 Unrealized loss—Equity

Revenues

401 _____ fees earned
402 _____ fees earned
403 _____ services revenue
404 _____ services revenue
405 Commissions earned
406 Rent earned
407 Dividends earned
408 Earnings from investment in _____
409 Interest revenue (or Interest earned)
410 Sinking fund earnings
413 Sales
414 Sales returns and allowances
415 Sales discounts

Cost of Sales

Cost of Goods Sold

502 Cost of goods sold
505 Purchases
506 Purchases returns and allowances
507 Purchases discounts
508 Transportation-in

Manufacturing

520 Raw materials purchases
521 Freight-in on raw materials
530 Factory payroll
531 Direct labor
540 Factory overhead
541 Indirect materials
542 Indirect labor
543 Factory insurance expired
544 Factory supervision
545 Factory supplies used
546 Factory utilities
547 Miscellaneous production costs
548 Property taxes on factory building
549 Property taxes on factory equipment
550 Rent on factory building
551 Repairs, factory equipment
552 Small tools written off
560 Depreciation of factory equipment
561 Depreciation of factory building

Standard Cost Variance

580 Direct material quantity variance
581 Direct material price variance

582 Direct labor quantity variance
583 Direct labor price variance
584 Factory overhead volume variance
585 Factory overhead controllable variance

Expenses

Amortization, Depletion, and Depreciation

601 Amortization expense, _____
602 Amortization expense, _____
603 Depletion expense, _____
604 Depreciation expense, Boats
605 Depreciation expense, Automobiles
606 Depreciation expense, Building _____
607 Depreciation expense, Building _____
608 Depreciation expense, Land improvements
609 Depreciation expense, Land improvements _____
610 Depreciation expense, Law library
611 Depreciation expense, Trucks
612 Depreciation expense, _____ equipment
613 Depreciation expense, _____ equipment
614 Depreciation expense, _____
615 Depreciation expense, _____

Employee-Related Expenses

620 Office salaries expense
621 Sales salaries expense
622 Salaries expense
623 _____ wages expense
624 Employees' benefits expense
625 Payroll taxes expense

Financial Expenses

630 Cash over and short
631 Discounts lost
632 Factoring fee expense
633 Interest expense

Insurance Expenses

635 Insurance expense, Delivery equipment
636 Insurance expense, Office equipment
637 Insurance expense, _____

Rental Expenses

640 Rent expense
641 Rent expense, Office space
642 Rent expense, Selling space
643 Press rental expense
644 Truck rental expense
645 _____ rental expense

Supplies Expenses

650 Office supplies expense
651 Store supplies expense

652 _____ supplies expense
653 _____ supplies expense

Miscellaneous Expenses

655 Advertising expense
656 Bad debts expense
657 Blueprinting expense
658 Boat expense
659 Collection expense
661 Concessions expense
662 Credit card expense
663 Delivery expense
664 Dumping expense
667 Equipment expense
668 Food and drinks expense
669 Gas, oil, and repairs expense
671 Gas and oil expense
672 General and administrative expense
673 Janitorial expense
674 Legal fees expense
676 Mileage expense
677 Miscellaneous expenses
678 Mower and tools expense
679 Operating expense
681 Permits expense
682 Postage expense
683 Property taxes expense
684 Repairs expense, _____
685 Repairs expense, _____
687 Selling expense
688 Telephone expense
689 Travel and entertainment expense
690 Utilities expense
691 Warranty expense
695 Income taxes expense

Gains and Losses

701 Gain on retirement of bonds
702 Gain on sale of machinery
703 Gain on sale of short-term investments
704 Gain on sale of trucks
705 Gain on _____
706 Foreign exchange gain or loss
801 Loss on disposal of machinery
802 Loss on exchange of equipment
803 Loss on exchange of _____
804 Loss on sale of notes
805 Loss on retirement of bonds
806 Loss on sale of investments
807 Loss on sale of machinery
808 Loss on _____
809 Unrealized gain—Income
810 Unrealized loss—Income

Clearing Accounts

901 Income summary
902 Manufacturing summary